CLARENCE BYRD
Athabasca University

IDA CHEN
Clarence Byrd Inc.

Study Guide to Byrd & Chen's Canadian Tax Principles

2013–2014 EDITION

Toronto

Vice-President, Editorial Director: Gary Bennett
Marketing Manager: Claire Varley
Acquisitions Editor: Megan Farrell
Supervising Developmental Editor: Suzanne Schaan
Developmental Editor: Suzanne Simpson Millar
Lead Project Manager: Avinash Chandra
Manufacturing Manager: Jane Schell
Production Editor: Lila Campbell
Cover Designer: Anthony Leung

10 9 8 7 6 5 4 3 2 1 [EB]

PREFACE

List Of 2013 Tax Rates And Credits For Your Use

A complete list of 2013 tax rates and credits to use when solving problems is available at the front of both Volumes 1 and 2, as well as on the Student CD-ROM as a .PDF file.

Available Study Tools And Resources

The inner front cover of Volume 1 describes the abundant study tools, resources and software that are available to users of *Canadian Tax Principles*.

ProFile Tax Preparation Software

For users of *Canadian Tax Principles*, we provide access to Intuit's professional tax preparation software, ProFile. Instructions on how to access this software are available on the inner back cover of Volume 1.

Web Site

Please check the web site periodically for additions or corrections to the textbook and Study Guide. The web site for *Canadian Tax Principles* can be found at:

www.pearsoncanada.ca/byrdchen/ctp2014

Content Of Study Guide

Your two volume textbook is accompanied by this Study Guide. The chapters of this Study Guide correspond to the chapters of *Canadian Tax Principles*. Each of these Study Guide chapters contains the following:

- Detailed guidance on how to work through the text and problems in the chapter.
- Detailed solutions to the Exercises and Self Study Problems in the textbook for the chapter.
- A list of learning objectives for the material in the chapter.

In addition, there are:

- Two sample personal tax returns and two Self Study Tax Software Problems in Chapters 4 and 11.
- A sample corporate tax return in Chapter 13.

Glossary

At the back of this Study Guide is a comprehensive Glossary that carefully defines more than 500 tax terms that are used throughout the text. Tied to this important resource, at the end of each chapter you will find a list of the Key Terms, without definitions, that were used in that chapter. This provides an additional resource for reviewing the text material in that, by reviewing this list, you can ensure that you are familiar with all of the concepts that are presented in the chapter.

To assist in this review, Glossary Flashcards and Key Terms Self-Tests for each Chapter are available in two places, on the Student CD-ROM and on the *Canadian Tax Principles* web site.

Using The Solutions

With respect to the problem solutions that are included in this book, the header at the top of each page identifies the solution on the page. The page numbers in this Study Guide have been numbered with the prefix "S-" to distinguish them from the page numbers of the textbook. We encourage you to attempt to solve each Exercise or Self Study Problem prior to consulting these solutions. It is our opinion that one of the most unfortunate misconceptions that many students have is the belief that simply reading through a solution is a learning experience. It is not!

We welcome any corrections or suggestions for additions or improvements. These can be e-mailed to us at:

byrdinc@sympatico.ca

July, 2013

Clarence Byrd, Athabasca University
Ida Chen, Clarence Byrd Inc.

CONTENTS

CHAPTER 1

Web Site

The web site for this book can be found at:

www.pearsoncanada.ca/byrdchen/ctp2014

Here you will find:

- Updates and corrections to the textbook and Study Guide
- Glossary Flashcards and Key Terms Self-Tests (also on your Student CD-ROM)
- Links to other relevant web sites
- Instructions on how to install the 2013 ProFile program and download updated sample tax returns and Cases when the updated ProFile software is available in January, 2014
- Instructions on how to access the FITAC/CTP Infobase on the Student CD-ROM

How To Work Through Chapter 1

We recommend the following approach in dealing with the material in this chapter:

The Canadian Tax System
- ❑ Read paragraph 1-1 to 1-12 (in the textbook).
- ❑ Do Exercises One-1 and One-2 (in the textbook) and check the solutions on page S-2 of this Study Guide. All solutions to Exercises and Self Study Problems can be found in this Study Guide and the page numbers all start with the prefix S-.
- ❑ Read paragraph 1-13 to 1-17.
- ❑ Do Exercise One-3 and check the solution in this Study Guide.
- ❑ Read paragraph 1-18 to 1-25.

Tax Policy Concepts
- ❑ Read paragraph 1-26 to 1-28.
- ❑ Do Exercise One-4 and check the solution in this Study Guide.
- ❑ Do Self Study Problem One-1 at the end of the textbook chapter on page 32 and check the solution in this Study Guide.
- ❑ Read paragraph 1-29 to 1-34.
- ❑ Do Self Study Problem One-2 and check the solution in this Study Guide.
- ❑ Read paragraph 1-35 to 1-43.
- ❑ Do Self Study Problem One-3 and check the solution in this Study Guide.

Income Tax Reference Materials
- ❑ Read paragraph 1-44 to 1-76.
- ❑ Do Self Study Problem One-4 and check the solution in this Study Guide.

Liability For Income Tax

❑ Read paragraph 1-77 to 1-90.
❑ Do Exercise One-5 and check the solution in this Study Guide.

Alternative Concepts Of Income

❑ Read paragraph 1-91 to 1-99.

Net Income For Tax Purposes

❑ Read paragraph 1-100 to 1-126.
❑ Do Exercises One-6 to One-8 and check the solutions in this Study Guide.
❑ Do Self Study Problems One-5 to One-7 and check the solutions in this Study Guide.

Net Income To Taxable Income

❑ Read paragraph 1-127 and 1-128.

Principles Of Tax Planning

❑ Read paragraph 1-129 to 1-148.
❑ Do Exercises One-9 and One-10 and check the solutions in this Study Guide.

To Complete This Chapter

❑ Review the Key Terms Used In This Chapter on page 30. Consult the Glossary for the meaning of any key terms you do not know.
❑ Review the Glossary Flashcards and complete the Key Terms Self-Test for the Chapter. These features can be found in two places, on your Student CD-ROM under the heading "Key Term Practice" and on the web site.
❑ Review the Learning Objectives of the Chapter found on page S-11 of this Study Guide.
❑ As a final review, we recommend that you view the PowerPoint Slides for Chapter 1 that are on your Student CD-ROM. If you do not have access to the Microsoft PowerPoint program, the PowerPoint Viewer program can be installed from the Student CD-ROM.

Practice Examination

❑ Write the Practice Examination for Chapter 1 that is on your Student CD-ROM. For this chapter only, the Examination has been printed and can also be found starting on page S-12. Mark your examination using the Practice Examination Solution that is on your Student CD-ROM.

Solution to Chapter One Exercises

Exercise One - 1 Solution

Max Jordan, the Jordan family trust, and Jordan Enterprises Ltd. could be required to file income tax returns. Jordan's Hardware, Jordan & Jordan and The Jordan Foundation are not taxable entities for income tax purposes.

Exercise One - 2 Solution

Under the GST legislation, all of the listed entities could be required to file a GST return. Where only individuals, corporations and trusts can be required to file an income tax return, the definition of a person (i.e., taxable entity) is much broader for GST purposes. As is explained in detail in Chapter 21, whether an entity is required to file a GST return is dependent on the level of commercial activity.

Exercise One - 3 Solution

Federal Tax Payable [(15%)($27,000)]	$4,050
Provincial Tax Payable [(7.5%)($27,000)]	2,025
Total Tax Payable [(15% + 7.5%)($27,000)]	$6,075

Exercise One - 4 Solution

Margie's HST paid totals $22,360 [(13%)($172,000)]. Based on her Taxable Income of $895,000, this would represent an effective rate of 2.5 percent ($22,360 ÷ $895,000).

Jane's HST paid totals $3,575 [(13%)($27,500)]. On her Taxable Income of $18,000, this would be an effective rate of 19.9 percent ($3,575 ÷ $18,000).

Exercise One - 5 Solution

She is not correct. Under ITA 2(3) she would be subject to Canadian taxes on employment income earned in Canada.

Exercise One - 6 Solution

Mr. Blanton's Net Income For Tax Purposes is calculated as follows:

Income Under ITA 3(a):		
Employment Income	$42,000	
Business Loss (See ITA 3(d) below)	Nil	$42,000
Income Under ITA 3(b):		
Taxable Capital Gains	$24,000	
Allowable Capital Losses	Nil	24,000
Balance From ITA 3(a) And (b)		$66,000
Subdivision e Deductions		(13,000)
Balance Under ITA 3(c)		$53,000
Deduction Under ITA 3(d):		
Business Loss		(15,000)
Net Income For Tax Purposes (Division B Income)		**$38,000**

Exercise One - 7 Solution

Ms. Stodard's Net Income For Tax Purposes would be calculated as follows:

Income Under ITA 3(a):		
Interest Income	$33,240	
Rental Loss (See ITA 3(d) below)	Nil	$33,240
Income Under ITA 3(b):		
Taxable Capital Gains	$24,750	
Allowable Capital Losses	(19,500)	5,250
Balance From ITA 3(a) And (b)		$38,490
Subdivision e Deductions		Nil
Balance Under ITA 3(c)		$38,490
Deduction Under ITA 3(d):		
Rental Loss		(48,970)
Net Income For Tax Purposes (Division B Income)		**Nil**

She would have a non-capital loss carry over of $10,480 ($38,490 - $48,970).

Exercise One - 8 Solution

Mrs. Bergeron's Net Income For Tax Purposes would be calculated as follows:

Income Under ITA 3(a):		
Employment Income	$42,680	
Business Loss (See ITA 3(d) below)	Nil	$42,680
Income Under ITA 3(b):		
Taxable Capital Gains	$27,400	
Allowable Capital Losses	(33,280)	Nil
Balance From ITA 3(a) And (b)		$42,680
Subdivision e Deductions		(8,460)
Balance Under ITA 3(c)		$34,220
Deduction Under ITA 3(d):		
Business Loss		(26,326)
Net Income For Tax Purposes (Division B Income)		**$ 7,894**

She would have an allowable capital loss carry over of $5,880 ($27,400 - $33,280).

Exercise One - 9 Solution

Mr. Chung is involved in income splitting, tax deferral, and possibly tax avoidance. He is getting the deduction from taxable income now and his wife will be taxed on the income in the future. All RRSP contributions normally create a tax deferral. The contribution will be deductible and the earnings on the contribution will accumulate on a tax free basis. However, all of these amounts will be taxable when they are withdrawn from the plan. There may also be tax avoidance. This will happen if his spouse is taxed at a lower rate than is currently applicable to Mr. Chung when the funds become taxable to her.

Exercise One - 10 Solution

As the dental plan is a benefit that can be received by Mr. Green without being taxed (private health care), tax avoidance is illustrated.

Self Study Solution One - 1

The HST is based on certain specified expenditures, not on the income level of the individual making the expenditure. In most cases, the proportion of an individual's income that is spent declines as the individual's level of income increases. This means that when a flat rate of tax is applied to a decreasing portion of the individual's income, the rate of taxation as a percentage of that income will decline.

For example, a 13 percent HST applied to $150,000 in expenditures made by a person with $250,000 in income would amount to only 7.8 percent of that person's income ($19,500 ÷ $250,000).

In contrast, that same 13 percent HST applied to $25,000 in expenditures made by a person with $20,000 in income would reflect a tax rate of 16.3 percent ($3,250 ÷ $20,000) of that person's income.

Self Study Solution One - 2

If tax simplification was the only objective, Mr. Right's proposal would be appropriate. However, such a system would be in conflict with other possible objectives of tax policy. For example, it would almost certainly be in conflict with the objective of fairness in that it would not provide for treating different types of income (capital gains vs. employment income) or people (the poor vs. the rich) in a suitable manner.

His system would also conflict with other objectives such as the goal of equity and after-tax income stability and the need for redistribution of income. In other words, in meeting the objective of simplicity, Mr. Right's system would ignore other possible objectives of a taxation system.

Self Study Solution One - 3

A. **Diamonds, South Africa**   In a monopoly, the tax will probably be entirely shifted to employees and/or consumers. The incidence shift will depend on competition in world markets and employment levels. If the international diamond market is price sensitive and there is high unemployment in South Africa, then the tax will be shifted almost entirely to employees.

 The shifting assumptions affect evaluation of the tax using the characteristics of a "good" tax system. A tax that is entirely shifted to employees is similar to one on wages and is non-neutral, as it affects the decisions of employees to continue working. Some employees will work less and thus increase the excess burden resulting from imposition of the tax.

B. **Diamonds, Sierra Leone**   The taxing authorities will find it difficult to enforce the tax, due to their inability to track diamond movements. Records maintained by the mine will likely be inaccessible, and those presented will be incomplete. The tax will not be effective and the tax revenue will be uncertain and inadequate.

C. **Principal Residences, Canada**   This exemption is non-neutral because investment decisions are affected by the tax preference. Given the choice of investing in real estate to hold for resale or a principal residence, both of which are likely to appreciate, a taxpayer will invest in a principal residence so that the gain on disposition is tax exempt.

 It is also vertically inequitable because it benefits high-income families who can invest in more expensive residences which have the potential of earning greater returns.

 This tax expenditure is spread among all taxpayers, and general tax revenue must be larger to compensate for the revenue foregone.

D. **Business Meals, Canada**   This restriction adds complexity to accounting for deductible expenses, as all business meals have to be accounted for and accumulated separately from other promotion expenses. The tax could be shifted to consumers, employees and/or shareholders. If it is shifted to consumers, it could be more advantageous to raise personal taxes so that incidence is more certain. If it is shifted to shareholders or employees, then it would be non-neutral as it could affect investment decision making and willingness to work.

E. **Head Tax**   A head tax is neutral as it does not affect economic choices. However, it is vertically inequitable, based on the ability to pay concept of equity, as all taxpayers, regardless of their income levels are taxed the same. The head tax is very inelastic. This tax serves the objectives of certainty, simplicity and ease of compliance. It could promote stability in the economy.

Self Study Solution One - 4

The principal other sources of information can be described as follows:

1. **Draft Legislation**   This legislation often provides the only information available with respect to announced budget changes that require application in the current taxation year. Explanatory notes are included with released draft legislation but are always set out separately.

2. **Income Tax Regulations**   These Regulations provide detailed guidance with respect to the implementation and administrative enforcement of the provisions of the *Income Tax Act*.

3. **International Tax Treaties**   These are a group of bilateral tax treaties between Canada and other countries. They are designed to avoid double taxation of taxpayers who pay taxes in more than one jurisdiction and to prevent international tax evasion.

4. **Income Tax Application Rules, 1971 (ITARs)**   These are a set of transitional rules that were introduced when the *Income Tax Act* was heavily revised at the end of 1971. The rules were largely designed to ensure that the provisions of the new *Act* were not applied retroactively.

5. **Interpretation Bulletins**   These Bulletins give the CRA's interpretations of particular sections of the law which it administers and provide a vehicle for announcing significant changes in departmental interpretation.

6. **Information Circulars**   These Circulars provide information with respect to procedural matters related to both the *Income Tax Act* and the Canada Pension Plan.

7. **Income Tax Technical News**   These newsletters are an occasional publication of the CRA which, like the technical interpretations, provide detailed guidance on various current issues. These newsletters are equivalent in value to Interpretation Bulletins.

8. **CRA News Releases, Tax Tips and Fact Sheets**   The CRA publishes News Releases on a variety of subjects. They are usually issued in advance of the relevant legislation or coverage in an Interpretation Bulletin or Information Circular.

9. **Guides And Pamphlets**   These non-technical publications provide guidance for the public on a variety of income tax issues (e.g., treatment of rental income).

10. **Advance Income Tax Rulings**   For a fee, the CRA will provide an Advance Income Tax Ruling on how it will tax a proposed transaction, subject to certain limitations and qualifications. These are rulings that are provided in response to requests from taxpayers.

11. **Technical Interpretations**   The CRA provides both written and telephone Technical Interpretations to the public free of charge. These Interpretations provide technical information on various current issues.

12. **Income Tax Folios**   A new CRA publication providing their interpretation of various technical issues related to income taxes. These will gradually replace the CRA's Interpretation Bulletins.

13. **Court Decisions**   Decisions by the Tax Court of Canada, the Federal Court and the Supreme Court on income tax cases serve to establish precedents for dealing with particular tax issues.

Self Study Solution One - 5

Case A

The Case A solution would be calculated as follows:

Income Under ITA 3(a):		
Employment Income	$46,200	
Business Income	13,500	$59,700
Income Under ITA 3(b):		
Taxable Capital Gains	$14,320	
Allowable Capital Losses	(23,460)	Nil
Balance From ITA 3(a) And (b)		$59,700
Spousal Support Payments (See Note)		(4,800)
Balance From ITA 3(c)		$54,900
Deduction Under ITA 3(d):		
Net Rental Loss		(2,350)
Net Income For Tax Purposes (Division B Income)		$52,550

Note   As indicated in the text, spousal support payments are a Subdivision e deduction.

In this Case, Christina has an unused allowable capital loss carry over of $9,140 ($14,320 - $23,460). The roulette winnings would not be included in income and the related expenses would not be deductible.

Case B

The Case B solution would be calculated as follows:

Income Under ITA 3(a):		
Employment Income	$64,000	
Interest Income	2,600	
Net Rental Income	4,560	$71,160
Income Under ITA 3(b):		
Taxable Capital Gains	$32,420	
Allowable Capital Losses	(29,375)	3,045
Balance From ITA 3(a) And (b)		$74,205
Deductible RRSP Contribution		(12,480)
Balance From ITA 3(c)		$61,725
Deduction Under ITA 3(d):		
Partnership Business Loss [(50%)($144,940)]		(72,470)
Net Income For Tax Purposes (Division B Income)		Nil

Note   As indicated in the text, deductible RRSP contributions are a Subdivision e deduction.

In this Case, Christina has an unused business loss carry over of $10,745 ($72,470 - $61,725).

Self Study Solution One - 6

Case A

The Case A solution would be calculated as follows:

Income Under ITA 3(a):		
Employment Income	$78,400	
Rental Income	8,400	$ 86,800
Income Under ITA 3(b):		
Taxable Capital Gains	$42,500	
Allowable Capital Losses	(16,300)	26,200
Balance From ITA 3(a) And (b)		$113,000
Subdivision e Deductions		(8,100)
Balance From ITA 3(c)		$104,900
Deduction Under ITA 3(d):		
Business Loss		(12,300)
Net Income For Tax Purposes (Division B Income)		$ 92,600

Ms. DeBoo has no loss carry overs at the end of the year.

Case B

Income Under ITA 3(a):		
Employment Income	$23,600	
Rental Income	16,000	$39,600
Income Under ITA 3(b):		
Taxable Capital Gains	$12,500	
Allowable Capital Losses	(18,600)	Nil
Balance From ITA 3(a) And (b)		$39,600
Subdivision e Deductions		(3,200)
Balance From ITA 3(c)		$36,400
Deduction Under ITA 3(d):		
Business Loss		(4,500)
Net Income For Tax Purposes (Division B Income)		$31,900

Ms. DeBoo has a carry over of $6,100 ($12,500 - $18,600) in unused allowable capital losses.

Case C

Income Under ITA 3(a):		
Employment Income	$33,400	
Rental Income	3,400	$36,800
Income Under ITA 3(b):		
Taxable Capital Gains	$21,400	
Allowable Capital Losses	(20,700)	700
Balance From ITA 3(a) and (b)		$37,500
Subdivision e Deductions		(12,400)
Balance From ITA 3(c)		$25,100
Deduction Under ITA 3(d):		
Business Loss		(42,300)
Net Income For Tax Purposes (Division B Income)		Nil

Ms. DeBoo would have a business loss carry over of $17,200 ($25,100 - $42,300).

Case D
The Case D solution would be calculated as follows:

Income Under ITA 3(a):		
Employment Income		$46,200
Income Under ITA 3(b):		
Taxable Capital Gains	$41,200	
Allowable Capital Losses	(43,400)	Nil
Balance From ITA 3(a) And (b)		$46,200
Subdivision e Deductions		(9,300)
Balance From ITA 3(c)		$36,900
Deduction Under ITA 3(d):		
Business Loss		(22,300)
Rental Loss		(32,400)
Net Income For Tax Purposes (Division B Income)		Nil

Ms. DeBoo would have a carry over of unused non-capital losses in the amount of $17,800 ($36,900 - $22,300 - $32,400) and of unused allowable capital losses in the amount of $2,200 ($41,200 - $43,400).

Self Study Solution One - 7

Case A

Income Under ITA 3(a):		
Employment Income	$45,000	
Income From Property	15,000	$60,000
Income Under ITA 3(b):		
Taxable Capital Gains	$25,000	
Allowable Capital Losses	(10,000)	15,000
Balance From ITA 3(a) And b)		$75,000
Subdivision e Deductions		(5,000)
Balance From ITA 3(c)		$70,000
Deduction Under ITA 3(d):		
Business Loss		(20,000)
Net Income For Tax Purposes (Division B Income)		$50,000

In this Case, there are no carry overs from the current year.

Case B

Income Under ITA 3(a):		
Employment Income	$17,000	
Income From Property	12,000	$29,000
Income Under ITA 3(b):		
Taxable Capital Gains	$22,000	
Allowable Capital Losses	(8,000)	14,000
Balance From ITA 3(a) And (b)		$43,000
Subdivision e Deductions		(6,000)
Balance From ITA 3(c)		$37,000
Deduction Under ITA 3(d):		
Business Loss		(42,000)
Net Income For Tax Purposes (Division B Income)		Nil

In this Case, Mr. Haynes' will have an unused business loss carry over from the current year of $5,000 ($42,000 - $37,000).

Case C

The Case C solution would be calculated as follows:

Income Under ITA 3(a):		
Employment Income	$24,000	
Income From Property	47,000	$71,000
Income Under ITA 3(b):		
Taxable Capital Gains	$22,000	
Allowable Capital Losses	(73,000)	Nil
Balance From ITA 3(a) And (b)		$71,000
Subdivision e Deductions		(4,000)
Balance From ITA 3(c)		$67,000
Deduction Under ITA 3(d):		
Business Loss		(48,000)
Net Income For Tax Purposes (Division B Income)		$19,000

In this Case, Mr. Haynes will have a carry over from the current period of unused allowable capital losses in the amount of $51,000 $73,000 - $22,000).

Case D

The Case D solution would be calculated as follows:

Income Under ITA 3(a):		
Employment Income	$18,000	
Income From Property	7,000	$25,000
Income Under ITA 3(b):		
Taxable Capital Gains	$13,000	
Allowable Capital Losses	(18,000)	Nil
Balance From ITA 3(a) And (b)		$25,000
Subdivision e Deductions		(12,000)
Balance From ITA 3(c)		$13,000
Deduction Under ITA 3(d):		
Business Loss		(20,000)
Net Income For Tax Purposes (Division B Income)		Nil

In this Case, Mr. Haynes has a carry over from the current year of unused business losses in the amount of $7,000 ($20,000 - $13,000) and of unused allowable capital losses in the amount of $5,000 ($18,000 - $13,000).

Chapter 1 Learning Objectives

After completing Chapter 1, you should be able to:

1. List some of the different bases that can be used by the various levels of government to assess taxes (paragraph [P hereafter] 1-1 through 1-6).

2. List all of the types of entities that are subject to paying federal income taxes and GST/HST (P 1-7 through 1-12).

3. Explain the relationship between the assessment of taxes at the federal level and the assessment of taxes at the provincial level (P 1-13 through 1-25).

4. List some of the ways that taxation is used to achieve economic objectives (P 1-26).

5. Describe the differences between progressive, regressive, and flat tax systems, including some of the advantages and disadvantages of each system (P 1-27 through 1-34).

6. Discuss the issue of who ultimately pays the cost of various types of taxes (P 1-35 and 1-36).

7. Explain the nature of tax expenditures (P 1-37 through 1-40).

8. Evaluate issues in tax policy on the basis of the qualitative characteristics of tax systems (P 1-41 through 1-43).

9. Describe the reference materials that are available on income tax databases (P 1-44 through 1-48).

10. Describe the general structure of the *Income Tax Act* (P 1-49 through 1-60).

11. List and explain the nature of other sources of income tax legislation (P 1-61 through 1-70).

12. Describe other sources of income tax information (P 1-71 through 1-76).

13. Describe the charging provisions of the *Income Tax Act* for residents and non-residents (P 1-77 through 1-90).

14. Describe, in general terms, the various views of income that are held by economists, accountants, and tax authorities (P 1-91 through 1-99).

15. Calculate Net Income For Tax Purposes by applying the rules found in Section 3 of the *Income Tax Act* (P 1-100 through 1-126).

16. Explain how Net Income For Tax Purposes is converted to Taxable Income (P 1-127 and 1-128).

17. Explain the principles of tax planning (P 1-129 through 1-132).

18. Explain and provide examples of tax avoidance or reduction, and tax deferral (P 1-133 through 1-140).

19. Explain and provide examples of income splitting (P 1-141 through 1-148).

Practice Examination For Chapter 1

In order to introduce you to the Practice Examinations that are found on your Student CD-ROM, we have included the Practice Examination for Chapter 1 in this Study Guide.

Since the material in this introductory chapter is quite general, this Examination is less difficult than the Examinations for subsequent chapters. However, we suggest you make a serious effort to write this Practice Examination as it will improve your ability to create an examination environment and understand how examinations are marked.

Create An Examination Environment

Your text and the accompanying Study Guide provide you with a large number of Exercises and Self Study Problems for which solutions are provided. These problems are designed to assist you with understanding the content of each Chapter. In contrast, the goal of this Practice Examination is to allow you to evaluate your ability to write the examinations in your tax course.

To get maximum benefits from this Practice Examination, you should write it under examination conditions. It is designed as a 90 minute examination and it should be written within that time constraint. You should make an effort to set aside 90 minutes of time during which you will not be interrupted. You should also pick a location where you will not be distracted by extraneous influences.

Materials To Be Used

The materials that you use while writing this Practice Examination should be consistent with the materials that will be available during the examinations that you will be writing in your tax course. These vary from course to course, and include the following possibilities:

- you may be allowed to bring a copy of the *Income Tax Act* into the examination room,
- you may be provided with the list of "Rates and Other Data" that is found in the front of your *Canadian Tax Principles* textbook and as a .PDF file on your Student CD-ROM,
- you may be allowed to bring a "cheat sheet" with various notes into the examination room, or
- you may be allowed to bring your *Canadian Tax Principles* textbook into the examination room.

You should determine, either from your course outline or directly from your instructor, which of these approaches applies in your situation. You should write this Practice Examination using only the materials permitted for your examination.

Types Of Questions

Different instructors use alternative types of questions on their examinations. This examination includes essay questions, true or false questions, and multiple choice questions. However, the majority of the marks on this examination are allocated to problems that are similar to the Exercises and Self Study Problems that are available in your *Canadian Tax Principles* text.

This content may not be consistent with the types of questions used by the instructor in the course you are taking (e.g., an instructor might choose to have an examination that contains only multiple choice questions, or only one comprehensive question). You should take this into consideration when you are evaluating your results on this examination.

How To Use The Marking Guides

For each question on this Practice Examination, we have provided information as to how marks would be allocated. In some cases, this allocation is very straightforward. For example, if a 12 mark question consists of 6 multiple choice questions, 2 marks will be allocated to each correct answer.

However, in other situations the allocation process is more complex. Consider, for example, an employment income calculation that has 11 separate components (i.e., salary, RPP contributions and so forth). If 15 grading marks were assigned to this problem, the marking guide could assign 1.36 marks (15 marks divided by 11 components) to each line or, alternatively, award more than one mark to some components. Both of these approaches can be awkward.

To resolve this problem, the marking guides that we provide in these more complex situations will be based on "grading points". In the preceding example, 11 grading points would be assigned to this question — one for each component in the calculation. These "grading points" would then be converted into the relevant mark. Continuing the example, if you had 8 of 11 components in the calculation correct, this result would be converted to a mark as follows:

$$[(8 \div 11)(15\%)] = 10.9\%$$

In the solution that we have provided for this Practice Examination, these grading points have been identified with highlighting the appropriate number or word.

Examination Content

The content of this examination, along with the marks and times for each question, are found in the following table.

Question	Type Of Question Or Subject	Marks	Time In Minutes
1	Essay Question	10	9.0
2	Essay Question	10	9.0
3	Essay Question	10	9.0
4 - 9	True Or False Questions	9	8.1
10 - 16	Multiple Choice Questions	21	18.9
17	Net Income For Tax Purposes	40	36.0
Total		100	90.0

Question 1 (10 Marks)

The goods and services tax is assessed at a single rate, applied to certain specified goods and services. Despite the use of a single rate, this tax is criticized for being a regressive tax. What is a regressive tax? Explain how a tax that is assessed at a single rate can be considered regressive.

Question 2 (10 Marks)

Describe the meaning of the term "person" as it is used in the *Income Tax Act*. Does this term have a different meaning under the GST legislation? Provide one example of an entity that would be taxable under the GST legislation, but not under the *Income Tax Act*.

Question 3 (10 Marks)

Your client, a government employee, would like to reduce his taxes. He is trying to decide whether he should contribute $5,000 to an RRSP this year. He has an RRSP as does his wife, a part time employee at a day care centre.

Briefly describe the basic goals of tax planning. What advice would you give your client regarding his RRSP contribution? Explain your conclusion.

Questions 4 Through 9 (9 Marks)

4. Both corporations and trusts are required to file income tax returns.

    True or False?

5. Partnerships, public corporations, private corporations, and trusts are required to file income tax returns.

    True or False?

6. The use of progressive income tax rates encourages tax evasion.

    True or False?

7. If a tax system has horizontal equity, individuals in the same economic circumstances will pay the same amount of taxes.

    True or False?

8. If there is a conflict between an international tax treaty and Canadian tax legislation, the Canadian tax legislation will prevail.

    True or False?

9. Canadian citizens are required to file a Canadian income tax return, without regard to where they currently live.

    True or False?

Questions 10 Through 16 (21 Marks)

10. Which of the following is not a taxable entity for income tax purposes?

    A. Lyton Inc., a Canadian private company.
    B. John Lyton, a Canadian resident.
    C. Joan Lyton, a Canadian citizen, living in Tokyo, Japan.
    D. The Lyton family trust.

11. Which of the following statements is correct?

    A. A progressive tax system encourages individuals to work harder.
    B. Tax expenditures are more costly to administer than program expenditures.
    C. Inelasticity is a desirable feature of a tax system.
    D. Regressive taxes are unfair to individuals with low incomes.

12. Which of the following tax reference materials is a legislative source?

    A. Interpretation Bulletins.
    B. International Tax Treaties.
    C. Information Circulars.
    D. Advance Income Tax Rulings.

13. With respect to taxation years, which of the following statements is not correct?

    A. Individuals can choose to have a non-calendar fiscal year.
    B. Corporations can choose to have a non-calendar fiscal year.
    C. Testamentary trusts can have a non-calendar fiscal year.
    D. Corporations can have a taxation year based on the calendar year.

14. With respect to Canadian income taxes on non-residents, which of the following statements is not correct?

    A. Non-residents must pay Canadian income taxes on employment income earned in Canada.
    B. Non-residents must pay Canadian income taxes on capital gains arising on dispositions of any Canadian property.
    C. Non-residents must pay Canadian income taxes on business income earned in Canada.
    D. Non-residents must pay Canadian income taxes on gains resulting from the sale of Canadian real property.

15. Fred Hopkins has employment income of $45,000, a business loss of $14,000, capital gains of $20,000, capital losses of $12,000, and subdivision deductions of $3,000. Fred's Net Income For Tax Purposes is equal to:

    A. $36,000
    B. $50,000
    C. $39,000
    D. $32,000

16. Which of the following will always result in tax avoidance?

    A. Making contributions to a registered retirement savings plan.
    B. Making contributions to an employer's registered pension plan.
    C. Making use of the lifetime capital gains deduction.
    D. Making maximum capital cost allowance deductions.

Question 17 (40 Marks)

The following four Cases make different assumptions with respect to the amounts of income and deductions of Ms. Salma Rizk for the current year:

	Case A	Case B	Case C	Case D
Employment Income	$35,000	$33,000	$16,000	$28,000
Income (Loss) From Business	(10,000)	(39,000)	22,000	15,000
Income (Loss) From Property	12,000	14,000	(21,000)	(36,000)
Taxable Capital Gains	42,000	36,000	32,000	21,000
Allowable Capital Losses	(18,000)	(42,000)	(69,000)	(27,000)
Subdivision e Deductions (RRSP)	(4,000)	(7,000)	(5,000)	(11,000)

Required For each Case, calculate Ms. Rizk's Net Income For Tax Purposes (Division B income). Indicate the amount and type of any loss carry overs that would be available at the end of the current year.

END OF EXAMINATION

CHAPTER 2

How To Work Through Chapter 2

We recommend the following approach in dealing with the material in this chapter:

Administration Of The Department
☐ Read paragraph 2-1 to 2-7 (in the textbook).

Filing Requirements For Living And Deceased Individuals
☐ Read paragraph 2-8 to 2-16.
☐ Do Exercise Two-1 (in the textbook) and check the solution on page S-17 in this Study Guide.
☐ Read paragraph 2-17 to 2-19.
☐ Do Exercise Two-2 and check the solution in this Study Guide.

Source Deductions
☐ Read paragraph 2-20 to 2-26.

Instalment Payments For Individuals
☐ Read paragraph 2-27 to 2-42.
☐ Do Exercises Two-3 to Two-5 and check the solutions in this Study Guide.
☐ Do Self Study Problem Two-1 at the end of the textbook chapter on page 66 and check the solution in this Study Guide.

Interest, Penalties And Balance Due Dates For Living And Deceased Individuals
☐ Read paragraph 2-43 to 2-54.
☐ Do Exercise Two-6 and check the solution in this Study Guide.
☐ Read paragraph 2-55 to 2-59.

Returns And Instalment Payments For Corporations
☐ Read paragraph 2-60 to 2-73.
☐ Do Exercises Two-7 and Two-8 and check the solutions in this Study Guide.

Due Date For Balance Owing For Corporations
☐ Read paragraph 2-74 and 2-75.
☐ Do Exercise Two-9 and check the solution in this Study Guide.
☐ Do Self Study Problems Two-2 to Two-4 and check the solutions in this Study Guide.

Interest And Penalties For Corporations
☐ Read paragraph 2-76 to 2-79.

Returns And Payments For Trusts
☐ Read paragraph 2-80 to 2-83.
☐ Do Self Study Problem Two-5 and check the solution in this Study Guide.

**General Administrative Issues,
Including Refunds, Assessments And Adjustments**
❑ Read paragraph 2-84 to 2-102.

Appeals And Notices Of Objection
❑ Read paragraph 2-103 to 2-115.
❑ Do Exercise Two-10 and check the solution in this Study Guide.
❑ Read paragraph 2-116 to 2-125.
❑ Do Self Study Problem Two-6 and check the solution in this Study Guide.

Tax Evasion, Avoidance, And Planning
❑ Read paragraph 2-126 to 2-139.

Collection And Enforcement
❑ Read paragraph 2-140 to 2-152.

Taxpayer Relief Provisions
❑ Read paragraph 2-153 to 2-156.

To Complete This Chapter
❑ Review the Key Terms Used In This Chapter on page 64. Consult the Glossary for the meaning of any key terms you do not know.
❑ Review the Glossary Flashcards and complete the Key Terms Self-Test for the Chapter. These features can be found in two places, on your Student CD-ROM under the heading "Key Term Practice" and on the web site.
❑ Review the Learning Objectives of the Chapter found on page S-24 and S-25 of this Study Guide.
❑ As a final review, we recommend that you view the PowerPoint Slides for Chapter 2 that are on your Student CD-ROM. The PowerPoint Viewer program can be installed from the Student CD-ROM.

Practice Examination
❑ Write the Practice Examination for Chapter 2 that is on your Student CD-ROM. Mark your examination using the Practice Examination Solution that is also on your Student CD-ROM.

Solution to Chapter Two Exercises

Exercise Two - 1 Solution
While Mr. Katarski's 2013 tax return does not have to be filed until June 15, 2014, his tax liability must be paid by April 30, 2014 in order to avoid the assessment of interest.

Exercise Two - 2 Solution
Sally Cheung's 2013 tax return must be filed by the later of six months after the date of her death and her normal filing date. As her husband has business income, her normal filing date is June 15, 2014. The later of the two dates would be August 15, 2014, six months after the date of her death. Her final return for 2014 would be due on June 15, 2015.

Exercise Two - 3 Solution
She is not required to make instalment payments as long as her current year (2013) net tax owing is less than $3,000.

Exercise Two - 4 Solution

As his net tax owing in the current year and one of the two preceding years is in excess of $3,000, he is required to make instalment payments. The minimum amount would be based on the preceding taxation year's net tax owing of $1,500, and would be $375 ($1,500 ÷ 4) per quarter.

Exercise Two - 5 Solution

The net tax owing amounts can be calculated as follows:

2011 $1,000 ($53,000 - $52,000)
2012 $7,000 ($59,000 - $52,000)
2013 $4,000 ($64,000 - $60,000)

As the net tax owing exceeds $3,000 in the current year and the first preceding year, instalments are required. The three alternatives for calculating instalment payments are as follows:

- Based on the estimate for the current year, the instalments would be $1,000 ($4,000 ÷ 4).
- Based on the estimate for the preceding year, the instalments would be $1,750 ($7,000 ÷ 4).
- Based on the second preceding year, the first two instalments would each be $250 ($1,000 ÷ 4). The second two instalments each be $3,250 [$7,000 - ($250)(2)]. The total instalments would be $7,000, the same amount as under the preceding alternative.

While the first two instalments are lower under the second preceding year alternative, the total for all the instalments under this alternative is $7,000, higher than the $4,000 total under the current year alternative. The current year alternative would be the best.

Exercise Two - 6 Solution

Given the size of her net tax owing, ITA 163.1 will not be applicable and there will be no penalties for late instalments. The penalty for late filing will be based on the number of **complete** months of non-payment, which is two. It will be equal to 7 percent of taxes payable (5 percent, plus 1 percent per month). If, in one of the three preceding taxation years she has committed a similar offence, the penalty could be 14 percent (10 percent, plus 2 percent per month).

Interest will be assessed on the deficient instalments, the balance owing on her filing date, and the penalty assessed for late filing. It will be assessed at the regular prescribed rate plus 4 percent for the period May 1 through July 20, 2014.

Exercise Two - 7 Solution

Not Small CCPC   If we assume that Madco Ltd. is not a small CCPC, the first two instalments would be due on the last day of January and February, 2013. They would be based on the second preceding year and would be $2,667 each ($32,000 ÷ 12). The remaining 10 instalments would be based on the preceding year, less the $5,334 paid in the first two instalments. The amount would be $5,367 [($59,000 - $5,334) ÷ 10] and the instalments would be due on the last day of each month for March to December, 2013.

Small CCPC   If we assume that Madco Ltd. is a small CCPC, the first instalment would be due on March 31, 2013. The amount would be based on the second preceding year and would equal $8,000 ($32,000 ÷ 4). The remaining three instalments would be based on the preceding year, less the amount paid in the first instalment. These payments would be equal to $17,000 [($59,000 - $8,000) ÷ 3]. These payments would be due on the last days of June, September, and December, 2013.

Exercise Two - 8 Solution

Not Small CCPC   If we assume that Fadco is not a small CCPC, the minimum instalments would be based on the estimated taxes payable for the taxation year ending November 30, 2013. The amount would be $1,417 ($17,000 ÷ 12) and the instalments would be due on the last day of each month beginning in December, 2012 and continuing to November, 2013. Note that, if the estimate of tax payable for 2013 is too low, interest will be assessed on the deficiency.

Small CCPC   If we assume that Fadco is a small CCPC, the instalments would be based on the estimated taxes payable for the taxation year ending November 30, 2013. The amount would be $4,250 ($17,000 ÷ 4). These amounts would be due on the last days of February, May, August, and November, 2013.

Exercise Two - 9 Solution

Radco Inc.'s tax return is due six months after the fiscal year end, on July 31, 2013. Unless Radco is able to claim the small business deduction, the final payment on their taxes must be made two months after their year end, on March 31, 2013. If they are eligible for the small business deduction, they can defer the final payment for an additional month, to April 30, 2013, provided their Taxable Income for the preceding taxation year did not exceed $500,000.

Exercise Two - 10 Solution

The notice of objection must be filed by the later of:

- 90 days after the date of mailing of the reassessment (August 13, 2015); or
- one year after the due date for filing the return that is being reassessed (April 30, 2015).

The later of these two dates is August 13, 2015.

Self Study Solution Two - 1

Need For Instalments

Instalments are required when an individual's "net tax owing" exceeds $3,000 in the current year and in either of the two preceding years. In somewhat simplified terms, "net tax owing" is defined as the combined federal and provincial taxes payable, less amounts withheld under ITA 153. Mr. Gore's estimated net tax owing for the three years under consideration is as follows:

2011 = $3,500 ($15,000 - $11,500)
2012 = Nil ($10,800 - $11,750)
2013 = $4,000 ($17,000 - $13,000)   Estimate

As Mr. Gore's net tax owing in 2013 (the current year) and his net tax owing in 2011 (one of the two preceding years) is greater than $3,000, he is required to make instalment payments.

Amounts

Note that the problem does not require the calculation of instalments under the three alternative methods, only the minimum instalments required.

The amount of the instalments could be based on the net tax owing for 2012 or 2013. In addition, the first two instalments could be based on the net tax owing for 2011, with the last two instalments based on the net tax owing for 2012, less the amounts paid in the first two instalments.

However, since net tax owing for 2012 is nil, the best solution for Mr. Gore is to use that year. This means that, even though Mr. Gore meets the requirements for making instalment payments, the minimum amount of the required instalments would be nil.

Due Dates
If Mr. Gore did have to pay instalments, the due dates would have been March 15, June 15, September 15 and December 15.

Self Study Solution Two - 2

Part A
There are three possible payment schedules that could be used by Amalmor Inc. in this situation. The amounts involved are calculated as follows:

Current Year Base   The payments could be 1/12th of the estimated taxes payable for the current year. This amount would be $7,917 ($95,000 ÷ 12).

Preceding Year Base   The payments could be 1/12th of the taxes that were paid in the immediately preceding year. This amount would be $6,667 ($80,000 ÷ 12).

Preceding And Second Preceding Years   A final alternative would be to base the first two payments on 1/12th of the taxes payable in the second preceding year, with the remaining ten payments based on 1/10th of the preceding year's total less the amounts paid in the first two instalments.

The first two instalments would be $5,208 ($62,500 ÷ 12), or a total of $10,416. In the remaining 10 months of the year, the 10 instalments would each be $6,958 [($80,000 - $10,416) ÷ 10].

The last alternative involves the same total as using the preceding year as a base. However, this alternative is preferable as it requires lower payments in the first two months which provides a small amount of tax deferral.

The instalments would be due on the last day of each month in 2013.

Part B
If we assume that Amalmor Inc. is a small CCPC, there would also be three alternative calculations:

Current Year Base   The payments could be 1/4 of the estimated taxes payable for the current year. This amount would be $23,750 ($95,000 ÷ 4).

Preceding Year Base   The payments could be 1/4 of the taxes that were paid in the immediately preceding year. This amount would be $20,000 ($80,000 ÷ 4).

Preceding And Second Preceding Years   A final alternative would be to base the first payment on 1/4 of the taxes paid in the second preceding year, with the remaining three payments based on the preceding year total, less the amounts paid in the first instalment. The first amount would be $15,625 ($62,500 ÷ 4). In the remaining 3 quarters of the year, the payments would be $21,458 [($80,000 - $15,625) ÷ 3].

The last alternative involves the same total as using the preceding year as a base. However, this alternative is preferable as it requires a lower first payment which provides a small amount of tax deferral.

These instalments would be due on the last days of March, June, September, and December, 2013.

Part C
If Amalcor is a public company, any remaining taxes payable must be paid within two months of the Company's year end. This is extended to three months for CCPCs that claim the small business deduction. Since in Part B, Amalcor is small CCPC, it would qualify for the extension.

Note that Amalcor would not have to qualify as a "small" CCPC to get the extension, it would just have to be able to claim the small business deduction which is available only to CCPCs. CCPCs and the small business deduction are covered in detail in Chapter 12.

Self Study Solution Two - 3

Case One

The net tax owing for each of the three years is:

2011 $5,306 ($23,540 - $18,234)

2012 $3,616 ($11,466 - $7,850)

2013   Nil ($25,718 - $27,346)

No instalments are required as the net tax owing for the current year is nil.

Case Two

The net tax owing for each of the three years is as follows:

2011 $1,820 ($23,540 - $21,720)

2012 $5,216 ($11,466 - $6,250)

2013 $3,885 ($25,718 - $21,833)

As the net tax owing for the current year and one of the two preceding years exceeds $3,000, instalment payments are required.

The best alternative would be to use the current year estimate. This would result in quarterly instalment payments of $971 ($3,885 ÷ 4)

While the first two instalments could be based on 2011, the last two payments would result in total instalments of $5,216. This is higher than the $3,885 that would be paid if the current year is used as the instalment base. This means that using the current year as the instalment base would be the best solution.

The payments would be due on March 15, June 15, September 15, and December 15, 2013.

Case Three

As the corporation's tax payable for both the current and the preceding year exceeds $3,000, instalments are required.

The best choice would be to use the previous year as the instalment base. As the corporation is a small CCPC, the instalments would be quarterly. The amount would be $2,867 ($11,466 ÷ 4).

The instalments would be due on the last days of March, June, September, and December, 2013.

Case Four

As the corporation's tax payable for both the current and the preceding year exceeds $3,000, instalments are required.

Given the assumption that the 2012 taxes payable were $32,560, the best choice is to use the current year as the base. Because the corporation is not a small CCPC, the instalments will be monthly. This would result in instalment payments of $2,143 ($25,718 ÷ 12).

While the first two instalments could be based on 2011 which had a lower taxes payable than the current year, the last 10 payments would have to result in instalments totaling $32,560. This is significantly higher than the $25,718 that would be paid if the current year is used as the instalment base.

The instalments would due at the end of each month beginning January, 2013.

Self Study Solution Two - 4

Case A
The individual's net tax owing in each of the three years is as follows:

2011 = $6,000 ($18,000 - $12,000)
2012 = $4,400 ($14,400 - $10,000)
2013 = $3,500 ($13,500 - $10,000)

As the individual's net tax owing is expected to exceed $3,000 in 2013 and was more than $3,000 in both 2011 and 2012, the payment of instalments is required.

Using the 2013 estimate would result in minimum instalment payments. Based on this year, the required quarterly instalments would be $875 ($3,500 ÷ 4).

They would be due on March 15, June 15, September 15, and December 15. They would total $3,500.

Case B
The individual's net tax owing in each of the three years is as follows:

2011 = $11,000 ($18,000 - $7,000)
2012 = Nil (Withholdings Exceed Tax Payable)
2013 = $4,500 ($13,500 - $9,000)

As the individual's net tax owing is expected to exceed $3,000 in 2013 and was more than $3,000 in 2011, the payment of instalments is required.

Using the 2012 net tax owing would result in minimum instalment payments. Based on this year, the required quarterly instalments would be nil.

Case C
The corporation's Tax Payable for the three years is as follows:

2011 = $18,000
2012 = $14,400
2013 = $13,500

As the corporation's tax payable for both the current and the preceding year exceeds $3,000, instalments are required.

Using the estimated Tax Payable for the current year would result in the minimum instalment payments. As the corporation is a small CCPC, the required instalments would be quarterly. The amount would be $3,375 ($13,500 ÷ 4).

They would be due on the last days of March, June, September, and December, 2013.

Case D
The corporation's Tax Payable for the three years is as follows:

2011 = $18,000
2012 = $14,400
2013 = $16,000

As the corporation's tax payable for both the current and the preceding year exceeds $3,000, instalments are required.

Using the estimated Tax Payable for 2012 would result in minimum instalment payments. As the corporation is not a small CCPC, the required instalments would be monthly. The amount would be $1,200 ($14,400 ÷ 12). They would be due on the last day of each month, beginning in January, 2013. While the first two instalments could have been based on 2011, this would not have been advantageous as the Tax Payable for that year of $18,000 is great than $14,400.

Self Study Solution Two - 5

The three taxable entities are individuals, corporations, and trusts. The required information for each is as follows:

Individuals For individuals, the taxation year is the calendar year. For individuals without business income, the filing deadline is April 30 of the following year. Individuals with business income, and their spouse or common-law partner, have an extended filing deadline of June 15.

If an individual dies after October, the due date of the return for the year of death is extended to 6 months after the date of death. Instalment payments for all individuals, if required, are to be made quarterly on March 15, June 15, September 15, and December 15.

Corporations Corporations can choose any fiscal year that does not exceed 53 weeks. The filing deadline is six months after the fiscal year end. In general, corporations must make instalments on the last day of each month. However, if the corporation qualifies as a small CCPC, quarterly instalments are required on the last day of the last month of each 3 month period in the corporation's taxation year.

Trusts
- **Testamentary** trusts can choose any fiscal year not exceeding 12 months. Their filing deadline is 90 days after the fiscal year end and they are not required to pay instalments.
- **Inter vivos** trusts must use a calendar year. They are also required to file within 90 days of the year end and quarterly instalment payments are required under the same rules as those used by individuals. However, this requirement appears to be waived on an administrative basis.

Self Study Solution Two - 6

With respect to resolving the dispute, a first step may involve nothing more than a call to the CRA to discuss the matter. If Mr. Coffee feels that there has been a misunderstanding that can be resolved by providing a more detailed explanation of the relevant facts, this may be the only step required. However, in some cases more formal steps will be necessary and they can be outlined as follows:

Notice of Objection As the reassessment relates to the previous year's tax return, it is within the three year time limit and, therefore, a legitimate procedure for the Minister. This means that within 90 days of the mailing date on the notice of reassessment or (as Mr. Coffee is an individual) one year from the due date for the return under reassessment, a notice of objection can be filed. This objection, or Form T400A, should be sent by registered mail and should explain the facts and reasons why Mr. Coffee does not agree with the reassessment.

Tax Court of Canada If there is an adverse decision on the notice of objection, Mr. Coffee has up to 90 days after the mailing date of the response to the notice of objection to appeal to the Tax Court of Canada. Alternatively, if he does not receive a response to his notice of objection within 90 days, he will then be able to appeal to the Tax Court of Canada. As the amount involved is only $5,000, it would probably be advisable for Mr. Coffee to choose the informal procedures.

Federal Courts If Mr. Coffee has elected the informal Tax Court of Canada procedures, no appeal of an adverse decision is possible. An appeal to the Federal Court - Appeals Division would, however, be possible if an adverse decision was rendered under the general procedures. In theory, an adverse decision by the Federal Court could be appealed to the Supreme Court of Canada. However, this can only happen if the Federal Court recommends it or the Supreme Court authorizes such action. This would be extremely unlikely given the amount involved.

If you are to become involved in representing Mr. Coffee's interest in this matter, a signed Consent Form, T1013, which would give you authorization to discuss the case with the CRA would have to be on file with the CRA.

Chapter 2 Learning Objectives

After completing Chapter 2, you should be able to:

1. Explain when an individual is required to file an income tax return (paragraph [P hereafter] P 2-8 through 2-13).

2. List the dates on which income tax returns must be filed by living and deceased individuals (P 2-14 through 2-19).

3. Explain the nature of, and need for, source deductions P 2-20 through 2-26).

4. Explain the circumstances which result in an individual having to make income tax instalment payments (P 2-27 through 2-31).

5. Calculate the amount of any income tax instalment payments required for individual taxpayers and determine their due date (P 2-32 through 2-42).

6. Explain how the prescribed interest rate is used to calculate interest on late or insufficient income tax payments for individuals (P 2-43 through 2-49).

7. Calculate the penalties that will be assessed for the late filing of individual income tax returns (P 2-50 through 2-54).

8. Identify the dates on which balances owing by living and deceased individuals are due (P 2-55 and 2-59).

9. Identify the dates on which income tax returns must be filed by corporations and the filing alternatives that are available (P 2-60 through 2-66).

10. Calculate the amount of income tax instalment payments required for corporations, including small CCPCs (P 2-67 through 2-73).

11. Identify the dates on which balances owing by corporations are due (P 2-74 and 2-75).

12. Calculate the interest and penalties that will be assessed on late tax payments and for the late filing of corporate income tax returns (P 2-76 through 2-79).

13. Explain the general filing and payment requirements for testamentary and inter vivos trusts (P 2-80 through 2-83).

14. Explain the circumstances in which a taxpayer is required to file an information return (P 2-84).

15. Explain when interest is paid on refunds and how it is calculated (P 2-85 through 2-90).

16. Describe the record keeping requirements of the CRA (P 2-91 and 2-92).

17. Describe the process of assessment, reassessment and adjustments to income tax returns for all taxpayers (P 2-93 through 2-102).

18. Explain the initial procedures for disputing an assessment and the procedures for filing a notice of objection (P 2-103 through 2-115).

19. Describe further appeals procedures, including those made to the Tax Court of Canada, the Federal Court of Appeals, and the Supreme Court of Canada (P 2-116 through 2-125).

20. Explain the difference between tax evasion, avoidance and planning, including the concepts involved in the General Anti-Avoidance Rule (P 2-126 through 2-139).

21. Describe the collection and enforcement procedures available to the CRA (P 2-140 through 2-145).

22. Describe some of the penalties that can be assessed including those applicable to tax preparers and promoters (P 2-146 through 2-152).

23. Briefly describe the taxpayer relief provisions (P 2-153 through 2-156).

CHAPTER 3

How To Work Through Chapter 3

We recommend the following approach in dealing with the material in this chapter:

Employment Income Defined
- ❑ Read paragraph 3-1 to 3-11 (in the textbook).
- ❑ Do Exercise Three-1 (in the textbook) and check the solution on page S-27 in this Study Guide.
- ❑ Do Self Study Problem Three-1 at the end of the textbook chapter on page 118 and check the solution in this Study Guide.
- ❑ Read paragraph 3-12 to 3-13.

Employee Versus Self-Employed
- ❑ Read paragraph 3-14 to 3-44.
- ❑ Do Self Study Problem Three-2 and check the solution in this Study Guide.

Salaries And Fringe Benefits
- ❑ Read paragraph 3-45 to 3-53.
- ❑ Do Exercise Three-2 and check the solution in this Study Guide.
- ❑ Read paragraph 3-54 to 3-60.
- ❑ Do Exercise Three-3 and check the solution in this Study Guide.
- ❑ Read paragraph 3-61 to 3-73.
- ❑ Do Exercise Three-4 and check the solution in this Study Guide.

GST/HST/PST On Taxable Benefits
- ❑ Read paragraph 3-74 to 3-75.
- ❑ Do Exercise Three-5 and check the solution in this Study Guide.

Board And Lodging
- ❑ Read paragraph 3-76 to 3-78.

Automobile Benefits (Standby Charge And Operating Cost Benefit)
- ❑ Read paragraph 3-79 to 3-116.
- ❑ Do Exercise Three-6 and check the solution in this Study Guide.
- ❑ Read paragraph 3-117 to 3-122.
- ❑ Do Exercise Three-7 and check the solution in this Study Guide.
- ❑ Read paragraph 3-123 to 3-124.
- ❑ Do Self Study Problems Three-3 and Three-4 and check the solutions in this Study Guide.

Allowances
- ❑ Read paragraph 3-125 to 3-137.
- ❑ Do Exercise Three-8 and Three-9 and check the solutions in this Study Guide.
- ❑ Read paragraph 3-138 to 3-142.
- ❑ Do Exercise Three-10 and check the solution in this Study Guide.

Employee Insurance Benefits
❑ Read paragraph 3-143 to 3-148.
❑ Do Exercise Three-11 and check the solution in this Study Guide.
❑ Read paragraph 3-149 to 3-151.

Loans To Employees
❑ Read paragraph 3-152 to 3-157.
❑ Do Exercise Three-12 and check the solution in this Study Guide.
❑ Read paragraph 3-158 to 3-162.
❑ Do Exercise Three-13 and check the solution in this Study Guide.
❑ Do Self Study Problem Three-5 and check the solution in this Study Guide.

Stock Option Benefits
❑ Read paragraph 3-163 to 3-177.
❑ Do Exercise Three-14 and check the solution in this Study Guide.
❑ Read paragraph 3-178 to 3-182.
❑ Do Exercise Three-15 and check the solution in this Study Guide.
❑ Do Self Study Problem Three-6 and Three-7 and check the solution in this Study Guide.

Other Inclusions
❑ Read paragraph 3-183 to 3-193.

Specific Deductions Including Salesperson's Expenses And Home Office Costs
❑ Read paragraph 3-194 to 3-210.
❑ Do Exercise Three-16 and check the solution in this Study Guide.
❑ Read paragraph 3-211 to 3-220.
❑ Do Self Study Problems Three-8 to Three-12 and check the solutions in this Study Guide.

To Complete This Chapter
❑ Review the Key Terms Used In This Chapter on page 117 of the text. Consult the Glossary for the meaning of any key terms you do not know.
❑ Review the Glossary Flashcards and complete the Key Terms Self-Test for the Chapter. These features can be found in two places, on your Student CD-ROM under the heading "Key Term Practice" and on the web site.
❑ Review the Learning Objectives of the Chapter found on page S-46 of this Study Guide.
❑ As a final review, we recommend that you view the PowerPoint Slides for Chapter 3 that are on your Student CD-ROM. The PowerPoint Viewer program can be installed from the Student CD-ROM.

Practice Examination
❑ Write the Practice Examination for Chapter 3 that is on your Student CD-ROM. Mark your examination using the Practice Examination Solution that is also on your Student CD-ROM.

Solution to Chapter Three Exercises

Exercise Three - 1 Solution
The bonus will be taxed in Mr. Neelson's hands in the year of receipt. This means that it will be included in his 2014 tax return. With respect to Neelson Inc., the bonus is not payable until more than 180 days after the September 30 fiscal year end. As a consequence, the Company will not be able to deduct the bonus in the year ending September 30, 2013, the year of declaration. It will be deducted in the year ending September 30, 2014, the year of payment.

Solution to Chapter Three Exercises

Exercise Three - 2 Solution

The tax consequences associated with each of the listed items are as follows:

Gift	Tax Consequence
$15 T-Shirt	No consequences as value is immaterial
$75 Birthday Gift	Taxable as it is a near cash gift
$400 Performance Reward	Taxable as it is performance related
$275 10-Year Award	Non-taxable as it is under $500
$300 Wedding Gift	These remaining three gifts qualify as non-taxable. However, their total value is $700 ($300 + $250 + $150). The $200 excess over $500 will be taxable.
$250 Weight Loss Award	
$150 Holiday Season Gift	

Exercise Three - 3 Solution

The tax consequences of the various items would be as follows:

- IT-470R indicates that discounts on employer merchandise are not a taxable benefit.
- It could be argued that these tuition fees involve "general employment-related training" as described in IT-470R. If the argument is successful, the payment would not be taxable to John. If unsuccessful, the $2,000 would be a taxable benefit.
- While IT-470R indicates that uniforms or special clothing is not a taxable benefit, it is unlikely that business clothing would fall into this category as it could be used for personal purposes. The $8,500 should be included in John's income as a taxable benefit.
- The $450 gift would not be taxable to John.
- ITA 6(1)(a) indicates that premiums on private health care plans are not a taxable benefit.

Exercise Three - 4 Solution

From Jill's point of view, the best alternative is probably the dental plan. Its value is significantly enhanced by the fact that it can be received without tax consequences. The annual vacation trip is clearly a taxable benefit. With respect to the $4,000 birthday gift, the $3,500 excess over the limit of $500 will be taxable. Note that the desirability of the dental plan would be affected by whether her spouse has a dental plan.

Exercise Three - 5 Solution

Ms. Correli's taxable benefit would be $4,725, the $4,500 cost of the trip, plus the additional $225 in GST.

Exercise Three - 6 Solution

As Mrs. Lee's employment related use is more than 50 percent of the total (16,000 out of 28,000), she is eligible for a reduction in the full standby charge. She is also eligible for the alternative one-half of the standby charge calculation of the operating cost benefit. Given these factors, the taxable benefit would be calculated as follows:

Standby Charge
$[(2\%)(12)(\$25,000 + \$1,250 + \$2,000)(12,000 \div 20,004*)]$ $4,067
Operating Cost Benefit - Lesser Of:
- $[(\$0.27)(12,000)] = \$3,240$
- $[(1/2)(\$4,067)] = \$2,034$ 2,034

Total Benefit $6,101

*$[(12 \text{ Months})(1,667)]$

Exercise Three - 7 Solution

The actual operating costs paid by the employer do not affect these calculations. Rounded to the nearest whole number, 325 days results in 11 months of availability. As Mr. Forthwith's employment related use is more than 50 percent, he is eligible for a reduction in the full standby charge. He is also eligible for the alternative one-half of the standby charge calculation of the operating cost benefit. Given these factors, the taxable benefit would be calculated as follows:

Standby Charge [(2/3)(12)($525 + $68)(11/12)(3,000 ÷ 18,337*)] $ 711
Operating Cost Benefit - Lesser Of:
- [($0.27)(3,000)] = $810
- [(1/2)($711)] = $356   356

Total Benefit	$1,067

*[(11)(1,667)]

Exercise Three - 8 Solution

Because the allowance is not based on kilometers driven, she will have to include the $3,600 allowance in her income. Because the allowance has been included in income, she can deduct the employment related portion of her actual automobile costs against this amount. This would be $1,936 [($7,150)(6,500 ÷ 24,000)]. The net inclusion would be $1,664 ($3,600 - $1,936).

Exercise Three - 9 Solution

As the milage allowance paid by the employer was based on the number of employment related kilometers driven, the $3,500 [(35,000 Km.)($0.10)] will not be included on his T4 Information Return and, as a consequence, it does not have to be included in his employment income. However, he will not be able to deduct his actual costs of owning and operating the automobile.

Mr. Lorenz's actual deductible costs total $11,900 [($5,400 + $15,000)(35,000/60,000)], well in excess of the allowance of $3,500. While Mr. Lorenz could attempt to include the allowance in income and deduct the actual costs, this approach could be disallowed by the CRA.

Exercise Three - 10 Solution

The hotel allowance would appear to be reasonable and would not be included in Ms. Ohm's T4. Given this, it will not be included in her net employment income. Even though her actual costs of $18,300 are in excess of the $16,400 allowance, it would be difficult for Ms. Ohm to argue that the $200 figure is not reasonable. Given this, she does not have the choice of including the $16,400 in income and deducting the actual amount of $18,300.

As the milage charge is based on kilometers, it will not be included in her T4. In addition, since the amount appears to be reasonable in terms of actual costs, she does not have the choice of including it in income and deducting the actual costs. In fact, it would not be to Ms. Ohm's advantage to do so as her actual costs would be $2,880 [($7,200)(9,400/23,500)], which is less than the $3,854 payment she received.

No amounts would be included in Ms. Ohm's net employment income and no amounts would be deductible.

Solution to Chapter Three Exercises

Exercise Three - 11 Solution

As his employer contributes to the plan and the contributions do not create a taxable benefit, the $5,250 in benefits received during the year will be included in his employment income. This will be reduced by the $600 [(2)($300)] in non-deductible contributions that he made during 2012 and 2013, leaving a net inclusion of $4,650 ($5,250 - $600).

Exercise Three - 12 Solution

Whether or not the loan qualifies as a home relocation loan would make no difference in the calculation of Mrs. Caldwell's taxable benefit. The only difference would be the availability of a deduction from Taxable Income in the case of the home relocation loan.

The ITA 80.4(1) benefit is calculated as follows:

The Lesser Of:
- [($100,000)(2%)(1/4) + ($100,000)(3%)(1/4) + ($100,000)(1%)(2/4)] = $1,750
- [($100,000)(2%)] = $2,000

The Lesser Of	$1,750
Less Interest Payment [($100,000)(1%)]	(1,000)
Net Benefit	$ 750

As this is a home purchase loan, the annual benefit cannot exceed the benefit that would result from applying the 2 percent rate that was in effect when the loan was made. Note that the 2 percent rate is not compared to the prescribed rate on a quarter-by-quarter basis, but on an annual basis. The lower figure of $1,750 would then be reduced by the $1,000 in interest paid.

Exercise Three - 13 Solution

In the absence of the interest free loan, the employee would borrow $125,000 at 5 percent, requiring an annual interest payment of $6,250. The after tax cash outflow associated with the employer providing sufficient additional salary to carry this loan would be calculated as follows:

Required Salary [$6,250 ÷ (1 - 0.42)]	$10,776
Corporate Tax Savings From Deducting Salary [($10,776)(26%)]	(2,802)
Employer's After Tax Cash Flow - Additional Salary	$ 7,974

Alternatively, if the loan is provided, the employee will have a taxable benefit of $2,500 [(2%)($125,000)], resulting in taxes payable of $1,050 [(42%)($2,500)]. To make this situation comparable to the straight salary alternative, the employer will have to provide the employee with both the loan amount and sufficient additional salary to pay the taxes on the imputed interest benefit. The amount of this additional salary would be $1,810 [$1,050 ÷ (1 - 0.42)]. The employer's after tax cash flow associated with providing the additional salary and the loan amount would be calculated as follows:

Required Salary [$1,050 ÷ (1 - 0.42)]	$1,810
Corporate Tax Savings From Deducting Salary [($1,810)(26%)]	(471)
After Tax Cost Of Salary To Cover Taxes On Benefit	$1,339
Employer's Lost Earnings [(7%)(1 - 0.26)($125,000)]	6,475
Employer's After Tax Cash Flow - Loan	$7,814

Given these results, providing the loan appears to be the better alternative.

Exercise Three - 14 Solution

At time of exercise, Mr. Guise will have an employment income benefit of $21,250 [($31.50 - $23.00)(2,500 Shares)]. As the option price at issue exceeded the fair market value at issue, Mr. Guise will be able to deduct $10,625 [(1/2)($21,250)] in the determination of Taxable Income. These results are summarized in the following table:

Fair Market Value Of Shares Acquired [(2,500)($31.50)]	$78,750
Cost Of Shares [(2,500)($23)]	(57,500)
ITA 7(1)(a) Employment Income Inclusion =	
Increase In Net Income For Tax Purposes	**$21,250**
ITA 110(1)(d) Deduction [(1/2)($21,250)]	(10,625)
Increase In Taxable Income	**$10,625**

In addition, there will be an allowable capital loss of $4,375 [($31.50 - $28.00)(2,500 Shares)(1/2)]. Mr. Guise will only be able to deduct this loss in 2013 to the extent that he has taxable capital gains on other dispositions. It cannot be deducted against the employment income inclusion.

Exercise Three - 15 Solution

There will be no tax consequences in either 2009 when the options are received, or in 2012, when the options are exercised. This latter result reflects the fact that the acquired shares are those of a Canadian controlled private corporation.

At the time the shares are sold in 2013, there will be an employment income benefit of $58,500 [($75.00 - $42.50)(1,800 Shares)]. As the option price of $42.50 was below the fair market value of $45 at the time the options were issued, there is no deduction under ITA 110(1)(d). Although she could have been eligible for the deduction under ITA 110(1)(d.1), she did not hold the shares for the required two years. These results are summarized in the following table:

Deferred Employment Income:	
Fair Market Value Of Shares Acquired [(1,800)($75)]	$135,000
Cost Of Shares [(1,800)($42.50)]	(76,500)
ITA 7(1)(a) Employment Income Inclusion =	
Increase In Net Income For Tax Purposes	**$ 58,500**
ITA 110(1)(d) Deduction (Option Price < FMV)	N/A
ITA 110(1)(d.1) Deduction (Held Less Than 2 Years)	N/A
Increase In Taxable Income	**$ 58,500**

When she sells the shares, she will have an allowable capital loss of $23,400 [($49.00 - $75.00)(1,800 Shares)(1/2)]. Ms. Van will only be able to deduct this loss in 2013 to the extent that she has taxable capital gains on other dispositions. It cannot be deducted against the employment income inclusion.

Exercise Three - 16 Solution

The potential deduction is $27,100 [$8,000 + (1/2)($12,000) + $13,100]. However, this total exceeds his commissions received and cannot be deducted under ITA 8(1)(f). If he deducts under ITA 8(1)(h), there is no limit on the total. However, he cannot deduct the advertising or the entertainment. Further, he cannot make any deduction under ITA 8(1)(h) if he makes any deduction under ITA 8(1)(f).

As the travel costs that are deductible under ITA 8(1)(h) exceed the $12,200 limited deduction under ITA 8(1)(f), his maximum deduction is the $13,100 in travel costs that can be deducted under ITA 8(1)(h).

Self Study Solution Three - 1

The required information for the four Cases included in this problem is as shown in the following table:

	Deduction - Empire Inc. Year Ending October 31	Inclusion-Ms. Betz Calendar Year
Case A	2013	2013
Case B	2013	2014
Case C	2014	2014
Case D	2013	2013

In Case A, the bonus is deducted when accrued because it is received within 180 days of Empire's 2013 year end. It is taxed when received.

In Case B, the bonus is deducted when accrued because it is received within 180 days of Empire's 2013 year end. It is taxed when received.

In Case C, the bonus is not paid within 180 days of Empire's year end. As a consequence, it cannot be deducted until the year ending October 31, 2014. However, as it is paid within 3 years of Empire's 2013 year end it is not a salary deferral arrangement. This means it does not have to be included in Ms. Betz's Taxable Income until 2014.

In Case D, the bonus is not paid until more than 3 years after the end of the calendar year in which Ms. Betz rendered the services. This makes it a salary deferral arrangement, resulting in Ms. Betz having to include it in her 2013 Taxable Income. Empire will deduct the bonus in the fiscal year ending October 31, 2013.

Self Study Solution Three - 2

Quantitative Considerations

If the individual's services are acquired as an employee, the 2013 costs would be as follows:

Basic Salary	$250,000
Company Benefits [($250,000)(8%)]	20,000
CPP (Maximum)	2,356
Employer's Share Of EI [(1.4)(1.88%)($47,400)]	1,248
Payroll Tax [(2%)($250,000)]	5,000
Total Cost	$278,604

This is very close to the $280,000 that would have to be paid to the individual if he is classified as an independent contractor.

Other Considerations

While the quantitative factors slightly favour employee classification, this is probably not the best choice. Other factors that should be considered:

- self-employed status relieves the company from any ongoing commitment beyond the period specified in the contract,
- Farnham Ltd. would not be legally responsible for any errors in the work of the engineer if he is self-employed,
- the fact that employment contracts usually require that salary and related benefits grow over time, and
- the added administrative costs of withholding amounts from his salary if he is an employee.

It would appear to be more advantageous to structure the arrangement so that this individual qualifies as an independent contractor.

Self Study Solution Three - 3

Acura TL

With employment related usage at more than 50 percent of the total, Ms. Vines can reduce the standby charge on the basis of actual personal usage and Ms. Vines can calculate the operating cost benefit as one-half of the standby charge which results in a lower benefit. The taxable benefit on this vehicle would be calculated as follows:

Standby Charge [(2%)($39,000 + $1,950 + $1,950)(5)(3,400 ÷ 8,335*)]	$1,750
Operating Cost Benefit - Lesser Of:	
• [(3,400)($0.27)] = $918	
• [(1/2)($1,750)] = $875	875
Total Benefit On Acura TL	$2,625

*[(5)(1,667)]

Ford Taurus

The $100 insurance included in the monthly lease payment is removed from the standby charge calculation as it is an operating cost.

As the car was driven more than 50 percent for employment related purposes, a reduction in the standby charge is available (but is nil in this case) and Ms. Vines can calculate the operating cost benefit as one-half of the standby charge which results in a lower benefit. The taxable benefit on this vehicle is calculated as follows:

Standby Charge [(2/3)(6)($699 - $100)(6/6)(10,002* ÷ 10,002*)]	$2,396
Operating Cost Benefit - Lesser Of:	
• [(14,600)($0.27)] = $3,942	
• [(1/2)($2,396)] = $1,198	1,198
Total Benefit On Ford Taurus	$3,594

*[(6)(1,667)] - since the numerator (personal kilometers of 14,600) cannot exceed the denominator, the effect of applying the reduction fraction is nil (10,002 ÷ 10,002).

Total Benefit

The total taxable benefit would be calculated as follows:

Total Benefit - Acura	$2,625
Total Benefit - Ford	3,594
Reimbursement To Company [($0.10)(3,400 Km + 14,600 Km)]	(1,800)
Total Taxable Benefit	$4,419

Notes:

- The taxable benefit calculation is not influenced by restrictions on the amount that the Company can deduct with respect to the Acura.
- Calculation of the operating cost benefits is not influenced by the employer's actual operating costs.

Self Study Solution Three - 4

Mr. Sam Stern

The taxable benefit for the president of the Company would be calculated as follows:

Standby Charge [(2%)($78,000)(8)]	$12,480
Operating Cost Benefit [(32,000)($0.27)]	8,640
Taxable Benefit	$21,120

As Mr. Stern did not drive the car more than 50 percent for employment related purposes, no reduction in the standby charge is available. Since his employment related use was not more than 50 percent, he cannot use the alternative calculation of the operating cost benefit.

Ms. Sarah Blue

The taxable benefit for the marketing vice president would be calculated as follows:

Standby Charge [(2/3)(12)($900)(12/12)(5,000/20,004)]	$1,800
Operating Cost Benefit - Lesser Of:	
• [(5,000)($0.27)] = $1,350	
• [(1/2)($1,800)] = $900	900
Taxable Benefit	$2,700

As employment related driving was more than 50 percent of the total, Ms. Blue can reduce the standby charge on the basis of actual personal usage. As the car was driven more than 50 percent for employment related purposes, Ms. Blue can calculate the operating cost benefit as one-half of the standby charge which results in a lower benefit.

Mr. John Stack

The taxable benefit for the finance vice president would be calculated as follows:

Standby Charge [(2%)($48,000)(12)(10,000/20,004]	$5,759
Operating Cost Benefit - Lesser Of:	
• [(10,000)($0.27)] = $2,700	
•](1/2)($5,759)] = $2,880	2,700
Payment For Use Of Company Car	(7,000)
Taxable Benefit	$1,459

Mr. Stack's employment related driving was more than 50 percent of the total and, as a consequence, he can reduce his standby charge on the basis of actual personal milage. Mr. Stack could have calculated the operating cost benefit as one-half of the standby charge, but this would have resulted in a higher benefit.

Mr. Alex Decker

The taxable benefit for the industrial relations vice president would be calculated as follows:

Standby Charge [(2/3)(12)($500)(10/12)(8,500/16,670)]	$1,700
Operating Cost Benefit - Lesser Of:	
• [(8,500)($0.27)] = $2,295	
• [(1/2)($1,700)] = $850	850
Taxable Benefit	$2,550

As Mr. Decker's employment related driving is more than 50 percent of the total, he can reduce his standby charge on the basis of actual personal milage. While the $10,000 deposit will affect the deductibility of the lease payments by the employer, it does not influence the calculation of the taxable benefit to Mr. Decker. As the car was driven more than 50 percent for employment related purposes, Mr. Decker can calculate the operating cost benefit as one-half of the standby charge which results in a lower benefit.

Tax Planning

With respect to the tax planning of management compensation, two points can be made. First, the question of providing company cars as a method of compensation should be examined on a case-by-case basis.

In situations where a car is owned by the Company and provided to an executive for a fairly long period of time, the taxable benefit assessed may exceed the value of the benefit. For example, over five years, the taxable benefit without regard for operating costs on Mr. Stern's Mercedes could total $93,600 [(2%)(60)($78,000)]. This is more than $15,000 in excess of the cost of the car.

With the limitations on the deductibility of CCA and leasing costs on cars, the after tax cost to the Company of owning and leasing luxury cars can be very high. While a complete analysis of this issue will depend on a number of variables, it is possible that some of these executives would be better off receiving additional amounts of salary and billing the Company for employment related mileage driven in their own cars.

The second point to be made here is that, except in situations where the car is kept for very short periods of time, the employee will be allocated a smaller taxable benefit if the Company were to lease the car rather than buy it. In general, monthly lease payments on a three year lease will tend to be between 2 percent and 2.5 percent of the capital cost of the car.

As the leasing standby charge is based on two-thirds of the monthly lease payment, it is clear that the standby charge under this type of arrangement will be less than the 2 percent per month that is assessed when the Company owns the car. However, for shorter lease terms, the lease payment will be a greater percentage of the capital cost and this relationship may reverse.

Other tax planning techniques would involve any procedure that would reduce the capital cost of purchased cars or the lease payments on leased cars. Such procedures would include high residual values on leasing arrangements and low trade in values assigned to old cars when new ones are purchased. In addition, it might be possible to reduce a taxable benefit, such as the one being allocated to Mr. Stern, by selling his car to a leasing company with an immediate leaseback arrangement. Although large refundable deposits on leasing arrangements would reduce the lease payment and therefore the standby charge, there would be a tax cost to the employer (see Chapter 6).

Self Study Solution Three - 5

Approach

The appropriate comparison in evaluating the interest free loan arrangement would be to determine the cost to the Company of providing the loan and then compare this amount with the cost of providing an equivalent benefit in the form of straight salary. The following analysis calculates the Company's lowest cost route to providing Mr. Malone with the financing required, assuming he is not a shareholder.

Cost Of Providing For Interest Payments On Commercial Loan

As the problem indicates, Mr. Malone can borrow on a loan at a rate of interest of 5 percent. This means that the annual interest payments on $200,000 would amount to $10,000. If the interest is deductible, the after tax cost of this interest would be reduced to $5,500 [($10,000)(1 - .45)].

Mr. Malone is in the 45 percent tax bracket and, if the interest is not deductible, $18,182 [$10,000 ÷ (1 - .45)] of before tax salary would be required to provide the necessary $10,000 in after tax funds. If the interest is deductible, the Company will only have to provide for the $5,500 after tax cost of the loan to Mr. Malone, an amount of $10,000 [$5,500 ÷ (1 - .45)]. The annual cost to the Company of providing for this alternative under both assumptions would be as follows:

	Not Deductible	Deductible
Gross Salary Increase [$10,000 ÷ (1 - .45)]	$18,182	
Gross Salary Increase [$5,500 ÷ (1 - .45)]		$10,000
Reduction In Corporate Taxes (At 40 Percent)	(7,273)	(4,000)
Net Cost To Company - Additional Salary	$10,909	$6,000

Cost Of Providing Interest Free Loan

Mr. Malone would be assessed a taxable benefit on the loan in the amount of imputed interest at the Regulation 4301 rate. The benefit would amount to $4,000 [(2%)($200,000)] for one year. In order to make the two alternatives comparable, if the interest is not deductible, it is necessary to recognize that Mr. Malone would pay an additional $1,800 [(45%)($4,000)] in taxes on this benefit and, as a consequence, the Company would have to pay him an additional $3,273 [$1,800 ÷ (1 - .45)] in salary to provide for this outflow of funds.

If the interest is deductible, the imputed interest would be deemed interest paid. As he is using all of the funds provided to produce investment income, the full amount would be deductible, resulting in no net change in taxes. If this is the case, this alternative only requires looking at the cost of the loan to the company.

The annual cost to the Company of the loan alternative under both assumptions can be calculated as follows:

	Not Deductible	Deductible
Gross Salary Increase [$1,800 ÷ (1 - .45)]	$ 3,273	N/A
Reduction In Corporate Taxes (At 40 Percent)	(1,309)	N/A
Lost Earnings On Funds Loaned (At 18 Percent)	36,000	$36,000
Corporate Taxes On Imputed Earnings (At 40 Percent)	(14,400)	(14,400)
Net Cost To Company - Loan	$23,564	$21,600

Conclusion

On the basis of the preceding analysis, it can be concluded that the Company should provide additional salary rather than providing Mr. Malone with an interest free loan of $200,000 whether or not his interest is deductible. This alternative results in a net annual cost to the Company which is either $12,655 ($23,564 - $10,909) or $15,600 ($21,600 - $6,000) lower. Given the very high earnings rate on funds used by Technocratic, this result is not unexpected.

Self Study Solution Three - 6

Case A

2011 In 2011, the year in which the options are issued, there would be no tax consequences for Ms. Wu.

2012 The tax consequences in 2012 would be as follows:

Fair Market Value At Exercise [(12,000)($31)]	$372,000
Cost Of Shares [(12,000)($22)]	(264,000)
Employment Income Inclusion = Increase In **Net Income For Tax Purposes**	$108,000
Deduction Under ITA 110(1)(d) [(1/2)($108,000)]	(54,000)
Increase In **Taxable Income**	$ 54,000

2013 When the shares are sold in 2013, the tax consequences would be as follows:

Proceeds Of Disposition [(12,000)($28)]	$336,000
Adjusted Cost Base [(12,000)($31)]	(372,000)
Capital Loss	($ 36,000)
Inclusion Rate	1/2
Allowable Capital Loss	($ 18,000)

Ms. Wu will only be able to deduct this loss in 2013 to the extent that she has taxable capital gains on other dispositions.

Case B

2011   There are no tax consequences in 2011.

2012   There are no tax consequences in 2012.

2013   In 2013, the employment income inclusion would be as follows:

Fair Market Value At Exercise [(12,000)($31)]	$372,000
Cost Of Shares [(12,000)($22)]	(264,000)
Employment Income Inclusion = Increase In **Net Income For Tax Purposes**	$108,000
Deduction Under ITA 110(1)(d) [(1/2($108,000)]	(54,000)
Increase In **Taxable Income**	$ 54,000

In addition there would be an allowable capital loss calculated as follows:

Proceeds Of Disposition [(12,000)($28)]	$336,000
Adjusted Cost Base [(12,000)($31)]	(372,000)
Capital Loss	($ 36,000)
Inclusion Rate	1/2
Allowable Capital Loss	($ 18,000)

Ms. Wu will only be able to deduct this loss in 2013 to the extent that she has taxable capital gains on other dispositions.

Self Study Solution Three - 7

Salary From Maritime Trust [(6/12)($105,000)]		$ 52,500
Salary From Bolten [(6/12)($90,000)]		45,000
Total Salaries		$ 97,500
Maritime Trust Stock Options:		
Market Price Of Shares [(5,000)($16)]	$80,000	
Option Price [(5,000)($15)]	(75,000)	5,000
Bolten Financial Services Stock Options (Note 1)		Nil
Automobile Benefit (Note 2):		
Standby Charge [(2%)($40,000)(4)(6,668/6,668)]	$3,200	
Operating Cost Benefit - Lesser Of:		
• [(10,000)($0.27)] = $2,700		
• [(1/2)($3,200)] = $1,600	1,600	4,800
Loan Benefit (Note 3)		2,000
Net Employment Income		$109,300

Notes:

1. As Bolten Financial Services is a Canadian controlled private corporation, the exercise of the options to purchase its common stock does not result in a taxable benefit at the time of exercise. When the shares are sold, he will have to include the difference between the option price and the fair market value at the time of exercise in employment income. Note that Mr. Jurgens will have a related deduction equal to $2,500 [(1/2)($5,000)] under ITA 110(1)(d) when the shares are sold. However, this is a deduction in the determination of Taxable Income and would not alter the amount of net employment income.

2. As Mr. Jurgens' employment related milage is more than 50 percent of the total milage, he can make use of the reduced standby charge formula. In this case, however, his personal usage exceeded the 6,668 [(4)(1,667)] kilometer maximum usage allowed by the reduction, so the reduction is nil. His employment related milage is more than 50 percent of the total and, as a consequence, he can elect to calculate the operating cost benefit as one-half of the standby charge. Since this is less than the amount determined through the usual calculation, it would be the operating cost benefit.

3. The imputed interest on the interest free loan must be included in employment income under the requirements of ITA 6(9), a benefit which is defined in ITA 80.4(1). The amount of the benefit is $2,000 [(2%)($200,000)(6/12)]. Note that there is a deduction under ITA 110(1)(j) for the amount of this benefit which relates to an interest free home relocation loan of $25,000. However, this is a deduction in the calculation of Taxable Income and will not affect the amount of net employment income.

4. The interest and dividend income is not included in the calculation of net employment income.

Self Study Solution Three - 8

Mr. Barth's net employment income for the year would be calculated as follows:

Gross Salary		$ 82,500
Additions:		
Bonus (Note One)	$20,000	
Automobile Benefit (Note Two)	7,520	
Counseling Benefit (Note Three)	1,500	
Imputed Interest Benefit (Note Four)	375	
Stock Option Benefit [($18 - $15)(1,000)] (Note Five)	3,000	32,395
		$114,895
Deductions:		
Registered Pension Plan Contributions	($3,200)	
Professional Dues	(1,800)	(5,000)
Net Employment Income		$109,895

Note One As the bonus is not payable until more than three years after the end of the employer's taxation year, it is a salary deferral arrangement and must be included in income under ITA 6(11).

Note Two Since Mr. Barth's employment related usage is not more than 50 percent, there is no reduction of the full standby charge. In addition, he cannot use the alternative calculation of the operating cost benefit. Given this, the automobile benefit is calculated as follows:

Standby Charge [(2%)($47,500)(10)]	$9,500
Operating Cost Benefit [(6,000)($0.27)]	1,620
Payments Withheld	(3,600)
Taxable Benefit	$7,520

Note Three IT-470R indicates that counseling services, with the exception of those items specified under ITA 6(1), are considered taxable benefits. The items specified under ITA 6(1)(a)(iv) are counseling with respect to mental or physical health or with respect to re-employment or retirement. As a consequence, the counseling on personal finances is a taxable benefit.

Note Four The imputed interest benefit is calculated as follows:

Taxable Benefit [($150,000)(2%)(3/12)]	$750
Reduction For Interest Paid	(375)
Net Addition To Employment Income	$375

Note Five Note that the problem asks for net "employment income". Although Mr. Barth is eligible for the ITA 110(1)(d) deduction of one-half the stock option benefit, it is a deduction in the calculation of Taxable Income and will not affect the amount of net employment income.

Note Six Other items and the reasons for their exclusion would be as follows:

- Any income tax withheld is not deductible.

- CPP contributions, EI premiums, and United Way donations create credits against taxes payable, but are not deductible in the determination of employment income.

- The payments for personal use of the company car are used in the calculation of the taxable benefit associated with this automobile.

Self Study Solution Three - 9

As Ms. Firth paid all of her own operating expenses, there is no taxable benefit for vehicle operating costs. However, she has to include the $7,200 car allowance in income. Given this, she can deduct a pro rata share of her actual expenses. The deduction would be $5,728 [($6,200)(85,000 km ÷ 92,000 km)].

Ms. Firth's total entertainment, meal, and travel expenses that would be deductible under ITA 8(1)(f) are as follows:

Entertainment Expenses [(1/2)($6,500)]	$3,250
Travel Meals [(1/2)($1,300)]	650
Lodging	3,500
Automobile Operating Costs [($6,200)(85,000 ÷92,000)]	5,728
Total Salesperson Expenses	$13,128

As this total is less than her commission income of $14,000, they can all be deducted under ITA 8(1)(f).

Ms. Firth's net employment income for the year would be calculated as follows:

Gross Salary		$72,000
Commission Income		14,000
Additions:		
Disability Insurance Receipts,		
Less Employee's Premium ($2,000 - $250)	$ 1,750	
Car Allowance	7,200	
Automobile Benefit (Note 1)	2,471	
Term Life Insurance Benefit [($1,350)(2/3)]	900	
Low Interest Loan Benefit [($400,000)(2%) - $3,000]	5,000	
Stock Option Benefit [(1,000)($7 - $5)] (Note 2)	2,000	
Travel Allowance	3,600	22,921
Deductions:		
Registered Pension Plan Contributions (Note 3)	($ 3,200)	
Salesperson Expenses (Preceding Calculation)	(13,128)	(16,328)
Net Employment Income		$92,593

Note 1 The personal benefit on the company car would be calculated as follows:

Reduced Standby Charge [(2%)($58,000)(11)(7,000/18,337*)]	$4,871
Operating Costs Benefit	Nil
Total Benefit	$4,871
Less: Payments Withheld By Employer	(2,400)
Taxable Benefit	$2,471

* [(1,667)(11)]

Note 2 Although Ms. Firth would qualify for the deduction of one-half of the stock option benefit under ITA 110(1)(d), it is a deduction from Taxable Income and would not affect the calculation of net employment income.

Note 3 Contributions made to a registered pension plan under the terms of the plan are deductible. The matching contributions made by the employer are not a taxable benefit.

Excluded Items Other items not included and the reason for their exclusion:

• Federal and provincial income taxes withheld are not deductible.

• The purchase of Canada Savings Bonds is a non-deductible capital expenditure. Any interest charged on the payroll deduction purchase is deductible from Net Income For Tax Purposes, but does not affect employment income.

• Employers can provide their employees with a non-cash gift with a value of less than $500 without creating a taxable benefit. The BlackBerry costs less than $500.

• The $2,500 membership to the Mountain Tennis Club paid by the Company for Ms. Firth is not a taxable benefit since the primary beneficiary appears to be the Company.

Self Study Solution Three - 10

Mr. Jones' net employment income would be calculated as follows:

Salary			$25,800
Taxable Benefit From Fishing Trip			2,450
Commission Income			
Sales Commissions		$47,700	
Deductions:			
Airline Tickets	($2,350)		
Office Supplies	(415)		
Client Entertainment			
[(50%)($1,750)]	(875)		
CCA (Note 1)	(2,520)		
Operating Costs (Note 2)	(5,040)	(11,200)	36,500
Net Employment Income			$64,750

Note 1   The deductible capital cost allowance on the car would be calculated as follows:

Full Capital Cost Allowance*	$ 3,600
Employment Related Usage Proportion (35,000/50,000)	70%
Deductible Amount	$ 2,520

*While this subject is not covered until Chapter 5, the maximum capital cost allowance would be calculated as follows:

$$\$3,600 = [(\$24,000)(30\%)(1/2)]$$

Note 2   As the car was used 30 percent on personal matters, only 70 percent of the $7,200 in operating costs would be deductible.

Other Notes

- The laptop computer is a capital expenditure and is not deductible as an expense. Since an employee cannot deduct CCA except for an automobile, musical instrument, or aircraft, the purchase of the laptop computer would not have any effect on either employment income or taxes payable.

- The payment for Blue Cross would be eligible for the medical expenses tax credit, but would not be deductible in the calculation of net employment income. The life insurance premiums would not have any effect on either employment income or taxes payable.

- Discounts for employees on merchandise normally sold by an employer are not generally considered to be a taxable benefit.

Self Study Solution Three - 11

Part A

As Mr. Worthy's income includes commissions, he has a choice of deducting his expenses under a combination of ITA 8(1)(f), (i), and (j) or, alternatively under a combination of ITA 8(1)(h), (h.1), (i), and (j).

Deductions under ITA 8(1)(f) are limited to the amount of commissions earned. Alternatively, traveling costs and motor vehicle costs other than capital costs can be deducted under ITA

8(1)(h) and ITA 8(1)(h.1). Deductions under these provisions are not limited to commission income. As discussed in the text, he cannot use both ITA 8(1)(f) and the combination of ITA 8(1)(h) and (h.1).

As the deduction under ITA 8(1)(f) is limited by commission income, alternative calculations are required to determine the maximum deduction. In the calculations which follow, we have minimized the effect of the commission income limit by listing any item that can be deducted under either ITA 8(1)(f) or ITA 8(1)(i) or (j) under the ITA 8(1)(i) and (j) column.

For example, house utilities and maintenance could be deducted under either ITA 8(1)(f) or 8(1)(i). We have included them under ITA 8(1)(i) in order to minimize the deductions that are limited by commission income.

The required calculations are as follows:

	ITA 8(1)(f) (Limited To $11,000)	ITA 8(1) (h) and (h.1)	ITA 8(1) (i) and (j)
Supplies			
Monthly Charge For Residential Line	-	-	-
Long Distance Telephone Charges	-	-	$ 400
Cellular Phone Airtime	-	-	800
Office Supplies	-	-	295
House Utilities	-	-	485
House Maintenance	-	-	255
Other Work Space In Home Costs			
House Insurance	$ 70	-	-
Property Taxes	265	-	-
Capital Cost Allowance - House	-	-	-
Mortgage Interest	-	-	-
Automobile Costs:			
Operating Costs [(80%)($2,700)]	2,160	2,160	-
Car Interest [(80%)($2,300)]	-	-	1,840
Car CCA [(80%)($2,450)]	-	-	1,960
Entertainment			
Deductible Portion [(50%)($2,550)]	1,275	-	-
Travel Costs			
Hotels	2,850	$2,850	-
Deductible Portion Of Meals [(50%)($900)]	450	450	-
Office Furniture			
Interest	-	-	-
Capital Cost Allowance	-	-	-
Total	$7,070	$5,460	$6,035

Using the preceding calculations, Mr. Worthy's minimum net employment income can be calculated as follows:

Salary		$65,000
Commissions	$11,000	
Expenses Under ITA 8(1)(f) - Limited To Commissions	(7,070)	3,930
Total		$68,930
Expenses Under ITA 8(1)(i) and (j)		(6,035)
Net Employment Income		$62,895

Expenses in excess of commission income cannot be deducted under ITA 8(1)(f). Since the total of the expenses is less than the commissions of $11,000, they can all be deducted. The deduction of automobile capital costs (CCA and financing costs) under ITA 8(1)(j) is permitted without regard to other provisions used.

Notes:

1. The monthly telephone charge is not deductible. The long distance charges and cellular telephone airtime to clients can be deducted. The deduction for supplies can be deducted under ITA 8(1)(f) or (i). They have been deducted under ITA 8(1)(i), which is not limited by the commission income.

2. Only 50 percent of entertainment and meals when traveling are deductible.

3. ITA 8(1)(f) prohibits the deduction of amounts associated with capital assets except as they are permitted under ITA 8(1)(j) and ITA 8(1)(p). These latter Paragraphs only permit interest or capital cost allowance to be deducted when it is related to an automobile, aircraft, or musical instrument. Therefore, the interest and the capital cost allowance on the house and the office furniture would not be deductible against employment income. This is a good illustration of the importance of distinguishing between employment income and business income. While these amounts cannot be deducted against employment income, they would likely be deductible against business income.

4. As the car is used 20 percent for personal purposes, this proportion of the operating costs, capital cost allowance, and interest costs will not be deductible.

5. The deduction for work space in the home costs has been split between ITA 8(1)(i) and (f). Since the maintenance portion can be deducted under ITA 8(1)(i) by any employee, it is not limited by the commission income. The insurance and property tax components are limited as they can only be deducted under ITA 8(1)(f). A limitation, which is not illustrated in this problem, prevents the deduction of home office costs from creating an employment loss. If any of the home office costs had not been deductible during the current year, they could be deducted against employment income in any subsequent year as long as a loss is not created or increased by their deduction.

6. Mr. Worthy's employer must sign Form T2200 certifying that Mr. Worthy is required to incur travel expenses and maintain his own work space. Mr. Worthy must retain this signed form with his records in order to deduct car and home office expenses.

Part B

If Mr. Worthy deducted the ITA 8(1)(f) expenses, they would be limited to his commission income of $4,000. Alternatively, he can use the combination of ITA 8(1)(h) and (h.1). His minimum net employment income under both alternatives can be calculated as follows:

	ITA 8(1)(f)	ITA 8(1)(h)(h.1)
Salary	$65,000	$65,000
Commissions	4,000	4,000
Expenses Under ITA 8(1)(f) - Limited To Commissions	(4,000)	Nil
Subtotal	$65,000	$69,000
Expenses Under ITA 8(1)(h) and (h.1)	Nil	(5,460)
Expenses Under ITA 8(1)(i) and (j)	(6,035)	(6,035)
Net Employment Income	$58,965	$57,505

Using the combination of ITA 8(1)(h), (h.1), (i), and (j) produces a lower net employment income figure. Note that when this approach is used, work space in the home costs are limited to utilities and maintenance. Further, there is no deduction for entertainment costs. However, this approach results in deductions totalling $1,460 ($5,460 - $4,000) more than the amount available using ITA 8(1)(f), (i), and (j) due to the effect of the commission income limit.

Self Study Solution Three - 12

Mitch Lesner's net employment income would be calculated as follows;

Item 1 - Signing Bonus (Note 1)	$10,000
Item 1 - Salary Received (Note 2)	62,550
Item 1 - RPP Contributions	(1,200)
Item 2 - Bonus Received (Note 2)	2,000
Item 6 - Employer Reimbursement Of CGA Dues (Note 3)	628
Item 6 - CGA Dues Paid (Note 3)	(785)
Item 9 - Housing Loss Reimbursement (Note 4)	1,300
Item 10 - Imputed Interest On Housing Loan (Note 5)	170
Item 11 - Stock Option Benefit (Note 6)	1,280
Item 12 - Automobile Benefit (Note 7)	741
Item 13 - Stationery And Supplies	(129)
Item 13 - Long Distance Calls	(74)
Item 13 - Home Office (Note 8)	(563)
Item 14 - Home Office Allowance (Note 9)	1,500
Net Employment Income	$77,418

Note 1   Amounts received prior to, during or after employment are required to be included in employment income when received.

Note 2   Salary and other forms of remuneration such as bonuses are included in income when received regardless of when earned.

Note 3   The reimbursement of employee professional dues is considered a taxable benefit, but the employee is generally entitled to an employment expense deduction for annual professional membership dues under ITA 8(1)(i).

Note 4   Employer-reimbursed housing losses fall into two categories – regular housing losses and eligible housing losses. Eligible housing losses occur when there is an eligible relocation which generally means a relocation or move the expenses of which would qualify for a moving expense deduction had they been paid by the employee. In this case the move is an eligible relocation meaning that the reimbursement qualifies as an eligible housing loss. The employer reimbursed $17,600 [(80%)($22,000)].   The taxable portion of the loss reimbursement is $1,300 [(1/2)($17,600 - $15,000)]. The remaining tax free amount of $16,300 can be calculated as ($17,600 - $1,300) or [$15,000 + (1/2)($17,600 - $15,000)].

Note 5   When an employee receives an interest-free or low interest loan an imputed interest benefit is calculated. The interest benefit is $170 [(1%)($200,000)(31/365)]. There is no reduction in that amount since Mitch is not required to repay any of the interest. As this loan would qualify as a home relocation loan, Mitch will claim a home relocation loan deduction in the calculation of Taxable Income. However, this would have no effect on the required net employment income calculation.

Note 6   Despite the fact that the option price was 20 percent below fair market value, the issuance of the stock options does not create employment income. However, when he exercises the option by purchasing shares, there is a benefit as follows:

Market Value At Exercise Date ($12,800 ÷ 80%)	$16,000
Option Price	(12,800)
Value of Benefit (200 Shares)	$ 3,200
Per Share Benefit ($3,200 ÷ 200)	$16 Per Share

As Oxford Associates is a CCPC, this benefit can be deferred until the shares are sold. As 80 shares are sold, there will be a 2013 net employment income inclusion of $1,280 [(80)($16)]. In addition there is a taxable capital gain of $1,280 {[1/2][$8,960 - (80/200)($16,000)]}. However, capital gains are not a component of net employment income.

Note 7   The kilometers driven in the year total 19,252 (19,414 – 162), of which 5,198 are personal and 14,054 (19,252 - 5,198) are employment related. Since the employment related driving accounts for more than 50 percent (14,054 ÷ 19,252 = 73%), a reduced standby charge is available. The automobile benefit would be calculated as follows:

Standby Charge [(2/3)(8)($430)(8/8)(5,198 ÷ 13,336*)]	$ 894
Operating Cost Benefit - Lesser Of:	
• [($0.27)(5,198)] = $1,403	
• [(1/2)($894)] = $447	447
Total Benefit	$1,341
Reimbursement To Employer [(8)($75)]	(600)
Net Benefit	$ 741

*[(8)(1,667)]

Note 8   Based on floor space, the home office occupies 8.5 percent of the apartment [100 ÷ 1,176]. The home office expenses that may be claimed for the period June 1 to November 30 are the following:

Rent Paid [(6)($960)]	$5,760
Electricity Paid [($870)(6 ÷ 8.5 Months)]	614
Paint	253
Total Eligible Expenses	$6,627
Home Office Use	8.5%
Deductible Expense	$ 563

Note 9   Allowances received are included in employment income unless the allowance is specifically excluded by ITA 6(1)(b). There is no exclusion for this allowance. The amount is $1,500 [(6)($250)].

Comments On Excluded Items

- Item 1 - Income taxes, CPP and EI withheld - These amounts are not deductible. The CPP and EI are eligible for a non-refundable tax credit that will reduce taxes payable.
- Item 2 - Bonus of $5,450 - Salaries and bonuses are not included in income until received. This amount will be included in employment income for 2014.
- Item 3 - Counselling services for mental health - Amounts paid are specifically excluded from benefit taxation.
- Item 4 - Private dental and hospital plan - Group medical plans are generally referred to as Private Health Insurance Plans. Premiums paid by employers are specifically excluded from benefit taxation.
- Item 5 - Employer contributions to an RPP do not result in a taxable benefit at the time of contribution.
- Item 7 - Wedding gifts - The CRA allows employers to make non-cash gifts totalling no more than $500 without including the amount in an employee's income. The employer's half of the gifts totalled $425.
- Item 8 - Squash club fees - Fees to clubs where the primary advantage is to the employer are not considered taxable.

- Item 13 - Home Office and other expenses:
  - No deduction may be claimed for the furniture and the computer by employees
  - Monthly phone charges are not deductible
  - Property insurance can only be claimed by employees earning commissions

Chapter 3 Learning Objectives

After completing Chapter 3, you should be able to:

1. Explain the basic concept of employment income (paragraph [P hereafter] 3-1 through 3-6).

2. Explain the reasons for using, and rules associated with, bonus arrangements for employees (P 3-7 through 3-13).

3. Distinguish between an employee and a self-employed individual earning business income and list the advantages and disadvantages of both classifications (P 3-14 through 3-44).

4. Explain how salaries and fringe benefits in general are taxed (P 3-45).

5. List the benefits that can be excluded from employment income under ITA 6(1)(a) and the benefits that must be included in income under the other Paragraphs in ITA 6(1) (P 3-46 through 3-48

6. Apply the content of IT-470R with respect to the tax status of the various employee benefits described in the Bulletin (P 3-49 through 3-60).

7. Explain the basic elements of tax planning for employee benefits (P 3-61 through 3-73).

8. Describe the effects of GST/HST/PST on taxable benefits (P 3-74 and 3-75).

9. Explain the treatment of board and lodging benefits (P 3-76 through 3-78).

10. Calculate the standby charge and operating cost benefits that apply to employees who are provided with an automobile that is leased or owned by their employer (P 3-79 through 3-122).

11. Explain basic tax planning for company cars (P 3-123 and 3-124).

12. Explain the tax treatment of allowances that are provided by employers to their employees for travel costs (P 3-125 through 3-142).

13. Describe the tax status of various types of insurance benefits that are provided by employers to their employees (P 3-143 through 3-151).

14. Calculate the tax consequences of low-rate or interest free loans to employees (P 3-152 through 3-162).

15. Calculate the tax consequences that result from employees receiving and exercising stock options, and from the subsequent sale of the acquired shares (P 3-163 through 3-182).

16. List and describe other inclusions in employment income (P 3-183 through 3-193).

17. List and describe specific deductions against employment income that are listed in ITA 8 (P 3-194 through 3-214).

18. Explain how deductible home office costs for employees are calculated (P 3-215 through 3-220).

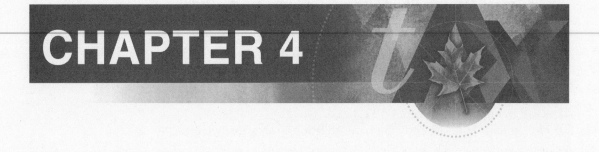

CHAPTER 4

How To Work Through Chapter 4

We recommend the following approach in dealing with the material in this chapter:

Taxable Income Of Individuals
☐ Read paragraph 4-1 to 4-12 (in the textbook).
☐ Do Exercise Four-1 (in the textbook) and check the solution on page S-58 in this Study Guide.
☐ Read paragraph 4-13.

Federal And Provincial Tax Payable Before Credits
☐ Read paragraph 4-14 to 4-26.
☐ Do Exercise Four-2 and check the solution in this Study Guide.
☐ Read paragraph 4-27 to 4-31.

Credits Against Tax Payable - Calculating The Amount
☐ Read paragraph 4-32 to 4-36.

Family Caregiver, Spousal, Eligible Dependant And Child Tax Credits
☐ Read paragraph 4-37 to 4-46.
☐ Do Exercise Four-3 and check the solution in this Study Guide.
☐ Read paragraph 4-47 to 4-59.

Basic Personal, Caregiver And Infirm Dependant Over 17 Tax Credits
☐ Read paragraph 4-60 to 4-65.
☐ Do Exercise Four-4 and check the solution in this Study Guide.
☐ Read paragraph 4-66 to 4-72.
☐ Do Exercise Four-5 and check the solution in this Study Guide.

Eligible Dependant vs. Caregiver vs. Infirm Dependant Over 17 Tax Credits
☐ Read paragraph 4-73 to 4-77.
☐ Do Exercise Four-6 and check the solution in this Study Guide.
☐ Read paragraph 4-78 to 4-81.
☐ Do Exercises Four-7 and Four-8 and check the solutions in this Study Guide.

Age, Pension, Canada Employment And Adoption Expenses Tax Credits
☐ Read paragraph 4-82 to 4-83.
☐ Do Exercise Four-9 and check the solution in this Study Guide.
☐ Read paragraph 4-84 to 4-96.
☐ Do Exercise Four-10 and check the solution in this Study Guide.

Public Transit Passes, Child Fitness, Children's Arts Credit, First Time Home Buyer's And Volunteer Firefighters Tax Credits
❑ Read paragraph 4-97 to 4-112.
❑ Do Exercise Four-10 and check the solution in this Study Guide.
❑ Read paragraph 4-113 to 4-117.

Charitable Donations Credit
❑ Read paragraph 4-118 to 4-132.
❑ Do Exercise Four-12 and check the solution in this Study Guide.

Medical Expense Credit And Refundable Medical Expense Supplement
❑ Read paragraph 4-133 to 4-143.
❑ Do Exercise Four-13 and check the solution in this Study Guide.
❑ Read paragraph 4-144 to 4-147.
❑ Do Exercise Four-14 and check the solution in this Study Guide.

Disability Credit
❑ Read paragraph 4-148 to 4-155.
❑ Do Exercise Four-15 and check the solution in this Study Guide.
❑ Read paragraph 4-156 to 4-159.

Education Related Credits Including Carry Forwards And Transfers
❑ Read paragraph 4-160 to 4-172.
❑ Do Exercise Four-16 and check the solution in this Study Guide.
❑ Read paragraph 4-173 to 4-181.
❑ Do Exercises Four-17 and Four-18 and check the solutions in this Study Guide.

Employment Insurance And Canada Pension Plan Tax Credits
❑ Read paragraph 4-182 to 4-188.

Credit Transfers To A Spouse Or Common-Law Partner
❑ Read paragraph 4-189 to 4-190.
❑ Do Exercise Four-19 and check the solution in this Study Guide.
❑ Do Self Study Problem Four-1 at the end of the textbook chapter beginning on page 181 and check the solution in this Study Guide.

Political Contributions Credit
❑ Read paragraph 4-191 to 4-193.
❑ Do Exercise Four-20 and check the solution in this Study Guide.

Labour Sponsored Funds Credit
❑ Read paragraph 4-194 to 4-196.
❑ Do Exercise Four-21 and check the solution in this Study Guide.
❑ Read paragraph 4-197 to 4-199.
❑ Do Self Study Problems Four-2 to Four-4 and check the solutions in this Study Guide.

Refundable Credits - GST, Working Income Tax Benefit, Canada Child Tax Benefit
❑ Read paragraph 4-200 to 4-212.
❑ Do Exercise Four-22 and check the solution in this Study Guide.
❑ Read paragraph 4-213 to 4-217.

EI And OAS Repayment (Clawback)
❑ Read paragraph 4-218 to 4-228.
❑ Do Exercise Four-23 and check the solution in this Study Guide.

Comprehensive Example
❑ Read paragraph 4-229.
❑ Do Self Study Problems Four-5 to Four-7 and check the solutions in this Study Guide.

Sample Personal Tax Return For Chapter 4
❑ Read the Sample Personal Tax Return For Chapter 4 found on page S-49 to S-53 of this Study Guide. The complete sample tax return is available on the Student CD-ROM in two formats, a T1 ProFile return file and a .PDF file. To view the files, access your Student CD-ROM and under the heading "Textbook Support Files", select the option "Tax Return Files".

In January, 2014, after the first 2013 filing version is released, the updated 2013 sample tax returns and updated Tax Software Problems will be available at:

www.pearsoncanada.ca/byrdchen/ctp2014

Tax Software Self Study Problem
❑ Read the Suggestions For Working With ProFile Software found on page S-53 to S-55 of this Study Guide.
❑ Do Tax Software Self Study Problem - Chapter 4 using the ProFile T1 Software. The Self Study Problem is on page S-56 to S-59 of this Study Guide. The condensed solution is on pages S-79 to S-80 of this Study Guide. The complete tax return is available on the Student CD-ROM.

To Complete This Chapter
❑ Review the Key Terms Used In This Chapter on page 179. Consult the Glossary for the meaning of any key terms you do not know.
❑ Review the Glossary Flashcards and complete the Key Terms Self-Test for the Chapter. These features can be found in two places, on your Student CD-ROM under the heading "Key Term Practice" and on the web site.
❑ Review the Learning Objectives of the Chapter found on page S-81 and S-82.
❑ As a final review, we recommend that you view the PowerPoint Slides for Chapter 4 that are on your Student CD-ROM. The PowerPoint Viewer program can be installed from the Student CD-ROM.

Practice Examination
❑ Write the Practice Examination for Chapter 4 that is on your Student CD-ROM. Mark your examination using the Practice Examination Solution that is also on your Student CD-ROM.

Sample Personal Tax Return For Chapter 4

The following example contains a T1 individual income tax return completed using the ProFile T1 Personal Income Tax Program for 2012 tax returns from Intuit Canada. As software for 2013 is not yet available, this example contains 2012 rates and credits.

The updated 2013 filing version of the ProFile software will be available in January, 2014. Non-filing versions will be available prior to that date, but include a number of 2013 draft forms that have not yet been updated. On installation, the program defaults to check for updates, so non-filing versions may be installed automatically. In January, 2014, after the first 2013 filing version is released, the updated 2013 version of this sample return will be available on the textbook web site at:

www.pearsoncanada.ca/byrdchen/ctp2014

This example is expanded in Chapter 11 to contain other components of Taxable Income and Tax Payable. In the following example, the relevant T1 schedule or ProFile form name is provided in square brackets to make it easier for users to find where the information is input.

Sample Files On Student CD-ROM

The complete sample tax return is available on the Student CD-ROM included with this book in two versions, a T1 ProFile return file and a .PDF file.

To View The Tax Return Files

To view the ProFile return files, you must have the ProFile program installed. For information on how to obtain the program for free, see the inside back cover of Volume 1.

To view the .PDF files, you must have the Adobe Reader program installed. This program can be installed for free from the Adobe website (www.adobe.com).

To view the files, insert your Student CD-ROM and you should see a splash page. Under the heading "Textbook Support Files" is the option to view "Tax Return Files". Select this option and you will see two drop-down lists.

- To view the T4, select "Chapter 4 - T4" from the PDF drop-down list.
- To view the ProFile file, select "Sample - Chapter 4" from the ProFile drop-down list.
- To view the .PDF file of the tax return, select "PDF Sample - Chapter 4" from the PDF drop-down list.

Tips To Increase The Benefits From Viewing The ProFile Files

When viewing the sample return ProFile file, we suggest the following:

- Press <F1> on any ProFile form or field to display related information in the help system. In ProFile dialog boxes, click the [?] symbol in the top right corner, then click any element for help on that item.
- By pressing <F4> you will open the Form Explorer. In the categories of forms appearing in the shaded box on the left, if you choose "A. Used" near the bottom of the column, all the forms that have calculations for the return will be shown. You can then double click on the form itself to view it.
- Right clicking on a number in a field shows a variety of options, including the form or schedule where the amount originated from.
- Clicking on "Show Auditor" under the "Audit" list will display any warnings or potential errors.

For students who would like more assistance in using the software, we have provided "Suggestions For Working With ProFile Software" in this Study Guide following this example.

Sample Problem Data

DISCLAIMER: All characters appearing in this example are fictitious. Any resemblance to real persons, living or dead, is purely coincidental.

George Pilot (SIN 527-000-145) is a married, semi-retired air force pilot living in Banff, Alberta. His wife, Deborah (SIN 130-692-544) was blinded three years ago when she fell while rock climbing.

They have been your clients for many years. George was born on February 24, 1961 and Deborah was born on April 10, 1965. They are both Canadian citizens.

After some discussion with George and Deborah, you confirm that they have never owned any foreign property. As he has for many years, George authorizes the CRA to provide information to Elections Canada and he authorizes you to e-file his return. They are currently living at 69 BBB Street in Banff, Alberta T9Z 0C0. Their home phone number is (403) 111-1111.

George and Deborah have three children:

- Bryan (SIN 527-000-947) was born on March 12, 2005 and had no income during the year.

- Janice (SIN 527-000-269) was born on June 6, 1999 and is in high school. She had income from babysitting totalling $400 during 2012.

- Willa (SIN 527-000-228) was born on January 22, 1993 and is attending university in Edmonton. Willa had Net Income of $3,300 during 2012.

George loves flying and was hired in February to fly fire bombers June 1 to September 30 for the provincial forest service fire control squad located in Banff.

George informs you that on February 12, 2012, he received $2 million from his mother's estate. Using some of these funds, George bought a house in Banff. The remainder of the funds were invested with his stockbroker, $$$$ Inc. In this Chapter 4 version of the example, assume there is no investment income from these funds.

Deborah had no income during the year. Only George will be filing a tax return.

George brings you the following receipts and documents:

1. A T4 (included on the Student CD - see "Chapter 4 - T4" from the PDF drop-down list).

2. A T2202A "Tuition And Education Amounts Certificate" for himself from Athabasca University. It showed he was a part time student for 6 months and paid $591 in tuition for 2012. [T2202]

3. A receipt for $1,000 from the Canadian Wildlife Federation dated December 3, 2012. [Donations]

4. A statement from the Banff Dental Clinic that he paid a total of $1,650 during 2012. This consisted of $850 for himself on November 24, and $200 each for Deborah, Bryan, Willa and Janice on December 15. [Medical]

5. One receipt for Bryan for a one week hockey camp in Edmonton. The registration fee of $650 includes $182 for accommodation and $193 for meals. A second receipt for Bryan of $200 for membership in the co-ed soccer club. This enabled Bryan to participate in the club's weekly games for four months of the year. [Dependants]

6. One receipt for Janice for an art appreciation and sculpture workshop course in Banff. The course is for 10 Saturdays in the fall and cost $600. [Dependants]

7. Twelve monthly bus passes that were purchased during 2012 by Janice for $30 per month. [OtherCredits]

8. An agreement of purchase and sale for a house at 69 BBB St. in Banff. The purchase price was $800,000 and the invoice for legal fees totalled $1,200. The deal closed March 31, 2012. George and his family had been living in a rented townhouse for the last 5 years. Prior to that George had owned a house, but it went to his ex-wife in the divorce settlement. Deborah has never owned a principal residence. [OtherCredits for the Home Buyers' Credit.]

9. An instalment statement for 2012 that showed that George had paid the CRA instalments of $1,500 on September 15 and December 15 ($3,000 in total). These were the instalments requested by the CRA for the year due to his self-employed income in the previous year. [OtherCredits]

Required: With the objective of minimizing George's Tax Payable, complete his 2012 tax return. Ignore any GST implications.

Sample Return

On the following page you will find George's T1 Summary. The complete return can be found on the Student CD-ROM.

2012 Tax Summary (Federal)

George-Chapter 4 Example

George-Chapter 4 Example

Total income

Employment *	101	19,000
Old Age Security	113	
CPP/QPP benefits	114	
Other pensions	115	
Split-pension amount	116	
Universal Child Care Benefit	117	
Employment Insurance	119	
Taxable dividends	120	
Interest	121	
Limited partnership	122	
RDSP	125	
Rental	126	
Taxable capital gains	127	
Support payments	128	
RRSP	129	
Other	130	
Self-employment *	135	
Workers' compensation and social assistance	147	
Total income	**150**	**19,000**

Net income

RPP	207	900
RRSP *	208	
Split-Pension Deduction	210	
Union and professional dues	212	110
UCCB repayment	213	
Child care expenses	214	
Disability supports deduction	215	
Business investment loss	217	
Moving expenses	219	
Support payments	220	
Carrying charges and interest	221	
CPP/QPP/PIPP *	222	
Exploration and development	224	
Employment expenses	229	
Social benefits repayment	235	
Other deductions *	231	
Net income	**236**	**17,990**

Taxable income

Canadian Forces personnel	244	
Home relocation loan	248	
Security options deductions	249	
Other payments deduction	250	
Losses of other years *	251	
Capital gains deduction	254	
Northern residents	255	
Additional deductions	256	
Taxable income	**260**	**17,990**

2013 Estimated

George-Chapter 4 Example

GST/HST credit	808 00
Child Tax Benefit	8,327 00
RRSP contribution limit	1,600 00

* More than one line is considered

Non-refundable tax credits

Basic personal amount	300	10,822
Age amount	301	
Spouse / eligible dependant *	303	12,822
Amount for children	367	4,382
Infirm/caregiver *	306	
CPP/QPP/PPIP/EI *	308	1,115
Volunteer firefighters' amount	362	
Canada employment amount	363	1,095
Public transit passes amount	364	360
Children's fitness amount	365	475
Children's arts amount	370	500
Home buyers/Home renovation *	369	5,000
Adoption expenses	313	
Pension income amount	314	
Disability amount	316	
Transfers *	318	7,546
Interest on student loans	319	
Tuition / education	323	
Medical expenses	332	1,011
Subtotal	**335**	**45,128**
Credit at 15%	338	6,769
Donations and gifts	349	
Non-refundable tax credits	**350**	**6,769**

Total payable

Federal tax	404	2,699
Non-refundable tax credits	350	6,769
Dividend tax credit	425	
Min. tax carry-over/other *	426	
Basic federal tax	**429**	
Non resident surtax		
Foreign tax credits / other	405	
Federal tax	**406**	
Political/inv. tax credit/other *	410	
Labour-sponsored tax credit	414	
Alternative minimum tax	417	
WITB Prepayment (RC210)	415	
Special Taxes	418	
Net federal tax	**420**	
CPP contributions payable	421	
EI self-employment	430	
Social benefits repayment	422	
Provincial/territorial tax	428	
Total payable	**435**	

Total credits

Income tax deducted *	437	2,000
QC or YT abatement *	440	
CPP/EI overpayment *	448	
Medical expense supplement	452	253
WITB (Schedule 6)	453	1,250
Other credits *	454	
GST/HST rebate	457	
Instalments	476	3,000
Provincial tax credits	479	
Total credits	**482**	**6,503**

Balance owing (refund)	(6,503)
Combined balance (refund)	(6,503)

Complete Return Available On Student CD-ROM

S - 52

Notes To The Chapter 4 Return

1. As Deborah has no income, her disability credit has been transferred to George.

2. Inheritances are not taxable.

3. Due to his nil Tax Payable, George's $1,000 charitable donation and his education related credits are all carried forward.

4. Since Willa is over 17 years of age, her medical expenses are reduced by 3 percent of her Net Income For Tax Purposes. Willa should file a return in order to receive the GST credit.

5. Due to his low Net Income For Tax Purposes, George is eligible for the refundable medical expense supplement and the working income tax benefit. Although George could consider carrying forward his medical expenses because his non-refundable tax credits are greater than his tax payable, if he did so, he would not receive the refundable medical expense supplement.

6. Both the hockey camp and the soccer club receipts qualify for the child fitness credit. However, since accommodation and meals do not qualify for the credit, the total credit base is $475 ($650 - $182 - $193 + $200), which is less than the annual maximum of $500.

7. The art course qualifies for the children's arts credit. The credit base is limited to the annual maximum of $500.

8. The Home Buyers' Tax Credit of $750 [(15%)($5,000)] is available since George had been living in a rented town house for five years and neither he nor Deborah had another principal residence. However, since George's non-refundable tax credits already exceed his Tax Payable, he cannot take advantage of this credit and it cannot be carried forward.

9. George has paid installments based on the CRA's Instalment Reminders. Given the amount of his refund, they were unnecessary. George should review his estimated net tax owing periodically in the future to determine whether instalments should be paid.

Suggestions For Working With ProFile Software

Before You Start

To get the maximum benefit from using the ProFile tax preparation software program, we strongly advise that you do the tutorial "Getting Started" included within the program under the Training tab. The data in the sample tax returns can be used in the tutorial.

Sample Tax Returns

Included in this Study Guide are sample tax returns for Chapters 4 and 11. The tax returns contain 2012 data as the 2013 version of the ProFile tax preparation software is not yet available. In January, 2014, after the first 2013 filing version is released, the updated 2013 sample tax returns and updated Tax Software Problems will be available at:

www.pearsoncanada.ca/byrdchen/ctp2014

Before completing the Tax Software Self Study Problem, you should review the ProFile files for the sample tax returns and ensure that you are familiar with how the data was entered into the program.

Creating A New T1 Return

To provide some guidance on how to use ProFile to create a simple new personal tax return, we suggest the following approach.

1. Start the ProFile software. Open a new file. Ensure that you have chosen the new file in the correct software (T1) and year (2012 or 2013 if the updated data is available).

2. By default, the software will open on the form "Info". Fill in the highlighted cells and answer all questions that are applicable. If you do not fill in the highlighted areas, ProFile will generate an audit message, At a minimum, you will need to have the following information:

    - Taxpayer's Social Insurance Number (SIN)
    - Taxpayer's first and last name
    - Address, city, province, and postal code
    - Telephone number
    - Taxpayer's birth date

    If applicable, you will also need to enter any relevant information for the spouse on the "Info" form. At a minimum, the following information will be necessary:

    - Spouse's Social Insurance Number (SIN)
    - Spouse's first and last name
    - Address, city, province, and postal code
    - Telephone number
    - Spouse's birth date

3. Using the Form Explorer (F4), go to the Dependant form and enter all relevant information about any dependants. At a minimum, the following information will be necessary:

    - Dependant's Social Insurance Number (SIN) if there is one
    - Dependant's first and last name
    - Dependant's relationship to the taxpayer
    - Dependant's birth date
    - Dependant's Net Income
    - Address, city, province, and postal code
    - Children's fitness or arts amount (if applicable)

    Note that if there are child care expenses, the information will flow here from T778. If the Dependant has tuition, education and textbook amounts and is not filing a tax return, the education related information should be entered on the Dependant form.

4. Using the Form Explorer (F4), open the relevant information slip form. Enter all relevant information in the appropriate forms. Some common information slip forms are:

    - T3 - Statement of Trust Income
    - T4 - Statement of Remuneration Paid
    - T5 - Statement of Investment Income
    - T2202 - Tuition and Education Amounts
    - T4AOAS - Statement of Old Age Security

5. Enter any other relevant income information on the appropriate forms. These forms may include the following:

    - S3Details - Capital Gains Entry
      (this form, not Schedule 3, must be used to input details on capital dispositions)
    - T2125 - Statement of Business Or Professional Activities
    - T2125Asset - T2125 Asset Details
    - T2125CCA - T2125 CCA Details
    - T776 - Statement of Real Estate Rentals
    - T776Asset - T776 Asset Details
    - T776CCA - T776 CCA Details

6. Enter any relevant deduction information on the appropriate forms. These forms may include the following:

- RRSP - RRSP Deduction
- T777 - Statement of Employment Expenses (Use the jump link to T777Details in upper right hand corner of form if applicable)
- T778 - Child Care Expense Deduction
- Support - Support Payments
- Auto - Motor Vehicle Expenses
- S4 - Statement of Investment Income
  (much of the information for this schedule will be carried forward from the T3, T5, and other information slips, but a few items such as carrying charges are entered directly on Schedule 4)
- LossNetCap - Net Capital Losses (carry forward information)
- LossNonCap - Non-Capital Losses (carry forward information)

7. Enter any relevant tax credit information on the appropriate forms. These forms may include the following:

   - Donations - Charitable Donations
   - Medical - Medical Expenses

8. Enter any remaining relevant information in the appropriate schedule. These schedules may include the following:

   - S2 - Federal Amounts Transferred From Your Spouse or Common-Law Partner (primarily used if spouse or common-law partner is not filing a tax return)
   - T1032 - Joint Election To Split Pension Income

9. Use the function "Show Auditor" under the "Audit" list to check for warnings or potential errors.

Tips For Using ProFile Software

- Press the F5 key or choose Spouse from the Form menu to display the return of the spouse.

- If you cannot determine where a specific slip or other information should be input, one way to search for the correct form is to open the Form Explorer (F4) and choose the "Key" mode icon in the top right corner of the menu. If you type a key word into the line above the listing of key words, the appropriate form may be found.

- Press the F4 key to view the Form Explorer. Choose the form "Summary" to see the tax data of both spouses on the same one page summary. (Second column will be blank for a single taxpayer.)

- If you want to print only the form you have on the screen, use the print icon identified with 1 in the tool bar. The other print icon opens the print selection screen for printing complete returns. If you want to print just one copy of the return, deselect the print sets you don't want on the print selection screen. Before you print the return, review the forms that have been selected in the print set to ensure that you will not be printing forms you do not require. If it is a coupled return, the print settings for the spouse should be reviewed before clicking on Print as both returns will be printed.

- Review marks can be used to flag information that should be reviewed. The cell with the review mark will be listed when the Show Auditor feature is turned on.

- A memo and/or a tape can be attached to a cell to provide backup information.

- To see the effect of various changes such as province of residence or a change in an RRSP contribution, you can use the "Snapshot/Variance" feature. Information on this feature is available from the Help menu. Note you must press the "Enter" key for the change to take effect. The data monitor at the bottom of the screen should show the new balance/refund. The difference can also be seen on the "Summary" form. If you open the Auditor (F9) and select the Variance tab you will see a detailed analysis of the changes.

Tax Software Self Study Problem - Chapter 4

DISCLAIMER: All characters appearing in this problem are fictitious. Any resemblance to real persons, living or dead, is purely coincidental.

Note The following problem contains 2012 (not 2013) information as software for 2013 is not yet available. If you have an updated 2013 version of ProFile installed on your computer, ensure that when you begin, you open a file for 2012, not 2013 as this data is for 2012. Shortly after the first filing version of the 2013 Intuit ProFile software is available in January, 2014, the updated 2013 version of this problem will be available on the textbook web site at:

www.pearsoncanada.ca/byrdchen/ctp2014

This Tax Software Self Study Problem is expanded in Chapter 11 to contain other components of Taxable Income and Tax Payable.

Ms. Eleanor Victoria's husband died two years ago. After her husband died, she moved from her house in Prince George, B.C., to a rented house in Victoria, B.C.

Ms. Victoria's widowed mother, Marjorie Vancouver lives with Ms. Victoria and takes care of the house, Ms. Victoria's younger daughter, Amy, and all of the household cooking. In addition to OAS benefits, Marjorie has a small income from her deceased husband's life insurance policy. She has never filed a tax return.

Diane Victoria, Eleanor's older daughter, is studying psychology at McGill University in Montreal. Her field is addiction research with a special emphasis on gambling. She does volunteer work at a gambling addiction treatment centre in Montreal in the summers. As Eleanor has paid for her tuition and living costs, Diane has agreed that any credits available should be transferred to her mother.

Diane has decided not to file a tax return this year as she is too busy with her studies and volunteer work. Her income was earned driving for a client of the addiction treatment centre who had lost his licence after being charged with impaired driving.

Late in December, 2012, Eleanor was notified that she had inherited $500,000 from an aunt. Eleanor loves her work and though she plans to travel more, she has no plans to retire.

Information concerning Ms. Victoria for 2012 is given on the following pages.

Required: With the objective of minimizing Ms. Victoria's Tax Payable, prepare the 2012 income tax return of Eleanor Victoria using the ProFile tax software program. List any assumptions you have made, and any notes and tax planning issues you feel should be discussed with Ms. Victoria.

Personal Information	
Title	Ms.
First Name	Eleanor
Last Name	Victoria
SIN	527-000-087
Date of birth (Y/M/D)	1964-05-15
Marital Status	Widowed
Canadian citizen?	Yes
Provide information to Elections Canada?	Yes
Own foreign property of more than $100,000 Canadian?	No

Taxpayer's Address

111 VVV Street Victoria, B.C. V4H 3W4

Phone number (250) 111-1111

Dependants	Child 1	Child 2	Mother
First Name	Diane	Amy	Marjorie
Last Name	Victoria	Victoria	Vancouver
SIN	527-000-293	None	527-000-483
Date of birth (Y/M/D)	1992-05-14	2000-10-11	1931-05-21
Net income	$2,300	Nil	$8,000

T2202A - (Diane)	Box	Amount
Tuition fees - for Diane Victoria (daughter)	A	7,000
Number of months in school - part-time	B	2
Number of months in school - full-time	C	8

T4	Box	Amount
Issuer - 1750 Canada Inc.		
Employment income	14	60,201.80
Employee's CPP contributions	16	2,306.70
Employee's EI premiums	18	839.97
RPP contributions	20	2,406.16
Pension adjustment	52	7,829.00
Income tax deducted	22	11,408.00
Union dues	44	748.59
Charitable donations	46	175.00

Eleanor and her family had the following medical expenses, all of which Eleanor paid for:

Patient	(Y/M/D)	Medical Expenses	Description	Am't
Eleanor	2012-08-15	Grace Hospital	Ambulance charge	392
Eleanor	2012-08-18	Paramed Home Health	Nursing care	1,350
Marjorie	2012-05-20	Dr. Zhang (Optometrist)	Contact lenses	110
Marjorie	2012-07-06	Pharmacy	Prescription	75
Diane	2012-09-01	Dr. Glassman	Physiotherapist	100
Amy	2012-05-11	Walk Right Foot Clinic	Orthotics	450
Amy	2012-01-23	Dr. Tamo	Dental Fees	1,120

Donor	Charitable Donation Receipts	Am't
Eleanor	Heart and Stroke	375
Eleanor	Terry Fox Foundation	50
Diane	Addiction Research Council of Canada	100

Solution to Chapter Four Exercises

Exercise Four - 1 Solution

The net effect of this home relocation loan on Taxable Income would be as follows:

Taxable Benefit Under ITA 80.4(1)(a) - Lesser Of:	
• [(4%)(2/4)($82,000) + (5%)(2/4)($82,000)] = $3,690	
• [(4%)(4/4)($82,000)] = $3,280	$3,280
Reduction For Payments Under ITA 80.4(1)(c) - [(2%)($82,000)]	(1,640)
Total ITA 80.4(1) Benefit	$1,640
ITA 110(1)(j) Deduction - Lesser Of:	
• ITA 80.4(1) Benefit = $1,640	
• [(4%)($25,000)(4/4)] = $1,000	(1,000)
Net Addition To Taxable Income	$ 640

Despite the fact that the prescribed rate has increased, the taxpayer can continue to use the rate in effect at the time the loan was made to calculate the taxable benefit. This can continue for a period of five years. Note that the ITA 110(1)(j) deduction is calculated as if the loan had been for $25,000 rather than $82,000.

Exercise Four - 2 Solution

The required Tax Payable would be calculated as follows:

Tax Payable On First $43,561 At 20.05 Percent (15.00% + 5.05%)	$8,734
Tax Payable On Next $3,139 ($46,700 - $43,561)	
At 31.15 Percent (22% + 9.15%)	978
Total Tax Payable Before Credits	$9,712

Her average rate of tax is 20.8 percent ($9,712 ÷ $46,700).

Exercise Four - 3 Solution

Assuming Johan's wife does not have a mental or physical infirmity, the required amount would be calculated as follows:

Basic Personal Amount	$ 11,038
Spousal Amount ($11,038 - $2,600)	8,438
Credit Base	$19,476
Rate	15%
Personal Tax Credits	$ 2,921

If there was a mental or physical infirmity, the amount would be calculated as follows:

Basic Personal Amount	$ 11,038
Spousal Amount ($11,038 + $2,040 - $2,600)	10,478
Credit Base	$21,516
Rate	15%
Personal Tax Credits	$ 3,227

Exercise Four - 4 Solution

As her father is active, Joan would be entitled to a caregiver tax credit in the amount of $634 {[15%][$4,490 - ($15,600 - $15,334)]}. If he were infirm, the base for the credit would be increased by the FCA, resulting in a credit of $940 {[15%)($4,490 + $2,040 - ($15,600 - $15,334)]}.

Exercise Four - 5 Solution

Harold would be entitled to an infirm dependant over 17 tax credit in the amount of $822 {[15%][$6,530 - ($7,600 - $6,548)]}. He could not claim the caregiver credit as his mother does not live with him. If his mother lived with him, Harold would be able to claim the full caregiver credit as his mother's income is below the income threshold of the caregiver credit.

Exercise Four - 6 Solution

As his mother is over 64 years of age, she does not have to be infirm to qualify for the caregiver credit. In addition, she qualifies for the eligible dependant credit. In these circumstances, ITA 118(4)(c) indicates that he cannot take the caregiver credit, in effect requiring that he take the eligible dependant credit. The value of this credit would be calculated as follows:

$$[(15\%)(\$11,038 - \$7,500)] = \$531$$

As his mother's income is below the $15,334 threshold for the caregiver credit, in the absence of the ITA 118(4)(c) restriction, he would have been eligible for $674, the full amount of the caregiver credit. This means that he will have an additional credit under ITA 118(1)(e) of $143 ($674 - $531). The combination of the eligible dependant credit and the ITA 118(1)(e) credit totals $674, the maximum caregiver credit.

Exercise Four - 7 Solution

ITA 118(4)(d) indicates that, if a taxpayer is entitled to the caregiver credit for a particular individual, the taxpayer cannot claim the infirm dependant over 17 credit for that individual. As his investment income is below the income threshold for the caregiver tax credit, the caregiver tax credit, including the FCA, for Suki's son would be calculated as follows:

$$[(15\%)(\$4,490 + \$2,040 - Nil)] = \$980$$

Exercise Four - 8 Solution

The son qualifies for the eligible dependant credit, the infirm dependant over 17 credit, and the caregiver tax credit. However, if the eligible dependant credit is taken for the daughter, the fact that this claim can only be made for one dependant means that the son is no longer eligible for this credit. This leaves the infirm dependant over 17 and caregiver credits for the son. In these circumstances, ITA 118(4)(d) requires that she claim the caregiver credit. As the son is dependent because of a physical disability, the family caregiver amount is added. Given these considerations, the maximum credits would be calculated as follows:

Basic Personal Amount	$ 11,038
Eligible Dependant - Daughter ($11,038 - $1,800)	9,238
Caregiver - Son ($4,490 + $2,040)	6,530
Child - Daughter	2,234
Credit Base	$29,040
Rate	15%
Total Credits	$ 4,356

Exercise Four - 9 Solution

Mr. Smythe's age credit would be $647 {[15%][$6,854 - (15%)($51,500 - $34,562)]}.

Exercise Four - 10 Solution

The adoption expenses tax credit would be calculated as follows:

Cost Of First China Trip (See Note)	?
Cost Of Second China Trip	$ 6,420
Chinese Orphanage Fee	1,600
Canadian Adoption Agency Fee	3,200
Legal Fees	2,700
Medical Costs (Qualify For Medical Expense Credit)	Nil
Total Eligible Expenses	$13,920

Note   Under existing legislation, the cost of the first China trip is clearly not deductible as it was made prior to opening of the provincial adoption file. Under the proposal contained in the 2013 budget, the cost of the first trip would be an eligible expenditure as they had already applied to a licensed adoption agency. However, it doesn't make any real difference in this solution as the base for the credit is limited to $11,669. Since the $5,000 employer reimbursement is a taxable benefit and included in employment income, it does not reduce the total eligible adoption expenses. This means that the maximum credit that can be claimed is $1,750 [(15%)($11,669)].

Exercise Four - 11 Solution

The maximum child fitness credit would be based on the lesser of:

- The $1,200 cost of the eligible program.
- The $500 overall limit.

The lesser figure of $500 would result in a tax credit of $75 [(15%)($500)].

If Buff qualified for the disability tax credit, the overall limit would be $1,000 ($500 + $500 supplement), resulting in a tax credit of $150 [(15%)($1,000)]. All of the $500 supplement is available as long as at least $100 was paid in physical fitness fees.

Exercise Four - 12 Solution

While Marion's credit base for 2013 is $48,750 [(75%)($65,000)], she chooses to claim only $10,000, leaving a carry forward of $90,000 ($100,000 - $10,000). If we assume that she is not eligible for the FDSC, the credit would be:

$200 At 15 Percent	$ 30
$9,800 ($10,000 - $200) At 29 Percent	2,842
Total Credit	$2,872

If we assume that Marion is eligible for the FDSC, the credit would be calculated as follows:

$200 At 40 (15 + 25) Percent	$ 80
$800 ($1,000 - $200) At 54 (29 + 25) Percent	432
$9,000 ($10,000 - $1,000) At 29 (29 + 0) Percent	2,610
Total Credit	$3,122

As you would expect, the difference between the two results is $250 [(25%)($1,000)]

Regular charitable donations can be carried forward for up to 5 years. As a result, the final year to claim any unused portion of her 2013 donation would be 2018. This would also be the limit for FDSC. Note, however, for donations made in 2014 through 2017, the FDSC would only be available until 2018.

Exercise Four - 13 Solution

Amount B Qualifying Expenses ($4,330 + $4,600)		$ 8,930
Amount C - Lesser Of:		
• [(3%)($150,000)] = $4,500		
• 2013 Threshold Amount = $2,152		(2,152)
Subtotal		$ 6,778
Amount D		
Max's Medical Expenses	$8,425	
Reduced By The Lesser Of:		
• $2,152		
• [(3%)($8,250)] = $248	(248)	8,178
Allowable Amount Of Medical Expenses		$14,956
Amount A The Appropriate Rate (Minimum Rate)		15%
Medical Expense Tax Credit		$ 2,243

Exercise Four - 14 Solution

The regular medical expense credit would be calculated as follows:

Medical Expenses	$6,250
Lesser Of:	
• [(3%)($26,400)] = $792	
• 2013 Threshold Amount = $2,152	(792)
Allowable Amount Of Medical Expenses	$5,458

The refundable supplement would be calculated as follows:

Lesser Of:	
• $1,142 (2013 Maximum)	
• [(25%)($5,458)] = $1,365	$1,142
Reduction [(5%)($26,400 - $25,278)]	(56)
Refundable Medical Expense Supplement	$1,086

Ms. Brunt's total Tax Payable (Refund) would be calculated as follows:

Tax Payable Before Credits [(15%)($26,400)]		$3,960
Non-Refundable Credits:		
Basic	$ 11,038	
Common-Law Partner	11,038	
Allowable Medical Expenses	5,458	
Total	$27,534	
Rate	15%	(4,130)
Tax Before Refundable Supplement		$ Nil
Refundable Medical Expense Supplement		(1,086)
Tax Payable (Refund)		($1,086)

Exercise Four - 15 Solution

John's income is too high to qualify for the refundable medical expense supplement. As Keith has no income, the regular disability credit can be transferred to John. However, as Keith is over 17, the disability supplement is not available. In addition to the disability credit, John will be able to take the caregiver credit and the family caregiver credit, as well as a credit for Keith's medical expenses. Since the caregiver credit is claimed, the infirm dependant over 17 credit is not available.

The total credits related to Keith would be as follows:

Transfer Of Keith's Disability - Regular Amount		$ 7,697
Caregiver (Includes Family Caregiver Amount)		6,530
Keith's Medical Expenses	$16,240	
Reduced By The Lesser Of:		
• $2,152		
• [(3%)(Nil)] = Nil	Nil	16,240
Total Credit Base		$30,467
Rate		15%
Total Credits Related To Keith		$ 4,570

Exercise Four - 16 Solution

Ms. Bright's education related tax credits would be calculated as follows:

Tuition Amount:		
Total (Including $1,000 Prepayment)	$3,200	
Ineligible Ancillary Fees ($400 - $250)	(150)	$3,050
Education Amount:		
Full Time [(4)($400)]	$1,600	
Part Time [(2)($120)]	240	1,840
Textbook Amount:		
Full Time [(4)($65)]	$ 260	
Part Time [(2)($20)]	40	300
Interest On Student Loan		325
Total Credit Base		$5,515
Rate		15%
Total Available Credits		$ 827

Exercise Four - 17 Solution

Income Tax Act Approach   The available education related credits for the year would be calculated as follows:

Tuition Amount	$4,800
Education Amount [(8)($400)]	3,200
Textbook Amount [(8)($65)]	520
Education Related Amounts From Current Year	$8,520
Rate	15%
Education Related Credits From Current Year	$1,278
Carry Forward Credit	300
Total Available Education Related Credits	$1,578

Tax Return Approach   The alternative calculation approach that is used in the tax return would be as follows:

Education Related Amounts From Current Year	
(Preceding Calculation)	$ 8,520
Carry Forward Amount	2,000
Total Available Education Related Amounts	$10,520
Rate	15%
Total Available Education Related Credits	$ 1,578

Kerri's Tax Payable before deducting education related credits would be $1,944 [(15%)($24,000 - $11,038)]. This is more than sufficient to absorb the available education related credits of $1,578 and, as a consequence, there would be no carry forward of credits.

Exercise Four - 18 Solution

The available education related credits for the year would be calculated as follows:

Tuition Amount	$23,500
Education And Textbook Amounts [(11)($400 + $65)]	5,115
Available Education Related Amounts (Maximum Transfer = $5,000)	$28,615
Rate	15%
Available Education Related Credits (Maximum Transfer = $750)	$ 4,292

Note that the transfer and carry forward amounts calculated in the following alternative approaches ignore his medical expense credit. If he is eligible for the refundable medical expense supplement, that supplement would also be ignored in the following calculations.

Income Tax Act Approach   The $750 maximum transfer of education related credits must be reduced by Jerry's Tax Payable, before deducting his medical expense credit, of $32 [(15%)($11,250 - $11,038)]. This will leave a maximum transfer of $718 ($750 - $32) and a carry forward credit of $3,542 ($4,292 - $32 - $718).

Tax Return Approach   The $5,000 maximum transfer of education related amounts must be reduced by $212 ($11,250 - $11,038)], the excess of Jerry's Taxable Income over his basic personal amount. This results in a maximum transfer of $4,788 ($5,000 - $212) and a carry forward amount of $23,615 ($28,615 - $212 - $4,788). Multiplying this by 15 percent gives the same $3,542 that we calculated under the alternative approach.

Exercise Four - 19 Solution

His tax credits would be calculated as follows:

Basic Personal Amount	$ 11,038
Spousal Amount ($11,038 - Nil)	11,038
Age [$6,854 - (15%)($42,000 - $34,562)]	5,738
Pension Income*	2,000
Spousal Age Transfer	6,854
Spousal Tuition, Education, and Textbook Transfer - Lesser Of:	
• [$2,200 + (4 Months)($400) + (4 Months)($65)] = $4,060	
• Maximum Transfer = $5,000	4,060
Credit Base	$40,728
Rate	15%
Total Credits	$ 6,109

* A payment from a life annuity purchased with funds in an RRSP is eligible pension income.

Exercise Four - 20 Solution

Ms. Unger's $487 credit would be calculated as follows:

	Contributions	Credit Rate	Tax Credit
First	$400	3/4	$300
Next	350	1/2	175
Remaining	35	1/3	12
Maximum Credit	$785		$487

Exercise Four - 21 Solution

The credit will be $450 [(15%)($3,000)]. As his acquisition is less than the $5,000 maximum, the full cost is eligible for the 15 percent federal credit.

Exercise Four - 22 Solution

The family working income totals $19,000 ($13,000 + $6,000). The working income tax benefit for 2013 would be calculated as follows:

Lesser Of:	
• [(25%)($19,000 - $3,000)] = $4,000	
• Maximum Benefit For Family = $1,797	$1,797
Reduction [(15%)($19,000 - $15,509)]	(524)
Working Income Tax Benefit	$1,273

Exercise Four - 23 Solution

Ms. Jacobi's income before deducting either the EI or OAS repayments would be as follows:

Net Employment Income	$60,000
EI Benefits	10,000
OAS Benefits	6,550
Income Before Deductions	$76,550

Dealing first with the EI repayment, Ms. Jacobi would have to repay $3,000, the lesser of:

- $3,000 [(30%)($10,000)]
- $5,190 [(30%)($76,550 - $59,250)]

Using this deduction, the clawback of her OAS payments would be the lesser of:

- $6,550, the OAS payments included in income, and
- $389 [(15%)($76,550 - $3,000 - $70,954)].

As a result, her Net Income For Tax Purposes would be as follows:

Income Before Deductions	$76,550
ITA 60(v.1) Deduction (EI)	(3,000)
ITA 60(w) Deduction (OAS)	(389)
Net Income For Tax Purposes	$73,161

Self Study Solution Four - 1

Federal Tax Before Credits

For all of the following Cases, the Federal Tax Before Credits would be calculated as follows:

Tax On First $43,561	$ 6,534
Tax On Next $34,439 ($78,000 - $43,561) At 22 Percent	7,577
Federal Tax Before Credits	$14,111

Case A

The solution to this Case can be completed as follows:

Federal Tax Before Credits (As Previously Calculated)		$14,111
Basic Personal Amount	($11,038)	
Eligible Dependant	(11,038)	
Child	(2,234)	
Tuition	(5,640)	
Education [(10)($120)]	(1,200)	
Textbook [(10)($20)]	(200)	
Credit Base	($31,350)	
Rate	15%	(4,703)
Federal Tax Payable		$ 9,408

Case B

The solution to this Case can be completed as follows:

Federal Tax Before Credits (As Previously Calculated)		$14,111
Basic Personal Amount	($11,038)	
EI	(891)	
CPP	(2,356)	
Canada Employment	(1,117)	
Credit Base	($15,402)	
Rate	15%	(2,310)
Charitable Donations (See Note)		(10,122)
Federal Tax Payable		$ 1,679

Note With a Net Income For Tax Purposes of $78,000, Ms. Sykes' maximum claim for charitable donations is $58,500 [(75%)($78,000)]. However, if this amount was claimed, the resulting credit would exceed her Tax Payable. By claiming $35,000, her credit will be $10,122 [(15%)($200) + (29%)($35,000 - $200)]. The unused donation of $115,000 ($150,000 - $35,000) can be carried forward for up to five years.

The $2,000,000 that she won in the lottery is not included in her Net Income For Tax Purposes.

Case C

The solution to this Case can be completed as follows:

Federal Tax Before Credits (As Previously Calculated)		$14,111
Basic Personal Amount	($11,038)	
Spousal ($11,038 - $7,600)	(3,438)	
Child Including FCA ($2,234 + $2,040)	(4,274)	
Transfer Of Disability	(7,697)	
Transfer Of Disability Supplement	(4,490)	
Caregiver - Harry [$4,490 - ($17,600 - $15,334)]	(2,224)	
Credit Base	($33,161)	
Rate	15%	(4,974)
Federal Tax Payable		$ 9,137

Ms. Sykes would claim the caregiver credit for Harry since Buff would have no Tax Payable. As Harry is a parent over the age of 64, he does not have to be infirm to qualify for the caregiver credit. However, as he is not infirm, the family caregiver amount is not added to this credit.

Case D

The solution to this Case can be completed as follows:

Federal Tax Before Credits (As Previously Calculated)		$14,111
Basic Personal Amount	($11,038)	
Spousal ($11,038 - $2,540)	(8,498)	
Child - Janice	(2,234)	
EI	(891)	
CPP	(2,356)	
Canada Employment	(1,117)	
Medical Expenses (See Note)	(8,399)	
Credit Base	($34,533)	
Rate	15%	(5,180)
Federal Tax Payable		$ 8,931

Note The claim for medical expenses is determined as follows:

Wanda, Buff, And Janice ($2,100 + $360 + $3,645)		$6,105
Lesser Of:		
• [(3%)($78,000)] = $2,340		
• 2013 Threshold Amount = $2,152		(2,152)
Mark's Medical Expenses	$4,520	
Reduced By The Lesser Of:		
• [(3%)($2,460)] = $74		
• 2013 Threshold Amount = $2,152	(74)	4,446
Total Medical Expense Claim		$8,399

Case E

The solution to this Case can be completed as follows:

Federal Tax Before Credits (As Previously Calculated)		$14,111
Basic Personal Amount	($11,038)	
Spousal Including FCA ($11,038 + $2,040 - $9,600)	(3,478)	
Children [(2)($2,234)]	(4,468)	
EI	(891)	
CPP	(2,356)	
Canada Employment	(1,117)	
Transfer Of Buff's Disability Amount	(7,697)	
Transfer Of Buff's Age Amount	(6,854)	
Transfer Of Buff's Pension Amount	(2,000)	
Transfer Of Education Related Amounts (See Note)	(5,000)	
Credit Base	($44,899)	
Rate	15%	(6,735)
Federal Tax Payable		$ 7,376

Note Buff's education related amounts are calculated as follows:

Tuition	$ 8,450
Education [(8)($400)]	3,200
Textbook [(8)(65)]	520
Total	$12,170

While Buff has $12,170 in education related amounts available and cannot make any use of them in determining his Tax Payable, the transfer is limited to $5,000. The unused amount of $7,170 ($12,170 - $5,000) can be carried forward indefinitely, but can only be claimed by Buff.

Self Study Solution Four - 2

Federal Tax Before Credits

For all of the following Cases, except Case G, the Federal Tax Before Credits would be calculated as follows:

Tax On First $43,561	$6,534
Tax On Next $11,439 ($55,000 - $43,561) At 22 Percent	2,517
Federal Tax Before Credits	$9,051

Case A

The solution for this Case would be as follows:

Federal Tax Before Credits (As Previously Calculated)		$9,051
Basic Personal Amount	($11,038)	
EI	(891)	
CPP	(2,356)	
Canada Employment	(1,117)	
Credit Base	($15,402)	
Rate	15%	(2,310)
Political Contributions Tax Credit		
[(3/4)($400) + (1/2)($350) + (1/3)($250)]		(558)
Federal Tax Payable		$ 6,183

Case B

Federal Tax Before Credits (As Previously Calculated)		$9,051
Basic Personal Amount	($11,038)	
Spousal ($11,038 - $4,650)	(6,388)	
Child - Eileen	(2,234)	
EI	(891)	
CPP	(2,356)	
Canada Employment	(1,117)	
Medical Expenses [$3,150 - (3%)($55,000)]	(1,500)	
Credit Base	($25,524)	
Rate	15%	(3,829)
Federal Tax Payable		$ 5,222

As family net income is greater than $48,118, Stanley Murphy is not eligible for the refundable medical expense supplement. Eileen's income does not affect the child tax credit or the medical expenses credit.

Case C

Federal Tax Before Credits (As Previously Calculated)		$9,051
Basic Personal Amount	($11,038)	
Spousal ($11,038 - $9,400)	(1,638)	
Caregiver Including FCA (Note 1)	(6,530)	
Transfer Of Albert's Disability	(7,697)	
Medical Expenses (Note 2)	(8,350)	
Credit Base	($35,253)	
Rate	15%	(5,288)
Federal Tax Payable		$3,763

Note 1   Albert qualifies for both the caregiver tax credit and the infirm dependant over 17 tax credit. In these circumstances, ITA 118(4)(d) effectively requires the use of the caregiver credit. As Albert is disabled, the family caregiver amount is included in the base for this credit.

Note 2   The base for the medical expense tax credit would be calculated as follows:

Expenses For Stanley And Helen		$1,250
Lesser Of:		
• [(3%)($55,000)] = $1,650		
• 2013 Threshold Amount = $2,152		(1,650)
Subtotal		$ Nil
Albert's Medical Expenses (Note 3)	$8,350	
Reduced By The Lesser Of:		
• [(3%)(Nil)] = Nil		
• 2013 Threshold Amount = $2,152	Nil	8,350
Base For Medical Expense Credit		$8,350

Case D

The solution for this Case can be completed as follows:

Federal Tax Before Credits (As Previously Calculated)		$9,051
Basic Personal Amount	($11,038)	
Spousal (Income Too High)	Nil	
Caregiver (Ahmed)	(4,490)	
EI	(891)	
CPP	(2,356)	
Canada Employment	(1,117)	
Interest On Student Loan	(375)	
Credit Base	$ 20,267	
Rate	15%	(3,040)
Federal Tax Payable		$ 6,011

Stanley would claim the caregiver credit for Ahmed, since Helen would have no Tax Payable after considering her basic personal, CPP, EI and employment income credit. As Ahmed is a parent over 64 years of age, he does not have to be infirm to qualify for the caregiver credit. Note that, because Ahmed is not infirm, the family caregiver amount is not added to this credit. There would be no credit available for Jaleh as she is not a parent of either Stanley or Helen and is not infirm.

Case E

The solution for this Case can be completed as follows:

Federal Tax Before Credits (As Previously Calculated)		$9,051
Basic Personal Amount	($11,038)	
Common-Law Partner ($11,038 - $4,500)	(6,538)	
Child [(2)($2,234)]	(4,468)	
EI	(891)	
CPP	(2,356)	
Canada Employment	(1,117)	
First Time Home Buyer (Maximum)	(5,000)	
Credit Base	($31,408)	
Rate	15%	(4,711)
Federal Tax Payable		$ 4,340

Case F

The solution for this Case is as follows:

Federal Tax Before Credits (As Previously Calculated)		$9,051
Basic Personal Amount	($11,038)	
Spousal ($11,038 - $5,050)	(5,988)	
EI	(891)	
CPP	(2,356)	
Canada Employment	(1,117)	
Transfer From Son (Note)	(5,000)	
Credit Base	($26,390)	
Rate	15%	(3,959)
Federal Tax Payable		$ 5,092

Note The transfer from the son is as follows:

Tuition Fees	$5,400
Base For Education Credit [(8 Months)($400)]	3,200
Base For Textbook Credit [(8 Months)($65)]	520
Total Amount Available	$9,120
Maximum Transfer	(5,000)
Carry Forward (For Albert's Use Only)	$4,120

Albert's Tax Payable is completely eliminated by his basic personal credit. He can transfer a maximum of $5,000 of his education, tuition and textbook amounts to his father. The remaining $4,120 can be carried forward indefinitely, but must be used by Albert.

Case G

The solution for this Case is as follows:

Tax [(15%)($42,400)]		$6,360
Basic Personal Amount	($11,038)	
Spousal Including FCA ($11,038 + $2,040 - $7,250)	(5,828)	
Age [$6,854 - (15%)($42,400 - $34,562)]	(5,678)	
Pension	(2,000)	
Spouse's Age	(6,854)	
Spouse's Disability	(7,697)	
Spouse's Pension (Limited To RPP Receipt)	(450)	
Credit Base	($39,545)	
Rate	15%	(5,932)
Federal Tax Payable		$ 428

As Helen is infirm, the family caregiver amount is added to the spousal credit. Helen's Registered Pension Plan receipt is eligible for the pension income credit, but the Old Age Security and Canada Pension Plan receipts are not. As Helen's income is below $34,562, there is no reduction in her age credit. Neither Stanley nor Helen's income is high enough to have an OAS clawback.

Self Study Solution Four - 3

Mr. Lane's federal tax payable (refund) would be calculated as follows:

Net Income For Tax Purposes And Taxable Income		$70,000
Tax On First $43,561		$ 6,534
Tax On Next $26,439 ($70,000 - $43,561) At 22 Percent		5,817
Federal Tax Before Credits		$12,351
Basic Personal Amount	($11,038)	
Eligible Dependant (Note 1)	(11,038)	
Child [(3)($2,234)]	(6,702)	
EI	(891)	
CPP (maximum)	(2,356)	
Canada Employment	(1,117)	
Public Transit Passes [(11)(2)($75)]	(1,650)	
Child Fitness [(2)($425)]	(850)	
Medical Expenses (Note 2)	(2,300)	
Credit Base	($37,942)	
Rate	15%	(5,691)
Federal Political Tax Credit [(3/4)($400) + (1/2)($50)]		(325)
Federal Tax Payable		$ 6,335
CPP Overpayment ($2,391 - $2,356)		(35)
Federal Tax Withheld		(10,100)
Federal Tax Payable (Refund)		($ 3,800)

Note 1   The eligible dependant amount can be claimed for either his 10 or 12 year old child. His 15 year old son would not be selected as he has Net Income For Tax Purposes of $8,200.

Note 2   Allowable medical expenses are as follows:

Minor Child's Medical Expenses	$4,400
Lesser Of:	
• [(3%)($70,000)] = $2,100	
• 2013 Threshold Amount = $2,152	(2,100)
Allowable Medical Expenses	$2,300

Since his 15 year old son is under 18 years of age, his allowable medical expenses are not affected by his Net Income For Tax Purposes. If he was 18 or older, they would be.

Self Study Solution Four - 4

Part A
The required Tax Payable calculation is as follows:

Taxable Income		$13,400
Less:		
Basic Personal Amount	($11,038)	
EI	(252)	
CPP	(490)	
Canada Employment	(1,117)	
Credit Base Before Education Related Amounts	($12,897)	
Tuition, Education And Textbook Amounts Claimed		
(Note 1)	(503)	(13,400)
Subtotal		Nil
Rate		15%
Federal Tax Payable (Refund)		Nil

Note 1   Marg has tuition, education and textbook amounts available totalling $10,020 [($400)(8 Months) + ($65)(8 Months) + $6,300]. Of this total, she will use $503 to reduce her current Tax Payable to nil. This leaves an unused amount of $9,517 ($10,020 - $503). Of this amount, $4,497 ($5,000 - $503) can be transferred to her father. This will leave her with a carry forward amount of $5,020 ($10,020 - $503 - $4,497).

Since her medical expenses were paid for by her father, she cannot claim them herself and they must be transferred to her father. Even if she had paid for them herself and claimed them, she would not increase the transfer to her father as the medical expense tax credit is not taken into consideration in determining the amount of education credits that can be transferred.

Part B
Mr. Barth's net employment income for the year would be calculated as follows:

Gross Salary		$ 82,500
Additions:		
Bonus (Note One)	$20,000	
Automobile Benefit (Note Two)	7,520	
Counseling Benefit (Note Three)	1,500	
Imputed Interest Benefit (Note Four)	375	
Stock Option Benefit [($18 - $15)(1,000)] (Note Five)	3,000	32,395
		$114,895
Deductions:		
Registered Pension Plan Contributions	($3,200)	
Professional Dues	(1,800)	(5,000)
Net Employment Income		$109,895

Note One   As the bonus is not payable until more than three years after the end of the employer's taxation year, it is a salary deferral arrangement and must be included in income under ITA 6(11).

Note Two   Since Mr. Barth's employment related usage is not more than 50 percent, there is no reduction of the full standby charge. In addition, he cannot use the alternative calculation of the operating cost benefit. Given this, the automobile benefit is calculated as follows:

Standby Charge [(2%)($47,500)(10)]	$9,500
Operating Cost Benefit [(6,000)($0.27)]	1,620
Payments Withheld	(3,600)
Taxable Benefit	$7,520

Note Three   IT-470R indicates that counseling services, with the exception of those items specified under ITA 6(1), are considered taxable benefits. The items specified under ITA 6(1)(a)(iv) are counseling with respect to mental or physical health or with respect to re-employment or retirement. As a consequence, the counseling on personal finances is a taxable benefit.

Note Four   The imputed interest benefit is calculated as follows:

Taxable Benefit [($150,000)(2%)(3/12)]	$750
Reduction For Interest Paid	(375)
Net Addition To Employment Income	$375

Note Five   As the option price was greater than the market price at the time the options were issued, one-half of this amount can be deducted in the determination of Taxable Income. The adjusted cost base of the stock option shares is equal to their fair market value at the exercise date ($18 per share). Since they were sold for $18 per share, there is no capital gain or loss.

Note Six   Other items and the reasons for their exclusion would be as follows:

- Any income tax withheld is not deductible.
- CPP contributions, EI premiums, and United Way donations create credits against taxes payable, but are not deductible in the determination of employment income.
- The payments for personal use of the company car are used in the calculation of the taxable benefit associated with this automobile.

Taxable Income

The loan to purchase a ski chalet would not be a home relocation loan and there would be no deduction from Taxable Income related to the interest benefit. Mr. Barth's Taxable Income would be calculated as follows:

Net Income For Tax Purposes = Net Employment Income	$109,895
Stock Option Deduction [(1/2)($3,000)]	(1,500)
Taxable Income	$108,395

Tax Payable

Mr. Barth's Tax Payable would be calculated as follows:

Tax On First $87,123		$16,118
Tax On Next $21,272 ($108,395 - $87,123) At 26 Percent		5,531
Federal Tax Before Credits		$21,649
Basic Personal Amount	($11,038)	
Spousal Including FCA		
($11,038 + $2,040 - $1,250)	(11,828)	
Spouse's Disability	(7,697)	
EI	(891)	
CPP	(2,356)	
Canada Employment	(1,117)	
Medical Expenses (Note Six)	(1,916)	
Marg's Education, Tuition And		
Textbook Transfer (See Part A)	(4,497)	
Credit Base	($41,340)	
Rate	15%	(6,201)
Charitable Donations [(15%)($200) + (29%)($2,000 - $200)]		(552)
Net Federal Tax		$ 14,896
Federal Income Tax Withheld During Year		(16,000)
Federal Tax Payable (Refund)		($ 1,104)

Note Six Allowable medical expenses are as follows:

John And Spouse Medical Expenses ($200 + $3,550)		$3,750
Reduced By The Lesser Of:		
• [(3%)($109,895)] = $3,297		
• 2013 Threshold Amount = $2,152		(2,152)
Marg's Medical Expenses	$720	
Reduced By The Lesser Of:		
• [(3%)($13,400)] = $402		
• 2013 Threshold Amount = $2,152	(402)	318
Allowable Medical Expenses		$1,916

Self Study Solution Four - 5

Extension of Tax Software Self Study Problem in Study Guide on page S-56

The required calculations for Eleanor's balance owing would be as follows:

Salary		$ 60,202
RPP Deduction		(2,406)
Union Dues		(749)
Net And Taxable Income		$ 57,047
Federal Tax On First $43,561		$6,534
Federal Tax On Next $13,486 ($57,047 - $43,561) At 22 Percent		2,967
Gross Federal Tax		$9,501
Basic Personal Amount	($11,038)	
Eligible Dependant - Amy	(11,038)	
Child - Amy	(2,234)	
Caregiver - Marjorie	(4,490)	
EI Premiums	(891)	
CPP Contributions	(2,356)	
Canada Employment	(1,117)	
Transfer Of Tuition, Education And Textbook - Lesser Of:		
• $5,000		
• [$7,000 + (8)($400) + (8)($65) + (2)($120)		
+ (2)($20)] = $11,000	(5,000)	
Medical Expenses (Note One)	(1,632)	
Credit Base	($39,796)	
Rate	15%	(5,969)
Charitable Donations [(15%)($200) +		
(29%)($175 + $375 + $50 - $200)]		(146)
Federal Tax Payable		$ 3,386
Tax Withheld		(11,408)
Balance Owing (Refund)		($ 8,022)

Note One Allowable medical expenses are as follows:

Eleanor And Minor Child (Amy) Medical Expenses		
($392 + $1,350 + $450 + $1,120)		$3,312
Reduced By The Lesser Of:		
• [(3%)($57,047)] = $1,711		
• 2013 Threshold Amount = $2,152		(1,711)
Balance Before Dependants 18 And Over		1,601
Marjorie's Medical Expenses ($110 + $75)	$185	
Reduced By The Lesser Of:		
• $2,152		
• [(3%)($8,000)] = $240	(240)	Nil
Diane's Medical Expenses	$100	
Reduced By The Lesser Of:		
• $2,152		
• [(3%)($2,300)] = $69	(69)	31
Allowable Medical Expenses		$1,632

Notes To Eleanor's Tax Return

- Diane transfers the $5,000 maximum education related credits to Eleanor and carries forward the remaining $6,000 ($11,000 - $5,000).

- Eleanor cannot claim the charitable donation made by Diane, but Diane can carry it forward for up to five years.

- Diane should file a tax return, otherwise she will not be eligible for the GST credit and she will not benefit from the RRSP deduction room created during the year. Filing a tax return will also make her education related tax credits and charitable donation tax credit easier to keep track of for carry forward purposes.

- Marjorie should file a tax return in order to receive the GST credit. However, she will need to obtain a Social Insurance Number to do so.

- Since Amy is under 18 and wholly dependent, Eleanor can claim the eligible dependant credit for Amy.

- Since the eligible dependant credit is taken for Amy, the fact that this claim can only be made for one dependant means that Marjorie is not eligible for this credit. As a result, Eleanor claimed the full caregiver credit for Marjorie as her income is well below the income threshold. Note that, because Marjorie is not infirm, the family caregiver amount is not added to this credit.

- Since Diane and Marjorie are over 17 years of age, their medical expenses are reduced by 3 percent of their Net Income For Tax Purposes. This means that none of Marjorie's medical expenses can be claimed by Eleanor.

Self Study Solution Four - 6

Part A

Mr. Strong's minimum Net Income For Tax Purposes would be calculated as follows:

Salary	$72,000
Additions:	
Employer's Disability Contribution (Not A Taxable Benefit)	Nil
Automobile Benefit (Note 1)	8,090
Tuition For Chants Course (Note 2)	600
Travel Costs (Note 3)	Nil
Home Relocation Loan Benefit (Note 4)	1,500
Deductions:	
RPP Contributions	(4,200)
Cost Of Tools - Maximum (Note 5)	(500)
Net Income For Tax Purposes	$77,490

Note 1   The automobile benefit would be calculated as follows:

Standby Charge [(2/3)(12)($565 - $40)(10/12)]	$3,500
Operating Cost Benefit [($0.27)(17,000)]	4,590
Total Benefits	$8,090

As Mr. Strong's employment related use was less than 50 percent, there is no reduction in the standby charge and he cannot use the alternative calculation of the operating cost benefit.

Note 2   Employer paid tuition is a taxable benefit unless it is for the benefit of that employer. While the spoken French course appears to be for the benefit of the employer, it would be difficult to argue that the employer would benefit from a course in 16th century liturgical chants.

Note 3   As the travel costs were reimbursed, there is no deduction. As long as the costs were reasonable, there would be no benefit from the reimbursement.

Note 4   The ITA 80.4(1) loan benefit would be $1,500, the lesser of:

- [($150,000)(2% - Nil)(1/4) + ($150,000)(1% - Nil)(2/4)] $1,500
- [($150,000)(2% - Nil)(3/4)] $2,250

Note 5   Mr. Strong can deduct the cost of tradesperson's tools that cost more than $1,117. However, the overall limit for this deduction is $500 per year.

Part B

Mr. Strong's minimum Taxable Income would be calculated as follows:

Net Income For Tax Purposes	$77,490
Home Relocation Loan Deduction (Note 6)	(250)
Taxable Income	$77,240

Note 6   The deduction would be $250, the lesser of:

- ITA 80.4(1) Benefit $1,500
- [($25,000)(2% - Nil)(1/4) + ($25,000)(1% - Nil)(2/4)] $ 250

Part C

Based on the Taxable Income calculated in Part B, Mr. Strong's Tax Payable would be calculated as follows:

Tax On First $43,561		$ 6,534
Tax On Next $33,679 ($77,240 - $43,561) At 22 Percent		7,409
Tax Before Credits		$13,943
Credits:		
Basic Personal Amount	($11,038)	
Spousal ($11,038 - $5,600)	(5,438)	
Child [(2)($2,234)]	(4,468)	
Caregiver (Note 7)	(4,490)	
EI Premiums	(891)	
CPP Contributions	(2,356)	
Canada Employment	(1,117)	
Monthly Transit Passes [($60)(2)(10)]	(1,200)	
Tuition (Note 8)	(600)	
Education And Textbook (Note 8)	Nil	
Medical Expenses (Note 9)	(3,998)	
Credit Base	($35,596)	
Rate	15%	(5,339)
Charitable Donations (Note 10)		
[(15%)($200) + (29%)($1,200 - $200)]		(320)
Federal Tax Payable		$ 8,284

Note 7 His mother's income is below the threshold for the caregiver credit. This means that Mr. Strong can claim the full amount of the caregiver credit. Note that because the mother is not infirm, the family caregiver amount is not available.

Note 8 When an employer reimburses tuition costs, the tuition credit can be claimed if the reimbursement is included in the employee's income. However, when there is employer reimbursement, without regard to whether the amount is included in income, none of the other education related credits can be claimed by the employee.

Note 9 The base for Mr. Strong's medical expense credit can be calculated as follows:

Mr. Strong, His Spouse, And Minor Children		
($1,250 + $2,300 + $850)		$4,400
Reduced By The Lesser Of:		
• [(3%)($77,490)] = $2,325		
• 2013 Threshold Amount = $2,152		(2,152)
Mother's Medical Expenses	$1,960	
Reduced By The Lesser Of:		
• $2,152		
• [(3%)($7,000)] = $210	(210)	1,750
Allowable Medical Costs		$3,998

Note 10 Mr. Strong cannot claim a credit for the $1,500 of donated services.

Note 11 Mr. Strong cannot claim the First Time Home Buyers' Credit as he owned a house within 4 years of purchasing the heritage home.

Self Study Solution Four - 7

Part A

Mr. Bosworth's minimum Net Income For Tax Purposes would be calculated as follows:

Salary	$180,000
Additions:	
Commissions	11,500
Bonus (Note 1)	Nil
Life Insurance Premiums (Employer's Contribution)	460
Automobile Benefit (Note 2)	6,800
Gift ($2,500, Less $500 Limit On Gifts)	2,000
Stock Option Benefit (Note 3)	13,000
Deductions:	
RPP Contributions	(5,200)
Employment Expenses (Note 4)	(20,371)
Net Income For Tax Purposes	**$188,189**

Note 1 As all of the bonus is being paid in 2014, none of it will be included in Mr. Bosworth's 2013 Net Income For Tax Purposes.

Note 2 The standby charge would be calculated as follows:

$$[(2/3)(12)(\$925 - \$75)(20,004 \div 20,004)] = \$6,800$$

As Mr. Bosworth's personal milage exceeds 20,004 kilometers, there is no reduction in the standby charge. There would be no operating cost benefit as Mr. Bosworth paid for all of the operating costs.

Note 3 The total employment income inclusion would be $13,000 [(5,000)($12.35 - $9.75)]. As the option price was equal to the market price at the time the options were issued, $6,500 [(1/2)($13,000)] can be deducted in the determination of Taxable Income.

Note 4 Potentially deductible expenses are as follows:

Car Operating Costs [(41,000 ÷ 62,000)($10,300)]	$ 6,811
Meals [(50%)($6,420)]	3,210
Hotels	10,350
Subtotal for ITA 8(1)(h) and (h.1)	**$20,371**
Advertising	12,400
Entertainment [(50%)($6,500)]	3,250
Total for ITA 8(1)(f) - Limited To Commissions	**$36,021**

All of these costs can be deducted under ITA 8(1)(f). However, the total deduction is limited to commission income which, for 2013, is only $11,500. Alternatively, the car operating costs, meals, and hotels, can be deducted under ITA 8(1)(h) and (h.1). As shown in the preceding table, this total would be $20,371. As Mr. Bosworth cannot simultaneously use ITA 8(1)(f) and the combination of ITA 8(1)(h) and (h.1), he will minimize his Net Income For Tax Purposes by deducting under the latter provisions.

Part B

Mr. Bosworth's minimum Taxable Income would be calculated as follows:

Net Income For Tax Purposes	$188,189
Stock Option Deduction [(1/2)($13,000)]	(6,500)
Taxable Income	**$181,689**

Part C

Based on the Taxable Income calculated in Part B, Mr. Bosworth's federal Tax Payable would be calculated as follows:

Tax On First $135,054		$28,580
Tax On Next $46,635 ($181,689 - $135,054) At 29 Percent		13,524
Tax Before Credits		$42,104
Credits:		
Basic Personal Amount	($11,038)	
Spouse ($11,038 - $6,450)	(4,588)	
Child Including FCA - Daughter	(4,274)	
Transfer Of Daughter's Disability	(7,697)	
Transfer Of Disability Supplement (Note 5)	Nil	
EI Premiums	(891)	
CPP Contributions	(2,356)	
Canada Employment	(1,117)	
Child Fitness ($400 + $500) (Note 6)	(900)	
Tuition - Andrew	(1,670)	
Education - Andrew [(4)($120)]	(480)	
Textbook - Andrew [(4)($20)]	(80)	
Transfer Of Son's Education Credits (Note 7)	(3,588)	
Medical Expenses (Note 8)	(14,514)	
Credit Base	($53,193)	
Rate	15%	(7,979)
Charitable Donations [(15%)($200) + (29%)($2,400 - $200)]		(668)
Federal Tax Payable		$33,457

Note 5 Since the daughter's attendant care costs that are included in the medical expenses total more than $7,120 ($4,490 + $2,630), the disability supplement is reduced to nil.

Note 6 Since the son is over 16 years old and not disabled, his fitness fees are not eligible for the fitness credit. Mr. Bosworth's credit is based on the $400 paid for his daughter, plus the $500 supplement that is available because she is under 18 and qualifies for the disability credit.

Note 7 The son's available education credits are as follows:

Tuition	$ 7,650
Ancillary Fees (Mandatory For All Students)	560
Tuition [(8)($400)]	3,200
Textbook [(8)($65)]	520
Total	$11,930

As the son has Net Income For Tax Purposes of $12,450, he must use $1,412 ($12,450 - $11,038) of this total. This means that the maximum transfer to his father will be $3,588 ($5,000 - $1,412).

Note 8 The base for Mr. Bosworth's medical expense credit can be calculated as follows:

Eligible Medical Expenses		
Andrew And His Spouse ($1,200 + $2,250)		$ 3,450
Daughter		11,250
Reduced By The Lesser Of:		
• [(3%)($188,189)] = $5,646		
• 2013 Threshold Amount = $2,152		(2,152)
Son's Medical Expenses	$2,340	
Reduced By The Lesser Of:		
• $2,152		
• [(3%)($12,450)] = $374	(374)	1,966
Allowable Medical Expenses		$14,514

Solution to Tax Software Self Study Problem - Chapter 4

This solution includes the Tax Summary from the ProFile T1 return. Note that this solution is based on a 2012 (not 2013) tax return. The complete tax return is available on the Student CD-ROM.

To view the files, access your Student CD-ROM. Under the heading "Textbook Support Files", select the option "Tax Return Files" and you will see two drop-down lists.

- To view the ProFile file, select "Chapter 4 SS Software Problem" from the ProFile drop-down list.

- To view the .PDF file, select "PDF Chapter 4 SS Software Problem" from the PDF drop-down list.

For more information on how to use the ProFile tax program, refer to the Chapter 4 sample tax return in this Study Guide.

Notes to tax return

- Diane transfers the $5,000 maximum education related credits to Eleanor and carries forward the remaining $6,000 [$7,000 + (8)($400) + (8)($65) + (2)($120) + (2)($20) - $5,000]. The carry forward can only be used by Diane.

- Eleanor cannot claim the charitable donation made by Diane, but Diane can carry it forward for up to five years.

- Diane should file a tax return, otherwise she will not be eligible for the GST credit and she will not benefit from the RRSP deduction room created during the year. Filing a tax return will also make her education related tax credits and charitable donation tax credit easier to keep track of for carry forward purposes.

- Marjorie should file a tax return in order to receive the GST credit.

- Since Amy is under 18 and wholly dependent, Eleanor claimed the eligible dependant credit for Amy.

- Eleanor claimed the full caregiver credit for Marjorie as her income is well below the income threshold. Note that, because Marjorie is not infirm, the family caregiver amount is not added to this credit.

- Since Diane and Marjorie are over 17 years of age, their medical expenses are reduced by 3 percent of their Net Income For Tax Purposes. This means that none of Marjorie's medical expenses can be claimed by Eleanor.

2012 Tax Summary (Federal)

Eleanor-Chapter 4 SS Problem

Eleanor-Chapter 4 SS Problem

Total income

Employment *	101	60,202
Old Age Security	113	
CPP/QPP benefits	114	
Other pensions	115	
Split-pension amount	116	
Universal Child Care Benefit	117	
Employment Insurance	119	
Taxable dividends	120	
Interest	121	
Limited partnership	122	
RDSP	125	
Rental	126	
Taxable capital gains	127	
Support payments	128	
RRSP	129	
Other	130	
Self-employment *	135	
Workers' compensation and social assistance	147	
Total income	**150**	**60,202**

Net income

RPP	207	2,406
RRSP *	208	
Split-Pension Deduction	210	
Union and professional dues	212	749
UCCB repayment	213	
Child care expenses	214	
Disability supports deduction	215	
Business investment loss	217	
Moving expenses	219	
Support payments	220	
Carrying charges and interest	221	
CPP/QPP/PIPP *	222	
Exploration and development	224	
Employment expenses	229	
Social benefits repayment	235	
Other deductions *	231	
Net income	**236**	**57,047**

Taxable income

Canadian Forces personnel	244	
Home relocation loan	248	
Security options deductions	249	
Other payments deduction	250	
Losses of other years *	251	
Capital gains deduction	254	
Northern residents	255	
Additional deductions	256	
Taxable income	**260**	**57,047**

2013 Estimated

Eleanor-Chapter 4 SS Problem

GST/HST credit		
Child Tax Benefit		1,163 00
RRSP contribution limit		11,488 00

* More than one line is considered

Non-refundable tax credits

Basic personal amount	300	10,822
Age amount	301	
Spouse / eligible dependant *	303	10,822
Amount for children	367	2,191
Infirm/caregiver *	306	4,402
CPP/QPP/PPIP/EI *	308	3,147
Volunteer firefighters' amount	362	
Canada employment amount	363	1,095
Public transit passes amount	364	
Children's fitness amount	365	
Children's arts amount	370	
Home buyers/Home renovation *	369	
Adoption expenses	313	
Pension income amount	314	
Disability amount	316	
Transfers *	318	5,000
Interest on student loans	319	
Tuition / education	323	
Medical expenses	332	1,632
Subtotal	**335**	**39,110**
Credit at 15%	338	5,867
Donations and gifts	349	146
Non-refundable tax credits	**350**	**6,013**

Total payable

Federal tax	404	9,561
Non-refundable tax credits	350	6,013
Dividend tax credit	425	
Min. tax carry-over/other *	426	
Basic federal tax	**429**	**3,548**
Non resident surtax		
Foreign tax credits / other	405	
Federal tax	**406**	**3,548**
Political/inv. tax credit/other *	410	
Labour-sponsored tax credit	414	
Alternative minimum tax	417	
WITB Prepayment (RC210)	415	
Special Taxes	418	
Net federal tax	**420**	**3,548**
CPP contributions payable	421	
EI self-employment	430	
Social benefits repayment	422	
Provincial/territorial tax	428	1,558
Total payable	**435**	**5,106**

Total credits

Income tax deducted *	437	11,408
QC or YT abatement *	440	
CPP/EI overpayment *	448	
Medical expense supplement	452	
WITB (Schedule 6)	453	
Other credits *	454	
GST/HST rebate	457	
Instalments	476	
Provincial tax credits	479	
Total credits	**482**	**11,408**

Balance owing (refund)	(6,302)
Combined balance (refund)	(6,302)

Complete Return Available On Student CD-ROM

S - 80

Chapter 4 Learning Objectives

Note Regarding Rates And Credits

A schedule of rates, brackets, credit amounts and other data is available at the beginning of both Volumes of this textbook (but not this Study Guide). We expect you to refer to this information when calculating the credits covered in this chapter (i.e., you are not expected to memorize the rates, brackets and credit bases).

After completing Chapter 4, you should be able to:

1. Calculate Taxable Income when an individual has basic deductions against Net Income For Tax Purposes. (paragraph [P hereafter] 4-1 through 4-13).

2. Calculate federal and provincial Tax Payable before the consideration of any tax credits (P 4-14 through 4-31).

3. Calculate the personal tax credits described in ITA 118(1) which include the:

    - family caregiver,
    - spousal,
    - eligible dependant,
    - child,
    - basic,
    - caregiver, and
    - infirm dependant over 17 credits (P 4-32 through 4-81).

4. Calculate the age tax credit (P 4-82 and 4-83).

5. Calculate the pension income tax credit (P 4-84 through 4-88).

6. Calculate the Canada employment tax credit (P 4-89 through 4-91).

7. Calculate the adoption expenses tax credit (P 4-92 through 4-96).

8. Calculate the public transit passes tax credit (P 4-97 through 4-101).

9. Calculate the child fitness and children's arts tax credits (P 4-102 through 4-112).

10. Calculate the first time home buyer's tax credit (P 4-113 through 4-115).

11. Calculate the volunteer firefighters tax credit (P 4-116 and 4-117).

12. Calculate the charitable donations tax credit, including the first-time donor's super tax credit, when the donation is in the form of cash (P 4-118 through 4-129).

13. Calculate the medical expense tax credit (P 4-133 through 4-143).

14. Calculate the refundable medical expense supplement (P 4-144 through 4-147).

15. Calculate the disability tax credit (P 4-148 through 4-159).

16. Calculate the education related tax credits including those related to tuition fees, examination fees, ancillary fees, education, textbook and student loan interest tax credits (P 4-160 through 4-172).

17. Calculate the amount of education related tax credits that can be carried forward or transferred to another individual (P 4-173 through 4-181).

18. Calculate the Employment Insurance and Canada Pension Plan credits (P 4-182 through 4-188).

19. List the types and amounts of tax credits that can be transferred to a spouse or common-law partner (P 4-189 through 4-190).

20. Calculate the political contributions tax credit (P 4-191 through 4-193).

21. Calculate the labour sponsored funds tax credit (P 4-194 through 4-196).

22. Explain the basic provisions of the refundable GST credit (P 4-200 through 4-207).

23. Calculate the working income tax benefit and WITB disability supplement (P 4-208 through 4-212).

24. Calculate the Canada child tax benefit (P 4-213 through 4-217).

25. Calculate the OAS and EI clawbacks (P 4-218 through 4-228).

26. Complete a simple personal tax return using the ProFile T1 tax preparation software program (page S-49 through S-55 in this Study Guide).

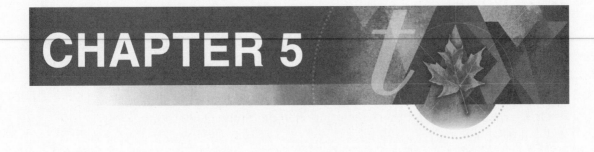

How To Work Through Chapter 5

We recommend the following approach in dealing with the material in this chapter:

Tax And Accounting Procedures Compared
❑ Read paragraph 5-1 to 5-11 (in the textbook).

Additions To Capital Cost
❑ Read paragraph 5-12 to 5-29.

Capital Cost Allowances - General Overview and Rates For Common Classes
❑ Read paragraph 5-30 to 5-32.
❑ Do Exercise Five-1 (in the textbook) and check the solution on page S-84 in this Study Guide.

Half-Year (a.k.a. First Year) Rules
❑ Read paragraph 5-33 to 5-37.
❑ Do Exercises Five-2 to Five-5 and check the solutions in this Study Guide.

Short Fiscal Periods
❑ Read paragraph 5-38 to 5-42.
❑ Do Exercise Five-6 and check the solution in this Study Guide.

Tax Planning Considerations
❑ Read paragraph 5-43 to 5-47.
❑ Do Exercise Five-7 and check the solution in this Study Guide.

Dispositions Of Depreciable Assets
❑ Read paragraph 5-48 to 5-56.
❑ Do Exercise Five-8 and check the solution in this Study Guide.

Recapture of Capital Cost Allowance
❑ Read paragraph 5-57 to 5-60.
❑ Do Exercise Five-9 and check the solution in this Study Guide.

Terminal Losses
❑ Read paragraph 5-61 to 5-65.
❑ Do Exercises Five-10 and Five-11 and check the solutions in this Study Guide.

Summary Of Tax Consequences
❑ Read paragraph 5-66.

CCA Schedule - Example
❑ Read paragraph 5-67 to 5-68.
❑ Do Self Study Problems Five-1 to Five-4 at the end of the textbook chapter on pages 228 to 230 and check the solutions in this Study Guide.

Separate Class Election And Other Special Situations
❑ Read paragraph 5-69 to 5-76.
❑ Do Exercise Five-12 and check the solution in this Study Guide.
❑ Read paragraph 5-77 to 5-80.

Cumulative Eligible Capital,
Including CEC Disposal Election, Business Terminations and Death
❑ Read paragraph 5-81 to 5-99.
❑ Do Exercise Five-13 and check the solution in this Study Guide.
❑ Do Self Study Problems Five-5 to Five-7 and check the solutions in this Study Guide.
❑ Read paragraph 5-100 to 5-102.
❑ Do Exercise Five-14 and check the solution in this Study Guide.
❑ Do Self Study Problem Five-8 and check the solution in this Study Guide.
❑ Read paragraph 5-103 to 5-106.

To Complete This Chapter
❑ Review the Key Terms Used In This Chapter on page 225. Consult the Glossary for the meaning of any key terms you do not know.
❑ Review the Glossary Flashcards and complete the Key Terms Self-Test for the Chapter. These features can be found in two places, on your Student CD-ROM under the heading "Key Term Practice" and on the web site.
❑ Review the Learning Objectives of the Chapter found on page S-101 of this Study Guide.
❑ As a final review, we recommend that you view the PowerPoint Slides for Chapter 5 that are on your Student CD-ROM. The PowerPoint Viewer program can be installed from the Student CD-ROM.

Practice Examination
❑ Write the Practice Examination for Chapter 5 that is on your Student CD-ROM. Mark your examination using the Practice Examination Solution that is also on your Student CD-ROM.

Solution to Chapter Five Exercises

Exercise Five - 1 Solution
The correct classes for each of the assets would be as follows:

Asset	Class
Taxicab	16
Manufacturing and processing equipment	29
Franchise with a limited life	14
Passenger vehicle with a cost of $120,000*	10.1
Water storage tank	6
Photocopy machine (office equipment not specifically listed elsewhere)	8
Leasehold improvements	13
Rental building*	1

*These two assets would have to be allocated to separate classes. In addition, as covered later in the Chapter, the taxpayer could elect to include the photocopy machine in a separate class if its capital cost is $1,000 or more.

Exercise Five - 2 Solution
CCA should have been $48,900 [($326,000)(1/2)(30%)]. The amount recorded was $6,520 [($326,000)(1/2)(4%)]. This error understated deductions and overstated income by $42,380 ($48,900 - $6,520).

Exercise Five - 3 Solution
The required CCA calculations would be as follows:

On 2008 Improvements ($52,000 ÷ 15)	$3,467
On 2013 Improvements [($31,000 ÷ 10)(1/2)]	1,550
2013 Capital Cost Allowance	$5,017

Exercise Five - 4 Solution
The required information would be calculated as follows:

January 1, 2013 UCC Balance		$212,000
Add: Additions	$37,400	
Deduct: Dispositions (Amount Of Deduction Given)	(18,300)	19,100
Deduct: One-Half Net Additions [(1/2)($19,100)]		(9,550)
CCA Base		$221,550
CCA [(20%)($221,550)]		(44,310)
Add: One-Half Net Additions		9,550
January 1, 2014 UCC Balance		$186,790

The maximum 2013 CCA is $44,310 and the January 1, 2014 UCC balance is $186,790.

Exercise Five - 5 Solution
The maximum CCA for the Class 14 asset would be $28,253 [($375,000 ÷ 10)(275 ÷ 365)]. Note that the half year rule is not applicable to Class 14 assets. However, the amount of CCA must be pro rated for the year, based on the number of days that the asset is owned. The January 1, 2014 UCC balance would be $346,747 ($375,000 - $28,253).

Exercise Five - 6 Solution
The maximum CCA for the year is $4,821 [(1/2)(20%)($115,000)(153/365)].

Exercise Five - 7 Solution
Following the general rule that, when less than the maximum CCA is to be deducted, the amounts deducted should be taken from the class(es) with the lowest rates, the required calculations would be as follows:

Required Total		$45,000
Maximum CCA - Class 1 [(4%)($426,000)]	($17,040)	
Maximum CCA - Class 8 [(20%)($126,000)]	(25,200)	(42,240)
Required Balance		$ 2,760

As they are both 30 percent declining balance classes, the remaining $2,760 could be taken from either Class 10 or Class 10.1. It would be advisable to use Class 10.1, as recapture is not recorded for this class. In addition, if the Class 10.1 vehicle is going to be disposed of in the near future, it could be better tax planning to take the maximum CCA for Class 10.1 of $6,300 [(30%)($21,000)] and reduce the Class 8 CCA to $21,660 ($45,000 - $6,300 - $17,040). Since there is no recapture for Class 10.1, this could increase aggregate future deductions of the other classes. Whether this would be advantageous depends on the anticipated proceeds of disposition.

Exercise Five - 8 Solution

Following the basic rule for dispositions, we would subtract from the Class 8 UCC the lesser of the proceeds of disposition ($23,000) and the capital cost of the individual asset ($18,000). Subtracting the lesser figure of $18,000 would leave a large positive balance in Class 8. As there are no other dispositions during the year, we can conclude that the balance will be positive at the end of the year. This fact, combined with the presence of many other assets in Class 8 means that there will be no recapture and no terminal loss. There will, however, be a taxable capital gain of $2,500 [(1/2)($23,000 - $18,000)].

Exercise Five - 9 Solution

The required information would be calculated as follows:

UCC Of The Class At The Beginning Of The Year	$24,883
Add: Acquisitions During The Year	Nil
Deduct: Dispositions During The Year - Lesser Of:	
• Capital Cost = $27,000	
• Proceeds Of Disposition = $28,500	(27,000)
Deduct: One-Half Net Additions	N/A*
Negative Ending Balance	($ 2,117)
Recapture Of CCA	2,117
January 1, 2014 UCC Balance	Nil

*This adjustment for one-half of the excess of additions over disposal deductions is only made when the net amount is positive.

The effect would be an addition to business income of $2,117 in recaptured CCA. While there would also be a taxable capital gain of $750 [(1/2)($28,500 - $27,000)], this would not be included in business income.

Exercise Five - 10 Solution

The required information would be calculated as follows:

UCC Of The Class At The Beginning Of The Year	$24,883
Add: Acquisitions During The Year	Nil
Deduct: Dispositions During The Year - Lesser Of:	
• Capital Cost = $54,000	
• Proceeds Of Disposition = $18,000	(18,000)
Ending Balance With No Remaining Assets	$ 6,883
Terminal Loss	(6,883)
January 1, 2014 UCC Balance	Nil

As there is a positive balance in Class 8 at the end of the year, but no remaining assets, there would be a terminal loss of $6,883. This loss is deducted in the calculation of net business income.

Exercise Five - 11 Solution

For accounting purposes, there would be a gain of $82,500 ($126,000 - $43,500), the full amount of which would be included in accounting Net Income. For tax purposes, there would be a capital gain of $29,000 ($126,000 - $97,000), of which one-half, or $14,500, would be included in income. The capital cost of $97,000 would be subtracted from the UCC, leaving a balance of $2,365,000. While this disposition would reduce the maximum CCA for the current and subsequent years, there would be no recapture (the balance in Class 8 is still positive) or terminal loss (there are still assets in Class 8).

Exercise Five - 12 Solution

Photocopiers would be included in Class 8, a 20 percent declining balance class. The following table compares the CCA if no election is made with the results if the separate class election is made.

	No Election 10 Copiers	With Election 2 Copiers	With Election 8 Copiers
January Acquisitions @ $20,000	$200,000	$40,000	$160,000
Dispositions	(6,000)	(6,000)	N/A
Terminal Loss		$34,000	
December Acquisitions @ $22,000	44,000	$44,000	
One-Half Net Additions	(119,000)	(22,000)	(80,000)
Base Amount For CCA Claim	$119,000	$22,000	$ 80,000
Class 8 CCA Rate	20%	20%	20%
CCA	$ 23,800	$ 4,400	$ 16,000

If no election is made, there will be a deduction for CCA of $23,800. Alternatively, if each machine is allocated to a separate class, there will be a deduction for CCA of $20,400 ($4,400 + $16,000). In addition, there will be a terminal loss of $34,000. The use of the election increases the total deductible amount by $30,600 [($4,400 + $16,000) + $34,000 - $23,800].

Exercise Five - 13 Solution

The required income inclusion can be calculated as follows:

	CEC Balance	CEC Deductions
2011 CEC Addition [(3/4)($85,600)]	$64,200	
CEC Amount [($64,200)(7%)]	(4,494)	$4,494
Balance January 1, 2012	$59,706	
CEC Amount [($59,706)(7%)]	(4,179)	4,179
Balance January 1, 2013	$55,527	
Proceeds From Sale [(3/4)($93,400)]	(70,050)	
Balance After Sale	($14,523)	$8,673

The negative balance in the CEC account after the sale is more than the total of the CEC deductions in the past two years ($8,673). Given this, the income inclusion will be as follows:

- $8,673 (the CEC deducted), plus
- $3,900 [(2/3)($14,523 - $8,673)].

As a result, $12,573 ($8,673 + $3,900) will be included in income in 2013. Note that the $3,900 income inclusion could also be calculated by taking one-half of the gain (similar to capital gains treatment) on the disposition [$3,900 = (1/2)($93,400 - $85,600)].

Exercise Five - 14 Solution

The following table compares the balance in the CEC account assuming the election is not made with the balance assuming the election is made:

	No Election	With Election
2012 Addition [(3/4)($514,000)]	$385,500	$385,500
CEC Amount [($385,500)(7%)]	(26,985)	(26,985)
January 1, 2013 CEC Balance	$358,515	$358,515
Proceeds Of Sale [(3/4)($296,000)]	(222,000)	Nil
Deemed Proceeds Of Sale [(3/4)($223,000)]	Nil	(167,250)
Balance After Sale	$136,515	$191,265
Taxable Capital Gain [(1/2)($296,000 - $223,000)]	N/A	$ 36,500

If no election is made, there will be no income inclusion and the only tax consequence of the disposition is a reduction in the current and future CEC amounts.

If an election is made, there would be a capital gain of $73,000 ($296,000 - $223,000), resulting in an income inclusion of $36,500 [(1/2)($73,000)] and a balance in the CEC account that is $54,750 ($191,265 - $136,515) higher. Note that this $54,750 equals three-quarters of the $73,000 capital gain that was recognized using the election.

Self Study Solution Five - 1

Part A

Note that the calculation of UCC balances is not required. The required calculation of the maximum CCA is as follows:

	Class 1	Class 8
Opening Balance And CCA Base	$876,000	$220,000
CCA Rate	4%	20%
Maximum CCA	$ 35,040	$ 44,000

Class 10.1	Porsche	Cadillac
Opening Balance And CCA Base	$25,500	$25,500
CCA Rate	30%	30%
Maximum CCA (**Class 10.1 = $15,300**)	$ 7,650	$ 7,650

Opening Balance - **Class 10**		$95,000
Additions	$122,000	
Dispositions - Lesser Of:		
• Cost = $118,000		
• Proceeds Of Disposition = $87,000	(87,000)	35,000
One-Half Net Additions [(1/2)($35,000)]		(17,500)
CCA Base		$112,500
CCA Rate		30%
Maximum CCA		$ 33,750

This gives a maximum amount for CCA of $125,795 ($35,040 + $44,000 + $13,005 + $33,750) for the taxation year.

Part B

Since Marion Enterprises only has Net and Taxable Income before CCA of $53,000, the business may wish to deduct less than the maximum CCA that is available to them. However, there is no question that the business will wish to deduct the $53,000 that is required to reduce the current year's Taxable Income to nil.

Further, it would be advisable to deduct an additional $39,000. This would create a business loss in 2013 of $39,000, which could then be carried back to claim refunds of taxes paid in the three preceding years. If we ignore the possibility of loss carry forwards, no additional CCA would be taken in 2013. Given this, the total deduction would be $92,000 ($53,000 + $39,000).

Assuming the 2013 CCA deduction is limited to $92,000, it would normally be deducted in the class or classes with the lowest rates. This would leave the unused amounts in classes with higher rates which, in turn, would maximize the amount that could be deducted in the first profitable years.

As they are both 30 percent declining balance classes, the remaining $12,960 could be taken from either Class 10 or both Class 10.1 assets. It would be advisable to use Class 10.1, as recapture is not recorded for this class. Since the Porsche will be sold, the maximum CCA should be deducted from the Class 10.1 of the Porsche.

If there were no plans to sell the Porsche, the decision of which car to take maximum CCA on would have to consider the estimated proceeds of disposition and the anticipated disposal date of each car. For example, if the Cadillac was to be sold for proceeds of $10,000, the fact that Class 10.1 does not allow terminal losses would have to be considered.

Taking this approach, the $92,000 would be deducted as follows:

Class 1 (Maximum Available)	$35,040
Class 8 (Maximum Available)	44,000
Class 10.1 - Porsche (Maximum Available)	7,650
Class 10.1 - Cadillac (Balance Required)	5,310
Total CCA	$92,000

This $92,000 CCA deduction would reduce 2013 Taxable Income to nil. In addition, it would create a loss carry back that could be used to eliminate the Taxable Income reported in the three preceding years, resulting in a refund of any taxes paid during that period.

Note that if there were immediate plans to sell the building for more than its opening UCC, this could affect the choice of Classes to deduct CCA from as any additional CCA taken on Class 1 would have to be added to income as recaptured CCA when the building is sold.

Self Study Solution Five - 2

Class 1

The required information is calculated as follows:

Opening Balance	$115,000
Additions	Nil
Dispositions - Lesser Of:	
• Cost = $190,000	
• Proceeds Of Disposition = $110,000	(110,000)
Balance Before Terminal Loss	$ 5,000
Terminal Loss	(5,000)
January 1, 2014 UCC Balance	Nil

Since the building sold is the last asset in the class, there is a terminal loss of $5,000. The proceeds of disposition for the building total $110,000 ($260,000 - $150,000). As the adjusted cost base of the land is equal to the proceeds of disposition, there is no gain on the disposition of the land.

Class 8

The required information is calculated as follows:

Opening Balance		$ 96,000
Additions	$52,000	
Dispositions - Lesser Of:		
• Cost = $75,000		
• Proceeds Of Disposition = $35,000	(35,000)	17,000
One-Half Net Additions [(1/2)($17,000)]		(8,500)
CCA Base		$104,500
CCA At 20 Percent		(20,900)
One-Half Net Additions		8,500
January 1, 2014 UCC Balance		$ 92,100

Class 10

The required information is calculated as follows:

Opening Balance		$ 6,700
Additions	$ 8,000	
Dispositions - Lesser Of:		
• Cost = $20,000		
• Proceeds = $25,000	(20,000)	(12,000)
One-Half Net Additions (Only If Positive)		N/A
Negative Ending Balance		($ 5,300)
Recapture		5,300
January 1, 2014 UCC Balance		Nil

As the cost of the used car is less than $30,000, its cost is added to Class 10. With respect to the retirement, only the capital cost of the truck sold is deducted from Class 10. The excess of the $25,000 proceeds over the capital cost of $20,000 is a $5,000 capital gain, one-half of which would be taxable. The $12,000 net deduction creates a negative balance in the class and, as a consequence, no CCA will be taken for 2013. However, the negative balance of $5,300 will have to be taken into income as recapture. Note that detailed coverage of capital gains is available in Chapter 8 of the text.

Class 29

The manufacturing and processing equipment in Class 29 is subject to straight-line CCA at 50 percent. After taking into consideration the half-year rule, this results in a three year straight-line write-off at 25%/50%/25%. The 2013 CCA on Class 29 is $50,000 [(50%)($100,000)]. Note that the 2012 CCA of $25,000 ($100,000 - $75,000) was calculated using 25 percent [(1/2)(50%)] of the capital cost.

This leaves a January 1, 2014 UCC balance of $25,000, all of which can be claimed as CCA in 2014.

Summary Of Results (Required)

The preceding results can be summarized as follows:

Terminal Loss - Class 1	($ 5,000)
CCA - Class 8	(20,900)
Recapture - Class 10	5,300
CCA - Class 29	(50,000)
Subtotal	($70,600)
Taxable Capital Gain - Class 10 [(1/2)($25,000 - $20,000)]	2,500
Decrease In Net Income For Tax Purposes	($68,100)

Self Study Solution Five - 3

2008 Solution

The required calculations are as follows:

Additions To Class [(20 Cars)($12,000)]	$240,000
One-Half Net Additions [(1/2)($240,000)]	(120,000)
CCA Base	$120,000
CCA [(30%)($120,000)(122/365)]	(12,033)
One-Half Net Additions	120,000
January 1, 2009 UCC Balance	$227,967

Note that one-half of the net additions for the year is deducted to provide the basis for calculating the 2008 CCA, and then added back to establish the opening UCC base for the next period. The other point that is illustrated in this first year is application of the short fiscal period rules. As the business was established on September 1, 2008, its operations were carried out for only 122 of the 365 days in that year. This means that only a proportionate share of the annual CCA charge may be taken. Note that it is the length of the taxation year, not the period of ownership of the assets, which establishes the fraction of the year for which CCA is to be recorded.

2009 Solution

The required calculations are as follows:

Opening Balance For The Class	$227,967
Additions [(5 Cars)($12,500)]	62,500
Dispositions - Lesser Of:	
• Capital Cost = 3 @ $12,000 = $36,000	
• Proceeds Of Disposition = $27,500	(27,500)
One-Half Net Additions [(1/2)($62,500 - $27,500)]	(17,500)
CCA Base	$245,467
CCA [(30%)($245,467)]	(73,640)
One-Half Net Additions	17,500
January 1, 2010 UCC Balance	$189,327

Here again, one-half of the net additions for the year are deducted in establishing the base for calculating CCA, with the same amount being added back to determine the opening UCC for the next period.

2010 Solution

The required calculations are as follows:

Opening Balance For The Class	$189,327
Dispositions - Lesser Of:	
• Capital Cost = 4 @ $12,000 = $48,000	
• Proceeds Of Disposition = $38,000	(38,000)
One-Half Net Additions	N/A
CCA Base	$151,327
CCA [(30%)($151,327)]	(45,398)
January 1, 2011 UCC Balance	$105,929

The calculations are simplified by the absence of additions to the delivery car fleet. To establish the CCA base, it is only necessary to deduct the proceeds of the dispositions. The new UCC is the CCA base, less the CCA for the period.

2011 Solution

The required calculations are as follows:

Opening Balance For The Class	$105,929
Dispositions - Lesser Of:	
• Capital Cost = 13 @ $12,000	
+ 3 @ $12,500 = $193,500	
• Proceeds Of Disposition = $128,000	(128,000)
Negative Ending Balance	($ 22,071)
Recaptured CCA (i.e. Recapture)	22,071
January 1, 2012 UCC Balance	Nil

The inability to replace the fleet cars in a timely fashion was a costly mistake in that the $22,071 in recapture will be included in the 2011 Net Income. In a more realistic situation, it is likely that actions would have been taken to delay the retirement of the older cars and, thereby, avoid the tax implications of recapture. Note also that when recapture occurs, the balance in the class for the next period is reduced to zero.

2012 Solution

The required calculations are as follows:

Opening Balance For The Class	Nil
Acquisitions [(25 Cars)($16,000)]	$400,000
One-Half Net Additions [(1/2)($400,000)]	(200,000)
CCA Base	$200,000
CCA [(30%)($200,000)]	(60,000)
One-Half Net Additions	200,000
January 1, 2013 UCC Balance	$340,000

As was the case in 2008 and 2009, one-half of the net additions must be deducted in establishing the base for CCA and then added back to determine the opening UCC balance for the next period.

2013 Solution

The required calculations are as follows:

Opening Balance For The Class	$340,000
Dispositions - Lesser Of:	
• Capital Cost = 2 @ $12,500	
+ 25 @ $16,000 = $425,000	
• Proceeds Of Disposition = $268,000	(268,000)
Balance Before Terminal Loss	$ 72,000
Terminal Loss	(72,000)
January 1, 2014 UCC Balance	Nil

After all of the assets in Class 10 have been retired there is still a $72,000 UCC balance. This results in a terminal loss that will be deducted in full from the Net Income of Golden Dragon Ltd. The terminal loss will also be deducted from the UCC balance leaving a January 1, 2014 balance of nil.

Self Study Solution Five - 4

Class 1 and Class 3 - Buildings

As the new non-residential building has been allocated to a separate Class 1 and is used 100 percent for non-residential purposes, it is eligible for an enhanced CCA rate. As no manufacturing and processing is involved, the enhanced rate will be 6 percent. Based on this, the maximum 2013 CCA amounts and January 1, 2014 UCC balances are as follows:

	Separate Class 1	Class 3
Addition	$258,000	N/A
One-Half Net Additions	(129,000)	
CCA Base/Opening UCC	$129,000	$1,562,000
Maximum CCA:		
[(6%)($129,000)]	(7,740)	
[(5%)($1,562,000)]		(78,100)
Add: One-Half Net Additions	129,000	N/A
January 1, 2014 UCC	$250,260	$1,483,900

Class 8 - Office Furniture And Equipment

The required calculations for this class would be as follows:

Opening Balance		$278,000
Additions	$72,000	
Disposition of Furniture - Lesser Of:		
• Capital Cost = $38,000		
• Proceeds Of Disposition = $42,000	(38,000)	
Disposition Due To Fire - Lesser Of:		
• Capital Cost = $18,000		
• Proceeds Of Disposition = $11,000	(11,000)	23,000
One-Half Net Additions [(50%)($23,000)]		(11,500)
CCA Base		$289,500
2013 CCA [(20%)($289,500)]		(57,900)
One-Half Net Additions		11,500
January 1, 2014 UCC Balance		$243,100

With respect to the sale that occurred during the year, there would be a capital gain of $4,000 ($42,000 - $38,000), one-half, or $2,000, of which would be included in the Company's Net Income For Tax Purposes.

Class 10 - Vehicles

The required calculations for this class would be as follows:

Opening Balance		$204,000
Additions	$63,000	
Disposition of Truck - Lesser Of:		
• Capital Cost = $37,000		
• Proceeds Of Disposition = $12,000	(12,000)	51,000
One-Half Net Additions [(50%)($51,000)]		(25,500)
CCA Base		$229,500
2013 CCA [(30%)($229,500)]		(68,850)
One-Half Net Additions		25,500
January 1, 2014 UCC Balance		$186,150

Class 13 - Leasehold Improvements

In general, leasehold improvements will be written off over the term of the lease on a straight line basis. For purposes of applying this calculation, the term of the lease includes the first renewal option beginning in a period after the improvements were made. In the case of the original improvements, the period to be used is 10 years. With respect to the improvements during the current period, the write-off period will be 8 years. Also note that Class 13 assets are subject to the first year rules on net additions. The required calculation is as follows:

Opening Balance	$106,250
Additions	58,000
CCA Base	$164,250
2013 CCA:	
• First Improvements ($125,000 ÷ 10)	(12,500)
• Current Improvements [($58,000 ÷ 8)(1/2)]	(3,625)
January 1, 2014 UCC Balance	$148,125

Class 29 - Manufacturing Equipment

The required calculations are as follows:

Opening Balance	$126,000
Disposition - Lesser Of:	
• Capital Cost = $504,000	
• Proceeds Of Disposition = $89,000	(89,000)
Balance Before Terminal Loss	$ 37,000
Terminal Loss	(37,000)
January 1, 2014 UCC Balance	Nil

After all of the assets in Class 29 have been retired there is still a $37,000 UCC balance. This results in a terminal loss that will be deducted in full from the Net Income of Burton Steel Ltd. The terminal loss will also be deducted from the UCC balance.

Class 50 - Computers

The required calculations are as follows:

Opening Balance	$11,000
Additions	17,000
One-Half Net Additions [(50%)($17,000)]	(8,500)
CCA Base	$19,500
2013 CCA [(55%)($19,500)]	(10,725)
One-Half Net Additions	8,500
January 1, 2014 UCC	$ 17,275

Summary Of The Results (Not Required)

The maximum CCA for the year ending December 31, 2013 and the January 1, 2014 UCC balances can be summarized as follows:

	Maximum CCA	UCC
Class 1	$ 7,740	$ 250,260
Class 3	78,100	1,483,900
Class 8	57,900	243,100
Class 10	68,850	186,150
Class 13	16,125	148,125
Class 29	Nil	Nil
Class 50	10,725	17,275

In addition, the following income effects resulted from the information provided in the problem:

Taxable Capital Gain On Class 8 Assets [(1/2)($4,000)]	$ 2,000
Terminal Loss On Class 29 Assets	(37,000)
Total Deduction	($35,000)

Self Study Solution Five - 5

The required schedule showing the relevant balances in the cumulative eligible capital account would be as follows:

	CEC Balance	CEC Deductions
2010 Addition [(3/4)($500,000)]	$375,000	
CEC Amount At 7 Percent	(26,250)	$26,250
CEC Balance, January 1, 2011	$348,750	
CEC Amount At 7 Percent	(24,413)	24,413
CEC Balance, January 1, 2012	$324,337	
CEC Amount At 7 Percent	(22,704)	22,704
CEC Balance, January 1, 2013	$301,633	
Proceeds From Sale [(3/4)($780,000)]	(585,000)	
Balance After Sale	($283,367)	$73,367

As can be seen in the preceding table, $73,367 of the negative balance reflects CEC deductions that have been made in previous years. This full amount will have to be included in 2013 income.

The remaining $210,000 ($283,367 - $73,367) reflects three-quarters of the $280,000 ($780,000 - $500,000) gain on the disposition. This will have to be converted to the one-half capital gains inclusion rate by multiplying by two-thirds. The result is $140,000 [(2/3)($210,000)]. Note that this is half of the gain on the disposition of the goodwill [(1/2)($780,000 - $500,000)].

This gives a total 2013 income inclusion of $213,367 ($73,367 + $140,000).

Self Study Solution Five - 6

Class 1 - Buildings (Existing And Separate Class)
As the new building has been allocated to a separate Class 1, two calculations are required here. The CCA on the existing Class 1 would be as follows:

Opening UCC Balance	$590,000
Disposition - Lesser Of:	
Proceeds = $290,000 ($440,000 - $150,000)	
Capital Cost = $300,000 ($475,000 - $175,000)	(290,000)
CCA Base	$300,000
Rate	4%
Maximum 2013 CCA	$ 12,000

Since the replacement building is new, used 100 percent for non-residential purposes and allocated to a separate Class 1, it qualifies for an enhanced CCA rate. As it is not used for manufacturing and processing, the enhanced rate is 6 percent. Using this rate, the CCA on the new building would be as follows:

Opening UCC Balance	Nil
Additions ($500,000 - $125,000)	$375,000
One-Half Net Additions	(187,500)
CCA Base	$187,500
Rate	6%
Maximum 2013 CCA	$ 11,250

Class 8 - Furniture

The required calculation here would be as follows:

Opening UCC Balance	$570,000
Additions	14,000
One-Half Net Additions	(7,000)
CCA Base	$577,000
Rate	20%
Maximum 2013 CCA	$115,400

Class 10 - Vehicles

The required calculations here would be as follows:

Opening UCC Balance	$61,000
Additions	22,000
One-Half Net Additions*	Nil
CCA Base	$83,000
Rate	30%
Maximum 2013 CCA	$24,900

*As the acquired truck was a depreciable property (it had a UCC balance) transferred from a non-arm's length person, the half-year rules do not apply to this acquisition. The shareholder's UCC does not affect the CCA calculations for Bartel Ltd.

Class 14 - Limited Life Franchise

The franchise would be allocated to Class 14 and amortized on a straight line basis over its legal life. The maximum 2013 CCA would be $20,000 ($120,000 ÷ 6). Note that the half-year rule is not applicable to Class 14.

CEC

The maximum deduction from the cumulative eligible capital account is calculated as follows:

Goodwill Purchased [(3/4)($92,000)]	$69,000
Unlimited Life Franchise [(3/4)($28,000)]	21,000
2011 Base	$90,000
CEC Amount At 7 Percent	(6,300)
January 1, 2012 Balance	$83,700
2012 Disposition [(3/4)($59,000)]	(44,250)
2012 Base	$39,450
CEC Amount At 7 Percent	(2,762)
January 1, 2013 Balance	$36,688
CEC Amount At 7 Percent	(2,568)
January 1, 2014 Balance (Not Required)	$34,120

Summary (Not Required)

The total deductible CCA and CEC write-off is as follows:

Class 1	$ 12,000
Class 1	11,250
Class 8	115,400
Class 10	24,900
Class 14	20,000
CEC Amount	2,568
Total CCA And CEC Deductible	**$186,118**

Self Study Solution Five - 7

Class 1 - Building

There were no additions or dispositions in this class. As a consequence, the maximum 2013 CCA would be $25,000 [(4%)($625,000)]. The January 1, 2014 UCC of Class 1 would be $600,000 ($625,000 - $25,000).

Class 8 - Office Furniture And Equipment

The required calculations for this class would be as follows:

Opening UCC Balance		$155,000
Additions	$27,000	
Dispositions - Lesser Of:		
• Capital Cost = $22,000		
• Proceeds Of Disposition = $35,000	(22,000)	5,000
One-Half Net Additions [(1/2)($5,000)]		(2,500)
CCA Base		$157,500
2013 CCA [(20%)($157,500)]		(31,500)
One-Half Net Additions		2,500
January 1, 2014 UCC Balance		$128,500

The sale of the furniture and equipment would result in a taxable capital gain that would be calculated as follows:

Proceeds Of Disposition	$35,000
Capital Cost	(22,000)
Capital Gain	$13,000
Inclusion Rate	1/2
Taxable Capital Gain	$ 6,500

Class 10 - Vehicles

The required calculations for this class would be as follows:

Opening UCC Balance		$118,000
Additions	$33,000	
Disposition of Truck - Lesser Of:		
• Capital Cost = $23,000		
• Proceeds Of Disposition = $8,500	(8,500)	
Disposition of Car - Lesser Of:		
• Capital Cost = $17,000		
• Proceeds Of Disposition = $8,000	(8,000)	16,500
One-Half Net Additions [(1/2)($16,500)]		(8,250)
CCA Base		$126,250
2013 CCA [(30%)($126,250)]		(37,875)
One-Half Net Additions		8,250
January 1, 2014 UCC Balance		$ 96,625

Note that the amount received from the insurance company on the destroyed vehicle is treated as proceeds from a disposition.

Class 12 - Tools

Tools that cost $500 or less are allocated to Class 12 where they are not subject to the half-year rule. This means that they are eligible for a write-off rate of 100 percent in the year of acquisition. As a consequence, the entire $34,000 can be deducted as CCA for 2013, leaving a nil January 1, 2014 UCC balance.

Class 13 - Leasehold Improvements

In general, leasehold improvements will be written off over the term of the lease on a straight line basis. For purposes of applying this calculation, the term of the lease would include the first renewal option, beginning in a period after the improvements were made. In the case of the original improvements, the period to be used is 12 years. With respect to the improvements during the current year, the write-off period will be 9 years. Also note that Class 13 assets are subject to the half-year rules on net additions. The required calculations are as follows:

Opening UCC Balance		$ 61,750
Additions		45,000
CCA Base		$106,750
CCA:		
• 2010 Improvements ($78,000 ÷ 12)	($6,500)	
• 2013 Improvements [($45,000 ÷ 9)(1/2)]	(2,500)	(9,000)
January 1, 2014 UCC Balance		$ 97,750

Class 29 - Manufacturing Equipment

The required calculations are as follows:

Opening UCC Balance	$217,000
Dispositions - Lesser Of:	
• Capital Cost = $752,000	
• Proceeds Of Disposition = $188,000	(188,000)
Balance Before Terminal Loss	$ 29,000
Terminal Loss	(29,000)
January 1, 2014 UCC Balance	Nil

After all of the assets in Class 29 have been retired there is still a $29,000 UCC balance. This results in a terminal loss that will be deducted in full from the Net Income of Atlantic Manufacturing Company.

Class 50 - Computer Hardware
The required calculations are as follows:

Opening UCC Balance	$ Nil
Additions	28,000
One-Half Net Additions	(14,000)
CCA Base	$14,000
2013 CCA [(55%)($14,000)]	(7,700)
One-Half Net Additions	14,000
January 1, 2014 UCC Balance	$20,300

Cumulative Eligible Capital
The required calculations for the sale of the licence would be as follows:

Opening Balance	Nil
Proceeds Of Disposition [($87,000)(3/4)]	($65,250)
Negative Balance	($65,250)
Addition To Balance	65,250
January 1, 2014 Balance	Nil

The proceeds are based on 75 percent of the amount received. Therefore, 75 percent of the proceeds of $87,000 would be deducted, thereby creating a negative balance for cumulative eligible capital in the amount of $65,250. As no CEC has been deducted in previous years, the entire negative balance in the cumulative eligible capital account would be multiplied by two-thirds (1/2 ÷ 3/4), resulting in an income inclusion of $43,500 [(1/2)($87,000)]. In effect, the entire $87,000 proceeds is being given capital gains treatment, with only one-half of this amount being included in income. The $65,250 will also be added back to the CEC balance, restoring the balance to nil.

Other Income Effects
In addition, the following income effects resulted from the information provided in the problem:

Taxable Capital Gain On Class 8 Assets [(1/2)($13,000)]	$ 6,500
Terminal Loss On Class 29 Assets	(29,000)
Income From License Sale [(2/3)($65,250)]	43,500
Total Inclusion	$21,000

Summary Of CCA And UCC Results (Not Required)
The maximum 2013 CCA and the January 1, 2014 UCC balances can be summarized as follows:

	Maximum CCA	UCC
Class 1	$ 25,000	$600,000
Class 8	31,500	128,500
Class 10	37,875	96,625
Class 12	34,000	Nil
Class 13	9,000	97,750
Class 29	Nil	Nil
Class 50	7,700	20,300

Self Study Solution Five - 8

Part A

The maximum CEC deductions for 2011, 2012, and 2013 would be calculated as follows:

	CEC Balance	CEC Deductions
Balance January 1, 2011	$2,345,000	
Acquisition [(3/4)($400,000)]	300,000	
Balance Before CEC Deduction	$2,645,000	
2011 CEC Amount [(7%)($2,645,000)]	(185,150)	$185,150
Balance January 1, 2012	$2,459,850	
Dispositions:		
Goodwill [(3/4)($240,000)]	(180,000)	
Franchise [(3/4)($160,000)]	(120,000)	
Balance Before CEC	$2,159,850	
2012 CEC Amount [(7%)($2,159,850)]	(151,190)	151,190
Balance January 1, 2013	$2,008,660	
Disposition [(3/4)($560,000)]	(420,000)	
Balance Before CEC	$1,588,660	
2013 CEC Amount [(7%)$1,588,660)]	(111,206)	111,206
Balance January 1, 2014	$1,477,454	$447,546

As shown in the preceding schedule, the maximum CEC deductions for the 3 years total $447,546.

Part B

As can be seen in the Part A table, the deductions for the dispositions always leave a positive CEC balance. This means that no amount will have to be included in CRI's Net Income For Tax Purposes as a result of the dispositions.

Part C

With respect to the 2012 disposals, ITA 14(1.01) cannot be used for disposals of goodwill. In addition, it cannot be used when the proceeds of disposition are less than the original cost of the eligible capital expenditure (a loss situation). Given this, the 2012 results cannot be altered through the use of this election.

As the proceeds resulting from the 2013 election exceed the cost of the eligible capital expenditure, ITA 14(1.01) can be used. Under this election, three-quarters of the original cost would be deducted from the CEC balance, changing the Part A results as follows:

Balance January 1, 2013	$2,008,660
Three-Quarters Of Cost [(3/4)($400,000)]	(300,000)
CEC Balance After Disposition	$1,708,660
2013 CEC Amount [(7%)($1,708,660)]	(119,606)
Balance January 1, 2014	$1,589,054
Proceeds Of Disposition	$560,000
Cost Of Franchise	(400,000)
Capital Gain	$160,000
Inclusion Rate	1/2
Taxable Capital Gain	$ 80,000

Use Of The Election
Without the election, there is a 2013 deduction of $111,206.

With the election, there is a taxable capital gain of $80,000 and a 2013 deduction of $119,606 equaling a net deduction of $39,606 ($80,000 - $119,606).

The probable reason for making this election would be that CRI has unused allowable capital losses from the current or previous years. By making this election the Company has created a taxable capital gain which will allow for the use of up to $80,000 in allowable capital losses. If this is not the case, using the election has added $71,600 ($111,206 - $39,606) to income.

Chapter 5 Learning Objectives

After completing Chapter 5, you should be able to:

1. Describe the differences between the accounting procedures used for depreciable assets and the tax procedures used for these assets (paragraph [P hereafter] 5-1 through 5-11).

2. Determine the types of costs that are included in the amounts that are added to depreciable asset classes (P 5-12 through 5-22).

3. Recall the basic available for use rules (P 5-23 through 5-25).

4. Recall the general rules for segregating depreciable assets into classes (P 5-26 through 5-28).

5. Recall the types of assets that must be allocated to separate classes (P 5-29).

6. Explain the basic elements of the CCA system (P 5-30 and 5-31).

7. Apply the rates and methods that are applicable to common CCA classes in order to determine the maximum CCA for the period (P 5-32).

8. Apply the half-year (first year) rules in the determination of maximum CCA for the period (P 5-33 through 5-37).

9. Apply the short fiscal period rules in the determination of maximum CCA for the period (P 5-38 through 5-42).

10. Explain the tax planning considerations that are involved when a business takes less than maximum CCA (P 5-43 through 5-47).

11. Determine the tax consequences associated with dispositions of depreciable assets, including recapture, terminal losses, and capital gains (P 5-48 through 5-68).

12. Apply the provisions relating to separate class elections and other special situations (P 5-69 through 5-80).

13. Apply the provisions relating to additions, amortization and dispositions of eligible capital expenditures (P 5-81 through 5-106).

CHAPTER 6

How To Work Through Chapter 6

We recommend the following approach in dealing with the material in this chapter:

Overview And Classification Of Business Income
❑ Read paragraph 6-1 to 6-16 (in the textbook).

Business Income Vs. Property Income
❑ Read paragraph 6-17 to 6-27.
❑ Do Exercise Six-1 (in the textbook) and check the solution on page S-104 in this Study Guide.

Business Income Vs. Capital Gains
❑ Read paragraph 6-28 to 6-42.
❑ Do Exercise Six-2 and check the solution in this Study Guide.

Business Income And GAAP
❑ Read paragraph 6-43 to 6-45.

Inclusions - Amounts Received And Receivable
❑ Read paragraph 6-46 to 6-53.

Reserves For Doubtful Debts, Undelivered Goods And Unpaid Amounts
❑ Read paragraph 6-54 to 6-61.
❑ Do Exercise Six-3 and check the solution in this Study Guide.
❑ Read paragraph 6-62.
❑ Do Exercise Six-4 and check the solution in this Study Guide.
❑ Read paragraph 6-63 to 6-64.
❑ Do Exercise Six-5 and check the solution in this Study Guide.
❑ Do Self Study Problems Six-1 and Six-2 at the end of the textbook chapter on page 280 and check the solutions in this Study Guide.

Other Inclusions
❑ Read paragraph 6-65.

Limitations On Deductions From Business And Property Income, Including Home Office Costs
❑ Read paragraph 6-66 to 6-93.
❑ Do Exercise Six-6 and check the solution in this Study Guide.
❑ Read paragraph 6-94 to 6-100.
❑ Do Exercise Six-7 and check the solution in this Study Guide.
❑ Do Self Study Problem Six-3 and check the solution in this Study Guide.
❑ Read paragraph 6-101 to 6-105.

Limitations On Deductions From Business, Property, And Employment Income - Reasonableness, Meals And Entertainment

❑ Read paragraph 6-106 to 6-114.

Restrictions On Automobile Costs

❑ Read paragraph 6-115 to 6-120.
❑ Do Exercise Six-8 and check the solution in this Study Guide.
❑ Read paragraph 6-121 to 6-128.
❑ Do Exercise Six-9 and check the solution in this Study Guide.
❑ Do Self Study Problems Six-4 and Six-5 and check the solutions in this Study Guide.

Leasing Property

❑ Read paragraph 6-129 to 6-131.
❑ Do Exercise Six-10 and check the solution in this Study Guide.

Illegal Payments, Fines And Penalties

❑ Read paragraph 6-132 and 6-133.

Specific Deductions From Business Income, Including Cost Of Sales

❑ Read paragraph 6-134 to 6-142.
❑ Do Exercise Six-11 and check the solution in this Study Guide.
❑ Do Self Study Problem Six-6 and check the solution in this Study Guide.
❑ Read paragraph 6-143 to 6-144.

Reconciliation Of Accounting Net Income And Net Income For Tax Purposes

❑ Read paragraph 6-145 to 6-150.
❑ Do Self Study Problems Six-7 to Six-9 and check the solutions in this Study Guide.

Taxation Year And Additional Business Income

❑ Read paragraph 6-151 to 6-158.
❑ Do Exercise Six-12 and check the solution in this Study Guide.
❑ Do Self Study Problem Six-10 and check the solution in this Study Guide.

Income For Farmers

❑ Read paragraph 6-159 to 6-167.
❑ Do Exercise Six-13 and check the solution in this Study Guide.
❑ Read paragraph 6-168 to 6-172.

Professional Income (Billed Basis Of Recognition)

❑ Read paragraph 6-173 to 6-175.
❑ Do Exercise Six-14 and check the solution in this Study Guide.
❑ Do Self Study Problems Six-11 and Six-12 and check the solutions in this Study Guide.

Sale Of A Business and SR&ED Expenditures

❑ Read paragraph 6-176 to 6-181.
❑ Do Exercise Six-15 and check the solution in this Study Guide.
❑ Read paragraph 6-182 and 6-183.
❑ Do Self Study Problem Six-13 and check the solution in this Study Guide.

To Complete This Chapter

❑ Do Self Study Problem Six-14 and check the solution in this Study Guide.
❑ Review the Key Terms Used In This Chapter on page 278. Consult the Glossary for the meaning of any key terms you do not know.
❑ Review the Glossary Flashcards and complete the Key Terms Self-Test for the Chapter. These features can be found in two places, on your Student CD-ROM under the heading "Key Term Practice" and on the web site.

❑ Review the Learning Objectives of the Chapter found on page S-124 of this Study Guide.
❑ As a final review, we recommend that you view the PowerPoint Slides for Chapter 6 that are on your Student CD-ROM. The PowerPoint Viewer program can be installed from the Student CD-ROM.

Practice Examination

❑ Write the Practice Examination for Chapter 6 that is on your Student CD-ROM. Mark your examination using the Practice Examination Solution that is also on your Student CD-ROM.

Solution to Chapter Six Exercises

Exercise Six - 1 Solution

With a single transaction, Joan's activity clearly does not fall within the general definition of operating a business. However, the real question is whether this transaction would be considered an adventure or concern in the nature of trade. As she is not behaving like a dealer and does not appear to have an intent to sell the song rights, it is unlikely that this transaction would be viewed as an adventure or concern in the nature of trade. This means that the royalties would be treated as property income, rather than business income. While this classification would not be important as long as she holds the rights, if there is a disposition of these rights, any gain would be treated as a capital gain, rather than as a fully taxable business gain.

Exercise Six - 2 Solution

Provided that she can demonstrate that her intent was to operate the building as a rental property, the gain should qualify as a capital gain. The fact that the offer was unsolicited would support this conclusion.

Exercise Six - 3 Solution

The Bad Debt Expense would be as follows:

2013 Estimate Of Future Bad Debts (Credit Allowance)	($18,400)
Increase In Expense To Eliminate Debit Balance In Allowance	
($17,200 Actual Write-Offs - $16,000 Allowance)	(1,200)
2013 Bad Debt Expense For Accounting Purposes	($19,600)

For tax purposes, the net decrease for the year will be the same $19,600 calculated as follows:

Add: 2012 Reserve For Tax Purposes		$ 16,000
Deduct:		
2013 Actual Write-Offs	($17,200)	
2013 Reserve For Tax Purposes	(18,400)	(35,600)
2013 Net Deduction For Tax Purposes		($19,600)

Exercise Six - 4 Solution

The amount to be included in net business income would be calculated as follows:

Cash Sales	$53,400
Accounts Receivable	26,300
Reserve For Undelivered Services	(5,600)
Reserve For Doubtful Accounts	(425)
Total Increase	$73,675

Exercise Six - 5 Solution

As some of the proceeds are not receivable for more than two years after the date of sale, a reserve can be deducted under ITA 20(1)(n) for the years 2013, 2014, and 2015. As December 31, 2016 is more than 36 months after the sale was made, no reserve can be deducted for 2016 or 2017. Note that the previous year's reserve is added to income before deducting the new reserve. The maximum reserve is based on the gross profit of $65,000. None of this profit will be recognized in 2013 as no proceeds are received. In 2014 and 2015, 25 percent of the profit will be recognized, with the remainder being in 2016 when no reserve can be deducted. The maximum reserve that can be deducted in each year, as well as the minimum income to be recognized in each year, is shown in the following schedule:

	Income	Proceeds Rec'd
2013 Reserve = [(100%)($65,000)] = $65,000	Nil	Nil
2014 Reserve = [(75%)($65,000)] = $48,750	$16,250	$ 30,000
2015 Reserve = [(50%)($65,000)] = $32,500	16,250	30,000
2016 Reserve = Nil	32,500	30,000
2017 Reserve = Nil (All Proceeds Received)	Nil	30,000
Totals	$65,000	$120,000

As December 31, 2016 is more than 36 months after the sale was made, no reserve can be deducted for 2016 or 2017. Note that the technically correct calculation of income involves adding back the previous year's reserve and deducting the new reserve. For example, the calculation for 2015 involves adding back the 2014 reserve of $48,750 and deducting the new reserve of $32,500 to calculate the income of $16,250 ($48,750 - $32,500).

Exercise Six - 6 Solution

As Ms. Johnson owns 30 percent of the common shares, she is clearly a specified shareholder under ITA 18(5). Her relevant equity balance would be $1,620,000 [(30%)($2,400,000) + (100%)($900,000)]. Given this, the disallowed interest would be calculated as follows:

Total Interest Paid To Ms. Johnson [(9%)($4,500,000)]	$405,000
Maximum Deductible Interest [(9%)(1.5)($1,620,000)]	(218,700)
Disallowed Interest	$186,300

Exercise Six - 7 Solution

The following work space in the home costs would be deductible in each of the three scenarios:

	Part A	Part B	Part C
Utilities	$2,400	$ 2,400	$ 2,400
Maintenance And Repairs	4,600	4,600	4,600
Property Taxes	Nil	5,200	5,200
House Insurance	Nil	2,300	2,300
Interest On Mortgage	Nil	Nil	7,800
House CCA	Nil	Nil	12,000
Subtotal	$7,000	$14,500	$34,300
Percentage	25%	25%	25%
Subtotal	$1,750	$ 3,625	$ 8,575
Employment/Business Related			
Long Distance Charges (100%)	590	590	590
Office Supplies	425	425	425
Maximum Deduction	$2,765	$ 4,640	$ 9,590

Exercise Six - 8 Solution

With respect to the amount of CCA, since the business commenced operations on September 15, 2013, the CCA is limited to the proportion of the year the business was in operation (108/365) and the first year rules would apply. The base amount for the CCA calculation is limited to the Class 10.1 maximum of $30,000. With respect to the interest, the car was financed for a total of 108 days with a limit of $10 per day. As a result, the amounts that can be deducted are as follows:

CCA [(1/2)(108/365)(30%)($30,000)]	$1,332
Interest Costs - Lesser Of:	
• Amount Paid = $1,200	
• [($10)(108 Days)] = $1,080	1,080
Total Deduction	$2,412

Exercise Six - 9 Solution

The amount he can deduct is limited to $2,229, the least of:

- $4,925 [($985)(5)];
- $4,080 [($800)(153/30)]; and
- $2,229 {[$4,925][$30,000 ÷ (85%)($78,000)]}.

Exercise Six - 10 Solution

For tax purposes, the lease would be treated as an operating lease, with the deduction being based only on the lease payments. Under Canadian GAAP, the lease would have to be treated as a purchase and capitalized. This is because during the lease term the lease transfers "substantially all of the benefits and risks of ownership related to the leased property from the lessor to the lessee". This means that the accounting deductions would be for amortization on the capitalized asset and interest costs on the associated liability.

Exercise Six - 11 Solution

The average per unit cost of $2.87 ($663,850 ÷ 231,000) is calculated as follows:

Price	Units	Total
$2.50	50,000	$125,000
$2.85	35,000	99,750
$2.95	62,000	182,900
$3.05	84,000	256,200
Totals	231,000	$663,850

The following calculations will be used in this solution.

Fair Market Value (Using Replacement Cost) [($3.10)(102,000)]	$316,200
Fair Market Value (Using Net Realizable Value) [(90%)($4.50)(102,000)]	413,100
FIFO Cost [(84,000)($3.05) + (102,000 - 84,000)($2.95)]	309,300
Average Cost [($2.87)(102,000)]	292,740

For tax purposes, the inventory value can be determined by any of the following methods.

Fair Market Value = Replacement Cost	$316,200
Fair Market Value = Net Realizable Value	413,100
Lower of FIFO Cost ($309,300) or Replacement Cost ($316,200)	309,300
Lower of FIFO Cost ($309,300) or Net Realizable Value ($413,100)	309,300
Lower of Average Cost ($292,740) or Replacement Cost ($316,200)	292,740
Lower of Average Cost ($292,740) or Net Realizable Value ($413,100)	292,740

Exercise Six - 12 Solution

Mr. Gelato's additional business income for 2013 will be $18,551 [($12,300)(184 Days ÷ 122 Days)]. The 184 days is for the period July 1 through December 31, while the 122 days is for the period March 1 through June 30. The total business income that Mr. Gelato will have to report for 2013 is $30,851 ($12,300 + $18,551).

Exercise Six - 13 Solution

For Ms. Morph, farming is clearly a secondary source of income. Given this, her farm losses will be restricted. The amount she can deduct for 2013 will be limited to $10,600 [$2,500 + (1/2)($18,700 - $2,500)]. The remaining $8,100 ($18,700 - $10,600) restricted farm loss is available for carry over.

Exercise Six - 14 Solution

Mr. Winters' income for the current year under the three alternatives would be as follows:

Cash Basis The cash basis income would be $252,000 ($35,000 + $57,000 + $160,000).

Billed Basis The billed basis income would be $220,000 ($35,000 + $185,000).

Accrual Basis The accrual basis income would be $245,000.

Exercise Six - 15 Solution

Mr. Nero would include in his business income the 2012 reserve of $3,800. He could then deduct the $5,250 ($53,450 - $48,200) loss on the receivables. The net tax effect for Mr. Nero would be a deduction in the determination of business income of $1,450 ($5,250 - $3,800).

Mr. Labelle would have to include the $5,250 difference between the face value and the price paid in income. Subsequent to the sale, 100 percent of any difference between the $53,450 face value of the receivables and amounts actually collected will be deductible when calculating Mr. Labelle's net business income.

Mr. Labelle could establish a new reserve for doubtful debts related to any uncollected receivables that are outstanding at the end of the year.

Self Study Solution Six - 1

The net deduction for bad debts in the calculation of 2013 business income would be calculated as follows:

Add:	
2012 Reserve For Doubtful Debts	$11,500
Recoveries Of 2012 Bad Debts During 2013	1,500
Deduct:	
Actual Bad Debt Write-Offs During 2013 ($8,800 - $700)	(8,100)
2013 Reserve For Doubtful Debts ($15,900 + $700)	(16,600)
2013 Net Deduction From Business Income	($11,700)

Note that the $700 that was due from Dr. Allworth's personal friend has been treated as part of the reserve for doubtful debts, rather than as part of the write-offs for the period. The $190 recovery in 2012 would have been included in income in 2012 and would not affect 2013 income.

Self Study Solution Six - 2

The results for 2013 and 2014 would be as follows:

	2013	2014
Cash Sales	$112,000	$146,000
Sales On Account	96,000	123,000
Reserve For Doubtful Debts:		
Add Prior Year Reserve	Nil	11,000
Deduct Current Year Reserve	(11,000)	(10,000)
Actual Write-Offs	Nil	(13,000)
Reserve For Unpaid Amounts*	N/A	Nil
Advances From Customers	12,000	16,000
Reserve For Undelivered Merchandise:		
Add Prior Year Reserve	Nil	12,000
Deduct Current Year Reserve	(12,000)	(16,000)
Net Effect	$197,000	$269,000

*In order to deduct a reserve for unpaid amounts on sales that are not of land, some part of the proceeds must be due more than two years after the date of the related sale. In this case, the proceeds are due 5 months after the sale and, as a consequence, no reserve for unpaid amounts can be deducted.

Self Study Solution Six - 3

Part A

Under ITA 18(12), the following conditions must be satisfied in order for expenses related to work space in a self-contained domestic establishment to be deductible:

- the work space is either the individual's principal place of business; or
- the work space is used exclusively for the purpose of earning income from business and is used on a regular and continuous basis for meeting clients, customers, or patients of the individual in respect of the business.

The deductible amount cannot exceed the individual's income from the business for the year. However, any amount not deductible because it is greater than the individual's income, can be deducted in any subsequent year provided there is sufficient income from the same business in that year. This provides for an unlimited carry forward of unused work space in home costs (see IT-514, *Work Space in Home Expenses*).

Part B

As the problem asks for "minimum" net business income, CCA on Billy's home should be included. However the necessary cost information is not provided to calculate the CCA on the house or the proportion of deductible property taxes and house insurance.

Since the work space at home is the only place where Billy teaches, it would represent his principal place of business. The calculation of business income to be reported in Billy's personal tax return is as follows:

Revenues		$3,700
Less: Expenses Other Than Work Space In Home Costs:		
Music Books	($ 250)	
Supplies	(1,000)	
Snacks (50 Percent)	(125)	
CCA (Note 1)	(490)	(1,865)
Income Before Home Work Space Costs		$1,835
Less: Home Work Space Costs (Note 2)]		(1,710)
Net Business Income		$ 125

Note 1 Maximum CCA amounts on the assets of the business (not including CCA on the house) for the short fiscal year would be calculated as follows (alternative calculations shown in the two columns):

	100%	Short Fiscal Year (275/365)
Class 8 [($5,000)(1/2)(20%)]	$500	$377
Class 12 [($300)(1/2)(100%)]	150	113
Total	$650	
Short Fiscal Year Factor	275/365	
Maximum 2013 CCA	$490	$490

Note 2 Note that the home related costs are only for the period beginning April 1, 2013, not the whole year. As a result, they do not have to be prorated for the short fiscal year. Using the information provided, the known work space in home costs would be calculated as follows:

Utilities For Home (Heat, Light, And Water)	$ 3,500
Mortgage Interest Paid	11,000
Repairs And Maintenance For Home	2,600
Property Tax	?
House Insurance	?
Total (Known) Costs For The Home	$17,100
Percentage Of Floor Space	10%
Deductible (Known) Home Work Space Costs	$ 1,710

Part C

There are a few issues that should be discussed with Billy.

- A portion of the property taxes and insurance on the home is deductible. These amounts were not provided and should be included to increase the amount deductible in 2013. Although work space in home costs cannot create a business loss, they can be carried forward and deducted from his business income in any future year.

- While it would be possible to claim CCA on his home in this problem if the information was provided, most tax advisors would discourage this. The problem is that, if he takes CCA, it could jeopardize the principal residence exemption on this property, resulting in the payment of taxes on a portion of the taxable capital gain that might arise on any future sale of the property, assuming real estate prices are increasing. This is discussed in more detail in Chapter 8. Note that if CCA on the house was taken, it would be included in the work space in home costs calculation, not the CCA calculation, and could not be taken if it created a business loss.

- The tuxedo is not deductible and is not a Class 8 asset since it is not "specialized clothing" and can be used for non-business purposes.

Self Study Solution Six - 4

Part A

In Part A(i), Ms. Wise is an employee and, because her income includes commissions, she can deduct expenses related to the production of employment income under ITA 8(1)(f), provided no deduction is made under ITA 8(1)(h) or ITA 8(1)(h.1).

Deductions under ITA 8(1)(f) are limited to the amount of commissions earned. Alternatively, traveling costs and motor vehicle costs other than capital costs can be deducted under ITA

8(1)(h) and ITA 8(1)(h.1). Deductions under these provisions are not limited to commission income.

The deduction of dues and other expenses under ITA 8(1)(i) and automobile capital costs (CCA and financing costs) under ITA 8(1)(j) is permitted without regard to other provisions used.

	ITA 8(1)(f) (Limited To $15,000)	ITA 8(1) (h) and (h.1)	ITA 8(1) (i) and (j)	Part A(ii)
Professional Dues	-	-	$ 600	$ 600
Automobile Costs:				
Operating Costs				
[(35,000/50,000)($6,000)]	$ 4,200	$ 4,200	-	4,200
Financing Costs				
[(35,000/50,000)($2,500)]	-	-	1,750	1,750
CCA (See Note)	-	-	5,355	5,355
Home Office Costs:				
Utilities [(40%)($3,550)]	-	-	1,420	1,420
Maintenance [(40%)($1,500)]	-	-	600	600
Insurance [(40%)($950)]	380	-	-	380
Property Taxes [(40%)($4,700)]	1,880	-	-	1,880
Interest [(40%)($13,500)]	-	-	-	5,400
CCA [($140,000)(4%)]	-	-	-	5,600
Travel Costs	23,000	23,000	-	23,000
Non-Deductible Meals				
[(50%)($8,000)]	(4,000)	(4,000)	-	(4,000)
Country Club Charges	12,000	-	-	12,000
Non-Deductible Membership Fees	(2,500)	-	-	(2,500)
Non-Deductible Meals				
[(50%)($9,500)]	(4,750)	-	-	(4,750)
Total	$30,210	$23,200	$9,725	$50,935

The deduction for home office costs has been split between ITA 8(1)(i) and (f). Since the utilities and maintenance portion can be deducted under ITA 8(1)(i), it is not limited by the commission income. The insurance and property tax components are limited as they are deducted under ITA 8(1)(f). A limitation, which is not illustrated in this problem, prevents the deduction of home office costs from creating an employment loss.

As the ITA 8(1)(f) amount is limited to the $15,000 in commission income, the total deduction using ITA 8(1)(f), (i) and (j), is $24,725 ($15,000 + $9,725).

The total deduction using ITA 8(1)(h), (h.1), (i) and (j), is $32,925 ($23,200 + $9,725). Note that when this approach is used, home office costs are limited to utilities and maintenance. Further, there is no deduction for entertainment costs. However, this approach results in deductions totaling $8,200 ($32,925 - $24,725) more than the amount available using ITA 8(1)(f), (i), and (j) due to the effect of the commission income limit.

Comparing Parts A (i) and A (ii), there is a difference of $18,010 ($50,935 - $32,925) between the maximum employee and self-employed calculations, illustrating the importance of the difference between being an employee and being self-employed. This problem is, of course, somewhat unrealistic in that, if Ms. Wise was an employee, it is likely that she would be compensated or reimbursed for at least part of her employment related expenses.

Note The car will be allocated to Class 10.1 at a value of $30,000, the 2012 limit. The excess of $23,000 will not be deductible. Maximum CCA for 2012 would have been $4,500 [(30%)(1/2)($30,000)]. The deductible amount for 2012 would have been this amount, multiplied by the portion of her total usage that was related to income producing activity.

The January 1, 2013 UCC would be $25,500 ($30,000 - $4,500) and maximum CCA for 2013 would have been $7,650 [(30%)($25,500)]. Note that, in determining the relevant UCC value, the full amount of maximum 2012 CCA was deducted, not just the portion that was actually deducted in that year. The deductible amount for 2013 equals $5,355 [(35,000/50,000)($7,650)].

Part B

As will be discussed in Chapter 8, capital gains on an individual's principal residence are, in general, not subject to income taxes. While a strict application of the relevant rules would remove from principal residence status the portion of Ms. Wise's home that was used for income producing activities, the administrative procedures of the CRA do not follow this approach. It appears that, as long as no CCA is taken on the work space portion of the home, 100 percent of the property will qualify as a principal residence. Given this, and the assumption that real estate prices are increasing, it would not be wise for Ms. Wise to take CCA on her office space.

Self Study Solution Six - 5

Part A

As the lease was entered into in 2012, the 2012 limits on deductibility apply for the life of the lease. The maximum deduction for automobile lease payments for 2012 would be the least of:

- $1,800
- $\left[\$800 \times \dfrac{31}{30}\right] - \text{Nil} - \left[(\$10,000 - \$1,000) \times 2\% \times \dfrac{31}{365}\right] - \$500 = \$312$
- $\left[\$1,800 \times \dfrac{\$30,000}{(85\%)(\$85,000)}\right] - \left[(\$10,000 - \$1,000) \times 2\% \times \dfrac{31}{365}\right] - \$500 = \$232$

The least of the three figures is $232 and this will be the maximum 2012 deduction for Borris Industries.

The maximum deduction for automobile lease payments for 2013 would be the least of:

- $[(\$1,800)(12)] = \$21,600$
- $\left[\$800 \times \dfrac{396}{30}\right] - \$232 - \left[(\$10,000 - \$1,000) \times 2\% \times \dfrac{396}{365}\right] - \$6,500 = \$3,633$
- $\left[\$21,600 \times \dfrac{\$30,000}{(85\%)(\$85,000)}\right] - \left[(\$10,000 - \$1,000) \times 2\% \times \dfrac{365}{365}\right] - \$6,000 = \$2,789$

The least of the three figures is $2,789 and this will be the maximum 2013 deduction for Borris Industries.

Part B

In 2012, the Mercedes was used solely for personal purposes. In 2013, it was used primarily (more than 50 percent) for employment purposes, so he is eligible for the reduced standby charge and the alternative operating cost benefit calculation. However, since Mr. Borris' personal usage exceeds 20,004 kilometers during the year, he cannot claim a reduction in the standby charge.

The taxable benefit that will be included in the Net Income For Tax Purposes of Mr. Borris for the two years is calculated as follows:

Standby Charge - No Reduction [(2/3)(1)($1,800)(1/1)]	$1,200
Operating Cost Benefit - No Alternative [($0.26)(2,500)]	650
Repayment	(500)
2012 Total Benefit	**$1,350**

Standby Charge - No Reduction [(2/3)(12)($1,800)(12/12)]	$14,400
Operating Cost Benefit - Lesser Of:	
• [(1/2)($14,400) = $7,200	
• [($0.27)(22,000)] = $5,940	5,940
Repayment [($500)(12)]	(6,000)
2013 Total Benefit	**$14,340**

Self Study Solution Six - 6

Valuation Basis
For tax purposes, the Company can use either fair market value or lower of cost and market. The inventory rules under GAAP are more restrictive as inventories must be measured using the lower of cost and net realizable value.

Market Determination - Two Possible Values
For tax purposes, the Company can measure market using either replacement cost or net realizable value. These values would be as follows:

Replacement Cost [($10.50)(22,000)]	$231,000

Net Realizable Value [($11.75)(22,000)]	$258,500

While it is not an acceptable practice under GAAP, the CRA will accept the use of market values, without regard to their relationship to cost.

Cost Determination
In the determination of cost, taxpayers are permitted to use specific identification (this would not appear to be practical here), a First In, First Out (FIFO) assumption, or Average Cost.

Using the First In, First Out method, the appropriate value for the ending inventory would be determined as follows:

17,000 Units At $12.50	$212,500
5,000 Units At $12.00	60,000
22,000 Units At FIFO Cost	**$272,500**

Based on average cost, the ending inventory value would be calculated as follows:

Number Of Units	22,000
Average Cost [($1,554,500 ÷ 136,000)]	11.43
22,000 Units At Average Cost	**$251,460**

Lower Of Cost And Market - Four Possible Values

For tax purposes, the possible values here would be as follows:

Lower Of Replacement Cost And FIFO Cost	$231,000
Lower Of Replacement Cost And Average Cost	231,000
Lower Of Net Realizable Value And FIFO Cost	258,500
Lower Of Net Realizable Value And Average Cost	251,460

For accounting purposes, only the last two values would be acceptable.

Self Study Solution Six - 7

The minimum net business income of Yossarian Tools would be calculated as follows::

Accounting Net Income	$298,000
Additions:	
Item 1 - Increase In Warranty Reserve	14,500
Item 2 - Parking Tickets	980
Item 4 - Amortization Expense	53,750
Item 6 - Contributions To Registered Charity (Note 1)	4,300
Item 9 - Golf Club Membership	1,400
Item 9 - 50% Of Business Meals (50% of $3,400)	1,700
Item 10 - Appraisal Costs (Note 2)	7,400
Item 11 - Fee Paid To Son (Note 3)	12,000
Subtotal	$394,030
Deduction:	
Item 4 - CCA	(62,000)
Net Business Income	$332,030

Note 1 Donations to charities cannot be deducted in the calculation of net business income. They will be the basis for a tax credit in the calculation of Tax Payable for Mr. Yossarian.

Note 2 The fees paid to appraise certain Company assets for sale would be added to the adjusted cost base of these assets.

Note 3 As it is extremely unlikely that 6 year olds will be buying power tools, it does not appear that the fee paid to Mr. Yossarian's son is reasonable. As a result it would not be deductible.

Other Items Further explanation related to the items not included in the preceding calculation of Net Business Income are as follows:

Item 3 As the landscaping costs have already been deducted in accounting Net Income, they do not require adjustment for tax purposes.

Item 5 While interest on late income tax instalments is clearly not deductible, there does not appear to be a similar prohibition against interest on late property taxes. We would note here that all fines and penalties are not deductible. This would not appear to include interest for late payment of municipal taxes.

Item 7 The tax treatment of such payments would be the same as the accounting treatment.

Item 8 The tax treatment of volume discounts would be the same as the accounting treatment.

Item 12 As the profits from the illegal business have already been included in accounting Net Income, they do not require adjustment for tax purposes.

Item 13 The tax treatment of the car lease and operating costs would be the same as the accounting treatment. As the monthly lease payment is less than $800, the list price is less than $35,294 ($30,000 ÷ 85%) and the car is used 100 percent for business purposes, no adjustment for tax purposes is required.

Self Study Solution Six - 8

The Net Income For Tax Purposes would be calculated as follows:

Accounting Income After Taxes	$340,000
Additions:	
Item 1 - Income Tax Expense	86,000
Item 2 - Donations To Charities (Note 1)	3,500
Item 3 - Amortization Expense	241,000
Item 5 - Amount Paid To Cousin (Note 2)	10,000
Item 7 - Warranty Reserve (Note 3)	9,000
Item 11 - Non-Deductible Meals And Entertainment (50% Of $13,500)	6,750
Item 12 - Amortization Of Bond Discount	1,800
Item 13 - Non-Deductible Lease Payments (Note 4)	13,037
Subtotal	$711,087
Deductions:	
Item 4 - Capital Cost Allowance	(389,000)
Item 9 - Issue Costs (Note 5)	(1,600)
Item 10 - Landscaping Costs	(11,000)
Net Income For Tax Purposes	$309,487

Note 1 The donations to registered charities will be deductible in the computation of Taxable Income, but not in the computation of Net Income For Tax Purposes. Charitable donations are a deduction for corporations, although they are the basis for a tax credit for individuals.

Note 2 Under ITA 67, this amount would be disallowed as not being reasonable in the circumstances.

Note 3 For tax purposes, warranty costs can only be deducted as incurred. Therefore, the $9,000 ($27,000 - $18,000) increase in the warranty reserve must be added back to accounting income.

Note 4 Under ITA 67.3, the deductible amount of the lease payments is limited to the least of:

- $18,000
- [($800)(365/30)] = $9,733
- {[$18,000][$30,000 ÷ (85%)($128,000)]} = $4,963

The non-deductible portion of the lease payments is $13,037 ($18,000 - $4,963).

Note 5 Under ITA 20(1)(e), issue costs must be amortized at the rate of 20 percent per year. As the full amount was treated as an asset in the accounting records, the required adjustment is a deduction of $1,600 [(20%)($8,000)].

Two of the items described in the problem did not require any adjustment. The explanations for these omissions are as follows:

Item 6 As the advertising was not directed at the Canadian market, it can be deducted for tax purposes and no adjustment is required.

Item 8 As the same bad debt estimates were used for tax purposes and accounting purposes, no adjustment is required with respect to bad debts.

Self Study Solution Six - 9

The Net Income For Tax Purposes of Darlington Inc. would be calculated as follows:

Accounting Income		$ 596,000
Additions:		
	Item 1 - Income Tax Expense	55,000
	Item 4 - Amortization Expense	623,000
	Item 4 - Taxable Capital Gain On Class 8 Disposition	
	[($550,000 - $400,000)(1/2)]	75,000
	Item 5 - Non-Deductible Meals And Entertainment	
	[(50%)($41,400)]	20,700
	Item 6 - Club Fees	2,500
	Item 7 - Property Taxes On Vacant Land	15,000
Subtotal		$1,387,200
Deductions:		
	Item 2 - Landscaping Costs	(95,000)
	Item 4 - Accounting Gain On Class 8 Disposition	(225,000)
	CCA (see CCA Calculations)	(925,750)
	Terminal Loss (See Class 10 CCA Calculation)	(113,000)
Net Income For Tax Purposes		$ 28,450

CCA Calculations

Class 1 - Buildings The required calculations for this class would be as follows:

Headquarters Building

January 1, 2013 UCC Balance	$1,000,000
CCA At 4 Percent	(40,000)
January 1, 2014 UCC Balance	$ 960,000

New Building (Separate Class)

Addition ($650,000 - $125,000)	$525,000
One-Half Net Additions	(262,500)
CCA Base	$262,500
CCA At 6 Percent	(15,750)
One-Half Net Additions	262,500
January 1, 2014 UCC Balance	$509,250

Class 8 - Office Furniture And Equipment The required calculations for this class would be as follows:

January 1, 2013 UCC Balance		$4,200,000
Additions	$700,000	
Dispositions - Lesser Of:		
• Proceeds = $550,000		
• Cost = $400,000	(400,000)	300,000
One-Half Net Additions		(150,000)
CCA Base		$4,350,000
CCA At 20 Percent		(870,000)
One-Half Net Additions		150,000
January 1, 2014 UCC Balance		$3,630,000

With respect to the sale that occurred during the year, there would be a capital gain of $150,000 ($550,000 - $400,000). One-half, or $75,000, is included in the Company's Net Income For Tax Purposes, and the accounting gain of $225,000 is deducted.

Class 10 - Vehicles   All of the cars were sold during the year for proceeds that totalled less than their capital cost and the UCC of the class. The remaining balance in the class of $113,000 ($800,000 - $687,000) is a terminal loss that is fully deductible.

Summary Of The Results   The maximum 2013 CCA and January 1, 2014 UCC balances can be summarized as follows:

Class	Maximum CCA	UCC
Class 1 - Main Class	$ 40,000	$ 960,000
Class 1 - Separate Class	15,750	509,250
Class 8	870,000	3,630,000
Class 10 (Terminal Loss = $113,000)	Nil	Nil
Total	$925,750	

In addition, there was a taxable capital gain on the sale of the Class 8 assets of $75,000 and a terminal loss in Class 10 of $113,000.

Other Notes

- Item 2 - Landscaping costs are fully deductible.

- Item 3 - ITA 19.01 provides for the full deduction of advertising costs in foreign periodicals directed at the Canadian market, provided 80 percent or more of their non-advertising content is original editorial content. If the original editorial content is less than 80 percent, the deduction is equal to 50 percent of the costs. Note that this applies only to periodicals and not other print or broadcast media.

- Item 7 - The property taxes on the vacant land are not deductible. They can be added to the cost of the land if the land was acquired for the purpose of earning either business or property income and may be deducted to the extent of any net income earned on the land.

Self Study Solution Six - 10

Part I

A. As covered in this Chapter 6, ITA 12(1)(l) requires inclusion of business income from a partnership. As explained in more detail in Chapter 18, Partnerships, each partner's share of partnership profits is considered personal income of each partner. The profit is calculated as though the partnership was an individual resident of Canada. Once determined, it is allocated as per the partnership agreement, with the allocated amount being included in the individual tax returns of each partner.

B. The basic rules of ITA 249.1(1) require that, in general, a partnership with members who are individuals use a December 31 fiscal year end. While ITA 249.1(4) allows a partnership to elect a fiscal year end other than December 31, this election requires complex adjustments for Additional Business Income that may or may not be worthwhile.

C. This question requires an analysis of whether the arrangement with the seamstresses is one of employment. This material is discussed in Chapter 3 which covers employment income. Detailed guidance can be found in the CRA Guide titled "Employee Or Self-Employed?" (RC4110).

    If the seamstresses are considered employees, source deductions will be required. In making this decision, the overriding consideration is the intent of the involved parties. Factors that can be considered in determining this intent include the following:

    Control   It appears that Montpetit does not exercise a large degree of control over the seamstresses. They are free to work when they choose and may provide their services to different payers at the same time. The seamstresses can choose to accept or refuse work from Montpetit.

    Ownership Of Tools And Equipment   The seamstresses provide the tools and equipment required for the work and the work is done in their homes, not in space provided by Montpetit.

    Ability To Subcontract Or Hire Assistants   It appears that Montpetit does not exercise control over who does the work as long as the quality is satisfactory.

    Financial Risk   Since the work is done for a set fee and the fabric and accessories are provided, there is no financial risk for seamstresses.

    Responsibility For Investment And Management   There is not enough information for this factor to be considered.

    Opportunity For Profit   Since the work is done for a set fee, a seamstress cannot increase her proceeds and hence the profit from a gown. Since the fabric and accessories are supplied and there would appear to be no other material expenditures needed for a gown, there is no opportunity to decrease expenses and increase profit on a gown. As a result, it does not appear that a profit could arise.

    In addition to these factors, the work is for a specific gown, not general sewing as part of an ongoing relationship.

    On balance, the seamstress contracts for the creation of designer gowns are likely contracts for service (self-employment contracts). Given this, source deductions would not be required.

Part II

A. The $800 legal fees are eligible capital expenditures. Three-quarters of the legal fees, or $600 [(75%)($800)], will be added to the cumulative eligible capital account. Seven percent of this account, or $42 [(7%)($600)], can be claimed as a deduction in calculating partnership Net Business Income.

B. The sewing machines are capital expenditures and cannot be deducted in the current year. However, a deduction will be available for CCA on these amounts. The sewing accessories can be deducted in the first year as they will be used and replaced in the same year.

C. While this point is not covered in the Business Income Chapter, because of its non-arm's length nature, interest paid to partners cannot be deducted in the determination of partnership income (see Chapter 18 on partnerships). Rather it will be treated as a drawing by the partners.

    The $10,000 contributions are of a capital nature and are not deductible in the calculation of personal Taxable Income.

D. The designer clothes held on consignment at year end are inventory of the partnership and are not deductible as cost of sales. The inventory will be valued either at lower of cost and market or, alternatively, market. The cost is given as $9,500 ($5,000 + $4,500) and the retail price is given as $26,000. It is likely that the net realizable value will be less than the full retail value, but the value cannot be determined with the information given.

E. The $15,000 payment for a limited term distribution right is a capital cost that cannot be currently deducted. However, it will be available for the deduction of CCA.

F. The payment of the annual membership is not deductible. The Crepe Suzette Diner expenses for entertainment of clients would be deductible, but they are subject to a 50 percent limitation, which means $750 [(50%)($1,500)] of these costs would be allowed as a business expense. The personal usage is not deductible.

Self Study Solution Six - 11

Christine's business income for the period ending December 31, 2013 can be calculated as follows:

Design Power
Statement of Income and Expenses
For the seven month period ended December 31, 2013

Revenues		
Revenue collected	$22,000	
Revenue billed	4,000	
Work-In-Progress (Note 1)	1,500	$27,500
Expenses		
Capital cost allowance (Note 2)	($2,383)	
Work space in home expenses [(20%)($6,400)]	(1,280)	
Legal and business license fees	(1,000)	
Meals and entertainment [(50%)($500)]	(250)	
Automobile expenses (Note 3)	(1,960)	
Office and computer supplies	(650)	
Printing sub-contract fees	(1,800)	(9,323)
Net Business Income		$18,177

Note 1 Visual designers are not eligible for the special rule under ITA 34 which allows some professionals to recognize revenues on a billed basis.

Note 2 CCA amounts are calculated as follows:

	Class 8 Furniture	Class 10 Car	Class 50 Computer	Class 12 Software
Additions	$2,000	$18,000	$5,000	$1,200
One-Half Net Additions	(1,000)	(9,000)	(2,500)	(600)
CCA Base	$1,000	$ 9,000	$2,500	$ 600
CCA Rate	20%	30%	55%	100%
CCA For Full Year	$ 200	$ 2,700	$1,375	$ 600
Deduct Non-Business Usage (Car)	N/A	(810)	N/A	N/A
Balance	$ 200	$ 1,890	$1,375	$ 600
Short Fiscal Period Factor	214/365	214/365	214/365	214/365
Deductible Amount	$ 117	$ 1,108	$ 806	$ 352

The non-business usage of the car is 30 percent. CCA is also restricted by the fact that Christine's taxation year only contains 214 days. Given these factors, the total maximum CCA for 2013 is $2,383 ($117 + $1,108 + $806 + $352). Note that the CCA calculation is based on the portion of the year since the inception of the business, not the portion of the year since the assets were acquired.

Note 3 The total automobile costs are $2,800 ($1,100 + $200 + $800 + $700). Since the interest is well below the $10 per day limit, there is no reduction in the amount of interest included in the preceding calculation. As the car is used 70 percent for business, the deduction is $1,960 [(70%)($2,800)]. No portion of the down payment is deductible.

Self Study Solution Six - 12

Carla's minimum net business income can be calculated as follows:

Carla Jensen
Statement Of Business Income
For Year Ending December 31, 2013

Revenues		
Revenue Collected	$105,000	
Increase In Billed Receivables		
($42,000 - $37,000)	5,000	$110,000
Expenses		
Building Operating Costs	($24,500)	
Vehicle Operating Costs	(7,200)	
Payments To Assistants	(13,500)	
Miscellaneous Office Costs	(3,750)	
Business Meals [(50%)($4,200)]	(2,100)	
CCA (Note 2)	(26,518)	
Terminal Loss For Class 10 (Note 3)	(4,955)	
CEC (Note 4)	(2,468)	($ 84,991)
Net Business Income		$ 25,009

Note 1 As Carla is a professional accountant she is eligible for the special rule under ITA 34 which allows her to recognize revenue on a billed basis. This means that she does not have to include her unbilled work-in-progress in her net business income.

Note 2 The total CCA deductible would be as follows:

Class 1 (Calculation Follows)	$13,560
Class 8 (Calculation Follows)	12,100
Class 50 (Calculation Follows)	495
Class 12 (Calculation Follows)	363
Total CCA	$26,518

Class 1 As the building is used 100 percent for non-residential purposes, it is eligible for the enhanced rate of 6 percent. This means that the maximum CCA for 2013 would be:

Class 1 [($226,000)(6%)]	$13,560

Class 8   The required calculations are as follows:

Opening Balance		$46,500
Additions	$34,000	
Disposal - Lesser Of:		
• Proceeds = $6,000		
• Cost = $18,000	(6,000)	28,000
One-Half Net Additions		(14,000)
CCA Base		$60,500
Rate		20%
Class 8 CCA		$12,100

Class 50   The CCA on the new computer would be calculated as follows:

Class 50 [(1/2)($1,800)(55%)]	$495

Class 12   The CCA on the applications software would be calculated as follows:

Class 12 [(1/2)($725)(100%)]	$363

Note 3   As the only vehicle used by the business was disposed of during 2013, there is no CCA for Class 10. However, as there is a balance left in the Class, there would be a terminal loss calculated as follows:

UCC Of The Class At The Beginning Of The Year	$17,255
Deduct: Dispositions During The Year - Lesser Of:	
• Capital Cost = $20,300	
• Proceeds Of Disposition = $12,300	(12,300)
Ending Balance With No Remaining Assets = Terminal Loss	$ 4,955

Note 4   Three-quarters of the $47,000 cost of the client list would be allocated to Cumulative Eligible Capital. The CEC deduction for 2013 would be $2,468 [($47,000)(3/4)(7%)].

Note 5   The car leasing costs would be wholly deductible as the monthly lease charge and the manufacturer's list price are within the limits.

Self Study Solution Six - 13

Part A

If the ITA 22 election is not made, the tax consequences for Ms. Close would be as follows:

Add: 2012 Reserve For Doubtful Debts		$8,000
Deduct Capital Loss:		
Proceeds Of Disposition	$107,000	
Adjusted Cost Base	(120,000)	
Capital Loss	($ 13,000)	
Non-Deductible One-Half	6,500	(6,500)
2013 Income Inclusion		$1,500

If the ITA 22 election is not made, the tax consequences to Mr. Phar would be as follows:

Proceeds Of Disposition (Amount Collected)	$100,000
Adjusted Cost Base	(107,000)
Capital Loss	($ 7,000)
Non-Deductible One-Half	3,500
2013 Deduction From Income	($ 3,500)

Note that, in the case of both Ms. Close and Mr. Phar, the allowable capital losses included in the preceding calculations could only be deducted against taxable capital gains. If they did not have taxable capital gains sufficient to absorb their allowable capital losses, Ms. Close would have an inclusion of $8,000, and Mr. Phar would have no deduction or inclusion.

Part B

If the ITA 22 election is made, the tax consequences for Ms. Close would be as follows:

Add: 2012 Reserve For Doubtful Debts	$ 8,000
Deduct: Business Loss ($120,000 - $107,000)	(13,000)
2013 Deduction From Income	($ 5,000)

If the ITA 22 election is made, the tax consequences to Mr. Phar would be as follows:

Add: Face Value - Price Paid ($120,000 - $107,000)	$13,000
Deduct: Actual Write-Offs ($120,000 - $100,000)	(20,000)
2013 Deduction From Income	($ 7,000)

As would always be the case, the use of the ITA 22 election improves the results for the vendor (Ms. Close). There is a $5,000 deduction as compared to a $1,500 inclusion when ITA 22 is not used.

In this case, Mr. Phar is also better off using ITA 22. He has a $7,000 deduction as compared to a $3,500 deduction when ITA 22 is not used. This result reflects the fact that the actual amount collected ($100,000) was less than the estimated fair value at the time of transfer ($107,000). If the actual proceeds had been more than $107,000, Mr. Phar would have been better off not using the ITA 22 election.

If, for example, the proceeds were $110,000, Mr. Phar would have had business income of $3,000 ($110,000 - $107,000) if he had used ITA 22. In the absence of ITA 22, he would have had a capital gain of $1,500 [(1/2)($110,000 - $107,000)].

Self Study Solution Six - 14

Net Employment Income

The Net Employment Income component of Net Income For Tax Purposes would be calculated as follows:

Salary	$68,000
Commissions	13,500
RPP Contributions	(2,800)
Professional Association Dues	(250)
Automobile Benefit (Note 1)	792
Home Office Costs (Note 2)	(596)
Meals And Entertainment [(1/2)($4,350)]	(2,175)
Net Employment Income	$76,471

Note 1 The automobile benefit would be calculated as follows:

Standby Charge [(2%)($32,000)(11)(4,500 ÷ 18,337)]	$1,728
Operating Cost Benefit - Lesser Of:	
• [($0.27)(4,500)] = $1,215	
• ($1,728 ÷ 2) = $864	864
Total Benefit Before Repayment	$2,592
Repayment	(1,800)
Taxable Benefit	$ 792

Note 2 As an employee, Ms. Compton cannot deduct any part of the mortgage interest or take CCA on the cost of the property. Any employee can deduct utilities and maintenance and, because Ms. Compton's employment income includes commissions, she can also deduct the property tax and insurance costs. The total available deduction is $596 [(15%)($2,450 + $1,100 + $425)].

Net Business Income

The Net Business Income component of Net Income For Tax Purposes would be calculated as follows:

Accounting Net Income		$53,500
Add:		
Amortization Expense	$12,800	
Non-Deductible Meals and		
Entertainment [(1/2)($6,000)]	3,000	15,800
Subtotal		$69,300
Deduct:		
CCA (Note 3)	($26,200)	
Landscaping Costs	(8,600)	(34,800)
Net Business Income		$34,500

Note 3 Maximum CCA would be calculated as follows:

Class 1 [(4%)($233,000)]			$ 9,320
Class 8			
Opening Balance		$41,500	
Additions	$13,400		
Disposals - Lesser Of:			
Cost = $12,000			
Proceeds = $8,600	(8,600)		
Net Additions	$ 4,800		
Portion Added To CCA Base	1/2	2,400	
CCA Base		$43,900	
Rate		20%	8,780
Class 10 [(30%)($27,000)]			8,100
Total			$26,200

Net Income For Tax Purposes And Taxable Income

Ms. Compton has no deductions in the calculation of Taxable income. Given this, her Net Income For Tax Purposes and Taxable Income are as follows:

Net Employment Income	$76,471
Net Business Income	34,500
Net Income For Tax Purposes And Taxable Income	$110,971

Federal Tax Payable

The required calculations are as follows:

Tax On First $87,123		$16,118
Tax On Next $23,848 ($110,971 - $87,123) At 26 Percent		6,200
Tax Before Credits		$22,318
Tax Credits:		
Basic Personal Amount	($11,038)	
Eligible Dependent (Allison - Note 4)	(11,038)	
Child (Allison)	(2,234)	
Caregiver, Including Family Caregiver (John - Note 4)	(6,530)	
Transfer Of John's Disability	(7,697)	
EI Premiums	(891)	
CPP Contributions	(2,356)	
Canada Employment	(1,117)	
Transfer Of Tuition, Education And Textbook - Lesser Of:		
• $5,000		
• [$2,850 + (4)($400) + (4)($65)] = $4,710	(4,710)	
Medical Expenses (Note 5)	(15,748)	
Public Transit Passes [(12)($60 + $25)] (Note 6)	(1,020)	
Total Credit Base	($64,379)	
Rate	15%	(9,657)
Charitable Donations		
[(15%)($200) + (29%)($1,250 - $200)]		(335)
Political Contributions [(3/4)($350)]		(263)
Federal Tax Payable		$12,063

Note 4 As the eligible dependant credit has been claimed for Allison, John is not eligible for this credit. Given this, he qualifies for both the infirm dependant over 17 credit and the caregiver credit. When this is the case, ITA 118(4)(d) deems the individual not to be a dependant, effectively requiring the use of the caregiver credit. As John is disabled, he also qualifies for the family caregiver amount.

Note 5 The claim for medical expenses is determined as follows:

Medical Expenses For Ms. Compton And Allison		
($4,220 + $2,180)		$ 6,400
Lesser Of:		
• [(3%)($110,971)] = $3,329		
• 2013 Threshold Amount = $2,152		(2,152)
Balance Before Dependants 18 And Over		$ 4,248
John's Medical Expenses	$11,500	
Reduced By The Lesser Of:		
• $2,152		
• [(3%)($Nil)] = Nil	Nil	11,500
Total Medical Expense Claim		$15,748

Note 6   The public transit pass credit is only applicable to dependants under the age of 19. As a result, John's passes do not qualify as a credit for Ms. Compton. Since John has no income, he would not be able to claim the public transit pass credit himself.

Chapter 6 Learning Objectives

After completing Chapter 6, you should be able to:

1. Classify property based on its use and determine what type of income will be produced while the asset is being held and when it is disposed of (paragraph [P hereafter] 6-1 through 6-16)

2. Describe the tax factors that can be affected by the classification of income as business or property (P 6-17 through 6-27).

3. Distinguish between business income and capital gains, including the criteria used by the courts in making this distinction (P 6-28 through 6-42).

4. Describe the major differences between net business income and Net Income as determined under GAAP (P 6-43 through 6-45).

5. Recall the various items that are included in net business income (P 6-46 through 6-53 and P 6-65).

6. Apply the system of reserves that can be used in determining net business income (P 6-54 through 6-64).

7. Apply the limitations on deductions that apply to business and property income, including those on home office costs (P 6-66 through 6-105).

8. Apply the limitations on deductions that apply to business, property and employment income, including those related to meals and entertainment and automobile costs (P 6-106 through 6-133).

9. Apply the inventory valuation procedures that are used for determining net business income (P 6-134 through 6-142).

10. Recall the deductions that are specified in the *Income Tax Act* for calculating net business income (P 6-143 through 6-144).

11. Reconcile accounting Net Income with net business income (P 6-145 through 6-153).

12. Recall the rules for determining taxation years and calculate additional business income for non-calendar fiscal years (P 6-154 through 6-158).

13. Apply the special provisions related to farm activities and farm losses (P 6-159 through 6-172).

14. Apply the special rule for unbilled work in process applicable to the income of some professionals (P 6-173 through 6-175).

15. Apply the provisions related to the disposition of inventories and accounts receivable in situations where a business is being sold (P 6-176 through 6-181).

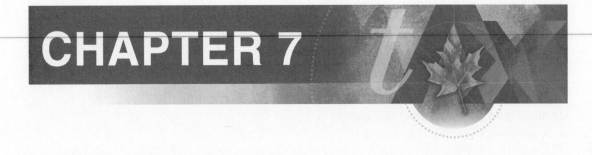

CHAPTER 7

How To Work Through Chapter 7

We recommend the following approach in dealing with the material in this chapter:

Property Income - General Concept
❏ Read paragraph 7-1 to 7-4 (in the textbook).

Interest As A Deduction (Including IT-533)
❏ Read paragraph 7-6 to 7-29.
❏ Do Self Study Problem Seven-1 at the end of the textbook chapter on page 341 and check the solution in this Study Guide.

Discount And Premium On Long-Term Issued Debt
❏ Read paragraph 7-30 to 7-36.
❏ Do Exercise Seven-1 (in the textbook) and check the solution on page S-127 in this Study Guide.
❏ Read paragraph 7-37 to 7-38.
❏ Do Exercise Seven-2 and check the solution in this Study Guide.

Interest Income - General Provisions
❏ Read paragraph 7-39 to 7-46.
❏ Do Exercise Seven-3 and check the solution in this Study Guide.

Discount And Premium On Long-Term Debt Holdings
❏ Read paragraph 7-47 to 7-48.

Prescribed Debt Obligations
❏ Read paragraph 7-49 to 7-51.
❏ Do Exercise Seven-4 and check the solution in this Study Guide.

Accrued Interest At Transfer
❏ Read paragraph 7-52 to 7-54.
❏ Do Exercise Seven-5 and check the solution in this Study Guide.

Payments Based On Production Or Use (Royalties)
❏ Read paragraph 7-55 to 7-57.

Rental Income
❏ Read paragraph 7-58 to 7-69.
❏ Do Exercise Seven-6 and check the solution in this Study Guide.
❏ Do Self Study Problem Seven-2 and check the solution in this Study Guide.

Cash Dividends From Taxable Canadian Corporations

❑ Read paragraph 7-70 to 7-85.
❑ Do Exercise Seven-7 and check the solution in this Study Guide.
❑ Read paragraph 7-86 to 7-98.
❑ Do Exercise Seven-8 and check the solution in this Study Guide.
❑ Read paragraph 7-99 to 7-100.

Comparison Of Investment Returns

❑ Read paragraph 7-101 to 7-103.
❑ Do Self Study Problems Seven-3 to Seven-6 and check the solutions in this Study Guide.

Income Trusts

❑ Read paragraph 7-104 to 7-122.
❑ Do Exercise Seven-9 and check the solution in this Study Guide.

Mutual Funds

❑ Read paragraph 7-123 to 7-133.
❑ Do Exercise Seven-10 and check the solution in this Study Guide.
❑ Do Self Study Problem Seven-7 and check the solution in this Study Guide.

Stock Dividends And Capital Dividends

❑ Read paragraph 7-134 to 7-137.
❑ Do Exercise Seven-11 and check the solution in this Study Guide.
❑ Read paragraph 7-138 and 7-139.

Foreign Source Income

❑ Read paragraph 7-140 to 7-143.
❑ Do Exercise Seven-12 and check the solution in this Study Guide.

Shareholder Benefits

❑ Read paragraph 7-144 to 7-146.

Tax Credits Revisited - Dividend And Foreign Tax Credits

❑ Read paragraph 7-147 to 7-150.

To Complete This Chapter

❑ Do Self Study Problems Seven-8 and Seven- 9 and check the solutions in this Study Guide.
❑ Review the Key Terms Used In This Chapter on page 340. Consult the Glossary for the meaning of any key terms you do not know.
❑ Review the Glossary Flashcards and complete the Key Terms Self-Test for the Chapter. These features can be found in two places, on your Student CD-ROM under the heading "Key Term Practice" and on the web site.
❑ Review the Learning Objectives of the Chapter found on page S-141 of this Study Guide.
❑ As a final review, we recommend that you view the PowerPoint Slides for Chapter 7 that are on your Student CD-ROM. The PowerPoint Viewer program can be installed from the Student CD-ROM.

Practice Examination

❑ Write the Practice Examination for Chapter 7 that is on your Student CD-ROM. Mark your examination using the Practice Examination Solution that is also on your Student CD-ROM.

Solution to Chapter Seven Exercises

Exercise Seven - 1 Solution

For tax purposes, in each of the years 2013, 2014, and 2015, Moreau would have a deduction for interest of $40,000 [(4%)($1,000,000)]. When the bonds are retired in 2015, there would be a loss of $15,000 ($1,000,000 - $985,000). The bonds are sold for more than 97 percent of their maturity amount. In addition, the four-thirds test is met since the effective interest rate of 4.6 percent is less than four-thirds of the coupon rate [(4%)(4/3) = 5.3%]. As a result, it would appear that this loss would be fully deductible. This gives a total deduction of $135,000 over the three year period [(3)($40,000) + $15,000].

For accounting purposes, interest expense would be $45,000 in each of the three years. This is made up of the annual payment of $40,000, plus amortization of the discount of $5,000 [(1/3)($1,000,000 - $985,000)]. Note that the total for the three year period would be the same $135,000 [(3)($45,000)] that was deducted for tax purposes.

Exercise Seven - 2 Solution

The tax consequences under each of the three assumptions would be as follows:

Money Lender In this case, there would be an income inclusion of $400,000 ($1,400,000 - $1,000,000) in the current year. The interest deduction for the year would be $180,000 [(18%)($1,000,000)].

No Deliberate Premium In this case, the premium would have no immediate tax consequences and there would be no tax consequences when the bonds mature. The interest deduction for the year would be $180,000 [(18%)($1,000,000)]. Given that the bonds are paid off for less than the proceeds from their issuance, this result provides the issuer of the bonds with a tax free capital receipt of $400,000.

Deliberate Premium In this case, the premium would be amortized at the rate of $40,000 per year ($400,000 ÷ 10). This means the interest deduction for the year would be $140,000 ($180,000 - $40,000).

Exercise Seven - 3 Solution

The total interest to be recorded on the instrument is $28,800 [($60,000)(8%)(6 years)]. It will be allocated as follows

Year	Interest Paid	Interest Reported
2013	Nil	Nil
2014	Nil	$ 4,800
2015	Nil	4,800
2016	$15,600	6,000
2017	Nil	3,600
2018	Nil	4,800
2019	13,200	4,800
Total	$28,800	$28,800

2013 As no anniversary date occurred and no interest was received during 2013, no interest will have to be included in Ms. Dumont's 2013 tax return.

2014 The first anniversary date occurs on September 30 and this requires the recognition of $4,800 [(8%)($60,000)] of interest.

2015 The second anniversary date occurs and this requires the recognition of an additional $4,800 of interest.

2016 An additional $4,800 will have to be recognized because of the third anniversary date. Also during this year, a payment of $15,600 [($4,800)(3.25)] is received. Of this total,

$14,400 [(3)($4,800)] has been recognized because of the three anniversary dates. This will require the recognition of an additional $1,200 ($15,600 - $14,400) in 2016, bringing the total for the year to $6,000 ($4,800 + $1,200).

2017   The anniversary date will require recognition of $4,800. However, only $3,600 of this amount will be included as $1,200 was received and recognized in 2016.

2018 $4,800 will be recognized on the anniversary date.

2019   A payment of $13,200 [(2.75)($4,800)] will be received. As $8,400 ($3,600 + $4,800) of the amount received has been recorded on the two anniversary dates, the total for 2019 will be $4,800 ($13,200 - $8,400).

Note that the total interest of $28,800 is equal to 8 percent of $60,000 for 6 years.

Exercise Seven - 4 Solution

With respect to the maturity amount, the interest to be included in the purchaser's tax return would be calculated as follows:

Year	Initial Balance	Interest At 7%	Closing Balance
2013	$204,075	$14,285	$218,360
2014	218,360	15,285	233,645
2015	233,645	16,355	250,000

Calculations of interest income with respect to the coupon payments are as follows:

Year	Initial Balance	Interest At 7%	Cash Received	Closing Balance
2013	$45,925	$3,215	($17,500)	$31,640
2014	31,640	2,215	(17,500)	16,355
2015	16,355	1,145	(17,500)	Nil

Exercise Seven - 5 Solution

Mr. Lay will have to include the full $6,000 received. However, under ITA 20(14) he is eligible for a deduction of $2,000 [($3,000)(4/6)], reflecting the interest that was accrued on the bonds at the time of purchase. The net amount of $4,000 will be included in his tax return.

Exercise Seven - 6 Solution

As the improvements will be added to her CCA base, her maximum available CCA on the rental property is $3,560 [(4%)(1/2)($185,000 - $42,000 + $35,000)]. Her maximum available CCA is not limited by the fact the property was purchased in September as the calendar year is considered the fiscal year for property income purposes for individuals. However, the maximum CCA that she can deduct will be limited to her net rental income before CCA of $2,100 ($7,200 - $5,100). Her net rental income is nil ($2,100 - $2,100).

Exercise Seven - 7 Solution

The Tax Payable by Mr. Johns would be calculated as follows:

Non-Eligible Dividends Received	$17,000
Gross Up At 25 Percent	4,250
Taxable Dividends	$21,250
Combined Federal/Provincial Tax Rate (29% + 12%)	41%
Tax Before Dividend Tax Credit	$8,713
Dividend Tax Credit [(2/3 + 30%)($4,250)]	(4,108)
Federal And Provincial Tax Payable	$ 4,605

The after tax retention is $12,395 ($17,000 - $4,605). Note that to calculate this amount, the taxes are deducted from the dividends received and not the grossed up taxable dividends.

Exercise Seven - 8 Solution

The Tax Payable by Ms. Holt would be calculated as follows:

Eligible Dividends Received	$15,000
Gross Up At 38 Percent	5,700
Taxable Dividends	$20,700
Combined Federal/Provincial Tax Rate (29% + 14.5%)	43.5%
Tax Before Dividend Tax Credit	$ 9,005
Dividend Tax Credit [(6/11 + 30%)($5,700)]	(4,819)
Federal And Provincial Tax Payable	$ 4,186

The after tax retention is $10,814 ($15,000 - $4,186). Note that to calculate this amount, the taxes are deducted from the dividends received and not the grossed up taxable dividends.

Exercise Seven - 9 Solution

John will include an additional $7,000 [(2,000)($5.00 - $1.50)] in his 2013 Net Income For Tax Purposes. His adjusted cost base will be increased by the $10,000 [(2,000)($5.00)] reinvestment of the distribution and reduced by the $3,000 [(2,000)($1.50)] return of capital.

The reinvestment of the $10,000 distribution will result in the acquisition of an additional 175.44 ($10,000 ÷ $57) units. The adjusted cost base calculations are as follows:

	Amount	Number Of Units
Original Investment	$110,000	2,000.00
Reinvestment Of Distribution	10,000	175.44
Tax Free Return Of Capital	(3,000)	N/A
Adjusted Cost Base/Number Of Units	$117,000	2,175.44

This will result in an average cost of $53.78 ($117,000 ÷ 2,175.44) per unit.

Exercise Seven - 10 Solution

Given the purchase price per unit is $13, the reinvestment will result in Ms. Tiompkins receiving 80.77 ($1,050 ÷ $13) additional units. This will leave her holding 3,580.77 units with an adjusted cost base of $40,425 ($39,375 + $1,050). Her adjusted cost base per unit after the reinvestment is $11.29 ($40,425 ÷ 3,580.77).

Exercise Seven - 11

Prior to the stock dividend, Mr. Morgna held 200,000 [(10%)(2,000,000)] shares with a total cost of $2,400,000 [($12)(200,000)]. The stock dividend would add 20,000 [(10%)(200,000)] to his total holding. With $15 per share added to the paid up capital of the corporation, he would have a stock dividend of $300,000 [($15)(20,000)].

Depending on whether this was an eligible or a non-eligible dividend, it would be grossed up by either 25 percent or 38 percent. There would also be a federal dividend tax credit of either 2/3 of the gross up or 6/11 of the gross up. Mr. Morgna's adjusted cost base per share would be $12.27 [($2,400,000 + $300,000) ÷ (200,000 + 20,000)]. Note that his percentage of ownership remains at 10 percent (220,000 ÷ 2,200,000).

Exercise Seven - 12 Solution

The federal Tax Payable on the amount received assuming it is foreign non-business income or business income would be calculated as follows:

	Non-Business Income	Business Income
Amount Received	$22,500	$22,500
Foreign Tax Withheld	7,500	7,500
Inclusion For Foreign Income	$30,000	$30,000
Deduction Of Excess Withholding		
[$7,500 - (15%)($30,000)]	(3,000)	N/A
Increase In Taxable Income	$27,000	$30,000
Rate	29%	29%
Tax Payable Before Credit	$ 7,830	$ 8,700
Foreign Tax Credit [(15%)($30,000)]	(4,500)	
Foreign Tax Credit (Amount Withheld)		(7,500)
Federal Tax Payable	$ 3,330	$ 1,200

Note that the total tax cost if the foreign income is business income is $8,700 ($7,500 + $1,200). This is the same amount that would have been paid by Norah on the receipt of $30,000 of Canadian source business income [(29%)($30,000) = $8,700].

Self Study Solution Seven - 1

Case A

The interest would be deductible as the direct use of the borrowed funds was to acquire the Bee Ltd. shares.

Case B

Since the proceeds exceed the borrowings, Ms. Burns has complete flexibility with respect to linking. She could allocate all of the $100,000 to property B or alternatively, $40,000 to property A, with the other $60,000 going to property B. Any other allocation totaling $100,000 would be acceptable.

Case C

When the value of the replacement property is less than the amount borrowed, the taxpayer must use a pro-rata allocation of the borrowed money. In this case, the result would be an allocation of $75,000 [($60,000 ÷ $80,000)($100,000)] to property A and an allocation of $25,000 [($20,000 ÷ $80,000)($100,000)] to property B.

Case D

Under ITA 20.1 (the disappearing source rules), the $60,000 balance will be deemed to be used to produce income. Therefore, he can continue to deduct the interest.

Self Study Solution Seven - 2

CCA And Recapture Calculations

As each of the properties has a cost in excess of $50,000, they must each be allocated to a separate Class 1. Based on this, the required calculations are as follows:

Property A	
January 1 UCC Balance - Property A	$121,500
Disposition - Lesser Of:	
• Proceeds Of Disposition = $172,000	
• Capital Cost = $136,000	(136,000)
Negative Ending Balance = Recapture	($ 14,500)

As Property A has been sold, no CCA can be taken for the current year.

Property B

January 1 UCC Balance - Property B	$143,000
CCA Rate	4%
Maximum CCA	$ 5,720

Property C

January 1 UCC Balance - Property C	$146,000
Disposition - Lesser Of:	
• Proceeds Of Disposition = $161,000	
• Capital Cost = $163,000	(161,000)
Negative Ending Balance = Recapture	($ 15,000)

As was the case with Property A, this Property has been sold and no CCA can be taken for the current year.

Property D

January 1 UCC Balance - Property D	$164,000
CCA Rate	4%
Maximum CCA	$ 6,560

Property E

Capital Cost Property E	$192,000
One-Half Net Additions	(96,000)
CCA Base	$ 96,000
Rate	4%
Maximum CCA	$ 3,840

Total Maximum CCA
This gives a total maximum CCA for Class 1 of $16,120 ($5,720 + $6,560 + $3,840).

Property Income
In calculating the net property income (loss) for Mr. Drake, the rules that restrict CCA deductions on rental properties must be taken into consideration. These rules are discussed in IT-195R4, "Rental Property - Capital Cost Restrictions". This Interpretation Bulletin makes it clear that in determining the maximum CCA deduction, net rental income, before CCA for all classes of rental properties, must first be determined. The maximum CCA deduction that can then be taken is limited to the amount that will reduce this balance to nil. Using this approach, net property income is calculated as follows:

	Rental Revenues	Cash Expenses
Property A	$ 6,200	$ 4,450
Property B	7,700	4,350
Property C	13,200	13,250
Property D	16,300	22,150
Property E	2,000	4,900
Totals	$45,400	$49,100

Income (Loss) Before CCA And Recapture ($45,400 - $49,100)	($ 3,700)
Recapture From Properties A And C ($14,500 + $15,000)	29,500
Rental Income Before CCA	$25,800
Maximum CCA	(16,120)
Net Property Income	$ 9,680

In addition to the net property income calculated above, there is also the taxable capital gain of $18,000 [(1/2)($172,000 - $136,000)] resulting from the sale of Property A.

Self Study Solution Seven - 3

Part A - Bonds
This amount would be calculated as follows:

Interest Received [(7.75%)($20,000)]	$1,550
Taxes At 38% (26% + 12%)	(589)
After Tax Return - Bonds	$ 961

Part B - Preferred Shares
This amount would be calculated as follows:

Dividends Received [(5%)($20,000)]	$1,000
Gross Up Of 38 Percent	380
Taxable Dividends	$1,380
Combined Tax Rate (26% + 12%)	38%
Tax Before Dividend Tax Credit	$ 524
Dividend Tax Credit [(6/11 + 30%)($380)]	(321)
Tax Payable	$ 203
Dividends Received	$1,000
Tax Payable	(203)
After Tax Return - Preferred Shares	$ 797

Conclusion
Based on after tax returns, the investment in bonds is the better alternative.

Self Study Solution Seven - 4

Guaranteed Investment Certificate
The required calculations for this investment are as follows:

Interest Received [($600,000)(4.5%)]	$27,000
Combined Federal/Provincial Tax Rate (29% + 12%)	41%
Tax Payable	$11,070
Interest Received	$27,000
Tax Payable	(11,070)
After Tax Return	$15,930

Preferred Shares
The required calculations for this investment are as follows:

Dividends Received [($600,000)(5.25%)]	$31,500
Gross Up of 38 Percent	11,970
Taxable Income	$43,470
Combined Federal/Provincial Tax Rate (29% + 12%)	41%
Tax Payable Before Dividend Tax Credit	$17,823
Federal/Provincial Dividend Tax Credit [($11,970)(6/11 + 28%)]	(9,881)
Total Tax Payable	$ 7,942

Dividends Received (Before Gross Up)	$31,500
Tax Payable	(7,942)
After Tax Return	$23,558

High Tech Shares

The required calculations for this investment are as follows:

Proceeds Of Disposition	$675,000
Adjusted Cost Base	(600,000)
Capital Gain	$ 75,000
Inclusion Rate	1/2
Taxable Capital Gain	$37,500
Combined Federal/Provincial Tax Rate (29% + 12%)	41%
Tax Payable	$15,375

Capital Gain Realized (100%)	$75,000
Tax Payable	(15,375)
After Tax Return	$59,625

Self Study Solution Seven - 5

The major considerations in deciding between the three alternative investment strategies are the after tax return and the certainty of the related cash flows.

Guaranteed Investment Certificate   As long as the certificate is purchased from a financial institution that is guaranteed by the federal government, there is virtually no risk that the principal or interest could be lost. Your combined federal and provincial tax rate for interest is 44 percent (29% + 15%). This means that the $100,000 investment would provide an after-tax amount calculated as follows:

Interest [($100,000)(5.5%)]	$5,500
Federal/Provincial Tax Payable [($5,500)(29% + 15%)]	(2,420)
After Tax Cash Flow	$3,080

Common Stock Purchase   If you invest the $100,000 in common stock, you will be exposing yourself to a greater risk and uncertainty of cash flows than the guaranteed investment certificate alternative. There is no guarantee that the stock will pay a dividend of $5,000 during the year. There is the possibility that more or less than $5,000 will be paid. In addition, the estimated market price of at least $106,000 on December 31, 2013 is not certain. The price on that date could be higher or lower.

Assuming that the stock does pay $5,000 in dividends and you sell the shares for $106,000 on December 31, 2013, your after tax return on the investment is as follows:

Dividends Received	$5,000
Gross Up [(38%)($5,000)]	1,900
Taxable Dividends	$6,900
Taxable Capital Gain [(1/2)($106,000 - $100,000)]	3,000
Taxable Income	$9,900
Combined Tax Rate (29% + 15%)	44%
Tax Payable Before Dividend Tax Credit	$4,356
Dividend Tax Credit [($1,900)(6/11 + 27%)]	(1,549)
Tax Payable	$2,807

Dividends Received	$5,000
Capital Gain (100%)	6,000
Tax Payable	(2,807)
After Tax Cash Flow	$8,193

Rental Property   If you invest the $100,000 in real estate, you will be choosing the highest risk alternative. Rental properties can require significant personal involvement if there are problems with the tenant or repairs become necessary. The transaction costs (e.g., real estate commissions and legal fees), would be much higher on this investment than on either of the other two. In addition, the real estate investment is the least liquid of the three alternatives and you might encounter difficulties in the disposition of this investment. The estimated net proceeds of $175,000 on December 31, 2013 is not certain. The net proceeds could be higher or lower.

Assuming that the property has the anticipated revenues and expenses and you net $175,000 when you sell the property on December 31, 2013, your after tax return on the investment is as follows:

Gross Rents	$13,200
Expenses	(9,600)
CCA (Property Sold Prior To Year End)	Nil
Net Rental Income	$ 3,600

In addition to this net rental income, you anticipate a capital gain of $10,000 ($175,000 - $165,000), of which one-half, or $5,000, would be included in your income. Based on these figures, the Tax Payable would be calculated as follows:

Net Rental Income	$3,600
Taxable Capital Gain	5,000
Taxable Income	$8,600
Tax Rate	44%
Tax Payable	$3,784

The total after tax cash flow would be as follows:

Net Rental Income	$ 3,600
Capital Gain (Cash Flow is 100% Of Gain)	10,000
Tax Payable	(3,784)
After Tax Cash Flow	$ 9,816

Conclusion   Based purely on after tax returns, it would appear that you should acquire the rental property. However, as previously indicated, this alternative involves the most risk and uncertainty.

In choosing between the guaranteed investment certificate and the shares of Norton Ltd., the after tax cash flows from the shares are considerably higher. However, the return on the shares is made up of dividends and a potential capital gain, both of which are more uncertain than the interest on the guaranteed investment certificate. Given this, the possibility of greater than anticipated dividends and/or capital gains must be weighed against the additional risk of lower than anticipated returns.

Other factors which may influence your decision are as follows:

- The funds are locked into the investment certificate and can only be withdrawn prior to maturity at a severe interest penalty, if at all.
- The investment in common stock would give you more flexibility if you should require some of the funds before the end of the year. All or some portion of the stockholding could be sold during the year.
- Any dividends or rent that is paid will be available for your use as at the payment date. The interest will not be available to you until maturity.

Self Study Solution Seven - 6

Mr. Shark's minimum Net Income For Tax Purposes would be calculated as follows:

Income From A Business Or Profession:		
Billed Revenues ($42,000 + $475,000 - $35,000)	$482,000	
Office Supplies And Office Expenses	(56,000)	
Travel Costs	(8,000)	
Meals And Entertainment [(1/2)($12,000)]	(6,000)	
CCA - Building [(1/2)(4%)($526,000)]	(10,520)	
CCA - Class 8 [(20%)($11,059)]	(2,212)	$399,268
Rental Income:		
Rents Received [(6)($4,000)]	$24,000	
Expenses Other Than CCA	(14,400)	
Rental Income Before CCA	$ 9,600	
CCA (Note)	(9,600)	Nil
Investment Income:		
Eligible Dividends Received	$18,000	
Gross Up Of 38 Percent	6,840	24,840
Net Income For Tax Purposes		$424,108

Note   The maximum available CCA on the rental portion of the property would be $10,520 [(1/2)(4%)($526,000)]. However, because CCA cannot be used to create or increase a rental loss, the deduction is limited in this case to the $9,600 of income before CCA.

Self Study Solution Seven - 7

Taxable Income And Tax Payable
The amount of taxable income and tax payable resulting from the two investments would be calculated as follows:

Real Property Distribution [($4.50)(5,000)]	$22,500	
Return Of Capital [($1.25)(5,000)]	(6,250)	$16,250
Infidelity Capital Gain [($2.00)(10,000)]	$20,000	
Non-Taxable One-Half	(10,000)	10,000
Infidelity Eligible Dividends [($2.75)(10,000)]	$27,500	
Dividend Gross Up [(38%)($27,500)]	10,450	37,950
Infidelity Interest [($2.25)($10,000)]		22,500
Taxable Income		$86,700
Tax Rate (29% + 11%)		40%
Tax Before Dividend Tax Credit		$34,680
Dividend Tax Credit [($10,450)(6/11 + 28%)]		(8,626)
Tax Payable		$26,054

Adjusted Cost Base - Real Property

The reinvestment of the $22,500 distribution at $52.00 per unit would acquire an additional 432.69 units. After recognizing these changes, the adjusted cost base per unit would be:

$49.01 [($250,000 + $22,500 - $6,250) ÷ (5,000 + 432.69)]

Adjusted Cost Base - Infidelity

The reinvestment of the $70,000 [($7.00)(10,000)] distribution at $83.00 per unit would acquire an additional 843.37 units. After recognizing these changes, the adjusted cost base per unit would be as follows:

$84.84 [($850,000 + $70,000) ÷ (10,000 + 843.37)]

Self Study Solution Seven - 8

The required calculations are as follows:

Net Employment Income

Salary	$64,000
RPP Contributions	(2,960)
Disability Benefits (Note 1)	4,945
Home Office Allowance [(12)($400)]	4,800
Home Office Expenses (Note 2)	(471)
Net Employment Income	$70,314

Property Income

Gross Rents	$42,000
Expenses Other Than CCA	(32,500)
Recapture of CCA (Note 3)	5,000
Rental Income Before CCA	$14,500
CCA (Note 3)	(14,500)
Net Rental Income	$ Nil
Zero-Coupon Bond Interest (Note 4)	5,445
Canadian Dividends Received	9,300
Gross Up On Canadian Dividends (38%)	3,534
Foreign Dividends - No Gross Up (Amount Before 15% Withholding)	5,600
Property Income	$23,879

Note 1 As the employer contributes to the plan and the contributions do not create a taxable benefit, the benefits received during the year will be included in employment income. Although the disability insurance premiums that Ms. Spring pays are not deductible, they would reduce the taxable portion of any amounts subsequently received under the plan. As a result, the amount to be included in employment income is $4,945 ($5,600 - $180 - $225 - $250).

Note 2 As Ms. Spring has no commission income, she can only deduct costs associated with electricity, water, maintenance, and repairs. The deductible amount is $471 [(15%)($1,340 + $1,800)].

Note 3 The recapture and maximum available CCA for 2013 would be calculated as follows:

January 1, 2013 UCC of Property A	$156,000
Disposals - Lesser Of:	
• Capital Cost ($245,000 - $40,000) = $205,000	
• Proceeds Of Disposition	
($201,000 - $40,000) = $161,000	(161,000)
Negative Ending Balance = Recapture Of CCA	($ 5,000)

Property A (Sold)	$ Nil
Property B [(4%)($276,000)]	11,040
New Property [(4%)(1/2)($322,000 - $75,000)]	4,940
Maximum CCA Available	$15,980

While there is $15,980 in CCA available, this deduction cannot be used to create a rental loss. This means that the maximum deduction is equal to $14,500, the amount of rental income before the deduction of CCA. Note that the recaptured CCA is included in Rental Income Before CCA.

Note 4 As no interest has been paid on this bond, interest will have to be accrued on its first anniversary date, December 31, 2013. As this is a prescribed debt obligation, interest will have to be accrued at the effective rate of 8 percent, resulting in an income inclusion of $5,445 [(8%)($68,058)].

Net Income For Tax Purposes And Taxable Income

There are no Taxable Income deductions available. As a consequence, Taxable Income is equal to Net Income For Tax Purposes.

Net Employment Income	$70,314
Property Income	23,879
Net Income For Tax Purposes And Taxable Income	$94,193

Tax Payable

Tax Payable would be calculated as follows:

Tax On First $87,123		$16,118
Tax On Next $7,070 ($94,193 - $87,123) At 26 Percent		1,838
Tax Before Credits		$17,956
Basic Personal Amount - Ms. Spring	($11,038)	
Eligible Dependant Including FCA - Mark (Note 5)	(13,078)	
EI Premiums	(891)	
CPP Contributions	(2,356)	
Canada Employment	(1,117)	
Transfer Of Amy's Education Credits (Note 6)	(5,000)	
Medical Expenses (Note 7)	(10,831)	
Credit Base	($44,311)	
Rate	15%	(6,647)
Subtotal		$11,309
Dividend Tax Credit [(6/11)($3,534)]		(1,928)
Foreign Tax Credit (Amount Withheld = 15%)		(840)
Federal Tax Payable		$ 8,541

Note 5 Amy is not eligible for the eligible dependant credit as she was not under 18 years of age at any time during the taxation year. This means that Mark is entitled to this credit as it is not taken for anyone else. This, in turn, means that neither the caregiver nor the infirm dependant over 17 credits can be used for Mark. Because Mark is infirm and has no income, Ms. Spring can claim the full amount of the eligible dependant credit, as well as the family caregiver amount. This amount would be $13,078 ($11,038 + $2,040).

Note 6 Amy's total education credits are $11,920 [$8,200 + (8)($400) + (8)($65)], well in excess of the maximum transfer of $5,000. Amy's Taxable Income of $7,300 is less than the basic personal credit amount. The maximum transfer of education related amounts is $5,000.

Note 7 The medical expense credit base would be calculated as follows:

Medical Expenses Of Ms. Spring		$ 962
Lesser Of:		
• [(3%)($94,193)] = $2,826		
• 2013 Threshold Amount = $2,152		(2,152)
Balance Before Dependants 18 And Over		Nil
Amy's Medical Expenses	$2,450	
Reduced By The Lesser Of:		
• $2,152		
• [(3%)($7,300)] = $219	(219)	2,231
Mark's Medical Expenses	$8,600	
Reduced By The Lesser Of:		
• $2,152		
• [(3%)(Nil)] = Nil	Nil	8,600
Medical Expense Tax Credit Base		$10,831

Self Study Solution Seven - 9

Net Business Income

Derek's Net Business Income is calculated as follows:

Accounting Net Income		$211,000
Additions:		
Amortization Expense	$18,000	
Meals And Entertainment (Note 1)	5,750	
Automobile Operating Costs - Personal (Note 2)	1,350	25,100
		$236,100
Deductions:		
Capital Cost Allowance		
Automobile (Note 3)	($ 3,234)	
Furniture And Fixtures (Note 4)	(9,300)	
Building [(6%)($450,000)] (Note 5)	(27,000)	(39,534)
Net Business Income For Tax Purposes		$196,566

Note 1   As the business deducted 100 percent of the meals and entertainment costs, the non-deductible one-half of this amount needs to be added back to arrive at Net Business Income For Tax Purposes.

Note 2   As the business deducted 100 percent of the automobile operating costs, the portion related to Derek's personal use must be added back. This amount would be $1,350 [($4,800)(9,000 ÷ 32,000)].

Note 3   The addition to UCC for the car would be limited to $30,000 and it would be allocated to a separate Class 10.1. Maximum CCA for 2013 would be $4,500 [(1/2)(30%)($30,000)]. However, the business can only deduct $3,234 [($4,500)(23,000 ÷ 32,000)].

Note 4   CCA for Class 8 would be calculated as follows:

UCC January 1, 2013	$42,000
Additions	12,000
Disposals (Lesser Of $10,000 Or $3,000)	(3,000)
One-Half Net Additions [(1/2)($12,000 - $3,000)]	(4,500)
Base For CCA	$46,500
Rate	20%
Class 8 CCA	$ 9,300

Note 5   As the building was acquired new and was used 100 percent for non-residential purposes, it is eligible for the 6 percent CCA rate. The fact that it was the only building owned by the business would result in it automatically being allocated to a separate class, but it must remain in a separate Class 1 to continue to qualify for the 6 percent rate.

Property Income

Derek's property income is calculated as follows:

Eligible Dividends On Breax	$ 8,000
Gross Up On Eligible Dividends [(38%)($8,000)]	3,040
Realco Income Trust Units [(5,000)($1.50)]	7,500
Debt Securities (Note 6)	12,000
Foreign Term Deposit (Note 7)	15,000
Total Property Income	$45,540

Note 6   Derek would have to recognize $8,000 [(8%)($100,000)] in interest on the July 1, 2013 anniversary of the debt security. In addition, because a $12,000 payment is received on December 31, 2013, he would have to recognize an additional $4,000 ($12,000, less the $8,000 recognized on the anniversary date).

Note 7   As non-business income is involved, the tax credit will be limited to $3,000 [(15%)($20,000)]. The remaining $5,000 ($8,000 - $3,000) can be deducted against the interest. This leaves an inclusion of $15,000 ($20,000 - $5,000).

Capital Gain

The adjusted cost base of the Breax shares that were sold was $52 ($130,000 ÷ 2,500). Given this, the capital gain on the Breax common shares would be calculated as follows:

Proceeds [($65)(1,000)]	$65,000
Adjusted Cost Base [($52)(1,000)]	(52,000)
Capital Gain	$13,000
Inclusion Rate	1/2
Taxable Capital Gain	$ 6,500

Net Income For Tax Purposes And Taxable Income

There are no Taxable Income deductions available. As a consequence, Taxable Income is equal to Net Income For Tax Purposes.

Net Business Income	$196,566
Total Property Income	45,540
Taxable Capital Gain	6,500
Net Income For Tax Purposes And Taxable Income	$248,606

Tax Payable

Tax Payable would be calculated as follows:

Tax On First $135,054		$28,580
Tax On Next $113,552 ($248,606 - $135,054) At 29 Percent		32,930
Tax Before Credits		$61,510
Tax Credits:		
Basic Personal Amount (Derek)	($11,038)	
Spouse ($11,038 - $9,500)	(1,538)	
Child		
Barbara	(2,234)	
Brad Including FCA ($2,234 + $2,040)	(4,274)	
Disability Transferred From Brad	(7,697)	
Disability Supplement For Brad	(4,490)	
Transit Passes [(2)($60)(11)] (Note 8)	(1,320)	
Child Fitness (Note 9)	(1,300)	
First Time Home Buyer	(5,000)	
Transfer Of Bill's Education Credits (Note 10)	(5,000)	
Medical Expenses (Note 11)	(18,848)	
Total Credit Base	($62,739)	
Rate	15%	(9,411)
Dividend Tax Credit On Eligible		
Dividends [(6/11)($3,040)]		(1,658)
Foreign Tax Credit [(15%)($20,000)]		(3,000)
Federal Tax Payable		$47,441

Note 8   Since Bill is over 18, Derek cannot claim his transit pass credit. Bill could claim it himself, but his Net Income For Tax Purposes is already less than his basic personal credit amount. As a result, claiming the transit pass credit would not result in less Tax Payable.

Note 9   Mr. Fontaine can claim the fitness fees of $400 for each child. In addition, he can claim the $500 supplement that is available because Brad is under 18 and qualifies for the disability credit. This results in a total of $1,300 [(2)($400) + $500].

Note 10   Bill's total education credits are $13,150 [$8,500 + (10)($400 + $65)], well in excess of the maximum transfer of $5,000. Bill's Net Income For Tax Purposes of $10,000 is less than the basic personal credit amount. The maximum transfer of education related amounts is $5,000.

Note 11   The base for the medical expense tax credit is calculated as follows:

Medical Expenses Of Derek, Emily, Brad And Barbara		
($1,400 + $1,600 + $11,400 + $2,300)		$ 16,700
Lesser Of:		
• [(3%)($248,606)] = $7,458		
• 2013 Threshold Amount = $2,152		(2,152)
Balance Before Dependants 18 And Over		$ 14,548
Bill's Medical Expenses	$4,600	
Reduced By The Lesser Of:		
• $2,152		
• [(3%)($10,000)] = $300	(300)	4,300
Medical Expense Tax Credit Base		$18,848

Chapter 7 Learning Objectives

After completing Chapter 7, you should be able to:

1. Explain the nature of property income (paragraph [P hereafter] 7-1 through 7-4).
2. Describe the rules applicable to the deductibility of interest payments and be able to apply these rules to various types of borrowing (P 7-5 through 7-29).
3. Apply the provisions relating to the treatment of discount and premium on long-term issued debt (P 7-30 through 7-38).
4. Calculate the taxable amount of interest income for both individuals and corporations (P 7-39 through 7-46).
5. Explain the tax treatment of discounts and premiums on long-term debt holdings (P 7-47 and 7-48).
6. Explain the tax treatment of prescribed debt obligations (P 7-49 through 7-51).
7. Apply the provisions related to accrued interest at the time of transfer of debt obligations (P 7-52 through 7-54).
8. Describe tax procedures for royalties and payments based on production or use (P 7-55 through 7-57).
9. Calculate net rental income (P 7-58 through 7-69).
10. Apply the gross up and tax credit procedures to determine the tax consequences of receiving eligible and non-eligible dividend income (P 7-70 through 7-100).
11. Compare the after-tax returns from various types of investments (P 7-101 through 7-103).
12. Discuss the provisions relating to investments in income trusts (P 7-104 through 7-122).
13. Discuss the provisions relating to investments in mutual funds (P 7-123 through 7-133).
14. Explain the general treatment of stock dividends and capital dividends (P 7-134 through 7-139).
15. Explain the general tax treatment of withholdings on foreign source business and non-business income (P 7-140 through 7-143).
16. Explain the general treatment of shareholder benefits (P 7-146 through 7-144).

CHAPTER 8

How To Work Through Chapter 8

We recommend the following approach in dealing with the material in this chapter:

Economic Background And General Rules For Capital Gains Taxation
❑ Read paragraph 8-1 to 8-30 (in the textbook).
❑ Do Exercises Eight-1 and Eight-2 (in the textbook) and check the solutions on page S-144 in this Study Guide.
❑ Read paragraph 8-31 to 8-36.

Identical Properties
❑ Read paragraph 8-37 to 8-38.
❑ Do Exercise Eight-3 and check the solution in this Study Guide.
❑ Do Self Study Problem Eight-1 at the end of the textbook chapter on page 394 and check the solution in this Study Guide.

Partial Dispositions And Warranties On Capital Assets
❑ Read paragraph 8-39 to 8-41.
❑ Do Exercise Eight-4 and check the solution in this Study Guide.
❑ Do Self Study Problem Eight-2 and check the solution in this Study Guide.

Capital Gains Reserves
❑ Read paragraph 8-42 to 8-61.
❑ Do Exercise Eight-5 and check the solution in this Study Guide.
❑ Do Self Study Problems Eight-3 and Eight-4 and check the solutions in this Study Guide.

Bad Debts On Sales Of Capital Property
❑ Read paragraph 8-62 to 8-63.
❑ Do Exercise Eight-6 and check the solution in this Study Guide.
❑ Do Self Study Problems Eight-5 and Eight-6 and check the solutions in this Study Guide.

Special Rule For Sales Of Real Property
❑ Read paragraph 8-64 to 8-71.
❑ Do Exercise Eight-7 and check the solution in this Study Guide.

Principal Residence
❑ Read paragraph 8-72 to 8-79.
❑ Do Exercises Eight-8 and Eight-9 and check the solutions in this Study Guide.
❑ Do Self Study Problem Eight-7 and check the solution in this Study Guide.
❑ Read paragraph 8-80 to 8-84.

Personal Use And Listed Personal Property
❑ Read paragraph 8-85 to 8-92.
❑ Do Exercise Eight-10 and check the solution in this Study Guide.
❑ Do Self Study Problem Eight-8 and check the solution in this Study Guide.

Gains And Losses On Foreign Currency
❑ Read paragraph 8-93 to 8-104.
❑ Do Exercise Eight-11 and check the solution in this Study Guide.
❑ Do Self Study Problem Eight-9 and check the solution in this Study Guide.

Options
❑ Read paragraph 8-105 to 8-110.

Deemed Dispositions - Change In Use Including Principal Residences
❑ Read paragraph 8-111 to 8-119.
❑ Do Exercise Eight-12 and check the solution in this Study Guide.
❑ Read paragraph 8-120 to 8-126.
❑ Do Exercise Eight-13 and check the solution in this Study Guide.
❑ Read paragraph 8-127 to 8-128.
❑ Do Exercise Eight-14 and check the solution in this Study Guide.
❑ Do Self Study Problems Eight-10 and Eight-11 and check the solutions in this Study Guide.
❑ Read paragraph 8-129 to 8-131.

Deemed Dispositions - Departures From Canada
❑ Read paragraph 8-132 to 8-133.
❑ Do Exercises Eight-15 and Eight-16 and check the solutions in this Study Guide.
❑ Do Self Study Problem Eight-12 and check the solution in this Study Guide.

Deferral Provisions On Small Business Investments
❑ Read paragraph 8-134 to 8-136.
❑ Do Exercise Eight-17 and check the solution in this Study Guide.
❑ Do Self Study Problem Eight-13 and check the solution in this Study Guide.

Deferral Provisions On Replacement Property For Capital Gains And CCA
❑ Read paragraph 8-137 to 8-153.
❑ Do Exercise Eight-18 and check the solution in this Study Guide.

Replacement Property - Combined Use Of Deferral Elections
❑ Read paragraph 8-154 to 8-165.
❑ Do Exercise Eight-19 and check the solution in this Study Guide.

Capital Gains And Tax Planning
❑ Read paragraph 8-166 to 8-168.
❑ Do Self Study Problems Eight-14 to Eight-16 and check the solutions in this Study Guide.

To Complete This Chapter
❑ Do Self Study Problems Eight-17 and Eight-18 and check the solutions in this Study Guide.
❑ Review the Key Terms Used In This Chapter on page 392 and 393. Consult the Glossary for the meaning of any key terms you do not know.
❑ Review the Glossary Flashcards and complete the Key Terms Self-Test for the Chapter. These features can be found in two places, on your Student CD-ROM under the heading "Key Term Practice" and on the web site.
❑ Review the Learning Objectives of the Chapter found on page S-174 of this Study Guide.
❑ As a final review, we recommend that you view the PowerPoint Slides for Chapter 8 that are on your Student CD-ROM. The PowerPoint Viewer program can be installed from the Student CD-ROM.

Practice Examination
❑ Write the Practice Examination for Chapter 8 that is on your Student CD. Mark your examination using the Practice Examination Solution that is also on your Student CD-ROM.

Solution to Chapter Eight Exercises

Exercise Eight - 1 Solution
The capital cost of this Class 1 asset would be $3,500,000 ($5,600,000 - $600,000 - $1,500,000). As it is used 100 percent for non-residential purposes and is in a separate Class 1, the maximum CCA in this first year would be $105,000 [(1/2)($3,500,000)(6%)].

Exercise Eight - 2 Solution
The total loss on the sale of 1,000 shares would be $8,500 [(1,000)($14.50 - $23.00)]. As she acquires 600 shares of identical property within 30 days of the sale, 60 percent (600/1,000) of the loss would be disallowed. This $5,100 [(60%)($8,500)] disallowed loss would be added to the adjusted cost base of the new shares. This gives a total adjusted cost base for the new shares of $13,350 [(600)($13.75) + $5,100], or $22.25 per share. The remaining capital loss of $3,400 will create an allowable capital loss of $1,700 [(1/2)($3,400)].

Exercise Eight - 3 Solution
The relevant average cost calculations are as follows:

Acquisition Date Or Sale Date	Shares Purchased (Sold)	Cost Per Share	Total Cost	Average Cost/Share
January 15, 2012	650	$23.50	$15,275	
March 12, 2012	345	24.25	8,366	
Subtotal	995		$23,641	$23.76
September 15, 2012	(210)	$23.76	(4,990)	
Subtotal	785		$18,651	
February 14, 2013	875	$26.75	23,406	
Subtotal	1,660		$42,057	$25.34
October 1, 2013	(340)	$25.34	(8,616)	
End Of Year Balances	1,320		$33,441	

Ms. Montrose's taxable capital gain for 2012 is calculated as follows:

Proceeds Of Disposition [($25.50)(210)]	$5,355
Adjusted Cost Base [($23.76)(210)]	(4,990)
Capital Gain	$ 365
Inclusion Rate	1/2
Taxable Capital Gain	$ 183

Ms. Montrose's taxable capital gain for 2013 is calculated as follows:

Proceeds Of Disposition [($29.50)(340)]	$10,030
Adjusted Cost Base [($25.34)(340)]	(8,616)
Capital Gain	$ 1,414
Inclusion Rate	1/2
Taxable Capital Gain	$ 707

Exercise Eight - 4 Solution
For 2012, there will be a taxable capital gain of $27,500 [(1/2)($292,000 - $237,000)]. During 2013, there will be an allowable capital loss of $2,400 [(1/2)($4,800)]. This allowable capital loss will only be deductible in the determination of 2013 Net Income For Tax Purposes, to the extent that there are 2013 taxable capital gains. Any undeducted loss is subject to the carry over provisions described in Chapter 11.

Exercise Eight - 5 Solution

Mr. Goodson's capital gain on this transaction is $71,800 ($382,000 - $293,000 - $17,200). The maximum reserve for 2012 is $56,387, the lesser of:

- [($71,800)($300,000 ÷ $382,000)] $56,387 (Reserve)
- [($71,800)(20%)(4 - 0)] $57,440 (Reserve)

His taxable capital gain for 2012 is $7,707 [(1/2)($71,800 - $56,387)]. For 2013, the maximum reserve is $43,080, the lesser of:

- [($71,800)($240,000 ÷ $382,000)] $45,110 (Reserve)
- [($71,800)(20%)(4 - 1)] $43,080 (Reserve)

Adding back the previous year's reserve and deducting the new reserve results in a taxable capital gain for 2013 of $6,654 [(1/2)($56,387 - $43,080)].

Exercise Eight - 6 Solution

For 2012, there will be an allowable capital loss of $7,500 [(1/2)($110,000 - $125,000)]. For 2013, there will be an allowable capital loss of $17,500 [(1/2)(Nil - $35,000)]. The total allowable capital loss of $25,000 ($7,500 + $17,500) over the two years is equivalent to the allowable capital loss that would have resulted if the property had been sold for cash of $75,000. The capital loss would equal $50,000 ($125,000 - $75,000) and the allowable capital loss would be $25,000 [(1/2)($50,000)].

These allowable capital losses will only be deductible against taxable capital gains. However, they can be carried over to other years in which the taxpayer has taxable capital gains and deducted in the determination of Taxable Income.

Exercise Eight - 7 Solution

A comparison of the tax effects for Part 1 and Part 2 is as follows:

	Part 1	Part 2
Building - Fair Market Value	$500,000	
Building - Deemed Proceeds		$615,000
UCC	(615,000)	(615,000)
Terminal Loss	($115,000)	Nil
Land - Fair Market Value	$750,000	
Land - Deemed Proceeds		
($1,250,000 - $615,000)		$635,000
Adjusted Cost Base	(425,000)	(425,000)
Capital Gain	$325,000	$210,000
Inclusion Rate	1/2	1/2
Taxable Capital Gain	$162,500	$105,000
Terminal Loss	(115,000)	Nil
Net Income Inclusion	$ 47,500	$105,000

Part 1 Explanation In the absence of the special rule, there would be a taxable capital gain of $162,500 on the land. This would be reduced by the $115,000 terminal loss on the building, resulting in a net income inclusion of $47,500.

Part 2 Explanation ITA 13(21.1)(a) modifies the results in such situations by deeming the proceeds of disposition for the building to be:

The Lesser Of:

- The FMV of the land and building $1,250,000
  Reduced By The Lesser Of:
  - The ACB of the land = $425,000
  - The FMV of the land = $750,000   (425,000) $825,000

- The Greater Of:
  - The FMV of the building = $500,000
  - The Lesser Of:
    The cost of the building = $930,000
    The UCC of the building = $615,000 $615,000

With the building proceeds at $615,000, the terminal loss is eliminated. The $635,000 deemed proceeds for the land result in a capital gain of $210,000. In effect, this eliminates the terminal loss of $115,000 by reducing the capital gain by the same amount (from $325,000 to $210,000) and increases the net income inclusion by one-half of this amount or $57,500 ($105,000 - $47,500).

Exercise Eight - 8 Solution

There would be no tax consequences due to the sales. There would be a capital gain on the first sale of $20,500 ($109,500 - $89,000). This gain could be eliminated by designating the first property as his principal residence for the six years 2004 through 2009. The gain reduction would be calculated as follows:

$$\left(\$20,500 \times \frac{(6+0)^{\,*}}{6} \right) = \$20,500 \quad \text{(Reduction, Not Gain)}$$

* Although the gain reduction formula includes a +1 in the numerator, the numerator cannot exceed the denominator as the gain reduction cannot be larger than the total capital gain.

The $26,000 ($178,000 - $152,000) capital gain on the second home could be eliminated by designating the second property as his principal residence for the years 2010 through 2013 and adding the plus one in the numerator. The gain reduction would be calculated as follows:

$$\left(\$26,000 \times \frac{(4+1)}{5} \right) = \$26,000 \quad \text{(Reduction, Not Gain)}$$

Exercise Eight - 9 Solution

The annual gain on the two properties can be calculated as follows:

	City Home	Cottage
Sales Price	$198,000	$143,500
Adjusted Cost Base	(126,000)	(85,000)
Total Capital Gain	$ 72,000	$ 58,500

Annual Gain - City Home ($72,000 ÷ 12)	$6,000
Annual Gain - Cottage ($58,500 ÷ 9)	$6,500

Given these amounts, the years 2006 through 2013 should be allocated to the cottage. When these eight years are combined with the plus one in the numerator of the reduction formula, the $58,500 gain on the cottage will be completely eliminated. This leaves the years 2002 through 2005 for the Ottawa house, resulting in the following gain reduction:

$$\left(\$72,000 \times \frac{(4+1)}{12} \right) = \$30,000 \quad \text{(Reduction, Not Gain)}$$

This will leave a total capital gain on the sale of the two properties of $42,000 ($72,000 - $30,000 + $58,500 - $58,500).

Exercise Eight - 10 Solution
The results would be as follows:

	Personal Use Property	Listed Personal Property
Gain On Sailboat ($68,000 - $43,000)	$25,000	
Gain On Oil Painting ($25,000 - $1,000)		$24,000
Loss On Personal Automobile	Nil	
Loss On Necklace ($23,000 - $46,000)		(23,000)
Capital Gain	$25,000	$ 1,000
Inclusion Rate	1/2	1/2
Net Taxable Capital Gain	$12,500	$ 500

The total taxable capital gain on the dispositions is equal to $13,000 ($12,500 + $500). While the loss on the automobile is not deductible as it is personal use property, the loss on the diamond necklace can be deducted against the gain on the oil painting because jewelry is listed personal property. The adjusted cost base of the oil painting is deemed to be $1,000 using the $1,000 floor rule.

Exercise Eight - 11 Solution
In 2012, as a result of his share purchase, Mr. Pratt will have an exchange gain of $612 [(450)(TT$68)(C$0.20 - C$0.18)]. As this qualifies as an ITA 39(2) foreign currency capital gain, he will only include $206 [(1/2)($612 - $200)] of this in his Net Income For Tax Purposes.

In 2013, there will be a capital gain on the sale of $792 {[(450)(TT$96)(C$0.16)] - [(450)(TT$68)(C$0.20)]}. None of this gain qualifies under ITA 39(2), so there would be no $200 exclusion. Mr. Pratt's 2013 Net Income For Tax Purposes will include $396, or one-half, of this gain.

Exercise Eight - 12 Solution
The change in use will trigger capital gains on the land and building as follows:

	Land	Building
Proceeds Of Disposition	$120,000	$111,000
Adjusted Cost Base	(20,000)	(23,000)
Capital Gain	$100,000	$ 88,000
Inclusion Rate	1/2	1/2
Taxable Capital Gain	$ 50,000	$ 44,000

For capital gains purposes, the new capital cost will be $111,000 for the building and $120,000 for the land.

As the change is from personal to business use and the fair market value is greater than the cost, the new UCC for the building will be its cost, plus one-half of the difference between the fair market value and the cost. The relevant CCA calculation is as follows:

Original Cost	$23,000
Bump Up [(1/2)($111,000 - $23,000)]	44,000
Cost For CCA Purposes	$67,000
One-Half Net Additions	(33,500)
CCA Base	$33,500
Rate	4%
2013 CCA	$ 1,340

Solution to Chapter Eight Exercises

Note that for individuals, the calendar year is considered the fiscal year for property income purposes. As a consequence, there is no adjustment for a short fiscal period in the year of acquisition. Also note that, while the half-year rules are generally not applicable to non-arm's length transfers, this exemption is only available when the property was used to produce business or property income prior to the transfer which is not the case here.

Exercise Eight - 13 Solution

No ITA 45(2) Election   The 2012 change in use would be treated as a deemed disposition/re-acquisition at the fair market value of $210,000. As the home was personal use property, the $10,000 loss ($210,000 - $220,000) would not be deductible.

The maximum CCA for 2012 would be $4,200 [($210,000)(4%)(1/2)]. This would result in a net rental income for 2012 of $4,800 ($21,600 - $12,600 - $4,200).

When the property is sold in 2013, she would have a taxable capital gain of $67,500 [($345,000 - $210,000)(1/2)]. In addition, there would be recapture of CCA of $4,200, the amount of CCA taken in 2012 for a total income inclusion of $71,700 ($67,500 + $4,200).

ITA 45(2) Election   If she did not take CCA in 2012, her net rental income would be $9,000, $4,200 higher than when no ITA 45(2) election is made. However, she could then elect under ITA 45(2) and this means that the property could continue to be designated as her principal residence in 2013. Given this, the capital gain could be eliminated by the principal residence deduction. In addition, there would be no recapture. This is clearly a better alternative.

Exercise Eight - 14 Solution

The maximum CCA for 2012 would be $7,500 [($375,000)(4%)(1/2)]. Deducting this amount would result in a 2012 net rental income of $2,300 ($9,800 - $7,500).

Because he has deducted CCA for this year, he cannot treat the property as his principal residence and, when he moves in on January 1, 2013, the change in use will create a deemed disposition/re-acquisition at the fair market value of $450,000. This will result in a taxable capital gain of $37,500 [($450,000 - $375,000)(1/2)]. There would also be recapture of the $7,500 of CCA taken in 2012.

When he sells the property at the end of the year for $510,000, there will be an additional taxable capital gain of $30,000 [($510,000 - $450,000)(1/2)]. However, as he lived in the condominium during 2013, this gain would be eliminated through the use of the principal residence exemption. This would leave a 2013 income inclusion of $45,000 ($37,500 + $7,500 + $30,000 - $30,000).

If he does not take CCA in 2012, his net rental income will be $9,800. However, if he makes the ITA 45(3) election, the unit can be designated as his principal residence for both 2012 and 2013. This means that there will be no additional income in 2013. This is clearly a better alternative as shown in the following table:

	No Election	ITA 45(3) Election
2012 Income	$ 2,300	$9,800
2013 Income	45,000	Nil
Total	$47,300	$9,800

Exercise Eight - 15 Solution

There would be a deemed disposition on his departure, leaving him liable for the taxes on a $55,000 [(1/2)($1,030,000 - $920,000)] taxable capital gain.

Exercise Eight - 16 Solution

As real property is exempt from the deemed disposition provision contained in ITA 128.1(4)(b), there would be no tax consequences with respect to the rental property at the time of Ms. Twain's departure. However, real property is Taxable Canadian Property and, as a consequence, as explained in Chapter 1, she would be liable for Canadian taxes on both recapture and capital gains resulting from a subsequent sale of the property, even after she becomes a non-resident.

Exercise Eight - 17 Solution

The capital gain would be calculated as follows:

Proceeds Of Disposition	$1,350,000
Adjusted Cost Base	(750,000)
Capital Gain	$ 600,000

As the lesser of the proceeds of disposition and the cost of the replacement shares is the $1,200,000 cost of the replacement shares, the maximum deferral would be $533,333 [($600,000)($1,200,000 ÷ $1,350,000)].

The adjusted cost base of the new shares would be calculated as follows:

Initial Cost	$1,200,000
Maximum Deferral	(533,3333)
Adjusted Cost Base	$ 666,667

Exercise Eight - 18 Solution

The Company would have to record recapture of $750,000 ($650,000 - $1,400,000) for 2012. This is reversed during 2013 by electing under ITA 13(4). Since the replacement cost of the new building exceeds the normal recapture of CCA, the amended recapture of CCA is nil. Using the ITA 13(4) formula, the amended 2012 recapture of CCA would be as follows:

UCC Balance			$650,000
Deduction:			
Lesser Of:			
• Proceeds Of Disposition = $1,400,000			
• Capital Cost = $1,500,000		$1,400,000	
Reduced By The Lesser Of:			
• Normal Recapture = $750,000			
• Replacement Cost = $2,350,000	(750,000)		(650,000)
Recapture Of CCA (Amended)			Nil

The result is that the UCC of the replacement building would be limited to $1,600,000 ($2,350,000 - $750,000). This also reflects the economic substance of the replacement transaction ($650,000 + $2,350,000 - $1,400,000 = $1,600,000).

Exercise Eight - 19 Solution

As the replacement did not occur until 2013, Hadfeld's 2012 tax return will include a capital gain of $225,000 ($950,000 - $725,000), of which one-half or $112,500 is taxable, and recapture of $101,850 ($725,000 - $623,150).

Since the cost of the replacement property exceeded the proceeds of disposition for the old property, these amounts can be reversed in 2013 through a 2012 amended return. The deemed capital cost and UCC of the new building are as follows:

Actual Capital Cost	$980,000
Capital Gain Reversed By Election ($950,000 - $725,000)	(225,000)
Deemed Capital Cost	$755,000
Recapture Reversed By Election ($725,000 - $623,150)	(101,850)
UCC	$653,150

Each of these amounts are $30,000 more than the old capital cost and UCC. This reflects the $30,000 ($980,000 - $950,000) over and above the insurance proceeds that the Company spent on replacing the building.

Self Study Solution Eight - 1

Acquisition Or Sale Date	Shares Purchased (Sold)	Cost Per Share	Total Cost	Average Cost/Share
October 15, 2007	5,500	$40.00	$220,000	
November 8, 2007	(1,500)	(40.00)	(60,000)	
December 12, 2009	3,200	79.00	252,800	
Subtotal	7,200		$412,800	$ 57.33
February 3, 2010	(2,600)	(57.33)	(149,058)	
Subtotal	4,600		$263,742	
January 15, 2011 Stock Dividend	460	99.00	45,540	
June 15, 2011	3,800	104.00	395,200	
Subtotal	8,860		$704,482	
December 23, 2012 Stock Dividend	886	125.00	110,750	
March 15, 2013 Balances	9,746		$815,232	

The taxable capital gain resulting from the November 8, 2007 sale of shares would be calculated as follows:

Proceeds Of Disposition [(1,500)($52)]	$78,000
Adjusted Cost Base [(1,500)($40)]	(60,000)
Capital Gain	$18,000
Inclusion Rate	1/2
Taxable Capital Gain	$ 9,000

The taxable capital gain resulting from the February 3, 2010 sale of shares would be calculated as follows:

Proceeds Of Disposition [(2,600)($94)]	$244,400
Adjusted Cost Base [(2,600)($57.33)]	
(See preceding table for per share adjusted cost base)	(149,058)
Capital Gain	$ 95,342
Inclusion Rate	1/2
Taxable Capital Gain	$ 47,671

The taxable capital gain resulting from the March 15, 2013 sale of shares would be calculated as follows:

Proceeds Of Disposition [(9,746)($174)]	$1,695,804
Adjusted Cost Base (Remainder)	(815,232)
Capital Gain	$ 880,572
Inclusion Rate	1/2
Taxable Capital Gain	$ 440,286

Self Study Solution Eight - 2

No recognition can be given to the warranty at the time the land is sold. This means that a taxable capital gain of $600,000 [(1/2)($2,600,000 - $1,400,000)] will result from this sale. However, since no reduction in the capital gain can be made to reflect potential outlays under the warranty, the subsequent outlays that are required under the warranty agreement will be treated as a capital loss. Thus, the $1,040,000 payment that is required in 2013 will result in a $520,000 [(1/2)($1,040,000)] allowable capital loss.

This allowable capital loss must first be deducted against taxable capital gains that occur in 2013. If such gains are not sufficient to absorb the loss, some or all of the $520,000 can be carried back to 2012 to be applied against the gain that was recognized when the sale occurred.

Any loss that is not carried back can be carried forward indefinitely and applied against future capital gains. (Loss carry overs are covered in Chapter 11.)

Self Study Solution Eight - 3

Total Gain
The total amount of the capital gain can be calculated as follows:

Proceeds Of Disposition		$500,000
Less:		
Adjusted Cost Base	$230,000	
Disposition Costs	20,000	250,000
Total Capital Gain		$250,000

The cash payment schedule is as follows:

	Payment	Balance Owing
Sale Price = Total Proceeds		$500,000
2013 Payment (40%)	$200,000	300,000
2019 Payment (60%)	300,000	Nil

Reserve Limits
As Miss Stevens has not received the entire proceeds in the year of sale, she is entitled under ITA 40(1) to establish a reserve. The reserve that would be available at the end of each year would be the lesser of:

- [(Capital Gain)(Proceeds Not Yet Due ÷ Total Proceeds)]
- [(Capital Gain)(20%)(4 - Number Of Preceding Years Ending After Disposition)]

The first of these limiting factors is based, as would be expected, on the pattern of collections. In contrast, the second factor serves to require that at least 20 percent of any gain be recognized in the year of disposition and each subsequent year, regardless of the pattern of cash collections.

2013 Gain
At the end of 2013 the two reserve calculations are as follows:

- [($250,000)($300,000 ÷ $500,000)] = $150,000
- [($250,000)(20%)(4 Years - 0 Years)] = $200,000

The lesser figure is $150,000, resulting in the following capital gain calculation:

Total Capital Gain	$250,000
Reserve	(150,000)
Capital Gain	$100,000
Inclusion Rate	1/2
Taxable Capital Gain For 2013	$ 50,000

2014 Gain

At the end of 2014, the two calculations provide equal results as follows:

- [($250,000)($300,000 ÷ $500,000)] = $150,000
- [($250,000)(20%)(4 Years - 1 Year)] = $150,000

This means the 2014 taxable capital gain would be calculated as follows:

Addition Of Previous Year's Reserve	$ 150,000
Deduction Of New Reserve	(150,000)
2014 Capital Gain And Taxable Capital Gain	Nil

2015, 2016, And 2017 Gains

In these three years no further proceeds are receivable and, as a consequence, the reserve calculation based on proceeds not receivable until after December 31 would remain unchanged at $150,000. However, results under the alternative calculation would decline as follows:

- 2015 [($250,000)(20%)(4 Years - 2 Years)] = $100,000
- 2016 [($250,000)(20%)(4 Years - 3 Years)] = $50,000
- 2017 [($250,000)(20%)(4 Years - 4 Years)] = Nil

Based on this, taxable capital gain for these three years will be calculated as follows:

	2015	2016	2017
Previous Year's Reserve	$150,000	$100,000	$50,000
New Reserve	(100,000)	(50,000)	Nil
Capital Gain	$ 50,000	$ 50,000	$50,000
Inclusion Rate	1/2	1/2	1/2
Taxable Capital Gain	$ 25,000	$ 25,000	$25,000

At this point, the entire taxable capital gain of $125,000 would have been taken into income as per the following schedule:

Year	Capital Gain	Taxable Capital Gain
2013	$100,000	$50,000
2014	Nil	Nil
2015	50,000	25,000
2016	50,000	25,000
2017	50,000	25,000
Total	$250,000	$125,000

2018 And 2019 Gains

As the entire taxable capital gain was taken into Net Income For Tax Purposes by the end of 2017, no further gains will be recognized in either 2018 or 2019.

Self Study Solution Eight - 4

Capital Gain

Without regard to the assumptions about the down payment, the total capital gain for Ms. Gerhardt is $750,000 ($1,350,000 - $600,000). The taxable capital gain is $375,000 [(1/2)($750,000)].

Reserve Limits

Under ITA 40(1)(a)(iii), the amount that can be deducted as a capital gains reserve is equal to the lesser of:

- [(Capital Gain)(Proceeds Not Yet Due ÷ Total Proceeds)]
- [(Capital Gain)(20%)(4 - Number Of Preceding Years Ending After Disposition)]

The second part of this formula serves to require that at least 20 percent of the gain be recognized in the year of disposition and each subsequent year, without regard to the pattern of cash collected.

Part A

The reserve percentage under the two components of ITA 40(1)(a)(iii) would be as follows:

Year	Proceeds Not Yet Due	20 Percent Formula
2013	55%	80%
2014	50%	60%
2015	45%	40%
2016	40%	20%
2017	35%	Nil

For the years 2013 and 2014, the proceeds not yet due calculation provides the lower figure. Based on this, the gains to be recognized in these two years would be calculated as follows:

2013 Capital Gain	$750,000
2013 Reserve [($750,000)(55%)]	(412,500)
Capital Gain	$337,500
Inclusion Rate	1/2
Taxable Capital Gain For 2013	$168,750

2013 Reserve	$412,500
2014 Reserve [($750,000)(50%)]	(375,000)
Capital Gain	$ 37,500
Inclusion Rate	1/2
Taxable Capital Gain For 2014	$ 18,750

In the years 2015 through 2017, the 20 percent formula provides the lower reserve. As a result, the reserves for these three years are as follows:

- 2015 [($750,000)(20%)(4 Years - 2 Years)] = $300,000
- 2016 [($750,000)(20%)(4 Years - 3 Years)] = $150,000
- 2017 [($750,000)(20%)(4 Years - 4 Years)] = Nil

Based on this, taxable capital gain for these three years will be calculated as follows:

	2015	2016	2017
Previous Year's Reserve	$375,000	$300,000	$150,000
New Reserve	(300,000)	(150,000)	Nil
Capital Gain	$ 75,000	$150,000	$150,000
Inclusion Rate	1/2	1/2	1/2
Taxable Capital Gain	$ 37,500	$ 75,000	$75,000

Part B

In this case, the reserve percentage components would be as follows:

Year	Proceeds Not Yet Due	20 Percent Formula
2013	85%	80%
2014	80%	60%
2015	75%	40%
2016	70%	20%
2017	65%	Nil

In this case, the 20 percent formula calculation provides the lower figure for the reserve in each of the 5 years. Using this as the basis for the reserve will result in the recognition of $150,000 [(20%)($750,000)] of the gain in each of the five years. The taxable amount in each year will be $75,000 [(1/2)($150,000)], for a total of $375,000 over the five years 2013 through 2017.

Summary

As shown in the following table, the entire $375,000 taxable capital gain has been recognized in both Cases over the first 5 years, regardless of when the total proceeds will be completely collected.

Year	Part A	Part B
2013	$168,750	$ 75,000
2014	18,750	75,000
2015	37,500	75,000
2016	75,000	75,000
2017	75,000	75,000
Gain Recognized	$375,000	$375,000

Self Study Solution Eight - 5

For 2012, Mrs. Simpkins would have a capital gain of $10,000 ($25,000 - $15,000), of which one-half is taxable, resulting in a taxable capital gain of $5,000. While this could have been reduced through the use of reserves, Mrs. Simpkins chose not to do so.

In 2013, the inability to collect the note payment would result in a capital loss of $10,000 (Nil - $10,000). The $5,000 allowable amount of this loss must first be applied against any taxable capital gains that are realized in 2013. If such gains are not sufficient to absorb the loss, all or part of the $5,000 can be carried back and applied against the taxable capital gain that was recognized in 2012 (assuming there were no 2012 allowable capital losses net against it).

Any loss that is not carried back can be carried forward indefinitely and applied against future capital gains. (Loss carry overs are covered in Chapter 11.)

Self Study Solution Eight - 6

2013 Results

The only tax consequence in this year is the capital gain that occurs on the sale. The gain, along with the maximum deductible reserve, would be calculated as follows:

Proceeds Of Disposition	$9,400,000
Adjusted Cost Base	(4,200,000)
Capital Gain	$5,200,000
Reserve - Lesser Of:	
• [($5,200,000)($8,000,000 ÷ $9,400,000)] = $4,425,532	
• [($5,200,000)(20%)(4 - 0)] = $4,160,000	(4,160,000)
Capital Gain	$1,040,000
Inclusion Rate	1/2
Taxable Capital Gain	$ 520,000

As no provision can be made for the estimated cost of the warranty, the total Net Income For Tax Purposes inclusion for 2013 would be $520,000.

2014 Results

During this year, Mr. Howard will include $480,000 [(6%)($8,000,000)] of interest in his Net Income For Tax Purposes.

In addition, Mr. Howard will include the 2013 reserve in income and deduct a new reserve for 2014. The calculations are as follows:

2013 Reserve	$4,160,000
2014 Reserve - Lesser Of:	
• [($5,200,000)($6,000,000 ÷ $9,400,000)] = $3,319,149	
• [($5,200,000)(20%)(4 - 1)] = $3,120,000	(3,120,000)
Capital Gain	$1,040,000
Inclusion Rate	1/2
Taxable Capital Gain	$ 520,000

The total Net Income For Tax Purposes inclusion for 2014 would be $1,000,000 ($480,000 + $520,000).

2015 Results

During this year, Mr. Howard will include $360,000 [(6%)($6,000,000)] of interest in his Net Income For Tax Purposes.

In addition, Mr. Howard will include the 2014 reserve in income and deduct a new reserve for 2015. The calculations are as follows:

2014 Reserve	$3,120,000
2015 Reserve - Lesser Of:	
• [($5,200,000)($4,000,000 ÷ $9,400,000)] = $2,212,766	
• [($5,200,000)(20%)(4 - 2)] = $2,080,000	(2,080,000)
Capital Gain	$1,040,000
Inclusion Rate	1/2
Taxable Capital Gain	$ 520,000

The total Net Income For Tax Purposes inclusion for 2015 would be $880,000 ($360,000 + $520,000).

2016 Results

During this year, Mr. Howard will include $240,000 [(6%)($4,000,000)] of interest in his Net Income For Tax Purposes.

As the warranty was on a capital asset, the payment of the $900,000 will be treated as a capital loss. In addition, Mr. Howard will include the 2015 reserve in income and deduct a new reserve for 2016. The calculations are as follows:

2015 Reserve	$2,080,000
2016 Reserve - Lesser Of:	
• [($5,200,000)($2,000,000 ÷ $9,400,000)] = $1,106,383	
• [($5,200,000)(20%)(4 - 3)] = $1,040,000	(1,040,000)
Capital Gain	$1,040,000
Capital Loss On Warranty	(900,000)
Net Capital Gain	$ 140,000
Inclusion Rate	1/2
Net Taxable Capital Gain	$ 70,000

The total Net Income For Tax Purposes inclusion for 2016 would be $310,000 ($240,000 + $70,000).

2017 Results

With the bankruptcy of the developer, no interest will be collected in 2017 and the balance of the loan must be written off as a bad debt, resulting in a capital loss of $2,000,000.

Mr. Howard will include the 2016 reserve of $1,040,000 in income, but no new reserve can be deducted as, with the write-off of the loan balance, no proceeds remain to be collected.

The net effect of these items is an allowable capital loss of $480,000 [(1/2)($1,040,000 - $2,000,000)]. Note that this loss can only be deducted in 2017 to the extent of taxable capital gains in that year. However, it can be carried back to be applied to the capital gains that were recognized in previous years.

Summary (Not Required)

The results can be summarized as follows:

Year	Interest	Taxable Gain (Allowable Loss)
2013	Nil	$ 520,000
2014	$ 480,000	520,000
2015	360,000	520,000
2016	240,000	70,000
2017	Nil	(480,000)
Totals	$1,080,000	$1,150,000

Self Study Solution Eight - 7

The gain on the English Bay property is $390,000 ($515,000 - $125,000) and the gain on the Whistler cottage is $280,000 ($320,000 - $40,000). However, we need to calculate the gain per year of ownership. This is necessary because the period of ownership for the two properties is not the same. For the English Bay property, the period is 25 years (1989 through 2013). For the Whistler cottage, the period is 20 years (1994 through 2013). The annual amounts would be as follows:

English Bay = [($515,000 - $125,000) ÷ 25] = $15,600

Cottage = [($320,000 - $40,000) ÷ 20] = $14,000

As the annual gain is greater on the English Bay property, this should be the designated principal residence for enough years to reduce the capital gain to nil. Because the exemption formula has an added year, the gain on this property can be completely eliminated by designating the 24 years 1989 through 2012 to this property. The exemption here would be calculated as follows:

$$[(24 + 1) ÷ 25][\$390,000] = \$390,000$$

This will leave the year 2013 to be used on the cottage, and the exemption here would be calculated as follows:

$$[(1 + 1) ÷ 20][\$280,000] = \$28,000$$

The total taxable capital gain to be recognized would be as follows:

Gain On English Bay	$390,000
Exemption On English Bay	(390,000)
Gain On Cottage	280,000
Exemption On Cottage	(28,000)
Total Capital Gain	$252,000
Inclusion Rate	1/2
Taxable Capital Gain	$126,000

Self Study Solution Eight - 8

Listed personal property consists of these specified items as listed in ITA 54:

(i)   print, etching, drawing, painting, sculpture, or other similar work of art,
(ii) jewelry,
(iii) rare folio, rare manuscript, or rare book,
(iv) stamp, or
(v)   coin.

Personal Use Property (Automobile, Boat, and Desk)

While gains on the disposition of personal use property are taxable, losses are not deductible. This means that, because there is a loss on this property, selling the sailboat would have no effect on Mr. Firenza's Net Income For Tax Purposes. However, the gains on both the automobile and the desk would be subject to tax. These gains would be calculated as follows:

	Automobile	Desk
Proceeds Of Disposition	$320,000	$2,200
Adjusted Cost Base		
($135,000 + $42,000)	(177,000)	
Adjusted Cost Base ($1,000 Floor)		(1,000)
Capital Gain	$143,000	$1,200
Inclusion Rate	1/2	1/2
Taxable Capital Gain	$ 71,500	$ 600

Listed Personal Property (Coin Collection, Manuscript, Painting)

With respect to listed personal property, gains are taxable and losses are deductible. However, the losses can only be deducted against gains resulting from the disposition of listed personal property. Given this, the addition to Mr. Firenza's Net Income For Tax Purposes would be calculated as follows:

Gain On Coin Collection ($23,500 - $17,600)	$5,900
Gain On Painting [(80%)($350,000) - $275,000]	5,000
Total Gain	$10,900
Loss On Manuscript (Note)	(10,900)
Addition to Net Income For Tax Purposes	Nil

Note The total loss on the manuscript is $33,500 ($8,500 - $42,000). However, it can only be deducted to the extent of the gains on other listed personal property dispositions. The remaining loss of $22,600 ($33,500 - $10,900) can be carried over to other years. As is discussed in Chapter 11, such losses can be carried back 3 years and forward for 7 years.

Self Study Solution Eight - 9

The taxable capital gain on the sale of securities and the conversion to Canadian dollars would be calculated as follows:

Proceeds Of Disposition [(5,000)(£32)($1.57)]	$251,200	
Adjusted Cost Base [(5,000)(£25)($1.64)]	(205,000)	
Capital Gain On Sale Of Securities		$46,200
Converted Dollars - June [(5,000)(£32)($1.62)]	$259,200	
Proceeds Of Disposition [(5,000)(£32)($1.57)]	(251,200)	
Capital Gain On Foreign Exchange	$ 8,000	
ITA 39(2) Deduction	(200)	
Net Foreign Exchange Gain		7,800
Total Capital Gains		$54,000
Inclusion Rate		1/2
Taxable Capital Gains		$27,000

There is a foreign exchange gain under ITA 39(2), resulting from the increase in the value of the British pound between June and December of 2013. As Mr. Levitt is an individual, he is eligible to deduct the first $200 of foreign exchange gains under ITA 39(2).

As the securities would be considered capital assets, this net foreign exchange gain of $7,800 would be a capital gain.

Mr. Levitt's income inclusion for 2013 would be $27,000.

Self Study Solution Eight - 10

2011 Results

As the 2011 change in use is from personal to business, the deemed disposition will take place at a value, for CCA purposes, of cost plus one-half of the excess of fair market value over cost [ITA 13(7)(b)]. Although Miss Coos previously owned this building, the half-year rule applies to this change in use because the building was not being used to produce business or property income prior its change in use. As the building is not used 90 percent or more for non-residential purposes, the enhanced CCA rates for buildings cannot be used.

Given this, the maximum CCA that can be deducted in 2011 can be calculated as follows:

Cost Of Building	$ 90,000
Bump Up On Transfer [(1/2)($120,000 - $90,000)]	15,000
Capital Cost For CCA Purposes Only	$105,000
Rental Portion	30%
Opening UCC	$ 31,500
One-Half Net Additions	(15,750)
CCA Base	$ 15,750
Maximum Class 1 CCA At 4 Percent	(630)
One-Half Net Additions	15,750
January 1, 2012 UCC	$ 30,870

The deemed disposition would result in a taxable capital gain on the building of $4,500 [(1/2)(30%)($120,000 - $90,000)]. As the $30,000 value of the land is unchanged, there is no capital gain on the land.

It is likely that Ms. Coos would designate this property as her principal residence for 2009 and 2010, thereby eliminating this gain from her income.

2012 Results

The required CCA calculation for 2012 is as follows:

Opening UCC	$30,870
Maximum CCA At 4 Percent	(1,235)
January 1, 2013 UCC	$29,635

2013 Results

In this year, the transfer is from business to personal use and, as a consequence, the disposition will result in a deduction from UCC in an amount equal to the lesser of 10 percent of the capital cost for CCA purposes ($105,000) and 10 percent of the fair market value of $140,000.

The required CCA calculation for 2013 is as follows:

Opening UCC	$29,635
Disposition - Lesser Of:	
• Capital Cost [(10%)($105,000)] = $10,500	
• UCC = $29,635	(10,500)
CCA Base	$19,135
Maximum CCA At 4 Percent	(765)
January 1, 2014 UCC	$18,370

The deemed disposition would result in a taxable capital gain of $1,000 [(1/2)(10%)($140,000 - $120,000)] on the building. As the market value of the land remains unchanged at $30,000, there would be no capital gain on the land.

Note that the $120,000 capital cost used in the calculation of the taxable capital gain is not the same as the $105,000 capital cost used in the calculation of CCA.

Self Study Solution Eight - 11

2012 Solution

As the property is being transferred from personal to business use and its fair market value is greater than its cost, ITA 13(7)(b) requires that, for the purposes of calculating CCA, the property be recorded at an amount equal to its cost, plus one-half of the excess of its fair market value over cost. The half-year rule is applicable as the personal residence was not used to produce business or property income. The UCC would be calculated as follows:

Cost Of Building ($176,000 - $83,000)	$ 93,000
Bump-Up On Transfer -	
{[1/2][($253,000 - $106,000) - ($176,000 - $83,000)]}	27,000
Capital Cost For CCA Purposes Only	$120,000
Rental Share	32%
Opening UCC	$ 38,400
One-Half Net Additions	(19,200)
CCA Base	$ 19,200
CCA [($19,200)(4%)]	(768)
One-Half Net Additions	19,200
January 1, 2013 UCC	$ 37,632

Based on the preceding information, the 2013 net rental income would be calculated as follows:

Rents [(12)($850)]	$10,200
Expenses [(32%)($5,600)]	(1,792)
CCA	(768)
Net Rental Income	$ 7,640

There would also be taxable capital gains on the land and the building, calculated as follows:

	Land	Building
Deemed Proceeds Of Disposition		
Land	$106,000	
Building ($253,000 - $106,000)		$147,000
Adjusted Cost Base/Capital Cost		
Land	(83,000)	
Building ($176,000 - $83,000)		(93,000)
Subtotal	$ 23,000	$ 54,000
Rental Share	32%	32%
Capital Gain	$ 7,360	$ 17,280
Inclusion Rate	1/2	1/2
Taxable Capital Gain	$ 3,680	$ 8,640

Note that the capital cost used for determining the capital gain on the building ($147,000) is not the same capital cost that was used for determining CCA ($120,000). For capital gains purposes, the fair market value is used. As shown in the CCA calculation, the value for CCA and UCC purposes is limited by ITA 13(7)(b) to its cost plus the bump up.

As Mr. Blake does not use the principal residence exemption, the increase in his Net Income For Tax Purposes would total $19,960 ($7,640 + $3,680 + $8,640).

2013 Solution

In this year, the transfer is from business to personal use and, as a consequence, the disposition will result in a deduction from UCC in an amount equal to the lesser of 11 percent of the capital cost for CCA purposes ($120,000) and 11 percent of the fair market value of $168,000 ($278,000 - $110,000). The calculations are as follows:

Opening UCC	$37,632
Plus: Additions (Improvements)	12,350
Less: Dispositions - Lesser Of:	
Cost [(11%)($120,000)] = $13,200	
Deemed Proceeds	
[(11%)($278,000 - $110,000)] = $18,480	(13,200)
One-Half Net Additions	Nil
CCA Base	$36,782
CCA [($36,782)(4%)]	(1,471)
January 1, 2014 UCC	$35,311

Based on the preceding information, the 2013 net rental income would be as follows:

Rents [(6)($850) + (6)($750)]	$9,600
Expenses {[(32%)($2,900)] + [(21%)($3,200)]}	(1,600)
CCA	(1,471)
Net Rental Income	$6,529

There would also be taxable capital gains on the land and building, calculated as follows:

	Land	Building
Deemed Proceeds Of Disposition		
Land	$110,000	
Building ($278,000 - $110,000)		$168,000
Adjusted Cost Base		
Land	(106,000)	
Building ($253,000 - $106,000)		(147,000)
Subtotal	$ 4,000	$ 21,000
Rental Share	11%	11%
Capital Gain	$ 440	$ 2,310
Inclusion Rate	1/2	1/2
Taxable Capital Gain	$ 220	$ 1,155

The increase in Mr. Blake's Net Income For Tax Purposes would total $7,904 ($6,529 + $220 + $1,155).

Self Study Solution Eight - 12

Mr. Vargo's taxable capital gain on deemed dispositions resulting from his departure from Canada would be calculated as follows:

Antique Sports Car ($46,000 - $32,000) (Note 1)	$ 14,000
Personal Automobile (Note 1)	Nil
Bank Of Nova Scotia Shares ($16,000 - $12,000)	4,000
Vargo Ltd. Shares ($17,000 - $23,000)	(6,000)
Coin Collection (Note 2)	Nil
Cottage (Note 3)	Nil
Capital Gain	$12,000
Inclusion Rate	1/2
Taxable Capital Gain On Departure	$ 6,000

Note 1   While losses on personal use property such as his personal automobile are not deductible, gains are taxable.

Note 2   While there is a listed personal property loss of $2,000 ($6,000 - $8,000) on the stamp collection, it can only be deducted against gains on listed personal property.

Note 3   Real property is exempted from the ITA 128.1(4)(b) deemed disposition requirement. However, as it is taxable Canadian property, a later sale of this land will attract Canadian income taxes, even though Mr. Vargo is no longer a Canadian resident.

Self Study Solution Eight - 13

Case A
The capital gain on the disposition is $60,000. As the cost of the replacement shares is only $90,000, the permitted deferral would be $54,000 [($90,000 ÷ $100,000)($60,000)]. The adjusted cost base of the replacement shares would be $36,000 ($90,000 - $54,000).

Case B
The capital gain on the disposition is $600,000. As the cost of the replacement shares is equal to the qualifying cost of the proceeds of disposition, the permitted deferral would be $600,000. This would leave the adjusted cost base of the replacement shares at $400,000 ($1,000,000 - $600,000). Note that the deferral election can be made because the replacement shares were acquired within 120 days after the end of the year.

Self Study Solution Eight - 14

2013 Results
For 2013, the insurance proceeds would create recaptured CCA, calculated as follows:

January 1, 2013 UCC Balance	$ 368,000
Disposition - Lesser Of:	
• Cost = $500,000	
• Proceeds Of Disposition = $490,000	(490,000)
Negative Closing Balance = Recapture	($ 122,000)
Recapture	122,000
January 1, 2014 UCC	Nil

The $122,000 in recapture would be taken into 2013 income and added back to the UCC to create a UCC balance of nil.

2014 Results
Using ITA 13(4), Trail Resources Ltd. would file an amended return for the 2013 taxation year. The revised recapture would be calculated as follows:

January 1, 2013 UCC Balance		$368,000
Deduction:		
Lesser Of:		
• Proceeds Of Disposition = $490,000		
• Capital Cost = $500,000	$490,000	
Reduced By The Lesser Of:		
• Normal Recapture = $122,000		
• Replacement Cost = $650,000	(122,000)	(368,000)
Recapture Of 2013 CCA (Amended)		Nil

The UCC of the new building will be adjusted for this change as follows:

Cost Of New Building	$ 650,000
Reversal Of Recapture - ITA 13(4) Election	(122,000)
UCC	$ 528,000

Given this, the required maximum CCA for 2014 and the January 1, 2015 UCC balance would be calculated as follows:

Opening UCC - Class 1	Nil
Addition Of UCC Of New Building	$528,000
One-Half Net Additions	(264,000)
Base For CCA	$264,000
Maximum CCA [($264,000)(6%)]	(15,840)
Add: One-Half Net Additions	264,000
UCC Balance, January 1, 2015	$512,160

The reasonableness of the CCA base calculation can be verified by noting that the $528,000 is equal to the initial UCC of $368,000, plus the cost of the new building of $650,000, less the insurance proceeds of $490,000. The half-year rule is applied to the net addition to Class 1.

Self Study Solution Eight - 15

Part A
The 2013 tax consequences would be as follows:

Land The Company would have a taxable capital gain on the Land calculated as follows:

Proceeds Of Disposition	$1,720,000
Adjusted Cost Base	(325,000)
Capital Gain	$1,395,000
Inclusion Rate	1/2
Taxable Capital Gain	$ 697,500

Building The Company would have a taxable capital gain and recapture calculated as follows:

Proceeds Of Disposition	$1,200,000
Capital Cost	(1,100,000)
Capital Gain	$ 100,000
Inclusion Rate	1/2
Taxable Capital Gain	$ 50,000

Opening UCC	$ 720,000
Deduct Disposition - Lesser Of:	
Capital Cost = $1,100,000	
Proceeds Of Disposition = $1,200,000	(1,100,000)
Negative Closing UCC Balance = Recapture	($ 380,000)
Recapture (Included In Income)	380,000
UCC - January 1, 2014	Nil

Equipment The Company would have recapture calculated as follows:

Opening UCC		$240,000
Deduct Disposition - Lesser Of:		
Capital Cost = $620,000		
Proceeds Of Disposition = $320,000		(320,000)
Negative Closing UCC Balance = Recapture		($ 80,000)
Recapture (Included In Income)		80,000
UCC - January 1, 2014		Nil

Part B

Land   With respect to the Land, the capital gain resulting from the use of the ITA 44(1) election would be the lesser of:

- $1,395,000 (regular capital gain); and
- $770,000 (the excess of the $1,720,000 proceeds of disposition for the old land over the $950,000 cost of the replacement land).

The taxable amount would be $385,000 [(1/2)($770,000)] and this would be included in the revised 2013 Net Income For Tax Purposes.

If the ITA 44(1) election is used in 2014, the deemed adjusted cost base of the replacement land would be calculated as follows:

Cost	$950,000
Capital Gain Reversed By Election ($1,395,000 - $770,000)	(625,000)
Deemed Adjusted Cost Base Of Replacement Land	$325,000

Note that the deemed adjusted cost base of the replacement land has been reduced to the actual adjusted cost base of the old land.

Building   If the ITA 44(1) election is used in 2014, the amended 2013 capital gain would be nil, the lesser of:

- $100,000 (regular capital gain); and
- Nil (reflecting the fact that there was no excess of the $1,200,000 proceeds of disposition for the old building over the $1,350,000 cost of the replacement building).

If the ITA 13(4) election is used in 2014, the amended 2013 recapture would be as follows:

January 1, 2013 UCC Balance			$720,000
Deduction:			
Lesser Of:			
• Proceeds Of Disposition = $1,200,000			
• Capital Cost = $1,100,000		$1,100,000	
Reduced By The Lesser Of:			
• Normal Recapture = $380,000			
• Replacement Cost = $1,350,000	(380,000)	(720,000)	
Recapture Of 2013 CCA (Amended)			Nil

If both elections are used in 2014, the UCC of the replacement building is calculated as follows:

Cost	$1,350,000
Capital Gain Reversed By Election	(100,000)
Deemed Capital Cost	$1,250,000
Recapture Reversed By Election	(380,000)
UCC - Replacement Building	$ 870,000

Note that the UCC for the new building is equal to the UCC of the old building ($720,000), plus the additional $150,000 ($1,350,000 - $1,200,000) in funds required for its acquisition.

Equipment   As this is a voluntary disposition, the ITA 13(4) and 44(1) elections can only be used on real property (land and buildings). They cannot be used on the equipment and, as a consequence, the $80,000 in recapture will not be altered in the amended return. As the elections cannot be used, both the capital cost and the UCC of the new equipment will be $475,000.

Part C

After the application of the ITA 44(1) election, there was a $770,000 capital gain on the land and no gain on the building. Some reduction of Net Income For Tax Purposes can be achieved under the ITA 44(6) election. However, the reduction is limited to the $150,000 difference between the $1,200,000 proceeds resulting from the sale of the old building, and the $1,350,000 cost of the replacement building. This would reduce the capital gain on the land by $150,000. The adjusted cost base of the replacement land would remain at $325,000.

This would still leave the capital gain on the building at nil. This can be shown as follows:

Deemed Proceeds Of Disposition ($1,200,000 + $150,000)	$1,350,000
Less: Cost Of Replacement Building	1,350,000
Capital Gain	Nil

Using this election, the amended 2013 Net Income For Tax Purposes would be reduced by $75,000 [(1/2)($150,000)]. It would be possible to further reduce the gain on the land by transferring more of the proceeds to the building. The result, however, would be a new gain on the building that would be equal to the gain reduction on the land.

With the use of this election, the deemed cost of the new building would be $1,100,000 [$1,350,000 - ($1,200,000 + $150,000 - $1,100,000)] and the UCC would be reduced to $720,000 ($1,100,000 - $380,000).

Also note that there is a cost involved with this election. While the Company has reduced its 2013 Net Income For Tax Purposes by one-half of the $150,000 capital gain, it has forgone future CCA for the full amount of $150,000. Under normal circumstances, this would not be advisable as the trade-off for the tax deferral is a substantial increase in future taxes.

Self Study Solution Eight - 16

Part A

The proceeds of disposition were greater than the relevant capital costs for all the destroyed and expropriated assets. As a result, with respect to Net Income For Tax Purposes, the 2013 tax effects related to the involuntary dispositions would be as follows:

	Old Land	Old Building	Old Contents
Proceeds Of Disposition	$723,000	$4,800,000	$1,256,000
Adjusted Cost Base - Capital Cost	(256,000)	(3,700,000)	(972,000)
Capital Gains	$467,000	$1,100,000	$ 284,000
Inclusion Rate	1/2	1/2	1/2
Taxable Capital Gains	$233,500	$ 550,000	$ 142,000

	Old Building	Old Contents
Opening UCC	$1,856,000	$ 72,000
Capital Cost (Less Than Proceeds)	(3,700,000)	(972,000)
Closing UCC	($1,844,000)	($900,000)
Recapture Of CCA	1,844,000	900,000
UCC - January 1, 2014	Nil	Nil

The increase in Net Income For Tax Purposes totals $3,669,500 ($233,500 + $550,000 + $142,000 + $1,844,000 + $900,000).

Part B

The revised amounts that would be included in the 2013 amended return would be as follows:

Land Under ITA 44(1), the revised 2013 capital gain would be $223,000, the lesser of:

- $467,000 (regular capital gain); and
- $223,000 (the excess of the $723,000 proceeds of disposition for the old land over the $500,000 cost of the new land).

The taxable amount of this capital gain will be $111,500 [(1/2)($223,000)].

The adjusted cost base of the replacement land is calculated as follows:

Cost	$500,000
Capital Gain Reversed By Election ($467,000 - $223,000)	(244,000)
Deemed Adjusted Cost Base Of Replacement Property	$256,000

Note that the deemed adjusted cost base of the replacement land has been reduced to the actual adjusted cost base of the old land.

Building Under ITA 44(1), the revised 2013 capital gain would be nil, the lesser of:

- $1,100,000 (regular capital gain); and
- Nil (reflecting the fact that there was no excess of the $4,800,000 proceeds of disposition for the old building over the $5,700,000 cost of the replacement building).

Under ITA 13(4), the revised 2013 recapture would be reduced from $1,844,000 to nil. The calculation is as follows:

January 1, 2013 UCC Balance		$1,856,000
Deduction:		
Lesser Of:		
• Proceeds Of Disposition = $4,800,000		
• Capital Cost = $3,700,000	$3,700,000	
Reduced By The Lesser Of:		
• Normal Recapture = $1,844,000		
• Replacement Cost = $5,700,000	(1,844,000)	(1,856,000)
Recapture Of 2013 CCA (Amended)		Nil

The UCC of the replacement building is calculated as follows:

Cost	$5,700,000
Capital Gain Reversed By Election ($1,100,000 - Nil)	(1,100,000)
Deemed Capital Cost	$4,600,000
Recapture Reversed By Election ($1,844,000 - Nil)	(1,844,000)
UCC	$2,756,000

Note that the UCC for the new building is equal to the UCC of the old building ($1,856,000), plus the additional $900,000 ($5,700,000 - $4,800,000) in funds paid by Fraser in excess of the insurance proceeds.

Building Contents   If this was a voluntary disposition, the building contents would not be "former business property" and would not qualify for either the ITA 13(4) election or the ITA 44(1) election. However, as this is an involuntary disposition, both elections are available.

Under ITA 44(1), the revised 2013 capital gain would be $23,000, the lesser of:

- $284,000 (regular capital gain); and
- $23,000 (the excess of the $1,256,000 proceeds of disposition for the old building contents over the $1,233,000 cost of the replacement contents)

The taxable amount of the gain will be $11,500 [(1/2)($23,000)].

Under ITA 13(4), the revised 2013 recapture would be reduced from $900,000 to nil. The calculation is as follows:

January 1, 2013 UCC Balance		$ 72,000
Deduction:		
Lesser Of:		
• Proceeds Of Disposition = $1,256,000		
• Capital Cost = $972,000	$972,000	
Reduced By The Lesser Of:		
• Normal Recapture = $900,000		
• Replacement Cost = $1,233,000	(900,000)	(72,000)
Recapture Of 2013 CCA (Amended)		Nil

The UCC of the replacement contents is calculated as follows:

Cost	$1,233,000
Capital Gain Reversed By Election ($284,000 - $23,000)	(261,000)
Deemed Capital Cost	$ 972,000
Recapture Reversed By Election ($900,000 - Nil)	(900,000)
UCC	$ 72,000

Note that the UCC for the new Class 8 assets is equal to the $72,000 UCC of the old Class 8 assets. Since the $1,233,000 cost of the replacement assets is less than the $1,256,000 in insurance proceeds, there is no increase in the UCC.

Comparison - Part A and Part B

A comparison of the increase in Net Income For Tax Purposes as reported in 2013 with the increase in Net Income For Tax Purposes in the amended return which applies the ITA 13(4) and 44(1) elections is as follows:

	Part A As Reported	Part B With Elections
Land - Taxable Capital Gain	$ 233,500	$111,500
Building - Taxable Capital Gain	550,000	Nil
Contents - Taxable Capital Gain	142,000	11,500
Building - Recaptured CCA	1,844,000	Nil
Contents - Recaptured CCA	900,000	Nil
Total Increase	$3,669,500	$123,000

Part C

As there was a $223,000 capital gain remaining on the land and no gain remaining on the building, a reduction of Net Income For Tax Purposes can be achieved under the ITA 44(6) election. In fact, the excess of replacement cost over the old cost for the building is sufficient that all of the gain can be eliminated on the land without creating a gain on the building. This is accomplished by electing under ITA 44(6) to transfer $223,000 of the land proceeds to the building proceeds. This will completely eliminate the $223,000 capital gain on the land and will increase the capital gain removed by elections on the building by $223,000. In turn, the deemed cost of the building will now be $4,377,000 ($4,600,000 - $223,000) and the UCC will be $2,533,000 ($4,600,000 - $1,844,000 - $223,000). The adjusted cost base of the land will remain at $256,000.

Note that this election is not made without a cost. Had the $223,000 been left as a capital gain, tax would have applied on only one-half of the total. While we have eliminated this $111,500 in income, we have given up future CCA for the full amount of the $223,000. In other words, we have given up $223,000 in future deductions in return for eliminating $111,500 of income in 2013. This makes the use of this election somewhat questionable. Factors that should be considered include whether capital gains are taxed at different rates than business income (corporations) and the anticipated future tax rates and timing of Taxable Income.

Self Study Solution Eight - 17

Business Income

The required calculations here would be as follows:

Net Cash Inflow	$53,000
January 1 Accounts Receivable	(10,000)
January 1 Inventories	(22,000)
January 1 Accounts Payable	14,000
June 30 Accounts Receivable	8,000
June 30 Inventories	18,000
June 30 Accounts Payable	(16,000)
Accrual Based Income	$45,000
Recapture On Sale Of Building ($250,000 - $211,000)	39,000
Terminal Loss On Furniture And Fixtures ($12,900 - $9,800)	(3,100)
Terminal Loss On Car ($25,075 - $18,000)	(7,075)
Net Business Income	$73,825

Since the capital cost of the Furniture and Fixtures and the Car was greater than their proceeds of disposition, the proceeds were used to calculate the terminal losses. There is no deduction for CCA as the assets were sold prior to the end of the year.

Employment Income

The required calculations here would be as follows:

Salary	$56,000
Bonus (Note 1)	Nil
RPP Contributions	(2,500)
Automobile Benefit (Note 2)	4,055
Net Employment Income	$57,555

Note 1 The bonus will not be included in 2013 employment income as it will not be paid until 2014.

Note 2 The automobile benefit would be calculated as follows:

Standby Charge [(2%)($62,000)(6)(4,000 ÷ 10,002)]	$2,975
Operating Cost Benefit - Lesser Of:	
• [(1/2)($2,975)] = $1,488	
• [(4,000)($0.27)] = $1,080	1,080
Total Benefit	$4,055

Property Income

The required calculations here would be as follows:

Eligible Dividends	$ 5,600
Gross Up On Eligible Dividends [(38%)($5,600)]	2,128
Interest On GICs	4,275
Income Trust Income Distribution ($6,800 - $2,600)	4,200
Mutual Fund Distribution [(1,000)($0.50)]	500
Fees To Professional Investment Counsellor	(875)
Total Property Income	$15,828

Net Taxable Capital Gains

The required calculations here would be as follows:

Gain On Building ($308,000 - $250,000)	$ 58,000	
Gain On Land ($125,000 - $50,000)	75,000	
Commissions	(17,320)	
Gain On Sale Of Property		$115,680
Gain On Income Trust Units [$63,000 - ($56,000 - $2,600)]		9,600
Loss On New World Equity Units [$9,000 - ($9,650 + $500)]	(	1,150)
Net Capital Gains		$124,130
Inclusion Rate		1/2
Net Taxable Capital Gains		$ 62,065

Net Income For Tax Purposes

The required calculations here would be as follows:

Net Business Income	$ 73,825
Net Employment Income	57,555
Property Income	15,828
Net Taxable Capital Gains	62,065
Net Income For Tax Purposes	$209,273

Taxable Income

As there are no Taxable Income deductions available, Ms. Barnes' Taxable Income is equal to her Net Income For Tax Purposes.

Federal Tax Payable

The required calculations here would be as follows:

Tax On First $135,054		$28,580
Tax On Next $74,219 ($209,273 - $135,054) At 29 Percent		21,524
Tax Before Credits		**$50,104**
Tax Credits:		
Basic Personal Amount	($11,038)	
Common-Law Partner		
($11,038 - $4,600)	(6,438)	
Child [(2)($2,234)]	(4,468)	
Caregiver Including FCA (Note 3)	(6,530)	
EI	(891)	
CPP	(2,356)	
Canada Employment	(1,117)	
Adoption Expenses (Note 4)	(15,669)	
Public Transit Passes (Note 5)	(3,600)	
Medical Expenses (Note 6)	(13,566)	
Total Credit Base	($65,673)	
Rate	15%	(9,851)
Subtotal		**$40,253**
Charitable Donations Credit		
[(15%)($200) + (29%)($1,600 - $200)]		(436)
Dividend Tax Credit [(6/11)($2,128)]		(1,161)
Federal Tax Payable		**$38,656**

Note 3 Alicia is eligible for both the infirm dependant over 17 and the caregiver tax credits. In these circumstances, ITA 118(4)(d), in effect, requires the use of the caregiver credit. Because Alicia is infirm, and her income is below the threshold for the caregiver credit, Laura can claim the full amount of the caregiver credit, as well as the family caregiver amount.

Note 4 The $11,669 maximum for the adoption expenses credit is applied to each child. Andrew's legal expenses are limited to $11,669, while all of Allison's $4,000 in legal expenses are eligible for the credit. This results in a total of $15,669 ($11,669 + $4,000) that can be claimed.

Note 5 The transit pass credit can be claimed for dependants under 19, and for a spouse or common-law partner. This means that Laura can claim the public transit passes credit for herself, Julia and their children. This would give her a credit base of $3,600 [(2)(12)($100) + (2)(12)($50)]. She cannot claim the pass for her mother. Since Alicia's income is less than the basic personal amount, she would have no Tax Payable to claim them against herself.

Note 6 Medical expenses can only be claimed by the taxpayer who pays them. If Alicia had paid her own medical expenses, she would no Tax Payable to claim them against. Since Laura paid Alicia's medical expenses, Laura can claim them. The medical expense credit base would be calculated as follows:

Medical Expenses Of Laura, Julia, Allison, And Andrew		$11,400
Lesser Of:		
• [(3%)($209,273)] = $6,278		
• 2013 Threshold Amount = $2,152		(2,152)
Subtotal		**$ 9,248**
Alicia's Medical Expenses	$4,600	
Reduced By The Lesser Of:		
• $2,152		
• [(3%)($9,400)] = $282	(282)	4,318
Medical Expense Tax Credit Base		**$13,566**

Note 7 Although Laura paid her mother's tuition fees and her mother is dependent on her, Alicia's education related credits cannot be transferred to her daughter. The transfers can only be made to a spouse, parent or grandparent. Alicia will carry forward any unused education related credits.

Self Study Solution Eight - 18

Employment Income

Lorenzo's commission income of $43,000 is large enough not to limit the deduction of his employment related expenses. The required calculations here would be as follows:

Salary	$136,000
Additions	
Commissions	43,000
One-Half Total Bonus (Amount Paid In 2013)	11,000
Expense Allowance [(12)($2,500)]	30,000
Stock Option Benefit [(500)($108 - $92)]	8,000
Deductions	
RPP Contributions	(4,200)
Professional Association Dues	(1,500)
Automobile Costs	
CCA (Note 1)	(6,120)
Operating Costs [(80%)($6,300)]	(5,040)
Hotel Costs	(9,700)
Airline And Other Transportation	(5,400)
Business Meals And Entertainment [(1/2)($9,300)]	(4,650)
Home Office Expenses (Note 2)	(978)
Net Employment Income	$190,412

Note 1 The 2013 CCA would be based on a UCC calculated as though 100 percent of the available CCA had been taken in 2012. The 100 percent CCA of the Class 10.1 vehicle for 2012 would be $4,500 [(1/2)(30%)($30,000 maximum)]. Using this figure, the deductible 2013 CCA would be $6,120 [(80%)(30%)($30,000 - $4,500)].

Note 2 As Lorenzo has commission income, he can deduct 12 percent of all of the costs except the mortgage interest. This will provide a deduction of $978 [(12%)($1,250 + $1,300 + $5,600)].

Property Income

The required calculations here would be as follows:

Net Rental Income (Note 3)	$ 8,870
Income Trust Distribution [(500)($2.40)]	1,200
Eligible Dividends	4,200
Gross Up On Eligible Dividends [(38%)($4,200)]	1,596
Total Property Income	$15,866

Note 3 As the change in use is from personal to business, the base for calculating CCA would be as follows:

Cost Of Building ($105,000 - $42,000)		$63,000
Fair Market Value At Change In Use		
($350,000 - $100,000)	$250,000	
Cost	(63,000)	
Increase In Value (Bump Up)	$187,000	
Inclusion Factor	1/2	93,500
Cost For UCC And CCA Purposes		$156,500
One-Half Net Additions		(78,250)
CCA Base		$ 78,250
Rate For Class 1		4%
CCA		$ 3,130

Using this CCA figure, net rental income for 2013 would be $8,870 ($12,000 - $3,130).

Net Taxable Capital Gains

The required calculations here would be as follows:

Stock Option Shares [(500)($115 - $108)]		$ 3,500
Sculpture (Note 4)		38,000
Change In Use:		
Cottage - Land ($100,000 - $42,000)	$ 58,000	
Cottage - Building ($250,000 - $63,000)	187,000	245,000
Real Property Income Trust (Note 5)		2,161
Land Sale ($180,000 - $78,000)	$102,000	
Reserve For Land Sale (Note 6)	(71,400)	30,600
Net Capital Gains		$319,261
Inclusion Rate		1/2
Net Taxable Capital Gains		$159,631

Note 4   As the actual adjusted cost base of this personal use property is less than $1,000, its deemed adjusted cost base is $1,000 (the floor). This results in a gain of $38,000 ($39,000 - $1,000).

Note 5   The $1,200 income trust distribution was used to acquired 20.51 additional units ($1,200 ÷ $58.50). Using this figure, the capital gain calculation would be:

Proceeds Of Distribution [(520.51)($60.25)]	$31,361
Adjusted Cost Base [(500)($56) + $1,200)]	(29,200)
Capital Gain	$ 2,161

Note 6   The gain on the land would be $102,000 ($180,000 - $78,000). The maximum reserve would be $71,400, the lesser of:

- $71,400 [($102,000)($126,000 ÷ $180,000)]
- $81,600 [($102,000)(20%)(4 - 0)]

Net And Taxable Income

The required calculations here would be as follows:

Net Employment Income	$190,412
Property Income	15,866
Net Taxable Capital Gains	159,631
Net Income For Tax Purposes	$365,909
Stock Option Deduction [(1/2)($8,000)]	(4,000)
Taxable Income	$361,909

Federal Tax Payable

The required calculations here would be as follows:

Tax On First $135,054		$28,580
Tax On Next $226,855 ($361,909 - $135,054) At 29 Percent		65,788
Tax Before Credits		$94,368
Tax Credits:		
Basic Personal Amount	($11,038)	
Spouse ($11,038 - $6,300)	(4,738)	
Child - Gianni	(2,234)	
Child Including FCA - Anita	(4,274)	
Transfer Of Anita's Disability	(7,697)	
Disability Supplement	(4,490)	
Transfer Of Education Credits (Note 7)	(5,000)	
Fitness Program (Note 8)	(1,500)	
Medical Expenses (Note 9)	(15,473)	
EI	(891)	
CPP	(2,356)	
Canada Employment	(1,117)	
Total Credit Base	($60,809)	
Rate	15%	(9,121)
Subtotal		$85,247
Charitable Donations Credit		
[(15%)($200) + (29%)($2,400 - $200)]		(668)
Dividend Tax Credit [(6/11)($1,596)]		(871)
Federal Tax Payable		$83,708

Note 7   The transfer of Maria's tuition, education and textbook credits would be $5,000, the lesser of:

• $5,000
• [$9,300 + (8)($400) + (8)($65)] = $13,020

Note 8   Mr. Desoto can claim the fitness fees to a maximum of $500 for each child. In addition, he can claim the $500 supplement that is available because his daughter is under 18, qualifies for the disability credit and the fitness fees paid for her are greater than $100. This results in a total of $1,500 [(2)($500) + $500].

Note 9   The base for the medical expense tax credit would be calculated as follows:

Total Medical Expenses	$17,625
Lesser Of:	
• [(3%)($365,909))] = $10,977	
• 2013 Threshold Amount = $2,152	(2,152)
Medical Expense Tax Credit Base	$15,473

Chapter 8 Learning Objectives

After completing Chapter 8, you should be able to:

1. Explain the economic basis for treating capital gains more favourably than other types of income (paragraph [P hereafter] 8-1 through 8-10).

2. Apply the general rules for the determination of gains and losses on the disposition of capital assets (P 8-11 through 8-36).

3. Calculate capital gains and losses on dispositions of identical properties (P 8-37 through 8-38).

4. Determine the tax consequences associated with partial dispositions of capital assets (P 8-39).

5. Calculate capital gains and losses on dispositions of capital assets with warranties attached (P 8-40 through P 8-41).

6. Apply the rules related to capital gains reserves (P 8-42 through 8-61).

7. Determine the tax consequences of a bad debt arising on debts acquired through the sale of capital assets (P 8-62 and 8-63).

8. Apply the special rule for sales of real property (P 8-64 through 8-71).

9. Apply the basic rules related to the reduction of taxation of capital gains arising from the disposition of a principal residence (P 8-72 through 8-81).

10. Describe the approaches available on the disposition of farm property that is also a principal residence (P 8-82 through 8-84).

11. Determine the tax consequences that result from dispositions of personal use property (P 8-85 through 8-89).

12. Determine the tax consequences that result from dispositions of listed personal property (P 8-90 through 8-92).

13. Determine the tax consequences that result from foreign currency transactions (P 8-93 through 8-104).

14. Determine the tax consequences that result from dispositions of options (P 8-105 through 8-110).

15. Determine the amount of capital gain or loss resulting from a change in the use of a capital asset (P 8-111 through 8-119).

16. Describe the principal residence elections that are available when there is a change in use (P 8-120 through 8-128).

17. Describe how an individual deals with the CCA on automobiles where the amount of employment or business usage changes over time. (P 8-129 through 8-131).

18. Explain the basic requirements for deemed dispositions on departures from Canada (P 8-132 through 8-133).

19. Apply the deferral provisions for capital gains arising on the disposition of small business investments (P 8-134 through 8-136).

20. Apply the deferral provisions for capital gains arising on voluntary and involuntary dispositions of property that is subsequently replaced (P 8-137 through 8-149).

21. Apply the deferral provisions for recapture arising on voluntary and involuntary dispositions of property that is subsequently replaced (P 8-150 through 8-165).

22. Explain the role of capital gains and losses in tax planning (P 8-166 through 8-168).

CHAPTER 9

How To Work Through Chapter 9

We recommend the following approach in dealing with the material in this Chapter:

Coverage And Organization Of Chapter 9
❑ Read paragraph 9-1 to 9-10 (in the textbook).

Inclusions - Pension Benefits, Retiring Allowances, And Death Benefits
❑ Read paragraph 9-11 to 9-19.

Inclusions - Deferred Income Plans, Scholarships, Social Assistance Payments
❑ Read paragraph 9-20 to 9-26.

Inclusions - Universal Child Care Benefits
❑ Read paragraph 9-27 to 9-29.

Deductions - CPP Contributions On Self-Employed Earnings
❑ Read paragraph 9-30 to 9-33.

Deductions - Moving Expenses
❑ Read paragraph 9-34 to 9-46.
❑ Do Exercise Nine-1 (in the textbook) and check the solution on page S-177 in this Study Guide.
❑ Do Self Study Problem Nine-1 at the end of the textbook chapter on page 460 to 461 and check the solution in this Study Guide.

Deductions - Child Care Expenses
❑ Read paragraph 9-47 to 9-60.
❑ Do Exercise Nine-2 and check the solution in this Study Guide.
❑ Do Self Study Problems Nine-2 and Nine-3 and check the solutions in this Study Guide.

Deductions - Disability Supports Deduction
❑ Read paragraph 9-61 to 9-68.
❑ Do Exercise Nine-3 and check the solution in this Study Guide.

Related Inclusions/Deductions - Employment Insurance Benefits
❑ Read paragraph 9-69 and 9-70.

Related Inclusions/Deductions - Pension Income Splitting
❑ Read paragraph 9-71 to 9-77.
❑ Do Exercise Nine-4 and check the solution in this Study Guide.
❑ Do Self Study Problems Nine-4 and Nine-5 and check the solutions in this Study Guide.

Related Inclusions/Deductions - Spousal And Child Support

❑ Read paragraph 9-78 to 9-87.
❑ Do Exercise Nine-5 and check the solution in this Study Guide.

Related Inclusions/Deductions - Annuity Payments Received

❑ Read paragraph 9-88 to 9-96.
❑ Do Exercise Nine-6 and check the solution in this Study Guide.

Registered Education Savings Plans (RESPs), CESGs and Registered Disability Savings Plans (RDSPs)

❑ Read paragraph 9-97 to 9-109.
❑ Do Exercise Nine-7 and check the solution in this Study Guide.
❑ Read paragraph 9-110 to 9-135.

Tax Free Savings Accounts (TFSAs)

❑ Read paragraph 9-136 to 9-140.
❑ Do Self Study Problem Nine-6 and check the solution in this Study Guide.

Non-Arm's Length Transfers Of Property - Inadequate Considerations (ITA 69)

❑ Read paragraph 9-141 to 9-155.
❑ Do Exercise Nine-8 and check the solution in this Study Guide.
❑ Read paragraph 9-156 to 9-158.
❑ Do Exercise Nine-9 and check the solution in this Study Guide.
❑ Do Self Study Problem Nine-7 and check the solution in this Study Guide.

Inter Vivos Transfers To A Spouse

❑ Read paragraph 9-159 to 9-166.
❑ Do Exercise Nine-10 and check the solution in this Study Guide.

Non-Arm's Length Transfers Of Depreciable Assets

❑ Read paragraph 9-167 to 9-171.
❑ Do Exercises Nine-11 and Nine-12 and check the solutions in this Study Guide.
❑ Do Self Study Problem Nine-8 and check the solution in this Study Guide.

Inter Vivos Transfer Of Farm Or Fishing Property To A Child

❑ Read paragraph 9-172 to 9-175.
❑ Do Exercise Nine-13 and check the solution in this Study Guide.

Deemed Dispositions - On Death

❑ Read paragraph 9-176 to 9-184.
❑ Do Exercise Nine-14 and check the solution in this Study Guide.
❑ Read paragraph 9-185.
❑ Do Self Study Problem Nine-9 and check the solution in this Study Guide.

Income Attribution

❑ Read paragraph 9-186 to 9-204.
❑ Do Exercises Nine-15 to Nine-17 and check the solutions in this Study Guide.
❑ Read paragraph 9-205 to 9-208.
❑ Do Self Study Problems Nine-10 to Nine-12 and check the solutions in this Study Guide.

Anti-Avoidance Provisions And Tax Planning

❑ Read paragraph 9-209 to 9-211.

To Complete This Chapter

❑ Do Self Study Problems Nine-13 and Nine-14 and check the solutions in this Study Guide.

❑ Review the Key Terms Used In This Chapter on page 459. Consult the Glossary for the meaning of any key terms you do not know.

❑ Review the Glossary Flashcards and complete the Key Terms Self-Test for the Chapter. These features can be found in two places, on your Student CD-ROM under the heading "Key Term Practice" and on the web site.

❑ Review the Learning Objectives of the Chapter found on page S-204 of this Study Guide.

❑ As a final review, we recommend that you view the PowerPoint Slides for Chapter 9 that are on your Student CD-ROM. The PowerPoint Viewer program can be installed from the Student CD-ROM.

Practice Examination

❑ Write the Practice Examination for Chapter 9 that is on your Student CD-ROM. Mark your examination using the Practice Examination Solution that is also on your Student CD-ROM.

Solution to Chapter Nine Exercises

Exercise Nine - 1 Solution

Ms. Chevlak cannot deduct the $1,300 house hunting trip. However, this amount can be reimbursed by her employer without creating a taxable benefit. Given these facts, the employer should reimburse this amount directly. The amount that can be deducted in 2013, and the amount to be carried forward would be calculated as follows:

Payment From Employer	$6,000
House Hunting Trip	(1,300)
Balance	$4,700
Moving Costs	(6,400)
Lease Penalty	(1,200)
Available Deduction	($2,900)
Income At New Location = Maximum Deduction	2,000
Carry Forward	($ 900)

The maximum moving expense deduction is limited to $2,000, the income at the new location. The remaining $900 can be carried forward and deducted against income earned at the new location in a subsequent year.

If a general moving allowance had been paid, all of the $6,000 would have been included in employment income with the same deductions of $7,600 ($6,400 + $1,200). After the $2,000 in income, this would have left $400 in income rather than a future deduction of $900. The $1,300 difference is the cost of the house hunting trip.

Exercise Nine - 2 Solution

The deduction will have to be made by the lower income spouse, Mr. Sampras. The deduction will be the least of the following amounts:

• The actual costs of $10,500.
• Annual Child Care Expense Amount of $15,000 [(1)($7,000) + (2)($4,000)].
• 2/3 of Mr. Sampras' earned income, an amount of $13,000 [(2/3)($14,000 + $5,500)].

The least of these three amounts is $10,500. Note that the universal child care benefit payments are not included in Mr. Sampras' earned income for this purpose.

Solution to Chapter Nine Exercises

Exercise Nine - 3 Solution

As Jose is not eligible for the disability tax credit, he will deduct the cost of full time attendant care under ITA 64. When combined with the other disability support costs and the reimbursement, the qualifying costs total $36,000 ($23,000 + $18,000 - $5,000). As this is less than his income from employment, he will be able to deduct the full amount of these costs as his disability supports deduction.

Exercise Nine - 4 Solution

In the absence of pension income splitting John would not pay any taxes for 2013. Joanna's Net Income For Tax Purposes before any OAS clawback would be $91,550 ($85,000 + $6,550). There would be an OAS clawback of $3,089 [(15%)($91,550 - $70,954), leaving Joanna with a Net and Taxable Income of $88,461 ($91,550 - $3,089). Based on this figure, her 2013 Amount Owing would be calculated as follows:

Tax Of First $87,123		$16,118
Tax On Next $1,338 ($88,461 - $87,123) At 26%		348
Total Before Credits		$16,466
Credits:		
Basic Personal	($11,038)	
Spousal ($11,038 - $6,550)	(4,488)	
Age [$6,854 - (15%)($88,461 - $34,562)	Nil	
Pension	(2,000)	
Spouse's Age	(6,854)	
Total	($24,380)	
Rate	15%	(3,657)
Federal Tax Payable		$12,809
OAS Clawback		3,089
Total Amount Owing		$15,898

If maximum pension splitting is used, it will give both Joanna and John Net and Taxable Income of $49,050 [($85,000 ÷ 2) + $6,550]. Since this is below the income threshold, there will be no clawback of OAS for Joanna or John. Based on these figures, the Amount Owing for both Joanna and John would be the same and calculated as follows:

Tax On First $43,561		$6,534
Tax On Next $6,293 ($49,050 - $43,561) At 22%		1,208
Total Before Credits		$7,742
Credits:		
Basic Personal	($11,038)	
Age [$6,854 - (15%)($49,050 - $34,562)	(4,681)	
Pension	(2,000)	
Total	($17,719)	
Rate	15%	(2,658)
Federal Tax Payable		$ 5,084
OAS Clawback		Nil
Total Amount Owing For Each		$ 5,084

With pension income splitting, the total amount owing by Joanna and John would be $10,168 [(2)($5,084)]. This is an improvement of $5,730 over the $15,898 that Joanna would have paid without income splitting. Further savings would be available at the provincial level.

Exercise Nine - 5 Solution

The total required child support is $9,000 [(6 Months)($1,500)] and Sandra's $12,000 [(3)($1,500 + $2,500)] in payments will be allocated to this requirement first. This means that $9,000 of her payment will not be deductible to her or taxable to Jerry. The remaining $3,000 ($12,000 - $9,000) will be considered a payment towards spousal support and will be deductible to Sandra and taxable to Jerry.

Exercise Nine - 6 Solution

A total of $63,492 [(4)($15,873)] in payments will be received from this annuity. The $15,873 will be included in his annual tax return. However, because the annuity was purchased with after tax funds, he is eligible for a deduction equal to:

$$\left[\frac{\$55,000}{\$63,492}\right][\$15,873] = \$13,750 \text{ Deduction}$$

As a result, Mr. Hollock's Net Income For Tax Purposes will increase by $2,123 ($15,873 - $13,750) each year.

Exercise Nine - 7 Solution

For 2012, the contributions to Jeanine's RESP total $1,700 ($500 + $1,200). This is within the $2,500 limit for contributions eligible for CESGs. This means that the 2012 CESG would be calculated as follows:

First $500 At 40 Percent	$200
Remaining $1,200 ($1,700 - $500) At 20 Percent	240
Total CESG For 2012	$440

For 2013, the contributions to Jeanine's RESP total $3,900 ($1,500 + $2,400). The CESG room is limited to $3,300 [(2)($2,500) - $1,700 from the previous year]. This means that $600 ($3,900 - $3,300) of the total contributions will not be eligible for CESGs. Given this, the 2013 CESG would be calculated as follows:

First $500 At 40 Percent	$200
Remaining $2,800 ($3,300 - $500) At 20 Percent	560
Total CESG For 2013	$760

If it is expected that annual contributions to Jeanine's RESP will be less than $2,500 in the future, this would suggest that Jeanine's father should limit his 2013 contribution to $900 and defer the extra $600 to the following year. In that year, it would be eligible for the CESG.

Exercise Nine - 8 Solution

Mr. Lipky's proceeds of disposition will be the amount received of $95,000, resulting in a capital loss of $5,000 ($95,000 - $100,000). His brother's adjusted cost base will be the fair market value of the land, or $75,000, and he will have no gain or loss on his sale at $75,000. In this case, the application of the ITA 69 rules has resulted in the potential loss of $20,000 ($95,000 - $75,000) not being available to either Carl Lipky or his brother.

Exercise Nine - 9 Solution

Under ITA 69(1.2), the proceeds of disposition in this case will be the greater of the $33,000 actual proceeds and the $211,000 fair market value of the property without considering the lease. The greater amount would be $211,000, resulting in a taxable capital gain for Mr. Bates of $89,000 [(1/2)($211,000 - $33,000)]. The adjusted cost base to the corporation would be the actual transfer price of $33,000. This would lead to double taxation on a subsequent sale of the property on the difference between $211,000 and $33,000.

Exercise Nine - 10 Solution

Part 1   If Mr. Schwartz does not elect out of ITA 73(1), his deemed proceeds of disposition will be equal to the $225,000 adjusted cost base of the land. There will be no tax consequences as a result of this transfer. The adjusted cost base to his spouse will be deemed to be $225,000, despite the fact that she paid $300,000 for the land.

Part 2   In order to elect out of ITA 73(1), Mr. Schwartz must record the gain on the land in his Net Income For Tax Purposes. This amount will be $37,500 [(1/2)($300,000 - $225,000)]. In this case, the adjusted cost base of the land to his spouse will be $300,000.

Exercise Nine - 11 Solution

Part 1   If Ms. Sharp does not elect out of ITA 73(1), the property will be transferred at the UCC of $110,000, without regard to the amount that her husband pays. There will be no tax consequences for Ms. Sharp as a result of this transfer. While the spouse would receive the property with a UCC of $110,000, the capital cost of $175,000 would be retained, with the difference being considered deemed CCA.

Part 2   If she elects out of ITA 73(1), the transfer will be made at $225,000, resulting in a capital gain of $50,000 ($225,000 - $175,000). In addition, she will have recapture of $65,000 ($175,000 - $110,000).

For capital gains purposes, the capital cost for Ms. Sharp's husband would be $225,000. However, for CCA and recapture purposes, ITA 13(7)(e) would deem the capital cost to be $200,000 [($175,000 + (1/2)($225,000 - $175,000)].

Exercise Nine - 12 Solution

As a result of this transaction, Ms. Lee will have recapture of $2,800 ($37,200 - $40,000). As this was a non-arm's length transfer at a value below the transferor's capital cost, ITA 13(7)(e) will deem the father's capital cost to be equal to Ms. Lee's capital cost of $53,000. The $13,000 difference between this value and the $40,000 he paid for the asset is treated as deemed CCA, resulting in a UCC value of $40,000.

This means that when he sells the asset, he will subtract the lesser of the $53,000 deemed capital cost and the $44,000 proceeds of disposition from the UCC of $40,000. This will result in recapture of $4,000 ($40,000 - $44,000).

Exercise Nine - 13 Solution

With respect to the land, the $280,000 paid is between the $250,000 adjusted cost base floor and the $325,000 fair market value ceiling. Therefore, the proceeds of disposition would be $280,000, resulting in a taxable capital gain for Mr. Nobel of $15,000 [(1/2)($280,000 - $250,000)]). The $280,000 would also be the adjusted cost base for his daughter.

With respect to the barn, as there was no consideration given, the transfer would take place at the UCC floor of $85,000. There would be no tax consequences for Mr. Nobel. With respect to his daughter, she would assume a UCC value of $85,000 but would retain the original capital cost of $115,000. The $30,000 difference would be considered deemed CCA.

Exercise Nine - 14 Solution

With respect to truck A, it would be transferred to her husband at its UCC value of $25,500 [(1/2)($51,000)]. No income would be included in Ms. Lardner's final tax return and, while the UCC value for the truck in Michel's hands would be the $25,500 transfer value, it would retain its original capital cost of $42,000 with the difference between the two values being treated as deemed CCA.

Truck B would be transferred to Melinda at its fair market value of $33,000. This means that the proceeds of disposition for the two trucks would be $58,500 ($25,500 + $33,000). This would result in recapture of $7,500 ($51,000 - $58,500) being included in Ms. Lardner's final tax return. The $33,000 transfer price would be the UCC value to Melinda. Since Ms. Lardner's original capital cost exceeds the $33,000 fair market value, Melinda would retain Ms. Lardner's $42,000 capital cost with the difference between the two values being treated as deemed CCA.

Exercise Nine - 15 Solution

ITA 73(1) provides for a tax free rollover of capital property to a spouse. The tax consequences for Mr. and Mrs. Moreau for the two years can be outlined as follows:

- 2012 for Mr. Moreau - none.
- 2012 for Mrs. Moreau - none.
- 2013 for Mr. Moreau - none.
- 2013 for Mrs. Moreau - total income of $12,950. She would have taxable dividends of $3,450 and the taxable capital gain of $9,500 [(1/2)($42,000 - $23,000)] attributed to her.

We suggest that it may be helpful for you to review Exercises Nine-10 and Nine-11 now as many students find the rules related to ITA 73(1) difficult to understand.

Exercise Nine - 16 Solution

There is no provision for a tax free transfer of shares to a child. The tax consequences for Norah and Nicki Moreau for the two years can be outlined as follows:

- 2012 for Nicki - none.
- 2012 for Norah - a taxable capital gain of $7,000 [(1/2)($37,000 - $23,000)].
- 2013 for Nicki - a taxable capital gain of $2,500 [(1/2)($42,000 - $37,000)].
- 2013 for Norah - taxable dividends of $3,450 attributed to her.

Exercise Nine - 17 Solution

Since Mr. Bronski does not elect out of ITA 73(1) by including a gain on his tax return at the time of the transfer, the income attribution rules will apply. Even if he did elect out of ITA 73(1), the rules would still apply as the loan does not bear interest at the prescribed rate.

There will be no tax consequences for either Mr. or Mrs. Bronski in 2012. Because the transfer is a tax free rollover, the adjusted cost base of the bonds to Mrs. Bronski will be $115,000. All of the 2013 interest income of $6,100 will be attributed to Mr. Bronski. In addition to the interest of $6,100, there would be a taxable capital gain of $7,000 [(1/2)($129,000 - $115,000)], which would also be attributed to Mr. Bronski. The total addition to Mr. Bronski's income for 2013 is $13,100 ($6,100 + $7,000). There will be no tax consequences for Mrs. Bronski in 2013.

Self Study Solution Nine - 1

The allowable moving expenses can be calculated as follows:

First Trip Hotel And Food After Acquiring		
New Residence (4 Days At $161)		$ 644
Selling Costs Of Old Residence ($9,500 + $1,400)		10,900
Acquisition Cost Of New Residence ($1,850 + $600)		2,450
Halifax Hotel And Food (3 days At $146)		438
Expenses Of Travel To Regina:		
Gasoline	$350	
Hotel (7 Days At $95)	665	
Food (7 Days At $51)	357	1,372
Moving Company Fees		3,800
Hotel And Food In Regina [(8 Days][$95 + $51)]		1,168
Total Allowable Expenses		$20,772
Employment Income In New Location		(10,500)
Carry Forward		$10,272

Notes:

1. With respect to the first trip, only the cost of meals and lodging that occurred after the acquisition of the new residence would be allowed. The airfare, the cost of car rentals, and the cost of meals and lodging prior to the acquisition of the new residence would not be deductible.

2. The taxes on the old home to the date of sale would not be an allowable moving expense.

3. Food and lodging costs near the old or new residences are limited to 15 days in total. For Ms. Fox, this would include 4 days on her first trip to Regina, the 3 days in Halifax, but only 8 of the 16 days during which she lived in a hotel on arriving in Regina. Note that the 7 days spent travelling to Regina are not included in the 15 day total.

4. The storage costs are deductible.

5. The unused moving cost balance of $10,272 can be carried forward and applied against employment income earned at the new location in a subsequent year.

Self Study Solution Nine - 2

Generally, the spouse with the lower income must claim the deduction for child care expenses. However, under certain circumstances, for example if this spouse is hospitalized, the spouse with the higher income can claim the deduction for the period of hospitalization.

The relevant calculations for determining the deductible costs for each individual are as follows:

	Mr. Pleasant	Mrs. Pleasant
Actual Costs (48 weeks at $100)	$ 4,800	$ 4,800
Annual Expense Limit [($4,000)(2) + ($7,000)(1)]	$15,000	$15,000
2/3 Of Earned Income For Child Care Expenses [(2/3)($99,000)] [(2/3)($18,000)]	$66,000	$12,000
Periodic Expense Limit [($100)(2)(6 weeks) + ($175)(1)(6 weeks)]	$ 2,250	N/A

There does not appear to be any requirement that actual child care costs claimed by the higher income spouse need to be limited to the specific amounts paid during the six week period of eligibility. This means that the lowest of the preceding figures for Mr. Pleasant would be the Periodic Expense Limit of $2,250. Note that Mr. Pleasant's earned income for child care cost purposes is his gross employment income, before the deduction of employment related expenses.

The lowest figure for Mrs. Pleasant is the actual costs of $4,800. This amount will be reduced by the $2,250 that was deducted by Mr. Pleasant. This results in a $2,550 ($4,800 - $2,250) deduction for Mrs. Pleasant.

Note that the universal child care benefit payments are not included in Mrs. Pleasant's earned income for this purpose.

Self Study Solution Nine - 3

The deductible actual costs are as follows:

Actual Costs Excluding Camp Costs (48 weeks At $260)	$12,480
Periodic Cost Limit For Camp Weeks [($100)(1)(4 weeks) + ($175)(1)(4 weeks) + ($250)(1)(4 weeks)]	2,100
Deductible Actual Costs	**$14,580**

Generally, the spouse with the lower income must claim the deduction for child care expenses. In this case, that would be Sue Brendal. However, under certain circumstances, the spouse with the higher income can claim a deduction that is subject to a weekly limitation.

One of these circumstances is when the lower income spouse is in attendance on a full time basis at a designated financial institution. This means that for the 5 week period that Sue is attending the accounting course, Maureen can deduct limited child care expenses.

The relevant calculations for determining the deductible costs for each individual are as follows:

	Maureen	**Sue**
Actual Costs And Limited Camp Costs	$14,580	$14,580
Annual Expense Limit [($4,000)(1) + ($7,000)(1) + ($10,000)(1)]	$21,000	$21,000
2/3 Of Earned Income [(2/3)($216,000)]	$144,000	
[(2/3)($24,000)]		$16,000
Periodic Expense Limit [($100)(1)(5 weeks) + ($175)(1)(5 weeks) + ($250)(1)(5 weeks)]	$ 2,625	N/A

The least of these amounts for Maureen is $2,625. You should note that there is no requirement that actual payments be allocated on the basis of the time that Sue was attending the accounting course.

The lowest figure for Sue is $14,580, the actual child care costs. Sue' deduction for the current year of $11,955 ($14,580 - $2,625) has been reduced by the amount claimed by Maureen.

Since Lori is 4 years old, it can be assumed that the support agreement was made after 1997 and the child support received is not taxable.

As Maureen is the higher income spouse, her 3 week stay in the hospital has no effect on the child care expense calculations.

Self Study Solution Nine - 4

Net And Taxable Income

John's Income	**No Split**	**With Split**
Pension Receipt	$ 64,000	$64,000
Net Rental Income	23,000	23,000
Pension Income To Fatima	N/A	(32,000)
Net And Taxable Income	**$87,000**	**$55,000**

Fatima's Income	**No Split**	**With Split**
Interest Income	$8,400	$ 8,400
Pension Income From John	N/A	32,000
Net And Taxable Income	**$8,400**	**$40,400**

Federal Tax Payable With No Pension Income Splitting

Without pension income splitting, John's Tax Payable would be calculated as follows:

Tax Of First $43,561		$6,534
Tax On Next $43,439 ($87,000 - $43,561) At 22%		9,557
Total Before Credits		$16,091
Credits:		
Basic Personal	($11,038)	
Spousal ($11,038 - $8,400)	(2,638)	
Pension	(2,000)	
Total	($15,676)	
Rate	15%	(2,351)
Federal Tax Payable - John		$13,740

Fatima's Tax Payable would be calculated as follows:

Tax Before Credits [(15%)($8,400)]	$ 1,260
Basic Personal Credit	(11,038)
Federal Tax Payable - Fatima	Nil

Federal Tax Payable With Pension Income Splitting

With pension income splitting, John's Tax Payable would be calculated as follows:

Tax On First $43,561		$6,534
Tax On Next $11,439 ($55,000 - $43,561) At 22%		2,517
Tax Before Credits		$9,051
Credits:		
Basic Personal	($11,038)	
Spousal	Nil	
Pension	(2,000)	
Total	($13,038)	
Rate	15%	(1,956)
Federal Tax Payable - John		$7,095

When maximum pension income splitting is used, Fatima's Tax Payable would be as follows:

Tax Before Credits [(15%)($40,400)]		$6,060
Credits:		
Basic Personal	($11,038)	
Pension	(2,000)	
Total	($13,038)	
Rate	15%	(1,956)
Federal Tax Payable - Fatima		$ 4,104

Comparison

Federal Tax Payable Without Income Splitting (John Only)	$13,740
Federal Tax Payable With Income Splitting ($7,095 + $4,104)	(11,199)
Savings With Pension Income Splitting	$ 2,541

Self Study Solution Nine - 5

Jean's Income	No Split	With Split
Pension Receipt	$168,000	$168,000
OAS	6,550	6,550
Pension Income To Carole	N/A	(84,000)
Net Income Before OAS Clawback	$174,550	$90,550
OAS Clawback (Note 1 and 2)	(6,550)	(2,939)
Net And Taxable Income	$168,000	$87,611

Carole's Income	No Split	With Split
Monthly Annuity [(12)($3,500)]	$42,000	$ 42,000
OAS	6,550	6,550
Pension Income From Jean	N/A	84,000
Net Income Before OAS Clawback	$48,550	$132,550
OAS Clawback (Note 3 and 4)	Nil	(6,550)
Net And Taxable Income	$48,550	$126,000

Note 1 Without pension income splitting, at Jean's income level, all of the $6,550 in OAS payments would be clawed back [(15%)($174,550 - $70,954) = $15,539].

Note 2 With pension income splitting, the OAS clawback would be $2,939 [(15%)($90,550 - $70,954)].

Note 3 Without pension income splitting, at Carole's income level, there would be no OAS clawback.

Note 4 With pension income splitting, all of the OAS received by Carole would be clawed back [(15%)($132,550 - $70,954) = $9,239].

Part A - Amount Owing With No Pension Income Splitting

Without pension income splitting, Jean's Amount Owing would be calculated as follows:

Tax Of First $135,054		$28,580
Tax On Next $32,946 ($168,000 - $135,054) At 29%		9,554
Total Before Credits		$38,134
Credits:		
Basic Personal	($11,038)	
Age [$6,854 - (15%)($168,000 - $34,562)]	Nil	
Pension	(2,000)	
Total	($13,038)	
Rate	15%	(1,956)
Federal Tax Payable		$36,178
OAS Clawback		6,550
Total Amount Owing - Jean		$42,728

Without pension income splitting, Carole's Amount Owing would be calculated as follows:

Tax On First $43,561		$6,534
Tax On Next $4,989 ($48,550 - $43,561 At 22 Percent		1,098
Total Before Credits		$7,632
Credits:		
Basic Personal	($11,038)	
Age [$6,854 - (15%)($48,550 - $34,562)	(4,756)	
Disability	(7,697)	
Total	($23,491)	
Rate	15%	(3,524)
Total Amount Owing (No Clawback) - Carole		$4,108

Part B - Amount Owing With Pension Income Splitting

With pension income splitting, Jean's Amount Owing would be calculated as follows:

Tax On First $87,123		$16,118
Tax On Next $488 ($87,611 - $87,123) At 26%		127
Tax Before Credits		$16,245
Credits:		
Basic Personal	$11,038)	
Age [$6,854 - (15%)($87,611 - $34,562)]	Nil	
Pension	(2,000)	
Total	($13,038)	
Rate	15%	(1,956)
Federal Tax Payable		$14,289
OAS Clawback		2,939
Total Amount Owing - Jean		$17,228

With pension income splitting, Carole's Amount Owing would be calculated as follows:

Tax On First $87,123		$16,118
Tax On Next $38,877 ($126,000 - $87,123) At 26%		10,108
Tax Before Credits		$26,226
Credits:		
Basic Personal	($11,038)	
Age [$6,854 - (15%)($126,000 - $34,562)]	Nil	
Disability	(7,697)	
Pension	(2,000)	
Total	($20,735)	
Rate	15%	(3,110)
Federal Tax Payable		$23,116
OAS Clawback		6,550
Total Amount Owing - Carole		$29,666

Comparison

The total amount owing for Jean and Carole in the absence of pension income splitting and with maximum pension income splitting would be calculated as follows:

	No Split	50:50 Split
Jean	$42,728	$17,228
Carole	4,108	29,666
Total Amount Owing	$46,836	$46,894

Maximum pension income splitting results in an amount owing that is $58 ($46,894 - $46,836) higher. While the splitting removed all of Jean's income from the 29 percent bracket, the 50:50 split resulted in Carole having all of her OAS payments clawed back and losing all of her age credit.

It is likely that, if pension income splitting was limited to an amount that would leave Carole's OAS payments clawback free, an improved result could be achieved with this planning technique.

Self Study Solution Nine - 6

The minimum Net Income For Tax Purposes for the Madison brothers would be calculated as follows:

	Arthur	Jules	Stanley
Net Employment Income	$ 6,000	$18,000	$73,000
Net Business Income (No Losses)	Nil	5,000	Nil
Net Property Income (No Losses)	8,000	Nil	11,000
Employment Insurance Received	3,000	Nil	Nil
Pension Benefits Received	Nil	3,000	Nil
Income Under ITA 3(a)	$17,000	$26,000	$84,000
Net Taxable Capital Gains - ITA 3(b)	2,813	Nil	Nil
Total Under ITA 3(a) And 3(b)	$19,813	$26,000	$84,000
Spousal Support Payments - ITA 3(c)	Nil	Nil	(4,800)
Total Under ITA 3(a), 3(b), 3(c)	$19,813	$26,000	$79,200
Business And Property Loss - ITA 3(d)	Nil	(4,000)	(12,000)
Net Income For Tax Purposes	$19,813	$22,000	$67,200

One-half of Arthur's capital gain is included in income. Jules Madison has a net capital loss carry over of $1,500 [(1/2)($17,000 - $14,000)]. Stanley Madison has a net capital loss carry over of $5,000 [(1/2)($10,000)]. While this is not a required part of the problem, these losses can be carried back three years and carried forward indefinitely.

The scholarship is exempt from income. While the charitable donations and tuition fees will generate credits against Tax Payable, they are not deductible in the computation of Net Income For Tax Purposes.

The contributions made by Arthur and Stanley to their TFSA are not deductible. The withdrawal from Stanley's TFSA is not taxable.

Self Study Solution Nine - 7

A. Sale For $75 Per Share
In this Case, the shares were transferred at a price that was below fair market value. However, John Bolton will have deemed proceeds under ITA 69(1)(b) equal to the fair market value of $525,000 [(5,000)($105)]. The result for John would be as follows:

Deemed Proceeds Of Disposition - ITA 69(1)(b)	$525,000
Adjusted Cost Base [(5,000)($45)]	(225,000)
Capital Gain	$300,000
Inclusion Rate	1/2
Taxable Capital Gain	$150,000

From the point of view of Alex Bolton, his cost base for the shares will be limited to the actual price paid of $375,000 [(5,000)($75)]. This means that, when Alex Bolton sells these shares, the difference between his proceeds of disposition per share of $105 and the price per share he paid of $75 would be taxed in his hands. In effect, any gain arising from a sales price of up to $105 will be subject to double taxation.

With respect to the subsequent sale by Alex, the results for him would be as follows:

Proceeds Of Disposition (Actual)	$525,000
Adjusted Cost Base (Actual)	(375,000)
Capital Gain	$150,000
Inclusion Rate	1/2
Taxable Capital Gain	$ 75,000

B. Sale For $125 Per Share

In this situation, the gain to be recorded by John Bolton would be based on $625,000 [(5,000)($125)], the actual amount received. The result for John would be as follows:

Proceeds Of Disposition (Actual)	$625,000
Adjusted Cost Base	(225,000)
Capital Gain	$400,000
Inclusion Rate	1/2
Taxable Capital Gain	$200,000

From the point of view of Alex Bolton, ITA 69(1)(a) would limit his adjusted cost base to $525,000, the fair market value of the shares at the time of purchase, despite the fact that John had to record the actual proceeds of $625,000. With respect to the subsequent sale by Alex, the results for him would be as follows:

Proceeds Of Disposition (Actual)	$525,000
Adjusted Cost Base - ITA 69(1)(a)	(525,000)
Capital Gain	Nil

C. Sale For $105 Per Share

In this Case, both the proceeds to John Bolton and the adjusted cost base to Alex Bolton will be equal to the amount paid for the shares as it is the fair market value. No double taxation will arise. The result for John would be the same as for Case A as follows:

Proceeds Of Disposition (Actual)	$525,000
Adjusted Cost Base [(5,000)($45)]	(225,000)
Capital Gain	$300,000
Inclusion Rate	1/2
Taxable Capital Gain	$150,000

With respect to the subsequent sale by Alex, the results for him would be as follows:

Proceeds Of Disposition (Actual)	$525,000
Adjusted Cost Base (Actual)	(525,000)
Capital Gain	Nil

D. Gift

In this Case, John Bolton will be deemed to have received proceeds equal to the fair market value of $525,000 and the adjusted cost base to Alex Bolton will also be equal to the fair market value. No double taxation will arise. The results will be the same as in Case C.

The result for John would be as follows:

Deemed Proceeds Of Disposition - ITA 69(1)(b)	$525,000
Adjusted Cost Base [(5,000)($45)]	(225,000)
Capital Gain	$300,000
Inclusion Rate	1/2
Taxable Capital Gain	$150,000

With respect to the subsequent sale by Alex, the results for him would be as follows:

Proceeds Of Disposition (Actual)	$525,000
Adjusted Cost Base - ITA 69(1)(c)	(525,000)
Capital Gain	Nil

Summary

These results can be summarized as follows:

	Taxable Capital Gain		
	John	Alex	Total
A. Sale For $75 (ACB = $375,000)	$150,000	$75,000	$225,000
B. Sale For $125 (ACB = $525,000)	200,000	Nil	200,000
C. Sale For $105 (ACB = $525,000)	150,000	Nil	150,000
D. Gift (ACB = $525,000)	150,000	Nil	150,000

Self Study Solution Nine - 8

Case One - FMV > Transferor's Capital Cost

As a result of this disposition, Jason will have a taxable capital gain of $34,000 [(1/2)($255,000 - $187,000)]. In addition, there will be recapture of $42,000 ($187,000 - $145,000). Jason's Net Income For Tax Purposes will increase by $76,000 ($34,000 + $42,000).

For capital gains purposes, the capital cost for his brother will be the transfer price of $255,000. However, because the fair market value of the asset was greater than its capital cost at the time of transfer, ITA 13(7)(e) will limit the capital cost for CCA and recapture purposes to the following amount:

$$[\$187,000 + (1/2)(\$255,000 - \$187,000)] = \$221,000$$

Case Two - FMV < Transferor's Capital Cost

As a result of this disposition, Christine will have recapture of $80,000 ($320,000 - $240,000) and her Net Income For Tax Purposes will increase by this amount. As the capital cost of the asset was greater than the proceeds of disposition, there will not be a capital gain on the transfer.

In this Case, where the fair market value of the asset is less than its capital cost, ITA 13(7)(e) deems the transferee's capital cost of the transferred asset to be equal to the transferor's capital cost, an amount of $520,000. This capital cost will be used for purposes of determining any capital gain and/or recapture on a future disposition.

The $200,000 ($520,000 - $320,000) difference between this value and the transfer price will be considered deemed CCA. The resulting UCC balance of $320,000 ($520,000 deemed capital cost - $200,000 deemed CCA) will be used by Christine's sister for calculating future CCA.

Self Study Solution Nine - 9

Case A - Transfer To Spouse At Death

Whenever a taxpayer dies, there is a deemed disposition of all of his property. If the transfer is to a spouse, the disposition is deemed to have taken place at the adjusted cost base of capital property other than depreciable property, or at the UCC of depreciable property. This would mean that there would be no immediate tax consequences associated with Mr. Caswell's death in this Case, where all of the property is transferred to his spouse.

With respect to the tax base of the various assets in the hands of his spouse, they would be unchanged by the transfer.

It is possible, after Mr. Caswell's death, for his legal representative to elect to have assets transferred to his spouse at fair market values. This would result in taxable capital gains and other income being included in his final tax return. Although the fair market value elections are available, the problem states that none were made.

Case B - Transfer To Son At Death

This Case is more complex and would follow the general rules applicable to transfers made at death to anyone other than a spouse. For both depreciable and non-depreciable property, other than farm property, the transfer will be deemed to have taken place at fair market value.

Farm Land

In the case of farm land that is being used by the taxpayer or a member of his family, ITA 70(9.01) permits a tax free transfer of such property to a child, at the time of death. The deemed proceeds would be Mr. Caswell's adjusted cost base, resulting in no tax consequences for his estate. As you would expect, the adjusted cost base to Mr. Caswell's son, John, would be the same $325,000 that was deemed to be the proceeds of the disposition on Mr. Caswell's death.

Rental Property

In the case of the rental property, the deemed proceeds would be $158,000, resulting in Taxable Income of $47,000 for Mr. Caswell's estate. This would be calculated as follows:

	Land	Building
Deemed Proceeds Of Disposition	$25,000	$133,000
Adjusted Cost Base/Capital Cost	(25,000)	(95,000)
Capital Gain	Nil	$ 38,000
Inclusion Rate	N/A	1/2
Taxable Capital Gain	Nil	$ 19,000
UCC		$ 67,000
Deduct Disposition - Lesser Of:		
• Capital Cost ($120,000 - $25,000) = $95,000		
• Deemed Proceeds ($158,000 - $25,000) = $133,000		(95,000)
Negative Closing UCC Balance = Recaptured CCA		($ 28,000)

The capital cost and UCC of the building for his son, John, is the fair market value of $133,000. The adjusted cost base of the land is unchanged at $25,000.

Shares

In the case of the General Industries shares and the shares of a Canadian controlled private corporation, the deemed proceeds would be the fair market value and this would also be John's adjusted cost base. The tax consequences to Mr. Caswell's estate would be as follows:

	General Industries	Caswell Enterprises
Deemed Proceeds	$350,000	$426,000
Adjusted Cost Base	(200,000)	(275,000)
Capital Gain	$150,000	$151,000
Inclusion Rate	1/2	1/2
Taxable Capital Gain	$ 75,000	$ 75,500

The adjusted cost base of the shares to Mr. Caswell's son would be their fair market value at the time of transfer.

Total Increase In Income - Case B
This gives a total increase in Net Income on Mr. Caswell's final return of $197,500 ($19,000 + $28,000 + $75,000 + $75,500).

Case C - Departure From Canada
With respect to the departure from Canada, ITA 128.1(4)(b) requires a deemed disposition of all property except real property, property used in a Canadian business, and excluded personal property [i.e., a variety of items specified under ITA 128.1(9)]. As both the farm land and rental property are exempt real property, the only deemed dispositions would be the shares of General Industries Ltd. and Caswell Enterprises. The relevant taxable capital gains on these shares were calculated for Case B.

Total Increase In Income - Case C
This gives a total increase in Mr. Caswell's Net Income of $150,500 ($75,000 + $75,500).

Self Study Solution Nine - 10

The general income attribution rules in ITA 74.1 apply to spouses, common-law partners, and non-arm's length individuals who are under 18 years of age. This means that the income on the bonds acquired by Mr. Langdon's wife and his 15 year child Pat would be attributed to him. The total amount would be $10,500 ($5,000 + $5,500).

A different income attribution rule, ITA 56(4.1) applies to loans made to any related party, if the loan is made for the purpose of producing property income. As the loan to Heather was not used to produce income, this attribution rule would not apply.

Self Study Solution Nine - 11

Note
As the farm would be considered qualified farm property, any capital gains arising from a disposition could be eligible for the lifetime capital gains deduction. If Long Consulting Ltd. is a qualified small business corporation, capital gains on the disposition of these shares could also be eligible for the lifetime capital gains deduction. As this deduction is not discussed until Chapter 11, the problem specifies that these possibilities should be ignored.

Long Consulting Ltd.
1. Gift To Spouse - ITA 73(1) Applies
ITA 73(1) permits transfers of a capital property to a spouse at its tax value (adjusted cost base or UCC). This means that the shares in Long Consulting Ltd. could be gifted to Mr. Long with no immediate tax consequences.

The tax basis for these shares for the spouse would remain at the adjusted cost base of $210,000.

Any dividends paid on the shares would be attributed to Mrs. Long.

If Mr. Long subsequently sell these shares for $525,000 ($50,000 more than the $475,000 fair market value at the time of the gift), the resulting taxable capital gain of $157,500, as calculated in the following table, would also be attributed to Mrs. Long.

Proceeds (Fair Market Value)	$525,000
Adjusted Cost Base	(210,000)
Capital Gain	$315,000
Inclusion Rate	1/2
Taxable Capital Gain	$157,500

2. Gift To Spouse - Elect Out Of ITA 73(1)
As an alternative, Mrs. Long could elect out of the provisions of ITA 73(1). Under ITA 69, the gift would be recorded as a disposition at the $475,000 fair market value. Mrs. Long would have an immediate taxable capital gain of $132,500 [(1/2)($475,000 - $210,000)] and Mr. Long's adjusted cost base would be $475,000. However, since the transfer is a gift, and Mr. Long does not use his own funds to purchase the shares, income attribution would apply to any dividends received by Mr. Long. In addition, if the property was subsequently sold by Mr. Long for $525,000, the resulting taxable capital gain of $25,000 [(1/2)(525,000 - $475,000)] would be attributed back to Mrs. Long.

3 And 4. Gift To Children
Under ITA 69, a gift to a related party is deemed to be a transfer at fair market value. Given this, a taxable capital gain of $132,500 [(1/2)($475,000 - $210,000) would result from a transfer to either child.

The adjusted cost base to the children would be the fair market value of $475,000.

Under the general income attribution rules, the dividend income paid on the shares given to Mary, who is under 18, would be attributed back to Mrs. Long. The problem specifies that the tax on split income should be ignored. However, as is discussed in Chapter 11, this dividend income would be subject to the tax on split income and, because of this, it would be exempt from the general income attribution rules.

As Barry is over 18, the gift would not result in attribution of dividends. We would also note that it would not be subject to the tax on split income.

There is no attribution of capital gains on assets transferred to children, without regard to their age. This means that, if the property was later sold for $525,000, the resulting taxable capital gain of $25,000 would be taxed in the hands of the child who received the gift.

Rental Property
1. Gift To Spouse - ITA 73(1) Applies
Here again, ITA 73(1) would permit a transfer to Mr. Long at tax values with no immediate tax consequences.

The tax cost of the building to Mr. Long would be the UCC of $125,000. However, Mr. Long would retain the capital cost of $190,000. With respect to the land, its adjusted cost base would be $100,000. This was Mrs. Long's tax cost and the current fair market value of the land.

As the transfer is a gift, income attribution rules would apply. This means that any net rental income would be attributed to Mrs. Long. If Mr. Long were to later sell the building for $325,000 ($50,000 more than its fair market value at the time of the gift), the following amounts would be attributed to Mrs. Long:

Capital Cost	$190,000
UCC	(125,000)
Recaptured CCA	$ 65,000

Proceeds Of Disposition	$325,000
Adjusted Cost Base	(190,000)
Capital Gain	$135,000
Inclusion Rate	1/2
Taxable Capital Gain	$ 67,500

Since we are assuming the value of the land on which the building was situated has not changed, the sale of the land by Mr. Long would have no tax consequences for Mrs. Long.

2. Gift To Spouse - Elect Out Of ITA 73(1)

Mrs. Long could also elect out of the provisions of ITA 73(1) and transfer the rental property at its fair market value. However, if she does, she would immediately be taxed on the recapture of $65,000, as well as the taxable capital gain of $42,500 [(1/2)($275,000 - $190,000)]. There would be no tax consequences related to the land as its tax cost is equal to its fair market value.

In this case, the cost of the building to Mr. Long for capital gains purposes would be $275,000. For CCA and recapture purposes, the value would be limited to $232,500 [$190,000 + (1/2)($275,000 - $190,000)]. His cost for the land would be $100,000.

Electing out of ITA 73(1) would not change the fact that the transfer is a gift to a spouse and, as a consequence, future rental income would be attributed to Mrs. Long.

If Mr. Long subsequently sells the building for $325,000, the additional taxable capital gain of $25,000 [(1/2)($325,000 - $275,000)] would also be attributed back to Mrs. Long. As we are assuming the value of the land remains at $100,000, there are no tax consequences associated with its sale.

3 And 4. Gift To Children

There is no exemption from the general rules of ITA 69 for transfers of depreciable property to children. As a consequence, Mrs. Long would be subject to taxation based on a disposition of the property at its fair market value of $275,000. This would result in immediate taxation on a $42,500 [(1/2)($275,000 - $190,000)] taxable capital gain, as well as on recapture of $65,000 ($190,000 - $125,000). There would be no tax consequences related to the land as its tax cost is equal to its fair market value.

The cost of the building to either of the children for capital gains purposes would be $275,000. The cost for the land would be $100,000. For CCA and recapture purposes, the value would be limited to $232,500 [$190,000 + (1/2)($275,000 - $190,000)].

If this property was given to Mary, the income attribution rules of ITA 74.1 would apply to any amount of property income subsequently earned. This would mean that until Mary reached 18 years of age, any property income from the rental property would be attributed to Mrs. Long. Alternatively, if the property was gifted to her son, Barry, all subsequent income would be taxed in his hands.

There is no attribution of capital gains on gifts to related children under 18. There would be no attribution of capital gains on a gift to either child. This means that if the property were later sold for $325,000 ($275,000 + $50,000), the $25,000 taxable capital gain would be taxed in the hands of the child who received the gift.

Dynamics Inc.

1. Gift To Spouse - ITA 73(1) Applies

As with the other properties, these shares could be given to Mr. Long and, under the provisions of ITA 73(1), no immediate tax consequences would arise.

The tax basis for Mr. Long would be unchanged at $212,000. Any dividend income on the shares would be attributed to Mrs. Long.

If Mr. Long were to subsequently sell the shares for $434,000 ($50,000 more that their $384,000 fair market value at the time of the gift), the income attribution rules of ITA 74.1 would require that the following taxable capital gain be attributed to the income of Mrs. Long:

Proceeds Of Disposition	$434,000
Adjusted Cost Base	(212,000)
Capital Gain	$222,000
Inclusion Rate	1/2
Taxable Capital Gain	$111,000

2. Gift To Spouse - Elect Out Of ITA 73(1)

Mrs. Long could elect out of ITA 73(1) by recording the $86,000 [(1/2)($384,000 - $212,000)] taxable capital gain at the time of the transfer to her spouse.

In this case the adjusted cost base to Mr. Long would be $384,000.

However, as long as the property was transferred as a gift, attribution would apply to both dividend income received by Mr. Long and to any further capital gains realized on a subsequent sale. If the property was subsequently sold for $434,000, Mr. Long would have a taxable capital gain of $25,000 [(1/2)($434,000 - $384,000)] that would be attributed back to Mrs. Long.

3 And 4. Gift To Children

In the case of a transfer to either of her children, ITA 69 would require that the gift be treated as a deemed disposition with the proceeds at the fair market value of $384,000. This would result in an immediate taxable capital gain of $86,000 [(1/2)($384,000 - $212,000)]

The tax base to the children would be the fair market value of $384,000.

A transfer to Mary would result in the application of the income attribution rules of ITA 74.1. This would mean that subsequent dividend income on these shares would be allocated to Mrs. Long until Mary reaches 18 years of age. If the shares were transferred to Barry, there would be no attribution of dividends. While we are ignoring this possibility, note that dividends on the shares of public companies are not subject to the tax on split income.

There is no attribution of capital gains on assets transferred to children, without regard to their age. This means that, if the property was later sold for $434,000, the resulting taxable capital gain of $25,000 [(1/2)($434,000 - $384,000)] would be taxed in the hands of the child who received the gift.

Farm Land

1. Gift To Spouse - ITA 73(1) Applies

As with all of the other properties, Mrs. Long could make a tax free transfer of the farm land to her husband under ITA 73(1).

The adjusted cost base to Mr. Long would remain unchanged at $80,000.

As farm income is considered to be business income rather than property income, there would be no attribution of any farm income that arises while Mr. Long is holding the property.

In the event of a subsequent sale of the farm land for $225,000 ($50,000 more than the fair market value at the time of transfer), the following taxable capital gain would be attributed to Mrs. Long under ITA 74.1:

Proceeds Of Disposition	$225,000
Adjusted Cost Base	(80,000)
Capital Gain	$145,000
Inclusion Rate	1/2
Taxable Capital Gain	$ 72,500

2. Gift To Spouse - Elect Out Of ITA 73(1)

Alternatively, Mrs. Long could elect out of ITA 73(1) and transfer the property at its fair market value of $175,000. This would result in an immediate taxable capital gain of $47,500 [(1/2)($175,000 - $80,000)].

In this case the adjusted cost base to Mr. Long would be $175,000.

A noted, farm income is business income and this would not be attributed to Mrs. Long

As the transfer was a gift, the income attribution rules would apply to subsequent capital gains on the property. If Mr. Long sells the property for $225,000, the resulting $25,000 [(1/2)($225,000 - $175,000)] taxable capital gain would be attributed back to Mrs. Long.

3 And 4. Gift To Children

ITA 73(3) permits the inter vivos transfer of farm property used by the taxpayer or her family to a child on a tax free basis. The deemed proceeds would be Mrs. Long's adjusted cost base, which means that Mrs. Long would incur no taxation at the time of the gift to either child.

The adjusted cost base to either child would be the same $80,000 that was deemed to be the proceeds of the disposition.

As noted in our discussion of the transfer of this property to Mr. Long, because farm income is business income rather than property income, there will be no attribution of farm income in the case of a transfer to either child.

On most transfers to related minors, there is no attribution of capital gains. This is a reflection of the fact that, unlike the rules for transfers to a spouse, there is no general rollover provision for transfers to related minors on a tax free basis. However, when a transfer is made to a related minor under the provisions of ITA 73(3) and the transfer value is below fair market value, ITA 75.1 requires that any subsequent gain resulting from a disposition by the transferee before they reach age 18 be attributed back to the transferor.

This means that, if the farm property is transferred to Mary and she sells the property for $225,000 before she reaches age 18, a taxable capital gain of $72,500 [(1/2)($225,000 - $80,000)] will be attributed to Mrs. Long. If the transfer was to Barry, this capital gain would not be attributed to Mrs. Long and would be taxed in his hands.

Self Study Solution Nine - 12

Summary

The results can be summarized as follows:

	Net Income For Tax Purposes		
	2012	2013	2014
Case A			
Dr. Bolt	Nil	$25,530	$37,500
Mr. Bolt	Nil	Nil	Nil

	Net Income For Tax Purposes		
	2012	2013	2014
Case B			
Dr. Bolt	Nil	$25,530	$37,500
Mr. Bolt	Nil	Nil	Nil
Case C			
Dr. Bolt	$20,000	Nil	Nil
Mr. Bolt	Nil	$25,530	$17,500
Case D			
Dr. Bolt	Nil	$25,530	$37,500
Mr. Bolt	Nil	Nil	Nil
Case E			
Dr. Bolt	$20,000	$25,530	$60,000
Mr. Bolt	Nil	Nil	Nil
Case F			
Dr. Bolt	$20,000	$25,530	Nil
Dolly Bolt	Nil	Nil	$17,500
Case G			
Dr. Bolt	$20,000	Nil	Nil
Dolly Bolt	Nil	$25,530	$17,500
Case H			
Dr. Bolt	$20,000	$25,530	Nil
Dirk Bolt	Nil	Nil	$17,500

In all Cases where the dividends are attributed back to Dr. Bolt, Dr. Bolt would claim the related dividend tax credit. The federal amount would be $3,835 [(6/11)(38%)($18,500)]. However, as the required refers to Net Income For Tax Purposes, no mention of this credit is required in the solution. The details of each Case are as follows:

Case A

With ITA 73(1) in effect, the December 31, 2012 transfer would be a deemed disposition at the adjusted cost base of $185,000. This means that Dr. Bolt would not record a capital gain at the time of the transfer and the adjusted cost base of the securities to Mr. Bolt would be $185,000. In 2013, the $25,530 in taxable dividends would be attributed back to Dr. Bolt and included in her Net Income For Tax Purposes for that year.

When Mr. Bolt sells the securities, the 2014 taxable capital gain of $37,500 [(1/2)($260,000 - $185,000)] would also be attributed back to Dr. Bolt.

None of these transactions would affect Mr. Bolt's Net Income For Tax Purposes in any of the three years under consideration.

Case B

With ITA 73(1) in effect, the December 31, 2012 transfer would still take place at the adjusted cost base of $185,000, and the resulting 2012, 2013, and 2014 results for both Dr. Bolt and Mr. Bolt would be identical to Case A.

Case C

With the decision to elect out of ITA 73(1) and payment of consideration equal to fair market value, the transfer will be recorded as a disposition at fair market value. This will result in a 2012 taxable capital gain for Dr. Bolt of $20,000 [(1/2)($225,000 - $185,000)] and an adjusted cost base to Mr. Bolt of $225,000. Given that the transfer was at fair market value and Dr. Bolt chose to elect out of ITA 73(1), there would be no attribution of either income or capital gains. The taxable dividends of $25,530 will be included in Mr. Bolt's 2013 Net Income For Tax Purposes, and the 2014 taxable capital gain of $17,500 [(1/2)($260,000 - $225,000)] will be included in his 2014 Net Income For Tax Purposes. The transfer would not affect Dr. Bolt's Net Income For Tax Purposes in either 2013 or 2014.

Case D

As ITA 73(1) continues to be applicable in this Case, the transfer would take place at the adjusted cost base of $185,000, and both eligible dividends and capital gains would be attributed back to Dr. Bolt. For both Dr. and Mr. Bolt, the results for all three years would be identical to those described in Case A.

Case E

When a taxpayer elects out of ITA 73(1) and a transfer is made for consideration that is less than fair market value, the provisions of ITA 69(1) are applicable to the transferor. Under these provisions, if a taxpayer disposes of a property for less than its fair market value, the proceeds of disposition are deemed to be the fair market value amount. This will result in Dr. Bolt recording a 2012 taxable capital gain of $20,000 [(1/2)($225,000 - $185,000)]. As the transfer is for consideration that is less than the fair market value of the securities, the income attribution rules will be applicable, resulting in the 2013 taxable dividends of $25,530 being included in Dr. Bolt's 2013 Net Income For Tax Purposes.

Despite the fact that ITA 69 deems Dr. Bolt's proceeds of disposition to be fair market value, Mr. Bolt's adjusted cost base would be the $140,000 that was actually paid. This means that, when the securities are sold in 2014 for $260,000, there will be a taxable capital gain of $60,000 [(1/2)($260,000 - $140,000)]. This will be attributed back to Dr. Bolt.

Note that the total gain that will be recognized by Dr. Bolt is $80,000 ($20,000 in 2012, plus $60,000 in 2014). This is $42,500 larger than the real taxable capital gain of $37,500 [(1/2)($260,000 - $185,000)]. This difference, resulting from the application of ITA 69 is based on:

- double taxation of the difference between Dr. Bolt's adjusted cost base of $185,000 and the $225,000 fair market value at the time of transfer [(1/2)($225,000 - $185,000) = $20,000]; and

- taxation of the difference between Dr. Bolt's adjusted cost base of $185,000 and the $140,000 price paid by Mr. Bolt [(1/2)($185,000 - $140,000) = $22,500]. This amount was taxed, despite the fact that Dr. Bolt could not recognize her real economic loss on the sale at $140,000.

Case F

Under ITA 69, a non-arm's length gift is deemed to be a disposition and acquisition to be recorded by both parties at fair market value. This means that Dr. Bolt would have to record a 2012 taxable capital gain of $20,000 [(1/2)($225,000 - $185,000)]. As a gift to a minor was involved, income attribution rules will apply and the 2013 taxable dividends of $25,530 will have to be included in the 2013 Net Income For Tax Purposes of Dr. Bolt. However, the attribution rules do not apply to capital gains when the attribution results from a transfer to someone under 18 years of age. As a consequence, Dolly Bolt will include a taxable capital gain of $17,500 [(1/2)($260,000 - $225,000)] in her 2014 Net Income For Tax Purposes. The transfer will have no effect on the 2012 and 2013 Net Income For Tax Purposes of Dolly Bolt, nor on the 2014 Net Income For Tax Purposes of Dr. Bolt.

Case G

The transfer at fair market value will result in Dr. Bolt recording a taxable capital gain of $20,000 [(1/2)($225,000 - $185,000)] in 2012. As the transfer is at fair market and the related loan requires interest at commercial rates, the income attribution rules are not applicable. This means that Dolly will include taxable dividends of $25,530 in her 2013 Net Income For Tax Purposes and a taxable capital gain of $17,500 [(1/2)($260,000 - $225,000)] in her 2014

Net Income For Tax Purposes. The transaction will have no effect on the 2013 and 2014 Net Income For Tax Purposes of Dr. Bolt, nor on the 2012 Net Income For Tax Purposes of Dolly Bolt.

Case H

As the transfer is at fair market value, Dr. Bolt will have a taxable capital gain of $20,000 [(1/2)($225,000 - $185,000)] included in her 2012 Net Income For Tax Purposes. Dirk's adjusted cost base for the securities will be $225,000, and the transfer will not affect his 2012 Net Income For Tax Purposes. As Dirk is not under 18 years of age, the attribution rules found in ITA 74.1(2) do not apply. However, ITA 56(4.1) indicates that income attribution applies in situations where an interest free or low interest loan has been given to a non-arm's length individual, and one of the main purposes of the loan is to reduce or avoid taxes. As Dirk has only limited income and would be in a lower tax bracket than Dr. Bolt, it is likely that this condition would apply in this Case.

As a result, the 2013 taxable dividends of $25,530 would be included in the 2013 Net Income For Tax Purposes of Dr. Bolt, rather than in the Net Income For Tax Purposes of her son. However, the 2014 taxable capital gain of $17,500 [(1/2)($260,000 - $225,000)] would not be attributed back to Dr. Bolt. Rather, it would be included in the 2014 Net Income For Tax Purposes of Dirk Bolt.

Self Study Solution Nine - 13

Net Employment Income

Carolyn's employment income would be calculated as follows:

Salary [(10 Months)($5,000)]	$50,000
RPP Contributions (Note 1)	(2,600)
Automobile (Note 2)	6,047
Travel Allowance (Note 3)	Nil
Moving Cost Allowance	10,000
Housing Loss Reimbursement (Note 4)	Nil
Housing Cost Allowance (Note 5)	7,500
Net Employment Income	$70,947

Note 1 While Carolyn's RPP contributions can be deducted, the matching contribution by her employer does not create a taxable benefit.

Note 2 The automobile benefit would be calculated as follows:

Standby Charge [(2%)($42,000)(9)(8,000 ÷ 15,003)]	$4,031
Operating Cost Benefit - Lesser Of:	
• [(1/2)($4,031)] = $2,016	
• [(8,000)($0.27)] = $2,160	2,016
Total Benefit	$6,047

Note 3 As the allowance appears to be reasonable, it does not have to be included in income. Given this, Carolyn cannot deduct her actual costs.

Note 4 As the housing loss reimbursement is less than $15,000, it does not have to be included in income.

Note 5 Assistance with higher housing costs related to a required move must be included in an employee's income.

Property Income

Carolyn's property income is calculated as follows:

Eligible Dividends Received	$ 5,800
Gross Up At 38 Percent	2,204
Recapture On Rental Property (Note 6)	20,000
Total Property Income	$28,004

Note 6 The fair market value of the rental building when it is bequeathed to Carolyn is $270,000 ($320,000 - $50,000). While this would be the UCC value that Carolyn would use to calculate CCA, because the fair market value of the property at the time of transfer is less than its capital cost, Carolyn must use her mother's capital cost of $300,000 ($400,000 - $100,000).

Carolyn's proceeds from the sale of the building is $290,000 ($340,000 - $50,000) and, when she subtracts the lesser of the capital cost and the proceeds from the $270,000 UCC, the result is recapture of $20,000 ($270,000 - $290,000).

Taxable Capital Gains

Carolyn's only capital gains will arise on the sale of the shares that were gifted to her by her parents. Note that her adjusted cost base for these shares will be their fair market value at the time of the gift.

Proceeds Of Disposition	$74,000
Adjusted Cost Base	(62,000)
Capital Gain	$12,000
Inclusion Rate	1/2
Taxable Capital Gain	$ 6,000

Other Income And Deductions

Carolyn's other income and other deductions amount is calculated as follows:

Spousal Support (Note 7)	$ 500
Moving Cost (Note 8)	(26,509)
Child Care Cost (Note 9)	(7,200)
Universal Child Care Benefit (Note 10)	Nil
Total Other Income And Deductions	($33,209)

Note 7 When the full amount of support is not paid, the first payments are deemed to be for child support. Given the total payments of $12,500 and the required child support of $12,000 [(12)($1,000)], Carolyn will include only $500 in her Net Income For Tax Purposes.

Note 8 Carolyn's deductible moving costs can be calculated as follows:

Selling Cost Of Lethbridge Property	$12,500
Legal Fees - Sale Of Lethbridge Property	600
Legal Fees - Purchase Of Edmonton Property	450
Storage Costs - February 15th Through March 10th	1,400
Cost Of Moving Belongings	7,250
Food And Lodging In Lethbridge And Edmonton (Limited To 15 Days At $250)	3,750
Simplified Meal Cost [(2)(3)($51)]	306
Simplified Milage [($.50)(506)]	253
Total	$26,509

As this amount is less than her income at her new job, she will be able to deduct the full amount of these expenses.

Note 9   Carolyn's deductible care costs would be the least of three amounts:

Actual Costs Plus Deductible Camp Costs

Edmonton Cost [(38)(($175)]	$6,650	
Camp [(2)($175 + $100)]	550	$7,200
Annual Limit ($7,000 + $4,000)		$11,000
Two-Thirds Earned Income		
[(2/3)($70,947 + $2,600 RPP)]		$49,031

The least of these three amounts is the actual cost of $7,200.

Note 10   In a single parent family, the parent has the option of including the total amount of the benefits received in the income of a dependant who qualifies for the eligible dependant tax credit. As a result, Carolyn will not include the UCCB in her net income.   The benefits will be considered income in the calculation of the eligible dependant credit.

Net Income For Tax Purposes

Carolyn's Net Income For Tax Purposes would be determined as follows:

Net Employment Income	$70,947
Property Income	28,004
Taxable Capital Gains	6,000
Other Income And Deductions	(33,209)
Net Income For Tax Purposes	$71,742

Taxable Income

As Carolyn has no Division C deductions, her Taxable Income would be equal to her Net Income For Tax Purposes.

Tax Payable

Carolyn's Tax Payable would be determined as follows:

Tax On First $43,561		$ 6,534
Tax On Next $28,181 ($71,742 - $43,561) At 22 Percent		6,200
Tax Before Credits		$12,734
Tax Credits:		
Basic Personal	($11,038)	
Eligible Dependant ($11,038 - $1,200)	(9,838)	
Child [(2)($2,234)]	(4,468)	
Fitness Credit (Maximum)	(500)	
EI Premiums	(891)	
CPP Contributions	(2,356)	
Canada Employment	(1,117)	
Medical Expenses (Note 11)	(5,448)	
Total Credit Base	($35,656)	
Rate	15%	(5,348)
Dividend Tax Credit [(6/11)($2,204)]		(1,202)
Charitable Donations [(15%)($200) + (29%)($600 - $200)]		(146)
Federal Tax Payable		$6,038

Note 11   The medical expenses eligible for the credit are as follows:

Total Medical Costs	$7,600
Lesser Of:	
• $2,152 [(3%)($71,742)]	
• 2013 Threshold Amount = $2,152	(2,152)
Medical Expense Tax Credit Base	$5,448

Self Study Solution Nine - 14

Net Employment Income
Chantale's employment income would be calculated as follows:

Salary	$90,000
RPP Contributions (Note 1)	(4,500)
Professional Dues	(1,200)
Automobile Benefit (Note 2)	9,071
Moving Allowance	6,000
Travel Allowance (Note 3)	Nil
Net Employment Income	$99,371

Note 1 The employer's matching contribution to the RPP would not be a taxable benefit.

Note 2 The automobile benefit would be calculated as follows:

Standby Charge [(2%)($28,000)(12)(18,000 ÷ 20,004)]	$6,047
Operating Cost Benefit - Lesser Of:	
• [(1/2)($6,047)] = $3,024	
• [(18,000)($0.27)] = $4,860	3,024
Total Benefit	$9,071

Note 3 As the allowance appears to be reasonable, it does not have to be included in income. Given this, Chantale cannot deduct her actual costs.

Property Income
As Chantale is divorced from her former husband the income attribution rules are no longer applicable. This means the eligible dividends would be included in her income and will result in an income inclusion calculated as follows:

Dividends Received	$1,500
Gross Up At 38 Percent	570
Taxable Dividends = Total Property Income	$2,070

Taxable Capital Gains
Here again, because income attribution no longer applies, the following capital gain would be included in Chantale's Net Income For Tax Purposes:

Proceeds Of Disposition	$34,400
Adjusted Cost Base	(26,000)
Capital Gain	$ 8,400
Inclusion Rate	1/2
Taxable Capital Gain	$ 4,200

Other Income And Deductions

Chantale's other income and other deductions amount is calculated as follows:

Spousal Support Received (Note 4)	$ 800
Moving Expenses (Note 5)	(12,850)
Child Care Costs (Note 6)	(11,000)
Universal Child Care Benefit (Note 7)	Nil
Total Other Income And Deductions	($23,050)

Note 4 As the required payments were not made in full, the payments that were made are first applied to child support. The taxable spousal support would be calculated as follows:

Total Payments	$8,000
Required Child Support [(12)($600)]	(7,200)
Taxable Spousal Support Received	$ 800

Note 5 As she is moving more the 40 kilometers closer to her work, moving costs are deductible. The deductible amounts are as follows:

Lease Cancellation Penalty	$ 1,200
Cost Of Storing Belongings	1,500
Cost Of Moving Belongings	6,400
Legal Fees On Purchase Of New Home	Nil
Food And Hotel In Ottawa (Limited To 15 Days At $250)	3,750
Deductible Moving Costs	$12,850

As this amount is less than her income at her new job location of $30,000 [(4/12)($90,000)], she will be able to deduct the full amount of these expenses. The costs of the house hunting trips are not deductible. In addition, because she did not own a home in Carleton Place, the legal costs of purchasing the new home are not deductible.

Note 6 The child care costs would be $11,000, the least of the following three amounts:

Actual Costs And Deductible Camp Costs		
Carleton Place [(32)(($300)]	$9,600	
Ottawa [(16)($350)]	5,600	
Camp [(4)($175) + (4)($100)]	1,100	$16,300
Annual Limit ($7,000 + $4,000)		$11,000
Two-Thirds Earned Income* [(2/3)($99,371 + $4,500 + $1,200)]		$70,047

*The income limit is based on gross employment income, without consideration of the RPP contributions or professional dues.

Note 7 In a single parent family, the parent has the option of including the total amount of the benefits received in the income of a dependant who qualifies for the eligible dependant tax credit. As a result, Ms. Bergeron will not include the UCCB in her net income. The benefits will be considered income in the calculation of the eligible dependant credit.

Net Income For Tax Purposes

Chantale's Net Income For Tax Purposes would be determined as follows:

Net Employment Income	$99,371
Property Income	2,070
Taxable Capital Gains	4,200
Other Income And Deductions	(23,050)
Net Income For Tax Purposes	$82,591

Taxable Income

As Chantale has no Division C deductions, her Taxable Income would be equal to her Net Income For Tax Purposes.

Tax Payable

Chantale's Tax Payable would be determined as follows:

Tax On First $43,561		$ 6,534
Tax On Next $39,030 ($82,591 - $43,561) At 22 Percent		8,587
Tax Before Credits		$15,121
Tax Credits:		
Basic Personal	($11,038)	
Eligible Dependant ($11,038 - $1,200)	(9,838)	
Child [(2)($2,234)]	(4,468)	
Transit Passes [(4)($100) + (4)($75)]	(700)	
EI Premiums	(891)	
CPP Contributions	(2,356)	
Canada Employment	(1,117)	
Medical Expenses (Note 8)	(11,398)	
Total Credit Base	($41,806)	
Rate	15%	(6,271)
Dividend Tax Credit [(6/11)($570)]		(311)
Balance Before Charitable Contributions		$ 8,539
Charitable Donations (Note 9)		(8,539)
Federal Tax Payable		Nil

Note 8   The medical expenses eligible for the credit are as follows:

Total Medical Costs	$13,550
Lesser Of:	
• $2,478 [(3%)($82,591)]	
• 2013 Threshold Amount = $2,152	(2,152)
Medical Expense Tax Credit Base	$11,398

Note 9   While Chantale has available a charitable donation of $200,000, the use of this credit is limited to 75 percent of her Net Income For Tax Purposes. This would be $61,943 [(75%)($82,591)].   However, using this total would create a credit of $17,935 [(15%)($200) + (29%)($61,943 - $200)]. As this is in excess of her Tax Payable, it would make no sense to claim the maximum because unused donations can be carried forward for five years.

The best solution would be to use an amount of these contributions that is sufficient to eliminate her federal Tax Payable. This amount would be $29,541. The credit would be $8,539 [(15%)($200) + (29%)($29,541 - $200)]. The required credit base is deter-mined by solving the following simple equation for X:

$$\$8,539 = [(29\%)(X - \$200) + (15\%)(\$200)]$$
$$X = [(\$8,539 + \$58 - \$30) \div 29\%]$$

This would leave a charitable donations carry forward of $170,459 ($200,000 - $29,541).

Chapter 9 Learning Objectives

After completing Chapter 9, you should be able to:

1. Identify the major other sources of income that are listed under Subdivision d of the *Income Tax Act* (paragraph [P hereafter] 9-1 through 9-19).

2. Identify the income inclusions from deferred income plans (P 9-20 and 9-21).

3. Apply the rules related to education assistance payments, social assistance, workers' compensation payments and the universal child care benefit (P 9-22 through 9-29).

4. Determine the deductible amount of CPP contributions on self-employed income (P 9-30 through 9-33).

5. Determine the deductible amount of moving expenses for an individual (P 9-34 through 9-46).

6. Determine the deductible amount of child care expenses (P 9-47 through 9-60).

7. Apply the provisions related to the disability supports deduction (P 9-61 through 9-68).

8. Apply the provisions related to EI benefits and repayments (P 9-69 and 9-70).

9. Explain the general rules for pension income splitting (P 9-71 through 9-77).

10. Explain the tax treatment of child support and spousal support payments and receipts (P 9-78 through 9-87).

11. Determine the taxable portion of annuity payments received (P 9-88 through 9-96).

12. Explain the provisions associated with Registered Education Savings Plans, Canada Education Savings Grants and Canada Learning Bonds (P 9-97 through 9-132).

13. Describe the major features of Registered Disability Savings Plans (P 9-133 through 9-135).

14. Describe the major features of Tax Free Savings Accounts (P 9-136 through 9-140).

15. Determine the tax consequences of non-arm's length transfers of property at values other than fair market value (P 9-141 through 9-158).

16. Describe the special rollover provisions applicable to inter vivos transfers of property to a spouse (P 9-159 through 9-166).

17. Determine the tax consequences of non-arm's length transfers of depreciable property (P 9-167 through 9-171).

18. Describe the special rollover provisions applicable to inter vivos transfers of farm or fishing property to a child (P 9-172 through 9-175).

19. Explain the basic requirements for deemed dispositions on death and any rollovers available at that time (P 9-176 through 9-185).

20. Apply the income attribution rules to inter vivos transfers of property to a spouse and to related individuals who are under the age of 18 (P 9-186 through 9-204).

21. Describe the income attribution rules applicable to transfers to other related parties (P 9-205 through 9-208).

22. Describe some of the anti-avoidance provisions that relate to the income attribution rules (P 9-209 and 9-210).

23. Describe some of the tax planning techniques that are available to mitigate the income attribution rules (P 9-211).

CHAPTER 10

How To Work Through Chapter 10

We recommend the following approach in dealing with the material in this Chapter:

Planning For Retirement
☐ Read paragraph 10-1 to 10-19 (in the textbook).

Registered Retirement Savings Plans (RRSPs)
☐ Read paragraph 10-20 to 10-39.
☐ Do Exercise Ten-1 (in the textbook) and check the solution on page S-207 in this Study Guide.
☐ Read paragraph 10-40.

RRSP Deduction Limit
☐ Read paragraph 10-41 to 10-51.
☐ Do Exercises Ten-2 and Ten-3 and check the solutions in this Study Guide.

Pension Adjustments (PAs)
☐ Read paragraph 10-52 to 10-54.
☐ Do Exercise Ten-4 and check the solution in this Study Guide.
☐ Read paragraph 10-55 to 10-62.
☐ Do Exercise Ten-5 and check the solution in this Study Guide.
☐ Do Self Study Problem Ten-1 at the end of the textbook chapter on page 522 and check the solution in this Study Guide.

Past Service Pension Adjustments (PSPAs) And Pension Adjustment Reversals
☐ Read paragraph 10-63 to 10-74.
☐ Do Self Study Problem Ten-2 and check the solution in this Study Guide.

Examples Of RRSP Deduction Calculations
☐ Read paragraph 10-75.
☐ Do Exercises Ten-6 and Ten-7 and check the solutions in this Study Guide.

Undeducted And Excess RRSP Contributions, Including Tax Planning For
☐ Read paragraph 10-76 to 10-81.
☐ Do Exercise Ten-8 and check the solution in this Study Guide.
☐ Read paragraph 10-82 to 10-85.
☐ Do Self Study Problem Ten-3 to Ten-5 and check the solutions in this Study Guide.

RRSP And RRIF Administration Fees
☐ Read paragraph 10-86.

RRSP Withdrawals, Voluntary Conversions And Involuntary Termination Due To Age Limitation
❑ Read paragraph 10-87 to 10-96.

Spousal RRSP
❑ Read paragraph 10-97 to 10-105.
❑ Do Exercise Ten-9 and check the solution in this Study Guide.

Home Buyers' Plan (HBP) And Lifelong Learning Plan (LLP)
❑ Read paragraph 10-106 to 10-116.
❑ Do Exercise Ten-10 and check the solution in this Study Guide.
❑ Read paragraph 10-117 to 10-125.
❑ Do Exercise Ten-11 and check the solution in this Study Guide.

RRSPs - Departure From Canada And Death Of The RRSP Registrant
❑ Read paragraph 10-126 to 10-141.
❑ Do Self Study Problem Ten-6 and check the solution in this Study Guide.

Registered Pension Plans (RPPs) And Pooled Registered Pension Plans (PRPPs)
❑ Read paragraph 10-142 to 10-162.

Registered Retirement Income Funds (RRIFs) - General Rules
❑ Read paragraph 10-163 to 10-173.
❑ Do Exercise Ten-12 and check the solution in this Study Guide.

RRIFs - Death Of The RRIF Registrant And Evaluation Of RRIFs
❑ Read paragraph 10-174 to 10-181.

Deferred Profit Sharing Plans And Profit Sharing Plans
❑ Read paragraph 10-182 to 10-191.

Transfers Between Plans And Retiring Allowances
❑ Read paragraph 10-192 to 10-195.
❑ Do Exercise Ten-13 and check the solution in this Study Guide.
❑ Do Self Study Problems Ten-7 and Ten-8 and check the solutions in this Study Guide.

Retirement Compensation Arrangements, Salary Deferral Arrangements And Individual Pension Plans
❑ Read paragraph 10-196 to 10-215.

To Complete This Chapter
❑ Do Self Study Problems Ten-9 and Ten-10 and check the solutions in this Study Guide.
❑ Review the Key Terms Used In This Chapter on page 519 to 520. Consult the Glossary for the meaning of any key terms you do not know.
❑ Review the Glossary Flashcards and complete the Key Terms Self-Test for the Chapter. These features can be found in two places, on your Student CD-ROM under the heading "Key Term Practice" and on the web site.
❑ Review the Learning Objectives of the Chapter found on page S-224 and S-225 of this Study Guide.
❑ As a final review, we recommend that you view the PowerPoint Slides for Chapter 10 that are on your Student CD-ROM. The PowerPoint Viewer program can be installed from the Student CD-ROM.

Practice Examination
❑ Write the Practice Examination for Chapter 10 that is on your Student CD-ROM. Mark your examination using the Practice Examination Solution that is also on your Student CD-ROM.

Solution to Chapter Ten Exercises

Exercise Ten - 1 Solution

Invested Inside RRSP

Deductible Contribution	$20,000
Dividends Received [(5)(5%)($20,000)]	5,000
Balance After Five Years	$25,000
Tax Payable [(40%)($25,000)]	(10,000)
Available For Vacation	$15,000

Invested Outside RRSP

Initial Investment [($20,000)(1 - .40)]	$12,000
After Tax Dividends [(5)(5%)($12,000)(1 - .22)]	2,340
Available For Vacation	$14,340

As this latter is $660 less than the after tax funds from the RRSP, Brian should make the $20,000 contribution to the RRSP.

Exercise Ten - 2 Solution

His Earned Income for RRSP purposes would be $70,500 ($56,000 + $2,500 + $12,000).

Exercise Ten - 3 Solution

Her Earned Income for RRSP purposes would be $54,500 ($82,000 + $3,000 - $12,500 - $18,000).

Exercise Ten - 4 Solution

The basic mechanism here is the Pension Adjustment (PA). Individuals who belong to an RPP or a DPSP have their RRSP Deduction Limit reduced by the amount of their PA for the previous year. PAs are designed to reflect the amount of contributions or benefits that have been accumulated in employer sponsored RPPs and DPSPs.

Exercise Ten - 5 Solution

The Pension Adjustment will be $6,400 ($2,300 + $1,800 + $2,300).

Exercise Ten - 6 Solution

The required calculations would be as follows:

Unused Deduction Room - End Of 2012	$4,800
Lesser Of:	
• 2013 RRSP Dollar Limit = $23,820	
• 18% Of 2013 Earned Income Of $38,000 = $6,840	6,840
2013 RRSP Deduction Limit	$11,640
RRSP Deduction Is Least Of:	
• RRSP Deduction Limit = $11,640	
• Available Contributions = $6,000	
• Amount Mr. Haslich Chooses To Deduct = $4,500	(4,500)
Unused RRSP Deduction Room - End Of 2013	$ 7,140

Assuming Mr. Haslich deducted only $4,500, he would have $1,500 ($6,000 - $4,500) in undeducted contributions that can be carried forward and deducted in a subsequent year.

If Mr. Haslich wanted to deduct his maximum RRSP deduction of $11,640, he would have to contribute an additional $5,640 ($11,640 - $6,000).

Exercise Ten - 7 Solution

The required calculations would be as follows:

Unused Deduction Room - End Of 2012	$10,750
Lesser Of:	
• 2013 RRSP Dollar Limit = $23,820	
• 18% Of 2012 Earned Income Of $66,530* = $11,975	11,975
Less 2012 PA	(4,800)
2013 RRSP Deduction Limit	$17,925
RRSP Deduction Is Lesser Of:	
• RRSP Deduction Limit = $17,925	
• Available Contributions = $19,760 ($6,560 + $13,200)	(17,925)
Unused RRSP Deduction Room - End Of 2013	Nil

*Earned Income = $6,530 - $18,000 + $75,600 + $2,400 (RPP)

Mr. Black's maximum RRSP deduction is $17,925. While he has no Unused RRSP Deduction Room, he has $1,835 ($19,760 - $17,925) in undeducted contributions that can be carried forward and deducted in a subsequent year in which there is sufficient RRSP deduction room.

Exercise Ten - 8 Solution

In 2011 and 2012, 18 percent of Ms. Brownell's $160,000 in earned income, is less than the RRSP dollar limit for those years. Her 2013 earned income is not relevant in this Exercise as it will not be used until 2014. Given this, the calculation of the excess amount of contributions is as follows:

2011 RRSP Dollar Limit	$22,970
2012 Contribution (July 1)	(23,800)
Excess Contribution For 2012 (Less Than $2,000)	($ 830)
2012 RRSP Dollar Limit	23,820
2013 Contribution (May 1)	(27,000)
Excess Contribution As Of May 1, 2013	($ 4,010)

As the excess contribution for 2012 was less than $2,000, there is no penalty for that year. There will be a 2013 penalty of $321 [(1%)($4,010)(8 Months)]. The fact that there is no RRSP deduction is not relevant to the penalty.

Exercise Ten - 9 Solution

As a spousal contribution was made in 2011, one of the two years prior to 2013, income attribution will apply. However, it will only apply to the extent of the $5,000 contribution made by Mrs. Garveau. This means that $5,000 of the withdrawal will be taxed in the hands of Mrs. Garveau, with the remaining $4,000 taxed in the hands of Mr. Garveau.

Exercise Ten - 10 Solution

Ms. DeBoo will have to repay $867 [(1/15)($18,000 - $5,000)] during 2013. Note that the voluntary payment that was made during 2012 did not reduce the fraction of the remaining balance that must be paid in 2013.

Exercise Ten - 11 Solution

There are no tax consequences associated with the withdrawal of $5,000. As he will have no education tax credit in either 2014 or 2015, his repayment period begins in 2015. As he makes the required payments of $500 ($5,000 ÷ 10) within 60 days of the end of each of the years 2015 through 2024, there are no tax consequences associated with his repayments.

Exercise Ten - 12 Solution

He has no required minimum withdrawal for 2013, the year the RRIF is established. His minimum withdrawal for 2014 will be $27,500 [$660,000 ÷ (90 - 66)].

Exercise Ten - 13 Solution

It would appear that Mr. Bartoli began working for his employer in 1976. Given this, he can rollover a total of $59,500 [($2,000)(20 Years Before 1996) + ($1,500)(13 Years Before 1989)] to his RRSP. The remainder of the retiring allowance will be taxed in 2013.

Self Study Solution Ten - 1

Mr. Barnes' 2012 Earned Income for RRSP purposes would be calculated as follows:

Salary	$55,000
Taxable Benefits	1,150
Union Dues	(175)
Net Employment Income	$55,975
Business Income	4,150
Rental Loss	(11,875)
Spousal Support Received	2,400
Earned Income	$50,650

Note that CPP and EI contributions do not reduce Earned Income for RRSP purposes.

Since Mr. Barnes has no undeducted RRSP contributions, his maximum deductible RRSP contribution for 2013 is equal to his RRSP Deduction Limit.

This is calculated for Part A (not a member of RPP or DPSP) and Part B (member of RPP) as follows:

	Part A	Part B
Unused Deduction Room - End Of 2012	$ 700	$ 700
Annual Addition - Lesser Of:		
• 2013 RRSP Dollar Limit = $23,820		
• 18% of 2012 Earned Income Of $50,650 = $9,117	9,117	9,117
Less 2012 PA	N/A	(4,200)
Maximum Deductible RRSP Contribution	$9,817	$5,617

Self Study Solution Ten - 2

Case A

The required 2013 PA would be calculated as follows:

Employer's Contribution To RPP	$3,200
Employer's Contribution To DPSP	1,100
Mr. Brokow's Contribution To RPP	1,500
PA	$5,800

Case B

The required 2013 PA would be calculated as follows:

$$[(9)(1.65\%)(\$52,000)] = \$7,722$$

Note that the contributions made during 2013 have no influence on the PA for a defined benefit RPP.

Case C
Bob's 2013 PSPA would be calculated as follows:

$$[(9)(1.10\%)(\$48,000)(2 \text{ Years})] = \$9,504$$

The 2013 PA will reflect the benefits earned during 2013.

Case D
Marianne's 2013 PSPA is based on the PAs that would have been reported in the relevant years, less the PAs actually reported. The calculation would be as follows:

$$[(9)(1.7\% - 1.4\%)(\$52,000)(2 \text{ Years})] = \$2,808$$

This $2,808 PSPA would reflect the increase in benefits that occurred in January, 2013. In addition to this PSPA, there would also be a PA based on her 2013 earnings, multiplied by the benefit factor of 9 and the new formula rate of 1.7 percent.

Self Study Solution Ten - 3

The excess RRSP contributions amount at the end of each month of 2013 would be calculated as follows:

	January	February	March To November	December
Undeducted Contributions At Beginning Of Month	$54,000	$54,000	$59,000	$59,000
Add: 2013 Contribution		5,000		
Deduct: 2013 Withdrawal				(35,000)
Undeducted Contributions At End Of Month	$54,000	$59,000	$59,000	$24,000
Deduct: Unused Deduction Room Carried Forward	(10,000)	(10,000)	(10,000)	(10,000)
Deduct: 2013 Increase In Unused Deduction Room	(9,000)	(9,000)	(9,000)	(9,000)
Deduct: $2,000 Cushion	(2,000)	(2,000)	(2,000)	(2,000)
Monthly Cumulative Excess	$33,000	$38,000	$38,000	$ 3,000
Penalty At 1 Percent Per Month	$ 330	$ 380	$ 380	$ 30

The total penalty for 2013 is $4,160 [($330)(1) + ($380)(10) + ($30)(1)].

Self Study Solution Ten - 4

Part A
Mr. Beasley's net employment income for 2012 would be $22,700, his gross salary of $24,000, reduced by his RPP contributions of $1,300.

Part B
The annual addition for 2013 would be the lesser of $23,820 and 18 percent of Earned Income for 2012. The latter amount would be calculated as follows:

Net Employment Income (Part A)	$22,700
Add Back RPP Contributions	1,300
Spousal Support	9,000
Net Rental Loss	(5,000)
Earned Income	$28,000
Percent	18%
Annual Addition (Less than $23,820)	$ 5,040

Note that the damage award, royalties on someone else's work, interest, dividends, and gift are not included in Earned Income for RRSP purposes. Mr. Beasley's maximum deductible RRSP contribution would be calculated as follows:

Opening Unused Deduction Room	Nil
Annual Addition	$ 5,040
Less 2012 PA	(2,600)
Maximum Deductible RRSP Contribution	$ 2,440

Part C

As Mr. Beasley has made no contributions prior to 2013, he has no undeducted contributions. In addition, he has interest income and dividends that are subject to current Tax Payable. Given this, as well as the fact that his damage award and separation gift leave him cash in excess of his needs, he should contribute the maximum deductible amount of $2,440 to his RRSP for 2013.

While he could deduct $2,440 of his total contribution in 2013, it would be advantageous to defer this deduction until 2014 when he expects to be in the maximum tax bracket. At the federal level, the tax savings will be $708 [(29%)($2,440)] in 2014, as compared to $366 [(15%)($2,440)] in 2013.

Given his available funds, Mr. Beasley should be advised to consider contributing the maximum allowable amount to a Tax Free Savings Account, as well as over contributing up to $2,000 to his RRSP. If he has made no contributions to his TFSA, in 2013 he could make a contribution of $25,500 ($5,000 per year from 2009 through 2012, and $5,500 for 2013).

With respect to his RRSP, as discussed in Chapter 10, he can over contribute up to $2,000 with no penalty. Although he would not be able to deduct these contributions, they would enjoy the benefit of having any income earned while in the plan compounded on a tax free basis. Further, any over contribution to his RRSP would be deductible in a future year with sufficient RRSP deduction room.

All of these contributions should be made as soon as possible in order to maximize the tax free earnings that will accrue inside of his RRSP and/or TFSA.

Self Study Solution Ten - 5

Ms. Stratton's net employment income would be calculated as follows:

Gross Salary	$130,000
Additions:	
Employer's Contributions For Life Insurance	96
Employer's Contribution To Provincial Health Insurance Plan	482
Trip To Bermuda ($5,000 - $500 Non-Cash Gift Exemption)	4,500
Deductions:	
RPP Contributions	(2,390)
Professional Dues	(225)
Net Employment Income	$132,463

The reasons for not including the other items given in the problem in the preceding calculation are as follows, identified by the relevant point number in the problem:

Point 1 - Income taxes withheld cannot be deducted in the calculation of Net Income For Tax Purposes or Taxable Income.

Point 1 - The EI and CPP contributions are eligible for tax credit treatment.

Point 1 - Contributions to registered charities create a credit against Tax Payable, but cannot be deducted in the calculation of net employment income.

Point 2 - Employer payments to employee dental plans and private health care plans are not a taxable benefit.

Point 2 - Employer payments to employee group income protection plans are not a taxable benefit.

Point 3 - Employer payments for membership fees in social or recreational clubs are generally not a taxable benefit to the employee, provided the facilities are used primarily for employment related purposes.

Point 5 - Reimbursed costs do not create a taxable benefit for an employee. Consistent with this, the reimbursed costs that have been incurred by an employee cannot be deducted.

Point 7 - Contributions to the RRSP can be deducted under Subdivision e, but not in the calculation of net employment income.

Point 7 - Contributions to a TFSA are not deductible.

Part B

Ms. Stratton's Earned Income would be calculated as follows:

Net Employment Income	$132,463
RPP Contributions Deducted	2,390
2013 Earned Income	$134,853

As the problem states that Ms. Stratton's 2012 Earned Income is equal to her 2013 Earned Income, $134,853 would also be her 2012 Earned Income. Using this figure, Ms. Stratton's 2013 RRSP Deduction Limit would be calculated as follows:

Unused Deduction Room - End of 2012	Nil
Annual Addition - Lesser Of:	
• 2013 RRSP Dollar Limit = $23,820	
• [(18%)($134,853)] = $24,274	$23,820
Less 2012 PA	(5,560)
2013 RRSP Deduction Limit	$18,260

As she has made a 2013 contribution of $20,000, she can deduct her RRSP Deduction Limit of $18,260. This will leave an undeducted contribution of $1,740 ($20,000 - $18,260).

Part C

The $20,000 contribution is still a good idea as she has contributed the maximum to her TFSA. Funds invested in an RRSP accumulate earnings on a tax free basis and, unless non-deductible contributions accumulate to more than $2,000, no penalty is applied. Further, contributions that are not deducted can be carried forward and are available for deduction in any subsequent year with sufficient RRSP deduction room. This means that Ms. Stratton will enjoy the benefits of tax free compounding without experiencing any unfavourable tax consequences.

Self Study Solution Ten - 6

Part A

Mr. Sabatini's minimum net employment income would be calculated as follows:

Salary	$ 58,000
Commissions	74,000
Registered Pension Plan Contributions	(3,500)
Net Disability Benefits (Note 1)	3,950
Life Insurance Premium Taxable Benefit [(50%)($3,000)]	1,500
Automobile Benefit (Note 2)	6,601
Stock Option Benefit [($23.50 - $12.50)(1,000 Shares)]	11,000
Golf And Country Club Costs (Note 3)	(3,400)
Net Employment Income	$148,151

Note 1   As Mr. Sabatini's employer has made contributions to the sickness and accident plan, the benefit of $4,500 is taxable. This is reduced by the payments of $550 [($100)(12 - 1)/2] that were made by Mr. Sabatini during the year, leaving a net benefit of $3,950.

Note 2   With respect to the standby charge, Mr. Sabatini's employment related usage is over 50 percent of the total and, as a consequence, he can reduce his standby charge to the extent of personal usage that is less than 1,667 kilometers per month. Also note that, as the car was not available during June, his standby charge would be based on 335 days of availability. This would be rounded to 11 months (335/30). Given this, the standby charge would be as follows:

$$[(\$68,000)(11 \text{ Months})(2\%)(7,000/18,337)] = \$5,711$$

As Mr. Sabatini's employment related use was over 50 percent of the total use, he could base his operating cost benefit on one-half of the standby charge. However, a lower benefit results from the regular $0.27 per kilometer calculation as follows:

$$\text{Operating Cost Benefit } [(\$0.27)(7,000)] = \$1,890$$

Given these two calculations, and the $1,000 payment that Mr. Sabatini made to his employer, the total automobile benefit is $6,601 ($5,711 + $1,890 - $1,000).

Note 3   Only 50 percent of the $6,800 country club entertainment costs can be deducted by Mr. Sabatini. The $5,000 membership fee would not be a taxable benefit and would not be deductible by his employer.

Other Notes

- The travel costs that the corporation reimbursed to Mr. Sabatini have no tax effect.
- The CPP and EI contributions are not deductible. They can be used to create credits against Tax Payable.
- Income taxes withheld are not deductible.
- Donations to a registered charity will create a credit against Tax Payable, but cannot be deducted in the determination of net employment income.
- Parking fees related to Mr. Sabatini's normal employment location are not deductible.
- Although he cannot deduct his share of the life insurance premiums, the life insurance proceeds will not be taxable.
- The use of frequent flyer points earned on employment related travel does not normally create a taxable benefit.
- The discounts on merchandise provided by the employer are not a taxable benefit.

Part B

Mr. Sabatini's 2012 Earned Income and maximum deductible 2013 RRSP contribution would be calculated as follows:

2012 Earned Income From Employment (Given)	$116,000
2012 Business Loss	(12,500)
2012 Rental Income	7,500
2012 Earned Income	**$111,000**

Unused Deduction Room - End Of 2012	Nil
Annual Addition - Lesser Of:	
• 2013 RRSP Dollar Limit = $23,820	
• 18% of 2012 Earned Income Of $111,000 = $19,980	$19,980
Less 2012 PA	(6,800)
2013 RRSP Deduction Limit	**$13,180**
RRSP Deduction For 2013	**$ 2,600**

While Mr. Sabatini has deduction room of $13,180, only the $2,600 contribution to his wife's plan can be deducted. His $10,000 contribution to his own RRSP is not relevant as it was deducted in the previous year.

Note that the stock option deduction from Taxable Income does not affect Earned Income.

Part C

Since the RRSP has no beneficiary specified, an amount equal to the fair market value of all the property held in the RRSP at the time of death will have to be reported on Mr. Sabatini's return for 2014, the year of death.

Part D

Since Mr. Sabatini's wife is the sole beneficiary, she can choose to transfer all the assets in the RRSP to an RRSP in her name. If this is done, there will be no tax consequences for either Mr. Sabatini or his wife. This would likely be the most tax advantageous arrangement for dealing with Mr. Sabatini's RRSP.

Note that there are also provisions that allow RRSPs to be transferred to a financially dependent child on a basis that shifts the tax burden to the child. Given Mr. Sabatini is receiving child support for an 8 year son, this approach might also be tax advantageous.

Self Study Solution Ten - 7

Part A

With respect to the retiring allowance, ITA 56(1)(a)(ii) requires that the entire $125,000 must be included in income. Then, to the extent that such amounts are transferred or contributed to an RRSP for which the taxpayer is the registrant, the taxpayer is entitled to a deduction under ITA 60(j.1), equal to $2,000 for each year of service prior to 1996 with the employer, plus an additional $1,500 for each year of service before 1989, for which the employee was not a member of an RPP or a DPSP. This provides for the following maximum deduction under ITA 60(j.1):

19 Years At $2,000 Per Year (1977 Through 1995)	$38,000
12 Years At $1,500 Per Year (1977 Through 1988)	18,000
Allowable Rollover	**$56,000**

Given this calculation, the maximum RRSP deduction that Mr. Colt would be allowed for 2013 would be calculated as follows:

Opening RRSP Deduction Room	$32,000
Annual Addition - Lesser Of:	
• 2013 RRSP Dollar Limit = $23,820	
• 18% of 2012 Earned Income Of $46,000 = $8,280	8,280
Less 2012 PA	(8,000)
RRSP Deduction Limit For 2013	$32,280
Retiring Allowance Rollover (See Preceding Calculation)	56,000
Maximum Deduction	$88,280

Part B
The $56,000 eligible portion of the retiring allowance can only be deducted if it is contributed to his RRSP. If Mr. Colt contributes only $50,000 to his RRSP, the remaining $6,000 ($56,000 - $50,000) cannot be deducted if it is contributed to a spousal RRSP.

Mr. Colt will be able to deduct contributions to the spousal RRSP of $32,280, his RRSP Deduction Limit. If he makes his planned RRSP contributions, he will have the following amount of non-deductible contributions:

Total Contributions	$125,000
Maximum Deduction Under ITA 60(j.1)	(50,000)
Maximum Deductible Spousal Contribution	(32,280)
Non-Deductible Contributions	$ 42,720

To the extent that non-deductible contributions exceed $2,000, they are subject to a heavy penalty of 1 percent per month. Unless Mr. Colt anticipates having Earned Income from another source in the future, overcontributing to his or the spousal RRSP would not be a good idea. Any over contribution would be taxable when it is withdrawn despite the fact that it was never deducted.

As a consequence, Mr. Colt should revise his planned RRSP contributions so that he contributes $56,000 to his RRSP and $32,280 to a spousal RRSP. This will maximize his RRSP deduction. As he will have additional unused funds available, it would be advisable for him to contribute the maximum amount to a Tax Free Savings Account (TFSA) for himself and his wife.

Self Study Solution Ten - 8

General Tax Planning Goals
The most desirable solution would be to find benefits that would be fully deductible to the Company and free of taxation for Mr. Jones. The only items that fall into this category would be:

- payments for private health care plans;
- payments for disability insurance;
- discounts on company merchandise; and
- annual non-cash gifts with a value of $500 or less.

Discounts on industrial engines are not likely to be of any value to Mr. Jones. However, Mr. Jones should arrange to have the Company provide private health care coverage, including a dental plan. The Company could also pay the premiums on a disability insurance plan without it becoming a taxable benefit to Mr. Jones at the time of payment (benefits received would be taxable). Finally, an annual non-cash gift with a value of $500 or less would be deductible to the company and received tax free by Mr. Jones.

Use Of RPP, DPSP, RRSP And Retiring Allowance

In terms of tax deferral, Mr. Jones should be included in the Company's Registered Pension Plan (RPP). Once he is admitted to the plan, both he and the Company should make the maximum contributions that are permitted under the terms of the plan. The limiting factor here is that these contributions cannot result in a Pension Adjustment that is in excess of the lesser of 18 percent of Mr. Jones' compensation for the year or the money purchase limit for the year under consideration ($24,270 for 2013).

While there is no indication that the Company has such an arrangement, a Deferred Profit Sharing Plan (DPSP) might also be useful. Whether or not Mr. Jones would be able to use such an arrangement would depend on the total employee/employer contributions to the Company's RPP. Contributions to a DPSP are included in the calculation of Mr. Jones' Pension Adjustment and, when combined with the RPP contributions, the total is subject to the limitation described in the preceding paragraph.

It would also be advisable for Mr. Jones to arrange for some of the compensation to be received in the form of a retiring allowance to be paid to a Registered Retirement Savings Plan (RRSP) at the end of the three years. Given his previous 11 year employment period with Martin was prior to 1996, a total of $28,000 [($2,000)(11) + $1,500 per year for the period 1985 through 1988], could be transferred on a tax free basis to this RRSP.

If the RRSP funds are subsequently withdrawn in the form of an annuity or transferred to a RRIF, the payments will be eligible for the pension income tax credit after Mr. Jones reaches age 65. The payments will also be eligible for the pension income splitting provisions. (See Chapter 9)

Housing Loan

The Company could provide a loan to Mr. Jones to purchase his new residence. As Mr. Jones is moving, he is eligible for a deduction of the benefit associated with a $25,000 interest free "home relocation" loan. Any additional low interest or interest free loan will result in imputed interest being added to Mr. Jones' Taxable Income without an offsetting deduction.

Note, however, that the prescribed rate for this purpose is currently at an historically low level of one percent. At this level, even if the loan is interest free, the relocation deduction is only $250 [(1%)($25,000)]. While this is not a significant benefit, the fact that the taxable benefit associated with amounts above $25,000 is very small could make a large interest free loan desirable. For example, on a $100,000 interest free loan, the benefit would only be $1,000, less the $250 deduction related to the relocation deduction.

Company Car

The Company could provide Mr. Jones with an automobile. In this case, Mr. Jones will be assessed for a personal benefit of a standby charge (24 percent per year of the capital cost or two-thirds of the lease payments, if he is not eligible for a reduction) and for operating costs (one-half of the standby charge or $0.27 per kilometer of personal use). Whether or not this will be desirable depends on an analysis of how Mr. Jones would actually use the car. In some cases, especially if the car has a list price of more than $30,000, the taxable benefit may exceed the actual benefit, making this an undesirable form of compensation.

Recreational Facilities

The Company could pay the dues for any recreational facilities that Mr. Jones might wish to use. While these amounts will not be treated as a taxable benefit to Mr. Jones, the payments will not be deductible to the Company. Given that both the Company and Mr. Jones will be subject to similar marginal tax rates, there would appear to be no significant advantage to this type of arrangement.

Moving Costs

The Company could provide assistance with the costs that will be incurred by Mr. Jones in moving to Hamilton. With respect to costs that Mr. Jones would be permitted to deduct, it makes little difference whether the Company pays the costs, or simply pays an equivalent amount in salary and lets Mr. Jones pay the costs and deduct them. However, certain types of moving costs that would not be deductible by Mr. Jones can be paid by the Company without creating a taxable benefit. An example of this would be compensation for a loss on a personal residence owned by Mr. Jones in Vancouver. (See Chapter 9)

Bonus And/Or Stock Options

If Martin Manufacturing has a year end after July 6, it can declare a bonus in the third year, but not pay it until the following calendar year. This will defer Mr. Jones' taxation of the bonus by one year without deferring Martin's deduction.

As an incentive, the Company could grant Mr. Jones options to purchase its stock. This would have no tax cost to the Company. The timing of the tax cost of the options for Mr. Jones could be delayed until after retirement.

Services As A Self-Employed Contractor Or Through A Corporation

Since Mr. Jones has been operating as a consultant, it may be possible to structure the project so that he will be considered an independent contractor rather than an employee. This would considerably increase the amount and type of expenditures that would be deductible by him and also create an opportunity to income split with his wife, if she could assist him in the project in some way. In considering this alternative it should be kept in mind that, if Mr. Jones is not an employee, some of the possibilities that have been previously discussed would no longer be feasible. For example, unless Mr. Jones is an employee, it would not be possible for him to be a member of the Company's RPP.

Another possibility would be for Mr. Jones to provide his services through a corporation. However, this would probably not be helpful. Given his relationship with Martin Manufacturing Company, any corporation would likely be viewed as a personal services business and taxed at full corporate rates. (Personal services corporations are covered in Chapter 12, Taxable Income And Tax Payable For Corporations.)

Self Study Solution Ten - 9

Part A - RRSP Contribution

In order to calculate the maximum deductible RRSP contribution, net employment income and net rental income must first be calculated.

Net Employment Income

The calculations required for 2012 (to be used in the RRSP earned income calculation) and 2013 would be as follows:

	2012	2013
Salary	$47,000	$53,000
Commissions	6,200	7,800
RPP Contributions	(1,800)	(1,950)
Work Space In Home Costs (Note 1)	(1,001)	(1,073)
Net Employment Income	$50,399	$57,777

Note 1 As an employee, Kerri cannot deduct either the listed mortgage interest or CCA on this office space. Because she has commission income, Kerri can deduct all of the other listed costs. Given this, the 2012 and 2013 deductions are as follows:

	2012	2013
Utilities And Maintenance	$1,850	$2,040
Insurance	625	715
Property Taxes	4,200	4,400
Total	$6,675	$7,155
Percentage Used	15%	15%
Deductible Amount	$1,001	$1,073

Net Rental Income

The calculations required for 2012 and 2013 would be as follows:

	2012	2013
Rents	$ 8,400	$13,800
Expenses Other Than CCA	(10,300)	(11,100)
Income (Loss) Before CCA	($ 1,900)	$ 2,700
CCA (Note 2)	N/A	(2,700)
Net Rental Income	($ 1,900)	Nil

Note 2 As CCA cannot be used to increase or create a rental loss, no deduction can be made in 2012. For 2013, the CCA maximum available deduction is $10,400 [(4%)($340,000 - $80,000)]. However, the actual deduction is limited to the $2,700 of rental income prior to the deduction of CCA.

RRSP Calculations

Determining the appropriate amount here requires the calculation of Earned Income for 2012. The calculation is as follows:

2012 Net Employment Income	$50,399
2012 RPP Contributions Deducted	1,800
Spousal Support Received [(12)($500)]	6,000
2012 Net Rental Loss	(1,900)
2012 Earned Income	$56,299

Using this figure, Ms. Sosteric's maximum 2013 deduction, along with the additional contribution required to make this deduction, would be calculated as follows:

Opening Unused Deduction Room	$ 6,200
Annual Addition - Lesser Of:	
• 2013 RRSP Dollar Limit = $23,820	
• 18% Of 2012 Earned Income Of $56,299 = $10,134	10,134
Less 2012 PA (Employee And Employer RPP Contributions)	(3,600)
Maximum RRSP Deduction	$12,734
Undeducted Contributions In Plan	(5,800)
Required Additional Contribution	$ 6,934

Part B - Net Income For Tax Purposes And Taxable Income

Other Required Information

While we can use several of the figures from Part A to calculate Net Income For Tax Purposes, two other items must be calculated before we can complete this figure.

Taxable Capital Gain And Dividends - Employer's Shares

The tax consequences related to buying, holding, and selling her employer's shares are as follows:

Proceeds Of Disposition [(5,000)($14.75)]	$73,750
Adjusted Cost Base [(5,000)($12.00)]	(60,000)
Capital Gain	$13,750
Inclusion Rate	1/2
Taxable Capital Gain	$ 6,875
Eligible Dividends [(5,000)($0.60)]	$3,000

Child Care Costs

Kerri's deductible child care costs are the least of three amounts:

Actual Costs   The actual costs were given as $8,600.

Annual Limit The annual limit is $11,000 ($7,000 for Barry and $4,000 for Kim).

Income Limit For this purpose, Ms. Sosteric's "earned income" is her gross employment income of $60,800 ($53,000 + $7,800). Two-thirds of this amount is $40,533.

The least of these figures is the actual costs of $8,600.

As Ms. Sosteric has no deductions applicable to the determination of Taxable Income, her 2013 Taxable Income is equal to her 2013 Net Income For Tax Purposes which is as follow:

Employment Income (Part A)	$57,777
Net Rental Income (Part A)	Nil
RRSP Deduction (Part A)	(12,734)
Spousal Support Received	6,000
Taxable Capital Gains	6,875
Eligible Dividends [(5,000)($0.60)]	3,000
Gross Up [(38%)($3,000)]	1,140
Child Care Costs	(8,600)
Universal Child Care Benefit (Note 3)	Nil
Net Income For Tax Purposes And Taxable Income	$53,458

Note 3   Single parents have the option of including the Universal Child Care Benefits received in the income of the child for whom the eligible dependant tax credit is claimed. As her children have no income of their own, including it in one of their incomes would not result in their paying taxes on this amount. While it would reduce the base for the eligible dependant credit, the rate for this credit is only 15 percent, whereas Ms. Sosteric's marginal federal tax rate is 22 percent. Given this it would be preferable to include the $1,200 in the income of the eligible dependant.

Part B - Tax Payable

The required calculations for her Tax Payable are as follows:

Tax On First $43,561		$6,534
Tax On Next $9,897 ($53,458 - $43,561) At 22 Percent		2,177
Tax Before Credits		$8,711
Tax Credits:		
Basic Personal Amount	($11,038)	
Eligible Dependant ($11,038 - $1,200)(Note 3)	(9,838)	
Child [(2)($2,234)]	(4,468	
EI Premiums	(891)	
CPP Contributions	(2,356)	
Canada Employment	(1,117)	
Medical Expenses (Note 4)	(1,016)	
Total Credit Base	($30,724)	
Rate	15%	(4,609)
Dividend Tax Credit [(6/11)($1,140)]		(622)
Federal Tax Payable		$3,480

Note 4 The base for Ms. Sosteric's medical expense tax credit would be calculated as follows:

Eligible Expenses	$2,620
Reduced By The Lesser Of:	
• [(3%)($53,458)] = $1,604	
• 2013 Reduction = $2,152	(1,604)
Base For Credit	$1,016

Self Study Solution Ten - 10

Part A - Spousal RRSP Contribution

As noted in the problem, we are to assume that Ahmed's 2012 Earned Income is equal to his 2013 Earned Income. In order to calculate the 2013 Earned Income, we need to calculate both net employment income and net rental income. These are the only components of Mr. Sidi's Earned Income.

Net Employment Income

Even though Ahmed is no longer an employee, he has employment income related to the exercise of his stock option shares. The calculations are as follows:

Exercise Date Value [(5,000)($21)]	$105,000
Option Price [(5,000)($15)]	(75,000)
Employment Income Inclusion	$ 30,000

There will be a deduction in the determination of Taxable Income equal to one-half of this inclusion or $15,000.

Net Rental Income

The required calculations here are as follows:

Revenues ($34,000 + $42,000 + $26,000)	$102,000
Recapture On Property A (Note 1)	138,000
Expenses Other Than CCA	
($29,000 + $37,000 + $23,000)	(89,000)
CCA (Note 1)	(38,240)
Net Rental Income	$112,760

Note 1   CCA on the rental properties would be calculated as follows:

	Property A	Property B	Property C
UCC On January 1	$422,000	$571,000	$385,000
Dispositions - Capital Cost	(560,000)	N/A	N/A
Subtotal	($138,000)	$571,000	$385,000
Recapture	138,000	N/A	N/A
Balance Subject To CCA	Nil	$571,000	$385,000
Rate	N/A	4%	4%
CCA	Nil	$ 22,840	$ 15,400

The total 2013 CCA would be $38,240 ($22,840 + $15,400).

RRSP Deduction
Since we are assuming that Ahmed's 2012 Earned Income is equal to his 2013 Earned Income, the required figure is calculated as follows:

Employment Income	$ 30,000
Net Rental Income	112,760
2012 Earned Income (Assumed To Be Equal To 2013)	$142,760

The maximum deductible spousal RRSP contribution for 2013 would be the lesser of $25,697 [(18%)($142,760)] and the 2013 RRSP Dollar Limit of $23,820. Using the lesser figure, the maximum deductible contribution would be $23,820.

Part B - Net Income For Tax Purposes
While the employment income and rental income figures from Part A are components of Net Income For Tax Purposes, other figures are needed to complete this Part B calculation.

Taxable Capital Gains
There will be a taxable capital gain on the sale of the shares, calculated as follows:

Proceeds Of Disposition [(5,000)($23)]	$115,000
Adjusted Cost Base [(5,000)($21)]	(105,000)
Capital Gain	$ 10,000
Inclusion Rate	1/2
Taxable Capital Gain	$ 5,000

In addition, there will be a capital gain on the sale of Property A, calculated as follows:

	Land	Building
Proceeds Of Disposition	$340,000	$620,000
Adjusted Cost Base/Capital Cost	(100,000)	(560,000)
Capital Gain	$240,000	$ 60,000

The total capital gain is $300,000 ($240,000 + $60,000). However, as the total proceeds were not collected in the year of sale, he can reduce his income inclusion through the use of a reserve.

Total Capital Gain ($240,000 + $60,000)	$300,000
Reserve - Lesser Of:	
• [($300,000)($864,000 ÷ $960,000)] = $270,000	
• [($300,000)(20%)(4 - 0)] = $240,000	(240,000)
Capital Gain	$ 60,000
Inclusion Rate	1/2
Taxable Capital Gain For 2013	$ 30,000

Minimum RRIF Withdrawal

For individuals under the age of 79, the minimum RRIF withdrawal can be based on dividing the fair market value of the assets in the plan at the beginning of the year by the number 90, less the registrant's age. However, the registrant can also base this calculation on the age of his spouse and, if the spouse is younger, this will minimize the required withdrawal. As Adrianna is aged 66, the minimum withdrawal would be $52,083 [$1,250,000 ÷ (90 - 66)].

Pension Income Splitting

The election to split CPP benefits is provided for in the Canada Pension Plan regulations and results in an actual split of the payments. The ITA 60.03 legislation allows certain other types of pension income to be split. Both payments of RPPs and withdrawals from RRIFs qualify for this split which is implemented solely on the tax returns. The total qualifying pension income for Ahmed is $138,083 ($86,000 + $52,083), one-half of which is $69,042.

Net Income For Tax Purposes

Based on the preceding calculations and the Other Information provided in the problem, Ahmed's 2013 minimum Net Income For Tax Purposes can be calculated as follows:

Employment Income - Part A	$ 30,000
Net Rental Income - Part A	112,760
Spousal RRSP Deduction - Part A	(23,820)
RPP Receipts (Pension Split)	86,000
CPP Receipts After Election To Split With Wife	5,500
Taxable Capital Gain - Option Shares	5,000
Taxable Capital Gain - Rental Property	30,000
Minimum RRIF Withdrawal (Pension Split)	52,083
Interest From Canadian Sources	18,000
Eligible Dividends Received	2,200
Gross Up [(38%)($2,200)]	836
Foreign Source Interest (100 Percent)	3,000
Net Income For Tax Purposes Before Pension Split	$321,559
Income Allocated To Wife [(1/2)($86,000 + $52,083)]	(69,042)
Net Income For Tax Purposes	$252,517

Part B - Taxable Income

Ahmed's Taxable Income would be calculated as follows:

Net Income For Tax Purposes	$252,517
Stock Option Deduction - Part A	(15,000)
Taxable Income	$237,517

Part B - Tax Payable

As the problem requires the minimum Tax Payable, Ahmed has claimed the credits for his son, the medical expenses and charitable donations. These could have been claimed by Adrianna. The required calculations are as follows:

Tax On First $135,054		$28,580
Tax On Next $102,463 ($237,517 - $135,054) At 29 Percent		29,714
Tax Before Credits		$58,294
Tax Credits:		
Basic Personal Amount	($11,038)	
Spousal (Note 2)	Nil	
Age (Net Income Too High)	Nil	
Caregiver Including FCA - Son	(6,530)	
Canada Employment (Stock Option Benefit)	(1,117)	
Pension Income	(2,000)	
Transfer Of Disability From Son	(7,697)	
Medical Expenses (Note 3)	(13,248)	
Total Credit Base	($41,630)	
Rate	15%	(6,245)
Charitable Donations		
[(15%)($200) + (29%)($4,000 - $200)]		(1,132)
Dividend Tax Credit On Eligible Dividends [(6/11)($836)]		(456)
Foreign Tax Credit (Foreign Tax Withheld < 15%)		(300)
Federal Tax Payable		$50,161

Note 2 While Adrianna has only $6,550 of OAS and the $5,500 in CPP benefits in her name, the added amounts resulting from the pension income splitting of more than $69,000 will be more than enough to eliminate the spousal tax credit. In addition, this additional income will use up all of her tax credits, preventing any transfers to Ahmed.

Note 3 The base for the medical expense tax credit is calculated as follows:

Ahmed And Adrianna ($2,500 + $3,100)		$5,600
Lesser Of:		
• [(3%)($252,517)] = $7,576		
• 2013 Threshold Amount = $2,152		(2,152)
Subtotal		$ 3,448
Son's Medical Expenses	$9,800	
Reduced By The Lesser Of:		
• $2,152		
• [(3%)(Nil)] = Nil	Nil	9,800
Allowable Amount Of Medical Expenses		$13,248

Part C - Pension Income Splitting

Given Ahmed's high Taxable Income, even after pension splitting, more than $100,000 is being taxed at the maximum 29 percent federal rate. Despite splitting the maximum amount of pension income, none of Adrianna's income is taxed at higher than 22 percent federally.

As a result, maximum pension income splitting appears to be advantageous if only federal tax rates are considered.

What should also be considered is the effect of the pension income splitting on the OAS clawback for Adrianna and the effect of provincial income taxes on both Ahmed and Adrianna. The effect of the OAS clawback and provincial taxes could make it more advantageous to reduce the amount of income splitting so that Adrianna's Net Income For Tax Purposes is below the OAS clawback income threshold.

While the ability to claim more medical expenses could be a factor in some pension income splitting analyses, it would have very little influence in this case given the high levels of Net Income involved.

Chapter 10 Learning Objectives

After completing Chapter 10, you should be able to:

1. Explain the general procedures used to provide tax deferral on retirement saving (paragraph [P hereafter] 10-1 through 10-16).

2. Describe the difference between a defined benefit pension plan and a defined contribution (a.k.a. money purchase) pension plan (P 10-17 through 10-19).

3. Describe the basic operation of RRSPs (P 10-20 through 10-40).

4. Understand the terms: RRSP Deduction Limit, Unused RRSP Deduction Room and RRSP Dollar Limit (P 10-41 through 10-48).

5. Calculate Earned Income for RRSP purposes (P 10-49 through 10-51).

6. Explain the concepts underlying Pension Adjustments (PAs) (P 10-52 through 10-63).

7. Explain the concepts underlying Past Service Pension Adjustments (PSPAs) (P 10-64 through 10-69).

8. Explain the concepts underlying Pension Adjustment Reversals (PARs) (P 10-70 through 10-74).

9. Calculate an individual's maximum RRSP deduction and Unused RRSP Deduction Room (P 10-75).

10. Apply the tax treatment for undeducted RRSP contributions (P 10-76 and 10-77).

11. Determine whether an individual has made "excess" contributions to an RRSP and identify associated tax planning issues including the use of TFSAs (P 10-78 through 10-85).

12. Recall the tax treatment of RRSP and RRIF administration fees (P 10-86).

13. Apply the provisions relating to RRSP withdrawals and voluntary conversions of RRSPs (P 10-87 through 10-94).

14. Apply the provisions relating to RRSP terminations due to the age limitation (P 10-95 through 10-96).

15. Apply the provisions associated with spousal RRSPs and identify associated tax planning issues (P 10-97 through 10-105).

16. Describe and apply the provisions of the Home Buyers' Plan (P 10-106 through 10-116).

17. Describe and apply the provisions of the Lifelong Learning Plan (P 10-117 through 10-125).

18. Apply the RRSP provisions relating to departure from Canada and death of the registrant (P 10-126 through 10-141).

19. Explain the general provisions associated with Registered Pension Plans (RPPs) (P 10-142 through 10-157).

20. Describe, in general terms, Pooled Registered Pension Plans (PRPPs) (P 10-158 through 10-162).

21. Describe the basic operation of RRIFs and the role that RRIFs play in tax planning for retirement (P 10-163 through 10-181).

22. Explain the general rules for Deferred Profit Sharing Plans (P 10-182 through 10-187).

23. Describe, in general terms, Profit Sharing Plans (P 10-188 and 10-191).

24. Describe the tax free transfers that can be made between various types of plans (P 10-192 and 10-193).

25. Apply the special rules associated with RRSP contributions and retiring allowances (P 10-194 and 10-195).

26. Explain the general provisions related to Retirement Compensation Arrangements (P 10-196 through 10-205).

27. Describe Salary Deferral Arrangements (P 10-206 through 10-213).

CHAPTER 11

How To Work Through Chapter 11

We recommend the following approach in dealing with the material in this Chapter:

Taxable Income Introduction And Overview
❏ Read paragraph 11-1 to 11-7 (in the textbook).

Lump-Sum Payments
❏ Read paragraph 11-8 to 11-13.

Loss Carry Over Provisions, Listed Personal Property Losses
❏ Read paragraph 11-14 to 11-35.
❏ Do Exercise Eleven-1 (in the textbook) and check the solution on page S-239 in this Study Guide.

Non-Capital Losses
❏ Read paragraph 11-36 to 11-38.
❏ Do Exercise Eleven-2 and check the solution in this Study Guide.
❏ Read paragraph 11-39 to 11-40.

Net Capital Losses (Including Special Rules At Death)
❏ Read paragraph 11-41 to 11-49.
❏ Do Exercise Eleven-3 and check the solution in this Study Guide.
❏ Read paragraph 11-50 to 11-54.
❏ Do Exercise Eleven-4 and check the solution in this Study Guide.

Allowable Business Investment Losses (ABILs)
❏ Read paragraph 11-55 to 11-62.
❏ Do Exercise Eleven-5 and check the solution in this Study Guide.
❏ Do Self Study Problem Eleven-1 at the end of the textbook chapter on page 577 and check the solution in this Study Guide.

Farm Losses
❏ Read paragraph 11-63 to 11-67.
❏ Do Exercise Eleven-6 and check the solution in this Study Guide.
❏ Do Self Study Problem Eleven-2 and check the solution in this Study Guide.

Lifetime Capital Gains Deduction
❏ Read paragraph 11-68 to 11-89.
❏ Do Exercise Eleven-7 and check the solution in this Study Guide.
❏ Read paragraph 11-90 to 11-97.
❏ Do Exercise Eleven-8 and check the solution in this Study Guide.
❏ Do Self Study Problem Eleven-3 and check the solution in this Study Guide.

Ordering Of Deductions And Losses
❏ Read paragraph 11-98 to 11-107.
❏ Do Exercise Eleven-9 and check the solution in this Study Guide.

Tax On Split Income (Kiddie Tax)
❏ Read paragraph 11-108 to 11-124.
❏ Do Exercise Eleven-10 and check the solution in this Study Guide.

Transfer Of Dividends To A Spouse Or Common-Law Partner
❏ Read paragraph 11-125.
❏ Do Exercise Eleven-11 and check the solution in this Study Guide.
❏ Do Self Study Problems Eleven-4 and Eleven-5 and check the solutions in this Study Guide.

Charitable Donations Credit - Gifts Of Capital Property
❏ Read paragraph 11-126 to 11-142.
❏ Do Exercise Eleven-12 and check the solution in this Study Guide.
❏ Read paragraph 11-143 to 11-145.
❏ Do Exercise Eleven-13 and check the solution in this Study Guide.
❏ Read paragraph 11-146 to 11-150.

Foreign Tax Credits Revisited
❏ Read paragraph 11-151 to 11-162.
❏ Do Exercise Eleven-14 and check the solution in this Study Guide.

Alternative Minimum Tax (AMT) And Read paragraph 11-161 to 11-175.
❏ Read paragraph 11-163 to 11-176.
❏ Do Exercise Eleven-15 and check the solution in this Study Guide.
❏ Do Self Study Problem Eleven-6 and check the solution in this Study Guide.

Comprehensive Tax Payable
❏ Read paragraph 11-177.
❏ Do Self Study Problems Eleven-7 to Eleven-11 and check the solutions in this Study Guide.

Sample Personal Tax Return For Chapter 11
❏ Read the Sample Personal Tax Return For Chapter 11 found on page S-228 to S-235 of this Study Guide. The complete sample tax returns are available on the Student CD-ROM included with the text in two formats, a T1 ProFile return file and a .PDF file. To view the files, access your Student CD-ROM and under the heading "Textbook Support Files", select the option "Tax Return Files".

Shortly after the first filing version of the 2013 Intuit ProFile software is available in January, 2014, the updated 2013 sample tax returns and updated Tax Software Problems will be available at:

www.pearsoncanada.ca/byrdchen/ctp2014

Tax Software Self Study Problem
❏ You may wish to review the Suggestions For Working With ProFile Software found on page S-53 to S-55 of this Study Guide.
❏ Do Tax Software Self Study Problem - Chapter 11 using the ProFile T1 Software. The Self Study Case is on page S-236 to S-239 of this Study Guide. The condensed solution is on page S-268 to S-270 of this Study Guide. The complete tax return is available on the Student CD-ROM included with the text in two formats, a T1 ProFile return file and a .PDF file.

To Complete This Chapter

❑ Review the Key Terms Used In This Chapter on page 576. Consult the Glossary for the meaning of any key terms you do not know.

❑ Review the Glossary Flashcards and complete the Key Terms Self-Test for the Chapter. These features can be found in two places, on your Student CD-ROM under the heading "Key Term Practice" and on the web site.

❑ Review the Learning Objectives of the Chapter found on page S-271 of this Study Guide.

❑ As a review, we recommend that you view the PowerPoint Slides for Chapter 11 that are on your Student CD-ROM. The PowerPoint Viewer program can be installed from the Student CD-ROM.

Practice Examination

❑ Write the Practice Examination for Chapter 11 that is on your Student CD-ROM. Mark your examination using the Practice Examination Solution that is also on your Student CD-ROM.

Sample Personal Tax Return For Chapter 11

The following example contains two scenarios (1) a single return without pension income splitting and (2) the returns of both spouses with pension income splitting. The T1 individual income tax returns have been completed using the ProFile T1 Personal Income Tax Program for 2012 tax returns from Intuit Canada. As software for 2013 is not yet available, this example contains 2012 rates and credits.

The updated 2013 filing version of the ProFile software will be available in January, 2014. Non-filing versions will be available prior to that date. They will include a number of 2013 draft forms that have not yet been updated. On installation, the program should be set to automatically check for updates, so non-filing versions may be installed automatically. Shortly after the first filing version is available, the updated 2013 version of this sample return will be available on the textbook web site at:

www.pearsoncanada.ca/byrdchen/ctp2014

For comparison purposes, you might find it useful to review the Chapter 4 version of this example. The Chapter 4 version also contains more information on how to view the files.

In the following example, the relevant T1 schedule or ProFile form name is provided in square brackets to make it easier for users to find where the information is input.

Sample Files On Student CD-ROM

The complete sample tax returns are available on the Student CD-ROM included with this book in two versions, a T1 ProFile return file and a .PDF file.

To View The Tax Return Files

Under the heading "Textbook Support Files" is the option to view "Tax Return Files". Select this option and you will see two drop-down lists.

• To view the T4, T4A and T5, select "Chapter 11 - T4_T4A_T5" from the the PDF drop-down list.

• To view the ProFile file, go to the ProFile drop-down list and select the file "Sample - Chapter 11 Without Split" or "Sample - Chapter 11 With Split".

• To view the .PDF file of the tax returns, go to the PDF drop-down list and select the file "PDF Sample - Chapter 11 Without Split" or "PDF Sample - Chapter 11 With Split".

Sample Problem Data

DISCLAIMER: All characters appearing in this example are fictitious. Any resemblance to real persons, living or dead, is purely coincidental.

George Pilot (SIN 527-000-145) is a married, semi-retired air force pilot living in Banff, Alberta. His wife, Deborah (SIN 130-692-544) was blinded three years ago when she fell while rock climbing.

They have been your clients for many years. George was born on February 24, 1961 and Deborah was born on April 10, 1965. They are both Canadian citizens.

After some discussion with George and Deborah, you confirm that they have never owned any foreign property. As he has for many years, George authorizes the CRA to provide information to Elections Canada and he authorizes you to e-file his return. They are currently living at 69 BBB Street in Banff, Alberta T9Z 0C0. Their home phone number is (111) 111-1111.

George and Deborah have three children:

- Bryan (SIN 527-000-947) was born on March 12, 2005 and had no income during the year.

- Janice (SIN 527-000-269) was born on June 6, 1999 and is in high school. She had income from babysitting totalling $400 during 2012.

- Willa (SIN 527-000-228) was born on January 22, 1993 and is attending university in Edmonton. Willa had Net Income of $3,300 during 2012.

George loves flying and was hired in February to fly fire bombers June 1 to September 30 for the provincial forest service fire control squad located in Banff. George informs you that on February 12, 2012, he received $2 million from his mother's estate. Using some of these funds, George bought a house in Banff. The remainder of the funds were invested with his stockbroker, $$$$ Inc.

Deborah, a voice teacher, adapted to her blindness quickly and required no outside help to take care of the family last year or for the first eight months of 2012. She decided to move temporarily to Edmonton with Willa to attend the music program at the University of Alberta.

During 2012, Deborah made a $50,000 loan to her brother, Andrew, who used the funds to expand his business. On December 15, 2012, Andrew paid her interest of $1,500 and principal of $5,000. Also during 2012, Deborah gave private voice lessons and earned a total of $3,200 in teaching fees. Deborah had no other income during the year. [S2 for Deborah's income in Part A. In Part B, Deborah's income is on S4 and T2125.]

George brings you the following receipts and documents:

1. A T4, T4A and a T5 (included on the Student CD - see "Chapter 11 - T4_T4A_T5" from the the PDF drop-down list)).

2. A T2202A "Tuition And Education Amounts Certificate" for himself from Athabasca University. It showed he was a part time student for 6 months and paid $591 in tuition for 2012. [T2202]

3. A receipt for $1,000 from the Canadian Wildlife Federation dated December 3, 2012. [Donations]

4. A statement from the Banff Dental Clinic that he paid a total of $1,650 during 2012. This consisted of $850 for himself on November 24, and $200 each for Deborah, Bryan, Willa and Janice on December 15. [Medical]

5. One receipt for Bryan for a one week hockey camp in Edmonton. The registration fee of $650 includes $182 for accommodation and $193 for meals. A second receipt for Bryan of $200 for membership in the co-ed soccer club. This enabled Bryan to participate in the club's weekly games for four months of the year. [Dependants]

6. One receipt for Janice for an art appreciation and sculpture workshop course in Banff. The course is for 10 Saturdays in the fall and cost $600. [Dependants]

7. Twelve monthly bus passes that were purchased during 2012 by Janice for $30 per month. [OtherCredits]

8. An agreement of purchase and sale for a house at 69 BBB St. in Banff. The purchase price was $800,000 and the invoice for legal fees totalled $1,200. The deal closed March 31, 2012. George and his family had been living in a rented townhouse for the last 5 years. Prior to that George had owned a house, but it went to his ex-wife in the divorce settlement. Deborah has never owned a principal residence. [OtherCredits for the First Time Home Buyers' Credit.]

9. An instalment statement for 2012 that showed that George had paid the CRA instalments of $1,500 on September 15 and December 15 ($3,000 in total). These were the instalments requested by the CRA for the year due to his self-employed income in the previous year. [OtherCredits]

10. A T2202A "Tuition And Education Amounts Certificate" for Deborah from the University of Alberta. It showed she was a full time student for 4 months and paid $2,600 in tuition for 2012. [S2 in Part A, T2202 in Part B.]

11. A T2202A "Tuition And Education Amounts Certificate" for Willa from the University of Alberta. It showed she was a full time student for 8 months and paid $5,200 in tuition for 2012. She had signed the certificate authorizing the transfer of all education related amounts to her father. [Dependant]

12. His 2011 Notice of Assessment that shows that his 2012 RRSP Deduction Limit is $13,979. He has no undeducted RRSP contributions from previous years. [RRSP]

13. A contribution receipt to a spousal RRSP (George contributed to Deborah's RRSP) for $2,000 from $$$$ Inc. dated February 20, 2013. [RRSP]

14. A receipt for $2,000 from George's 40 year old sister, Shirley Burns (SIN 527-000-582) for child care. She took care of Bryan after school during 2012 while Deborah was in Edmonton. [T778]

15. A receipt for Janice, an accomplished trombone player, from the Peak Music Camp in Whistler, B.C. The receipt for $1,600 was for two weeks of intensive music instruction at the camp. This fee also included $400 in accommodations and $325 for meals. [T778]

16. A receipt for $2,148 from the Mountain Moving Company dated April 1, 2012. The invoice showed that the fee was charged to pack and move George's household effects from 123 CCC Avenue, Calgary to his new house in Banff, a total of 125 kilometers. George's new home is 5 kilometers from the Alberta Fire And Brimstone Control offices. George and his family made the move in his truck. Since George has no travel receipts, he agrees that you should use the simplified method to calculate his moving costs. [T1M]

17. George brings in TFSA Statements for himself, Deborah and Willa. They show that he made a $5,000 contribution to each TFSA on February 20, 2012. It also shows that Willa withdrew $3,000 from her TFSA on December 15, 2012.

Other Information

During your discussion with George, you note the following information:

1. On January 8, 2012, George sold his 1971 Ford Mustang for $50,000. The car was driven only on sunny Sunday afternoons. Its original price in 1996 was $6,000, and George reconditioned it over the years at a cost of $12,000. [S3Details]

2. At the beginning of 2012, George has a net capital loss carry forward of $2,580 [(1/2)($5,160)] from 2010. [LossNetCap]

3. During 2012, he paid $6,000 in spousal support to his ex-wife, Marilyn (SIN 527-000-103), pursuant to a written agreement. [Support payments]

4. For the last two years, in the winter months, George gives private flying lessons. His statement of income of this unincorporated business, Pilot's Flying School, for the fiscal year ended December 31, 2012 is as follows:

Pilot's Flying School

Lesson fees	$40,200
Plane rentals	$ 9,600
Business meals and entertainment	3,250
Licenses and fees	1,650
Office expenses	550
Accounting fees	300
Amortization of laptop computer and software	900
Total expenses	$ 16,250
Net Income	$ 23,950

On April 15, 2012, George purchased a laptop computer and various software that will be used solely for his Flying School. The laptop cost $1,900 and the software costs totalled $800. Prior to this, George had not been using a computer for business purposes. [T2125]

5. George owns a commercial property at 999 JJJ Avenue, Edmonton, Alberta T9Z 0C0. The property was 10 years old when he purchased it on February 15, 2010 for $600,000 of which $160,000 was allocated to the land. Shortly after George purchased the building, the major tenant went bankrupt and he had rental losses for 2010 and 2011. No capital additions were made since the building's acquisition. The financial information for the property, for the year ended December 31, 2012, is as follows [Rental]:

Rental income	$46,700
Mortgage interest	$19,500
Maintenance and repairs	5,100
Management and administration fees	8,200
Legal fees	1,000
Property taxes	11,750
Total expenses	$45,550
Net Income before amortization	$ 1,150

Required:

A. Complete George's 2012 tax return, assuming he does not elect to pension income split and Deborah does not file a tax return. Include in your notes in his file any tax planning points you should discuss with him. Ignore any GST implications.

B. Calculate the maximum tax savings that are available if George elects to split his pension income with Deborah.

Notes To The Chapter 11 Return

Part A - Only George Is Filing A Return With No Pension Splitting

1. As in this version of the problem, Deborah has interest income of $1,500 and professional fees of $3,200, the spousal credit base is decreased by this amount on Schedule 2. Note that the principal repayment of $5,000 is not income. Deborah's disability credit has been transferred to George, as well as all of her education related tax credits since they

total less than $5,000.

2. Inheritances are not taxable.

3. Since Willa is over 17 years of age, her medical expenses are reduced by 3 percent of her Net Income For Tax Purposes. Willa's education related credits total more than $5,000. As a result, her transfer to George is limited to the $5,000 maximum. Only Willa can claim the unused credits in the future. Willa should file a return in order to receive the GST credit and to keep track of her education related credits carry forward.

4. George is not eligible for the refundable medical expense supplement or the working income benefit in this version of the example as his income is too high. Given 3 percent of his Net Income is greater than the medical expense threshold, the only allowable medical expenses are those of Willa.

5. Both the hockey camp and the soccer club receipts qualify for the child fitness credit. However, since accommodation and meals do not qualify for the credit, the total credit base is $475 ($650 - $182 - $193 + $200), which is less than the annual maximum of $500. Although the hockey camp could qualify as child care costs, it would be limited to $100 (the weekly maximum), as opposed to the $275 that is eligible for the fitness credit.

6. The art course qualifies for the children's arts credit. The credit base is limited to the annual maximum of $500.

7. The Home Buyers' Tax Credit of $750 [(15%)($5,000)] is available since George had been living in a rented town house for five years and neither he nor Deborah had another principal residence.

9. The Industry Code must be chosen from the list near the top right corner of the T2125. The appropriate choice is 611690, "All Other Schools And Instruction".

8. On the T2125, the non-deductible portion of business meals and entertainment of $1,625 (50% of $3,250) has been excluded. The laptop computer has been allocated to CCA Class 50 (55 percent). The software has been allocated to CCA Class 12 (100 percent).

9. George has claimed his net capital loss carry forward of $2,580 as his taxable capital gains were well in excess of this amount.

10. Since Deborah was in full time attendance at the University of Alberta, George could have deducted child care costs of up to $3,200 [(2)($100)(16 weeks)]. The deduction for child care costs is limited to $100 per week for overnight camp fees. Since there does not appear to be a physical activity component at the music camp, none of the fees would be eligible for the fitness credit. The camp fees would likely be eligible for the children's arts credit, but the maximum credit of $500 has already been claimed for Janice. The $2,000 paid to Shirley Burns is totally deductible. This results in maximum deductible child care costs of $2,200.

11. Form T1M, Claim For Moving Expenses should be filled out to calculate the deductible moving expenses. George cannot deduct the legal fees related to the purchase of his new home because he had been living in a rented townhouse in Calgary. On Form T1M, since the "Simplified Method" box is checked, the program calculates the allowable deduction for milage using the 2012 Alberta rate on Line 2.

12. Since the rental property has been showing a loss since its acquisition, no CCA could have been taken prior to 2012. As a result, the beginning of the year UCC of the building will be George's original allocation of $440,000 ($600,000 - $160,000 land cost). The CCA for 2012 is limited to $1,150, the amount that reduces his rental income to nil.

13. If he has sufficient funds, George should contribute the maximum deductible for 2013 of $17,098 [see RRSPLimit form] to a spousal RRSP as soon as possible. Since George is already getting a pension and Deborah appears to have little income, a spousal RRSP

would offer more opportunity for future income splitting. Although the pension income splitting legislation allows for some flexibility, the maximum split is 50 percent. With a spousal RRSP, Deborah can be taxed on 100 percent of the funds from her RRSP.

14. George should consider opening RESPs for Bryan and Janice if he has not already done so. How much he should contribute will depend on many factors (see the text), but it is probably advisable that he contribute enough to take advantage of the Canada Education Savings Plan each year if he has sufficient funds.

15. Deborah has created some RRSP contribution room with her professional income. George should consider whether Deborah should contribute to her own RRSP. Funds for George's RRSP and the RESPs should probably have priority given George's higher tax bracket and the Canada Education Savings Plan.

16. Since TFSA contributions are not deductible and withdrawals are not taxable, the TFSAs will not have an effect on any of the tax returns. George should review the TFSAs with a view to contributing the maximum on an ongoing basis and replacing any withdrawals in the following calendar year.

Part B - Tax Savings With Pension Splitting

The notes to Part A with no pension income splitting are also relevant in this scenario.

In creating Deborah's tax return, the following forms and schedules were filled in:

- T2202 - Tuition slips
- T2125 - Statement of Business or Professional Activities
- T1032 - Joint Election To Split Income (originated from George's return)
- Schedule 4 - Statement of Investment Income

Deborah claims the medical expenses for all the family except Willa. Since 3 percent of Deborah's Net Income is less than the threshold, this enables her to make a claim where George cannot. Willa's medical expenses could have been claimed by Deborah as well, but since she is getting a refund while George must pay, it is more advantageous to have George claim Willa's medical expenses.

In addition, although we do not cover provincial tax rules in the text, if you examine Deborah's Alberta tax credits [AB428], you will see that she does not utilize all of her non-refundable Alberta tax credits. If she claims Willa's medical credit, it will not decrease her Alberta tax payable as it is already nil. Claiming Willa's medical credit will decrease George's Alberta tax payable.

The tax savings of $2,360 can be seen by comparing the Tax Summary for the couple with and without pension income splitting.

Combined Balance Owing - No Pension Splitting	$4,272
Combined Balance Owing - With Pension Splitting	(2,319)
Tax Savings	$1,953

Note that the tax savings have been decreased due to the Family Caregiver Amount. When George claims the spousal credit for Deborah in Part A, he is eligible for the Family Caregiver Amount. In Part B, Deborah can only claim the basic personal amount and the Family Caregiver Amount is not available to the family unit.

Printed Summaries

On the following pages you will find:

- for Part A - the T1 Summary for George,
- for Part B - the T1 Summary for both George and Deborah.

The complete returns for Part A and Part B can be found on the Student CD-ROM.

Pilot, George-Chap 11 Non-split   SIN: 527 000 145
Summary

Without pension income split
2012 Tax Summary (Federal)

George-Chap 11 Non-split

George-Chap 11 Non-split

Total income

Employment *	101	19,000
Old Age Security	113	
CPP/QPP benefits	114	
Other pensions	115	42,000
Split-pension amount	116	
Universal Child Care Benefit	117	
Employment Insurance	119	
Taxable dividends	120	5,796
Interest	121	532
Limited partnership	122	
RDSP	125	
Rental	126	
Taxable capital gains	127	16,000
Support payments	128	
RRSP	129	
Other	130	
Self-employment *	135	25,553
Workers' compensation and social assistance	147	
Total income	**150**	**108,881**

Net income

RPP	207	900
RRSP *	208	2,000
Split-Pension Deduction	210	
Union and professional dues	212	110
UCCB repayment	213	
Child care expenses	214	2,200
Disability supports deduction	215	
Business investment loss	217	
Moving expenses	219	2,211
Support payments	220	6,000
Carrying charges and interest	221	
CPP/QPP/PIPP *	222	1,265
Exploration and development	224	
Employment expenses	229	
Social benefits repayment	235	
Other deductions *	231	
Net income	**236**	**94,195**

Taxable income

Canadian Forces personnel	244	
Home relocation loan	248	
Security options deductions	249	
Other payments deduction	250	
Losses of other years *	251	2,580
Capital gains deduction	254	
Northern residents	255	
Additional deductions	256	
Taxable income	**260**	**91,615**

2013 Estimated — George-Chap 11 Non-split

GST/HST credit		
Child Tax Benefit		630 00
RRSP contribution limit		17,098 00

* More than one line is considered

Non-refundable tax credits

Basic personal amount	300	10,822
Age amount	301	
Spouse / eligible dependant *	303	8,122
Amount for children	367	4,382
Infirm/caregiver *	306	
CPP/QPP/PPIP/EI *	308	2,380
Volunteer firefighters' amount	362	
Canada employment amount	363	1,095
Public transit passes amount	364	360
Children's fitness amount	365	475
Children's arts amount	370	500
Home buyers/Home renovation *	369	5,000
Adoption expenses	313	
Pension income amount	314	2,000
Disability amount	316	
Transfers *	318	17,006
Interest on student loans	319	
Tuition / education	323	1,431
Medical expenses	332	101
Subtotal	**335**	**53,674**
Credit at 15%	338	8,051
Donations and gifts	349	262
Non-refundable tax credits	**350**	**8,313**

Total payable

Federal tax	404	17,414
Non-refundable tax credits	350	8,313
Dividend tax credit	425	871
Min. tax carry-over/other *	426	
Basic federal tax	**429**	**8,231**
Non resident surtax		
Foreign tax credits / other	405	
Federal tax	**406**	**8,231**
Political/inv. tax credit/other *	410	
Labour-sponsored tax credit	414	
Alternative minimum tax	417	
WITB Prepayment (RC210)	415	
Special Taxes	418	
Net federal tax	**420**	**8,231**
CPP contributions payable	421	2,530
EI self-employment	430	
Social benefits repayment	422	
Provincial/territorial tax	428	2,513
Total payable	**435**	**13,273**

Total credits

Income tax deducted *	437	6,000
QC or YT abatement *	440	
CPP/EI overpayment *	448	
Medical expense supplement	452	
WITB (Schedule 6)	453	
Other credits *	454	
GST/HST rebate	457	
Instalments	476	3,000
Provincial tax credits	479	
Total credits	**482**	**9,000**
Balance owing (refund)		4,273
Combined balance (refund)		4,273

Complete Return Available On Student CD-ROM

S - 234

Pilot, George-Chap 11 Split   SIN: 527 000 145
Summary

With pension income split
2012 Tax Summary (Federal)

Total income

		George-Chap 11 Split	Deborah
Employment *	101	19,000	
Old Age Security	113		
CPP/QPP benefits	114		
Other pensions	115	42,000	
Split-pension amount	116		21,000
Universal Child Care Benefit	117		
Employment Insurance	119		
Taxable dividends	120	5,796	
Interest	121	532	1,500
Limited partnership	122		
RDSP	125		
Rental	126		
Taxable capital gains	127	16,000	
Support payments	128		
RRSP	129		
Other	130		
Self-employment *	135	25,553	3,200
Workers' compensation and social assistance	147		
Total income	**150**	**108,881**	**25,700**

Net income

		George-Chap 11 Split	Deborah
RPP	207	900	
RRSP *	208	2,000	
Split-Pension Deduction	210	21,000	
Union and professional dues	212	110	
UCCB repayment	213		
Child care expenses	214	2,200	
Disability supports deduction	215		
Business investment loss	217		
Moving expenses	219	2,211	
Support payments	220	6,000	
Carrying charges and interest	221		
CPP/QPP/PIPP *	222	1,265	
Exploration and development	224		
Employment expenses	229		
Social benefits repayment	235		
Other deductions *	231		
Net income	**236**	**73,195**	**25,700**

Taxable income

		George-Chap 11 Split	Deborah
Canadian Forces personnel	244		
Home relocation loan	248		
Security options deductions	249		
Other payments deduction	250		
Losses of other years *	251	2,580	
Capital gains deduction	254		
Northern residents	255		
Additional deductions	256		
Taxable income	**260**	**70,615**	**25,700**

2013 Estimated

	George-Chap 11 Split	Deborah
GST/HST credit		
Child Tax Benefit	630 00	
RRSP contribution limit	17,098 00	576

* More than one line is considered

Non-refundable tax credits

		George-Chap 11 Split	Deborah
Basic personal amount	300	10,822	10,822
Age amount	301		
Spouse / eligible dependant *	303		
Amount for children	367	4,382	
Infirm/caregiver *	306		
CPP/QPP/PPIP/EI *	308	2,380	
Volunteer firefighters' amount	362		
Canada employment amount	363	1,095	
Public transit passes amount	364	360	
Children's fitness amount	365	475	
Children's arts amount	370	500	
Home buyers/Home renovation *	369	5,000	
Adoption expenses	313		
Pension income amount	314	2,000	2,000
Disability amount	316		7,546
Transfers *	318	5,000	
Interest on student loans	319		
Tuition / education	323	1,431	4,460
Medical expenses	332	101	679
Subtotal	**335**	**33,546**	**25,507**
Credit at 15%	338	5,032	3,826
Donations and gifts	349	262	
Non-refundable tax credits	**350**	**5,294**	**3,826**

Total payable

		George-Chap 11 Split	Deborah
Federal tax	404	12,546	3,855
Non-refundable tax credits	350	5,294	3,826
Dividend tax credit	425	871	
Min. tax carry-over/other *	426		
Basic federal tax	**429**	**6,381**	**29**
Non resident surtax			
Foreign tax credits / other	405		
Federal tax	**406**	**6,381**	**29**
Political/inv. tax credit/other *	410		
Labour-sponsored tax credit	414		
Alternative minimum tax	417		
WITB Prepayment (RC210)	415		
Special Taxes	418		
Net federal tax	**420**	**6,381**	**29**
CPP contributions payable	421	2,530	
EI self-employment	430		
Social benefits repayment	422		
Provincial/territorial tax	428	2,380	
Total payable	**435**	**11,291**	**29**

Total credits

		George-Chap 11 Split	Deborah
Income tax deducted *	437	4,000	2,000
QC or YT abatement *	440		
CPP/EI overpayment *	448		
Medical expense supplement	452		
WITB (Schedule 6)	453		
Other credits *	454		
GST/HST rebate	457		
Instalments	476	3,000	
Provincial tax credits	479		
Total credits	**482**	**7,000**	**2,000**
Balance owing (refund)		4,291	(1,971)
Combined balance (refund)		2,320	

Complete Return Available On Student CD-ROM

S - 235

Tax Software Self Study Problem - Chapter 11

DISCLAIMER: All characters appearing in this problem are fictitious. Any resemblance to real persons, living or dead, is purely coincidental.

Note This Tax Software Self Study Problem is an expansion of the Chapter 4 version. The following problem contains 2012 (not 2013) information as software for 2013 is not yet available. Shortly after the first filing version of the 2013 Intuit ProFile software is available in January, 2014, the updated 2013 version of this problem will be available on the textbook web site at:

www.pearsoncanada.ca/byrdchen/ctp2014

Ms. Eleanor Victoria's husband died two years ago. After her husband died, she moved from her house in Prince George, B.C., to a rented house in Victoria, B.C.

Ms. Victoria's widowed mother, Marjorie Vancouver lives with Ms. Victoria and takes care of the house, Ms. Victoria's younger daughter, Amy, and all of the household cooking. In addition to OAS benefits, Marjorie has a small income from her deceased husband's life insurance policy. She has never filed a tax return.

Diane Victoria, Eleanor's older daughter, is studying psychology at McGill University in Montreal. Her field is addiction research with a special emphasis on gambling. She does volunteer work at a gambling addiction treatment centre in Montreal in the summers. As Eleanor has paid for her tuition and living costs, Diane has agreed that any credits available should be transferred to her mother.

Diane has decided not to file a tax return this year as she is too busy with her studies and volunteer work. Her income was earned driving for a client of the addiction treatment centre who had lost his licence after being charged with impaired driving.

Late in December, 2012, Eleanor was notified that she had inherited $500,000 from an aunt. Eleanor loves her work and though she plans to travel more, she has no plans to retire.

Information concerning Ms. Victoria for 2012 is given on the following pages.

Required:

A. Prepare the 2012 income tax return of Eleanor Victoria using the ProFile tax software program. List any assumptions you have made, and any notes and tax planning issues you feel should be placed in the file.

B. Calculate the maximum deductible contribution Ms. Victoria can make to her RRSP for the 2013 taxation year. What advice would you give Ms. Victoria concerning the various deferred savings plans available to her given the funds from her inheritance?

Personal Information	
Title	Ms.
First Name	Eleanor
Last Name	Victoria
SIN	527-000-087
Date of birth (Y/M/D)	1964-05-15
Marital Status	Widowed
Canadian citizen?	Yes
Provide information to Elections Canada?	Yes
Own foreign property of more than $100,000 Canadian?	No

Taxpayer's Address

111 VVV Street Victoria, B.C. V4H 3W4	
Phone number (250) 111-1111	

Dependants	Child 1	Child 2	Mother
First Name	Diane	Amy	Marjorie
Last Name	Victoria	Victoria	Vancouver
SIN	527-000-293	None	527-000-483
Date of birth (Y/M/D)	1992-05-14	2000-10-11	1931-05-21
Net income	$2,300	Nil	$8,000

T2202A - (Diane)	Box	Amount
Tuition fees - for Diane Victoria (daughter)	A	7,000
Number of months in school - part-time	B	2
Number of months in school - full-time	C	8

T4	Box	Amount
Issuer - 1750 Canada Inc.		
Employment income	14	60,201.80
Employee's CPP contributions	16	2,306.70
Employee's EI premiums	18	839.97
RPP contributions	20	2,406.16
Pension adjustment	52	7,829.00
Income tax deducted	22	11,408.00
Union dues	44	748.59
Charitable donations	46	175.00

Eleanor and her family had the following medical expenses, all of which Eleanor paid for:

Patient	(Y/M/D)	Medical Expenses	Description	Am't
Eleanor	2012-08-15	Grace Hospital	Ambulance charge	392
Eleanor	2012-08-18	Paramed Home Health	Nursing care	1,350
Marjorie	2012-05-20	Dr. Zhang (Optometrist)	Contact lenses	110
Marjorie	2012-07-06	Pharmacy	Prescription	75
Diane	2012-09-01	Dr. Glassman	Physiotherapist	100
Amy	2012-05-11	Walk Right Foot Clinic	Orthotics	450
Amy	2012-01-23	Dr. Tamo	Dental	1,120

Donor	Charitable Donation Receipts	Am't
Eleanor	Heart and Stroke	375
Eleanor	Terry Fox Foundation	50
Diane	Addiction Research Council of Canada	100

T3	Box	Amount
Issuer - Global Strategy Financial		
Foreign country - United States		
Capital gains	21	982.22
Foreign non-business income	25	310.94

T4A	Box	Amount
Issuer - 3601 Canada Inc. (Survivor benefit from husband)		
Pension	16	22,249.44
Income tax deducted	22	3,510.78

T4A(P)	Box	Amount
Survivor benefit	15	4,823.28
Income tax deducted	22	Nil

T5	Box	Slip 1	Slip 2
Issuer		Scotia Bank	Bank of Montreal
Actual amount of eligible dividends	24		1,603.00
Taxable amount of eligible dividends	25		2,212.14
Interest from Canadian sources	13	509.45	

RRSP information	(Y/M/D)	Amount
Issuer of receipt - Scotia Bank	2013-02-10	2,620.00
Unused deduction room at the end of 2011		1,665.00
Earned income for 2011		38,873.00
Pension adjustment for 2011		4,376.00

Child	Child Care Expenses	No. of weeks	Amount
Amy	Croft Computer Camp (14 days overnight)	2	1,000
Amy	Y Day Camp (July)	3	400

Neither of the camps would issue a receipt that qualified for either the child fitness credit or the children's arts credit.

Eleanor did not sell her house in Prince George when she moved to Victoria as it was her intention to move back into it within three years. It has been rented on a month-to-month lease since November, 2011. She claimed a rental loss of $4,250 in 2011.

Real Estate Rental	Amount
Address - 222 PPP Street, Prince George, B.C. V4H 3W4	
Gross rents (12 months for 2012)	15,600.00
Property taxes	2,190.00
Insurance	1,093.27
Interest on mortgage	5,377.58
Payment on principal	3,688.95
Plumbing repairs	290.94
Snow plow annual contract	300.00
Lawyer's fees for new lease	172.54
Hydro (during vacancy)	288.34
Building purchased October 1, 2009 for $168,900 - UCC beginning of year	168,900.00
Washer/dryer purchased May 9, 2011 for $921 - UCC beginning of year	921.00
Stove and refrigerator purchased August 17, 2012	1,500.00

Solution to Chapter Eleven Exercises

Exercise Eleven - 1 Solution
Mr. Smothers will have a listed personal property loss carry forward from 2012 of $5,500 [(1/2)($89,000 - $100,000)]. This can only be applied against the 2013 taxable gain on listed personal property of $2,000 [(1/2)($5,000 - $1,000)]. Based on this, his Net and Taxable Income would be calculated as follows:

Income Under ITA 3(a)	$62,000
Income Under ITA 3(b) ($2,000 - $2,000)	Nil
Net Income And Taxable Income	$62,000

In this case, the listed personal property loss carry forward of $3,500 ($5,500 - $2,000) can only be applied against taxable capital gains on listed personal property.

If the sale had been of shares, Mr. Smothers would have had a regular net capital loss carry forward of $5,500 from 2012. His Net and Taxable Income would be calculated as follows:

Income Under ITA 3(a)	$62,000
Income Under ITA 3(b)	2,000
Net Income	$64,000
Loss Carry Forward (Limited To Taxable Capital Gains)	(2,000)
Taxable Income	$62,000

In this case, the $3,500 net capital loss carry forward can be applied against any taxable capital gains.

Exercise Eleven - 2 Solution
The required calculation is as follows:

Amount E ($58,000 + $2,200)	$60,200
Amount F ($35,000 + $13,000)	(48,000)
Amount D	(2,200)
Non-Capital Loss	$10,000

Note that this is the excess of the business loss of $58,000, over the $48,000 in positive sources of income for the year. The additional farm loss of $2,200 would be allocated to a separate loss balance. It is included in the E component and then deducted in the D component. Since it is less than $2,500, the farm loss is fully deductible, without regard to whether it is restricted.

Exercise Eleven - 3 Solution

Her minimum 2013 Net Income For Tax Purposes will be $10,000 ($40,000 - $30,000). She can reduce her Taxable Income to nil by deducting $10,000 of the $15,000 net capital loss. This will leave a non-capital loss carry over of nil and a net capital loss carry forward of $5,000 ($15,000 - $10,000).

However, since she does not anticipate future capital gains, she will want to use as much of her net capital loss carry forward as she can. As the amount of this net capital loss carry forward is less than the current year's taxable capital gain, she can apply all of it in 2013. To do so, she will convert $5,000 of her non-capital (rental) loss to a non-capital loss carry over. This will leave a net capital loss carry forward of nil and a non-capital loss carry over of $5,000, calculated as follows:

Amount E ($30,000 + $15,000)	$45,000
Amount F [ITA 3(c) Income]	(40,000)
Non-Capital Loss Carry Over	$ 5,000

This alternative will also leave her Taxable Income at nil. Note this solution ignores the effect of her tax credits.

Exercise Eleven - 4 Solution

The carry forward must be applied on an adjusted basis to eliminate the 2013 taxable capital gain. To implement this, the $7,500 amount (three-quarter basis) must be adjusted to $5,000 (one-half basis). The $2,000 taxable capital gain will use $2,000 of the adjusted 1990 carry forward, leaving $3,000. This amount must be adjusted back to the 3/4 inclusion rate. The resulting $4,500 [(3/2)($3,000)] can be applied against any other type of income in 2013 or, if there is not sufficient other income in that year, against any other type of income in 2012 (amended return). This can be verified using the 100 percent figures, which give the same $4,500 [(3/4)($10,000 - $4,000)] amount.

Exercise Eleven - 5 Solution

The Allowable Business Investment Loss for the year would be calculated as follows:

Actual Loss On Disposition	$50,000
Disallowed By Lifetime Capital Gains Deduction Use	(26,000)
Business Investment Loss	$24,000
Inclusion Rate	1/2
Allowable Business Investment Loss	$12,000

All of the $12,000 can be deducted against Mr. Latvik's employment income. With respect to the disallowed $26,000, it becomes an ordinary capital loss, of which $18,000 can be deducted against the current year's capital gains on the publicly traded securities. This leaves a net capital loss carry over of $4,000 [(1/2)($26,000 - $18,000)].

Exercise Eleven - 6 Solution

It appears that Ms. Bodkin's farming activities are a subordinate source of income. Given this, the deduction of the 2013 loss would be limited to $17,500 [$2,500 + (1/2)($32,500 - $2,500)]. The remaining $18,500 ($36,000 - $17,500) is a restricted farm loss carry forward.

In 2014, $3,500 of this carry forward can be deducted against the 2014 farm income. This leaves a restricted farm loss carry forward of $15,000 ($18,500 - $3,500). Ms. Bodkin's 2014 Net Income For Tax Purposes is $88,500 ($85,000 + $3,500) and her 2014 Taxable Income is $85,000 ($85,000 + $3,500 - $3,500).

Exercise Eleven - 7 Solution

The annual gains limit is **$26,000** ($42,000 - $16,000). This is calculated using the ITA 110.6 formula of A - B where:

The A component of the formula would be equal to **$42,000**, the lesser of:

- $74,000 ($114,000 + $42,000 - $82,000); and
- $42,000.

The B component would be **$16,000**, the sum of:

- $13,000*; and
- $3,000.

    *The amount by which $45,000, exceeds $32,000 ($114,000 - $82,000 + $42,000 - $42,000).

Note that the net taxable capital gain on non-qualified property was $32,000 ($114,000 - $82,000). The mechanics of the B component of the formula are such that the first $32,000 of the $45,000 net capital loss deduction was charged against these gains and did not erode the annual gains limit. Only the remaining $13,000 ($45,000 - $32,000) served to reduce the annual gains limit.

To make maximum use of her lifetime capital gains deduction, it would be advisable for Ms. Slovena to deduct only $32,000 of the net capital loss carry forward. If she did this, the B component would be $3,000 and her annual gains limit would increase to $39,000 [$42,000 - (Nil + $3,000)]. Although she would have used $13,000 ($39,000 - $26,000) more of her lifetime capital gains deduction, her tax liability for 2013 would not change and she would have a net capital loss carry forward of $13,000 ($45,000 - $32,000) that could be applied against any type of capital gain for an unlimited period of time.

Exercise Eleven - 8 Solution

His maximum lifetime capital gains deduction is $223,500, the least of the following:

Available Deduction   His remaining deduction would be $357,000 ($375,000 - $5,000 - $13,000).

Annual Gains Limit   In the absence of capital gains on non-qualified property in any of the years under consideration, the simplified version of this calculation can be used. The annual gains limit for 2013 would be the qualified taxable capital gain of $255,000 [(1/2)($510,000)], reduced by the net capital loss carry forward deducted of $31,500 [(1/2)($63,000)]. This leaves a net amount of $223,500 ($255,000 - $31,500).

Cumulative Gains Limit   In the absence of capital gains on non-qualified property in 2006 and 2008, the annual gains limits for 2006 and 2008 would simply be the amount of the taxable capital gains on qualified property in those years. Given this, the required calculation would be as follows:

Sum Of Annual Gains Limits ($5,000 + $13,000 + $223,500)	$241,500
Previous Years' Capital Gains Deduction ($5,000 + $13,000)	(18,000)
Cumulative Net Investment Loss	Nil
Cumulative Gains Limit	$223,500

Exercise Eleven - 9 Solution

Alan's Net Income For Tax Purposes would be calculated as follows:

Income Under ITA 3(a):		
Business Income	$12,000	
Employment Income	56,000	
Farming Income	3,500	$71,500
Income Under ITA 3(b):		
Taxable Capital Gains		9,000
Net Income For Tax Purposes		$80,500

Alan's Taxable Income is as follows:

Net Income For Tax Purposes	$80,500
Loss Carry Forwards:	
Restricted Farm Losses (Limited to farming income)	(3,500)
Net Capital Losses (Limited to taxable capital gains)	(9,000)
Non-Capital Losses (All)	(36,000)
Taxable Income	$32,000

Loss Carry Forwards

• Restricted farm loss carry forward ($8,000 - $3,500)	$ 4,500
• Net capital loss carry forward ($20,000 - $9,000)	$11,000
• Non-capital loss carry forward	Nil

Exercise Eleven - 10 Solution

The regular Tax Payable would be calculated as follows:

Income Sources:	
Taxable Non-Eligible Dividends [(125%)($15,000)]	$18,750
Contract Income	12,200
Taxable Eligible Dividends [(138%)($5,600)]	7,728
Deduction For Split Income - Taxable Non-Eligible Dividends	(18,750)
Net Income For Tax Purposes = Taxable Income	$19,928
Rate	15%
Tax Payable Before Credits	$ 2,989
Basic Personal Credit [(15%)($11,038)]	(1,656)
Dividend Tax Credit - Eligible Dividends [(6/11)(38%)($5,600)]	(1,161)
Regular Tax Payable	$ 172

The Tax Payable on split income would be calculated as follows:

Split Income - Taxable Non-Eligible Dividends	$18,750
Rate	29%
Tax Payable Before Dividend Tax Credit	$ 5,438
Dividend Tax Credit [(2/3)(25%)($15,000)]	(2,500)
Tax Payable On Split Income	$ 2,938

The total Tax Payable would be $3,110 ($172 + $2,938).

Exercise Eleven - 11 Solution

Without the transfer, Mr. Ho's wife would have income of $11,730 [(138%)($8,500)] and, as her income is greater than $11,038, he would have no spousal tax credit. With the transfer, he would be eligible for the full $1,656. Given this, the analysis of his position at the federal level is as follows:

Additional Taxes On Dividends [(29%)(138%)($8,500)]	$3,402
Increase In Spousal Tax Credit	(1,656)
Dividend Tax Credit [(6/11)(38%)($8,500)]	(1,762)
Tax Increase (Decrease)	($ 16)

As there is a very small decrease in federal Tax Payable, the election would be marginally desirable. Note that the election would leave Mr. Ho's wife with no Taxable Income and no Tax Payable. Even without the election, Mrs. Ho would have no Tax Payable given her basic personal credit and the availability of the dividend tax credit.

Exercise Eleven - 12 Solution

With the gift being made at $85,000, Ms. Felder will have a taxable capital gain of $11,500 [(1/2)($85,000 - $62,000)], plus recapture of $34,000 ($62,000 - $28,000), for a total Net Income For Tax Purposes of $45,500. Given this, her maximum credit base would be calculated as follows:

75% Of Net Income For Tax Purposes [(75%)($45,500)]	$34,125
25% Of Taxable Capital Gain [(25%)($11,500)]	2,875
25% Of Recaptured CCA [(25%)($34,000)]	8,500
Charitable Donations Credit Base Limit (Equals Income From Donation)	$45,500

This base results in a potential credit of $13,167 [(15%)($200) + (29%)($45,500 - $200)]. While this amount could be used, she does not have sufficient Tax Payable to utilize the whole potential credit. Her federal Tax Payable for the year would be calculated as follows:

Tax On First $43,561	$6,534
Tax At 22 Percent On Remaining $1,939 ($45,500 - $43,561)	427
Tax Before Credits	$6,961
Basic Personal Credit	(1,656)
Federal Tax Payable Before Donations Credit	$5,305

In order to reduce her Tax Payable to nil, Ms. Felder should use a sufficient amount of her charitable donations credit base to produce a tax credit of $5,305. To arrive at the credit base that will result in this tax credit, the following equation must be solved for X:

$5,305 = [(15%)($200)] + [(29%)(X - $200)]
$5,305 - $30 + $58 = [(29%)(X)]

Solving this equation for X provides a value of $18,390 which equals the amount of her donation that produces the $5,305 [(15%)($200) + (29%)($18,390 - $200)] credit that will reduce her federal Tax Payable to nil. This leaves a carry forward of $66,610 ($85,000 - $18,390).

Exercise Eleven - 13 Solution

None of the capital gain will be included in Mr. Radeem's Net Income For Tax Purposes. This means that his Taxable Income for 2013 will consist of his employment income of $90,000. Based on the fair market value of the donated shares, Mr. Radeem's maximum base for his charitable donations tax credit would be $67,500 [(75%)($90,000)]. If he were to use this amount, his 2013 charitable donations tax credit would be $19,547 [(15%)($200) + (29%)($67,500 - $200)]. However, he does not need this amount to reduce his Tax Payable to nil:

Tax On First $87,123	$16,118
Tax At 26 Percent On Remaining $2,877 ($90,000 - $87,123)	748
Tax Before Credits	$16,866
Tax Credits (Given)	(4,000)
Tax Payable Before Donations Credit	$12,866

In order to reduce his Tax Payable to nil, Mr. Radeem should use a sufficient amount of his charitable donations credit base to produce a tax credit of $12,866. To arrive at the credit base that will result in this tax credit, the following equation must be solved for X:

$12,866 = [(15%)($200)] + [(29%)(X - $200)
$12,866 - $30 + $58 = [(29%)(X)]

Solving this equation for X provides a value of $44,462 which equals the amount of his donation that will produce the $12,866 [(15%)($200) + (29%)($44,462 - $200)] credit that will reduce his federal Tax Payable to nil. This leaves a carry forward of $65,538 ($110,000 - $44,462).

Exercise Eleven - 14 Solution

Ms. Cheung's Net Income For Tax Purposes and Taxable Income would be as follows:

Net Rental Income	$44,000
Net Taxable Capital Gains	2,500
Foreign Non-Business Income	3,500
Net Income For Tax Purposes	$50,000
Net Capital Loss Carry Forward	(2,500)
Adjusted Division B Income	$47,500
Non-Capital Loss Carry Forward	(4,000)
Taxable Income	$43,500

Ms. Cheung's credit for foreign tax paid would be the lesser of the foreign tax withheld of $385 [(11%)($3,500)] and an amount determined by the following formula:

$$\left[\frac{\text{Foreign Non} - \text{Business Income}}{\text{Adjusted Division B Income}}\right][\text{Tax Otherwise Payable}]$$

In this formula, the Adjusted Division B Income would be $47,500 (as shown in the preceding table). Note that, because the non-capital loss is not deducted here, this is not the same as her Taxable Income of $43,500.

Ms. Cheung's Tax Otherwise Payable would be calculated as follows (note that the foreign tax credit is not subtracted in this calculation):

Tax Before Credits [(15%)($43,500)]	$6,525
Basic Personal Credit	(1,656)
Tax Otherwise Payable	$4,869

Using this information, the formula amount would be $359 [($3,500 ÷ $47,500)($4,869)]. As this is less than the $385 withheld, this would be the foreign tax credit. Based on this, Ms. Cheung's actual federal Tax Payable would be calculated as follows:

Tax Before Credits [(15%)($43,500)]	$6,525
Basic Personal Credit	(1,656)
Foreign Tax Credit	(359)
Federal Tax Payable	$4,510

Exercise Eleven - 15 Solution
Mr. Blouson's regular Tax Payable would be calculated as follows:

Tax On First $43,561	$ 6,534
Tax At 22 Percent On $41,439 ($85,000 - $43,561)	9,117
Total	$15,651
Basic Personal Credit	(1,656)
Dividend Tax Credit [(6/11)(38%)($20,000)]	(4,145)
Regular Federal Tax Payable	$ 9,850

For alternative minimum tax purposes, his adjusted taxable income would be as follows:

Regular Taxable Income	$85,000
30 Percent Of Capital Gains [(30%)(2)($22,500)]	13,500
Dividend Gross Up [(38%)($20,000)]	(7,600)
Adjusted Taxable Income	$90,900

Calculation of the alternative minimum tax would be as follows:

Adjusted Taxable Income	$90,900
Basic Exemption	(40,000)
Amount Subject To Tax	$50,900
Rate	15%
Minimum Tax Before Credit	$ 7,635
Basic Personal Credit	(1,656)
Alternative Minimum Tax	$ 5,979

Mr. Blouson would not pay the alternative minimum tax as $5,979 is less than the regular Tax Payable of $9,850. Note that the $50,000 RRSP deduction does not affect the alternative minimum tax calculation.

Self Study Solution Eleven - 1

The calculation of Miss Atwater's Taxable Income for 2012 would be as follows:

Net Rental Income	$34,200
Interest Income	4,000
Net Income For Tax Purposes And Taxable Income	$38,200

The corresponding calculation for 2013 is as follows:

Net Rental Income	$ 35,200	
Interest Income	4,200	$39,400
Allowable Business Investment Loss [(1/2)($170,000)]		(85,000)
Net Income For Tax Purposes And Taxable Income		Nil

There is a deemed disposition of the shares for proceeds of nil due to the bankruptcy of the company. As the capital loss relates to the shares of a small business corporation, it is a Business Investment Loss. This means that, in contrast to other types of capital losses, the allowable portion can be deducted against any source of income. The total Allowable Business Investment Loss (ABIL) that is available for deduction in 2013 is $85,000 [(1/2)($170,000)].

As the ABIL was recognized in 2013, it must first be used to reduce that year's income to nil. Note that, because of this rule, she cannot deduct a smaller amount in order to have sufficient income to absorb her basic personal tax credit. This will use up $39,400 of the $85,000 total and leave a balance of $45,600 to be carried over to other years.

In carrying this amount back to 2012, the optimum solution would leave $10,822 of Taxable Income so that Miss Atwater can take advantage of her basic personal tax credit. Note that the calculation of the optimum carry back uses the basic personal amount of the carry back year, not the current year.

This means that she needs a loss carry back deduction of $27,378 ($38,200 - $10,822) in 2012. This deduction will leave a Taxable Income of $10,822. As planned, the taxes on this amount will be eliminated by the basic personal credit.

A carry back of $27,378 to 2012 leaves a carry forward balance of $18,222 ($45,600 - $27,378) to be used in future years.

The undeducted Allowable Business Investment Loss can be deducted against other sources of income in the 10 (not 20) year carry forward period. If it has not been utilized within the 10 years, it then becomes a net capital loss carry forward, deductible for an unlimited number of future periods, but only against net taxable capital gains.

Self Study Solution Eleven - 2

2010 Analysis

Mr. Fox's Net Income For Tax Purposes and Taxable Income would be calculated as follows:

ITA 3(a)		
Employment Income	$18,000	
Business Income	14,500	
Taxable (Grossed Up) Dividends	6,250	$38,750
ITA 3(b)		
Taxable Capital Gains	$ Nil	
Allowable Capital Losses [(1/2)($3,600)]	(1,800)	Nil
ITA 3(c)		$38,750
ITA 3(d)		
Farm Loss (See Note)		(4,250)
Net Income For Tax Purposes And Taxable Income		$34,500

Note Given that Mr. Fox is only a part time farmer, his deductible farm loss would be restricted as follows:

Total Farm Loss		$6,000
Deductible Amount:		
First $2,500	($2,500)	
One-Half Of $3,500 ($6,000 - $2,500)	(1,750)	(4,250)
Restricted Farm Loss Carry Forward		$1,750

As noted in the problem, none of the losses can be carried back before 2010. This would leave the following carry forward balances at the end of 2010:

- Restricted Farm Loss Carry Forward $1,750
- Net Capital Loss Carry Forward [(1/2)($3,600)] $1,800

2011 Analysis

Mr. Fox's Net Income For Tax Purposes and Taxable Income would be calculated as follows:

ITA 3(a)		
Employment Income	$16,000	
Taxable (Grossed Up) Dividends	8,156	$24,156
ITA 3(b)		
Taxable Capital Gains [(1/2)($7,400)]	$ 3,700	
Allowable Capital Losses	Nil	3,700
ITA 3(c)		$27,856
ITA 3(d)		
Business Loss		(39,000)
Net Income For Tax Purposes		Nil
2010 Net Capital Loss Carry Forward (Less Than $3,700)		(1,800)
Taxable Income		Nil

Mr. Fox does not have the option to retain $15,000 in Taxable Income to utilize his tax credits. A non-capital loss carry over is only available after the current year's income is reduced to nil.

Since there are taxable capital gains this year, and the problem states that Mr. Fox would like to deduct the maximum amount of his net capital loss carry forwards, the net capital loss carry forward of $1,800 is added to the balance of the non-capital loss. The non-capital loss for the year would be calculated as follows:

Business Loss	$39,000
2010 Net Capital Loss Deducted	1,800
ITA 3(c) Income	(27,856)
Non-Capital Loss Carry Over For 2011	$12,944

This non-capital loss will be carried back to 2010, resulting in the following amended Taxable Income for that year:

2010 Taxable Income (As Reported)	$34,500
Non-Capital Loss Carry Back From 2011	(12,944)
2010 Amended Taxable Income	$21,556

This carry back leaves Mr. Fox with more than his required $15,000 in Taxable Income. There would be the following carry forward balances at the end of 2011:

- Restricted Farm Loss Carry Forward (unchanged) $1,750

2012 Analysis

Mr. Fox's Net Income For Tax Purposes and Taxable Income would be calculated as follows:

ITA 3(a)		
Employment Income	$19,000	
Business Income	34,000	
Farming Income	8,000	
Taxable (Grossed Up) Dividends	10,000	$71,000
ITA 3(b)		
Taxable Capital Gains [(1/2)($6,300)]	$ 3,150	
Allowable Capital Losses	Nil	3,150
ITA 3(c)		$74,150
ITA 3(d)		Nil
Net Income For Tax Purposes		$74,150
Farm Loss Carry Forward (Less Than $8,000)		(1,750)
Taxable Income		$72,400

Given the deduction of the farm loss carry forward, there are no loss carry overs remaining at the end of 2012.

2013 Analysis

Mr. Fox's Net Income For Tax Purposes and Taxable Income would be calculated as follows:

ITA 3(a)		
Employment Income	$12,000	
Taxable (Grossed Up) Dividends	12,656	$24,656
ITA 3(b)		
Taxable Capital Gains	$ Nil	
Allowable Capital Losses [(1/2)($6,000)]	(3,000)	Nil
ITA 3(c)		$24,656
ITA 3(d)		
Business Loss	($52,000)	
Farm Loss	(2,000)	(54,000)
Net Income For Tax Purposes And Taxable Income		Nil

The non-capital loss carry over for the year would be calculated as follows:

Business Loss	$52,000
ITA 3(c) Income	(24,656)
Non-Capital Loss Carry Over	$27,344
Farm Loss (Unrestricted)	2,000
Total Loss Carry Over For 2013	$29,344

Although technically, the farm loss is accounted for separately from the non-capital loss, since the farm loss is less than $2,500 it is treated as an unrestricted farm loss and can be applied against all types of income. Given the carry over rules are the same, we have treated this farm loss as part of the non-capital loss carry over. The entire loss carry over could be carried back to 2012, but the problem requires that losses be carried back to the earliest possible year. As a result, some of this loss must be carried back to 2010. Since Mr. Fox requires $15,000 in Taxable Income to fully utilize his tax credits, the maximum carry back to 2010 is $6,556, calculated as follows:

2010 Taxable Income (As Amended)	$21,556
Non-Capital Loss Carry Back From 2013	(6,556)
2010 Amended Taxable Income (Minimum)	$15,000

This carry back leaves Mr. Fox with his required $15,000 in Taxable Income. The remaining loss carry over of $22,788 ($29,344 - $6,556) can be carried back to 2012.

There would be a $3,000 net capital loss carry over for 2013. This entire amount can be carried back to 2012, since the carry back is less than the $3,150 taxable capital gains recorded in 2012.

This will result in the following amended Taxable Income for that year:

2012 Taxable Income (As Reported)	$72,400
Non-Capital Loss Carry Back From 2013	(22,788)
Net Capital Loss Carry Back From 2013	(3,000)
2012 Amended Taxable Income	$46,612

There are no loss carry forwards remaining at the end of 2013.

Self Study Solution Eleven - 3

Mr. Cox's minimum Net Income For Tax Purposes and Taxable Income would be calculated as follows:

Net Employment Income	$76,000
Net Taxable Capital Gains [(1/2)($75,000 - $32,000)]	21,500
Interest Expense	(17,000)
Net Income For Tax Purposes	$80,500
Lifetime Capital Gains Deduction (See Note)	(4,500)
Net Capital Loss Carry Forward Deducted	Nil
Taxable Income	$76,000

Note The lifetime capital gains deduction is $4,500, the least of:

Amount Available [(1/2)($750,000)]	$375,000
Used In 2011 [(1/2)($5,000)]	(2,500)
Amount Remaining	**$372,500**

As the only net taxable capital gains in 2013 are on qualified property, the simplified version of the annual gains limit formula can be used:

Net Taxable Capital Gains [(1/2)($75,000 - $32,000)]	21,500
Net Capital Loss Carry Forward Deducted	Nil
Annual Gains Limit	**$21,500**

Sum Of Annual Gains Limits ($2,500 + $21,500)	$24,000
Amounts Deducted In Previous Years	(2,500)
CNIL	(17,000)
Cumulative Gains Limit	**$ 4,500**

It would have been possible for Mr. Cox to deduct $4,500 of the net capital loss carry forward instead of the available lifetime capital gains deduction. The carry forward period on net capital losses is unlimited and it can be applied against any type of capital gain. In contrast, the lifetime capital gains deduction can only be used for certain types of capital gains. As a result, use of the lifetime capital gains deduction is probably the better alternative.

Self Study Solution Eleven - 4

Part A - Taxable Income

Mr. and Mrs. Bahry's Taxable Income would be calculated as follows:

	Mr. Bahry	Mrs. Bahry
Old Age Security Benefits (See Note)	$ 6,550	$ 6,550
Registered Pension Plan Receipts	12,340	820
Registered Retirement Income Fund Receipts	N/A	1,000
Canada Pension Plan Receipts	3,690	830
Dividends Received	1,600	336
Gross Up On Dividends (38 Percent)	608	128
Interest On Savings Accounts	1,239	2,500
Net Taxable Capital Gain	Nil	Nil
Net Income For Tax Purposes And Taxable Income	$26,027	$12,164

Note Neither Mr. nor Mrs. Bahry would have to repay any OAS benefits as both Net Income figures are well below the threshold income of $70,954.

Mrs. Bahry cannot transfer her dividends under ITA 82(3) as the transfer would give her Net Income of $11,700 ($12,164 - $336 - $128) and this would not increase or create a spousal credit.

Part A - Tax Credits

Mrs. Bahry must include the $128 gross up on her dividends in her Taxable Income, which decreases the amount of tax credits she can transfer. She must decrease the amount of the age and pension credits she can transfer by the excess of her Taxable Income (including the dividends) over the basic personal amount. As a result, she cannot claim the dividend tax credit. Since Mr. Bahry is not eligible for the ITA 82(3) election, her dividend tax credit will be lost.

Credits Available For Transfer:		
Age		$6,854
Pension (On $820 + $1,000 Only)		1,820
Total Available		$8,674
Reduced By Excess Of:		
Mrs. Bahry's Net Income	($12,164)	
Over Basic Personal Credit Amount	11,038	(1,126)
Available For Transfer		$7,548

Mr. Bahry's maximum tax credits would be as follows:

Basic Personal Amount	$11,038
Spousal (Mrs. Bahry's Net Income Is Too High)	Nil
Age (No Reduction Required)	6,854
Pension	2,000
Transfers From Mrs. Bahry (See Preceding)	7,548
Credit Base	$27,440
Rate	15%
Total	$ 4,116
Dividend Tax Credit [(6/11)($608)]	332
Charitable Donations (See Note)	
[(15%)($200) + (29%)($1,210 + $300 - $200)]	410
Total Credits	$ 4,858

Note Charitable donations can be claimed by either spouse, as long as the total donations are less than 75 percent of the claiming spouse's Net Income For Tax Purposes. As Mrs. Bahry has no Tax Payable, Mr. Bahry will claim her charitable donations. It is usually advantageous for one spouse to claim all the charitable donations if they total more than $200, as the low rate of credit is only applied once.

Part A - Loss Carry Overs

Neither Mr. Bahry's allowable capital loss of $1,988 [(1/2)($3,975)] nor Mrs. Bahry's allowable capital loss of $160 [(1/2)($820 - $500)] can be deducted in 2013. They can be carried back three years and carried forward indefinitely to be applied against taxable capital gains.

Part B - Pension Income Splitting

Since Mr. and Mrs. Bahry are both in the lowest tax bracket and neither has any OAS clawback, the optimum use of pension income splitting would accomplish the following objectives:

- it would permit Mrs. Bahry to claim her dividend tax credit, and
- it would permit Mrs. Bahry to fully utilize her pension income tax credit.

Self Study Solution Eleven - 5

Part A

Mr. and Mrs. Dalton's Taxable Income would be calculated as follows:

	Mr. Dalton	Mrs. Dalton
Old Age Security Benefits	$ 6,550	$ 6,550
Registered Pension Plan Receipts	Nil	62,000
RRIF Income	1,640	12,420
Interest On Government Bonds	1,420	2,580
Non-Eligible Dividends Received	3,420	460
Gross Up On Dividends (25 Percent)	855	115
Net Income Before Clawback	$13,885	$84,125
Social Benefits Repayment (Note 1)	Nil	(1,976)
Net Income For Tax Purposes And Taxable Income Before Any Transfer Of Dividends	$13,885	$82,149

Note 1 Mr. Dalton would not have to repay any of his OAS benefits as his Net Income is well below the threshold income of $70,954. Mrs. Dalton's social benefits repayment would be $1,976, the lesser of:

- $6,550, and
- [(15%)($84,125 - $70,954)] = $1,976.

Mr. Dalton's Tax Payable would be calculated as follows:

Federal Tax Before Credits [(15%)($13,885)]		$2,083
Tax Credits		
Basic Personal	$11,038	
Other (Transferred To Mrs. Dalton)	Nil	
Total Base	$11,038	
Rate	15%	(1,656)
Dividend Tax Credit [(2/3)($855)]		(570)
Federal Tax Payable		Nil

The transfer to Mrs. Dalton would be calculated as follows:

Credits Available For Transfer:		
Age		$ 6,854
Pension (Limited To RRIF Receipts)		1,640
Disability		7,697
Total Available		$16,191
Reduced By Excess Of:		
Mr. Dalton's Net Income	($13,885)	
Over Basic Personal Credit Amount	11,038	(2,847)
Available For Transfer		$13,344

The amount owing for Mrs. Dalton would be calculated as follows:

Tax On First $43,561	$ 6,534	
Tax On Next $38,588 ($82,149 - $43,561) At 22 Percent	8,489	$15,023
Tax Credits		
Basic Personal	($11,038)	
Spousal Including FCA ($13,078 - $13,885)	Nil	
Age {$6,854 - [(15%)($82,149 - $34,562)]}	Nil	
Pension	(2,000)	
Transfer From Spouse (Preceding Calculation)	(13,344)	
Credit Base	($26,382)	
Rate	15%	(3,957)
Charitable Donations [(15%)($200) +		
(29%)($350 + $960 - $200)] (Note 2)		(352)
Dividend Tax Credit [(2/3)($115)]		(77)
Federal Tax Payable		$ 10,637
OAS Clawback		1,976
Amount Owing		$12,613

Note 2   Charitable donations can be claimed by either spouse, as long as the total donations are less than 75 percent of the claiming spouse's Net Income For Tax Purposes. As Mr. Dalton has no Tax Payable, Mrs. Dalton will claim his charitable donations. It is usually advantageous for one spouse to claim all the charitable donations if they total more than $200, as the low rate of credit is only applied once.

Part B - Eligibility For Transfer

Mrs. Dalton cannot currently take the spousal credit because Mr. Dalton's Net Income is more than the $13,078 base for this credit which includes the family caregiver amount. However, Mr. Dalton can transfer his dividends under ITA 82(3) as the transfer would leave Mr. Dalton with Net Income of $9,610 ($13,885 - $3,420 - $855). This is below the $13,078 base for the spousal credit with the FCA and, as a result, the transfer would create a spousal tax credit.

Part C

If all of Mr. Dalton's dividends are transferred to Mrs. Dalton, their new Taxable Income figures would be calculated as follows:

	Mr. Dalton	Mrs. Dalton
Net Income Before Clawback As Per Part A	$13,885	$84,125
Dividend Transfer	(3,420)	3,420
Gross Up Transfer	(855)	855
Net Income After Dividend Transfer Before Clawback	$ 9,610	$88,400
Social Benefits Repayment (Note 3)	Nil	(2,617)
Net Income For Tax Purposes And Taxable Income	$ 9,610	$85,783

Note 3   Mr. Dalton would not have to repay any of his OAS benefits as his Net Income is well below the threshold income of $70,954. Mrs. Dalton's social benefits repayment would be $2,617, the lesser of:

- $6,550, and
- [(15%)($88,400 - $70,954)] = $2,617.

As Mr. Dalton's revised income figure is below the basic personal credit of $11,038, his Tax Payable would continue to be nil. The transfer to Mrs. Dalton would be calculated as follows:

Credits Available For Transfer:

Age	$ 6,854
Pension (Limited To RRIF Receipts)	1,640
Disability	7,697
Total Available	$16,191

Reduced By Excess Of:

Mr. Dalton's Net Income	($ 9,610)	
Over Basic Personal Credit Amount	11,038	(Nil)
Available For Transfer		**$16,191**

With respect to Mrs. Dalton, her amount owing would be calculated as follows:

Tax On First $43,561	$6,534	
Tax On Next $42,222 ($85,783 - $43,561) At 22%	9,289	$15,823
Tax Credits		
Basic Personal	$11,038	
Spousal Including FCA ($13,078 - $9,610)	3,468	
Age {$6,537 - [(15%)($85,783 - $34,562)]}	Nil	
Pension	2,000	
Transfer From Spouse (Preceding Calculation)	16,191	
Credit Base	$32,697	
Rate	15%	(4,905)
Charitable Donations [(15%)($200) +		
(29%)($350 + $960 - $200)]		(352)
Dividend Tax Credit [(2/3)($115 + $855)]		(647)
Federal Tax Payable		$9,919
OAS Clawback		2,617
Amount Owing		**$12,536**

The use of the ITA 82(3) dividend transfer has decreased Mrs. Dalton's federal Tax Payable by $718 ($10,637 - $9,919). However, it has increased the OAS clawback by $641 ($2,617 - $1,976). Overall, the net effect is a decrease in the amount owing of $77 ($718 - $641). Given this small improvement, the transfer may not be worth the additional work required.

Self Study Solution Eleven - 6

Regular Tax Payable

The minimum regular Taxable Income and Tax Payable calculations would be as follows:

	Cheryl	Alma	Irene
Employment And Business Income	$ 60,800	$42,000	$ 22,900
Dividends Received	26,300	Nil	29,400
Non-Eligible Dividend Gross Up (25%)	6,575	Nil	7,350
Taxable Capital Gains	9,100	Nil	450,000
Retiring Allowance	Nil	58,000	Nil
RRSP Deductions (Note 1)	(2,344)	(58,000)	Nil
Net Income For Tax Purposes	$100,431	$42,000	$509,650
Lifetime Capital Gains Deduction	(9,100)	Nil	(375,000)
Taxable Income	$ 91,331	$42,000	$134,650

Federal Tax (Note 2)	$ 17,212	$ 6,300	$ 28,475
Basic Personal Credit	(1,656)	(1,656)	(1,656)
Dividend Tax Credit (2/3 of Gross Up)	(4,383)	Nil	(4,900)
Regular Federal Tax Payable	$ 11,173	$ 4,644	$ 21,919

Note 1 Cheryl's 2013 RRSP Deduction Room is calculated as follows:

Lesser Of:
- 2013 RRSP Dollar Limit = $23,820
- 18% Of 2012 Earned Income Of $60,800 = $10,944 $10,944

Less 2012 PA	(8,600)
2013 RRSP Deduction Limit	$ 2,344

Although she contributed $3,500, her RRSP deduction is limited to $2,344 and she has $1,156 ($3,500 - $2,344) in undeducted contributions that can be carried forward and deducted in a subsequent year in which there is sufficient RRSP deduction room.

Note 2 The federal Tax Payable, before the dividend tax credit, is as follows:

	Taxable Income	Federal Tax Calculations	Federal Tax
Cheryl	$ 91,331	$16,118 + (26%)($4,208)	$17,212
Alma	$ 42,000	(15%)($42,000)	$ 6,300
Irene	$134,650	$16,118 + (26%)($47,527)	$28,475

Alternative Minimum Tax Payable

The alternative minimum tax (AMT) calculations would be as follows:

	Cheryl	Alma	Irene
Regular Taxable Income	$91,331	$42,000	$134,650
30% Of Capital Gains (Note)	5,460	Nil	270,000
Dividend Gross Up	(6,575)	Nil	(7,350)
Adjusted Taxable Income	$90,216	$42,000	$397,300
AMT Exemption	(40,000)	(40,000)	(40,000)
AMT Base	$50,216	$ 2,000	$357,300
Rate	15%	15%	15%
Federal AMT Before Credit	$ 7,532	$ 300	$ 53,595
Basic Personal Credit	(1,656)	(1,656)	(1,656)
Federal AMT	$ 5,876	Nil	$ 51,939
Regular Federal Tax Payable	(11,173)		(21,919)
Additional Tax Required	Nil		$ 30,020

Note The 30 percent capital gain inclusion can be calculated by taking 30 percent of double the taxable capital gain.

The excess of AMT over regular tax payable for Irene can be carried forward for seven years and applied against any future excess of regular Tax Payable over the alternative minimum tax.

Self Study Solution Eleven - 7

Part A - Net Income For Tax Purposes

Ms. Worthmore's minimum Taxable Income is calculated as follows:

Employment Income

Gross Salary - Intra Graphics	$73,532	
Gross Salary - Lindworth Inc.	2,500	
RPP Contributions	(1,233)	$74,799

Income From Property

Eligible Dividend Attribution (Note One)	$ 182	
Gross Up [(38%)($182)]	69	
Non-Eligible Dividends From Lindworth	4,325	
Gross Up [(25%)($4,325)]	1,081	5,657

Taxable Capital Gains

Attribution From Husband (Note Two)	$ 1,144	
Transfer To Jayne (Note Three)	122	
Lackmere Shares (Note Four)	394	
Agricultural Land (Note Five)	9,000	10,660

Other Income And Deductions

Spousal Support Payments [($225)(12)]	($ 2,700)	
RRSP Deduction (Note Six)	(6,849)	(9,549)
Net Income For Tax Purposes		**$81,567**

Note One   There would be income attribution for the $182 [($3.50)(52)] in dividends received by Mr. Dalton on the shares received as a gift.

Note Two   In the case of transfers to a spouse, unless an election is made not to have Section 73 apply, the property is transferred at the adjusted cost base of the transferor. There is no recognition of capital gains at the time of transfer. However, when Mr. Dalton sells the shares on August 31, 2013, there would be attribution of taxable capital gains in the amount of $1,144 [($56 - $12)(52)(1/2)].

Note Three   In the case of a gift to a minor child, it is treated as a deemed disposition at fair market value. This results in a taxable capital gain at the time of transfer in the amount of $122 [($27 - $18)(27)(1/2)].

Note Four   The taxable capital gain on the Lackmere Ltd. shares would be computed using the average value for the shares. The average value would be calculated as follows:

122 Shares At $92	$11,224
178 Shares At $71	12,638
Total Cost	$23,862
Average Cost ($23,862 ÷ 300 Shares)	$ 79.54

Based on this, the gain would be calculated as follows:

Proceeds Of Disposition [(122)($86)]	$10,492
Adjusted Cost Base [(122)($79.54)]	(9,704)
Capital Gain	$ 788
Inclusion Rate	1/2
Taxable Capital Gain	$ 394

Note Five   When there is a non-arm's length transfer of property for consideration of less than fair market value, ITA 69 deems that, for the transferor, the transfer takes place at fair market value. Given this, the taxable capital gain would be calculated as follows:

Deemed Proceeds Of Disposition (FMV)	$28,000
Adjusted Cost Base	(10,000)
Capital Gain	$18,000
Inclusion Rate	1/2
Taxable Capital Gain	$ 9,000

Note Six Ms. Worthmore's 2012 Earned Income (assumed to be equal to the 2013 figure) is as follows:

Gross Salary - Intra	$73,532
Gross Salary - Lindworth	2,500
Spousal Support Paid And Deducted [(12)($225)]	(2,700)
Earned Income	$73,332

Ms. Worthmore's maximum deductible 2013 RRSP contribution is calculated as follows:

Unused Deduction Room - End of 2012	Nil
Lesser Of:	
• 2013 RRSP Dollar Limit = $23,820	
• [(18%)($73,332)] = $13,200	$13,200
Less 2012 PA	(6,351)
Maximum Deductible RRSP Contribution	$ 6,849

This means the excess contribution of $651 ($7,500 - $6,849) can be carried forward and deducted in future years.

Part B - Taxable Income

As Ms. Worthmore has no deductions from her Net Income For Tax Purposes, her 2013 Taxable Income would $81,567, the same amount as her 2013 Net Income For Tax Purposes

Part C - Tax Payable

Ms. Worthmore's federal Tax Payable can be calculated as follows:

Tax On First $43,561		$ 6,534
Tax On Next $38,006 ($81,567 - $43,561) At 22 Percent		8,361
Gross Federal Tax Payable		$14,895
Basic Personal Amount	($11,038)	
Spousal [$11,038 - ($750 + $2,475)]	(7,813)	
Child [(3)($2,234)]	(6,702)	
CPP Contribution	(2,356)	
EI Premiums	(891)	
Canada Employment	(1,117)	
Transfer Of Spouse's Tuition, Education and		
Textbook - Lesser of:		
• $5,000		
• [$2,300 + (4)($400) + (4)($65)] = $4,160	(4,160)	
Medical Expenses (Note Eight)	(10,954)	
Credit Base	($45,031)	
Rate	15%	(6,755)
Eligible Dividend Tax Credit [(6/11)($69)]		(38)
Non-Eligible Dividend Tax Credit [(2/3)($1,081)]		(721)
Charitable Donations [(15%)($200) + (29%)($342 - $200)]		(71)
Political Contributions [(3/4)($100)]		(75)
Federal Tax Payable		$ 7,235

Note Seven   Ms. Worthmore can claim all of the medical expenses of her husband and daughters, Joyce and June without taking into consideration June's income, as she is under 18 years of age. Allowable medical expenses are as follows:

John Dalton, Joyce And June Medical Expenses ($1,056 + $2,200 + $9,850)	$13,106

Threshold - Lesser Of:
   [(3%)($81,567)] = $2,447
   2013 Limit Of $2,152
	(2,152)

Allowable Medical Expenses	$10,954

Self Study Solution Eleven - 8

Taxable Income

Mr. Slater's Net Income For Tax Purposes And Taxable Income would be calculated as follows:

Employment Income - Salary		$ 35,000
Proprietorship Income ($28,300 - $2,300 - Note One)		26,000
Property Income:		
Interest On Savings Account	$ 4,450	
Interest On Loans To Friends	12,000	
Eligible Canadian Dividends	44,000	
Gross Up [($44,000)(38%)]	16,720	
Dividends From U.S. Corporations		
(Before Withholding, No Gross Up)	10,000	87,170
Taxable Capital Gain [(1/2)($111,500 - $23,000)]		44,250
CPP Benefits		5,100
Old Age Security Benefits (Note Three)		6,550
Restricted Farm Loss (Note Two)		(5,750)
Net Income Before OAS Repayment		$198,320
OAS Repayment (Note Three) - Lesser Of:		
• $6,550		
• $19,105 [(15%)($198,320 - $70,954)]		(6,550)
Net Income For Tax Purposes And Taxable Income		$191,770

Note One   The drawings from the proprietorship have no effect on the Taxable Income of Mr. Slater. Funds invested are capital and not deductible. The proprietorship income of $28,300 is reduced by the interest of $2,300 on the proprietorship bank loan.

Note Two   Since Mr. Slater's farming operation is a subordinate source of income, his farm loss would be restricted as follows:

Farm Revenues	$36,000
Farm Expenses	(45,000)
Total Farm Loss	($ 9,000)
Deductible Portion [$2,500 + (1/2)($9,000 - $2,500)]	5,750
Restricted Farm Loss Carry Over	($ 3,250)

The $3,250 restricted farm loss carry over could be carried back to the preceding 3 years and forward for 20 years, to be deducted against farming income.

Note Three Even though Mr. Slater did not receive the $6,550, it must be included in income and deducted because he has received an information return which includes the amount.

Tax Payable

Mr. Slater's federal Tax Payable would be calculated as follows:

Tax On First $135,054		$28,580
Tax On Next $56,716 ($191,770 - $135,054) At 29 Percent		16,448
Gross Federal Tax		$45,028
Tax Credits:		
Basic Personal Amount	($11,038)	
Spousal, Including FCA	(13,078)	
Mr. Slater's Age		
{$6,854 - [(15%)($191,770 - $34,562)]}	Nil	
Spouse's Disability	(7,697)	
Canada Employment	(1,117)	
Credit Base	($32,930)	
Rate	15%	(4,940)
Charitable Donations		
[(15%)($200) + (29%)($2,700 - $200)]		(755)
Subtotal = Tax Otherwise Payable For Foreign Tax Credit		$39,333
Dividend Tax Credit [(6/11)($16,720)]		(9,120)
Foreign Tax Credit (Note Four)		(1,500)
Federal Political Contributions Tax Credit (Note Five)		(350)
OAS Clawback		6,550
OAS Withheld		(6,550)
Federal Tax Payable		$28,363

Note Four The federal foreign tax credit will be the lesser of the foreign tax actually paid of $1,500 and an amount determined by the following formula:

$$\left[\frac{\text{Foreign Non-Business Income}}{\text{Adjusted Division B Income}}\right][\text{Tax Otherwise Payable}]$$

The Tax Otherwise Payable is equal to federal Tax Payable before the dividend tax credit and political contributions tax credit is deducted (the Subtotal in the preceding table). This amount would be $2,051 [($10,000 ÷ $191,770)($39,333)], leaving the actual taxes of $1,500 as the lesser amount.

Note Five The political contributions tax credit can be calculated as follows:

3/4 Of First $400	$300
1/2 Of The Next $100	50
Total Credit	$350

Other Notes

- The gambling income would not be taxable as Mr. Slater's activity is not extensive enough to be considered a business given his winnings and funds lost in gambling.
- Inheritances are capital receipts and do not constitute Taxable Income.
- The life insurance premiums are not deductible.
- The mortgage payments on his personal residence are not deductible.

Self Study Solution Eleven - 9

Deemed Dispositions Immediately Before Death

Immediately before the time of Mrs. Steele's death, there is a deemed disposition of all of her capital property. If the beneficiary is a spouse, the deemed proceeds of disposition will, in general, be equal to the tax cost of the property (ACB or UCC). If Andrea's representatives choose to do so, they can elect out of this rollover and record the transfer at fair market value. For the transfers to her daughter, the deemed proceeds of disposition must be equal to fair market value.

Principal Residence To Daughter

The bequest of the family home to her daughter would result in a capital gain of $134,600 ($344,000 - $209,400). As it appears to have been Mrs. Steele's principal residence, the application of the principal residence exemption formula to this amount would result in a deduction of the maximum amount of $134,600.

Other Properties At Death

Under ITA 70(6), property may be transferred at death to a spouse on the basis of adjusted cost base or its UCC. This means that the Rolston Inc. shares, the painting, and the assets of the boutique can be transferred to Mr. Steele with no tax effects in Mrs. Steele's final return. The adjusted cost base and UCC of these properties to Mr. Steele will be the same amounts that applied to Mrs. Steele, prior to her death.

Although the AGF Industries shares would also be eligible for a tax free rollover, it would not be advantageous to do so as there is an unrealized capital loss on these shares. It would be preferable for the legal representative of Mrs. Steele to elect in the final return to have the AGF Industries shares transferred to Mr. Steele at fair market value in order to utilize the capital loss. Electing out of ITA 70(6) is implemented in the final tax return and does not require the filing of a form.

There is no rollover available for the rental property as that is being transferred to her daughter. There is a taxable capital gain for the rental property on both the building and the land and recaptured CCA on the building.

The allowable capital loss on the shares and taxable capital gain and recaptured CCA on the deemed disposition of the rental property can be calculated as follows:

	AGF Shares	Land	Building
Fair Market Value	$ 7,900	$164,000	$235,000
Adjusted Cost Base/Capital Cost	(10,600)	(92,000)	(183,000)
Capital Gain (Loss)	($ 2,700)	$ 72,000	$ 52,000
Inclusion Rate	1/2	1/2	1/2
Taxable Capital Gain (Loss)	($ 1,350)	$ 36,000	$ 26,000

	Building
Capital Cost	$183,000
UCC	(144,800)
Recapture Of CCA	$ 38,200

Mortgage Interest - Attribution

With respect to the mortgage interest received by Mr. Steele, it was earned on mortgages given to him by Mrs. Steele and, as a consequence, it would be attributed to her up until her death on June 3, 2013. This means that $886 [(154/365)($2,100)] of the $2,100 would be included in her income. As attribution from a spouse ceases when the transferor spouse dies, the remaining $1,214 ($2,100 - $886) would be included in Mr. Steele's income. When this is combined with his $425 boutique salary, his total income for the year is $1,639. His income for the whole year, not just prior to Mrs. Steele's death, will decrease the spousal credit available on Mrs. Steele's final return.

Net Income For Tax Purposes And Taxable Income

Mrs. Steele's minimum Taxable Income would be calculated as follows:

Business Income		$55,200
Property Income:		
Eligible Dividends Received	$1,090	
Gross Up [(38%)($1,090)]	414	
Interest	2,025	
Mortgage Interest Attributed From Spouse	886	
Rent Revenues	41,200	
Rental Expenses (Note One)	(24,650)	
Recaptured CCA On Rental Property	38,200	59,165
Net Taxable Capital Gains:		
Taxable Capital Gains On Rental Property		
($26,000 + $36,000)	$62,000	
Allowable Capital Loss On AGF Industries Shares	(1,350)	60,650
Net Income		$175,015
Net Capital Loss Carry Forward (Note Two)		(76,500)
Taxable Income		$ 98,515

Note One   As there was a deemed disposition of the rental property immediately before the time of Mrs. Steele's death, no CCA can be taken for 2013.

Note Two   In the year of death, any capital losses and capital loss carry forwards can be deducted against any type of income, not just capital gains, as long as the lifetime capital gains deduction has not been claimed. As a result, although she has net taxable capital gains of only $60,650, she can deduct her total net capital loss carry forward of $76,500.

Tax Payable

Mrs. Steele's minimum federal Tax Payable would be calculated as follows:

Tax On First $87,123		$16,118
Tax On Remaining $11,392 ($98,515 - $87,123) At 26 Percent		2,962
Gross Federal Tax		$19,080
Basic Personal Amount	($11,038)	
Spousal ($11,038 - $1,639)	(9,399)	
Credit Base	($20,437)	
Rate	15%	(3,066)
Dividend Tax Credit [(6/11)(38%)($1,090)]		(226)
Federal Tax Payable		$15,788

Self Study Solution Eleven - 10

Extension of Tax Software Self Study Problem in Study Guide on page S-236

Part A

Rental Income   Since Eleanor is currently renting out her house, but plans to move back into it, no CCA is taken on the Class 1 building to preserve her principal residence status. Since she had a rental loss in the previous year, and the cost is equal to the UCC, no CCA has been taken on the building. Her CCA on the appliances would not affect her principal residence election and should be taken. The payments on principal are not deductible.

If she chose to take CCA on the building, the maximum potential CCA for the year would be $6,756 [(4%)($168,900)] since the first year one-half rule does not apply to her second year of rental. The maximum deductible CCA on the building would be limited to the net rental income after the CCA on the appliances of $5,553 ($5,887 - $334). This would reduce her Tax Payable for 2013, but she would no longer be eligible for the principal residence gain reduction on the property. In addition, the CCA would be recaptured on a subsequent sale if the proceeds were greater than the UCC.

Given her inheritance, she should have more than sufficient funds to pay her income taxes without taking CCA on her rental property. As a result, she should preserve her ability to claim the principal residence gain reduction by not taking CCA on the house.

Eleanor's net rental income can be calculated as follows:

Gross Rental Income		$15,600
Less Expenses:		
Less Expenses:		
Property Taxes	($2,190)	
Insurance	(1,093)	
Interest	(5,378)	
Maintenance And Repairs ($291 + $300)	(591)	
Legal Fees	(173)	
Utilities	(288)	(9,713)
Rental Income Before CCA		$ 5,887
CCA On Class 8 Assets {[20%][$921 + (1/2)($1,500)]}		(334)
Net Rental Income		$ 5,553

The calculations for Eleanor's Net Income For Tax Purposes and Taxable Income are as follows:

Salary	$60,202	
RPP Deduction	(2,406)	
Union Dues	(749)	$57,047
CPP Survivor Benefits		4,823
Pension Income		22,249
Eligible Dividends	$1,603	
Gross Up Of Dividends [(38%)($1,603)]	609	2,212
Interest Income ($509 + $311)		820
Rental Income		5,553
Taxable Capital Gains [(1/2)($982)]		491
RRSP Deduction (Note One)		(2,620)
Child Care Expenses (Note Two)		(600)
Net And Taxable Income		$89,975

Note One The maximum RRSP deduction for 2013 would be calculated as follows:

Unused Deduction Room From 2012	$1,665
Lesser Of:	
• 2013 RRSP Dollar Limit = $23,820	
• [(18%)($38,873)] = $6,997	6,997
Less 2012 Pension Adjustment	(4,376)
Maximum Available Deduction For 2013	$4,286

While Eleanor had a potential deduction of $4,286, her actual deduction is limited to her contribution of $2,620. This will leave her with unused deduction room of $1,666 ($4,286 - $2,620).

Note Two   The Croft Computer Camp was an overnight camp which means that the deductible costs are limited to $100 per week, a total of $200 [(2)($100)]. In contrast, there is no limit on the costs of day camps. This provides for the deduction of the entire $400 cost of the Y Day Camp.

Eleanor's minimum federal Tax Payable is calculated as follows:

Federal Tax On First $87,123		$16,118
Federal Tax On Next $2,852 ($89,975 - $87,123) At 26 Percent		742
Gross Federal Tax		$16,860
Basic Personal Amount	($11,038)	
Eligible Dependant - Amy	(11,038)	
Child	(2,234)	
Caregiver - Marjorie	(4,490)	
EI Premiums	(891)	
CPP Contributions	(2,356)	
Canada Employment	(1,117)	
Transfer Of Tuition, Education And Textbook - Lesser Of:		
• $5,000		
• [$7,000 + (8)($400) + (8)($65) + (2)($120) + (2)($20)] = $11,000	(5,000)	
Pension	(2,000)	
Medical Expenses (Note Two)	(1,191)	
Credit Base	($41,355)	
Rate	15%	(6,203)
Charitable Donations [(15%)($200) + (29%)($175 + $375 + $50 - $200)]		(146)
Dividend Tax Credit [(6/11)($609)]		(332)
Federal Tax Payable		$10,179
Provincial Tax Payable (Given)		4,500
Tax Withheld ($11,408 + $3,511)		(14,919)
Balance Owing (Refund)		($ 240)

Note Two   Allowable medical expenses are as follows:

Eleanor And Minor Child (Amy) Medical Expenses ($392 + $1,350 + $450 + $1,120)		$3,312
Threshold - Lesser Of: [(3%)($89,975)] And $2,152		(2,152)
Subtotal		$1,160
Marjorie's Medical Expenses ($110 + $75)	$185	
Reduced By The Lesser Of:		
• $2,152		
• [(3%)($8,000)] = $240	(240)	Nil
Diane's Medical Expenses	$100	
Reduced By The Lesser Of:		
• $2,152		
• [(3%)($2,300)] = $69	(69)	31
Allowable Medical Expenses		$1,191

Notes To Eleanor's Tax Return

- ~~Diane transfers the $5,000 maximum education related credits to Eleanor and carries~~ forward the remaining $6,000 [$7,000 + (8)($400) + (8)(65) + (2)($120) + (2)($20) - $5,000].

- Eleanor cannot claim the charitable donation made by Diane, but Diane can carry it forward for up to five years.

- Diane should file a tax return, otherwise she will not be eligible for the GST credit and she will not benefit from the RRSP deduction room created during the year. Filing a tax return will also make her education related tax credits and charitable donation tax credit easier to keep track of for carry forward purposes.

- Eleanor's mother, Marjorie, should file a tax return in order to receive the GST credit.

- Since Amy is under 18 and wholly dependent, Eleanor claimed the eligible dependant credit for Amy.

- Eleanor claimed the full caregiver credit for Marjorie as her income is well below the income threshold. Note that, because Marjorie is not infirm, the family caregiver amount is not added to this credit.

- Since Diane and Marjorie are over 17 years of age, their medical expenses are reduced by 3 percent of their Net Income For Tax Purposes. This means that none of Marjorie's medical expenses can be claimed by Eleanor.

- With the inflow of funds from the inheritance, Eleanor should review her debt outstanding and pay off any balances that have non-deductible interest, such as credit card balances. Although it is not exactly a tax planning point, Eleanor should compare the after tax cost of the interest she is paying on her rental property mortgage with the after tax yields that she can obtain on her investments to determine whether she should pay off her mortgage.

Part B

Eleanor's 2013 Earned Income is calculated as follows:

Salary	$60,202	
Union Dues	(749)	$59,453
Rental Income (See Part A)		5,553
Earned Income		$65,006

The maximum deductible RRSP contribution that Eleanor can make for 2014 is calculated as follows:

Unused Deduction Room From 2013 (Part A)	$ 1,666
Lesser Of:	
• 2014 RRSP Dollar Limit = $24,270	
• [(18%)($65,006)] = $11,701	11,701
Less Her 2013 PA (From T4)	(7,829)
Maximum 2014 RRSP Contribution	$ 5,538

Note that if Eleanor chooses to deduct CCA on her rental building and reduces her net rental income to nil, her maximum deductible RRSP contribution will be reduced by $1,000 [(18%)($5,553)]. This is another reason she should not take CCA on the rental building.

Given her inheritance, Eleanor should contribute the maximum deductible RRSP contribution as early in 2014 as possible.

Eleanor should open an RESP for Amy if she has not already done so. How much she should contribute will depend on many factors (see the text), but she should request that her accountant create a contribution schedule that will maximize Canada Education Savings Plan contributions and optimize RESP contributions.

Eleanor should open TFSAs for herself, Diane and Marjorie and contribute the maximum to each (see the text). Since the contributions are not deductible and the withdrawals are not taxable, the TFSAs will not have an effect on any of the tax returns.

If Eleanor still has funds to invest, she can overcontribute $2,000 to her RRSP without penalty, which she should do for as long as she plans to have earned income for RRSP purposes sufficient to deduct the $2,000 in the future. This will allow her to take advantage of the tax free earnings in the RRSP.

Self Study Solution Eleven - 11

Net Employment Income

Katherine's Net Employment Income would be calculated as follows:

Salary	$85,000
Loan Benefit (Note 1)	1,500
RPP Contribution	(2,875)
Net Employment Income	$83,625

Note 1 The loan benefit is $1,500 [(1%)($150,000)(4/4)]. Note that, because this is a housing loan to an employee, Katherine can calculate the benefit as using the lesser of the prescribed rate at the time the loan is granted (1 percent) and the current rate (2 percent). This privilege is available during the first five years of the loan.

Income From Rental Properties

Katherine's rental income from the two properties would be $8,600 ($2,900 + $5,700), calculated as follows:

	Property A	Property B
2013 Rents	$26,400	$28,800
2013 Expenses Other Than CCA	(23,500)	(23,100)
Income Before CCA	$ 2,900	$ 5,700
CCA	Nil	Nil
Net Rental Income	$ 2,900	$ 5,700

As there is a deemed disposition of these properties immediately before the time of Ms. O'Hara's death, CCA cannot be deducted for 2013.

Dispositions Of Darcy Inc. Shares

Since the problem requires the minimum Net Income For Tax Purposes, Mick (as executor) would not elect out of the ITA 73(1) spousal rollover and the gift of 2,500 shares to Mick would have no immediate tax consequences. However, the gifts to her two children and the sale to her daughter will be recorded at the current fair market value of $14. This will result in a taxable capital gain as follows:

Proceeds Of Disposition [(7,500)($14)]	$105,000
Adjusted Cost Base [(7,500)($120,000 ÷ 10,000)]	(90,000)
Capital Gain	$ 15,000
Inclusion Rate	1/2
Taxable Capital Gain	$ 7,500

Income On Securities

Katherine would include the following amounts in her 2013 Net Income For Tax Purposes:

Darcy Inc. Dividends The dividends on the Darcy Inc. shares that were gifted to Katherine's husband and her minor son, Sean, will be attributed to her. The amount would $4,500 [(5,000)($0.90)]. The dividends on the shares gifted to Sylvia and purchased by Sylvia would not be subject to income attribution and would be included in Sylvia's 2013 Net Income For Tax Purposes.

Barton Income Trust Distributions Katherine's income inclusion here would be $12,000 [(12,000)($1.50 - $0.50)].

Fidel Mutual Fund Distributions Katherine's income inclusion here would $8,000 [(8,000)($1.00)].

Tax Consequences Of Katherine's Death

There would be a deemed disposition of all of Katherine's capital property immediately before the December 31, 2013 date of her death. The tax consequences would be as follows:

Principal Residence The bequest of the principal residence to Sean would result in a capital gain of $38,000 ($510,000 - $472,000). However, application of the principal residence exemption formula to this amount would result in an exemption of the maximum amount of $38,000.

Barton Income Trust Units As there is no general rollover of capital property to children, the fact that Katherine gave all of these units to Sean and Sylvia will result in a taxable capital gain. These units had an original cost of $16.75 per share ($201,000 ÷ 12,000), but previous returns of capital had reduced the adjusted cost base to $15.00 per share ($180,000 ÷ 12,000) on January 1, 2013. This was further reduced to $14.50 by the $0.50 return of capital that was distributed in 2013. Given this, the taxable capital gain would be $18,000 [(1/2)(12,000)($17.50 - $14.50)].

Rental Property A Under ITA 70(6), there is a tax free rollover of capital property to a spouse and Mick would not elect out of ITA 70(6). Given this, there would be no tax consequences resulting from the bequest of rental property A to Mick O'Hara. He would be deemed to have acquired the building with a capital cost of $326,000 and a UCC of $297,000, with the difference being treated as deemed CCA. The land would be deemed to be acquired at its adjusted cost base of $50,000.

Rental Property B The results of this disposition are as follows:

	Land	Building
Fair Market Value	$60,000	$495,000
Capital Cost	(60,000)	(347,000)
Capital Gain	Nil	$148,000
Inclusion Rate	N/A	1/2
Taxable Capital Gain	Nil	$ 74,000

	Building
Capital Cost	$347,000
UCC	(311,000)
Recapture Of CCA	$ 36,000

Fidel Mutual Fund Units With the reinvestment of the 2013 distribution, the adjusted cost base of these units would be $80,000 [$72,000 + (8,000)($1)]. The reinvestment of the distribution would result in the acquisition of 800 new units

($8,000 ÷ $10.00), giving a total holding of 8,800 units. Since the problem requires the minimum Net Income For Tax Purposes, Mick, as executor for Katherine's estate, would elect out of the ITA 70(6) rollover in order to allow her to claim the allowable capital loss. The loss would be calculated as follows:

Fair Market Value [(8,800)($8.30)]	$73,040
Adjusted Cost Base	(80,000)
Capital Loss	($ 6,960)
Inclusion Rate	1/2
Allowable Capital Loss	($ 3,480)

Part A - Net Income For Tax Purposes And Taxable Income

The required calculations here are as follows:

Net Employment Income		$ 83,625
Net Rental Income ($2,900 + $5,700)		8,600
Recapture On Rental Property B		36,000
Net Taxable Capital Gains:		
Darcy Inc. Shares	$ 7,500	
Barton Income Trust Units	18,000	
Rental Property B	74,000	
Fidel Mutual Fund Units	(3,480)	96,020
Attributed Dividends On Darcy Inc. Shares		4,500
Gross Up Of 38 Percent		1,710
Barton Income Trust Distributions		12,000
Fidel Mutual Fund Distribution		8,000
Net Income For Tax Purposes		$250,455
Net Capital Loss Carry Forward		(10,000)
Taxable Income		$240,455

Part A - Tax Payable

The required calculations here would be as follows:

Tax On First $135,054		$28,580
Tax On Next $105,401 ($240,455 - $135,054) At 29 Percent		30,566
Tax Before Credits		$59,146
Tax Credits:		
Basic Personal	($11,038)	
Child (Sean)	(2,234)	
Employment Insurance	(891)	
Canada Pension Plan	(2,356)	
Canada Employment	(1,117)	
Transfer - Sylvia's Tuition, Education, And Textbook		
Lesser Of (Note 2):		
• $5,000		
• [$8,150 + (11)($400) + (11)($65)] = $13,265	(5,000)	
Medical Expenses (Note 3)	(3,232)	
Total Credit Base	($25,868)	
Rate	15%	(3,880)
Dividend Tax Credit [(6/11)($1,710)]		(933)
Federal Tax Payable		$54,333

Note 2 Sylvia owned a total of 5,000 shares of Darcy Inc., 2,500 that were gifted to her and 2,500 that she purchased. Sylvia's Net Income from the eligible dividends received from Darcy Inc. totalled $6,210 [(5,000)($.90)(138%)]. Her Tax Payable is completely eliminated by her basic personal credit. She can transfer a maximum of $5,000 of her education, tuition and textbook amounts to be claimed on her deceased mother's tax return. The remaining $8,265 can be carried forward indefinitely, but must be used by Sylvia.

Note 3 The base for the medical expense tax credit would be calculated as follows:

Unreimbursed Medical Expenses Of Katherine, Mick, And Sean		
[(50%)($3,700 + $2,420 + $300)]		$3,210
Reduced By The Lesser Of:		
• [(3%)($250,455)] = $7,514		
• 2013 Limit Of $2,152		(2,152)
Subtotal		$1,058
Sylvia's Medical Expenses (No Reimbursement)	$2,360	
Reduced By The Lesser Of:		
• [(3%)($6,210)] = $186		
• $2,152	(186)	2,174
Medical Expense Tax Credit Base		$3,232

Part B - Mike O'Hara's Net Income For Tax Purposes

The results with respect to rental property A would be as follows:

	Land	Building
Proceeds Of Disposition	$75,000	$395,000
Adjusted Cost Base	(50,000)	(326,000)
Capital Gain	$25,000	$ 69,000
Inclusion Rate	1/2	1/2
Taxable Capital Gain	$12,500	$ 34,500

Capital Cost		$326,000
UCC		(297,000)
Recapture Of CCA		$ 29,000

There would be no capital gain or loss on the Fidel Mutual Fund units as the transfer to Mick occurred at the December 31, 2013 fair market value.

The total increase in Mick's Net Income For Tax Purposes due to the sales would be $76,000 ($12,500 + $34,500 + $29,000).

Solution to Tax Software Self Study Problem - Chapter 11

This solution includes the Tax Summary from the ProFile T1 return. Note that this solution is based on a 2012 (not 2013) tax return. The complete tax return is available on the Student CD-ROM.

To view the files, access your Student CD-ROM. Under the heading "Textbook Support Files", select the option "Tax Return Files" and you will see two drop-down lists.

- To view the ProFile file, select "Chapter 11 SS Software Problem" from the ProFile drop-down list.

- To view the .PDF file, select "PDF Chapter 11 SS Software Problem" from the PDF drop-down list.

For more information on how to use the ProFile tax program, refer to the Chapter 4 sample tax return in this Study Guide.

Notes to tax return

- Diane transfers the $5,000 maximum education related credits to Eleanor and carries forward the remaining $6,000 [$7,000 + (8)($400) + (8)($65) + (2)($120) + (2)($20) - $5,000]. The carry forward can only be used by Diane.

- Eleanor cannot claim the charitable donation made by Diane, but Diane can carry it forward for up to five years.

- Diane should file a tax return, otherwise she will not be eligible for the GST credit and she will not benefit from the RRSP deduction room created during the year. Filing a tax return will also make her education related tax credits and charitable donation tax credit easier to keep track of for carry forward purposes.

- Eleanor's mother, Marjorie should file a tax return in order to receive the GST credit.

- Since Amy is under 18 and wholly dependent, Eleanor claimed the eligible dependant credit for Amy.

- Eleanor claimed the full caregiver credit for Marjorie as her income is well below the income threshold.

- Since Diane and Marjorie are over 17 years of age, their medical expenses are reduced by 3 percent of their Net Income For Tax Purposes. This means that none of Marjorie's medical expenses can be claimed by Eleanor.

- The Croft Computer Camp was an overnight camp which means that the deductible costs are limited to $100 per week, a total of $200 [(2)($100)]. In contrast, there is no limit on the costs of day camps. This provides for the deduction of the entire $400 cost of the Y Day Camp.

- Since Eleanor is currently renting out her house, but plans to move back into it, no CCA is taken on the Class 1 building to preserve her principal residence status. Since she had a rental loss in the previous year, and the cost is equal to the UCC, no CCA has been taken on the building. Her CCA on the Class 8 assets would not affect her principal residence election and should be taken. The payments on principal are not deductible.

  If she chose to take CCA on the building, the maximum potential CCA for the year would be $6,756 [(4%)($168,900)] since the first year one-half rule does not apply to the second year of rental. The maximum deductible CCA on the building would be limited to the net rental income after the CCA on the Class 8 assets of $5,553 ($5,887 - $334). This would reduce her Tax Payable for 2012, but she would no longer be eligible for the principal residence gain reduction on the property. In addition, the CCA would be recaptured on a subsequent sale if the proceeds were greater than the UCC.

Given her inheritance, she should have more than sufficient funds to pay her income taxes without taking CCA on her rental property. As a result, she should preserve her ability to claim the principal residence gain reduction by not taking CCA on the house.

- With the inflow of funds from the inheritance, Eleanor should review her debt outstanding and pay off any balances that have non-deductible interest, such as credit card balances. Although it is not exactly a tax planning point, Eleanor should compare the after tax cost of the interest she is paying on her rental property mortgage with the after tax yields that she can obtain on her investments to determine whether she should pay off her mortgage.

Part B

The maximum deductible RRSP contribution that Eleanor can make for 2013 is calculated as $5,538 by the program on the form "RRSPLimit". To access the form, press <F4> and type "rrsplimit" in the form box.

Note that if Eleanor chooses to deduct CCA on her rental building and reduce her net rental income to nil, her maximum deductible RRSP contribution will be reduced by $1,000 [(18%)($5,553)]. This is another reason she should not take CCA on the rental building.

Given her inheritance, Eleanor should contribute the maximum deductible RRSP contribution as early in 2013 as possible.

Eleanor should open an RESP for Amy if she has not already done so. How much she should contribute will depend on many factors (see the text), but she should request that her accountant create a contribution schedule that will maximize Canada Education Savings Plan contributions and optimize RESP contributions.

Eleanor should open TFSAs for herself, Diane and Marjorie and contribute the maximum to each (see the text). Since the contributions are not deductible and the withdrawals are not taxable, the TFSAs will not have an effect on any of the tax returns.

If Eleanor still has funds to invest, she can overcontribute $2,000 to her RRSP without penalty, which she should do for as long as she plans to have earned income for RRSP purposes sufficient to deduct the $2,000 in the future. This will allow her to take advantage of the tax free earnings in the RRSP.

2012 Tax Summary (Federal)

Eleanor-Chapter 11 SS Problem

Eleanor-Chapter 11 SS Problem

Total income

Employment *	101	60,202
Old Age Security	113	
CPP/QPP benefits	114	4,823
Other pensions	115	22,249
Split-pension amount	116	
Universal Child Care Benefit	117	
Employment Insurance	119	
Taxable dividends	120	2,212
Interest	121	820
Limited partnership	122	
RDSP	125	
Rental	126	5,553
Taxable capital gains	127	491
Support payments	128	
RRSP	129	
Other	130	
Self-employment *	135	
Workers' compensation and social assistance	147	
Total income	**150**	**96,351**

Net income

RPP	207	2,406
RRSP *	208	2,620
Split-Pension Deduction	210	
Union and professional dues	212	749
UCCB repayment	213	
Child care expenses	214	600
Disability supports deduction	215	
Business investment loss	217	
Moving expenses	219	
Support payments	220	
Carrying charges and interest	221	
CPP/QPP/PIPP *	222	
Exploration and development	224	
Employment expenses	229	
Social benefits repayment	235	
Other deductions *	231	
Net income	**236**	**89,977**

Taxable income

Canadian Forces personnel	244	
Home relocation loan	248	
Security options deductions	249	
Other payments deduction	250	
Losses of other years *	251	
Capital gains deduction	254	
Northern residents	255	
Additional deductions	256	
Taxable income	**260**	**89,977**

2013 Estimated   Eleanor-Chapter 11 SS Problem

GST/HST credit		
Child Tax Benefit		505 00
RRSP contribution limit		5,538 00

*   More than one line is considered

Non-refundable tax credits

Basic personal amount	300	10,822
Age amount	301	
Spouse / eligible dependant *	303	10,822
Amount for children	367	2,191
Infirm/caregiver *	306	4,402
CPP/QPP/PPIP/EI *	308	3,147
Volunteer firefighters' amount	362	
Canada employment amount	363	1,095
Public transit passes amount	364	
Children's fitness amount	365	
Children's arts amount	370	
Home buyers/Home renovation *	369	
Adoption expenses	313	
Pension income amount	314	2,000
Disability amount	316	
Transfers *	318	5,000
Interest on student loans	319	
Tuition / education	323	
Medical expenses	332	1,234
Subtotal	**335**	**40,713**
Credit at 15%	338	6,107
Donations and gifts	349	146
Non-refundable tax credits	**350**	**6,253**

Total payable

Federal tax	404	16,988
Non-refundable tax credits	350	6,253
Dividend tax credit	425	332
Min. tax carry-over/other *	426	
Basic federal tax	**429**	**10,403**
Non resident surtax		
Foreign tax credits / other	405	
Federal tax	**406**	**10,403**
Political/inv. tax credit/other *	410	
Labour-sponsored tax credit	414	
Alternative minimum tax	417	
WITB Prepayment (RC210)	415	
Special Taxes	418	
Net federal tax	**420**	**10,403**
CPP contributions payable	421	
EI self-employment	430	
Social benefits repayment	422	
Provincial/territorial tax	428	4,373
Total payable	**435**	**14,776**

Total credits

Income tax deducted *	437	14,919
QC or YT abatement *	440	
CPP/EI overpayment *	448	
Medical expense supplement	452	
WITB (Schedule 6)	453	
Other credits *	454	
GST/HST rebate	457	
Instalments	476	
Provincial tax credits	479	
Total credits	**482**	**14,919**

Balance owing (refund)	(143)
Combined balance (refund)	(143)

Complete Return Available On Student CD-ROM

S - 270

Chapter 11 Learning Objectives

After completing Chapter 11, you should be able to:

1. Recall the specified deductions from Net Income For Tax Purposes in the calculation of Taxable Income (paragraph [P hereafter] 11-1 through 11-7).

2. Apply the rules related to lump-sum payments (P 11-8 through 11-13).

3. Recall the general rules for the treatment of losses and loss carry overs (P 11-14 through 11-29).

4. Explain the treatment of losses on personal use property (P 11-30).

5. Apply the loss carry over provisions applicable to losses on listed personal property (P 11-31 through 11-35).

6. Apply the loss carry over provisions applicable to non-capital losses (P 11-36 through 11-40).

7. Apply the loss carry over provisions applicable to net capital losses (P 11-41 through 11-44).

8. Apply the rules for the conversion of a net capital loss carry over to a non-capital loss carry over (P 11-45 through 11-49).

9. Explain the special rules for net capital losses that are applicable to deceased taxpayers (P 11-50 through 11-54).

10. Explain the special features associated with Allowable Business Investment Losses (P 11-55 through 11-62).

11. Apply the loss carry over provisions applicable to regular and restricted farm losses (P 11-63 through 11-67).

12. Apply the provisions of the lifetime capital gains deduction (P 11-68 through 11-97).

13. Describe the importance of the ordering of deductions and losses in computing Net Income For Tax Purposes and Taxable Income (P 11-98 through 11-107).

14. Describe Basic Federal Tax Payable (P 11-108 through 11-113).

15. Calculate the amount of federal Tax Payable on split income (P 11-114 through 11-124).

16. Apply the provisions for the transfer of dividends to a spouse or common-law partner (P 11-125).

17. Calculate the charitable donations tax credit for donations of various types of property (P 11-126 through 11-150).

18. Calculate foreign business and non-business income tax credits (P 11-151 through 11-162).

19. Apply the provisions associated with the alternative minimum tax (P 11-163 through 11-176).

20. Review a personal tax return completed using the ProFile T1 tax preparation software program (page S-228 through S-235 in this Study Guide).

Web Site

The web site for this book can be found at:

www.pearsoncanada.ca/byrdchen/ctp2014

Here you will find:

- Updates and corrections to the textbook and Study Guide
- Glossary Flashcards and Key Terms Self-Tests (also on your Student CD-ROM)
- Links to other relevant web sites
- Instructions on how to install the 2013 ProFile program and download updated sample tax returns and Cases when the updated ProFile software is available in January, 2014
- Instructions on how to access the FITAC/CTP Infobase on the Student CD-ROM

How To Work Through Chapter 12

We recommend the following approach in dealing with the material in this Chapter:

Computation Of Net Income For Corporations
- [ ] Read paragraph 12-1 to Figure 12-1 (in the textbook).
- [ ] Do Exercise Twelve-1 (in the textbook) and check the solution on page S-274 in this Study Guide. All solutions to Exercises and Self Study Problems can be found in this Study Guide and the page numbers all start with the prefix S-.
- [ ] Do Self Study Problem Twelve-1 at the end of the textbook chapter on page 637 and check the solution in this Study Guide.

Deductions Available For Corporations In The Computation Of Taxable Income
- [ ] Read paragraph 12-5 to Figure 12-2.

Dividends Received From Other Corporations
- [ ] Read paragraph 12-10 to 12-12.
- [ ] Do Exercise Twelve-2 and check the solution in this Study Guide.

Dividends Received - Other Situations Including Stop Loss Rules
- [ ] Read paragraph 12-13 to 12-22.
- [ ] Do Exercise Twelve-3 and check the solution in this Study Guide.
- [ ] Read paragraph 12-23.
- [ ] Do Self Study Problem Twelve-2 and check the solution in this Study Guide.

Non-Capital Loss Carry Over For A Corporation
- [ ] Read paragraph 12-24 to 12-30.
- [ ] Do Exercises Twelve-4 and Twelve-5 and check the solutions in this Study Guide.

Ordering Of Taxable Income Deductions
❑ Read paragraph 12-31 to 12-36.
❑ Do Self Study Problems Twelve-3 and Twelve-4 and check the solutions in this Study Guide.

Geographical Allocation Of Income To Permanent Establishments
❑ Read paragraph 12-37 to 12-44.
❑ Do Self Study Problem Twelve-5 and check the solution in this Study Guide.

Federal Tax Payable For Corporations
❑ Read paragraph 12-45 to 12-52.
❑ Do Exercise Twelve-6 and check the solution in this Study Guide.

Provincial Tax Payable For Corporations
❑ Read paragraph 12-53 to 12-63.

Other Goals Of The Corporate Tax System
❑ Read paragraph 12-64 to 12-65.

Small Business Deduction - Definitions And Calculation
❑ Read paragraph 12-66 to 12-100.
❑ Do Exercise Twelve-7 and check the solution in this Study Guide.

Elimination Of The Small Business Deduction For Large CCPCs
❑ Read paragraph 12-101 to 12-111.
❑ Do Exercise Twelve-8 and check the solution in this Study Guide.

Personal Services Corporations, Professional Corporations And Management Companies
❑ Read paragraph 12-112 to 12-120.

Manufacturing And Processing Profits Deduction
❑ Read paragraph 12-121 to 12-139.
❑ Do Exercise Twelve-9 and check the solution in this Study Guide.

General Rate Reduction
❑ Read paragraph 12-140 to 12-147.
❑ Do Exercise Twelve-10 and check the solution in this Study Guide.
❑ Read paragraph 12-148 to 12-153.
❑ Do Exercise Twelve-11 and check the solution in this Study Guide.
❑ Do Self Study Problems Twelve-6 to Twelve-9 and check the solutions in this Study Guide.

Foreign Income Tax Credits For Corporations
❑ Read paragraph 12-154 to 12-165.
❑ Do Exercise Twelve-12 and check the solution in this Study Guide.
❑ Do Self Study Problem Twelve-10 and check the solution in this Study Guide.

To Complete This Chapter
❑ Review the Key Terms Used In This Chapter on pages 635 and 636. Consult the Glossary for the meaning of any key terms you do not know.
❑ Review the Glossary Flashcards and complete the Key Terms Self-Test for the Chapter. These features can be found in two places, on your Student CD-ROM under the heading "Key Term Practice" and on the web site.
❑ Review the Learning Objectives of the Chapter found on page S-289 of this Study Guide.
❑ As a review, we recommend that you view the PowerPoint Slides for Chapter 12 that are on your Student CD-ROM. If you do not have access to the Microsoft PowerPoint program, the PowerPoint Viewer program can be installed from the Student CD-ROM.

Solution to Chapter Twelve Exercises

Exercise Twelve - 1 Solution

Item 1   You would add the accounting loss of $5,600 ($48,300 - $53,900). You would also add the recapture of CCA of $13,700 ($34,600 - $48,300), for a total addition of $19,300.

Item 2   As goodwill is not amortized for accounting purposes and there was no impairment during the year, no adjustment of the accounting figures is required. However, when the goodwill is added to the CEC balance, it would be subject to amortization at a rate of 7 percent per year. This means that you would subtract CEC amortization of $9,450 [($180,000)(3/4)(7%)].

Item 3   You would add the charitable donations of $15,000.

Item 4   You would deduct the premium amortization of $4,500.

Exercise Twelve - 2 Solution

Net Income For Tax Purposes	$263,000
Dividends Received	(14,200)
Charitable Donations	(8,600)
Non-Capital Loss Carry Forward (All)	(82,000)
Net Capital Loss Carry Forward*	(14,250)
Taxable Income	$143,950

*While there is a net capital loss of $18,000 available, the actual deduction is limited to the current year's taxable capital gains of $14,250. The remaining net capital loss carry forward is $3,750 ($18,000 - $14,250).

Exercise Twelve - 3 Solution

Although Loren has held the shares for more than 365 days, it owns more than 5 percent of the shares. As a result, this transaction would be subject to the stop loss rules. The deductible loss would be calculated as follows:

Proceeds Of Disposition [($21.15)(1,000)]	$21,150
Adjusted Cost Base [($25.30)(1,000)]	(25,300)
Total Loss	($ 4,150)
Disallowed Portion [($2.16)(1,000)]	2,160
Capital Loss	($ 1,990)
Inclusion Rate	1/2
Allowable Capital Loss	($ 995)

Exercise Twelve - 4 Solution

Hacker's Net Income For Tax Purposes for 2013 would be nil, the business and property income of $63,500, less the allowable business investment loss of $75,750 [(1/2)($151,500)].

The net capital loss carry over balance at the end of the year would be $7,650 [(1/2)($23,100 - $38,400)].

The non-capital loss carry over would be calculated as follows:

Amount E (The ABIL)	$75,750
Amount F - ITA 3(c) Income	(63,500)
Non-Capital Loss At End Of Year	$12,250

Exercise Twelve - 5 Solution

The non-capital loss balance at the end of the year would be calculated as follows:

Amount E		
ABIL		$ 5,250
Dividends Received And Deducted		48,000
Net Business Loss		273,000
Net Capital Loss Carry Forward Deducted*		13,500
Total		$339,750
Amount F - ITA 3(c) Income:		
Dividends	($48,000)	
Interest	(27,200)	
Net Taxable Capital Gains		
[(1/2)($111,000 - $84,000)]	(13,500)	(88,700)
Non-Capital Loss At End Of Year		$251,050

*Limited to net taxable capital gains of $13,500 [(1/2)($111,000 - $84,000)]. There is a net capital loss carry forward of $5,500 ($19,000 - $13,500) at the end of the year.

Exercise Twelve - 6 Solution

The percentage of Taxable Income earned in each province would be calculated as follows:

	Gross Revenues		Wages And Salaries	
	Amount	Percent	Amount	Percent
Ontario	$1,303,000	44.6%	$ 52,000	31.5%
Manitoba	896,000	30.7%	94,000	57.0%
Not Related To A Province	724,000	24.7%	19,000	11.5%
Total	$2,923,000	100.0%	$165,000	100.0%

The average of the two percentages applicable for income not related to a province is 18.1%, leaving an average for income related to a province of 81.9%. Given this, federal Tax Payable can be calculated as follows:

Base Amount Of Part I Tax [(38%)($226,000)]	$85,880
Federal Tax Abatement [(10%)(81.9%)($226,000)]	(18,509)
General Rate Reduction [(13%)($226,000)]	(29,380)
Federal Tax Payable	$37,991

Exercise Twelve - 7 Solution

As a CCPC throughout the year and with no associated companies, Kartoom is eligible for the full amount of the $500,000 annual business limit. The amount eligible for the small business deduction will be $292,857, the least of:

Active Business Income	**$425,000**
Adjusted Taxable Income (See following calculation)	**$292,857**
Annual Business Limit	**$500,000**
Net Income For Tax Purposes	$570,000
Dividends Received	(85,000)
Non-Capital Loss Carry Forward	(160,000)
Taxable Income	$325,000
100/28 Times Foreign Non-Business Tax Credit	
[(100/28)(15%)($60,000)]	(32,143)
Adjusted Taxable Income	$292,857

Exercise Twelve - 8 Solution

The B component of the ITA 125(5.1) reduction formula is $2,925 [(.00225)($11,300,000 - $10,000,000)]. Given this, the required reduction would be calculated as follows:

$$[(\$500,000)(\$2,925 \div \$11,250)] = \underline{\underline{\$130,000}} \textbf{ Reduction}$$

This reduction leaves the annual business limit at $370,000 ($500,000 - $130,000).

The foreign non-business income tax credit is equal to $5,400 [(15%)($36,000)]. The small business deduction for Largely Small Inc. is equal to 17 percent of the least of:

• Active Business Income ($1,233,000 - $36,000)		$1,197,000
• Taxable Income ($1,233,000 - $914,000)	$319,000	
Less 100/28 Times Non-Business Income FTC		
Of $5,400	(19,286)	$ 299,714
• Reduced Annual Business Limit ($500,000 - $130,000)		$ 370,000

The small business deduction is equal to $50,951 [(17%)($299,714)].

Exercise Twelve - 9 Solution

The small business deduction for Marion Manufacturing would be equal to 17 percent of the least of:

• Canadian Active Business Income		$411,000
• Taxable Income ($462,000 - $310,000)	$152,000	
Less 4 Times Business Income FTC Of $3,150	(12,600)	$139,400
• Annual Business Limit		$500,000

Based on this, the small business deduction would be $23,698 [(17%)($139,400)].

The M&P deduction would be equal to 13 percent of the lesser of:

• M&P Profits	$411,000	
Less Amount Eligible For Small Business Deduction	(139,400)	$271,600
• Taxable Income ($462,000 - $310,000)	$152,000	
Less:		
Amount Eligible For Small Business Deduction	(139,400)	
4 Times Business FTC Of $3,150	(12,600)	
Aggregate Investment Income (Taxable Capital Gain)	(30,000)	$ Nil

The M&P profits deduction would be equal to nil.

It would have been possible to increase the small business deduction to the full $411,000 of active business income by increasing Taxable Income to $422,600 ($411,000 + $12,600). This could be accomplished by limiting the deduction for charitable donations to $39,400 ($462,000 - $422,600). The remaining unclaimed donations of $270,600 ($310,000 - $39,400) could be carried forward for up to five years.

Although this increases Taxable Income and the total Tax Payable for the year, there could still be an ultimate tax savings with this approach, as the small business deduction cannot be carried forward, while charitable donations can be. As the Exercise states that Marion expects large increases in income in the future, this approach would be advantageous if Marion's expectations turn out to be correct.

Exercise Twelve - 10 Solution
The federal Tax Payable for Marchand Inc. would be calculated as follows:

Base Amount Of Part I Tax [(38%)($320,000)]	$121,600
Federal Tax Abatement [(10%)($320,000)]	(32,000)
M&P Deduction [(13%)($180,000)]	(23,400)
General Rate Reduction [(13%)($320,000 - $180,000)]	(18,200)
Federal Tax Payable	$ 48,000

As you would expect, the overall tax rate is equal to 15 percent ($48,000 ÷ $320,000).

Exercise Twelve - 11 Solution
The federal Tax Payable for Redux Ltd. would be calculated as follows:

Base Amount Of Part I Tax [(38%)($200,000)]	$76,000
Federal Tax Abatement [(10%)($200,000)]	(20,000)
Small Business Deduction (Note One)	(23,800)
M&P Deduction (Note Two)	(650)
General Rate Reduction (Note Three)	(7,150)
Federal Tax Payable	$24,400

Note One   The small business deduction would be equal $23,800, 17 percent of $140,000, the least of:

Active Business Income	$200,000
Taxable Income	200,000
Business Limit	140,000

Note Two   The M&P deduction would be equal to $650, 13 percent of $5,000, the lesser of:

• M&P Profits	$145,000	
Amount Eligible For Small Business Deduction	(140,000)	$ 5,000
• Taxable Income	$200,000	
Amount Eligible For Small Business Deduction	(140,000)	$60,000

Note Three   The general rate reduction would be calculated as follows:

Taxable Income	$200,000
Amount Eligible For The SBD	(140,000)
Amount Eligible For The M&P Deduction	(5,000)
Full Rate Taxable Income	$ 55,000
Rate	13%
General Rate Reduction	$ 7,150

Exercise Twelve - 12 Solution
The Taxable Income figure would be calculated as follows:

Net Income For Tax Purposes	$146,000
Dividends Received	(30,000)
Non-Capital Loss Carry Forward	(75,000)
Net Capital Loss Carry Forward	(25,000)
Taxable Income	$ 16,000

Starting with this figure, the required calculation of Part I Tax Payable would be as follows:

Base Amount Of Part I Tax [(38%)($16,000)]	$6,080
Federal Tax Abatement [(88%)(10%)($16,000)]	(1,408)
General Rate Reduction [(13%)($16,000)]	(2,080)
Foreign Business Income Tax Credit (See Note)	(879)
Part I Tax Payable	$1,713

Note   The foreign business income tax credit would be $879, the least of:

- The amount withheld $3,000

- $\left[\dfrac{\$20,000}{\$146,000 - \$30,000 - \$25,000}\right]$ [$6,080 - $2,080] $879

- $6,080 - $2,080 $4,000

The unused foreign business tax amount of $2,121 ($3,000 - $879) can be carried back 3 years and forward for 10 years. In calculating the allowable tax credit for such carry overs, these unused amounts will be added to the foreign tax paid factor in the calculation of the foreign business income tax credit.

Self Study Solution Twelve - 1

1. The required adjustments would be:

    - Add: Amortization expense of $254,000.
    - Deduct: CCA of $223,000.

2. The required adjustment would be:

    - Deduct: Premium amortization of $2,000.

3. The capital gain on this sale is $40,000 ($120,000 - $80,000). Because only $48,000 ($120,000 - $72,000) of the proceeds are outstanding at the end of the current year, a reserve can be deducted. The reserve will be the lesser of:

    - $16,000 [($40,000)($48,000 ÷ $120,000)]
    - $32,000 [($40,000)(20%)(4 - 0)]

    The deduction of the lesser value of $16,000 will leave a capital gain of $24,000 ($40,000 - $16,000). Based on this, the required adjustments are:

    - Deduct: Accounting gain of $67,000 ($120,000 - $53,000).
    - Add: Taxable capital gain of $12,000 [(1/2)($24,000)].

    There is no recapture on this disposition as the Company still owns Class 43 assets, and there is a positive balance in the class at the end of the year.

4. The required adjustments would be:

    - Add: Membership fees of $8,000.
    - Add: Non-deductible entertainment expenses of $6,000 [(50%)($12,000)].

5. The required adjustment would be:

    - Add: Charitable donations of $11,000.

6. The required adjustments would be:

    - Add: Accounting loss of $16,000 ($23,000 - $39,000).
    - Add: Recapture of $23,000 (Nil - $23,000).

Self Study Solution Twelve - 2

The minimum Net Income For Tax Purposes and Taxable Income of Margo Ltd. would be calculated as follows:

Pre-Tax Accounting Income		$ 31,940
Additions:		
Inventory Reserve (Item 1)	$15,000	
Property Taxes On Vacant Land (Item 2)	1,200	
Amortization Expense	35,600	
Accounting Write-Down Of Goodwill (Item 3)	1,700	
Charitable Donations	19,800	
Taxable Capital Gain [(1/2)($30,500 - $21,000)]		
(Item 5)	4,750	
Warranty Provision	5,500	
Social Club Membership Fees	7,210	
Interest On Late Income Tax Instalments	1,020	
Foreign Taxes Withheld (Item 6)	270	
Premium On Share Redemption	480	92,530
Deductions:		
CCA (Item 7)	($78,000)	
Amortization Of Cumulative Eligible Capital (Note)	(1,785)	
Accounting Gain On Sale Of Investments (Item 5)	(9,500)	(89,285)
Net Income For Tax Purposes		**$ 35,185**
Deductions:		
Charitable Donations	($19,800)	
Dividends	(3,000)	(22,800)
Taxable Income		**$ 12,385**

Notes

Legal Fees While penalties and interest related to income tax balances are not deductible, the costs of appealing an assessment can be deducted. The fees related to general corporate matters would also be deductible.

Cumulative Eligible Capital The cumulative eligible capital account has an addition of $25,500 [(3/4)($34,000)] for the goodwill acquired. Amortization for the year is $1,785 [(7%)($25,500)].

Self Study Solution Twelve - 3

The required calculation of Net Income For Tax Purposes and Taxable Income is as follows:

ITA 3(a) Dividends		$ 33,500
ITA 3(b) Taxable Capital Gains	$9,600	
Allowable Capital Losses	(4,425)	5,175
ITA 3(c)		$ 38,675
ITA 3(d) Business Loss		(141,800)
Net Income For Tax Purposes		Nil
Dividends Received		($ 33,500)
Net Capital Loss Carry Forward		
(Limited To Net Taxable Capital Gains)		(5,175)
Charitable Donations		Nil
Taxable Income		Nil

The carry forward balances available at the end of the year are as follows:

Net Capital Loss Carry Forward

Beginning Balance	$10,500
Used During Year	(5,175)
Net Capital Loss Carry Forward	$ 5,325

Charitable Donations Carry Forward

Beginning Balance	$1,350
Added During Year	5,400
Used During Year	Nil
Unused Charitable Donations	$6,750

Non-Capital Loss Carry Forward

Balance Under E	
Dividends	$ 33,500
Business Loss	141,800
Net Capital Loss Carry Forward Deducted	5,175
Subtotal	$180,475
Balance Under F - Income Under ITA 3(c)	(38,675)
Non-Capital Loss Carry Forward	$141,800

As per the policy of the Company, this solution minimizes the net capital loss carry forward. In the absence of this policy, alternative solutions could minimize the charitable donations carry forward or the non-capital loss balance.

Self Study Solution Twelve - 4

2010 Analysis

Net And Taxable Income

Net Income For Tax Purposes and Taxable would be calculated as follows:

Business Income	$95,000
Dividends	12,000
Net Income For Tax Purposes	**$107,000**
Dividends	(12,000)
Charitable Donations	(21,400)
Taxable Income	**$ 73,600**

There would be a current year net capital loss of $5,000 [(1/2)($10,000)].

Loss Carry Forward

At the end of 2010, there would be a net capital loss carry forward of $5,000 [(1/2)($10,000)].

2011 Analysis

Net And Taxable Income

Both Net Income For Tax Purposes and Taxable Income would be nil as shown in the following calculation:

Business Loss	($205,000)
Dividends	42,000
Net Income For Tax Purposes	**Nil**
Dividends	(42,000)
Taxable Income	**Nil**

This would leave a non-capital loss balance of $205,000, calculated as follows:

Amount E ($205,000 + $42,000)	$247,000
Income Under ITA 3(c) - Dividends	(42,000)
Non-Capital Loss for 2011	$205,000

There would also be a current year net capital loss of $7,000 [(1/2)($14,000)].

Carry Back And 2010 Amended Return

Of the total non-capital loss of $205,000, $73,600, can be carried back to 2010, resulting in the following amended return for that year:

Taxable Income As Previously Reported	$73,600
Non-Capital Loss Carry Back From 2011	(73,600)
Amended 2010 Taxable Income	Nil

Carry Forwards

After the carry back, the following carry forward balances would be available at the end of 2011:

• Charitable Donations	$ 4,600
• Non-Capital Loss Carry Forward ($205,000 - $73,600)	$131,400
• Net Capital Loss Carry Forward ($5,000 + $7,000)	$ 12,000

2012 Analysis

Net And Taxable Income

Net Income For Tax Purposes and Taxable would be calculated as follows:

Business Income	$ 69,500
Taxable Capital Gains [(1/2)($9,000)]	4,500
Dividends	28,000
Net Income For Tax Purposes	**$102,000**
Dividends	(28,000)
Charitable Donations	(8,000)
Taxable Income Before Carry Forwards	$ 66,000
Net Capital Loss Carry Forward (Limited To Taxable Capital Gains)	(4,500)
Charitable Donations Carry Forward (All)	(4,600)
Non-Capital Loss Carry Forward (Note)	(56,900)
Taxable Income	**Nil**

Note The amount of the non-capital loss carry forward that was deducted was the amount required to reduce the 2012 Taxable Income to nil.

While the various balances carried forward from 2011 could be used in any order that Linden chooses, it is the policy of the Company to minimize its net capital loss balance. Also, since the charitable donations can only be carried forward for 5 years, it is more advantageous to deduct the charitable donations rather than more of the non-capital loss carry forward as the non-capital loss carry forward has a 20 year carry forward period.

Loss Carry Forwards

After the preceding allocation of losses, the following balances remain:

- Non-Capital Loss Carry Forward ($131,400 - $56,900) $74,500
- Net Capital Loss Carry Forward ($12,000 - $4,500) $ 7,500

2013 Analysis

Net And Taxable Income

Net Income For Tax Purposes and Taxable would be calculated as follows:

Business Income	$90,000
Taxable Capital Gains [(1/2)($10,000)]	5,000
Dividends	32,000
Net Income For Tax Purposes	**$127,000**
Dividends	(32,000)
Charitable Donations	(22,000)
Taxable Income Before Carry Forwards	$ 73,000
Net Capital Loss Carry Forward	
(Limited To Taxable Capital Gains)	(5,000)
Non-Capital Loss Carry Forward	
(Amount That Reduces Taxable Income To Nil)	(68,000)
Taxable Income	**Nil**

Loss Carry Forwards

After the preceding allocation of losses, the following balances remain:

- Non-Capital Loss Carry Forward ($74,500 - $68,000) $6,500
- Net Capital Loss Carry Forward ($7,500 - $5,000) $2,500

Self Study Solution Twelve - 5

From the descriptions in the problem, it would appear that each of the provincial warehouses of the Sundean Company would qualify as a permanent establishment. As a consequence, the allocation to each of the five provinces would be based on the following calculations:

Province	Gross Revenues		Salaries And Wages	
	Amount	Percent	Amount	Percent
Alberta	$ 1,886,940	18%	$ 261,870	21%
British Columbia	2,306,260	22%	274,340	22%
Nova Scotia	1,362,790	13%	174,580	14%
Saskatchewan	1,257,960	12%	99,760	8%
Ontario	3,669,050	35%	436,450	35%
Total	$10,483,000	100%	$1,247,000	100%

The province by province average of the two percentages calculated above, and the allocation of the total Taxable Income of $1,546,000 would be as follows:

Province	Revenues	Wages	Average	Taxable Income
Alberta	18%	21%	19.5%	$ 301,470
British Columbia	22%	22%	22.0%	340,120
Nova Scotia	13%	14%	13.5%	208,710
Saskatchewan	12%	8%	10.0%	154,600
Ontario	35%	35%	35.0%	541,100
Total	100%	100%	100.0%	$1,546,000

Self Study Solution Twelve - 6

Kannon's Part I tax payable for the year would be calculated as follows:

Base Amount Of Part I Tax [(38%)($473,000)]	$179,740
Federal Tax Abatement [(10%)(88.6%)($473,000)] (Note One)	(41,908)
Small Business Deduction (Note Two)	(42,689)
General Rate Reduction (Note Three)	(28,846)
Part I Tax Payable	$ 66,297

Note One The federal tax abatement must be reduced because of the foreign business income. The percentage would be calculated as follows:

Canadian Wages And Salaries As Percentage Of Total
($560,000 + $642,000) ÷ $1,298,000   92.6%

Canadian Gross Revenues As Percentage Of Total
($1,200,000 + $1,232,000) ÷ $2,879,000   84.5%

Based on these calculations, the percentage of income on which the federal tax abatement would be available is 88.6 percent [(92.6% + 84.5%) ÷ 2].

Note Two Since Kannon's Taxable Capital Employed In Canada during 2012 was greater than $10 million, its small business deduction is reduced. The B component of the ITA 125(5.1) reduction formula is $5,600 [(.00225)($12,488,890 - $10,000,000)]. Given this, the required reduction would be calculated as follows:

[($500,000)($5,600 ÷ $11,250)] = $248,889 **Reduction**

The small business deduction is equal to 17 percent of the least of:

- Canadian Active Business Income $440,000
- Taxable Income   473,000
- Reduced Annual Business Limit ($500,000 - $248,889)   251,111

The small business deduction would be $42,689 [(17%)($251,111)].

Note Three The general rate reduction would be calculated as follows:

Taxable Income	$473,000
Amount Eligible For Small Business Deduction	(251,111)
Full Rate Taxable Income	$221,889
Rate	13%
General Rate Reduction	$ 28,846

Self Study Solution Twelve - 7

The Taxable Income and Tax Payable for the Serendipity Shop Corp. for the year would be calculated as follows:

Net Income For Tax Purposes		$240,000
Deductions:		
Dividends	($20,000)	
Donations	(48,000)	(68,000)
Taxable Income		$172,000
Base Amount Of Part I Tax [(38%)($172,000)]		$ 65,360
Federal Tax Abatement [(10%)($172,000)]		(17,200)
Small Business Deduction (Note)		(22,950)
General Rate Reduction [(13%)($172,000 - $135,000)]		(4,810)
Part I Federal Tax Payable		$ 20,400

Note   The small business deduction is based on the least of the following:

Active business income	$220,000
Taxable Income	172,000
Allocated annual business limit	135,000

The small business deduction is equal to $22,950 [(17%)($135,000)].

Self Study Solution Twelve - 8

Part A - Net Income For Tax Purposes

The minimum Net Income For Tax Purposes for Borscan Inc. would be calculated as follows:

Accounting Income Before Taxes		$1,275,000
Additions:		
Taxable Capital Gain - Building		
[(1/2)($625,000 - $500,000 - $100,000)]	$ 12,500	
Taxable Capital Gain - Land ($100,000 - $100,000)	Nil	
Recaptured CCA ($500,000 - $350,000)	150,000	
Amortization Expense	255,000	
Interest And Penalties - Late Payment	500	
Charitable Donations	13,500	431,500
		$1,706,500
Deductions:		
Capital Cost Allowance	($287,000)	
Results Of Discontinued Operations		
(From Income Statement)	(25,000)	
Amortization Of Cumulative Eligible Capital		
[(7%)($85,000)]	(5,950)	(317,950)
Net Income For Tax Purposes		$1,388,550

Part B - Taxable Income

The minimum Taxable Income for Borscan Inc. would be calculated as follows:

Net Income For Tax Purposes	$1,388,550
Dividends Received	(25,000)
Charitable Donations	(13,500)
Net Capital Loss Carry Forward (Note)	(12,500)
Non-Capital Loss Carry Forward	(35,000)
Taxable Income	$1,302,550

Note The net capital loss carry forward can be used only to the extent of the taxable capital gain for the year, resulting in a deduction of $12,500. This leaves a remaining net capital loss carry forward of $17,500 ($30,000 - $12,500).

Part C - Tax Payable

The minimum federal Tax Payable for Borscan Inc. is as follows:

Base Amount Of Part I Tax [(38%)($1,302,550)]	$494,969
Federal Tax Abatement [(10%)($1,302,550)]	(130,255)
General Rate Reduction [(13%)($1,302,550)]	(169,332)
Federal Tax Payable	$195,382

Self Study Solution Twelve - 9

Part A - Net Income

Net Income For Tax Purposes for Industrial Tools Ltd. would be calculated as follows:

Accounting Income Before Taxes		$2,305,000
Additions:		
Taxable Capital Gain On Building (Note)	$ 37,500	
Taxable Capital Gain On Land ($200,000 - $200,000)	Nil	
Recaptured CCA ($875,000 - $625,000)	250,000	
Charitable Donations	28,000	
Interest And Penalties	2,500	
Warranty Reserve	20,000	
Amortization Expense	478,000	816,000
		$3,121,000
Deductions:		
CEC Amount [(7%)($115,000)]	($ 8,050)	
Accounting Gain On Building (Given)	(225,000)	
CCA	(523,000)	(756,050)
Net Income For Tax Purposes		$2,364,950

Note The taxable capital gain on the building would be calculated as follows:

Proceeds Of Disposition ($1,150,000 - $200,000)	$950,000
Adjusted Cost Base ($1,075,000 - $200,000)	(875,000)
Capital Gain	$ 75,000
Inclusion Rate	1/2
Taxable Capital Gain	$ 37,500

As its value has not changed, there is no capital gain on the land.

Part B - Taxable Income

Taxable Income for Industrial Tools Ltd. would be calculated as follows:

Net Income For Tax Purposes	$2,364,950
Dividends Received	(42,000)
Charitable Donations	(28,000)
Net Capital Loss Carry Forward (Note)	(37,500)
Taxable Income	$2,257,450

Note   The net capital loss carry forward can be used only to the extent of the taxable capital gain for the year, resulting in a deduction of $37,500. This leaves a remaining net capital loss carry forward of $52,500 ($90,000 - $37,500).

Part C - Tax Payable

Federal Tax Payable for Industrial Tools Ltd. would be calculated as follows:

Base Amount Of Part I Tax [(38%)($2,257,450)]	$857,831
Federal Tax Abatement [(10%)($2,257,450)]	(225,745)
General Rate Reduction [(13%)($2,257,450)]	(293,469)
Federal Part I Tax Payable	$338,617

Self Study Solution Twelve - 10

Part A - Net Income For Tax Purposes

The minimum Net Income For Tax Purposes would be calculated as follows:

Accounting Income Before Taxes	$530,400
Accounting Gain On Sale Of Shares	(22,900)
Taxable Capital Gain [(1/2)($22,900)]	11,450
Donations To Registered Canadian Charity	18,700
Net Income For Tax Purposes	$537,650

Part B - Taxable Income

The minimum Taxable Income would be calculated as follows:

Net Income For Tax Purposes	$537,650
Donations To Registered Canadian Charity	(18,700)
Dividends From Taxable Canadian Corporations	(9,400)
Non-Capital Loss Carry Forward	(21,950)
Net Capital Loss Carry Forward*	(11,450)
Taxable Income	$476,150

*While there is a net capital loss carry forward of $13,500, the deduction is limited to $11,450, the taxable gain that was recognized during the current year. This leaves a net capital loss carry forward of $2,050.

Part C - Tax Payable

The minimum federal Part I Tax Payable is as follows:

Base Amount Of Part I Tax [(38%)($476,150)]	$180,937
Federal Tax Abatement [(10%)(90%)($476,150)] (Note One)	(42,854)
Small Business Deduction (Note Two)	Nil
M&P Deduction (Note Three)	(51,136)
General Rate Reduction (Note Four)	(10,764)
Foreign Non-Business Tax Credit (Assumed Equal To Withheld)	(4,845)
Foreign Business Tax Credit (Assumed Equal To Withheld)	(20,700)
Part I Tax Payable	$ 50,638

Note One No income would be allocated to Manitoba as there are no permanent establishments in that province. However, the Manitoba sales would be included in the Ontario total, as the Manitoba customers are serviced through that province. Based on this, the allocation would be as follows:

Gross Revenues	Amount	Percent
Ontario And Manitoba	$5,725,000	91.0
New York	565,000	9.0
Total	$6,290,000	100.0

Salaries And Wages	Amount	Percent
Ontario	$3,540,000	89.0
New York	438,000	11.0
Total	$3,978,000	100.0

Average Ontario Percent [(91.0% + 89.0%) ÷ 2]	90.0%
Average New York Percent [(9.0% + 11.0%) ÷ 2]	10.0%
Total	100.0%

Based on the preceding calculations, the federal tax abatement would be $42,854 [(10%)(90%)($476,150)].

Note Two There is no small business deduction in the calculation of Part I tax, as Mercury Manufacturing Company is not Canadian controlled.

Note Three The M&P deduction would be equal to $51,136. This amount is 13 percent of $393,350, which is the lesser of:

M & P Profits (Given)		$410,000
Taxable Income	$476,150	
Less 4 Times Foreign Business Tax Credit [(4)($20,700)]	(82,800)	$393,350

Note Four The general rate reduction would be calculated as follows:

Taxable Income	$476,150
Amount Eligible For The M&P Deduction	(393,350)
Full Rate Taxable Income	$ 82,800
Rate	13%
General Rate Reduction	$ 10,764

Part D - Foreign Tax Credits

To calculate the M&P deduction, both the foreign business and non-business tax credits must first be calculated without considering the general rate reduction. This is necessary as otherwise there would be a circular calculation that could not be solved since the general rate reduction calculation requires the income eligible for the M&P deduction and the calculation of the M&P deduction uses the foreign business tax credit.

Although the foreign non-business tax credit is not used directly in the M&P deduction calculation, it is required to calculate the foreign business tax credit which is used.

In Part C of this problem, it is assumed that the credits are equal to the foreign tax withheld so that the alternative calculations were not necessary.

Using the amounts from Part C, the actual foreign tax credits can be calculated as follows:

Foreign Non-Business Tax Credit The Tax Otherwise Payable for this calculation would be $127,319 ($180,937 - $42,854 - $10,764). The credit would be lesser of:

- The Amount Withheld $4,845

- $\left(\dfrac{\text{Foreign Non-Business Income}}{\text{Adjusted Net Income}} \right)$ (Part I Tax Otherwise Payable)

$\left(\dfrac{\$32,300}{\$537,650 - \$11,450 - \$9,400} \right)(\$127,319)$ $7,957

The lesser figure would be the actual withholding of $4,845.

Foreign Business Tax Credit The credit would be the least of:

- The Amount Withheld $20,700

- $\left(\dfrac{\text{Foreign Business Income}}{\text{Adjusted Net Income}} \right)$ (Part I Tax Otherwise Payable)

$\left(\dfrac{\$64,200}{\$537,650 - \$11,450 - \$9,400} \right)(\$180,937 - \$10,764)$ $21,140

- Tax Otherwise Payable, Less The Foreign Non-Business Tax Credit
  [($180,937 - $10,764) - $4,845] $165,328

The least of these three figures would be the U.S. taxes withheld of $20,700.

Chapter 12 Learning Objectives

After completing Chapter 12, you should be able to:

1. Calculate a corporation's Net Income For Tax Purposes (paragraph [P hereafter] 12-1 to 12-4).

2. List the deductions that are available to corporations in calculating Taxable Income (P 12-5 to 12-9).

3. Apply the treatment for different types of dividends received, including the application of the stop loss rules (P 12-10 to 12-23).

4. Calculate the non-capital loss carry over for a corporation (P 12-24 to 12-30).

5. Determine the optimum ordering of the deductions available in calculating corporate Taxable Income (P 12-31 to 12-36).

6. Allocate corporate Taxable Income to specific provinces (P 12-37 to 12-44).

7. Apply the basic corporate tax rate and explain the effect of the federal tax abatement and the general rate reduction (P 12-45 to 12-52).

8. Calculate provincial Tax Payable for a corporation using a supplied schedule of rates and other data (P 12-53 to 12-63).

9. List the important non-revenue raising goals of the corporate tax system (P 12-64 and 12-65).

10. Explain the rules for determining which corporations and what amounts of income are eligible for the small business deduction (P 12-66 to 12-89).

11. Calculate the amount of the small business deduction (P 12-90 to 12-100).

12. Calculate the reduction in the small business deduction that is applicable to large CCPCs (P 12-101 to 12-111).

13. Identify personal services corporations and explain their tax treatment (P 12-112 to 12-118).

14. Identify professional corporations and management companies and explain their tax treatment (P 12-119 and 12-120).

15. Calculate the manufacturing and processing profits deduction for all types of corporations (P 12-121 to 12-139).

16. Calculate the general rate reduction that is available to all corporations and the specific application of the general rate reduction to CCPCs (P 12-140 to 12-153).

17. Calculate the foreign non-business (property) and business income tax credits for corporations and apply the rules that deal with any excess of foreign tax withheld over the foreign tax credit (P 12-154 to 12-165).

CHAPTER 13

How To Work Through Chapter 13

We recommend the following approach in dealing with the material in this Chapter:

Integration
- ❏ Read paragraph 13-1 to 13-24 (in the textbook).
- ❏ Do Exercises Thirteen-1 and Thirteen-2 (in the textbook) and check the solutions on page S-280 in this Study Guide.
- ❏ Do Self Study Problem Thirteen-1 at the end of the textbook chapter on page 684 and check the solution in this Study Guide.

Refundable Tax On Aggregate Investment Income
- ❏ Read paragraph 13-25 to 13-38.

Additional Refundable Tax On Investment Income (ART)
- ❏ Read paragraph 13-39 to 13-42.
- ❏ Do Exercise Thirteen-3 and check the solution in this Study Guide.
- ❏ Read paragraph 13-43 to 13-47.

Refundable Portion Of Part I Tax
- ❏ Read paragraph 13-48 to 13-68.
- ❏ Do Exercise Thirteen-4 and check the solution in this Study Guide.

Refundable Part IV Tax On Dividends Received
- ❏ Read paragraph 13-69 to 13-96.
- ❏ Do Exercise Thirteen-5 and check the solution in this Study Guide.
- ❏ Read paragraph 13-97 and 13-98.

Refundable Dividend Tax On Hand (RDTOH)
- ❏ Read paragraph 13-99 to 13-123.
- ❏ Do Exercises Thirteen-6 and Thirteen-7 and check the solutions in this Study Guide.

Working Through Large Corporate Problems
- ❏ Read paragraph 13-124 and 13-125.
- ❏ Do Self Study Problems Thirteen-2 and Thirteen-3 and check the solutions in this Study Guide.

Designation Of Eligible Dividends
- ❏ Read paragraph 13-126 to 13-133.

CCPCs And Their GRIP
- ❏ Read paragraph 13-134 to 13-140.
- ❏ Do Exercise Thirteen-8 and check the solution in this Study Guide.

Non-CCPCs And Their LRIP

❏ Read paragraph 13-141 to 13-144.

Part III.1 Tax On Excessive Eligible Dividend Designations (EEDDs)

❏ Read paragraph 13-145 to 13-153.
❏ Do Self Study Problems Thirteen-4 to Thirteen-7 and check the solutions in this Study Guide.

Sample Corporate Tax Return

❏ Read the Sample Corporate Tax Return found on page S-292 to S-296 of this Study Guide. The complete sample tax return is available on your Student CD-ROM included with the text in two formats, a T2 ProFile return file and a .PDF file. To view the files, access your Student CD-ROM and under the heading "Textbook Support Files", select the option "Tax Return Files".

In January, 2014, after the first 2013 filing version is released, the updated 2013 sample tax returns and updated Tax Software Problems will be available at:

www.pearsoncanada.ca/byrdchen/ctp2014

To Complete This Chapter

❏ Review the Key Terms Used In This Chapter on page 683. Consult the Glossary for the meaning of any key terms you do not know.
❏ Review the Glossary Flashcards and complete the Key Terms Self-Test for the Chapter. These features can be found in two places, on your Student CD-ROM under the heading "Key Term Practice" and on the web site.
❏ Review the Learning Objectives of the Chapter found on page S-313 of this Study Guide.
❏ As a review, we recommend that you view the PowerPoint Slides for Chapter 13 that are available on your Student CD-ROM. If you do not have access to the Microsoft PowerPoint program, the PowerPoint Viewer program can be installed from the Student CD-ROM.

Sample Corporate Tax Return

The following simplified example contains a T2 corporate income tax return completed using the ProFile T2 corporate tax preparation program from Intuit Canada. It contains 2012 (not 2013) information as the current Profile software release does not support fiscal periods ending after April 30, 2013. Shortly after the first filing version of the 2013 Intuit ProFile software is available in January, 2014, the updated 2013 version of this problem will be available on the textbook web site at:

www.pearsoncanada.ca/byrdchen/ctp2014

As this example is designed to illustrate corporate tax return calculations, limited GIFI (General Index of Financial Information) data has been included. The relevant T2 schedule or form name is provided in square brackets to make it easier to find where the information is input.

Sample Files On Student CD-ROM

The complete sample tax return is available on the Student CD-ROM included with this book in two versions, a T2 ProFile return file and a .PDF file.

To View The Tax Return Files

To view the ProFile return files, you must have the ProFile program installed. For information on how to obtain the program for free, see the inside back cover of Volume 1.

To view the .PDF files, you must have the Adobe Reader program installed. This program can be installed for free from the Adobe website (www.adobe.com).

To view the files, insert your Student CD-ROM and you should see a splash page. Under the heading "Textbook Support Files", is the option to view "Tax Return Files ". Select this option and you will see two drop-down lists.

- To view the ProFile file, select the file "Sample T2 - Chapter 13" from the ProFile drop-down list.

- To view the .PDF file, select the file "PDF Sample T2 - Chapter 13" from the PDF drop-down list.

Tips To Increase The Benefits From Viewing The ProFile Files

When viewing the sample return file, we offer the following suggestions:

- Press <F1> on any ProFile form or field to display related information in the help system. In ProFile dialog boxes, click the [?] symbol in the top right corner, then click any element for help on that item.

- By pressing <F4> you will open the Form Explorer. In the categories of forms appearing in the shaded box on the left, if you choose "A. Used" near the bottom of the column, all the forms that have calculations for the return will be shown. You can then double click on the form itself to view it.

- Right clicking on a number in a field shows a variety of options, including the form or schedule where the amount originated from.

- If you cannot determine where information should be input, one way to search for the correct form is to open the Form Explorer (F4) and choose the "Key" mode icon in the top right corner of the menu. If you type a key word into the line above the listing of key words, the appropriate form may be found.

- Clicking on "Show Auditor" under the "Audit" list will display any warnings or potential errors.

Sample Problem Data

The government's Crown Copyright does not permit us to use fake Business Numbers in software examples. To reduce the number of ProFile's error messages because of this, we have used NR (for not registered) in the Business Number field.

MetroFaux Inc. is a Canadian controlled private corporation based in Saskatoon that manufactures metal and composite office furniture. Its head office is located at 123 ABC Avenue, Saskatoon, SK S7G 1A1, phone number (306)111-1111. The signing officer and contact person is the President of the company, Jack Saskatoon. MetroFaux Inc. was incorporated on August 28, 1977.

Most of its income is earned from active business in Canada. The Company has no associated corporations.

As at December 31, 2011, the following information applied to MetroFaux Inc:

Taxable Capital Employed In Canada [Info]	$7,420,000
RDTOH [T2, line 460]	Nil
Dividends Declared And Paid During 2011	Nil
GRIP Balance [Schedule 53]	276,000

During the taxation year ending December 31, 2012, the condensed before tax Income Statement of MetroFaux Inc. was prepared in accordance with the International Financial Reporting Standards (IFRS). In condensed form it is as follows:

MetroFaux Inc.
Condensed Income Statement
Year Ending December 31, 2012

Sales	$3,980,000	
Gain On Building Sale	160,000	$4,140,000
Amortization Expense	$ 607,000	
Other Expenses Excluding Taxes	1,773,000	2,380,000
Accounting Income Before Taxes		$1,760,000

Preliminary GIFI Procedures

On the ProFile schedule titled "Info", answer the Filing question "Complete return from GIFI?" with No. Ignore the GIFI requirements except as follows:

- On GIFI Schedule 125 (Income Statement), input the total sales as "Trade sales of goods and services" (Code 8000) and the Gain On Building Sale as "Realized gains / losses on disposal of assets" (Code 8210) from the drop down menu under Revenues. Input the Amortization Expense as "Amortization of tangible assets" (Code 8670) and the Other Expenses as "Other expenses" (Code 9270) from the drop down menu under Operating Expenses.

- On GIFI Schedule 100 (Balance Sheet), input the Net Income figure as "Cash and deposits" (Code 1000) in order to make the total assets equal to the total liabilities and equity.

Although this will not properly complete the GIFI statements, it will eliminate the warning messages that would otherwise be generated when the Net Income figure and Amortization Expense are input on Schedule 1. These GIFI entries will have no effect on the calculations in the tax return.

To prevent audit warnings, S141, "Notes Checklist", has to be completed. Assume there are no notes to the financial statements and answer "No" to any other relevant questions.

Since the return is not being completed using the GIFI statements, the Net Income of $1,760,000 must be input on line A on Schedule 1.

Other Information:

1. Expenses include interest and penalties of $2,300 resulting from late installments and a failure to file the 2011 tax return within the prescribed time period. [Schedule 1]

2. Expenses include a deduction for charitable donations to the Cancer Research Society in the amount of $15,000. [Schedule 2]

3. Revenues include eligible dividends of $36,000 from Canadian Tax Save Inc., a taxable Canadian corporation. MetroFaux Inc. has no association with Canadian Tax Save Inc. and considers the dividends portfolio dividends. [Schedule 3. Note that under the GRIP/LRIP double column, "Column F deduction type" = s. 112 and X must be placed in the "Indicate eligible dividends" column.]

4. The Company paid $100,000 in taxable eligible dividends during 2012. [Schedule 3]

5. The Company has available a non-capital loss carry over from the previous year of $56,000 [S4Supp]. The net capital loss carry forward from 2009 is $22,500 (1/2 of $45,000). [Schedule 4 - note 100 percent figures are used for the capital loss]

6. During 2012, the Company earned $97,000 of interest income on bonds purchased in 2011 that mature in 2016. [Schedule 7]

7. Amortization expense on the Income Statement amounts to $607,000 The opening UCC balance was $905,000 for Class 8, $800,000 for Class 10 and $429,000 for Class 29. The only fixed asset acquisition was $100,000 in Class 29 manufacturing equipment. There were no dispositions in Classes 8 or 10. [Schedule 8 flows to Schedule 1]

8. The Gain On Building Sale resulted from the sale of a building for proceeds of $792,000 of which $120,000 was allocated to the land. The building at 456 DEF Street, Regina, Saskatchewan S7G 1A1, was acquired on August 28, 2003 for $764,000, of which $100,000 was allocated to the land. The sales office of the Company had been located in this building and the sales office has subsequently moved to leased space in Saskatoon. As the Company leases all of its other buildings and equipment, the building was the only asset in Class 1. The Undepreciated Capital Cost of this class prior to the disposition of the building was $514,000. [Schedules 1, 6 and 8]

9. The beginning balance in the Company's Cumulative Eligible Capital account is $90,000. There were no acquisitions or dispositions that affected this account during the year. [Schedule 10]

10. Information related to Canadian manufacturing and processing activities for the year is as follows: [Schedule 27]

Cost of capital [(10% of $6,000,000) + ($200,000 in rental costs)]	$ 800,000
Portion of capital used in M&P activities	500,000
Cost of labour	1,000,000
Portion of labour used in M&P activities	760,000

11. All of the common shares of MetroFaux Inc. are held by the president, Jack Saskatoon (SIN 527-000-582). [Schedule 50]

12. The beginning balance in the Company's capital dividend account is nil [CDA]. Note that capital dividends are covered in detail in Chapter 14.

13. The Company paid one federal income tax instalment of $212,000 on September 1, 2012 [TaxPaid].

Required: Prepare the federal corporate tax return for MetroFaux Inc. for the 2012 taxation year using the ProFile T2 corporate software program.

Notes On Sample Corporate Tax Return

Loss Carry Forwards

The losses of prior taxation years deducted in the calculation of Taxable Income consist of the non-capital loss of $56,000 and a $14,000 net capital loss. As calculated on Schedule 4, the net capital loss carry forward deduction is limited by the $28,000 capital gain for the year and leaves a capital loss carry forward of $17,000. Note Schedule 4 uses the 100 percent amounts. There is no non-capital loss carry forward remaining.

Building Sale

The $160,000 Gain On Building Sale is deducted on Schedule 1 as the tax effects of the disposition are included in Net Income For Tax Purposes. As calculated on Schedule 6, the taxable capital gain on the building sale is $14,000 [(1/2)($792,000 - $764,000)].

As calculated on Schedule 8, the recapture of CCA on the building is equal to $150,000 ($664,000 - $514,000). This is shown as an addition on Schedule 1, separate from the CCA.

Aggregate Investment Income

As calculated on Schedule 7, Part 1, the aggregate investment income of $97,000 consists of:

- the taxable capital gains of $14,000, less
- the $14,000 net capital loss carry forward claimed, plus
- net property income of $133,000 (dividends received of $36,000 plus interest income of $97,000), less
- taxable dividends deductible of $36,000.

This figure is used in calculating the refundable portion of Part I tax.

Active Business Income

As calculated on Schedule 7, Part 5, income from active business carried on in Canada of $1,159,000 is Net Income For Tax Purposes of $1,306,000 less the sum of:

- the taxable capital gains of $14,000, plus
- net property income of $133,000 (dividends received of $36,000 plus interest income of $97,000).

This figure is used in the small business deduction calculation and in Schedule 27 for the M&P deduction.

M&P Labour

As the grossed up M&P Labour of $1,013,333 [(100/75)($760,000)] is greater than the $1,000,000 Cost of Labour, M&P Labour in the Schedule 27, Part 7 calculation is limited to $1,000,000. As mentioned in the text, although the effect of the federal M&P deduction has been negated by the general rate reduction, there are still provincial M&P tax reductions available. In this example, MetroFaux Inc. is eligible for the Saskatchewan M&P tax reduction. (See Schedule 404.)

Capital Dividend Account

The balance in the Capital Dividend Account is $14,000 [(1/2)($692,000 - $664,000)]. A tax free capital dividend of $14,000 could have been paid if form T2054 had been filed. (See Chapter 14.)

GRIP

As no dividends were declared or paid during 2011, no eligible dividends could have been paid. As a result, Schedule 53 has no amount on line 300, "Eligible dividends paid in the previous tax year".

Tax Summary

Corporation name   MetroFaux Inc.

Tax year ending 2012-12-31

Taxable income

Net income for tax purposes			1,507,000
Charitable donations and gifts	-		15,000
Taxable dividends	-		36,000
Losses of prior years	-		70,000
Other adjustments	±		
Taxable income	=		1,386,000

Part I tax

38% of taxable income			526,680
Surtax	+		
Recapture of investment tax credit	+		
Refundable tax on CCPC investment income	+		6,467
Active business income		1,360,000	
Small business deduction	-		85,000
Federal tax abatement	-		138,600
Manufacturing and processing deduction	-		91,000
Additional deduction - credit unions	-		
Foreign tax credits	-		
Investment tax credit	-		
Other deductions and credits	-		11,570
Part I tax	=		206,977

Tax payable

Part I tax			206,977
Taxable dividends received	36,000		
GRIP at the end of the tax year	880,080		
LRIP at the end of the tax year			
Part III.1 tax		+	
Part IV tax		+	12,000
Other federal tax payable		+	
Subtotal		=	218,977
Provincial and territorial tax (except AB,QC)		+	102,320
Provincial tax on large corporations (NB,NS)		+	
Tax payable		+	321,297
Tax instalments paid		-	212,000
Investment tax credit refund		-	
Taxable dividends paid	100,000		
Dividend refund		-	33,333
Other refundable credits		-	
Balance owing (refund) on federal return		=	75,964
Provincial income tax (AB,QC)			
Capital and other provincial taxes		+	
Tax instalments and credits		-	
Other provincial taxes		=	
Total balance owing (refund)			75,964

Provincial tax

	% Provincial allocation	Taxable income	Income tax	Capital and other provincial taxes	Tax instalments and credits	Net provincial tax
Newfoundland						
Prince Edward Island						
Nova Scotia						
New Brunswick						
Ontario						
Manitoba						
Saskatchewan	100.0000	1,386,000	102,320			102,320
British Columbia						
Yukon Territory						
Northwest Territories						
Nunavut						
Schedule 5 provincial tax payable			102,320			
Alberta						
Québec						
Totals			102,320			102,320

Loss continuity

	Current year carry back	Carryforward end of year
Capital		17,000
Non-capital		
Farm		
Restricted farm		
Limited partnership		
Listed personal property		

Other carryforwards

Capital dividend account	14,000
Refundable dividend tax on hand (net of dividend refund)	4,534
Unused Part 1.3 tax credit	
Unused surtax credits	
Foreign business tax credits	
Donations and gifts	
Investment tax credits	
Ontario S510 (CMT) losses	
Ontario S510 (CMT) credit	

Complete Return Available On Student CD-ROM

S - 296

Solution to Chapter Thirteen Exercises

Exercise Thirteen - 1 Solution

If she incorporates, the corporation will pay taxes of $15,000 [(15%)($100,000)], leaving $85,000 to be distributed as dividends. Her individual Tax Payable on these non-eligible dividends would be calculated as follows:

Dividends Received	$ 85,000
Gross Up [(25%)($85,000)]	21,250
Grossed Up Dividends	$106,250
Personal Tax Rate	45%
Tax Before Credit	$ 47,813
Dividend Tax Credit [(2/3 + 30%)($21,250)]	(20,542)
Tax Payable On Dividends	$ 27,271

The net after tax retention would be $57,729 ($85,000 - $27,271). This compares to $55,000 [($100,000)(1 - .45)] retained if a corporation is not used. While the provincial dividend tax credit is below the 33-1/3 percent that is required for full integration, this is more than offset by the fact that the corporate tax rate is only 15 percent, well below the 20 percent required by full integration. The result is that the use of a corporation reduces taxes in this situation.

Exercise Thirteen - 2 Solution

If he incorporates, the corporation will pay taxes of $30,000 [(30%)($100,000)], leaving $70,000 to be distributed as dividends. His individual Tax Payable on these eligible dividends would be calculated as follows:

Dividends Received	$70,000
Gross Up [(38%)($70,000)]	26,600
Grossed Up Dividends	$96,600
Personal Tax Rate	42%
Tax Before Credit	$40,572
Dividend Tax Credit [(6/11 + 28%)($26,600)]	(21,957)
Tax Payable On Dividends	$18,615

The net after tax retention would be $51,385 ($70,000 - $18,615). This compares to $58,000 [($100,000)(1 - .42)] retained if a corporation is not used. Clearly the use of a corporation is not desirable in this situation. While the corporate tax rate of 30 percent is greater than the required 27.54 percent, the real problem here is the fact that the provincial dividend tax credit of 28 percent is significantly below the required 45.5 percent.

Exercise Thirteen - 3 Solution

Zircon's Taxable Income would be calculated as follows:

Net Income For Tax Purposes	$281,000
Dividends From Taxable Canadian Corporations	(22,000)
Net Capital Loss Carry Forward	(26,000)
Non-Capital Loss Carry Forward	(23,000)
Taxable Income	$210,000

Zircon's amount eligible for the small business deduction of $198,000 is the least of active business income of $198,000, Taxable Income of $210,000, and the annual business limit of $500,000.

Given these calculations, Zircon's additional refundable tax on investment income would be calculated using the lesser of:

Aggregate Investment Income		
Taxable Capital Gains	$46,000	
Net Capital Loss Deducted	(26,000)	
Interest Income	15,000	$35,000
Taxable Income	$210,000	
Amount Eligible For SBD	(198,000)	$12,000

The additional refundable tax on investment income would be $800 [(6-2/3%)($12,000)]. Note that the Taxable Income limit is $23,000 ($35,000 - $12,000) less than the Aggregate Investment Income. This difference is the result of the deduction of the $23,000 non-capital loss carry forward.

Exercise Thirteen - 4 Solution

If Ms. Nicastro receives the income directly, she will retain $54,000 [($100,000)(1 - .46)]. Alternatively, if the investments are transferred to a corporation, the results would be as follows:

Corporate Investment Income	$100,000
Corporate Tax At 48 Percent	(48,000)
After Tax Income	$ 52,000
Dividend Refund (Note)	26,000
Non-Eligible Dividends Paid To Ms. Nicastro	$ 78,000

Note As explained in the note to the example in Paragraph 13-63, in determining the dividend refund when you are paying out all of the corporate income, it is calculated by taking one-half of the after tax income [(1/2)($52,000)]. When this is added to the after tax income to provide a total dividend, this amount will be equal to one-third of the total dividends [($26,000 = (1/3)($78,000)]

Non-Eligible Dividends Received	$ 78,000
Gross Up Of 25 Percent	19,500
Personal Taxable Income	$ 97,500
Personal Tax Rate	46%
Tax Payable Before Dividend Tax Credit	$ 44,850
Dividend Tax Credit [(2/3 + 37%)($19,500)]	(20,215)
Personal Tax Payable With Corporation	$ 24,635
Non-Eligible Dividends Received	$ 78,000
Personal Tax Payable	(24,635)
After Tax Cash Retained With Corporation	$ 53,365

Conclusion On Deferral   The use of a corporation results in the prepayment of taxes in that the corporate tax, prior to any refund, is $48,000. This is $2,000 more than the $46,000 she would pay on direct receipt of the income.

Conclusion On Tax Savings   After tax retention is somewhat smaller when the income is flowed through a corporation ($53,365 vs. $54,000). There is clearly no advantage, either in terms of tax deferral or tax reduction, resulting from the use of a corporation.

Exercise Thirteen - 5 Solution

The amount of Part IV Tax Payable would be calculated as follows:

Tax On Portfolio Investments [(1/3)($14,000)]	$4,667
Tax On Emerald Inc. Dividends	Nil
Tax On Ruby Inc. Dividends [(30%)($15,000)]	4,500
Part IV Tax Payable	$9,167

Exercise Thirteen - 6 Solution

The refundable amount of Debut Inc.'s Part I tax for the current year would be the least of the following three figures:

Foreign Non-Business Income (100 Percent)		$15,000
Taxable Capital Gains [(1/2)($38,250)]		19,125
Net Rental Income		6,500
Interest Income		9,200
Net Capital Loss Carry Forward Deducted		(9,000)
Aggregate Investment Income Under ITA 129(4)		$40,825
Rate		26-2/3%
Amount Before Foreign Income Adjustment		$10,887
Deduct Excess Of:		
Foreign Non-Business Tax Credit	($ 750)	
Over 9-1/3 Percent Of Foreign Non-Business		
Income [(9-1/3%)($15,000)]	1,400	Nil
Amount Under ITA 129(3)(a)(i)		**$10,887**
Taxable Income ($121,825 - $22,000 - $9,000)		$ 90,825
Deduct:		
Amount Eligible For The Small Business Deduction ($8,500 ÷ 17%)		(50,000)
[(100/35)($750)] Foreign Non-Business Tax Credit		(2,143)
Adjusted Taxable Income		$ 38,682
Rate		26-2/3%
Amount Under ITA 129(3)(a)(ii)		**$ 10,315**
Amount Under ITA 129(3)(a)(iii) = Part I Tax Payable (Given)		**$18,903**

The least of these three amounts is $10,315, and this would be the refundable portion of Part I tax for the year.

Exercise Thirteen - 7 Solution

The balance in the RDTOH account of Quan Imports would be as follows:

Opening Balance	$12,500	
Less: Previous Year's Dividend Refund [($6,000)(1/3)]	(2,000)	$10,500
Part I Refundable Addition [(26-2/3%)($24,000)]	$ 6,400	
Part IV Tax On Portfolio Dividends [(1/3)($6,000)]	2,000	8,400
Closing Balance - RDTOH		$18,900

The dividend refund would be $5,000, the lesser of one-third of the $15,000 dividend paid and the $18,900 balance in the RDTOH account.

Exercise Thirteen - 8 Solution

Since Taxable Income is greater than Aggregate Investment Income (comparison used in F in the following table), the 2013 ending balance in GRIP will be calculated as follows:

C - GRIP Balance At End Of 2012		$365,000
D - Taxable Income	$960,000	
E - Income Eligible For SBD ($38,250 ÷ 17%)	(225,000)	
F - Aggregate Investment Income		
($65,000 + $23,000 - $14,000)	(74,000)	
Adjusted Taxable Income	$661,000	
Rate	72%	475,920
G - Eligible Dividends Received		85,000
I - Eligible Dividends Designated in 2012		(140,000)
GRIP At End Of 2013		$785,920

The eligible dividends paid during 2013 will be deducted from the GRIP in 2014.

Self Study Solution Thirteen - 1

The required calculations would be as follows:

Corporate Taxes

Corporate Income	$500,000
Corporate Taxes [(27%)($500,000)]	(135,000)
Income Available For Dividends	$365,000

Personal Taxes On Dividends

Dividend Income	$365,000
Gross Up (38%)	138,700
Taxable Dividends	$503,700

Tax Payable Before Dividend Tax Credit	
[(29% + 16%)($503,700)]	$226,665
Dividend Tax Credit [(6/11 + 4/11)($138,700)]	(126,091)
Personal Tax Payable	$ 100,574

Total Taxes On Corporate Flow Through

Corporate Taxes	$135,000
Personal Taxes	100,574
Total Taxes	$235,574

Total Taxes On Income Earned Directly

Income For The Year	$500,000
Combined Federal/Provincial Tax Rate (29% + 16%)	45%
Personal Tax Payable	$225,000

As combined corporate and personal taxes are $10,574 ($235,574 - $225,000) more on income flowed through the corporation, integration is not working perfectly. Although the corporate tax rate of 27 percent is below the 27.54 percent rate required for perfect integration, this is more than offset by the fact that the provincial dividend tax credit is only 36.4 percent (4/11), well below the 45.5 percent rate that is required for perfect integration.

Self Study Solution Thirteen - 2

Part A - FOL's Dividend Refund

The ending RDTOH balance for FOL would be as follows:

Refundable Dividend Tax On Hand - End Of Previous Year	$2,000
Refundable Portion Of Part I Tax [(26-2/3%)($7,000)]	1,867
Refundable Dividend Tax On Hand - Ending	$3,867

As FOL has no foreign investment income or deductions for loss carry overs, the calculation of the addition to the RDTOH for the refundable portion of Part I tax is based solely on the interest income.

The dividend refund would be $3,867, the lesser of:

- One-Third Of Taxable Dividends Paid [(1/3)($75,000)] $25,000

- Refundable Dividend Tax On Hand $ 3,867

Part B - SHI's Part IV Tax Payable

The Part IV tax for SHI would be calculated as follows:

Portfolio Dividends [(1/3)($8,000)]	$2,667
SHI's Share Of FOL's Dividend Refund (100%) - Part A	3,867
Part IV Tax Payable	$6,534

Part C - SHI's Dividend Refund

SHI's aggregate investment income totals $35,625, the sum of $12,000 in interest income and $23,625 [(1/2)($47,250)] in taxable capital gains. This means that the ending RDTOH balance for SHI would be as follows:

Refundable Dividend Tax On Hand - End Of Previous Year	$10,000
Refundable Portion Of Part I Tax [(26-2/3%)($35,625)]	9,500
Part IV Tax Payable (Part B)	6,534
Refundable Dividend Tax On Hand - Ending	$26,034

The dividend refund would be $16,667, the lesser of:

- One-Third Of Taxable Dividends Paid [(1/3)($50,000)] $16,667

- Refundable Dividend Tax On Hand $26,034

Note that the appropriate calculation of the refundable portion of Part I tax would require selecting the least of the amounts described in ITA 129(3)(a)(i), (ii), and (iii). This problem does not contain sufficient information to calculate ITA 129(3)(a)(ii) or (iii) and as a result, you are asked to assume that the refundable portion of Part I tax is the amount determined under ITA 129(3)(a)(i).

Self Study Solution Thirteen - 3

Part IV Refundable Tax
The Part IV Tax Payable for Burton Investments Ltd. would be calculated as follows:

Puligny's Dividend Refund	$12,500
Burton's Percentage Of Ownership	52%
Part IV Tax Payable On Puligny's Dividends	$ 6,500
Part IV Tax Payable On Portfolio Dividends From	
Bank Of Montreal [(1/3)($13,480)]	4,493
Part IV Tax Payable	$10,993

Part I Refundable Tax
As the interest received appears to be related to temporary balances resulting from the Company's normal business activities, it would be viewed as active business income, and would not influence the following calculations.

The refundable portion of the Part I tax would be the least of the following amounts:

Aggregate Investment Income [(1/2)($18,000)]	$ 9,000
Rate	26-2/3%
ITA 129(3)(a)(i)	$ 2,400
Taxable Income	$62,800
Amount Eligible For Small Business Deduction	(40,000)
Total	$22,800
Rate	26-2/3%
ITA 129(3)(a)(ii)	$ 6,080
ITA 129(3)(a)(iii) Part I Tax Payable - Given	$12,560

The refundable portion of Part I tax is equal to $2,400, which is the least of the preceding three amounts.

RDTOH
The end of year balance in the Refundable Dividend Tax On Hand account can be calculated as follows:

RDTOH Balance - End Of Preceding Year	$22,346
Dividend Refund For The Preceding Year	(7,920)
Opening Balance	$14,426
Part IV Tax Payable	10,993
Refundable Part I Tax	2,400
RDTOH Balance - End Of The Year	$27,819

Dividend Refund
The dividend refund will be $7,500, the lesser of:

- $7,500, one-third of the $22,500 of the dividends paid; and
- $27,819, the balance in the RDTOH account.

Self Study Solution Thirteen - 4

Part A - Part I Tax Payable
The required calculations to determine Part I federal Tax Payable are as follows:

Net Income For Tax Purposes	$473,900
Dividends ($108,000 + $56,000)	(164,000)
Taxable Income	$309,900

Base Amount Of Part I Tax [(38%)($309,900)]	$117,762
Federal Tax Abatement [(10%)($309,900)]	(30,990)
Small Business Deduction (Note One)	(36,771)
Additional Refundable Tax On Investment Income (Note Two)	6,240
General Rate Reduction (Note Three)	Nil
Part I Federal Tax Payable	$ 56,241

Note One The small business deduction is 17 percent of the least of the following three amounts:

1. Active Business Income	$216,300
2. Taxable Income (no foreign tax credit adjustment)	$309,900
3. Allocated Annual Business Limit ($500,000 - $200,000)	$300,000

The lowest of these figures is the active business income of $216,300 and this gives a small business deduction of $36,771 [(17%)($216,300)].

Note Two The aggregate investment income of $93,600 is calculated as follows:

Interest On Government Bonds	$ 36,300
Taxable Capital Gains	57,300
Aggregate Investment Income	$ 93,600

The ITA 123.3 refundable tax (ART) is 6-2/3 percent of the lesser of:

1. Aggregate Investment Income		$93,600
2. Taxable Income	$309,900	
Deduct: Amount Eligible For The SBD	(216,300)	$93,600

The ITA 123.3 tax on aggregate investment income is $6,240 [(6-2/3%)($93,600)].

Note Three The general rate reduction would be calculated as follows:

Taxable Income	$309,900
Amount Eligible For The Small Business Deduction	(216,300)
Aggregate Investment Income (Note Two)	(93,600)
Full Rate Taxable Income	Nil
Rate	13%
General Rate Reduction	Nil

Part B - Part IV Tax Payable
The required calculation of the Part IV Tax Payable on the portfolio investment dividends is as follows:

Part IV Tax [($56,000)(1/3)]	$18,667

Part C - RDTOH Balance

The ending balance in the Refundable Dividend Tax On Hand account is as follows:

RDTOH, End Of The Preceding Year	Nil
Dividend Refund For The Preceding Year	Nil
Opening Balance	Nil
Refundable Portion Of Part I Tax (Note Four)	$24,960
Part IV Tax (See Part B)	18,667
RDTOH Balance - December 31, 2013	$43,627

Note Four   Using amounts calculated in Part A, the amount of refundable Part I tax is $24,960, the least of three amounts, calculated as follows:

- Amount Under ITA 129(3)(a)(i) [(26-2/3%)($93,600)] $24,960
- Amount Under ITA 129(3)(a)(ii) [(26-2/3%)($309,900 - $216,300)] $24,960
- Amount Under ITA 129(3)(a)(iii) Part I Tax Payable $56,241

Part D - GRIP Balance

Since Taxable Income is greater than Aggregate Investment Income, the December 31, 2013 GRIP balance would be calculated as follows:

GRIP Balance At End Of 2012		$ 59,000
Taxable Income	$309,900	
Income Eligible For SBD	(216,300)	
Aggregate Investment Income	(93,600)	
Adjusted Taxable Income	Nil	
Rate	72%	Nil
Eligible Dividends Received		56,000
Eligible Dividends Designated in 2012		Nil
GRIP At End Of 2013		$115,000

Part E - Dividend Refund

The dividend refund for the year would be $10,800, the lesser of:

- One-third of taxable dividends paid [($32,400)(1/3)] = $10,800
- Ending RDTOH Balance (Part C) = $43,627

Part F - Total Federal Tax Payable

The required calculation to determine federal Tax Payable is as follows:

Part I Tax (Part A)	$56,241
Part IV Tax (Part B)	18,667
Dividend Refund (Part E)	(10,800)
Federal Tax Payable	$64,108

Self Study Solution Thirteen - 5

Part A - Part I Tax Payable

The Part I Tax Payable is calculated as follows:

Base Amount Of Part I Tax [(38%)($503,500)]	$191,330
Federal Tax Abatement [(10%)(72.95%)($503,500)]	(36,730)
Small Business Deduction [(17%)($200,000 Which Was Given)]	(34,000)
Additional Refundable Tax On Investment Income (Note One)	7,363
General Rate Reduction (Note Three)	(25,097)
Foreign Non-Business Income Tax Credit (Given)	(8,250)
Foreign Business Income Tax Credit (Given)	(34,300)
Part I Tax Payable	$ 60,316

Note One   The aggregate investment income of $110,450 is calculated as follows:

Interest On Loan To Subsidiary	$ 43,250
Foreign Investment Income	55,000
Taxable Capital Gains	24,500
Net Capital Losses Claimed	(12,300)
Aggregate Investment Income (Note Two)	$110,450

The ITA 123.3 refundable tax (ART) is 6-2/3 percent of the lesser of:

1. Aggregate Investment Income		$110,450
2. Taxable Income	$503,500	
Deduct: Amount Eligible For The SBD	(200,000)	$303,500

The ITA 123.3 tax on aggregate investment income is $7,363 [(6-2/3%)($110,450)].

Note Two   The definition contained in ITA 129(4.1) excludes income from property that is incidental to carrying on an active business and, as a consequence, we have left out the $5,050 of term deposit interest. With respect to the interest on the loan to the subsidiary, if the subsidiary had deducted the $43,250 in computing active business income eligible for the small business deduction, ITA 129(6) would have deemed this interest to be active business income rather than investment income. However, the problem notes that the subsidiary was not involved in the production of active business income and, as a consequence, the interest from the subsidiary is included in the above calculation of aggregate investment income.

Note Three   The general rate reduction is based on the amount of Taxable Income that is not subject to other types of favourable tax treatment. The reduction would be as follows:

Taxable Income	$503,500
Amount Eligible For The Small Business Deduction (Given)	(200,000)
Aggregate Investment Income (Note One)	(110,450)
Full Rate Taxable Income	$193,050
Rate	13%
General Rate Reduction	$ 25,097

Part B - Part IV Tax Payable

The Part IV Tax Payable would be calculated as follows:

One-Third Of Portfolio Dividends Received [(1/3)($19,600)]	$ 6,533
Share Of Dividend Refund Included In Dividends From Subsidiary [(75%)($12,750)]	9,563
Part IV Tax Payable	$16,096

Part C - RDTOH Balance

The refundable portion of Part I tax would be the least of the following three amounts:

Aggregate Investment Income (See Note One)		$110,450
Rate		26-2/3%
Total		$ 29,453
Deduct Excess Of:		
Foreign Non-Business Tax Credit	($8,250)	
Over 9-1/3% Of Foreign Non-Business Income		
[(9-1/3%)($55,000)]	5,133	(3,117)
Amount Under ITA 129(3)(a)(i)		**$ 26,336**
Taxable Income		$503,500
Deduct:		
Amount Eligible For The Small Business Deduction		(200,000)
[(100/35)($8,250)] Foreign Non-Business Tax Credit		(23,571)
[(4)($34,300)] Foreign Business Tax Credit		(137,200)
Total		$142,729
Rate		26-2/3%
Amount Under ITA 129(3)(a)(ii)		**$ 38,061**
Amount Under ITA 129(3)(a)(iii) = Part I Tax Payable		**$60,316**

The least of these three amounts is $26,336, the amount calculated under ITA 129(3)(a)(i).

The ending balance in the Refundable Dividend Tax On Hand account is as follows:

RDTOH Balance - End Of The Preceding Year	$23,500	
Dividend Refund For The Preceding Year	(9,600)	$13,900
Refundable Portion Of Part I Tax	$26,336	
Part IV Tax Payable (Part B)	16,096	42,432
RDTOH Balance - December 31, 2013		$56,332

Part D - Dividend Refund

Note that the dividend refund is calculated on the basis of dividends paid, not dividends declared. The dividend refund for the year would be $36,333, the lesser of:

- One-third of taxable dividends paid during the year
  {[1/3][$25,000 + (3)($28,000)]} = $36,333

- RDTOH Balance - December 31, 2013 = $56,332

Self Study Solution Thirteen - 6

Part A - Net And Taxable Income

The calculation of Acme Imports' Net Income For Tax Purposes and Taxable Income would be as follows:

Accounting Income Before Taxes		$232,300
Additions:		
Amortization Expense	$20,000	
Charitable Donations	25,000	
Taxable Capital Gain On Sale Of Equipment		
[(1/2)($84,500 - $62,000)]	11,250	
Golf Club Membership	2,800	
50 Percent Of Business Meals And Entertainment	3,360	
Share Issue Costs [(80%)($950)]	760	
Costs Of Supplementary Letters Patent	7,000	
Interest On Mortgage For The Land	12,300	82,470
Deductions:		
CCA (Note One)	($38,800)	
Gain On Sale Of Equipment ($84,500 - $27,500)	(57,000)	
Cumulative Eligible Capital On Customer List		
And Letters Patent [($183,000 + $7,000)(3/4)(7%)]	(9,975)	(105,775)
Net Income For Tax Purposes		**$208,995**
Charitable Donations		(25,000)
Dividends From Sarco Ltd.		(24,000)
Taxable Income		**$159,995**

Note One   The maximum CCA on the equipment would be calculated as follows:

Opening UCC	$256,000	
Disposition - Lesser Of:		
Proceeds Of Disposition = $84,500		
Capital Cost = $62,000	(62,000)	
CCA Base	$194,000	
Rate - Class 8	20%	
CCA	$ 38,800	

Several of the items in this problem need further comment. These are as follows:

- **Item 4**   With respect to the costs of issuing shares, IT-341R3 indicates that these amounts are deductible under ITA 20(1)(e). However, such amounts have to be deducted over at least five years at a maximum rate of 20 percent per year. With respect to the costs of acquiring supplementary letters patent, they are considered to be an eligible capital expenditure, three-quarters of which must be added to the cumulative eligible capital account, and amortized at 7 percent.

- **Item 6**   Only 50 percent of the $6,720 in charges at the local golf and country club are deductible.

- **Item 7**   The cars provided to the principal shareholder and to the manager of the Company will result in their being assessed for a substantial taxable benefit. However, the costs are fully deductible to the Company.

- **Item 10**   The fees paid to the site consultant are deductible as indicated in ITA 20(1)(dd). ITA 18(3.1) disallows the deduction of interest on financing related to land during construction. The $12,300 interest on the $244,000 mortgage on the land would be capitalized and is not deductible.

Part B - Active Business Income
The active business income of Acme is as follows:

Net Income For Tax Purposes		$208,995
Dividends		(24,000)
Aggregate Investment Income:		
Interest Revenue	($10,000)	
Taxable Capital Gain	(11,250)	(21,250)
Active Business Income		$163,745

Part C - Federal Tax Payable
The calculation of Acme Ltd.'s federal Tax Payable would be as follows:

Base Amount Of Part I Tax [(38%)($159,995]	$ 60,798
Federal Tax Abatement [(10%)($159,995)]	(16,000)
Small Business Deduction (Note Two)	(27,199)
Additional Refundable Tax On Investment Income (Note Three)	Nil
General Rate Reduction (Note Four)	Nil
Part I Tax Payable	$ 17,599
Part IV Tax Payable (Note Five)	3,000
Dividend Refund (No Dividends Declared)	Nil
Federal Tax Payable	$ 20,599

Note Two   Since none of the annual business limit has been allocated to Sarco, the small business deduction is 17 percent of the least of the following three amounts:

1. Active Business Income (Part B) $163,745
2. Taxable Income (no foreign tax credit adjustment) $159,995
3. Annual Business Limit $500,000

The lowest of these figures is the Taxable Income of $159,995 and this gives a small business deduction of $27,199 [(17%)($159,995)].

Note Three   The ITA 123.3 refundable tax (ART) is 6-2/3 percent of the lesser of:

1. Aggregate Investment Income (Part B) $21,250

2. Taxable Income $159,995
   Deduct: Amount Eligible For The SBD (159,995) Nil

Since the income eligible for the small business deduction is equal to Taxable Income, there is no ITA 123.3 tax on investment income payable.

Note Four   The general rate reduction would be nil, calculated as follows:

Taxable Income	$159,995
Amount Eligible For The Small Business Deduction	(159,995)
Aggregate Investment Income (Part B)	(21,250)
Full Rate Taxable Income	Nil
Rate	13%
General Rate Reduction	Nil

Note Five   Acme would have to pay a Part IV tax equal to its share of the dividend refund received from Sarco Ltd. This amount would be $3,000 [(60%)($5,000)].

Part D - RDTOH Balance

The amount of refundable Part I tax will be the least of the following three amounts. In this problem, the calculation of these amounts is greatly simplified by the absence of foreign non-business income. The calculations are as follows:

ITA 129(3)(a)(i)   This amount would be $5,667, 26-2/3 percent of aggregate investment income of $21,250 ($10,000 + $11,250).

ITA 129(3)(a)(ii)   This amount would be nil, 26-2/3 percent of Taxable Income, reduced by the amount of income that is eligible for the small business deduction [(26-2/3%)($159,995 - $159,995)].

ITA 129(3)(a)(iii)   This amount would be Part I Tax Payable of $17,599.

The least of these amounts is nil, so there would be no refundable portion of Part I tax.

The ending balance in this account would be calculated as follows:

RDTOH, End Of The Preceding Year	Nil
Refundable Portion Of Part I Tax	Nil
Part IV Tax Payable (Note Five)	$3,000
RDTOH Balance - December 31, 2013	$3,000

Self Study Solution Thirteen - 7

Part A - Net And Taxable Income

Brasco's minimum Net Income For Tax Purposes and Taxable Income would be calculated as follows:

Active Business Income (Given)		$171,000
Net Taxable Capital Gains (Given)		36,000
Canadian Source Interest Income		2,200
Eligible Portfolio Dividends		15,800
Foreign Source Investment Income (Gross Amount)		4,500
Non-Eligible Dividends From Subsidiary		37,800
Net Income For Tax Purposes		**$267,300**
Dividends Received:		
Portfolio	($15,800)	
Subsidiary	(37,800)	(53,600)
Charitable Donations		(11,900)
Non-Capital Loss Carry Forward Deducted		(25,800)
Net Capital Loss Carry Forward Deducted (Note One)		(36,000)
Taxable Income		**$140,000**

Note One   Note that the net capital loss carry forward is limited to the taxable capital gains. This will leave a net capital loss carry forward of $28,500 ($64,500 - $36,000) for subsequent periods.

Part B - Tax Payable (FTC = Amount Withheld)

Assuming the foreign non-business tax credit is equal to the amount withheld, Brasco's Tax Payable would be calculated as follows:

Base Amount Of Part I Tax [(38%)($140,000)]	$53,200
Federal Tax Abatement [(10%)($140,000)]	(14,000)
Small Business Deduction (Note Two)	(21,250)
Additional Refundable Tax On Investment Income (Note Three)	447
General Rate Reduction (Note Four)	(1,079)
Foreign Non-Business Tax Credit (Given As Amount Withheld)	(675)
Part I Tax Payable	$16,643
Part IV Tax Payable (Note Five)	17,867
Total Tax Payable	$34,510
Dividend Refund (Note Eight)	(13,000)
Net Federal Tax Payable	$21,510

Note Two   The small business deduction is 17 percent of the least of the following three amounts:

1. Active Business Income (Given)		$171,000
2. Taxable Income	$140,000	
Deduct:		
[(100/28)($675)] Foreign Non-Business Tax Credit (	2,411)	$137,589
3. Allocated Annual Business Limit (Given)		$125,000

The lowest of these figures is the allocated annual limit of $125,000 and this gives a small business deduction of $21,250 [(17%)($125,000)].

Note Three   The aggregate investment income of $6,700 is calculated as follows:

Taxable Capital Gains	$36,000
Net Capital Loss Carry Forward Deducted	(36,000)
Canadian Interest	2,200
Foreign Investment Income	4,500
Aggregate Investment Income	$ 6,700

The ITA 123.3 refundable tax (ART) is 6-2/3 percent of the lesser of:

1. Aggregate Investment Income		$ 6,700
2. Taxable Income	$140,000	
Deduct: Amount Eligible For The SBD	(125,000)	$15,000

The ITA 123.3 tax on aggregate investment income is $447 [(6-2/3%)($6,700)].

Note Four   The general rate reduction is based on the amount of Taxable Income that is not subject to other types of favourable tax treatment. The reduction would be calculated as follows:

Taxable Income	$140,000
Amount Eligible For The Small Business Deduction (Note Two)	(125,000)
Aggregate Investment Income (Note Three)	(6,700)
Full Rate Taxable Income	$ 8,300
Rate	13%
General Rate Reduction	$ 1,079

Note Five   The calculation of Part IV Tax Payable would be as follows:

Part IV Tax Transfer From Masco [(60%)($21,000)]	$12,600
Part IV Tax On Portfolio Dividends [(1/3)($15,800)]	5,267
Part IV Tax Payable	$17,867

Note Six   The refundable portion of Part I tax will be the least of the following three amounts:

Aggregate Investment Income (Note Three)		$ 6,700
Rate		26-2/3%
		$ 1,787
Deduct Excess Of:		
Foreign Non-Business Tax Credit	($675)	
Over 9-1/3% Of Foreign Non-Business Income		
[(9-1/3%)($4,500)]	420	(255)
Amount Under ITA 129(3)(a)(i)		$ 1,532

Taxable Income	$140,000
Deduct:	
Amount Eligible For The Small Business Deduction	(125,000)
[(100/35)($675)] Foreign Non-Business Tax Credit	(1,929)
Adjusted Taxable Income	$ 13,071
Rate	26-2/3%
Amount Under ITA 129(3)(a)(ii)	$ 3,486

Amount Under ITA 129(3)(a)(iii) = Part I Tax Payable	$ 16,643

The least of these three amounts would be $1,532, the amount calculated under ITA 129(3)(a)(i).

Note Seven   The Balance in the RDTOH would be calculated as follows:

RDTOH Balance - End Of The Preceding Year	$ 7,000	
Dividend Refund For The Preceding Year	Nil	$ 7,000
Refundable Portion Of Part I Tax (Note Six)	$ 1,532	
Part IV Tax (Note Five)	17,867	19,399
RDTOH Balance - December 31, 2013		$26,399

Note Eight   The dividend refund would be equal to the lesser of:

- One-third of taxable dividends paid [(1/3)($39,000)] = $13,000
- RDTOH Balance - December 31, 2013 (Note Seven) = $26,399

The lesser of these two figures is $13,000 and that would be the refund for the year.

Part C - GRIP Balance

Since Taxable Income is greater than Aggregate Investment Income, the 2013 ending balance in GRIP will be calculated as follows:

GRIP Balance At End Of 2012		$126,000
Taxable Income	$140,000	
Income Eligible For SBD	(125,000)	
Aggregate Investment Income	(6,700)	
Adjusted Taxable Income	$ 8,300	
Rate	72%	5,976
Eligible Dividends Received		15,800
Eligible Dividends Designated in 2012		Nil
GRIP At End Of 2013		$147,776

The eligible dividends paid during 2013 will be deducted from the GRIP in 2014.

Part D - Foreign Tax Credit

If you cannot assume that the foreign tax credit is equal to the amount withheld, the actual foreign tax credit is a complex calculation in this situation. The use of foreign taxes paid as credits against Canadian Tax Payable is limited by a formula that includes the "tax otherwise payable". In the case of foreign taxes paid on non-business income, the "tax otherwise payable" in the formula includes the ART that is assessed under ITA 123.3 and the general rate reduction. This creates a problem in that the calculation of the ART and the general rate reduction include the amount eligible for the small business deduction [ITA 123.3(b)]. In turn, the determination of the amount eligible for the small business deduction requires the use of the foreign tax credits for foreign taxes paid on non-business and business income [ITA 125(1)(b)(i) and (ii)].

To solve this circular calculation, for the purpose of calculating the small business deduction, the foreign tax credit for taxes paid on non-business income is calculated using a "tax otherwise payable" figure that does not include the ART under ITA 123.3 or the general rate reduction. This means that in situations where foreign non-business income, the small business deduction, and the ART are involved, the following procedures should be used:

1. Calculate the foreign non-business tax credit using a "tax otherwise payable" that excludes both the ART and the general rate reduction. This initial version of the foreign non-business tax credit will be used only for determining the small business deduction, with the actual credit available calculated after the ART and the general rate reduction have been determined.

2. Calculate the amount eligible for the small business deduction using the number determined in step 1.

3. Calculate the ART and the general rate reduction using the amount eligible for the small business deduction determined in step 2.

4. Calculate the actual foreign non-business tax credit using a "tax otherwise payable" figure that includes the ART and the general rate reduction.

The initial version of the foreign non-business tax credit (Step 1) will be the lesser of the actual tax paid of $675, and an amount determined by the following formula:

$$\left(\frac{\text{Foreign Non-Business Income}}{\text{Adjusted Net Income}}\right)(\text{Part I Tax Otherwise Payable Excluding The ART And GRR})$$

$$= \left(\frac{\$4,500}{\$267,300 - \$53,600 - \$36,000}\right)(\$53,200 - \$14,000)$$

$$= \$993$$

Part I tax otherwise payable in the preceding formula does not include the ART under ITA 123.3 or the general rate reduction. Adjusted Net Income in the formula is Net Income For Tax Purposes minus deductible dividends and the net capital loss carry forward claimed in the current year. In this case, the actual tax paid of $675 will be the credit. This means that the previously calculated small business deduction will be unchanged (Note 2, Step 2) and, in turn, the ART (Note 3, Step 3) and general rate reduction (Note 4, Step 3) will be unchanged.

We can now calculate the actual foreign non-business tax credit which takes into consideration the ART and the general rate reduction (Step 4). It is the lesser of the actual taxes paid of $675 and an amount determined by the following formula:

$$\left(\frac{\text{Foreign Non-Business Income}}{\text{Adjusted Net Income}} \right) (\text{Part I Tax Otherwise Payable Including The ART And GRR})$$

$$= \left(\frac{\$4,500}{\$267,300 - \$53,600 - \$36,000} \right) (\$53,200 - \$14,000 + \$447 - \$1,079)$$

$$= \$977$$

In this calculation, the actual taxes paid of $675 will again be the credit.

Chapter 13 Learning Objectives

After completing Chapter 13, you should be able to:

1. Explain the goal of integration in the design of the Canadian corporate tax system (paragraph [P hereafter] 13-1 to 13-6).

2. Calculate after-tax income retained from eligible and non-eligible dividends received (P 13-7 to 13-14).

3. Demonstrate how the dividend gross up and tax credit procedures work to implement integration with respect to business income (P 13-15 to 13-24).

4. List the components of aggregate investment income as it is defined in ITA 129(4) and describe the basic concept of refundable taxes (P 13-25 to 13-38).

5. Calculate the additional refundable tax (ART) on the investment income of a CCPC (P 13-39 to 13-47).

6. Calculate the Part I refundable tax on the investment income of a CCPC (P 13-48 to 13-68).

7. Apply the provisions related to the Part IV refundable tax on private corporations, including those related to dividends from a connected corporation (P 13-69 to 13-98).

8. Calculate the balance in the Refundable Dividend Tax On Hand (RDTOH) account and the dividend refund (P 13-99 to 13-123).

9. Use a logical approach to deal with comprehensive calculations of corporate Taxable Income and Tax Payable (P 13-124 to 13-125).

10. Explain how the gross up and tax credit procedures for eligible dividends improve integration (P 13-126 to 13-133).

11. Explain and apply the eligible dividend designation calculations relevant to CCPCs and their GRIP (P 13-134 to 13-140).

12. Explain and apply the eligible dividend designation calculations relevant to non-CCPCs and their LRIP (P 13-141 to 13-144).

13. Describe and calculate the Part III.1 tax on excessive eligible dividend designations (EEDD) (P 13-145 to 13-153).

How To Work Through Chapter 14

We recommend the following approach in dealing with the material in this chapter:

Acquisition Of Control Rules, Including Effect On Loss Carry Forwards
❑ Read paragraph 14-1 to 14-21 (in the textbook).
❑ Do Exercise Fourteen-1 (in the textbook) and check the solution on page S-316 in this Study Guide.
❑ Read paragraph 14-22 to 14-24.
❑ Do Exercise Fourteen-2 and check the solution in this Study Guide.
❑ Read paragraph 14-25 to 14-34.
❑ Do Exercise Fourteen-3 and check the solution in this Study Guide.
❑ Do Self Study Problems Fourteen-1 and Fourteen-2 at the end of the textbook chapter on page 731 to 732 and check the solutions in this Study Guide.

Associated Companies
❑ Read paragraph 14-35 to 14-50.
❑ Do Exercise Fourteen-4 and check the solution in this Study Guide.
❑ Do Self Study Problems Fourteen-3 and Fourteen-4 and check the solutions in this Study Guide.

Investment Tax Credits And SR&ED Expenditures By CCPCs
❑ Read paragraph 14-51 to 14-60.
❑ Do Exercise Fourteen-5 and check the solution in this Study Guide.
❑ Read paragraph 14-61 to 14-63.
❑ Do Exercise Fourteen-6 and check the solution in this Study Guide.

Refundable Investment Tax Credits
❑ Read paragraph 14-64 to 14-69.
❑ Do Exercise Fourteen-7 and check the solution in this Study Guide.
❑ Do Self Study Problem Fourteen-5 and check the solution in this Study Guide.
❑ Read paragraph 14-70 to 14-73.

Shareholders' Equity Under GAAP
❑ Read paragraph 14-74 to 14-76.

Paid Up Capital
❑ Read paragraph 14-77 to 14-80.
❑ Do Exercise Fourteen-8 and check the solution in this Study Guide.

Tax Basis Retained Earnings
❑ Read paragraph 14-81 to 14-89.

Capital Dividend Account
❑ Read paragraph 14-90 to 14-93.
❑ Do Exercise Fourteen-9 and check the solution in this Study Guide.
❑ Do Self Study Problem Fourteen-6 and Fourteen-7 and check the solutions in this Study Guide.

Distributions Of Corporate Surplus Through Cash, Stock And In Kind Dividends
❑ Read paragraph 14-94 to 14-105.
❑ Do Exercise Fourteen-10 and check the solution in this Study Guide.
❑ Read paragraph 14-106 to 14-108.
❑ Do Exercise Fourteen-11 and check the solution in this Study Guide.

Capital Dividends
❑ Read paragraph 14-109 to 14-113.

ITA 84(1) Deemed Dividends - Increase In PUC
❑ Read paragraph 14-114 to 14-118.
❑ Do Exercise Fourteen-12 and check the solution in this Study Guide.
❑ Read paragraph 14-119.

ITA 84(2) Deemed Dividends - On Winding-Up
❑ Read paragraph 14-120 to 14-124.
❑ Do Exercise Fourteen-13 and check the solution in this Study Guide.

ITA 84(3) Deemed Dividends - Redemption, Acquisition, Or Cancellation Of Shares
❑ Read paragraph 14-125 to 14-128.
❑ Do Exercise Fourteen-14 and check the solution in this Study Guide.

ITA 84(4) And ITA 84(4.1) Deemed Dividends
❑ Read paragraph 14-129 to 14-134.
❑ Do Exercise Fourteen-15 and check the solution in this Study Guide.
❑ Do Self Study Problem Fourteen-8 and check the solution in this Study Guide.

To Complete This Chapter
❑ Review the Key Terms Used In This Chapter on page 730. Consult the Glossary for the meaning of any key terms you do not know.
❑ Review the Glossary Flashcards and complete the Key Terms Self-Test for the Chapter. These features can be found in two places, on your Student CD-ROM under the heading "Key Term Practice" and on the web site.
❑ Review the Learning Objectives of the Chapter found on page S-330 of this Study Guide.
❑ As a review, we recommend that you view the PowerPoint Slides for Chapter 14 that are available on your Student CD-ROM. If you do not have access to the Microsoft PowerPoint program, the PowerPoint Viewer program can be installed from the Student CD-ROM.

Solution to Chapter Fourteen Exercises

Exercise Fourteen - 1 Solution

No Acquisition Of Control   Net Income For Tax Purposes for 2013 is $289,000 and, if there was no acquisition of control, the total $135,000 non-capital loss carry forward could be deducted. This would result in a 2013 Taxable Income of $154,000 ($289,000 - $135,000).

Acquisition Of Control   If there was an acquisition of the control on January 1, 2013, Net Income For Tax Purposes would still be $289,000 ($42,000 + $247,000). However, in this case, the non-capital loss carry forward could only be used to the extent of the pen business income of $42,000. This means that Taxable Income would be $247,000 ($289,000 - $42,000) with a non-capital loss carry forward of $93,000 ($135,000 - $42,000).

Exercise Fourteen - 2 Solution

The tax consequences of the acquisition of control procedures are as follows:

Land   As the fair market of the land is less than its adjusted cost base, ITA 111(4)(c) will require that it be written down to its fair market value of $215,000. This will result in an allowable capital loss of $39,000 [($293,000 - $215,000) ÷ 2].

Class 8 Assets   As the fair market value of this property is less than its UCC, ITA 111(5.1) requires that it be written down to its fair market value. The $92,000 ($276,000 - $184,000) write-down will be treated as CCA to be deducted in the deemed taxation year. For capital gains purposes, the property will retain its original capital cost of $416,000.

Cumulative Eligible Capital   Three-quarters of the fair market value of these assets is $168,750 [(3/4)($225,000)]. As this is less than the CEC balance of $216,000, the balance will have to be reduced by $47,250 ($216,000 - $168,750). The write-down amount will be treated as a CEC deduction under ITA 20(1)(b).

Exercise Fourteen - 3 Solution

It would clearly be desirable to elect to have a deemed disposition of the non-depreciable assets. This could be achieved by electing to have a deemed disposition of the non-depreciable assets for $650,000. This would result in a $75,000 taxable capital gain [(1/2)($650,000 - $500,000)] on the deemed disposition. This will leave $35,000 ($110,000 - $75,000) of the net capital loss carry forward.

This $35,000 could be eliminated by electing to have a deemed disposition of the depreciable property at an elected value of $470,000. This election would produce the required taxable capital gain of $35,000 [(1/2)($470,000 - $400,000)].

The election would also produce recapture of $50,000 ($400,000 - $350,000). As this is $5,000 ($50,000 - $45,000) greater than the operating loss, this would result in Taxable Income and Tax Payable. However, the ability to use the remaining $35,000 net capital loss carry forward is probably worth the cost of the Tax Payable on the extra $5,000 of income. In addition, the election would result in increased future CCA.

Exercise Fourteen - 4 Solution

Top And Middle   Top and Middle are associated under ITA 256(1)(a) as Top controls Middle.

Top And Bottom   Top and Bottom are associated under ITA 256(1)(b) as they are both controlled by the same person, Mr. Top. He controls Top directly. In addition, he controls Bottom through a combination of direct ownership, indirect ownership, and deemed ownership. His majority interest would be calculated as follows:

Direct Interest in Bottom	5%
Indirect Interest Through Top Company [(100%)(10%)]	10%
Indirect Interest Through Control Of Middle Company	35%
Deemed Interest Through Son - ITA 256(1.3)	15%
Deemed Interest Through Options - ITA 256(1.4)	10%
Controlling Interest	75%

Middle And Bottom   Middle and Bottom are associated under ITA 256(1)(b) as they are both controlled by the same person, Mr. Top. Mr. Top controls Middle indirectly through Top. He controls Bottom through a combination of direct and indirect control, as described in the discussion of Top and Bottom.

Exercise Fourteen - 5 Solution

With respect to the $125,000 in apprentice salaries, the investment tax credit is available on an annual salary maximum of $20,000 per apprentice. As a result, there will be a $10,000 [(5)(10%)($20,000)] credit against 2013 federal Tax Payable. This $10,000 credit will be added to income in 2014. With respect to the $3,000,000 in capital expenditures, there will be a 2013 credit against federal Tax Payable of $300,000 [(10%)($3,000,000)]. The $300,000 credit will not influence the calculation of 2013 CCA. This amount will be $750,000 [(50%)(1/2)($3,000,000)].

In 2014, the $300,000 credit will be deducted from the January 1, 2014 UCC, leaving a balance of $1,950,000 ($3,000,000 - $750,000 - $300,000). Given this, 2014 CCA will be $975,000 [(50%)($1,950,000)].

Exercise Fourteen - 6 Solution

For 2013, the annual limit would be $2,250,000, calculated as follows:

[$8 million – (10)($560,000)][($40 million – $2,500,000) ÷ $40 million] = $2,250,000

Exercise Fourteen - 7 Solution

As Sci-Tech has Taxable Income of less than $500,000 in the previous year, and its Taxable Capital Employed in Canada is less than $10 million, the Company's annual expenditure limit is not reduced from the maximum value of $3,000,000.

Given the $3,000,000 annual expenditure limit for the 35 percent rate, the total amount of investment tax credits available can be calculated as follows:

Qualified Property [(10%)($123,000)]		$ 12,300
SR&ED Current Expenditures [(35%)($1,200,000)]		420,000
SR&ED Capital Expenditures:		
1st $1,800,000 [(35%)($3,000,000 - $1,200,000)]	$630,000	
Remaining $700,000		
[(20%)($2,500,000 - $1,800,000)]	140,000	770,000
Total Available Amount		$1,202,300

The refund available would be as follows:

Qualified Property [(40%)($12,300)]	$ 4,920
SR&ED Current Expenditures [(100%)($420,000)]	420,000
SR&ED Capital Expenditures [(40%)($770,000)]	308,000
Total Refund Available	$732,920

The non-refunded investment tax credit of $469,380 ($1,202,300 - $732,920) can be carried forward 20 years to be applied against Tax Payable. There was no Tax Payable in the last three years so it cannot be carried back.

The cost of the qualified property will be reduced in the following year by the refundable investment tax credit of $4,920. The $420,000 tax credit on current SR&ED expenditures will be added to income in the following taxation year.

The treatment of the refundable investment tax credit on SR&ED capital expenditures of $308,000 will depend on whether they qualify for immediate deduction or, alternatively, are treated as an asset subject to CCA (see Supplementary Reading No. 4, SR&ED Expenditures if you are interested in this issue). If they are immediately deductible, the $308,000 will be added to income in the following year. If they are capitalized, the cost of the property subject to CCA will be reduced in the following year by $308,000.

Exercise Fourteen - 8 Solution

The adjusted cost base of the shares would be determined as follows:

	Number of Shares	Cost/Share	Total Cost
First Purchase	2,400	$1.10	$2,640
Second Purchase	3,850	$1.82	7,007
Totals	6,250		$9,647

The adjusted cost base for all of the investor's shares is $9,647. The adjusted cost base per share would be $1.54 ($9,647 ÷ 6,250).

The PUC for the investor's shares would be calculated as follows:

	Number of Shares	PUC/Share	Total PUC
First Sale	100,000	$1.10	$110,000
Second Sale	50,000	$1.35	67,500
Third Sale	30,000	$1.82	54,600
Total PUC Of Outstanding Shares	180,000		$232,100

Number Of Shares (From First Table)	6,250
PUC Per Share [$232,100 ÷ 180,000 Shares]	$ 1.29
PUC For Investor's Shares	$8,063

Exercise Fourteen - 9 Solution

The balance in the capital dividend account as at December 31, 2013 would be as follows:

2009 Capital Gain [(1/2)($22,000)]	$11,000
2012 Capital Dividend Received	8,200
2013 Sale Of Goodwill [(3/4)($42,000 - $37,000)(2/3)]	2,500
2013 Capital Dividend Paid	(16,000)
Balance - End Of 2013	$ 5,700

Exercise Fourteen - 10 Solution

Jean will receive 50 new shares [(5%)(1,000)] with a fair market value of $1,250 [(50)($25)]. This $1,250 non-eligible dividend will be grossed up to a taxable amount of $1,563 [($1,250)(125%)]. As a result, his Net Income For Tax Purposes will increase by $1,563. The receipt of this dividend will generate a credit against Jean's federal Tax Payable of $208 [(2/3)(25%)($1,250)].

Prior to the stock dividend, the adjusted cost base of Jean's shares was $18,000 [(1,000)($18)]. The $1,250 dividend will be added to this amount, resulting in a new adjusted cost base of $19,250. When the 50 new shares are added to his total holding, the adjusted cost base per share will be $18.33 ($19,250 ÷ 1,050).

Exercise Fourteen - 11 Solution

The dividend declaration will be treated as a disposition of capital property with an adjusted cost base of $6,300,000 [(150,000)($42)] for proceeds of disposition of $7,650,000 [(150,000)($51)]. This will result in an increase in Cloutier Ltd.'s 2013 Net Income For Tax Purposes of $675,000 [(1/2)($7,650,000 - $6,300,000)].

Sandrine Cloutier will have received a dividend of $1,147,500 [(15%)(150,000)($51)]. This will result in an inclusion in her 2013 Net Income For Tax Purposes of $1,434,375 [(125%)($1,147,500)]. In addition, the dividend will generate a credit of $191,250 [(2/3)(25%)($1,147,500)] against her 2013 federal Tax Payable.

Exercise Fourteen - 12 Solution

This transaction will result in an ITA 84(1) deemed dividend for all shareholders as follows:

PUC Of New Shares [(40,000)($12.70)]	$508,000
Increase In Net Assets	(450,000)
ITA 84(1) Deemed Dividend	$ 58,000

This would be allocated to all 166,000 (126,000 + 40,000) shares outstanding, on the basis of $0.35 per share. This would be a taxable dividend, subject to either the eligible or non-eligible dividend gross up and tax credit procedures. The $0.35 per share dividend would also be added to the adjusted cost base of all 166,000 shares.

With the addition of $0.35 resulting from the ITA 84(1) deemed dividend to the original issue price of $10.50, the adjusted cost base of these shares is now $10.85 per share. Mr. Uni's sale of 5,000 shares at $13.42 per share would result in a taxable capital gain calculated as follows:

Proceeds Of Disposition [($13.42)(5,000)]	$67,100
Adjusted Cost Base [($10.85)(5,000)]	(54,250)
Capital Gain	$12,850
Inclusion Rate	1/2
Taxable Capital Gain	$ 6,425

Exercise Fourteen - 13 Solution

The analysis of the $2,350,000 distribution would be as follows:

Cash Distributed	$2,350,000
PUC Of Shares	(250,000)
Total ITA 84(2) Deemed Dividend	$2,100,000
ITA 83(2) Capital Dividend	(340,000)
ITA 88(2)(b) Taxable Dividend	$1,760,000

To the extent the Company has a balance in its GRIP account, some amount of the $1,760,000 dividend could be designated as eligible. Any remainder will be taxed as a non-eligible dividend. The wind-up results in a disposition of the shares. The tax consequences of this disposition are as follows:

Cash Distributed	$2,350,000
ITA 84(2) Deemed Dividend	(2,100,000)
ITA 54 Proceeds Of Disposition	$ 250,000
Adjusted Cost Base	(250,000)
Capital Gain	Nil

As shown by the preceding calculation, there would be no capital gain on the disposition.

Exercise Fourteen - 14 Solution

The redemption transaction would have no tax consequences for Ms. Tandy. The tax consequences to Jesuiah Tandy resulting from the redemption of his shares would be as follows:

Proceeds Of Redemption [(15,000)($11.75)]	$176,250
PUC [(15,000)($8.25)]	(123,750)
ITA 84(3) Deemed Dividend	$ 52,500
Gross Up Of 25 Percent	13,125
Taxable Dividend	$ 65,625

Proceeds Of Redemption [(15,000)($11.75)]	$176,250
ITA 84(3) Deemed Dividend	(52,500)
ITA 54 Proceeds Of Disposition	$123,750
Adjusted Cost Base [(15,000)($7.90)]	(118,500)
Capital Gain (PUC - ACB)	$ 5,250
Inclusion Rate	1/2
Taxable Capital Gain	$ 2,625

Both the taxable dividend and the taxable capital gain would be included in the Jesuiah's Net Income For Tax Purposes. The non-eligible dividend qualifies for a federal dividend tax credit of $8,750 [(2/3)($13,125)].

Exercise Fourteen - 15 Solution

To the extent of the $225,000 PUC reduction, the dividend will be treated as a tax free distribution. The tax consequences will be a reduction in the PUC of these shares to $225,000 ($450,000 - $225,000), as well as an adjusted cost base reduction to $400,000 ($625,000 - $225,000). The $105,000 ($330,000 - $225,000) excess of the distribution over the PUC reduction will be an ITA 84(4) deemed dividend, subject to either the eligible or non-eligible dividend gross up and tax credit procedures. As it will be taxed as a dividend, this part of the distribution will not be subtracted from the adjusted cost base of the shares.

Self Study Solution Fourteen - 1

Part A - Non-Capital And Net Capital Losses

Net Business Loss The net business loss for the period to March 31, 2013 would be as follows:

Loss As Per March 31, 2013 Income Statement	($23,000)
Required Accounts Receivable Adjustment ($45,000 - $33,000)	(12,000)
Building Election - Recaptured CCA ($285,000 - $270,000)	15,000
Fixtures And Equipment - Deemed CCA ($95,000 - $90,000)	(5,000)
Vehicles Election - Recaptured CCA ($87,000 - $80,000)	7,000
Net Business Loss For Period Ending March 31, 2013	($18,000)

Net And Taxable Income Net Income For Tax Purposes and Taxable Income for the period ending March 31, 2013, calculated as per the ITA 3 rules, would be as follows:

ITA 3(a) - Non-Capital Income (Positive Amounts Only)		Nil
ITA 3(b) - Net Taxable Capital Gains (Losses):		
Elections Under ITA 111(4)(e):		
Gain On Land [(1/2)($420,000 - $275,000)]	$ 72,500	
Gain On Building [(1/2)($320,000 - $285,000)]	17,500	
Required Write-Down - ITA 111(4)(c) And (d)		
Loss On Temporary Investments		
[(1/2)($53,000 - $23,000)]	(15,000)	75,000
ITA 3(c) - Total		$ 75,000
ITA 3(d) - Business Loss For The Period		(18,000)
Net Income For Tax Purposes		$ 57,000
Net Capital Loss Carry Forward		
(Limited To Amount Included Under ITA 3(b)		(75,000)
Taxable Income		Nil

Lost Net Capital Loss   The net capital loss that would be lost would be calculated as follows:

From 2011 [(1/2)($68,000)]	$34,000
From 2012 [(1/2)($85,000)]	42,500
Net Capital Loss Balance At March 31, 2013	$76,500
Amount Deducted In 2013	(75,000)
Net Capital Loss Lost On Acquisition of Control	$ 1,500

Non-Capital Loss Carry Forward   The non-capital loss carry forward would be calculated as follows:

Net Business Loss For Period	$ 18,000
Net Capital Loss Deducted	75,000
Subtotal	$ 93,000
Income Under ITA 3(c)	(75,000)
Non-Capital Loss For The Period Ending March 31, 2013	$ 18,000
Non-Capital Loss Carry Forward From 2011	63,500
Non-Capital Loss Carry Forward From 2012	78,500
Non-Capital Loss Carry Forward At March 31, 2013	$160,000

Part B - Loss Carry Forward In 2013

The April 1 to December 31, 2013 Net Income For Tax Purposes would be $78,000 ($123,000 - $45,000). Note that there is no restriction against deducting the current year loss on bread operations against other sources of income. However, none of the non-capital loss carry forward of $160,000 can be used as these losses can only be applied against income in the bread operations. This leaves the 2013 Taxable Income equal to the Net Income For Tax Purposes of $78,000. The non-capital loss carry forward at December 31, 2013 is unchanged at $160,000.

Part C - Loss Carry Forward In 2014

The $40,000 loss on the figurines must be deducted from the profits of the bread operations to produce a Net Income For Tax Purposes of $171,000 ($211,000 - $40,000). As this income is entirely from bread operations, all of the $160,000 non-capital loss carry forward can be deducted, leaving a Taxable Income of $11,000. There is no remaining non-capital loss carry forward at December 31, 2014.

Self Study Solution Fourteen - 2

Part A

As a result of the acquisition of control, LF will have a deemed taxation year end on April 30, 2013. This results in a short January 1, 2013 through April 30, 2013 taxation year for LF. The effects of this include:

- An additional year will be counted towards the expiry of the non-capital losses.
- If CCA is to be taken, it will have to be calculated for a short fiscal period.
- All of the usual year end procedures (timing of bonuses, inclusion of reserves, etc.) will have to be carried out.
- For the first year after the acquisition of control, LF can choose a new fiscal year end, on any date up to 53 weeks after the deemed year end.

Other implications are as follows:

- Any net capital loss balance that that remains cannot be used after the deemed year end.
- Any non-capital loss balance that is carried forward can only be used against profits earned in the same or a similar line of business.
- The manufacturing equipment, because its fair market value is less than its UCC, will have to be written down to the $285,000 UCC value. The $90,000 ($375,000 - $285,000) amount of the write down will be treated as deemed CCA.

Part B

The land, Class 1 assets, and Class 8 assets all have fair market values in excess of their tax values. If the deemed disposition election is made and the fair market value of these assets is used as the elected value, the results would be as follows:

Asset	Recapture	Capital Gain
Land ($925,000 - $450,000)	N/A	$475,000
Class 1 ($650,000 - $515,000)	$135,000	Nil
Class 8 ($15,000 - $10,000)	5,000	Nil
Total Income	$140,000	$475,000

Part C

If the Companies believe that they will be able to generate sufficient income to use the non-capital loss carry forward in future periods, they will not want to make elections that will result in any unneeded pre-acquisition income. If the elections are made, the losses will increase the adjusted cost base or UCC balance of the assets the elections are made on. In the case of the land, the increased cost will not be of benefit until the land is sold. In the case of the depreciable assets, the increased UCC will only be deductible at the applicable rates of 4 or 20 percent. Alternatively, a non-capital loss carry forward can be deducted in full, as soon as the Companies have sufficient appropriate income to absorb it.

The situation with net capital losses is different. If such losses are not used during the short fiscal period prior to the acquisition of control, they will be lost forever. Given this, it would be appropriate to make an election that would absorb the $65,000 net capital loss from 2011. This will require a capital gain of $130,000 [(2)($65,000)] which can be created by electing a deemed disposition on the land at a value of $580,000. This election will create a taxable capital gain of $65,000 [(1/2)($580,000 - $450,000)].

Given the required write-down of the manufacturing equipment, the Net Business Loss would be calculated as follows:

Operating Loss To April 30, 2013 (Given)	($ 55,000)
Deemed CCA On Class 29 ($375,000 - $285,000)	(90,000)
Net Business Loss For The Period Ending April 30, 2013	($145,000)

Using this figure, along with the results of the election on the land, Net and Taxable Income would be calculated as follows:

ITA 3(a) Non-Capital Income (Positive Amounts Only)	Nil
ITA 3(b) Net Taxable Capital Gains	
Election Under ITA 111(4)(e) On Land	$ 65,000
ITA 3(c) Total	$ 65,000
ITA 3(d) Net Business Loss For The Period	(145,000)
Net Income For Tax Purposes	Nil
Net Capital Loss Carry Forward (See Following)	($ 65,000)
Taxable Income	Nil

The non-capital loss carry forward at April 30, 2013 would be calculated as follows:

Net Business Loss For The Period	$145,000
Net Capital Loss Deducted	65,000
Subtotal	$210,000
Income Under ITA 3(c)	(65,000)
Non-Capital Loss For The Period Ending April 30, 2013	$145,000
Carry Forward From 2011	180,000
Carry Forward From 2012	140,000
Non-Capital Loss Carry Forward	$465,000

The net capital loss balance from 2011 would be eliminated by the $65,000 carry forward deduction, leaving a balance of nil to be carried forward.

Part D

If there is uncertainty with respect to the ability of OLC and LF to generate income in the same or similar line of business in amounts sufficient to absorb the non-capital loss carry forward, additional elections should be made to absorb as much of this balance as possible. This would require elections on all of the assets with capital gains or recapture. Under this approach Net Business Income would be calculated as follows:

Operating Loss To April 30, 2013 (Given)	($ 55,000)
Deemed CCA On Class 29 ($375,000 - $285,000)	(90,000)
Class 1 - Recaptured CCA	135,000
Class 8 - Recaptured CCA	5,000
Net Business Loss For The Period Ending April 30, 2013	($ 5,000)

The resulting Net and Taxable Income amounts would be calculated as follows:

ITA 3(a) - Non-Capital Income (Positive Amounts Only)	Nil
ITA 3(b) - Net Taxable Capital Gains (Losses):	
Capital Gain On Land [(1/2)($925,000 - $450,000)]	$237,500
ITA 3(c) - Total	$237,500
ITA 3(d) - Business Loss For The Period	(5,000)
Net Income For Tax Purposes	$232,500
Net Capital Loss Carry Forward (All)	(65,000)
Subtotal	$167,500
Non-Capital Loss Carry Forward	
(Maximum Needed To Reduce Income To Nil)	(167,500)
Taxable Income	Nil

Under this Part D approach, the non-capital loss carry forward at April 30, 2013 would be calculated as follows:

Net Business Loss For The Period	$ 5,000
Net Capital Loss Deducted	65,000
Subtotal	$ 70,000
Income Under ITA 3(c)	(237,500)
Non-Capital Loss For The Period Ending April 30, 2013	Nil
Carry Forward From 2011	$180,000
Carry Forward From 2012	140,000
Non-Capital Loss Carry Forward Deducted For The Period Ending April 30, 2013	(167,500)
Non-Capital Loss Carry Forward	$152,500

As in Part C, the net capital loss from 2011 is eliminated by the $65,000 loss carry forward deduction.

Self Study Solution Fourteen - 3

Part A

By virtue of ITA 256(1)(a), John Fleming and Eric Flame are related by the fact that they are married to persons who are connected by a blood relationship (their wives). In addition, under ITA 256(1.5) a person who owns shares in two or more corporations shall be, as a shareholder of one of the corporations, deemed to be related to himself as a shareholder of the other corporation(s).

Given this, Fleming Ltd. and Lartch Inc. are associated under ITA 256(1)(d). John Fleming controls Fleming Ltd., is a member of a related group (John Fleming and Eric Flame) that controls Lartch Inc., and owns more than 25 percent of the voting shares of Lartch Inc.

In a similar fashion, Flame Ltd. is associated with Lartch Inc. under ITA 256(1)(d), as Eric Flame controls Flame Ltd., is a member of a related group (John Fleming and Eric Flame) that controls Lartch Inc., and owns more than 25 percent of Lartch Inc.

Based on these associations, Fleming Ltd. and Flame Ltd. are associated under ITA 256(2), as they are both associated with a third corporation, Lartch Inc.

Part B

Mr. and Mrs. Cuso are a group with respect to both Male Ltd. and Female Inc. [ITA 256(1.2)(a) - two or more persons holding shares in the same corporation]. As a group, they control both Male Ltd. and Female Inc. Therefore, the two Companies are associated under ITA 256 (1)(b). The fact that Mr. and Mrs. Cuso are related is not relevant.

Part C

Ms. Jones and Miss Lange are a group that controls Alliance Ltd. However, they do not control Breaker Inc., as Mrs. Kelly (not a member of the group that controls Alliance Ltd.) owns 50 percent of the shares. Therefore, Alliance Ltd. and Breaker Inc. are not associated.

Part D

While they are not related, Mr. Martin and Mr. Oakley constitute a group [ITA 256(1.2)(a)] with respect to both Martin Inc. and Oakley Ltd. As both Martin Inc. and Oakley Ltd. are controlled by the same group, the two Companies are associated under ITA 256(1)(b).

Part E
The two Companies are related, but not associated. While Lily and James are related, they are not a group with respect to the two Companies and there is no cross-ownership of shares.

Self Study Solution Fourteen - 4

Case 1
As a group, Mr. Jones and Mr. Twitty control both Jones Ltd. and Twitty Inc. As a consequence, these two Companies would be associated under ITA 256(1)(b).

Case 2
Ms. Wynette controls Wynette Enterprises Ltd., and is related to each member of the group that controls Lynn Inc. In addition, Ms. Wynette has the necessary 25 percent plus cross-ownership in Lynn Inc. As a consequence, Wynette Enterprises Ltd. and Lynn Inc. are associated under ITA 256(1)(d).

Case 3
A group, consisting of Mr. Travis and Mr. Cash, has control of both Cowboys Ltd. and Horses Inc. Therefore, Cowboys Ltd. and Horses Inc. are associated under ITA 256(1)(b).

Case 4
As Randy's Boots Inc. controls Hill Inc., those two companies are associated under ITA 256(1)(a).

As Mr. Nelson owns 80 percent of the shares of Willie's Hits Ltd., he controls that company. This gives him control over the 20 percent of Hill Inc. shares that are owned by Willie's Hits.

However, Mr. Nelson does not control Randy's Boots, and this means that his indirect interest in Hill Inc. through Randy's Boots of 24 percent [(30%)(80%)] is the product of the two ownership percentages.

As a result, his overall interest in Hill Inc. is only 44 percent (20% + 24%), which is not sufficient to give him control over Hill. Therefore, Willie's Hits Ltd. and Hill Inc. are not associated and Willie's Hits Ltd. and Randy's Boots Inc. are not associated.

Case 5
Ms. Parton controls Alpha Company, is related to each member of the group (Ms. Parton and her spouse) that control Beta Company, and has cross-ownership of Beta Company in excess of 25 percent. This means that these two Companies are associated under ITA 256(1)(d).

Her spouse controls Centra Company, is related to each member of the group (the spouse and Ms. Parton) that controls Beta Company, and has the necessary cross-ownership of at least 25 percent of Beta Company shares. This means that these two Companies are also associated under ITA 256(1)(d).

As they are not controlled by the same individual or group, Alpha Company and Centra Company are not associated under ITA 256(1). However, as they are both associated with the same third corporation (Beta Company), Alpha and Centra would be associated under ITA 256(2). Note that ITA 256(2) allows Alpha and Centra to avoid association, provided Beta elects not to be associated with either Company. This will mean, however, that Beta will have a business limit for the period of nil.

Case 6
For the purposes of determining associated companies, Ms. Gale is deemed to own the 30 percent interest in Norton Music Inc. that is held by her minor child [ITA 256(1.3)] and the 20

percent interest in Norton Music Inc. for which she holds an option [ITA 256(1.4)]. When this is combined with her own interest of 10 percent, she would be considered to control Norton Music Inc. As she controls both Kristal Enterprises Ltd. and Norton Music Inc., these Companies are associated under ITA 256(1)(b).

Self Study Solution Fourteen - 5

Case A

With respect to the $292,500 in apprentice salaries, the investment tax credit is available on an annual salary maximum of $20,000 per apprentice. As a result, there will be a $26,000 [(13)(10%)($20,000)] credit against 2012 federal Tax Payable. This $26,000 credit will be added to income in 2013.

With respect to the $1,600,000 in capital expenditures, there will be a 2012 credit against federal Tax Payable of $160,000 [(10%)($1,600,000)].

The $160,000 credit will not influence the calculation of 2012 CCA. This amount will be $160,000 [(20%)(1/2)($1,600,000)].

In 2013, the $160,000 credit will be deducted from the January 1, 2013 UCC, leaving a balance of $1,280,000 ($1,600,000 - $160,000 - $160,000). Given this, 2013 CCA will be $256,000 [(20%)($1,280,000)].

Case B

For 2013, the annual limit would be $1,170,560, calculated as follows:

[$8 million − (10)($672,000*)][($40 million − $3,420,000) ÷ $40 million] = $1,170,560.

*Greater of $500,000 and the corporation's Taxable Income for the preceding year

Case C

RAR's annual expenditure limit would be calculated as follows:

[$8 million − (10)($500,000*)][($40 million − $1,500,000) ÷ $40 million] = $2,887,500

*Greater of $500,000 and the corporation's Taxable Income for the preceding year

The amount of SR&ED Expenditure that would be eligible for the 35 percent rate can be calculated as follows:

Annual Expenditure Limit	$2,887,500
SR&ED Current Expenditures - All Eligible	(1,560,000)
SR&ED Capital Expenditures - Portion Eligible	$1,327,500

The total amount of investment tax credits available can be calculated as follows:

Qualified Property [(10%)($187,000)]		$ 18,700
SR&ED Current Expenditures [(35%)($1,560,000)]		546,000
SR&ED Capital Expenditures:		
At 35% Rate [(35%)($1,327,500)]	$464,625	
At 20% Rate - Remaining $632,500		
[(20%)($1,960,000 - $1,327,500)]	126,500	591,125
Total Available Amount		$1,155,825

RAR is a qualifying corporation. The refund available would be as follows:

	Rate	ITC	Refund
Qualified Property	40%	$ 18,700	$ 7,480
SR&ED Current Expenditures	100%	546,000	546,000
SR&ED Capital Expenditures	40%	591,125	236,450
Total Refund Available			$789,930

The non-refunded investment tax credit of $365,896 ($1,155,825 - $789,930) can be carried forward 20 years to be applied against Tax Payable. There was no Tax Payable in the last three years so it cannot be carried back.

The cost of the qualified property will be reduced in the following year by the refundable investment tax credit of $7,480. The $546,000 tax credit on current SR&ED expenditures will be added to income in the following taxation year.

The treatment of the refundable investment tax credit on SR&ED capital expenditures of $236,450 will depend on whether they qualify for immediate deduction or, alternatively, are treated as an asset subject to CCA (see Supplementary Reading No. 4, SR&ED Expenditures if you are interested in this issue).

Any portion that is immediately deductible will be added to income in the following year. Any portion that is capitalized will reduce the cost of the property subject to CCA in the following year.

> **Note On 2014 Changes**   This solution is correct for the 2013 taxation year. However, in 2014 and subsequent years, capital expenditures will no longer qualify for SR&ED investment tax credits. This will result in a different solution for this case.

Self Study Solution Fourteen - 6

Part A - CCPC

Assuming Hemingway Industries is a CCPC, the changes in the capital dividend account during the year are as follows:

Property	Proceeds	Adjusted Cost Base	Selling Costs	Gain (Loss)
1	$ 8,100	($ 4,200)	($ 200)	$3,700
2	7,900	(3,950)	(375)	3,575
3	2,200	(4,300)	(700)	(2,800)
4	1,900	(3,450)	(260)	(1,810)
Totals	$20,100	($15,900)	($1,535)	$2,665

The net capital gain for the year is $2,665. One-half of this amount, or $1,333, would be added to the capital dividend account.

Part B - Private Corporation

Assuming Hemingway Industries is a private corporation, but not a CCPC, the changes in the capital dividend account during the year would be the same as in Part A.

Self Study Solution Fourteen - 7

The December 31, 2013 balance in the capital dividend account is calculated as follows:

2002 Capital Gain [(1/2)($343,500 - $225,000)]	$ 59,250
2003 Life Insurance Proceeds	162,000
2005 Capital Loss [(1/2)($150,000 - $220,000)]	(35,000)
2007 Capital Dividend Received	26,000
2011 Franchise Sale [(3/4)($320,000 - Nil)(2/3)]	160,000
Capital Dividends Paid [(3)($45,000)]	(135,000)
Balance December 31, 2013	$237,250

Self Study Solution Fourteen - 8

Part A(i)

There would be an ITA 84(1) deemed dividend calculated as follows:

Increase In PUC - Preferred Shares	$11,000
Increase In Net Assets (Decrease In Liabilities)	(10,000)
ITA 84(1) Deemed Dividend	$ 1,000

This $1,000 deemed dividend is applicable to all 1,000 of the Preferred Shares that are now outstanding. A pro rata share of the dividend, $1 per share, will be added to the adjusted cost base of all of the Preferred Shares that are outstanding. All of the preferred stock investors will be taxed on the deemed dividend of $1 per share which will be subject to the 25 percent gross up and tax credit procedures.

Part A(ii)

This investor's taxable capital gain would be calculated as follows:

Proceeds Of Disposition		$5,500
Adjusted Cost Base:		
Original Cost	($4,100)	
ITA 84(1) Dividend [(250)($1)]	(250)	(4,350)
Capital Gain		$ 1,150
Inclusion Rate		1/2
Taxable Capital Gain		$ 575

Part B

As noted in ITA 84(1)(a), a stock dividend is not considered to be a deemed dividend under ITA 84. However, the $780 addition to Paid Up Capital will be considered to be a regular dividend under the definition in ITA 248(1). The holders of the common shares will have a dividend of $1.30 ($780 ÷ 600) per share, and this will be grossed up to a taxable dividend of $1.63 [($1.30)(125%)] per share. The federal dividend tax credit will be equal to $0.22 per share [($1.30)(25%)(2/3)]. For individuals holding the common shares, the adjusted cost base of their holding would be increased by $1.30, multiplied by the number of shares held prior to the stock dividend.

Part C

As the increase in Paid Up Capital is equal to the increase in net assets, there is no deemed dividend or any other tax consequences in this Part. This is verified in the following calculation:

Increase In PUC [(250/500)($11,000)]		$ 5,500
Increase In Net Assets:		
New Assets Acquired	$17,500	
Increase In Liabilities	(12,000)	(5,500)
ITA 84(1) Deemed Dividend		Nil

Part D

The ITA 84(3) deemed dividend would be calculated as follows:

Redemption Proceeds [(100 Shares)($32)]	$3,200
PUC [(100 Shares)($15,600 ÷ 600)]	(2,600)
ITA 84(3) Deemed Dividend	$ 600
Gross Up Of 25 Percent	150
Taxable Dividend	$ 750

In addition, there would be a taxable capital gain calculated as follows:

Redemption Proceeds	$3,200
ITA 84(3) Deemed Dividend	(600)
Deemed Proceeds Of Disposition	$2,600
Adjusted Cost Base [(100)($15)]	(1,500)
Capital Gain	$1,100
Inclusion Rate	1/2
Taxable Capital Gain	$ 550

The total increase in Taxable Income would be $1,300 ($750 + $550). As all of this individual's shares have been redeemed, information on changes in the adjusted cost base is not relevant. The taxable dividend will be eligible for a federal dividend tax credit of $100 [(2/3)($150)].

Chapter 14 Learning Objectives

After completing Chapter 14, you should be able to:

1. Explain the need for, and the tax implications of, a deemed year end when there has been an acquisition of control (paragraph [P hereafter] 14-1 to 14-13).

2. Apply the provisions related to charitable donations and loss carry forwards when there has been an acquisition of control (P 14-14 to 14-21).

3. Explain the treatment of unrecognized losses at a deemed year end resulting from an acquisition of control (P 14-22 to 14-34).

4. Apply the associated companies rules (P 14-35 to 14-50).

5. Apply the general rules applicable to investment tax credits and SR & ED expenditures by CCPCs (P 14-51 to 14-63).

6. Apply the provisions related to refundable investment tax credits (P 14-64 to 14-68).

7. Apply the carry over rules for investment tax credits, as well as describe the influence of an acquisition of control on their availability (P 14-69 to 14-73).

8. Explain the relationship between tax basis Shareholders' Equity and Shareholders' Equity as presented under GAAP (P 14-74 to 14-76).

9. Explain the concept of, and calculate the amount of, Paid Up Capital (P 14-77 to 14-80).

10. Identify and explain the major components of Tax Basis Retained Earnings (P 14-81 to 14-89).

11. Explain the objectives of, and list the major components of, the capital dividend account (P 14-90 to 14-93).

12. List the various types of dividends used to distribute corporate surplus (P 14-94 to 14-98).

13. Apply the procedures related to the declaration and payment of cash dividends (P 14-99 to 14-102).

14. Apply the procedures related to the declaration and payment of stock dividends (P 14-103 to 14-105).

15. Apply the procedures related to the declaration and payment of dividends in kind (P 14-106 to 14-108).

16. Apply the procedures related to the declaration and payment of capital dividends (P 14-109 to 14-113).

17. Explain and apply the procedures related to ITA 84(1) deemed dividends when there has been an increase in PUC (P 14-114 to 14-119).

18. Explain and apply the procedures related to ITA 84(2) deemed dividends on winding up (P 14-120 to 14-124).

19. Explain and apply the procedures related to ITA 84(3) deemed dividends on redemption, acquisition or cancellation of shares (P 14-125 to 14-128).

20. Explain and apply the procedures related to ITA 84(4) and 84(4.1) deemed dividends (P 14-129 to 14-134).

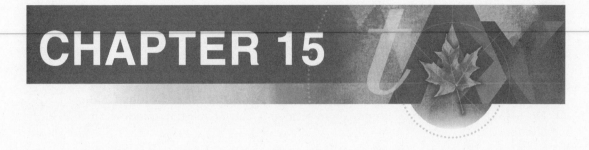

CHAPTER 15

How To Work Through Chapter 15

We recommend the following approach in dealing with the material in this chapter:

The Decision To Incorporate - Tax Considerations
❑ Read paragraph 15-1 to 15-9 (in the textbook).

Other Advantages And Disadvantages Of Incorporation
❑ Read paragraph 15-10 to 15-11.
❑ Do Self Study Problem Fifteen-1 at the end of the textbook chapter on page 788 and check the solution on page S-339 to S-341 in this Study Guide.

Basic Example Data - Tax Reduction And Deferral
❑ Read paragraph 15-12 to 15-24.

Public Companies - Tax Reduction And Deferral
❑ Read paragraph 15-25 to 15-34.
❑ Do Exercise Fifteen-1 (in the textbook) and check the solution on page S-332 and S-333 in this Study Guide.

CCPCs - Active Business Income - Tax Reduction And Deferral
❑ Read paragraph 15-35 to 15-47.
❑ Do Exercise Fifteen-2 and check the solution in this Study Guide.

CCPCs - Non-Dividend Investment Income - Tax Reduction And Deferral
❑ Read paragraph 15-48 to 15-51.
❑ Do Exercise Fifteen-3 and check the solution in this Study Guide.
❑ Do Self Study Problem Fifteen-2 and check the solution in this Study Guide.

CCPCs - Dividend Income - Tax Reduction And Deferral
❑ Read paragraph 15-52 to 15-56.

Conclusions On Tax Reductions And Deferrals
❑ Read paragraph 15-57 to 15-59.
❑ Do Exercises Fifteen-4 and Fifteen-5 and check the solutions in this Study Guide.
❑ Do Self Study Problem Fifteen-3 and check the solution in this Study Guide.

Provincial Taxes And Integration
❑ Read paragraph 15-60 to 15-78.
❑ Do Self Study Problem Fifteen-4 and check the solution in this Study Guide.

Tax-Free Dividend Calculations
❑ Read paragraph 15-79 to 15-90.

Solution to Chapter Fifteen Exercises

Income Splitting
❑ Read paragraph 15-91 to 15-101.
❑ Do Self Study Problem Fifteen-5 and check the solution in this Study Guide.

Shareholder Benefits Including Loans
❑ Read paragraph 15-102 to 15-124.
❑ Do Exercises Fifteen-6 to Fifteen-8 and check the solutions in this Study Guide.
❑ Do Self Study Problems Fifteen-6 and Fifteen-7 and check the solutions in this Study Guide.

Management Compensation - General Principles
❑ Read paragraph 15-125 to 15-131.

Salary Vs. Dividend Decisions For The Owner-Manager
❑ Read paragraph 15-132 to 15-162.
❑ Do Exercise Fifteen-9 and check the solution in this Study Guide.

Salary Vs. Dividends - Use Of Tax Credits
❑ Read paragraph 15-163 to 15-179.
❑ Do Exercises Fifteen-10 and Fifteen-11 and check the solutions in this Study Guide.

Salary Vs. Dividends - Conclusion
❑ Read paragraph 15-180 to 15-181.
❑ Do Self Study Problems Fifteen-8 and Fifteen-9 and check the solutions in this Study Guide.

To Complete This Chapter
❑ Review the Key Terms Used In This Chapter on page 787. Consult the Glossary for the meaning of any key terms you do not know.
❑ Review the Glossary Flashcards and complete the Key Terms Self-Test for the Chapter. These features can be found in two places, on your Student CD-ROM under the heading "Key Term Practice" and on the web site.
❑ Review the Learning Objectives of the Chapter found on page S-353 of this Study Guide.
❑ As a review, we recommend that you view the PowerPoint Slides for Chapter 15 that are available on your Student CD-ROM. If you do not have access to the Microsoft PowerPoint program, the PowerPoint Viewer program can be installed from the Student CD-ROM.

Solution to Chapter Fifteen Exercises

Exercise Fifteen - 1 Solution
As the new corporation would not be allocated any part of the annual business limit, all of the $100,000 would be taxed at full corporate rates:

Corporate Income	$100,000
Corporate Taxes [(25%)($100,000)]	(25,000)
Available For Eligible Dividends	$ 75,000
Eligible Dividends Received By Ms. Ashley	$ 75,000
Gross Up At 38 Percent	28,500
Taxable Dividends	$103,500
Ms. Ashley's Tax Rate	45%
Tax Payable Before Dividend Tax Credit	$ 46,575
Dividend Tax Credit [(6/11 + 44%)($28,500)]	(28,085)
Tax Payable	$ 18,490

Dividends Received	$75,000
Tax Payable	(18,490)
After Tax Retention	$56,510

This Exercise uses the highest provincial dividend tax credit and the lowest provincial corporate tax rate, both of which are favourable to the use of a corporation. Because of this, the after tax retention with the use of a corporation is $1,510 ($56,510 - $55,000) higher than it would be if the income was received directly.

Exercise Fifteen - 2 Solution

Mr. Slater's combined tax rate on income earned by the unincorporated business is 43 percent (29% + 14%). If he incorporates, all of the $126,000 will be eligible for the small business deduction. This means it will be taxed at a rate of 14 percent (38% - 10% - 17% + 3%). Mr. Slater's tax rate on non-eligible dividend income is 28.75 percent [(125%)(43%) - (2/3 + 1/3)(25%)].

Using these tax rates, a comparison of the income retained with and without the use of a corporation is as follows:

	With Corporation	Without Corporation
Business Income	$126,000	$126,000
Tax Rate	14%	43%
Tax Payable	$ 17,640	$ 54,180
Business Income	$126,000	$126,000
Tax Payable	(17,640)	(54,180)
Maximum Non-Eligible Dividend Payable	$108,360	N/A
Personal Tax On Dividends [(28.75%)($108,360)]	(31,154)	N/A
Income Retained By Mr. Slater	$ 77,206	$ 71,820

There is clearly a significant amount of tax deferral with respect to income left in the corporation. His Tax Payable on direct receipt of the $126,000 of business income would be $54,180, far higher than the $17,640 that would be paid by the corporation. There would also be a tax savings as the $77,206 in income retained using the corporation is $5,386 greater than the $71,820 in income retained without the use of the corporation.

Exercise Fifteen - 3 Solution

Mr. Slater's combined tax rate on interest income earned outside the corporation is 43 percent (29% + 14%). If he incorporates, the interest income will not be eligible for the small business deduction or the general rate reduction, and it will be subject to the ART. This means that, if the investments are transferred to a corporation, the interest will be taxed at a rate of 46-2/3 percent (38% - 10% + 6-2/3% + 12%). Mr. Slater's tax rate on non-eligible dividends received is 28.75 percent [(125%)(43%) - (2/3 + 1/3)(25%)].

Using these tax rates, a comparison of the income retained with and without the use of a corporation is as follows:

	With Corporation	Without Corporation
Interest Income	$126,000	$126,000
Tax Rate	46-2/3%	43%
Tax Payable	$ 58,800	$ 54,180

Solution to Chapter Fifteen Exercises

	With Corporation	Without Corporation
Interest Income	$126,000	$126,000
Tax Payable	(58,800)	(54,180)
Net Corporate Income Before Dividend Refund	$ 67,200	N/A
Maximum Dividend Refund (See Note)	33,600	
Maximum Dividend Payable	$ 100,800	
Personal Tax On Dividends [(28.75%)($100,800)]	(28,980)	
Income Retained By Mr. Slater	$ 71,820	$ 71,820

Note The dividend refund is the lesser of one-third of dividends paid and the balance in the RDTOH account. The available cash would support a dividend of $100,800 [(3/2)($67,200)], including a dividend refund of $33,600 [(1/3)($100,800)]. The balance in the RDTOH account is also $33,600 [($126,000)(26-2/3 Percent)]

As the corporate tax rate is higher than the 43 percent rate applicable to the direct receipt of interest income, the corporation does not provide any deferral on amounts left within the corporation. In this case, incorporation requires prepayment of taxes.

In this example, the results with a corporation are identical to those when a corporation is not used. The reason for this is that the after refund corporate tax rate is 20 percent [($58,800 - $33,600) ÷ $126,000] and the dividend tax credit is equal to the gross up. You will recall that these are the conditions that are required for perfect integration when non-eligible dividends are being paid.

With respect to the total amount of taxes paid, the use of a corporation in this example makes no difference. After tax retention is the same without regard to whether a corporation is used.

Exercise Fifteen - 4 Solution
Direct Receipt If the income is received directly, the total Tax Payable will be as follows:

Eligible Dividends Received	$46,000	
Gross Up At 38 Percent	17,480	$ 63,480
Non-Eligible Dividends Received	$87,000	
Gross Up At 25 Percent	21,750	108,750
Taxable Dividends		$172,230
Interest Income		32,000
Taxable Income		$204,230
Personal Tax Rate (29% + 15%)		44%
Tax Payable Before Dividend Tax Credit		$ 89,861
Dividend Tax Credit		
[(6/11 + 1/3)($17,480)]	($15,361)	
[(2/3 + 1/3)($21,750)]	(21,750)	(37,111)
Personal Tax Payable		$ 52,750

The after tax retention can be calculated as follows:

Cash Received ($46,000 + $87,000 + $32,000)	$165,000
Tax Payable	(52,750)
After Tax Retention	$112,250

Transfer To Corporation If the investments are transferred to a corporation, the tax rate on the interest income is 46-2/3 percent (38% - 10% + 6-2/3% + 12%). Given this, the corporate taxes will be as follows:

Part IV Tax On Dividends Received [(1/3)($46,000) + $29,000]	$44,333
Tax On Interest Income [(46-2/3%)($32,000)]	14,933
Corporate Tax Payable Before Refund	$59,266

As this Tax Payable is larger than the Tax Payable that would be paid on the direct receipt of income, the use of a corporation would not provide for any deferral of taxes. However, as the client needs all of the income produced by these investments, the use of a corporation to defer taxes is not an issue.

As this would be a new corporation, it would have no RDTOH balance at the beginning of the year. The RDTOH balance prior to the dividend refund would be calculated as follows:

Part IV Addition	$44,333
Part I Addition [(26-2/3%)($32,000)]	8,533
RDTOH Balance	$52,866

The cash available for paying dividends would be $105,734 ($165,000 - $59,266). This represents two-thirds of $158,601, a dividend that would generate a dividend refund of $52,867. As this is equal to the $52,866 balance in the RDTOH (with a $1 rounding difference), this amount of dividends can be paid.

The eligible dividends received by the corporation will be added to the GRIP balance, leaving $46,000 in this account. This means that $46,000 in dividends could be designated as eligible for the enhanced dividend gross up and tax credit procedures. The remainder of the dividends paid of $112,601 ($158,601 - $46,000) would be non-eligible.

This would result in personal taxes as follows:

Eligible Dividends Received	$46,000	
Gross Up At 38 Percent	17,480	$ 63,480
Non-Eligible Dividends Received	$112,601	
Gross Up At 25 Percent	28,150	140,751
Taxable Dividends		$204,231
Personal Tax Rate		44%
Tax Payable Before Dividend Tax Credit		$ 89,862
Dividend Tax Credit		
[(6/11 + 1/3)($17,480)]	($15,361)	
[(2/3 + 1/3)($28,150)]	(28,150)	(43,511)
Personal Tax Payable		$ 46,351

After tax retention with the use of a corporation would be $112,250 ($46,000 + $112,601 - $46,351). As this is exactly the same amount that would be retained on direct receipt of income, there would appear to be little point in going to the trouble of forming a corporation to hold the client's investments.

Exercise Fifteen - 5 Solution

The client's combined tax rate on direct receipt of income is 45 percent (29% + 16%). Based on this, the after tax amount retained on direct receipt of income can be calculated as follows:

Capital Gain	$92,000
Personal Taxes On Taxable Capital Gain [(45%)(1/2)($92,000)]	(20,700)
After Tax Retention - Direct Receipt	$71,300

If the investments are transferred to a CCPC, the aggregate investment income will be $46,000. The applicable tax rate will be 46-2/3% (38% - 10% + 6-2/3% + 12%). Based on this, the maximum distribution that can be made would be calculated as follows:

Available Cash	$92,000
Corporate Tax Payable [(46-2/3%)($46,000)]	(21,467)
Tax Free Capital Dividend [(1/2)($92,000)]	(46,000)
Available For Taxable Dividend	$24,533
Dividend Refund (See Note)	12,267
Taxable Dividend (Non-Eligible)	$36,800

Note The available cash would support a dividend of $36,800 [(3/2)($24,533)], including a refund of $12,267 [(1/3)($36,800)]. As this is the same amount as the $12,267 [(26-2/3%)($46,000)] balance in the RDTOH, this amount of dividends can be paid.

The client's tax rate on non-eligible dividend income is 31.25 percent [(125%)(45%) - (2/3 + 1/3)(25%)]. Based on this, the net after tax retention when a corporation is used would be as follows:

Tax Free Capital Dividend Received	$46,000
Non-Eligible Dividend Received	36,800
Tax Payable On Non-Eligible Dividend Received [(31.25%)($36,800)]	(11,500)
After Tax Cash Retained - With Corporation	$71,300

As this is exactly the same amount that would be retained on direct receipt of the income, there would appear to be little point in going to the trouble of forming a corporation to hold the client's investments.

Note that, as the client needs all of the income produced by these investments, the use of a corporation to defer taxes is not an issue.

Exercise Fifteen - 6 Solution

It is likely that Ms. Rourke will have to include the $50,000 principal amount of the loan in her Net Income For Tax Purposes in 2013. She owns more than 10 percent of the shares, making her a specified employee. This means she does not qualify for the exception under ITA 15(2.4)(a). While she is an employee, it is unlikely that this type of loan would be generally available to all employees and, as a consequence, it is likely that she received the loan because of her position as a shareholder. This means that she does not qualify for the acquisition of an automobile exception under ITA 15(2.4)(d). If the loan is included in income, she will be entitled to a $50,000 deduction under ITA 20(1)(j) when she repays the loan in 2017.

In the unlikely event that the loan is not included in income and ITA 15(2) does not apply, she will have to include imputed interest at the prescribed rate for the period of the loan. Her shareholder benefit for 2013 is $250 [(1%)($50,000)(6/12)]. The imputed interest rate and benefit will vary as the prescribed rate changes. Note, however, if imputed interest is assessed, some portion of the amount may be deductible as it relates to the acquisition of an automobile to be used in employment duties.

Exercise Fifteen - 7 Solution

If the loan is repaid on January 1, 2014, it will not be included in two consecutive Generic Inc. Balance Sheets. As a consequence, the principal amount will not have to be included in Ms. Fisk's income. However, as it is an interest-free loan, she will be assessed with a taxable benefit on the loan. The amount would be $1,890 [($162,000)(2% - Nil)(7/12)].

If the loan is not repaid until December 31, 2014, it will appear in two consecutive Generic

Inc. Balance Sheets. This means the $162,000 in principal will have to be included in Ms. Fisk's income for the taxation year ending December 31, 2013. However, there will be no imputed interest benefit based on the loan's low rate of interest. In addition, when the loan is repaid, the payment can be deducted from Net Income For Tax Purposes for the taxation year ending December 31, 2014.

Exercise Fifteen - 8 Solution

Mr. Hasid will repay 25 percent of the loan, or $30,750 on October 31, 2014. This will leave an outstanding balance of $92,250 ($123,000 - $30,750) until October 31, 2015.

If Granted As Employee

Provided Mr. Hasid receives the loan in his capacity as an employee of Hasid Ltd., the loan is one of the exceptions listed under ITA 15(2). This means that the principal amount will not have to be included in income. However, as the loan is interest free, a taxable benefit will arise. It will be calculated by applying the prescribed rate of 2 percent to the principal of the loan for all periods that it is outstanding.

The amounts for 2013 would be $410 [($123,000)(2% - Nil)(2/12)] and $2,358 {[($123,000)(2% - Nil)(10/12)] + [($92,250)(2% - Nil)(2/12)]} for 2014. The taxable benefit calculations for 2015 to 2017 would be calculated in a similar fashion.

If Granted As Shareholder

If Mr. Hasid cannot claim that he received the loan in his capacity as an employee of Hasid Ltd., $92,250 will be included in his income for 2013. The remaining $30,750 would not be included in income as it will have been repaid before Hasid Ltd.'s second year end. However, this balance will attract an interest benefit of $102.50 [($30,750)(2%)(2/12)] in 2013, and $512.50 [($30,750)(2%)(10/12)] in 2014.

As the remaining balance is repaid in 2015 through 2017, the payments can be deducted under ITA 20(1)(j) in the year they are repaid.

Exercise Fifteen - 9 Solution
(1) Salary Compensation

If the full $550,000 is paid out as salary, it will be deductible and will reduce the Company's Taxable Income to nil. This means that no corporate taxes will be paid. This salary payment will result in Ms. Broad having Taxable Income of $550,000. Given this, her Tax Payable will be calculated as follows:

Federal Tax On First $135,054	$ 28,580
Federal Tax On Remaining	
$414,946 ($550,000 - $135,054) At 29%	120,334
Provincial Tax At 10 Percent Of $550,000	55,000
Tax Payable Before Credits	$203,914
Personal Tax Credits (Given)	(3,800)
Total Tax Payable	$200,114

Based on the preceding Tax Payable, Ms. Broad's after tax retention would be $349,886 ($550,000 - $200,114), ignoring CPP contributions and the Canada employment credit.

(2) Dividend Compensation

As dividends are not deductible for tax purposes, corporate taxes will have to be paid prior to the payment of any dividends. While the $50,000 of income in excess of the annual business limit of $500,000 would not get the small business deduction, it would be eligible for the general rate reduction of 13 percent. Given this, the corporate rate on this income would be 29% (38% - 10% - 13% + 14%). On income eligible for the small business deduction, the rate would be 15% (38% - 10% - 17% + 4%). Using these rates, corporate taxes would be calculated as follows:

Income Not Eligible For SBD [(29%)($50,000)]	$14,500
Income Eligible For SBD [(15%)($500,000)]	75,000
Corporate Tax Payable	$89,500

After payment of these taxes, the maximum dividend that could be paid would be $460,500 ($550,000 - $89,500).

The fact that the corporation's Taxable Income was in excess of the annual business limit of $500,000 will create an addition to the GRIP of $36,000 [(72%)($550,000 - $500,000)]. Given this, $36,000 of the dividend can be designated as eligible, leaving a non-eligible dividend of $424,500 ($460,500 - $36,000). The grossed up taxable dividends would be calculated as follows:

Total Eligible And Non-Eligible Dividends Received	$460,500
Gross Up:	
Eligible Dividends [(38%)($36,000)]	13,680
Non-Eligible Dividends [(25%)($424,500)]	106,125
Taxable Dividends	$580,305

Personal taxes on this dividend would be calculated as follows:

Federal Tax On First $135,054	$ 28,580
Federal Tax On Remaining	
$445,251 ($580,305 - $135,054) At 29%	129,123
Provincial Tax At 10 Percent Of $580,305	58,031
Taxes Payable Before Credits	$215,734
Personal Tax Credits (Given)	(3,800)
Dividend Tax Credit:	
Eligible Dividends [(6/11 + 30%)($13,680)]	(11,566)
Non-Eligible Dividends [(2/3 + 30%)($106,125)]	(102,588
Personal Tax Payable	$ 97,780

The after tax retention would be equal to $362,720 ($460,500 - $97,780).

Exercise Fifteen - 10 Solution

Required Salary   Ms. Mortell's combined tax rate on additional salary is 45 percent (29% + 16%). In order to have $30,000 in after tax funds, she would have to receive salary of $54,545 [$30,000 ÷ (1 - .45)].

Required Dividend   Ms. Mortell's tax rate on non-eligible dividends is 33-1/3 percent [(125%)(45%) - (2/3 + 25%)(25%)]. In order to have $30,000 in after tax funds, she would have to receive dividends of $45,000 [$30,000 ÷ (1 - .3333)].

Tax Cost Of Salary   The net tax cost of paying salary can be calculated as follows:

Tax Payments On Receipt Of Salary [(45%)($54,545)]	$24,545
Tax Savings To Corporation [(14%)($54,545)]	(7,636)
Net Tax Cost Of Salary Alternative	$16,909

Tax Cost Of Dividend   As the dividend payment would not be deductible, its payment would not change corporate taxes. This means that the only tax cost would be the $15,000 [($45,000)(33-1/3%)] in personal taxes that Ms. Mortell would pay on the dividends received.

Conclusion   As the tax cost associated with the payment of salary is larger, the dividend alternative would be preferable.

Exercise Fifteen - 11 Solution

Salary Alternative - As the available cash is less than Taxable Income, some corporate taxes will have to be paid since there is insufficient cash to pay a salary equivalent to Taxable Income. To determine the maximum salary that can be paid (X), it is necessary to solve the following equation:

$$X = \$18,500 - [(15\%)(\$21,500 - X)]$$
$$X - 0.15X = [\$18,500 - (15\%)(\$21,500)]$$

$$X = \underline{\$17,971}$$

Corporate taxes of \$529 [(15%)(\$21,500 - \$17,971)] would have to be paid. The total cash outflow equals the cash available of \$18,500 (\$17,971 + \$529).

Given this salary, Mr. Fargo would be subject to the following personal Tax Payable:

Tax Payable Before Credits [(15% + 10%)(\$17,971)]	\$4,493
Available Tax Credits (Given)	(3,950)
Personal Tax Payable - Salary	\$ 543

Given the preceding Tax Payable, Mr. Fargo's after tax retention on salary would be \$17,428 (\$17,971 - \$543), ignoring the Canada employment credit.

Dividend Alternative - As dividends are not deductible, corporate taxes would have to be paid on the full \$21,500. These taxes would be \$3,225 [(15%)(\$21,500)], leaving an amount available for dividends of \$15,275 (\$18,500 - \$3,225). As no individual taxes would be payable on this amount of dividends, the full \$15,275 would be retained.

Given these calculations, it is clear that the preferred approach is to pay the maximum salary. Note, however, some combination of dividends and salary may provide an even better result.

Self Study Solution Fifteen - 1

Advantages Of Incorporation

Among the more commonly cited advantages of incorporation would be the following:

Tax Deferral   If the rate of tax applicable to the corporation is less than the rate applicable to the individual, there will be deferral of some taxation until funds are paid out of the corporation. This would apply in this case, as Mr. Copley's corporation would be eligible for the small business deduction. This would mean that his corporate tax rate would be around 14 percent in an average rate province. As he is currently paying a marginal rate in the neighbourhood of 45 percent on the income from the unincorporated business, this would represent a significant deferral.

Tax Reduction   The various integration provisions in the *Income Tax Act* attempt to eliminate any difference in the amount of after tax income that would be retained by an individual receiving pre tax income directly from its source and the after tax amount that would result from that same income source being directed through a corporation. The integration provisions are based on a notional corporate tax rate of 20 percent. As Mr. Copley's corporate income will be eligible for the small business deduction and will be taxed at around 14 percent (in an average rate province), the combined corporate and personal tax that will be paid if the income goes through the corporation will generally be lower than the taxes that he would pay on direct receipt of income.

Income Splitting   With a proper structuring of the ownership of the corporation, income can be channeled into the hands of other members of Mr. Copley's family. This can be in the form of either salary or dividends, and will be subject to what we would assume to be significantly lower rates of taxation.

Lifetime Capital Gains Deduction   The $750,000 deduction is available on the disposition of shares in a qualified small business corporation. Properly structured, incorporation could permit all members of his family access to the lifetime capital gains deduction. To qualify, the corporation must be a Canadian controlled private corporation and have at least 90 percent of the fair market value of its assets being used in an active business in Canada. In addition, the shares have to be held for at least 24 months prior to their disposition, unless the person holding the shares oper- ated the business as a sole proprietorship or partnership prior to transferring the business to the corporation. This could represent a significant advantage of incorpo- rating his business.

Employee Benefits   While Mr. Copley's organization may be somewhat small to make this feasible, the corporation can be used to establish various retirement programs, as well as group life and health insurance packages.

Estate Planning   A corporation can be useful in estate planning, particularly with respect to freezing the asset values in the estate (see Chapters 17 and 19).

Limited Liability   An investor in a corporation is, in general, not liable to the credi- tors for the debts of the corporation. In the case of large publicly traded corporations this is a very real and important consideration. However, in the case of a small owner-managed business such as Mr. Copley's, it is unlikely that creditors would extend significant sums without getting his personal guarantee for repayment.

However, limited liability could be important if his business is exposed to any type of product liability risk.

Liquidation Losses   If the business is unsuccessful and must be liquidated, the loss on corporate shares would be deductible as an allowable business investment loss. This means that one-half of the total amount could be deducted against any other income. However, it would require further analysis to ensure that this would involve a greater amount of deductions than would be the case if the business were liquidated in its present unincorporated form.

Disadvantages Of Incorporation
A list of the disadvantages associated with incorporation would include the following:

Administrative Costs   There will be higher legal, accounting and other costs associ- ated with meeting the various reporting requirements that are necessary for the startup and maintenance of a corporation.

Losses   The losses of the corporation cannot be offset against other personal income that the shareholders might have. Further, allowable capital losses of corporations can only be deducted against the corporation's taxable capital gains.

Termination   If the corporation is terminated, there is no available rollover for trans- ferring the assets back to Mr. Copley. Taxation will occur at fair market values. There is a further possibility of double taxation in that, while the corporation will be taxed on the disposition of its assets, the shareholder may be taxed on the same amounts when he disposes of his shares.

Higher Taxes   Under advantages we noted that there could be a tax reduction asso- ciated with a corporation earning income that is eligible for the small business deduction. On the other hand, if the corporation earns income that is not eligible for the small business deduction, there will be a significant extra payment of combined corporate and personal income tax when such income flows through the corporation in the form of dividends to its shareholders.

Winding Up Procedures   Because of its status as a separate legal entity, the procedures associated with winding up an incorporated business are significantly more complex than those associated with terminating an unincorporated enterprise.

Conclusions On Incorporation

In evaluating the preceding advantages and disadvantages, a recommendation that Mr. Copley incorporate his business seems to be appropriate. He does not appear to need all of the income produced by the business for personal living expenses and, as a consequence, the ability to defer income within the corporation is attractive. Further, his eligibility for the small business deduction will result in a reduction in taxes, even on amounts that are withdrawn from the corporation. Other major advantages related to incorporating Mr. Copley's business are the excellent opportunities that will be available to split income between the various members of his family and for estate planning, especially considering the lifetime capital gains deduction.

Self Study Solution Fifteen - 2

Part A - Direct Personal Investment

Mrs. Martin's marginal tax rate is 46 percent (29% + 17%). If Mrs. Martin invests the $200,000 as an individual, the after tax return can be calculated as follows:

Interest Income (All Taxable)	$14,000
Interest Received	$14,000
Personal Tax Payable At 46 Percent	(6,440)
After Tax Retention	$ 7,560

Part B - Investment Through Private Company

If Mrs. Martin invests the $200,000 through her private company, any dividends paid will be non-eligible. The after tax return would be as follows:

Interest Income	$14,000
Corporate Taxes At 50 Percent	(7,000)
Net Corporate Income Before Dividend Refund	$ 7,000
Maximum Dividend Refund (See Note)	3,500
Maximum Non-Eligible Dividend Payable	$10,500
Gross Up At 25 Percent	2,625
Taxable Dividend	$13,125
Personal Tax Rate	46%
Personal Tax Payable Before Dividend Tax Credit	$ 6,038
Dividend Tax Credit [(2/3 + 25%)($2,625)]	(2,406)
Personal Tax Payable	$ 3,632
Dividends Received	$10,500
Personal Tax Payable	(3,632)
After Tax Retention	$ 6,868

Note The available cash would support a dividend of $10,500 [(3/2)($7,000)], including a dividend refund of $3,500 [(1/3)($10,500)]. As this is less than the $3,733 [(26-2/3%)($14,000)] balance in the RDTOH, this amount of dividends can be paid. There is additional refundable tax of $233 ($3,733 - $3,500) that is available, but only on the payment of additional dividends.

The difference between the two alternatives is $692 ($7,560 - $6,868) in favour of direct personal investment.

Self Study Solution Fifteen - 3

Part A - Direct Personal Investment

Mr. Martin's marginal tax rate is 46 percent (29% + 17%). If Mr. Martin invests the $200,000 as an individual, the after tax return can be calculated as follows:

Eligible Dividends Received	$14,000
38 Percent Gross Up	5,320
Taxable Dividend	$19,320
Personal Tax Rate	46%
Personal Tax Payable Before Dividend Tax Credit	$ 8,887
Dividend Tax Credit [(6/11 + 25%)($5,320)]	(4,232)
Personal Tax Payable	$ 4,655

Dividends Received	$14,000
Personal Tax Payable	(4,655)
After Tax Retention - Direct Receipt	$ 9,345

Part B - Investment Through Private Company

If Mr. Martin invests the $200,000 through his private company, the eligible dividends received would be classified as portfolio dividends, subject to Part IV tax at 33-1/3 percent. There would also be an addition to the corporation's GRIP account of $14,000 (notice that eligible dividends are not multiplied by 72 percent for the GRIP addition). The after tax retention on the flow through the corporation would be as follows:

Eligible Dividends Received	$14,000
Part IV Tax At 33-1/3 Percent (Portfolio Dividends)	(4,667)
Earnings Retained By Corporation	$ 9,333
Refund When Dividends Paid	4,667
Eligible Dividends Paid (See Note)	$14,000

Note As the dividend payment is equal to the GRIP balance, the full amount of $14,000 can be designated as eligible for the enhanced gross up and tax credit procedure. Also note that the dividend refund would be equal to the $4,667 balance in the RDTOH resulting from the payment of Part IV tax on the receipt of the dividends.

At this point, the corporation has paid no net amount of taxes and will be paying exactly the same amount of eligible dividends that it received. This will result in Mr. Martin paying exactly the same amount of taxes that he would have paid on direct receipt of the dividends. With the use of a corporation, the after tax retention would be identical to the after tax retention resulting from direct receipt of the dividends.

Self Study Solution Fifteen - 4

Approach 1 (Joins Partnership As Individual)

Cora's share of the partnership income would $70,000 [(10%)($700,000)]. Cora's Tax Payable resulting from this approach would be calculated as follows:

Tax On First $43,561 At 23 Percent (15% + 8%)	$10,019
Tax On Next $26,439 ($70,000 - $43,561)	
At 34 Percent (22% + 12%)	8,989
Tax Payable Before Credits	$19,008
Personal Tax Credits - Given	(3,342)
Personal Tax Payable	$15,666

Business Income	$70,000
Personal Tax Payable	(15,666)
After Tax Retention - Alternative 1	$54,334

Approach 2 (All Dividends)

The total corporate taxes would be calculated as follows:

First $50,000 At 15 Percent	$ 7,500
Remaining $20,000 At 27 Percent	5,400
Corporate Tax Payable	$12,900

If all of the after tax income is paid out, the resulting dividend will be $57,100 ($70,000 - $12,900).

As $20,000 of the corporation's income was taxed at the general rate, there would be a GRIP balance of $14,400 [(72%)($20,000)]. This means that of the total dividend of $57,100, $14,400 could be designated as eligible, with the remaining $42,700 ($57,100 - $14,400) being non-eligible. Based on this, Cora's Taxable Income would be as follows:

Eligible Dividend	$14,400
Gross Up On Eligible Dividend At 38 Percent	5,472
Non-Eligible Dividend	42,700
Gross Up On Non-Eligible Dividend At 25 Percent	10,675
Total Taxable Income	$73,247

Based on this Taxable Income, her Tax Payable would be as follows:

Tax On First $43,561 At 23 Percent (15% + 8%)	$10,019
Tax On Remaining $29,686 ($73,247 - $43,561)	
At 34 Percent (22% + 12%)	10,093
Tax Payable Before Credits	$20,112
Personal Tax Credits - Given	(3,342)
Dividend Tax Credit = Gross Up ($5,472 + $10,675)	(16,147)
Personal Tax Payable	$ 623

Business Income	$70,000
Corporate Tax Payable	(12,900)
Personal Tax Payable	(623)
After Tax Retention - Alternative 2	$56,477

Approach 3 (Salary And Dividends)

With the payment of $20,000 in salaries to reduce corporate income to her $50,000 share of the small business deduction, corporate taxes would be $7,500 [(15%)($50,000)]. This would leave $42,500 ($70,000 - $20,000 - $7,500) for the payment of dividends.

Since no income was taxed at the general rate, the GRIP balance would be nil. This means that the total dividend of $42,500 would be non-eligible. Cora's Taxable Income would be calculated as follows:

Salary	$20,000
Non-Eligible Dividend	42,500
Gross Up On Non-Eligible Dividend At 25 Percent	10,625
Taxable Income	$73,125

Her Tax Payable would be calculated as follows:

Tax On First $43,561 At 23 Percent (15% + 8%)	$10,019
Tax On Next $29,564 ($73,125 - $43,561) At 34 Percent (22% + 12%)	10,052
Tax Payable Before Credits	$20,071
Personal Tax Credits - Given	(3,342)
Dividend Tax Credit = Gross Up	(10,625)
Personal Tax Payable	$ 6,104

Business Income	$70,000
Corporate Tax Payable After Salary [(15%)($70,000 - $20,000)]	(7,500)
Personal Tax Payable	(6,104)
After Tax Retention - Alternative 3	$56,396

Evaluation

The after tax amount retained for each of the three approaches is as follows:

Approach 1 (Joins Partnership As Individual)	$54,334
Approach 2 (All Dividends)	56,477
Approach 3 (Salary And Dividends)	56,396

In this analysis, Approach 1 provides the lowest amount of after tax retention. While they both provide a somewhat better after tax cash flow than Approach 1, there is very little difference between Approaches 2 and 3. However, Approach 2 does provide the largest amount of after tax retention and would be the best approach if nothing else is considered.

Other factors to consider:

- While Approach 2 provides the largest amount of after tax retention, there is some question as to whether the tax savings of $2,143 ($56,477 - $54,334) would justify the cost of establishing and maintaining a corporation.

- If the effect of CPP was considered, she would pay two times the annual maximum in Approach 1, no CPP in Approach 2 and in Approach 3 both Cora and her corporation would pay less than the annual maximum. Paying CPP contributions would allow her to receive CPP payments in the future, but would incur a liability at the present time.

- If the Canada employment credit was considered, it would only be applicable in Approach 3.

- If Cora wanted to participate in the Employment Insurance program on a voluntary basis, it would only be available to her in Approach 1 as a self-employed individual.

- If she wanted to contribute to an RRSP or deduct child care costs, she would need earned income. Dividends are not a component of earned income for either purpose. Earned income would be $70,000 in Approach 1 and $20,000 in Approach 3.

- Depending on the province, there could be additional payroll costs that her corporation would have to pay in Approach 3.

- The opportunity for income splitting is much easier with a corporation given that family members could buy shares that entitle them to share in the dividends. Income splitting through the partnership would be much more difficult given that, for the most part, the family members would have to be involved in partnership activity.

- Although an advantage of incorporation is the availability of the lifetime capital gains deduction, given the current situation, it is questionable whether her corporation could be sold for much of a gain given how important her personal services are to its value.

Self Study Solution Fifteen - 5

Part A - Tax Payable With Corporation

The business income of the corporation would be calculated as follows:

Management Fees		$82,900
Expenses:		
Mr. Ashley's Salary	($18,400)	
Office Salaries	(25,400)	
Office Rent	(8,180)	
CCA On Office And Dental Equipment	(5,700)	
Other Business Expenses	(2,170)	(59,850)
Business Income		$23,050
Rate On Active Business Income		14%
Tax Payable On Active Business Income		$ 3,227

Tax Payable on the dividends and investment income would be calculated as follows:

Interest Income	$21,600
Net Rental Income ($34,600 - $27,800)	6,800
Aggregate Investment Income	$28,400
Rate On Investment Income	47%
Part I Tax On Investment Income	$13,348
Part IV Tax On Dividends Received [(1/3)($13,900)]	4,633
Tax Payable On Property Income	$17,981

Given the preceding taxes on property income, the RDTOH balance is as follows:

Part I Refundable Amount [(26-2/3%)($28,400)]	$ 7,573
Part IV Refundable Amount [(1/3)($13,900)]	4,633
RDTOH Balance	$12,206

The eligible dividends received by the corporation will be added to the GRIP balance, leaving $13,900 in this account (note that the amount received is added, not the amount received multiplied by 72 percent). This means that $13,900 in dividends could be designated as eligible for the enhanced dividend gross up and tax credit procedures.

Given the preceding calculations, the maximum eligible and non-eligible dividend that could be paid is as follows:

Business Income	$23,050
Taxes On Business Income	(3,227)
Interest Income	21,600
Net Rental Income	6,800
Taxes On Property Income	(17,981)
Eligible Dividends	13,900
Balance Before Refund	$44,142
Dividend Refund (See Note)	12,206
Available For Dividends	$56,348
Eligible Dividends (GRIP Balance)	(13,900)
Non-Eligible Dividends (Remainder)	$42,448

Note   The dividend refund is the lesser of one-third of dividends paid and the RDTOH balance. If the full $1 for every $3 of dividends was available, a dividend refund of $22,071 [(1/3)($66,213)] would be received. However, the refund is limited by the RDTOH balance of $12,206.

With respect to the eligible dividends, $8,340 [(60%)($13,900)] would go to Mr. Ashley, and $5,560 [(40%)($13,900)] would go to Dr. Ashley. With respect to the non-eligible dividends, $25,469 [(60%)($42,448)] would go to Mr. Ashley, and $16,979 [40%)($42,448)] would go to Dr. Ashley. The resulting Tax Payable would be as follows:

	Dr. Ashley	Mr. Ashley
Salary	Nil	$18,400
Eligible Dividends ($13,900)	$ 5,560	8,340
Gross Up At 38 Percent	2,113	3,169
Non-Eligible Dividends ($42,448)	16,979	25,469
Gross Up At 25 Percent	4,245	6,367
Taxable Income	$28,897	$61,745
Tax Rate	47%	30%
Tax Payable Before Dividend Tax Credit	$13,582	$18,524
Dividend Tax Credits:		
Eligible Dividends [(6/11 + 25%)(Gross Up)]	(1,681)	(2,521)
Non-Eligible Dividends [(2/3 + 25%)(Gross Up)]	(3,891)	(5,836)
Tax Payable	$ 8,010	$ 10,167

This would leave after tax balances available to Dr. and Mr. Ashley as follows:

Ashley Management Services	Nil
Dr. Ashley ($5,560 + $16,979 - $8,010)	$14,529
Mr. Ashley ($18,400 + $8,340 + $25,469 - $10,167)	42,042
After Tax Retention	$56,571

Part B - Balances With No Corporation

If Dr. Ashley had received all of the amounts involved directly, her Tax Payable and net retention could be calculated as follows:

Business Income ($23,050 + $18,400 Salary To Husband)	$41,450
Interest Income	21,600
Rental Income (Net)	6,800
Eligible Dividends	13,900
Gross Up At 38 Percent	5,282
Taxable Income	$89,032
Tax Rate	47%
Tax Before Dividend Tax Credit	$41,845
Dividend Tax Credit [(6/11 + 25%)($5,282)]	(4,202)
Tax Payable	$37,643
Income Received ($41,450 + $21,600 + $6,800 + $13,900)	$83,750
Tax Payable	(37,643)
After Tax Retention	$46,107

It is clear from these calculations that the use of the management company has had a positive effect on after tax retention of income. Without the corporation, Dr. Ashley would have ended up with only $46,107. This compares to a total of $56,571 for Mr. and Dr. Ashley when the corporation is used, an improvement of $10,464.

You should note, however, that Dr. Ashley could have paid a salary to her husband without using a corporation. This would have significantly improved the results in Part B.

The problem asked you to ignore personal tax credits, the Canada employment tax credit, CPP contributions and GST. Personal tax credits would have made only a small difference, as Dr. Ashley would be able to claim the spousal credit in full if Mr. Ashley had no income.

While it is clear the Canada employment tax credit would favour paying Mr. Ashley salary, the advantage or disadvantage of CPP contributions is less clear cut. Although GST is not covered in detail until Chapter 21, we noted in Chapter 12 that the GST/HST legislation has made management companies for GST exempt services such as dentistry less attractive.

Self Study Solution Fifteen - 6

2010

As this loan is not repaid until 2013, more than one year after the end of the corporate year in which it was extended to Miss Stone, it will have to be included in Miss Stone's 2010 income. If Miss Stone does not include it in 2010, it will have to be included retroactively. Note, however, because the loan is included in income, there is no need to calculate a taxable benefit related to imputed interest on the loan.

2011

ITA 15(2.4) allows a company to provide an employee who is also a shareholder with a loan to acquire a car to be used for company business without the principal of the loan being treated as a taxable benefit. Given Miss Stone's responsibilities, it is reasonable to assume the loan was made because of her employment with the Company, not her shareholding. While the repayment period must be reasonable, it would appear that the four year term of the loan would meet that requirement. However, the loan is interest free and this will require Miss Stone to record a taxable benefit for imputed interest on the outstanding loan balance. The rate for imputing such interest is established in ITR 4301.

The imputed interest is deductible under ITA 8(1)(j) to the extent that the automobile is used for employment purposes. It would appear that the interest benefit would be at least partially offset by the ITA 8(1)(j) interest deduction.

2012

Home loans are also one of the exceptions covered in ITA 15(2.4). Since housing loans are generally available to senior employees, Miss Stone did not receive the housing loan because she is a shareholder. As a consequence, the loan principal will not be included in Miss Stone's income. The ITA 110(1)(j) deduction would not be available since the loan is a home purchase loan and not a home relocation loan.

The term of the loan would appear reasonable for a home loan. However, as the loan is interest free, Miss Stone will have to include a taxable benefit for imputed interest in her income. The amount of the benefit would be based on the ITR 4301 rate. Because she received the loan in her capacity as an employee, the benefit can be calculated under ITA 80.4(1). This means that for the first five years of the loan, the benefit calculation will use a rate no higher than the prescribed rate that prevailed when the loan was made. Should the rate go down, the employee is entitled to use the lower prescribed rate for the benefit calculation.

The bonus will not have to be included in Miss Stone's income until it is received in 2013.

2013

As noted, the $32,000 bonus will be included in this year's income. Of the $32,000 returned to the Company in 2013, the $28,000 viewed as a repayment of the 2010 loan can be deducted from 2013 income under ITA 20(1)(j). The tax treatment of the remaining $4,000 ($32,000 - $28,000) returned would depend on how the funds were accounted for by the Company. If it is considered a payment on the house loan, it will decrease the balance on which imputed interest is calculated. If it is considered a loan from Miss Stone, there are no tax consequences to her, or for the corporation, as there is no requirement for imputed interest to be calculated on loans by shareholders to corporations.

The non-eligible dividend, after a gross up of 25 percent, will be taken into 2013 income.

ITA 15(2.4)(c) indicates that loans made to a shareholder, who is an employee, to acquire shares in the lending corporation or a corporation related to the lending corporation, are not subject to the general rule. However, it appears that the acquired shares were those of an unrelated company. As a consequence, the principal of this loan will be included in Miss Stone's 2013 Net Income For Tax Purposes. No interest will have to be imputed on this loan. Miss Stone will be able to deduct any repayments of the loan when they occur, and the unallocated $4,000 she paid to the Company in March could be considered a repayment of this loan.

Self Study Solution Fifteen - 7

Alternative Treatments

The tax consequences here will depend on whether the loan was given to Mr. Blaine in his capacity as an employee or, alternatively, in his capacity as a shareholder. Note that this loan would not qualify for a home relocation loan deduction as it can be assumed that the property that he is acquiring is not 40 kilometers closer to his work since the house seller is a neighbour and he bicycles to work.

Treatment As Shareholder Loan

If similar loans are not available to the other employees of Blaine Enterprises, it is likely that the CRA will take the view that Mr. Blaine received the loan in his capacity as a shareholder. If this is the case and the loan is included in the Balance Sheet of Blaine Enterprises at two consecutive year ends, the principal amount of the loan will have to be included in Mr. Blaine's Net Income For Tax Purposes in the year of the loan. In this situation, having the company grant the loan has basically the same tax consequences for Mr. Blaine as having the company pay a similar amount of salary. There are, however, two differences:

- When the loan is repaid, the repayment can be deducted under ITA 20(1)(j). In contrast, the receipt of salary cannot be reversed.
- Mr. Blaine's salary of $57,000 does not provide sufficient earned income to allow him to make maximum RRSP contributions. Paying salary would increase his earned income and allow him to make additional RRSP contributions.

Note that since Arthur is receiving a salary of $57,000, he is already eligible for the Canada employment tax credit and paying the maximum CPP contributions so these factors are not relevant.

Treatment As Employee Loan

If similar loans are available to the other employees of Blaine Enterprises, Mr. Blaine can argue that he received the loan in his capacity as an employee. Provided there is a reasonable plan for repayment of the loan, he will not have to include the principal amount of the loan in his Net Income For Tax Purposes. However, he would be assessed a taxable benefit in the amount of imputed interest on the outstanding loan balance. The interest rate to be used in this calculation would be the prescribed rate (ITR 4301).

Evaluation

There would not appear to be any significant advantage to this arrangement if Mr. Blaine is required to include the loan in income because he has received it as a shareholder.

However, if he can claim that he received the loan in his capacity as an employee, the analysis will depend on the relationship between the prescribed rate and the rate that Mr. Blaine would have to pay if he financed his new home with a conventional mortgage. Currently (2013), the prescribed rate for the purpose of computing the taxable benefit on employee loans is a very low one percent, well below any current rate for home mortgages. Given this, it would appear that if the loan principal can be kept out of his income, having his company provide the loan would be an effective form of tax planning for Mr. Blaine.

Self Study Solution Fifteen - 8

Relevance Of Tax Brackets

Ms. Lusk's Taxable Income of $44,385 puts her in the 22 percent federal tax bracket. She will stay in this bracket for the next $42,738 ($87,123 - $44,385) of Taxable Income. Given that she only requires an additional $10,000 of after tax funds, there is no possibility that the required salary or dividend payment would push her into the 26 percent bracket. Any additional Taxable Income amounts will be taxed at a combined federal/provincial rate of 32 percent (22% + 10%).

Required Salary

Given the applicable rate of 32 percent, Ms. Lusk will need $14,706 in additional salary [$10,000 ÷ (1 - .32)] in order to have $10,000 in after tax funds.

Required Dividend

Ms. Lusk's combined tax rate on non-eligible dividends would be as follows:

$$[(125\%)(32\%) - (2/3 + 1/3)(25\%)] = 15\%$$

With a tax rate of 15 percent on non-eligible dividends, a dividend of $11,765 would be required to provide an after tax amount of $10,000 [$10,000 ÷ (1 - .15)].

Tax Cost Of Salary Alternative

Since salary payments are deductible to her corporation, this payment will result in a tax savings to the corporation. When this savings is combined with the taxes that will be paid at the personal level by Ms. Lusk, the net tax cost of this alternative can be calculated as follows:

Tax Cost To Ms. Lusk [(32%)($14,706)]		$4,706
Tax Savings To Lusk Esthetics [(13%)($14,706)]		(1,912)
Net Tax Cost Of Salary Alternative		$2,794

Tax Cost Of Dividend Alternative

The personal Tax Payable on the dividend would be calculated as follows:

Non-Eligible Dividends Received	$11,765
Gross Up At 25 Percent	2,941
Taxable Income	$14,706
Tax Rate (22% + 10%)	32%
Tax Payable Before Dividend Tax Credit	$ 4,706
Dividend Tax Credit [(2/3 + 1/3)($2,941)]	(2,941)
Personal Tax Payable On Dividend Alternative	$ 1,765

Subtracting the $1,765 from the $11,765 dividend received leaves the required $10,000 in after tax funds.

As dividends cannot be deducted by the corporation, the payment of the $11,765 dividend does not alter corporate Tax Payable. This means that the tax cost associated with this alternative would simply be the $1,765 of personal taxes paid by Ms. Lusk.

Conclusion

Since the dividend alternative has a tax cost of $1,765, while the salary alternative has a net tax cost of $2,794, the dividend alternative has the lower combined tax cost.

Self Study Solution Fifteen - 9

Part A - All Salary

As salary payments can be deducted by the corporation, the entire $27,500 can be paid as salary. Given this deduction, no taxes would be paid by the Company. With a salary payment of $27,500, Mr. Bedford's after tax cash balance would be as follows:

Salary Payment		$27,500
Tax Before Credits [(25%)($27,500)]	($ 6,875)	
Personal Tax Credits (Given)	3,750	(3,125)
After Tax Cash Retained (All Salary)		$24,375

Part B - All Dividends

The tax rate for Bedford Inc. would be 15% (38% - 10% - 17% + 4%). As dividend payments are not deductible to the Company, taxes of $4,125 [(15%)($27,500)] will have to be paid, leaving a maximum of $23,375 to be used for the payment of dividends. When this is paid, the after tax retention by Mr. Bedford will be as follows:

Non-Eligible Dividends Received	$23,375
Gross Up At 25 Percent	5,844
Taxable Dividends	$29,219
Personal Tax Rate	25%
Tax Payable Before Credits	$ 7,305
Personal Tax Credits (Given)	(3,750)
Dividend Tax Credit [(2/3 + 30%)($5,844)]	(5,649)
Tax Payable	Nil

Dividends Received	$23,375
Tax Payable	Nil
After Tax Cash Retained (All Dividends)	$23,375

Part C - Possible Improvement

While Mr. Bedford's Tax Payable is nil in Part B, subtracting personal and dividend tax credits from the tax balance gives a negative $2,094. This means that the all dividend approach leaves unused tax credits. While not conclusive, this suggests that there may be a better solution than either all salary or all dividends.

Part D - Salary/Dividend Combination

To examine the possibility of an optimum solution using both salary and dividends, consider the result that occurs when $1,000 in salary is paid in lieu of some dividends. Because the deductible salary payment would reduce corporate taxes, dividends would only have to be decreased by $850.00 [($1,000)(1 - 0.15)]. The tax effects of this switch can be calculated as follows:

Increase In Salary	$1,000.00
Decrease In Dividend	(850.00)
Decrease In Dividend Gross Up [(25%)($850.00)]	(212.50)
Decrease In Mr. Bedford's Taxable Income	($ 62.50)
Personal Tax Rate	25%
Decrease In Tax Payable Before Dividend Tax Credit	($ 15.63)
Decrease In Dividend Tax Credit	
= Increase In Tax Payable [(2/3 + 30%)($212.50)]	205.42
Net Increase In Personal Tax Payable	$ 189.79

The rate on a $1,000 increase in salary is 18.979% ($189.79 ÷ $1,000). Applying this rate to the unused credits of $2,094 (see Part C), gives a required increase in salary of $11,033 ($2,094 ÷ .18979).

Based on this payment of salary, corporate taxes and funds available for dividend payments would be calculated as follows:

Pre-Salary Corporate Taxable Income	$27,500
Salary	(11,033)
Corporate Taxable Income	$16,467
Corporate Tax At 15 Percent	(2,470)
Available For Dividends	$13,997

After tax retention at the personal level would be calculated as follows:

Non-Eligible Dividends Received	$13,997
Gross Up At 25 Percent	3,499
Taxable Dividends	$17,496
Salary	11,033
Mr. Bedford's Taxable Income	$28,529
Personal Tax Rate	25%
Tax Payable Before Credits	$ 7,132
Personal Tax Credits (Given)	(3,750)
Dividend Tax Credit [(2/3 + 30%)($3,499)]	(3,382)
Tax Payable	Nil

Amounts Received ($11,033 + $13,997)	$25,030
Personal Tax Payable	Nil
After Tax Cash Retained (Salary And Dividends)	$25,030

The comparative results for the three alternatives are as follows:

All Salary	$24,375
All Dividends	$23,375
Salary/Dividend Combination	$25,030

The combination of salary and dividends will produce the maximum after tax cash retention for Mr. Bedford. It is a $655 ($25,030 - $24,375) improvement over the all salary solution and a $1,655 ($25,030 - $23,375) improvement over the all dividend solution.

Part E - Other Factors
Other factors that might be considered include:

- The Canada employment tax credit was ignored in the calculations as it is not a credit against provincial taxes. However, it would allow the first $1,117 of salary to be received with a nil federal tax cost.

- If the effect of CPP was considered, both Mr. Bedford and Bedford Inc. would pay CPP contributions if salary was paid. Paying CPP contributions would allow him to receive CPP payments in the future, but would require both a personal and a corporate cash outflow at the present time.

- Dividend payments are not Earned Income for purposes of making RRSP contributions or deducting child care costs (which may be very important to Mr. Bedford given his triplets and the fact his wife likely has an extremely high income).

- Mr. Bedford should consider declaring a bonus (a form of salary) to be paid after the end of the calendar year if he does not need the cash immediately. This would defer the personal taxes without affecting corporate taxes as long as the bonus was paid within 180 days of December 31.

- If he has a CNIL balance, dividend payments will serve to reduce this constraint on the life-time capital gains deduction.

- In the future, if Bedford Inc. has benefits for employees, such as a private health services plan, this could make being an employee (by taking salary) more advantageous. However, it would be necessary to determine if his wife already has equivalent benefits for this to be a factor.

- Though not relevant in this problem, some provinces have payroll taxes which could be incurred.

Chapter 15 Learning Objectives

After completing Chapter 15, you should be able to:

1. Explain how a corporation can be used to reduce taxes, defer taxes, and facilitate income splitting (paragraph [P hereafter] 15-1 to 15-9).

2. Describe other advantages and disadvantages of incorporation (P 15-10 and 15-11).

3. Use various personal and corporate tax rates in the calculation of after-tax retention of earnings flowed to a corporation (P 15-12 to 15-24).

4. Calculate the amount of tax reduction and tax deferral that is available to the use of a public corporation (P 15-25 to 15-34).

5. Calculate the amount of tax reduction and tax deferral that is available to the use of a CCPC earning active business income (P 15-35 to 15-40).

6. Explain the advantages of bonusing down to the owner of a CCPC eligible for the small business deduction (P 15-41 to 15-47).

7. Calculate the amount of tax reduction and tax deferral that is available to the use of a CCPC earning investment income other than dividends (P 15-48 to 15-51).

8. Calculate the amount of tax reduction and tax deferral that is available to the use of a CCPC earning dividend income (P-52 to 15-56).

9. Summarize the tax reduction and tax deferral that is available to the use of various types of corporations earning different types of income (P 15-57 to 15-59).

10. Identify the effect of provincial taxes on the decision to incorporate (P 15-60 to 15-78).

11. Explain why large amounts of dividends can be received on a tax free basis by individuals with no other source of income (P 15-79 to 15-90).

12. Describe and calculate the benefits that can be achieved by using a corporation to implement income splitting (P 15-91 to 15-101).

13. Determine the tax consequences of various shareholder benefits, including loans (P 15-102 to 15-124).

14. Explain the principles of management compensation in the context of an owner-managed corporation (P 15-125 to 15-131).

15. Describe the basic trade-off between the payment of salary and the payment of dividends for the owner-manager (P 15-132 to 15-138).

16. Calculate the appropriate choice between salary and dividends, taking into consideration factors other than federal tax savings (P 15-139 to 15-162).

17. Optimize the salary/dividend mix when all tax credits are not utilized or there is a limited amount of cash in the corporation (P 15-163 to 15-179).

18. Summarize the various non-tax factors that must be taken into consideration in making salary vs. dividend decisions (P 15-180 and 15-181).

CHAPTER 16

How To Work Through Chapter 16

We recommend the following approach in dealing with the material in this chapter:

Rollovers Under Section 85 - General Rules For The Transfer
❑ Read paragraph 16-1 to 16-30 (in the textbook).

Transfer Price Rules Applicable To All Assets
❑ Read paragraph 16-31 to 16-36.

Accounts Receivable (Transfer Price Rules)
❑ Read paragraph 16-37 to 16-40.

Inventories And Non-Depreciable Capital Property (Transfer Price Rules)
❑ Read paragraph 16-41 to 16-49.
❑ Do Exercise Sixteen-1 (in the textbook) and check the solution on page S-355 in this Study Guide.

Disallowed Capital Losses (Transfer Price Rules)
❑ Read paragraph 16-50 to 16-61.

Depreciable Property (Transfer Price Rules)
❑ Read paragraph 16-62 to 16-69.
❑ Do Exercise Sixteen-2 and check the solution in this Study Guide.

Terminal Losses Disallowed (Transfer Price Rules)
❑ Read paragraph 16-70 to 16-73.

Eligible Capital Property (Transfer Price Rules)
❑ Read paragraph 16-74 to 16-80.
❑ Do Exercise Sixteen-3 and check the solution in this Study Guide.

Disallowed Deductions On CEC Dispositions (Transfer Price Rules)
❑ Read paragraph 16-81 to 16-90.
❑ Do Self Study Problems Sixteen-1 and Sixteen-2 at the end of the textbook chapter on page 834 and 835 and check the solutions in this Study Guide.

Consideration Received By The Transferor (Shareholder)
❑ Read paragraph 16-91 to 16-92.
❑ Do Exercise Sixteen-4 and check the solution in this Study Guide.

Assets Acquired By The Corporation
❑ Read paragraph 16-93 to 16-100.

Paid Up Capital Of Issued Shares And PUC Reduction
❑ Read paragraph 16-101 to 16-112.
❑ Do Exercise Sixteen-5 and check the solution in this Study Guide.
❑ Do Self Study Problem Sixteen-3 and check the solution in this Study Guide.

Section 85 Rollovers - Comprehensive Example
❑ Read paragraph 16-113 to 16-127.
❑ Do Exercise Sixteen-6 and check the solution in this Study Guide.
❑ Do Self Study Problems Sixteen-4, 5, 6, and 7 and check the solutions in this Study Guide.

Gift To Related Person - Section 85
❑ Read paragraph 16-128 to 16-142.
❑ Do Exercise Sixteen-7 and check the solution in this Study Guide.
❑ Do Self Study Problem Sixteen-8 and check the solution in this Study Guide.

Excess Consideration (Shareholder Benefits) - Section 85
❑ Read paragraph 16-143 to 16-146.
❑ Do Exercise Sixteen-8 and check the solution in this Study Guide.
❑ Do Self Study Problem Sixteen-9 and check the solution in this Study Guide.

Dividend Stripping - ITA 84.1
❑ Read paragraph 16-147 to 16-164.
❑ Do Exercise Sixteen-9 and check the solution in this Study Guide.
❑ Do Self Study Problem Sixteen-10 and check the solution in this Study Guide.

Capital Gains Stripping - ITA 55(2)
❑ Read paragraph 16-165 to 16-181.
❑ Do Exercise Sixteen-10 and check the solution in this Study Guide.
❑ Do Self Study Problem Sixteen-11 and check the solution in this Study Guide.

To Complete This Chapter
❑ Review the Key Terms Used In This Chapter on page 833. Consult the Glossary for the meaning of any key terms you do not know.
❑ Review the Glossary Flashcards and complete the Key Terms Self-Test for the Chapter. These features can be found in two places, on your Student CD-ROM under the heading "Key Term Practice" and on the web site.
❑ Review the Learning Objectives of the Chapter found on pages S-378 and S-379 of this Study Guide.
❑ As a review, we recommend that you view the PowerPoint Slides for Chapter 16 that are available on your Student CD-ROM. If you do not have access to the Microsoft PowerPoint program, the PowerPoint Viewer program can be installed from the Student CD-ROM.

Solution to Chapter Sixteen Exercises

Exercise Sixteen - 1 Solution
With respect to the inventories, the $125,000 is both the floor and the ceiling, making this the only possible elected value. The transfer would result in a loss of $15,000 ($140,000 - $125,000), an amount that would be fully deductible as a business loss [ITA(23)]. With respect to the land, the floor would be the boot of $150,000 and the ceiling would be the fair market value of $350,000. Electing the minimum amount would result in a taxable capital gain of $20,000 [($150,000 - $110,000)(1/2)].

Exercise Sixteen - 2 Solution

With respect to the Class 1 property, the range would be from a floor of $250,000 (the boot) to a ceiling of $475,000 (fair market value). Election of the $250,000 floor value would result in recapture of $70,000 ($220,000 - $150,000) and a taxable capital gain of $15,000 [($250,000 - $220,000)(1/2)].

The range for the Class 10 asset would be from a floor of $10,000 (the boot) to a ceiling of $12,000 (fair market value). Electing the minimum value of $10,000 would result in recapture of $2,000 ($10,000 - $8,000).

Exercise Sixteen - 3 Solution

The beginning 2013 CEC balance would be calculated as follows:

2012 Addition [(3/4)($135,000)]	$101,250
2012 CEC [(7%)($101,250)]	(7,088)
Opening 2013 Balance	$ 94,162

Four-thirds of this amount would be $125,549. However, the floor would be established by the boot of $135,000. The ceiling would be the fair market value of $175,000.

With the election at $135,000, three-quarters of this amount would be subtracted from the CEC balance, leaving a negative balance of $7,088 ($94,162 - $101,250). As this negative amount is equal to the $7,088 that was deducted in the previous year, the full amount must be included in 2013 income.

Exercise Sixteen - 4 Solution

The adjusted cost base amounts would be calculated as follows:

Elected Value	$62,000
ACB Of Note (Fair Market Value)	(51,000)
Available For Shares	$11,000
ACB Of Preferred Shares*	(11,000)
ACB Of Common Shares (Residual)	Nil

*Remainder available as it is less than the fair market value of $53,000.

Exercise Sixteen - 5 Solution

The adjusted cost base amounts would be calculated as follows:

Elected Value	$114,000
ACB Of Note (Fair Market Value)	(83,000)
Available For Shares	$31,000
ACB Of Preferred Shares*	(31,000)
ACB Of Common Shares (Residual)	Nil

*Remainder available as it is less than the fair market value of $97,000.

The total PUC reduction would be calculated as follows:

Increase In Legal Stated Capital ($97,000 + $54,000)		$151,000
Less The Excess Of:		
Total Elected Value	($114,000)	
Over The Total Non-Share Consideration	83,000	(31,000)
PUC Reduction		$120,000

Note that this reduction is equal to the deferred gain on the election ($234,000 - $114,000). The PUC reduction would be allocated on the basis of fair market values as follows:

Preferred Stock [($120,000)($97,000 ÷ $151,000)]	$ 77,086
Common Stock [($120,000)($54,000 ÷ $151,000)]	42,914
Total PUC Reduction	$120,000

Subsequent to applying this reduction, the remaining PUC of the two classes of shares would be as follows:

	Preferred Stock	Common Stock
Legal Stated Capital	$97,000	$54,000
PUC Reduction (From Preceding)	(77,086)	(42,914)
Total PUC	$19,914	$11,086

Note that the sum of these two figures equals $31,000 ($19,914 + $11,086), the total adjusted cost base of the preferred and common shares, as well as the difference between the elected value of $114,000 and the total non-share consideration of $83,000.

Exercise Sixteen - 6 Solution

Part 1   The adjusted cost base of all of the consideration will total the elected value of $275,000. It will be allocated as follows:

Elected Value	$275,000
Non-Share Consideration ($83,000 + $17,000)	(100,000)
Adjusted Cost Base Of All Shares	$175,000
Adjusted Cost Base Of Preferred Shares (FMV)	(125,000)
Adjusted Cost Base Of Common Shares (Residual)	$ 50,000

Part 2   The PUC of the shares issued must be reduced as follows:

Increase In Legal Stated Capital ($125,000 + $925,000)		$1,050,000
Less The Excess Of:		
Elected Value	($275,000)	
Over The Non-Share Consideration	100,000	(175,000)
PUC Reduction		$ 875,000

This PUC reduction would be split between the preferred and common shares on the basis of their fair market values:

Preferred Stock [($125,000/$1,050,000)($875,000)]	$104,167
Common Stock [($925,000/$1,050,000)($875,000)]	770,833
Total PUC Reduction	$875,000

Subsequent to applying this reduction, the remaining PUC of the two classes of shares would be as follows:

	Preferred Stock	Common Stock
Legal Stated Capital	$125,000	$925,000
PUC Reduction (From Preceding)	(104,167)	(770,833)
Total PUC	$ 20,833	$154,167

Part 3 The tax consequences of the preferred stock redemption would be as follows:

Proceeds Of Redemption	$125,000
PUC Of The Preferred Shares	(20,833)
ITA 84(3) Deemed Dividend (Non-Eligible)	$104,167

Proceeds Of Redemption	$125,000
ITA 84(3) Deemed Dividend	(104,167)
ITA 54 Deemed Proceeds Of Disposition	$ 20,833
Adjusted Cost Base	(125,000)
Capital Loss	($104,167)
Inclusion Rate	1/2
Allowable Capital Loss	($ 52,084)

The grossed up non-eligible dividend of $130,209 [(125%)($104,167)] would qualify for a federal dividend tax credit of $17,361 [(2/3)(25%)($104,167)]. The allowable capital loss is only deductible against taxable capital gains.

Exercise Sixteen - 7 Solution

The calculation of the gift is as follows:

Fair Market Value Of Property Transferred		$110,000
Less The Greater Of:		
• FMV Of Consideration Received = $65,000 ($50,000 + $15,000)		
• Elected Amount = $50,000		(65,000)
Excess = Gift To Daughter		$ 45,000

Given this gift, the tax consequences of the transfer for Ms. Bellows are as follows:

Deemed Elected Value = Deemed Proceeds Of Disposition ($50,000 + $45,000)	$95,000
Adjusted Cost Base	(50,000)
Capital Gain	$45,000
Inclusion Rate	1/2
Taxable Capital Gain	$22,500

The adjusted cost base of her preferred shares would be calculated as follows:

Elected Value (Original)	$50,000
Non-Share Consideration	(50,000)
Adjusted Cost Base Of Preferred Shares	Nil

As shown in the following calculation, there would be no PUC reduction for the preferred shares issued to Ms. Bellows:

Increase In Legal Stated Capital		$15,000
Less Excess Of:		
Deemed Elected Value	($95,000)	
Over Non-Share Consideration	50,000	(45,000)
PUC Reduction		Nil

PUC Of Preferred Shares ($15,000 - Nil)	$15,000

The fair market value of the common shares issued to the daughter is $46,000 ($110,000 + $1,000 - $50,000 - $15,000).

The sale of the shares for their fair market value would result in the following taxable capital gains:

	Preferred	Common
Proceeds (Fair Market Value)	$15,000	$46,000
Adjusted Cost Base	Nil	(1,000)
Capital Gain	$15,000	$45,000
Inclusion Rate	1/2	1/2
Taxable Capital Gain	$ 7,500	$22,500

If the property had simply been sold for its $110,000 fair market value, there would have been a $30,000 [(1/2)($110,000 - $50,000) taxable capital gain. Using ITA 85, Ms. Bellows' total taxable capital gain on the transfer and sale of the preferred shares is also $30,000 ($22,500 + $7,500). However, because the common shares held by the daughter have increased in value by the $45,000 amount of the gift, with their adjusted cost base remaining at $1,000, there is an additional $22,500 taxable capital gain on the sale of her daughter's common shares. This reflects the fact that the $45,000 amount of the gift has been subject to double taxation.

Exercise Sixteen - 8 Solution

The immediate tax consequences of the transfer would be a taxable capital gain on the property and an ITA 15(1) shareholder benefit. These would be calculated as follows:

Elected Value Of Property	$217,000
Adjusted Cost Base	(123,000)
Capital Gain	$ 94,000
Inclusion Rate	1/2
Taxable Capital Gain On Property	$ 47,000

Fair Market Value Of Consideration ($195,000 + $75,000)	$270,000
Fair Market Value Of Property	(217,000)
ITA 15(1) Shareholder Benefit	$ 53,000

The total effect on Net Income For Tax Purposes is as follows:

Taxable Capital Gain	$ 47,000
Shareholder Benefit	53,000
Total Addition To Net Income For Tax Purposes	$100,000

The ITA 15(1) benefit of $53,000 would be added to the adjusted cost base of the acquired property, resulting in the following ACB for the preferred shares:

Elected Value	$217,000
ACB Of Non-Share Consideration (Fair Market Value)	(195,000)
Available For Shares	$ 22,000
ITA 15(1) Shareholder Benefit	53,000
ACB Of Preferred Shares	$ 75,000

Solution to Chapter Sixteen Exercises

There will be a PUC reduction of $53,000 calculated as follows:

Increase In Legal Stated Capital		$75,000
Less Excess, If Any, Of:		
Total Elected Value	($217,000)	
Over The Non-Share Consideration	195,000	(22,000)
ITA 85(2.1) PUC Reduction		$53,000

This will leave a PUC of $22,000 ($75,000 - $53,000). As this is equal to the $22,000 increase in net assets ($217,000 - $195,000), there is no ITA 84(1) deemed dividend.

Sale Of Shares   If the preferred shares are sold for $75,000, the results would be as follows:

Proceeds Of Disposition	$75,000
Adjusted Cost Base	(75,000)
Capital Gain On Sale	Nil

Redemption Of Shares   If the preferred shares were redeemed for their fair market value of $75,000, the results would be as follows:

Redemption Proceeds	$75,000
PUC	(22,000)
ITA 84(3) Deemed Dividend (Non-Eligible)	$53,000
Proceeds Of Disposition	$75,000
ITA 84(3) Deemed Dividend	(53,000)
Adjusted Proceeds Of Disposition	$22,000
Adjusted Cost Base	(75,000)
Capital Loss	($53,000)
Inclusion Rate	1/2
Allowable Capital Loss On Redemption	($26,500)

The non-eligible dividend would have a taxable value of $66,250 [(125%)($53,000)] and would qualify for a federal dividend tax credit of $8,833 [(2/3)(25%)($53,000)]. The allowable capital loss could only be deducted in the current year to the extent of any taxable capital gains.

Exercise Sixteen - 9 Solution

Miss Cole (an individual) has sold shares of a subject corporation to a purchasing corporation, both corporations do not deal with Miss Cole at arm's length, and the two corporations are connected subsequent to the sale. As a consequence, ITA 84.1 is applicable. Given this, the tax consequences of this transaction to Miss Cole are as follows:

Increase In Legal Stated Capital		$317,000
Less Excess, If Any, Of:		
PUC And ACB Of Subject Shares	($125,000)	
Over The Non-Share Consideration	450,000	Nil
PUC Reduction		$317,000
PUC Of New Shares ($317,000 - $317,000)		Nil

Increase In Legal Stated Capital		$317,000
Non-Share Consideration		450,000
Total		$767,000
Less The Sum Of:		
PUC And ACB Of Subject Shares	($125,000)	
PUC Reduction	(317,000)	(442,000)
ITA 84.1 Deemed Dividend (Non-Eligible)		$325,000
Elected Proceeds Of Disposition For Subject Shares		$767,000
ITA 84.1 Deemed Dividend		(325,000)
Deemed Proceeds For Capital Gains Purposes		$442,000
ACB Of Subject Shares		(125,000)
Capital Gain		$317,000
Inclusion Rate		1/2
Taxable Capital Gain		$158,500
ACB Of New Shares ($767,000 - $450,000)		$317,000

The grossed up non-eligible dividend of $406,250 [(125%)($325,000)] would qualify for a federal dividend tax credit of $54,167 [(2/3)(25%)($325,000)]. In addition, there would be a taxable capital gain of $158,500 that would be eligible for the lifetime capital gains deduction. If Miss Cole claims the deduction, she may need to pay alternative minimum tax.

Economic Analysis Miss Cole is attempting to realize a capital gain of $642,000 ($767,000 - $125,000). However, her non-share consideration was $450,000, $325,000 more than the adjusted cost base of the Cole Inc. shares. ITA 84.1 acts to convert this from a capital gain to a deemed dividend. Note that the remaining $317,000 ($642,000 - $325,000) is allowed to flow through as a capital gain. This reflects the fact that Miss Cole did not attempt to take out the full $767,000 fair market value of the shares in the form of non-share consideration.

Exercise Sixteen - 10 Solution
A deductible dividend has been paid in conjunction with an arm's length sale of shares, and it would appear that the dividend payment served to eliminate the potential capital gain on the transaction. As a consequence, ITA 55 is applicable and the tax consequences of the transaction are as follows:

Dividends Received	$750,000
Dividends Attributable To Safe Income (Tax Free)	(225,000)
Deemed Proceeds Of Disposition	$525,000
Actual Proceeds Of Disposition	90,000
Total Proceeds Of Disposition	$615,000
Adjusted Cost Base Of Shares	(75,000)
Capital Gain	$540,000
Inclusion Rate	1/2
Taxable Capital Gain	$270,000

The $225,000 of dividends paid from safe income will be deducted in calculating Taxable Income, resulting in no tax cost.

Self Study Solution Sixteen - 1

Part A - No Election

The disposition of a business is a capital transaction and, in the absence of special provisions, any resulting gain or loss must be treated as a capital gain or loss. With respect to the Inventories, a special provision in ITA 23 indicates that, when such assets are sold as part of the disposition of a business, the sale is deemed to be in the ordinary course of carrying on business and any resulting gain or loss is considered business in nature. ITA 23 automatically applies in the disposition of a business and no election is required on the part of the vendor.

ITA 22 provides for a similar treatment of Accounts Receivable. However, a joint election by the vendor and purchaser is required before this business income treatment is applicable. In the absence of this election, losses on Accounts Receivable are treated as capital losses.

If the assets are transferred at fair market values, the Taxable Income resulting from the transfer can be calculated as follows:

Inventories - Business Income ($88,000 - $73,000)	$15,000
Furniture And Fixtures - Recaptured CCA ($45,000 - $38,000)	7,000
Goodwill [(3/4)($150,000 - Nil)(2/3)]	75,000
Taxable Income	$97,000

When the $112,500 [(3/4)($150,000)] proceeds for the goodwill is subtracted from the Cumulative Eligible Capital balance, a business income inclusion is created. As no amounts have been deducted under ITA 20(1)(b), this amount is reduced from a three-quarters inclusion to a one-half inclusion, by multiplying the negative balance by 2/3 (1/2 ÷ 3/4).

There is also an allowable capital loss of $3,000 [(1/2)($51,000 - $45,000)] on the disposition of the Accounts Receivable. However, it is a superficial loss in that the property is re-acquired within 30 days by an affiliated person (the new corporation would be affiliated with Ms. Flack). ITA 40(2)(g) deems such losses to be nil. This loss would be added to the tax cost of the Accounts Receivable on the corporation's books.

Part B - ITA 22 And ITA 85 Elections

The cash is not eligible to be transferred under ITA 85, but can be transferred to the corporation without a rollover. All of the other assets can be transferred at elected values under ITA 85. Under the provisions of this Section, the tax consequences would be as follows:

Accounts Receivable If the Accounts Receivable are transferred under ITA 85, the maximum value that can be elected is the fair market value of $45,000. This will result in a capital loss of $6,000 (allowable amount of $3,000). However, this loss will be disallowed under ITA 40(2)(g) because the transfer is to a corporation that will be controlled by Ms. Flack.

Inventories The Inventories can be transferred at an elected value of $73,000, resulting in no Taxable Income on the transfer.

Furniture And Fixtures The Furniture And Fixtures can be transferred at their UCC of $38,000, resulting in no Taxable Income on the transfer.

Goodwill The Goodwill can be transferred at a nominal value of $1, resulting in no significant Taxable Income on the transfer.

An alternative with respect to the Accounts Receivable would be to transfer these assets under the provisions of ITA 22. If Ms. Flack and her corporation were to make this joint election, the $6,000 loss resulting from transferring these assets to the corporation would be fully deductible as a business loss. As it is not a capital loss, it would not be disallowed and Ms. Flack would be able to deduct the full $6,000 against any other source of income in the year of transfer. As ITA 22 is a joint election, the corporation would have to include the $6,000 in income, but could then deduct actual bad debts as they occur. Using the ITA 22 election is the preferable approach to the transfer of these Accounts Receivable.

Self Study Solution Sixteen - 2

Part A - Assets To Be Transferred

Of the assets in the Balance Sheet, Cash is not among the eligible assets listed in ITA 85(1.1). This is of no consequence as the tax value of cash is always equal to its carrying value and can be transferred to the corporation without a rollover.

Accounts Receivable could be transferred under Section 85, but are usually transferred to the corporation under the provisions of ITA 22. ITA 22 is used for two reasons. First, it means that any loss on the transfer will be a fully deductible business loss, rather than a capital loss that will be disallowed on a transfer to a corporation controlled by the transferor under ITA 40(2)(g). In addition, the use of the ITA 22 joint election to make the transfer will permit the transferee corporation to deduct any additional bad debts as business losses, rather than capital losses.

There is a potential terminal loss on the transfer of the equipment as the fair market value of the equipment is less than the UCC of the class. Given this, ITA 13(21.2) prevents the use of ITA 85(1) for the transfer. In addition, ITA 13(21.2) disallows the loss on any transfer to an affiliated person. This problem can be avoided if Ms. Speaks sells the equipment to a non-affiliated person. However, if the business requires the equipment, she will have to sell it to the corporation and she will not be able to make immediate use of the terminal loss at the time of the transfer.

Part B - Minimum Transfer Values

The minimum transfer values for the assets to be included in the rollover would be as follows:

Inventories (Cost)	$261,000
Land (Adjusted Cost Base)	196,000
Building (UCC)	103,600
Goodwill (Nominal Value)	1

Note   The Goodwill has been given a nominal elected value to ensure that it is specifically included in the transfer. A failure to do this could result in the Goodwill being assessed on the basis of a transfer at fair market value.

Part C - Tax Consequences

The tax consequences of the Section 85 transfers with respect to both Ms. Speaks and Speaks Inc. can be described as follows:

Inventories   The cost of the Inventories to Speaks Inc. would be the transfer price of $261,000. As this was the cost of the Inventories, there would be no tax consequence to Ms. Speaks.

Land   The cost of the Land to Speaks Inc. would be the transfer price of $196,000. As this was the adjusted cost base of the Land, there would be no tax consequence to Ms. Speaks.

Building   The capital cost of the Building to Speaks Inc. would be $155,500, and Speaks Inc. would be deemed to have taken CCA in the amount of $51,900. As the net value of the transfer is equal to UCC, there would be no tax consequence to Ms. Speaks.

Goodwill   The cost of the Goodwill to Speaks Inc. will be $1, and three-quarters of this amount will be added to the Company's Cumulative Eligible Capital balance. There would be no material tax consequence to Ms. Speaks resulting from this transfer.

If Ms. Speaks chose to include the Equipment in the rollover, the capital cost of the Equipment to Speaks Inc. would be its fair market value of $32,500. Ms. Speaks will have a terminal loss of $34,500 ($67,000 - $32,500) that she will not be able to deduct. The $34,500 loss will be placed in the same CCA class from which it was removed. Ms. Speaks will continue to take CCA on this class until the Equipment is disposed of by Speaks Inc.

Self Study Solution Sixteen - 3

Case A

Immediate Tax Consequences   The $230,000 elected value becomes the proceeds of disposition. As this amount is equal to the adjusted cost base of the land, there are no immediate tax consequences resulting from the transfer.

ACB Of The Land   The ACB of the land to the corporation would be equal to the elected value of $230,000.

ACB Of Shares   The ACB of the shares issued by the corporation would be calculated as follows:

Elected Value	$230,000
Fair Market Value Of Non-Share Consideration	Nil
ACB Of Shares	$230,000

PUC Of Shares   The required PUC reduction and resulting PUC would be calculated as follows:

Legal Stated Capital Of Shares		$660,000
Less Excess, If Any, Of:		
Elected Value	($230,000)	
Over The Non-Share Consideration	Nil	(230,000)
PUC Reduction		$430,000
PUC Of Shares ($660,000 - $430,000)		$230,000

Case B

Immediate Tax Consequences   The elected value of $500,000 becomes proceeds of disposition. As this value exceeds the $230,000 adjusted cost base of the land, there is a taxable capital gain of $135,000 [(1/2)($500,000 - $230,000).

ACB Of The Land   The ACB of the land to the corporation will be equal to the elected value of $500,000.

ACB Of Shares   The ACB of the shares issued by the corporation would be calculated as follows:

Elected Value	$500,000
Fair Market Value Of Non-Share Consideration	Nil
ACB Of Shares	$500,000

PUC Of Shares   The required PUC reduction and resulting PUC would be calculated as follows:

Legal Stated Capital Of Shares		$660,000
Less Excess, If Any, Of:		
Elected Value	($500,000)	
Over The Non-Share Consideration	Nil	(500,000)
PUC Reduction		$160,000

PUC Of Shares ($660,000 - $160,000)	$500,000

Case C

Immediate Tax Consequences   The elected value of $500,000 becomes proceeds of disposition. As this value exceeds the $230,000 adjusted cost base of the land, there is a taxable capital gain of $135,000 [(1/2)($500,000 - $230,000).

ACB Of The Land   The ACB of the land to the corporation will be equal to the elected value of $500,000.

ACB Of Shares   The ACB of the shares issued by the corporation would be calculated as follows:

Elected Value	$500,000
Fair Market Value Of Non-Share Consideration	(500,000)
ACB Of Shares	Nil

PUC Of Shares   The required PUC reduction and resulting PUC would be calculated as follows:

Legal Stated Capital Of Shares		$160.000
Less Excess, If Any, Of:		
Elected Value	($500,000)	
Over The Non-Share Consideration	500,000	Nil
PUC Reduction		$160,000

PUC Of Shares ($160,000 - $160,000)	Nil

Self Study Solution Sixteen - 4

Part A - Tax Consequences Of The Transfer

As the $1,241,100 elected price was equal to the sum of the capital cost of the Land and the UCC of the Building ($315,000 + $926,100), there would be no tax consequences associated with the transfer of these assets. However, the corporation will be deemed to have acquired these assets at their old tax values to Mr. Dix, not at their fair market values at the time of transfer.

Under ITA 85(1)(f), the adjusted cost base of the non-share consideration is equal to its fair market value of $1,241,100. The problem does not specify whether preferred shares, common shares, or a combination of both were issued. Under ITA 85(1)(g), the adjusted cost base of any preferred shares received is the lesser of their fair market value and the total elected value, reduced by the non-share consideration.

As the $1,241,100 elected value is equal to the non-share consideration provided by the corporation, the adjusted cost base of any preferred shares would be nil. Under ITA 85(1)(h), the adjusted cost base of any common shares issued would be the elected value, reduced by any non-share consideration and any amounts allocated to preferred stock. This value would also be nil.

Part B - Tax Consequences Of Debt Retirement And Share Sale

As the debt was paid off at face value, this amount would be equal to Mr. Dix's adjusted cost base, and he would have no gain or loss. However, the shares have an adjusted cost base of nil and, as a consequence, he would have a capital gain equal to the entire proceeds of disposition of $894,000 ($894,000 - Nil). This would result in a taxable capital gain of $447,000 [(1/2)($894,000)].

As the corporation is a qualified small business corporation, Mr. Dix would be eligible for the $750,000 ($375,000 taxable amount) lifetime capital gains deduction. However, Mr. Dix would still have to pay taxes on a $72,000 ($447,000 - $375,000) taxable capital gain and he may need to pay alternative minimum tax.

Self Study Solution Sixteen - 5

Part A - ACB Of The Shares

The adjusted cost base of the shares would be as follows:

Total Elected Value	$467,000
Non-Share Consideration ($122,000 + $128,000)	(250,000)
Adjusted Cost Base Preferred And Common Shares	$217,000
Allocated To Preferred Shares (FMV)	(150,000)
Adjusted Cost Base Of Common Shares (Residual)	$ 67,000

Part B - PUC Of The Shares

The legal stated capital of the preferred and common shares would be their respective fair market values of $150,000 and $326,000. The PUC reduction required under ITA 85(2.1) would be calculated as follows:

Increase In Legal Stated Capital ($150,000 + $326,000)		$476,000
Less Excess Of:		
Total Elected Value	($467,000)	
Over The Total Non-Share Consideration	250,000	(217,000)
Reduction In Paid Up Capital		$259,000

Note that this total reduction is equal to the deferred gain on the election ($726,000 - $467,000). The PUC reduction would be allocated on the basis of fair market values as follows:

Preferred Stock [($259,000)($150,000 ÷ $476,000)]	$ 81,618
Common Stock [($259,000)($326,000 ÷ $476,000)]	177,382
Total PUC Reduction	$259,000

Subsequent to applying this reduction, the remaining PUC of the two classes of shares would be as follows:

	Preferred Shares	Common Shares
Legal Stated Capital	$150,000	$326,000
PUC Reduction	(81,618)	(177,382)
PUC	$ 68,382	$148,618

Note that the combined PUC of the two classes of shares is $217,000 ($68,382 + $148,618). This is the same amount as the combined ACB of the two classes of shares ($150,000 + $67,000).

Part C - Tax Consequences Of Redemption

The tax consequences to Mr. Lardner, if the corporation redeemed both classes of shares at their respective fair market values, would be calculated as follows:

	Preferred Shares	Common Shares
Redemption Proceeds	$150,000	$326,000
PUC (See Preceding Calculations)	(68,382)	(148,618)
ITA 84(3) Deemed Dividend	$ 81,618	$177,382
Redemption Proceeds	$150,000	$326,000
ITA 84(3) Deemed Dividend	(81,618)	(177,382)
Deemed Proceeds Of Disposition	$ 68,382	$148,618
Adjusted Cost Base (Part A)	(150,000)	(67,000)
Capital Gain (Loss)	($ 81,618)	$ 81,618

Mr. Lardner would have a deemed non-eligible dividend of $259,000 ($81,618 + $177,382). The grossed up non-eligible dividend of $323,750 [(125%)($259,000)] would qualify for a federal dividend tax credit of $43,167 [(2/3)(25%)($259,000)]. He has a net capital gain of nil ($81,618 - $81,618).

Self Study Solution Sixteen - 6

Part A - Assets To Be Transferred

Given the stated wishes of Mr. Fleck, he should transfer the following assets under ITA 85 using the indicated elected values:

	Elected Values	Fair Market Values
Equipment (At Tax Value)	$ 62,000	$ 66,000
Land (At Cost Plus $40,000)	146,000	185,000
Building (At Tax Value)	178,000	323,000
Goodwill (Note)	2	95,000
Totals	$386,002	$669,000

Note It is prudent to add at least a nominal elected value for goodwill. A failure to do so could result in the application of ITA 69, with the transfer assessed to the transferor at fair market value. Although a value of $1 can be used, we have used $2 in order to eliminate some rounding problems.

The following explanations are required:

Cash As cash as not an eligible property under ITA 85(1.1), it cannot be transferred under ITA 85(1). However, this is of no consequence as the fair market value of cash is always equal to its tax value.

Accounts Receivable Accounts Receivable should never be transferred under ITA 85(1) as the result will be a capital loss, which will be disallowed under ITA 40(2)(g). Rather, the Accounts Receivable should be transferred using a joint election under ITA 22. This will result in a fully deductible business loss on the transfer.

Land   The Land is transferred at a value that is $40,000 in excess of cost in order to create a taxable capital gain that will allow the deduction of Mr. Fleck's net capital loss carry forward. The same $40,000 gain could have been created by electing to transfer the Building at a value $40,000 in excess of its cost. However, this would have resulted in recapture rather than capital gains. As recapture could not be eliminated by using his net capital loss carry forward, this result would not be consistent with Mr. Fleck's desire not to have tax consequences resulting from the transfer of assets to Fleck Ltd.

Other Assets   The other assets (Equipment, Building, and Goodwill) have been transferred at their tax values in order to avoid other tax consequences resulting from the transfer.

Part B - Fair Market Value Of Common Shares
The fair market value of the common shares would be calculated as follows:

Fair Market Value Of Assets Transferred		$669,000
Non-Share Consideration:		
Old Debt	($123,000)	
New Debt	(77,000)	(200,000)
Fair Market Value Of Common Shares		$469,000

Part B - Adjusted Cost Base Of Common Shares
The adjusted cost base of the shares would be calculated as follows:

Total Elected Value	$386,002
Fair Market Value Of Non-Share Consideration	(200,000)
Adjusted Cost Base Of Common Shares	$186,002

Part B - PUC Of The Common Shares
The PUC reduction for the shares would be calculated as follows:

Increase In Legal Stated Capital (Fair Market Value)		$469,000
Less Excess Of:		
Total Elected Value	($386,002)	
Over The Non-Share Consideration	200,000	(186,002)
PUC Reduction For Common Shares		$282,998

Based on this, the reduced value for PUC would be calculated as follows:

Increase In Legal Stated Capital	$469,000
PUC Reduction	(282,998)
PUC Of Common Shares	$186,002

Part C - Tax Consequences Of Redemption
If one-half of the shares were redeemed for their fair market value of $234,500 [(1/2)($469,000)], the tax consequences would be as follows:

Redemption Proceeds	$234,500
PUC [(1/2)($186,002)]	(93,001)
ITA 84(3) Deemed Dividend	$141,499

Redemption Proceeds		$234,500
ITA 84(3) Deemed Dividend		(141,499)
Proceeds Of Disposition		$93,001
Adjusted Cost Base [(1/2)($186,002)]		(93,001)
Capital Gain		Nil

This $141,499 deemed dividend is consistent with an economic analysis of the transaction. Assets with a total fair market value of $669,000 were transferred at an elected value of $386,002. This resulted in the deferral of a gain of $282,998 ($669,000 - $386,002). With the sale of one-half of the common shares, $141,499 [(1/2)($282,998)] of this gain must be recognized.

The grossed up non-eligible dividend of $176,874 [(125%)($141,499)] would qualify for a federal dividend tax credit of $23,583 [(2/3)(25%)($141,499)].

Self Study Solution Sixteen - 7

Part A - Use Of ITA 22
Accounts Receivable could be transferred under Section 85, but are usually transferred to the corporation under the provisions of ITA 22. ITA 22 is used for two reasons. First, it means that any loss on the transfer will be a fully deductible business loss, rather than a capital loss that will be disallowed on a transfer to a corporation controlled by the transferor under ITA 40(2)(g). In addition, the use of the ITA 22 joint election to make the transfer will permit the transferee corporation to deduct any additional bad debts as business losses, rather than capital losses.

As a result, the Accounts Receivable should be transferred at $85,000 using the ITA 22 joint election. This will result in a fully deductible business loss of $3,000 for Miss Brock. If we assume that a $3,000 reserve was deducted at year end ($88,000 - $85,000), this will have to be added back to income in the following year. However, any difference between the $88,000 face value and amounts actually collected will be fully deductible.

Part B - Elected Values
The values that should be elected under ITA 85 on the other assets in order to eliminate any current Tax Payable on the transfer, are as follows:

Asset	Tax Value	FMV	Elected
Inventory	$174,000	$208,000	$174,000
Equipment (Cost = $420,000)	234,000	317,000	234,000
Goodwill (See Note)	Nil	350,000	1
Total Assets Transferred	$408,000	$875,000	$408,001

Note It is prudent to add at least a nominal elected value for goodwill. A failure to do so could result in the application of ITA 69, with the transfer assessed to the transferor at fair market value.

Part C - ACB Of Consideration
The total elected value would become the adjusted cost base of the consideration received by Miss Brock. It would be allocated to the individual items as follows:

Total Elected Value	$408,001
Non-Share Consideration ($95,000 + $75,000)	(170,000)
Available For Preferred And Common Stock	$238,001
Adjusted Cost Base - Preferred Stock (Maximum Of Fair Market Value)	(225,000)
Adjusted Cost Base - Common Stock (Residual)	$ 13,001

Part D - PUC Calculations

The calculation of PUC would begin with the legal stated capital associated with the two classes of shares, which is their fair market value. This would be $225,000 for the preferred stock and $480,000 for the common stock, a total of $705,000. ITA 85(2.1) would require a reduction in this total as follows:

Increase In Legal Stated Capital ($225,000 + $480,000)		$705,000
Less Excess Of:		
Total Elected Value	($408,001)	
Over The Total Non-Share Consideration	170,000	(238,001)
Reduction In PUC		$466,999

Note that this reduction is equal to the deferred gain on the election ($875,000 - $408,001 from Part B). The PUC reduction would be allocated on the basis of fair market values as follows:

Preferred Stock [($466,999)($225,000 ÷ $705,000)]	$149,042
Common Stock [($466,999)($480,000 ÷ $705,000)]	317,957
Total PUC Reduction	$466,999

Subsequent to applying this reduction, the remaining PUC of the two classes of shares would be as follows:

	Preferred Stock	Common Stock
Legal Stated Capital	$225,000	$480,000
PUC Reduction (From Preceding)	(149,042)	(317,957)
Total PUC	$ 75,958	$162,043

Note that the total PUC of $238,001 ($75,958 + $162,043) is equal to the difference between the total elected value for the assets of $408,001 and the non-share consideration received by Miss Brock of $170,000.

Part E - Tax Consequences Of Redemption

The tax consequences for Miss Brock on the redemption of the preferred and common shares would be calculated as follows:

	Preferred Stock	Common Stock
Redemption Proceeds	$225,000	$480,000
Paid Up Capital	(75,958)	(162,043)
ITA 84(3) Deemed Dividend	$149,042	$317,957
Redemption Proceeds	$225,000	$480,000
ITA 84(3) Deemed Dividend	(149,042)	(317,957)
ITA 54 Deemed Proceeds Of Disposition	$ 75,958	$162,043
Adjusted Cost Base	(225,000)	(13,001)
Capital Gain (Loss)	($149,042)	$149,042

Miss Brock would have a deemed non-eligible dividend of $466,999 ($149,042 + $317,957). This is also the amount of the gain that was deferred through the use of Section 85 ($875,000 - $408,001 from Part B).

The grossed up non-eligible dividend of $583,749 [(125%)($466,999)] would qualify for a federal dividend tax credit of $77,833 [(2/3)(25%)($466,999)]. There would be a net capital gain of nil ($149,042 - $149,042).

Self Study Solution Sixteen - 8

Part A

As the fair market value of the consideration received by Mr. Cheng was less than the fair market value of the assets transferred, it would appear that Mr. Cheng is attempting to make a gift to his daughter Sarah. Making this a reasonable conclusion is the fact that she is the only common shareholder the new corporation.

ITA 85(1)(e.2) requires that any gift amount be added to the elected value with the total being used as the proceeds of disposition without any increase in the adjusted cost base of the shares received.

The amount of the gift and the tax consequences of the transfer to Mr Cheng would be calculated as follows:

Fair Market Value Of Assets Transferred	$1,658,000
Less The Greater Of:	
• Fair Market Value Of Consideration Received ($160,000 + $947,000 + $200,000) = $1,307,000	
• Elected Value = $1,107,000	(1,307,000)
Gift To Daughter	$ 351,000

Deemed Elected Value = Deemed Proceeds Of Disposition ($1,107,000 + $351,000)	$1,458,000
Tax Values Of Assets Transferred	(1,107,000)
Difference Taken Into Income = Gift	$ 351,000

Of the deemed elected value, $1,107,000 can be allocated to the tax values of the assets transferred with no tax consequences. The additional $351,000 must be added to the transfer value of one or more of the assets and, depending on the asset, could result in business income, recapture, or capital gains. The most favourable allocation would be to assets where a capital gain would arise, limited by the fact that the allocated value cannot exceed fair market value.

Recording the land at its fair market value of $430,000 would create a capital gain of $233,000 ($430,000 - $197,000) and use up this amount of the $351,000 required addition. The remaining $118,000 ($351,000 - $233,000) would then be allocated to the building by recording the transfer at $728,000 ($610,000 + $118,000). The result here would be a capital gain of $6,000 ($728,000 - $722,000) and recapture of $112,000 ($722,000 - $610,000).

The increase in his Net Income For Tax Purposes as a result of the transfer would be equal to $231,500 [$112,000 + (1/2)($233,000 + $6,000)].

The adjusted cost base of the preferred shares received by Mr. Cheng would be calculated as follows:

Elected Value (Original)	$1,107,000
Non-Share Consideration ($160,000 + $947,000)	(1,107,000)
Adjusted Cost Base Of Preferred Shares	Nil

The PUC reduction for the preferred shares received by Mr. Cheng would be calculated as follows:

Increase In Legal Stated Capital		$200,000
Excess, If Any Of:		
Deemed Elected Value		
($1,107,000 + $351,000)	($1,458,000)	
Over Non-Share Consideration	1,107,000	(351,000)
PUC Reduction		Nil
PUC Of Preferred Shares ($200,000 - Nil)		$200,000

Part B

The tax consequences to Mr. Cheng of having his shares redeemed on January 1, 2013 would be as follows:

Proceeds Of Redemption	$200,000
PUC Of Shares	(200,000)
ITA 84(3) Deemed Dividend	Nil
Proceeds Of Disposition	$200,000
ITA 84(3) Deemed Dividend	(Nil)
Adjusted Proceeds Of Disposition	$200,000
Adjusted Cost Base Of Shares	Nil
Capital Gain (Loss)	$200,000
Inclusion Rate	1/2
Taxable Capital Gain	$100,000

Part C

If Sarah Cheng sells her shares for $401,000, the tax consequences would be as follows:

Proceeds Of Disposition	$401,000
Adjusted Cost Base Of Shares	(10,000)
Capital Gain	$391,000
Inclusion Rate	1/2
Taxable Capital Gain	$195,500

Economic Analysis (Not Required)

If Mr. Cheng had simply sold his business assets for their fair markets value on January 1, 2013, he would have had a combination of business income and capital gains totalling $551,000 ($1,658,000 - $1,107,000). Using the procedures described above, the result has been recapture and capital gains of $351,000 on the transfer and a capital gain of $200,000 on the redemption of the preferred shares. While the composition of the income is different, the overall result is the same $551,000 ($351,000 + $200,000).

However, there is an impact on his daughter. The $351,000 gift added to the value of her shares with no corresponding increase in the adjusted cost base of the shares. In effect, this has become a component of the $391,000 capital gain that was recorded when she sold her shares.

At the time of the rollover, Sarah's shares had a fair market value of $361,000, her investment of $10,000, plus the $351,000 gift. While the post rollover gain of $40,000 ($401,000 - $361,000) had nothing to do with the gift, $351,000 of the gain could have been avoided. In effect, this gain is being tax twice, once in the Sarah's hands and once in her father's hands.

Overall, the procedures used in this situation resulted in Mr. Cheng being taxed on the same amount of income as would have been the case without the ITA 85(1) rollover. In addition, his daughter paid taxes on an additional capital gain of $391,000 ($195,500 taxable amount) that would not have occurred without the inappropriate use of ITA 85(1).

Self Study Solution Sixteen - 9

Part A

The immediate tax consequences of the transfer would be a taxable capital gain on the land and an ITA 15(1) shareholder benefit. These would be calculated as follows:

Elected Value Of Land	$105,000
Adjusted Cost Base	(85,000)
Capital Gain	$ 20,000
Inclusion Rate	1/2
Taxable Capital Gain On Land	$ 10,000

Fair Market Value Of Consideration ($429,000 + $439,000)	$868,000
Fair Market Value Of Transferred Assets	(668,000)
ITA 15(1) Shareholder Benefit	$200,000

The total effect on Net Income For Tax Purposes is as follows:

Taxable Capital Gain	$ 10,000
Shareholder Benefit	200,000
Total Addition To Net Income For Tax Purposes	$210,000

As Ms. Gilmour has a $10,000 net capital loss carry forward, this can be deducted in the calculation of her Taxable Income.

The adjusted cost base of the preferred shares would be calculated as follows:

Elected Value ($48,000 + $105,000 + $276,000)	$429,000
Non-Share Consideration	(429,000)
Available For Shares	Nil
ITA 15(1) Shareholder Benefit	200,000
Adjusted Cost Base Of Shares	$200,000

The PUC of the preferred shares would be calculated as follows:

Increase In Legal Stated Capital		$439,000
Less The Excess, If Any Of:		
Elected Value	($429,000)	
Over The Non-Share Consideration	429,000	Nil
PUC Reduction		$439,000
PUC ($439,000 - $439,000)		Nil

Part B

The tax values for the assets transferred can be described as follows:

Depreciable Assets The tax cost for these assets will be the elected value of $48,000. However, they will retain their original capital cost of $87,000 for recapture and capital gains calculations. The $39,000 difference will be deemed to be CCA taken.

Land The adjusted cost base of the land will be the elected value of $105,000. (Note that the rules in ITA 13(7)(e) to limit the capital cost on non-arm's length transfers do not apply to non-depreciable assets.)

Building The tax cost for this asset will be the elected value of $276,000. However, the building will retain its original capital cost of $378,000 for recapture and capital gains calculations. The $102,000 difference will be deemed to be CCA taken.

Part C-1   Sale Of Shares

If the shares were sold for their fair market value, the results would be as follows:

Proceeds Of Disposition	$439,000
Adjusted Cost Base	(200,000)
Capital Gain	$239,000
Inclusion Rate	1/2
Taxable Capital Gain	$119,500

Part C-2   Redemption Of Shares

Alternatively, if the shares were redeemed, the results would be:

Proceeds Of Redemption	$439,000
PUC	Nil
ITA 84(3) Deemed Dividend	$439,000
Proceeds Of Disposition	$439,000
ITA 84(3) Deemed Dividend	(439,000)
Adjusted Proceeds Of Disposition	$ Nil
Adjusted Cost Base	(200,000)
Capital Loss	($200,000)
Inclusion Rate	1/2
Allowable Capital Loss	($100,000)

The allowable capital loss could only be deducted to the extent of Ms. Gilmour's 2014 taxable capital gains.

As a further point, notice that the total income of $239,000 resulting from the sale is the same as the total income resulting from the redemption ($439,000 - $200,000). However, because of the higher tax rate on dividends vs. capital gains, as well as the possibility that Ms. Gilmour cannot use any, or all, of her allowable capital loss in 2014, the redemption result is much less favourable from a tax point of view.

Self Study Solution Sixteen - 10

Part A - Tax Consequences Of Share Transfer

In the absence of ITA 84.1, the Section 85 rollover would have resulted in a capital gain of $750,000. This is based on the elected value of $825,000, less the adjusted cost base of $75,000 [(75%)($100,000)]. However:

- There has been a sale by a Canadian resident (Ms. Chisholm) of shares in a subject corporation (DML).

- The purchaser of the subject corporation (Dorlaine Inc.) does not deal at arm's length with the Canadian resident (Ms. Chisholm).

- Immediately after the disposition, the subject corporation (DML) and the purchaser corporation (Dorlaine Inc.) are connected (Dorlaine Inc. controls DML).

As a consequence, the provisions of ITA 84.1 are applicable. This means that there will be a reduction of Paid Up Capital under ITA 84.1(1)(a) as follows:

Increase In Legal Stated Capital Of Dorlaine Inc.		$200,000
Less Excess, If Any, Of:		
Greater Of PUC And ACB Of DML Shares	($ 75,000)	
Over The Non-Share Consideration	700,000	Nil
PUC Reduction		$200,000

The PUC of the Dorlaine Inc. shares would be nil ($200,000 - $200,000).

The transfer would result in an ITA 84.1(1)(b) deemed dividend that would be calculated as follows:

Increase In Legal Stated Capital Of Dorlaine Inc.		$200,000
Non-Share Consideration		700,000
Total		$900,000
Less The Sum Of:		
PUC Of DML Shares	($ 75,000)	
PUC Reduction Under ITA 84.1(1)(a)	(200,000)	(275,000)
ITA 84.1(1)(b) Deemed Dividend (Non-Eligible)		$625,000

The capital gain on the disposition of the DML shares would be calculated as follows:

Proceeds Before Adjustment Of DML Shares (Elected Value)	$825,000
Deemed ITA 84.1(1)(b) Dividend	(625,000)
Adjusted Proceeds Of Disposition (ITA 54)	$200,000
ACB Of DML Shares	(75,000)
Capital Gain	$125,000
Inclusion Rate	1/2
Taxable Capital Gain	$ 62,500

The tax consequences of transferring the DML shares are:

- a deemed non-eligible dividend of $625,000, which would be grossed up to $781,250 [(125%)($625,000)] and would qualify for a federal dividend tax credit of $104,167 [(2/3)(25%)($625,000)]; and

- a taxable capital gain of $62,500, which would be eligible for the lifetime capital gains deduction as DML is a qualified small business corporation.

If Ms. Chisholm had elected the same $825,000 value, but limited her non-share consideration to $75,000 (the PUC and ACB of the DML shares), there would have been no deemed dividend. Under this approach, she would have realized a $750,000 capital gain, which would be eligible for the lifetime capital gains deduction, and still retained control of her Company.

Part B - Tax Consequences Of Death

At Ms. Chisholm's death, there would be a deemed disposition of all of her capital property at its fair market value, $200,000 in the case of the Dorlaine Inc. shares. The adjusted cost base of these shares would be calculated as follows:

Value Elected In Section 85 Rollover	$825,000
Fair Market Value Of Non-Share Consideration	(700,000)
Adjusted Cost Base Of Dorlaine Inc. Shares	$125,000

Given this, the taxable capital gain on the deemed disposition would be calculated as follows:

Deemed Proceeds Of Disposition (Fair Market Value)	$200,000
Adjusted Cost Base	(125,000)
Capital Gain	$ 75,000
Inclusion Rate	1/2
Taxable Capital Gain	$ 37,500

Because of the large amount of investments transferred to Dorlaine Inc., it would not be a qualified small business corporation. As a result, none of the taxable capital gain would be eligible for the lifetime capital gains deduction.

Self Study Solution Sixteen - 11

Scenario One

As the value elected for the ITA 85 rollover was equal to the adjusted cost base of the shares, there would be no tax consequences associated with the transfer of shares. The redemption would normally result in a deemed dividend under ITA 84(3). However, as the redemption was in conjunction with a disposition of the property to an arm's length purchaser, ITA 55(2) alters this conclusion as follows:

Redemption Proceeds	$2,397,000
Paid Up Capital Of Preferred Shares	(479,000)
ITA 84(3) Deemed Dividend	$1,918,000
Amount Deemed Not To Be A Dividend	
Under ITA 55(2)(a) ($1,918,000 - $372,000)	(1,546,000)
Remaining ITA 84(3) Deemed Dividend (Tax Free)	$ 372,000

Redemption Proceeds	$2,397,000
ITA 84(3) Deemed Dividend	(372,000)
ITA 54 Deemed Proceeds Of Disposition	$2,025,000
Adjusted Cost Base	(479,000)
Capital Gain	$1,546,000
Inclusion Rate	1/2
Taxable Capital Gain	$ 773,000

The overall result would be a $372,000 tax free dividend and a taxable capital gain of $773,000.

Scenario Two

As a dividend has been paid in conjunction with a disposition of property to an arm's length party, ITA 55(2) is applicable. This legislation is designed to prevent capital gains strips. As a result, the following calculation is required for the dividend received by Gaynor:

Dividends Received From Oldhouse	$1,918,000
Dividend Attributable To Safe Income (Tax Free)	(372,000)
Deemed Proceeds Of Disposition Under ITA 55(2)(b)	$1,546,000
Actual Proceeds Of Disposition From Varafon Inc.	479,000
Total Proceeds Of Disposition	$2,025,000
Adjusted Cost Base	(479,000)
Capital Gain	$1,546,000
Inclusion Rate	1/2
Taxable Capital Gain	$ 773,000

The results here are the same as in Part A.

Chapter 16 Learning Objectives

After completing Chapter 16, you should be able to:

1. Describe the type of situation where ITA 85 is applicable (paragraph [P hereafter] 16-1 to 16-4).

2. Explain the general rules that are applicable to the transferor and the transferee under ITA 85 (P 16-5 to 16-11).

3. Describe the types of consideration that can be received by the transferor under ITA 85 (P 16-12 to 16-14).

4. Describe the procedures required for making the ITA 85 election (P 16-15 to 16-17).

5. Calculate the range of values that can be used in a transfer under the provisions of ITA 85 (P 16-18 to 16-30).

6. Apply the general rules applicable to all assets that determine the range of values that can be used in a transfer under the provisions of ITA 85 (P 16-31 to 16-36).

7. Apply the detailed rules for the transfer of accounts receivable, inventories, and non-depreciable capital property under ITA 85 (P 16-37 to 16-49).

8. Describe the rules related to the disallowance of capital losses arising on transfers of non-depreciable capital property to affiliated persons and associated tax planning issues (P 16-50 to 16-61).

9. Apply the detailed rules for the transfer of depreciable assets under ITA 85 (P 16-62 to 16-69).

10. Describe the rules related to the disallowance of terminal losses arising on transfers of depreciable capital property to affiliated persons and associated tax planning issues (P 16-70 to 16-73).

11. Apply the detailed rules for the transfer of eligible capital property under ITA 85 (P 16-74 to 16-80).

12. Describe the rules related to the disallowance of deductions arising on transfers of eligible capital property to affiliated persons and associated tax planning issues (P 16-81 to 16-89).

13. Summarize the transfer price rules for all assets under ITA 85 (P 16-90).

14. Calculate the amount of the elected value that will be allocated to each component of the consideration received by the transferor under ITA 85 (P 16-91 and 16-92).

15. Calculate the amount of the elected value that will be allocated to each of the assets acquired by the transferee under ITA 85 (P 16-93 to 16-100).

16. Calculate the Paid Up Capital of the shares received by the transferor in an ITA 85 rollover (P 16-101 to 16-112).

17. Apply the ITA 85 rules to situations involving the incorporation of an unincorporated business (P 16-113 to 16-127).

18. Identify situations where the ITA 85 rules on gifts to related persons are applicable and make the appropriate adjustments that are required by these rules (P 16-128 to 16-142).

19. Identify situations where the ITA 85 rules on benefits to the transferor are applicable and make the appropriate adjustments that are required by these rules (P 16-143 to 16-146).

20. Identify situations where ITA 84.1 (dividend stripping rules) is applicable (P 16-147 to 16-154).

21. Apply the ITA 84.1 rules to situations involving dividend stripping (P 16-155 to 16-164).

22. Identify situations where ITA 55(2) (capital gains stripping rules) is applicable (P 16-165 to 16-168).

23. Apply the ITA 55(2) rules to situations involving capital gains stripping (P 16-169 to 16-181).

CHAPTER 17

How To Work Through Chapter 17

Introduction
- ❑ Read paragraph 17-1 to 17-3 (in the textbook).

Share For Share Exchanges (ITA 85.1)
- ❑ Read paragraph 17-4 to 17-12.
- ❑ Do Exercise Seventeen-1 (in the textbook) and check the solution on page S-380 in this Study Guide.
- ❑ Read paragraph 17-13 to 17-14.
- ❑ Do Self Study Problems Seventeen-1 and Seventeen-2 at the end of the textbook chapter on pages 886 and 887 and check the solutions in this Study Guide.

Exchange Of Shares In A Reorganization (ITA 86)
- ❑ Read paragraph 17-15 to 17-30.
- ❑ Do Exercises Seventeen-2 to Seventeen-4 and check the solutions in this Study Guide.
- ❑ Do Self Study Problem Seventeen-3 and check the solution in this Study Guide.

Gift To Related Party - ITA 86(2) (Benefit Rule)
- ❑ Read paragraph 17-31 to 17-41.
- ❑ Do Exercise Seventeen-5 and check the solution in this Study Guide.

Using ITA 86 - Practical Considerations And Tax Planning Considerations
- ❑ Read paragraph 17-42 to 17-48.
- ❑ Do Self Study Problems Seventeen-4 and Seventeen-5 and check the solutions in this Study Guide.

Amalgamations (ITA 87)
- ❑ Read paragraph 17-49 to 17-67.
- ❑ Do Exercise Seventeen-6 and check the solution in this Study Guide.

Winding-Up Of A 90 Percent Owned Subsidiary
- ❑ Read paragraph 17-68 to 17-83.
- ❑ Do Exercise Seventeen-7 and check the solution in this Study Guide.
- ❑ Read paragraph 17-84 to 17-86.
- ❑ Do Exercise Seventeen-8 and check the solution in this Study Guide.
- ❑ Read paragraph 17-87 to 17-88.

Tax Planning Considerations - Amalgamation Vs. Winding-Up
- ❑ Read paragraph 17-89 to 17-95.
- ❑ Do Self Study Problem Seventeen-6 and check the solution in this Study Guide.

Winding-Up Of A Canadian Corporation
❑ Read paragraph 17-96 to 17-108.
❑ Do Exercise Seventeen-9 and check the solution in this Study Guide.
❑ Do Self Study Problem Seventeen-7 and check the solution in this Study Guide.

Convertible Properties
❑ Read paragraph 17-109 to 17-115.

Sale Of An Incorporated Business - Assets Vs. Shares
❑ Read paragraph 17-116 to 17-155.
❑ Do Self Study Problem Seventeen-8 and check the solution in this Study Guide.

To Complete This Chapter
❑ Review the Key Terms Used In This Chapter on page 885. Consult the Glossary for the meaning of any key terms you do not know.
❑ Review the Glossary Flashcards and complete the Key Terms Self-Test for the Chapter. These features can be found in two places, on your Student CD-ROM under the heading "Key Term Practice" and on the web site.
❑ Review the Learning Objectives of the Chapter found on page S-399 and S-400 of this Study Guide.
❑ As a review, we recommend that you view the PowerPoint Slides for Chapter 17 that are available on your Student CD-ROM. If you do not have access to the Microsoft PowerPoint program, the PowerPoint Viewer program can be installed from the Student CD-ROM.

Solution to Chapter Seventeen Exercises

Exercise Seventeen - 1 Solution
This transaction involves a share for share exchange that meets the conditions of ITA 85.1. Unless Ms. Alee opts out of this rollover provision in her income tax return, the tax consequences of this transaction for Ms. Alee would be as follows:

• Ms. Alee would be deemed to have disposed of her Aayee Ltd. shares at a value equal to their adjusted cost base of $450,000. As a consequence, there would be no capital gain on the disposition.
• Ms. Alee would be deemed to have acquired her Global Outreach Inc. shares at a cost equal to the adjusted cost base of the Aayee Ltd. shares, or $450,000.
• The adjusted cost base of the Aayee Ltd. shares that have been acquired by Global Outreach Inc. would be deemed to be the lesser of their fair market value and their paid up capital. In this case, the $450,000 paid up capital amount is the lower figure.
• The PUC of the Global Outreach Inc. shares that have been issued to Ms. Alee would be $450,000, the PUC of the Aayee Ltd. shares that were given up.

Exercise Seventeen - 2 Solution
The required PUC reduction on the redeemable preferred shares would be calculated as follows:

Increase In Legal Stated Capital		$1,300,000
Less The Excess, If Any, Of:		
PUC Of Common Shares	($1,000,000)	
Over The Non-Share Consideration	1,000,000	Nil
PUC Reduction		$1,300,000

This means that the redeemable preferred shares would have a PUC of nil ($1,300,000 - $1,300,000).

The adjusted cost base of the redeemable preferred shares would be calculated as follows:

Adjusted Cost Base Of Common Shares	$1,000,000
Non-Share Consideration	(1,000,000)
Adjusted Cost Base Of Redeemable Preferred Shares	Nil

Because Sam took back cash equal to his PUC and ACB, there would be no ITA 84(3) deemed dividend and no capital gain or loss. These calculations would be as follows:

PUC Of New Shares	Nil
Plus Non-Share Consideration	$1,000,000
Proceeds Of Redemption Under ITA 84(5)(d)	$1,000,000
PUC Of Old Shares	(1,000,000)
ITA 84(3) Deemed Dividend	Nil

Adjusted Cost Base Of New Shares	Nil
Plus Non-Share Consideration	$1,000,000
Proceeds Of Disposition Under ITA 86(1)(c)	$1,000,000
ITA 84(3) Deemed Dividend	Nil
Adjusted Proceeds	$1,000,000
Adjusted Cost Base Of Old Shares	(1,000,000)
Capital Gain (Loss)	Nil

Exercise Seventeen - 3 Solution

The required PUC reduction on the redeemable preferred shares would be calculated as follows:

Increase In Legal Stated Capital		$1,300,000
Less The Excess, If Any, Of:		
PUC Of Common Shares	($1,000,000)	
Over The Non-Share Consideration	1,000,000	Nil
PUC Reduction		$1,300,000

This means that the redeemable preferred shares would have a PUC of nil ($1,300,000 - $1,300,000).

The adjusted cost base of the redeemable preferred shares would be calculated as follows:

Adjusted Cost Base Of Common Shares	$1,250,000
Non-Share Consideration	(1,000,000)
Adjusted Cost Base Of Redeemable Preferred Shares	$ 250,000

Because Sam took back cash equal to his PUC and less than his ACB, there would be no ITA 84(3) deemed dividend and no capital gain or loss. These calculations would be as follows:

PUC Of New Shares	Nil
Plus Non-Share Consideration	$1,000,000
Proceeds Of Redemption Under ITA 84(5)(d)	$1,000,000
PUC Of Old Shares	(1,000,000)
ITA 84(3) Deemed Dividend	Nil

Adjusted Cost Base Of New Shares	$ 250,000
Plus Non-Share Consideration	1,000,000
Proceeds Of Disposition Under ITA 86(1)(c)	$1,250,000
ITA 84(3) Deemed Dividend	Nil
Adjusted Proceeds	$1,250,000
Adjusted Cost Base Of Old Shares	(1,250,000)
Capital Gain (Loss)	Nil

Exercise Seventeen - 4 Solution

The required PUC reduction on the redeemable preferred shares would be calculated as follows:

Increase In Legal Stated Capital		$1,100,000
Less The Excess, If Any, Of:		
PUC Of Common Shares	($1,000,000)	
Over The Non-Share Consideration	1,200,000	Nil
PUC Reduction		$1,100,000

This means that the redeemable preferred shares would have a PUC of nil ($1,100,000 - $1,100,000).

The adjusted cost base of the redeemable preferred shares would be calculated as follows:

Adjusted Cost Base Of Common Shares	$1,250,000
Non-Share Consideration	(1,200,000)
Adjusted Cost Base Of Redeemable Preferred Shares	$ 50,000

Because the non-share consideration was greater than the PUC of the old shares, the resulting ITA 84(3) deemed dividend and the capital loss would be calculated as follows:

PUC Of New Shares	Nil
Plus Non-Share Consideration	$1,200,000
Proceeds Of Redemption Under ITA 84(5)(d)	$1,200,000
PUC Of Old Shares	(1,000,000)
ITA 84(3) Deemed Dividend (Non-Eligible)	$ 200,000

Adjusted Cost Base Of New Shares	$ 50,000
Plus Non-Share Consideration	1,200,000
Proceeds Of Disposition Under ITA 86(1)(c)	$1,250,000
ITA 84(3) Deemed Dividend	(200,000)
Adjusted Proceeds	$1,050,000
Adjusted Cost Base Of Old Shares	(1,250,000)
Capital Gain (Loss)	($ 200,000)

The taxable amount of the non-eligible dividend would be $250,000 [(125%)($200,000)]. It would qualify for a federal dividend tax credit of $33,333 [(2/3)(25%)($200,000)]. The allowable capital loss would be $100,000 [(1/2)($200,000)].

Exercise Seventeen - 5 Solution

The amount of the gift can be calculated as follows:

Fair Market Value Of Shares [(80%)($1,600,000)]	$1,280,000
Consideration Received ($300,000 + $800,000)	(1,100,000)
Gift To Daughter	$ 180,000

As a gift is present in this transaction, ITA 86(2) is applicable.

The PUC reduction on the new shares would be calculated as follows:

Increase In Legal Stated Capital		$800,000
Less The Excess, If Any, Of:		
PUC Of Common Shares [(80%)($250,000)]	($200,000)	
Over The Non-Share Consideration	300,000	Nil
PUC Reduction		$800,000

This means that the redeemable preferred shares would have a PUC of nil ($800,000 - $800,000).

Under ITA 86(2)(e), the adjusted cost base of the redeemable preferred shares would be calculated as follows:

Adjusted Cost Base Of Common Shares		$200,000
Deduct:		
Non-Share Consideration	($300,000)	
Gift	(180,000)	(480,000)
Adjusted Cost Base Of Preferred Shares		Nil

Given the $180,000 gift, the ITA 84(3) deemed dividend and the capital gain would be calculated as follows:

PUC Of New Preferred Shares	Nil
Plus Non-Share Consideration	$300,000
Proceeds Of Redemption Under ITA 84(5)(d)	$300,000
PUC Of Shares Given Up	(200,000)
ITA 84(3) Deemed Dividend (Non-Eligible)	$100,000

Proceeds Of Disposition Under ITA 86(2)(c) - Lesser Of:	
• Fair Market Value Of Shares Given Up = $1,280,000	
• Non-Share Consideration Plus Gift	
($300,000 + $180,000) = $480,000	$480,000
Less ITA 84(3) Deemed Dividend	(100,000)
Adjusted Proceeds	$380,000
Adjusted Cost Base Of Shares Given Up	(200,000)
Capital Gain	$180,000

The taxable amount of the non-eligible dividend would be $125,000 [(125%)($100,000)]. It would qualify for a federal dividend tax credit of $16,667 [(2/3)(25%)($100,000)]. The taxable capital gain would be $90,000 [(1/2)($180,000)].

Her total gain of $280,000 ($100,000 + $180,000) reflects the excess of the $300,000 in non-share consideration over the $200,000 PUC and adjusted cost base of the old shares, plus the $180,000 gift. Ms. Reviser would also have a deferred gain of $800,000, the excess of fair market value of the preferred shares over their PUC and adjusted cost base of nil.

If Ms. Reviser had sold her common shares before the rollover, she would have had a capital gain of $1,080,000 ($1,280,000 - $200,000).

An additional gain relates to the daughter's shares. Before this transaction, the fair market value of her holding was $320,000 [(20%)($1,600,000)]. This holding now has a value of $500,000. This is the $1,600,000 total value of Janrev Inc. prior to the transaction, less the cash of $300,000, less the fair market value of the preferred shares of $800,000. As there is no increase in her adjusted cost base, this extra $180,000 ($500,000 - $320,000) represents a deferred gain that will be taxed if her shares are redeemed or if she chooses to sell them.

Exercise Seventeen - 6 Solution

As Upton Inc. has a clear majority of the shares in Amalgo Inc., it would appear that they have acquired control of Downer Ltd. As the acquisition of control rules would be applicable, there would be a deemed year end for both Companies that coincides with the amalgamated year end. The non-capital loss carry forward of Downer Ltd. will be flowed through to the amalgamated company, Amalgo Inc. However, because of the acquisition of control, the net capital loss carry forward cannot be used. In addition, for the non-capital loss to be used, Amalgo Inc. would have to continue the business in which the loss occurred and the loss carry forward could only be applied against profits in that business.

Exercise Seventeen - 7 Solution

Subsequent to an ITA 88(1) winding-up, the parent company can deduct subsidiary losses in its first taxation year beginning after that date. This would be the year beginning on September 16, 2013.

Side's loss is deemed to occur in Park's taxation year that includes Side's year end. This would be the year ending September 15, 2013. This means that it will expire, after 20 taxation years, at the end of Park's taxation year ending September 15, 2033.

Exercise Seventeen - 8 Solution

Under ITA 88(1), a limited bump-up of non-depreciable capital assets is available. The basic limit would be calculated as follows:

Adjusted Cost Base Of Lorne Inc. Shares	$1,200,000
Tax Values Of Lorne Inc.'s Net Assets	
At Winding-Up ($500,000 - $75,000)	(425,000)
Dividends Paid By Lorne Since Acquisition	Nil
Excess	$ 775,000

However, this basic amount cannot exceed the difference between the fair market value of the non-depreciable capital assets at the time of the share acquisition and their tax cost at that time. This amount would be $130,000 ($270,000 - $140,000). The bump-up in the Land value is limited to that amount, resulting in the following tax values for Lorne's assets at the time of the ITA 88(1) winding-up:

Cash	$120,000
Land ($140,000 + $130,000)	270,000
Depreciable Assets - At UCC	240,000
Total Assets	$630,000

Note that the remaining $645,000 ($775,000 - $130,000) of the excess is lost as a result of this wind up.

Exercise Seventeen - 9 Solution

Given the size of the proceeds, the balance in the RDTOH account will clearly be less than one-third of the dividends to be declared. Given this, the total distribution to shareholders will be $912,000 ($865,000 + $47,000).

The taxable dividend component of the total distribution to the shareholders is calculated as follows:

Total Distribution	$912,000
Paid Up Capital	(88,000)
ITA 84(2) Deemed Dividend On Winding-Up	$824,000
Capital Dividend Account (Election Required)	(26,000)
Non-Eligible Dividend Subject To Tax	$798,000

The non-eligible dividend will be grossed up to $997,500 [(125%)($798,000)]. The shareholders will also have a federal dividend tax credit of $133,000 [(2/3)(25%)($798,000)]

As shown in the following calculation, the shareholders will not have a capital gain on the disposition of their shares:

Total Distribution To Shareholders	$912,000
ITA 84(2) Deemed Dividend	(824,000)
Deemed Proceeds Of Disposition	$ 88,000
Adjusted Cost Base Of Shares	(88,000)
Capital Gain	Nil

Self Study Solution Seventeen - 1

It would appear that this is a share for share exchange that meets the conditions of ITA 85.1. Unless Jenny opts out of this rollover provision in her income tax return, the tax consequences of this transaction for her would be as follows:

- Jenny would be deemed to have disposed of her Jenny's Cupcakes Inc. shares at a value equal to their adjusted cost base of $125,000. As a consequence, there would be no capital gain on the disposition.

- Jenny would be deemed to have acquired her London Speciality Bakeries Ltd. shares at a cost equal to the $125,000 adjusted cost base of the Jenny's Cupcakes Inc. shares.

- The adjusted cost base of the Jenny's Cupcakes Inc. shares that have been acquired by London Speciality Bakeries Ltd. would be deemed to be the lesser of their fair market value ($725,000) and their paid up capital. In this case, the $125,000 paid up capital amount is the lower figure.

- The PUC of the London Speciality Bakeries Ltd. shares that have been issued to Jenny would be $125,000, the PUC of the Jenny's Cupcakes Inc. shares that were given up.

It is important to note that Jenny could opt out of ITA 85.1 by including a taxable capital gain of $300,000 [($725,000 - $125,000)(1/2)] in her income tax return. If Jenny's Cupcakes Inc. is a qualified small business corporation and Jenny still has room to use her lifetime capital gains deduction, this will be a better alternative.

By opting out and recognizing the taxable capital gain, the adjusted cost base of the London

Speciality Bakeries shares would be $725,000, resulting in a much lower capital gain on a subsequent sale of these shares.

How much tax this would cost her would depend on how much of her $750,000 lifetime capital gains deduction she has available. Alternative minimum tax considerations could also be a factor.

Self Study Solution Seventeen - 2

Part A - ITA 85.1 Applies

Sarah elected to transfer her business using ITA 85(1) at a value of $842,000. Given that she took back non-share consideration of $360,000, the adjusted cost base of her Hartman shares would be calculated as follows:

Elected Value	$842,000
Non-Share Consideration	(360,000)
Adjusted Cost Base Of Common Shares	$482,000

The PUC of these shares would be calculated as follows:

Increase in Legal Stated Capital		$1,200,000
Less Excess, If Any, Of:		
Elected Value	($842,000)	
Non-Share Consideration	360,000	(482,000)
PUC Reduction		$ 718,000
PUC Of Common Shares ($1,200,000 - $718,000)		$ 482,000

Using these values for the Hartman shares, if Sarah does not opt out of ITA 85.1, the tax consequences would be as follows:

- Sarah would be deemed to have disposed of her Hartman shares at a value equal to their adjusted cost base of $482,000. Given this, there would be no capital gain on the disposition.

- Sarah would be deemed to have acquired her Grande Ltd. shares at a cost equal to the $482,000 adjusted cost base of her Hartman shares.

- The PUC of the Grande Ltd. shares that have been issued to Sarah would be $482,000, the PUC of the Hartman shares that were given up.

Part A - Opting Out Of ITA 85.1

Sarah can opt out of ITA 85.1 by including a $1,109,000 [(1/2)($2,700,000 - $482,000)] taxable capital gain in her income tax return. This may be desirable in that it will allow her to make use of her $625,000 net capital loss carry forward. However, the disadvantage of opting out of ITA 85.1 is that she will have to pay taxes on the net taxable capital gain of $484,000 ($1,109,000 - $625,000).

Because all of her shares are involved in the exchange, she has no choice as to the amount of the gain to be recognized.

Part B - ACB For Grande Ltd.

The adjusted cost base of the Hartman shares in the hands of Grande would be the lesser of their $2,700,000 fair market value and their PUC. In this case, the PUC amount of $482,000 is lower and will be the adjusted cost base amount.

Part C - Alternative Solutions

There are two possible solutions that would make full use of the $625,000 net capital loss carry forward and minimize the current payment of taxes.

Alternative One   Sarah could use ITA 85(1) to exchange the shares at an elected value of $1,732,000. If this value was elected, the resulting taxable capital gain would be equal to the required amount of $625,000 [(1/2)($1,732,000 - $482,000)]. Note that this would leave the adjusted cost base of the acquired shares at the elected value of $1,732,000. If ITA 85.1 were used, this value would be the $482,000 PUC of the shares.

Alternative Two   Each share of Hartman Inc. has a fair market value of $450 ($2,700,000 ÷ 6,000) and an adjusted cost base of $80.33 ($482,000 ÷ 6,000). This means that each share that is sold to Grande would generate a taxable capital gain of $184.84 [(1/2)($450 - $80.33)]. Given this, selling 3,382 of these shares to Grande would result in a taxable capital gain of $625,128.88 [(3,382)($184.84)]. This would be largely eliminated by the application of the $625,000 net capital loss carry forward. The remaining 2,618 (6,000 - 3,382) shares of Hartman could then be exchanged for Grande Ltd. shares on a tax free basis under either of ITA 85(1) or ITA 85.1.

Self Study Solution Seventeen - 3

Part A - PUC Of New Preferred Shares

The PUC of the new preferred shares would be reduced under ITA 86(2.1) as follows:

Legal Stated Capital Of Preferred Shares		$99,000
Less The Excess, If Any, Of:		
PUC Of Shares Given Up	($99,000)	
Non-Share Consideration	69,000	(30,000)
Reduction In PUC		$69,000

Given this reduction, the resulting PUC of the new preferred shares would be as follows:

Legal Stated Capital Of Preferred Shares	$99,000
Reduction In PUC	(69,000)
PUC Of Preferred Shares	$30,000

Part B - ACB Of New Preferred Shares

The adjusted cost base of the new preferred shares would be calculated as follows:

Adjusted Cost Base Of Shares Given Up	$99,000
Non-Share Consideration	(69,000)
Adjusted Cost Base Of Preferred Shares	$30,000

Part C - Proceeds Of Redemption And Disposition

As the PUC of the shares given up is equal to their ACB, the proceeds of redemption would be equal to the proceeds of disposition. The amount would be calculated as follows:

Adjusted Cost Base And PUC Of Preferred Shares	$30,000
Non-Share Consideration	69,000
Proceeds Of Redemption And Disposition Of Shares Given Up	$99,000

Part D - ITA 84(3) Deemed Dividend

As the proceeds of redemption is equal to the PUC of the shares given up, there would be no ITA 84(3) deemed dividend. As the proceeds of disposition is equal to the adjusted cost base of the shares given up, there would be no capital gain.

Part E - Redemption Of Preferred Shares

If the preferred shares were redeemed for $381,000, the tax consequences would be as follows:

Redemption Proceeds	$381,000
Paid Up Capital Of Preferred Shares	(30,000)
ITA 84(3) Deemed Dividend (Non-Eligible)	$351,000
Proceeds Of Disposition	$381,000
ITA 84(3) Deemed Dividend	(351,000)
Adjusted Proceeds Of Disposition	$ 30,000
Adjusted Cost Base Of Preferred Shares	(30,000)
Capital Gain	Nil

There would be a taxable non-eligible dividend of $438,750 [(125%)($351,000)], which would qualify for a federal dividend tax credit of $58,500 [(2/3)(25%)($351,000)].

Part F - Sale Of Preferred Shares

If the preferred shares were sold for $381,000, the tax consequences would be as follows:

Proceeds Of Disposition	$381,000
Adjusted Cost Base Of Preferred Shares	(30,000)
Capital Gain	$351,000
Inclusion Rate	1/2
Taxable Capital Gain	$175,500

Self Study Solution Seventeen - 4

Part A

Gift To Jack   This transaction involves a gift of $320,000 to Mr. Mark's son, Jack, calculated as follows:

Fair Market Value Of Common Shares Given Up [(80%)($2,400,000)]	$1,920,000
Fair Market Value Of Preferred Shares Received	(1,600,000)
Gift	$ 320,000

It is fair to assume that this amount is a gift to Jack, as he is the only remaining holder of common shares in Markit Ltd.

PUC Of New Preferred Shares   The PUC reduction required under ITA 86(2.1) would be calculated as follows:

Legal Stated Capital Of New Shares		$8,000
Deduct:		
PUC Of Old Shares	($8,000)	
Non-Share Consideration	Nil	(8,000)
PUC Reduction		Nil
PUC Of Preferred Shares ($8,000 - Nil)		$8,000

As the required PUC reduction is nil, the PUC of the new shares would be equal to the $8,000 PUC of the old shares.

Adjusted Cost Base Of New Preferred Shares   This amount would be calculated as follows:

Adjusted Cost Base Of Old Shares		$ 8,000
Deduct:		
Non-Share Consideration	$ Nil	
Gift	(320,000)	(320,000)
Adjusted Cost Base Of New Shares		$ Nil

Proceeds Of Redemption For Old Common Shares - ITA 84(5)(d)   For purposes of determining any ITA 84(3) deemed dividend on the redemption of the old shares, the proceeds of redemption would be as follows:

PUC Of New Preferred Shares	$8,000
Non-Share Consideration	Nil
Proceeds Of Redemption	$8,000

As this amount is equal to the old PUC, there is no ITA 84(3) deemed dividend on the transaction.

Proceeds Of Disposition For Old Common Shares - ITA 86(2)(c)   For purposes of determining any capital gain on the redemption of the old common shares, the proceeds of disposition would be the lesser of the $1,920,000 fair market value of the old common shares and the following amount:

Non-Share Consideration	$ Nil
Gift	320,000
Proceeds Of Disposition	$320,000

Using the lesser figure of $320,000, there would be a taxable capital gain on the transaction calculated as follows:

Proceeds Of Disposition	$320,000
ITA 84(3) Deemed Dividend	Nil
Adjusted Proceeds Of Disposition	$320,000
Adjusted Cost Base	(8,000)
Capital Gain	$312,000
Inclusion Rate	1/2
Taxable Capital Gain	$156,000

The total potential gain on this transaction is $1,912,000 ($1,920,000 - $8,000). If there had been no gift to his son, all of this gain could have been deferred until there was a disposition of the new preferred shares.

Part B

This transaction will not alter the total fair market value of the Company and, as a consequence, the value of Jack's common shares will increase by the $320,000 amount of the gift. There will be no corresponding increase in the amount of the tax cost of these shares and, as a consequence, this value will be taxed when Jack sells the common shares. As this value has already been taxed in the hands of Mr. Mark, there will be double taxation on this amount.

Part C

If Mr. Mark's preferred shares were redeemed at their fair market value of $1,600,000, the tax consequences would be as follows:

Redemption Proceeds	$1,600,000
PUC	(8,000)
ITA 84(3) Deemed Dividend (Non-Eligible)	$1,592,000

Redemption Proceeds	$1,600,000
Deemed ITA 84(3) Dividend	(1,592,000)
Adjusted Proceeds Of Disposition	$ 8,000
Adjusted Cost Base	(Nil)
Capital Gain	$ 8,000
Inclusion Rate	1/2
Taxable Capital Gain	$ 4,000

The overall tax consequences of the redemption would be as follows:

Taxable Dividend [($1,592,000)(125%)]	$1,990,000
Taxable Capital Gain	4,000
Income Inclusion	$1,994,000

The deemed non-eligible dividend would qualify for a federal dividend tax credit of $265,333 [(2/3)($1,592,000)(25%)].

Note that Mr. Mark's dividends and capital gains from the rollover total $1,912,000 ($312,000 + $1,592,000 + $8,000). This is equal to the $1,912,000 [(80%)($2,400,000) - $8,000] capital gain that would have resulted from a sale of his shares at fair market value. From his point of view, the redemption result is less favourable in that part of the gain is in the form of more heavily taxed non-eligible dividends. In addition, if his son were to sell his shares, there would be additional income subject to tax of $320,000.

Self Study Solution Seventeen - 5

Approach One - No Gift = ITA 86(1)

Part A(i)   There is no gift involved in this approach, which can be verified as follows:

Fair Market Value Of Shares Given Up [(90%)($900,000)]		$810,000
Fair Market Value Of Consideration:		
Non-Share Consideration	($ 90,000)	
FMV Of Preferred Shares	(720,000)	(810,000)
Gift To Daughter		Nil

Since no gift is involved in the rollover, ITA 86(1) applies.

Part A(ii)   Since Mr. Long purchased the shares directly from Mr. Seto, the total paid up capital of the common shares remains at $100,000. The PUC of the new preferred shares would be calculated as follows:

Legal Stated Capital Of Preferred Shares		$234,000
Less The Excess, If Any, Of:		
PUC Of Common Shares Given Up		
[(90%)($100,000)]	($90,000)	
Over The Non-Share Consideration	90,000	Nil
PUC Reduction		**$234,000**

Legal Stated Capital Of Preferred Shares	$234,000
Reduction In PUC	(234,000)
PUC Of Preferred Shares	**Nil**

Part A(iii)   The adjusted cost base of these shares is calculated as follows:

Adjusted Cost Base Of Common Shares Given Up	
[(90%)$360,000)]	$324,000
Non-Share Consideration	(90,000)
Adjusted Cost Base Of Preferred Shares	**$234,000**

Part A(iv)   The ITA 84(3) deemed dividend calculation would be as follows:

PUC Of Preferred Shares	Nil
Plus Non-Share Consideration	$90,000
Proceeds Of Redemption - ITA 84(5)(d)	$90,000
PUC Of Common Shares Redeemed [(90%)($100,000)]	(90,000)
ITA 84(3) Deemed Dividend	**Nil**

Part A(v)   The capital gain (loss) calculation would be as follows:

Adjusted Cost Base Of Preferred Shares	$234,000
Plus Non-Share Consideration	90,000
Proceeds Of Disposition - ITA 86(1)(c)	$324,000
Deduct: ITA 84(3) Deemed Dividend	Nil
Adjusted Proceeds Of Disposition - ITA 54	$324,000
Adjusted Cost Base Of Common Shares Given Up	
[(90%)($360,000)]	(324,000)
Capital Gain	**Nil**

Approach Two - Gift = ITA 86(2)

Part A(i)   There is a gift involved in this approach, calculated as follows:

Fair Market Value Of Shares Given Up [(90%)($900,000)]		$810,000
Fair Market Value Of Consideration:		
Non-Share Consideration	($ 50,000)	
FMV Of Preferred Shares	(660,000)	(710,000)
Gift To Daughter		**$100,000**

As Mr. Long's daughter holds the remaining common shares, it is reasonable to assume that this $100,000 in value accrues to her. This means that the provisions of ITA 86(2) will be applicable if this approach is used.

Part A(ii)   Since Mr. Long purchased the shares directly from Mr. Seto, the total paid up capital of the common shares remains at $100,000. The PUC of the preferred shares would be calculated as follows:

Legal Stated Capital Of Preferred Shares		$40,000
Less The Excess, If Any, Of:		
PUC Of Common Shares Given Up		
[(90%)($100,000)]	($90,000)	
Over The Non-Share Consideration	50,000	(40,000)
PUC Reduction		**Nil**

Legal Stated Capital Of Preferred Shares	$40,000
Reduction In PUC	Nil
PUC Of Preferred Shares	**$40,000**

Part A(iii)   Under the provisions of ITA 86(2), the adjusted cost base of the new preferred shares would be calculated as follows:

Adjusted Cost Base Of Common Shares Given Up		
[(90%)($360,000)]		$324,000
Deduct:		
Non-Share Consideration	($ 50,000)	
Amount Of Gift	(100,000)	(150,000)
Adjusted Cost Base Of Preferred Shares		**$174,000**

Part A(iv)   The ITA 84(3) deemed dividend calculation would be as follows:

PUC Of Preferred Shares	$40,000
Plus Non-Share Consideration	50,000
Proceeds Of Redemption - ITA 84(5)(d)	$90,000
PUC Of Common Shares Redeemed	(90,000)
ITA 84(3) Deemed Dividend	**Nil**

Part A(v)   The capital gain (loss) calculation would be as follows:

Proceeds Of Disposition - ITA 86(2)(c) - Lesser Of:	
• FMV Of Common Shares = $810,000	
• Non-Share Consideration Plus Gift	
($50,000 + $100,000) = $150,000	$150,000
Less: ITA 84(3) Deemed Dividend	Nil
Adjusted Proceeds Of Disposition - ITA 54	$150,000
Adjusted Cost Base Of Common Shares Given Up	
[(90%)($360,000)]	(324,000)
Capital Loss [Disallowed By ITA 86(2)(d)]	**($174,000)**

Part B   If the preferred shares were sold for their fair market value of $720,000 or $660,000, the results would be as follows:

	Approach 1	Approach 2
Proceeds Of Disposition	$720,000	$660,000
Adjusted Cost Base	(234,000)	(174,000)
Capital Gain	$486,000	$486,000
Inclusion Rate	1/2	1/2
Taxable Capital Gain	$243,000	$243,000

Part C   If the preferred shares were redeemed at their fair market value of $720,000 or $660,000, the results would be as follows:

	Approach 1	Approach 2
Proceeds Of Redemption	$720,000	$660,000
PUC	Nil	(40,000)
ITA 84(3) Deemed Dividend (Non-Eligible)	$720,000	$620,000
Proceeds Of Redemption	$720,000	$660,000
ITA 84(3) Deemed Dividend	(720,000)	(620,000)
Adjusted Proceeds Of Disposition	Nil	$ 40,000
Adjusted Cost Base Of Preferred Shares	(234,000)	(174,000)
Capital Loss	($234,000)	($134,000)
Taxable Non-Eligible Dividend (125% Of Deemed Dividend)	$900,000	$775,000
Dividend Tax Credit (2/3 Of Gross Up)	$120,000	$103,333

Part D - Approach 1   If Mr. Long had simply sold the shares prior to any reorganization, the result would have been a capital gain of $486,000 ($810,000 - $324,000). While no current income was recognized as a result of the reorganization, this same amount of income was deferred until the preferred shares were either sold or redeemed. This is demonstrated in the preceding calculations which show a capital gain on a sale of $486,000 in Part B, as well as a net gain of $486,000 ($720,000 - $234,000) on redemption in Part C.

Part D - Approach 2   No current income would be assessed to Mr. Long as a result of the reorganization transaction. He would retain the $50,000 note along with the preferred stock with a fair market value of $660,000. The $486,000 ($660,000 - $174,000) deferred capital gain on these shares would be the same as the deferred capital gain that was present on his previous holding of common shares.

As a final point, the fair market value of his daughter's shares has increased by the $100,000 of the gift with no corresponding increase in their tax value. While he has succeeded in freezing his estate, in effect, this approach will result in the $100,000 amount of the gift being subject to tax in his daughter's hands, with no compensating benefit available to his daughter or himself.

Self Study Solution Seventeen - 6

Use Of Section 87

If ITA 87 is used, the tax consequences are as follows:

- The land will flow through to the amalgamated corporation at its adjusted cost base of $175,000. No capital gain or loss will be recorded.

- As the subsidiary is 100 percent owned, the ITA 88(1) bump-up provision is available. The bump-up will be the lesser of:

Adjusted Cost Base Of Lynn Shares		$390,000
Deduct:		
Lynn's Cost For Land	($175,000)	
Dividends Paid By Lynn	Nil	(175,000)
1st Value		$215,000
Value Of Land At Acquisition Of Lynn		$390,000
Adjusted Cost Base Of Land		(175,000)
2nd Value		$215,000

This will leave the adjusted cost base of the land at $390,000 ($175,000 + $215,000).

Use Of Section 88(1)

If ITA 88(1) is used, the tax consequences are as follows:

- Lynn will have proceeds of disposition equal to the adjusted cost base of the land of $175,000. No capital gain or loss will be recorded.

- Ricon Ltd. will have the same bump-up on the land as calculated under the ITA 87 approach. The adjusted cost base of the land will also be the same $390,000 that was calculated in the ITA 87 solution.

Conclusion

Both approaches result in a bump-up of $215,000 and an adjusted cost base for the land of $390,000. It does not appear to make any difference which of the two alternative approaches is used.

Self Study Solution Seventeen - 7

Part A - Funds Available For Distribution

The taxable capital gains and active business income (recapture) at the corporate level can be calculated as follows:

Asset	Taxable Capital Gains	Active Business Income
Inventories	Nil	Nil
Taxable Capital Gains:		
On Land [(1/2)($1,553,750 - $778,750)]	$387,500	Nil
On Building [(1/2)($1,591,250 - $1,093,750)]	248,750	
Recapture On Building ($1,093,750 - $732,500)		$361,250
Totals	$636,250	$361,250

As it appears there are no deductions from Net Income For Tax Purposes, this figure and Taxable Income would both be equal to $997,500 ($636,250 + $361,250). As the active business income is less than the $500,000 annual business limit, there will be no addition to the General Rate Income Pool Balance. The taxable capital gains are not eligible for addition to the GRIP balance. Tax Payable would be calculated as follows:

Federal Tax On Business Income [(28% - 17%)($361,250)]	$ 39,738
Federal Tax On Investment Income [(28% + 6-2/3%)($636,250)]	220,567

Part I Federal Tax Payable	$260,305
Provincial Tax On Business Income [(4%)($361,250)]	14,450
Provincial Tax On Investment Income [(12%)($636,250)]	76,350
Total Tax Payable	$351,105

The taxable capital gains will result in an addition to the Refundable Dividend Tax On Hand account. This will leave a balance in this account as follows:

RDTOH Balance Prior To Asset Dispositions	$ 33,750
Addition: The Least Of:	
• [(26-2/3%)($636,250)] = $169,667	
• [(26-2/3%)($997,500 - $361,250)] = $169,667	
• Part I Federal Tax Payable = $260,305	169,667
Ending RDTOH Balance	$203,417

The amount available for distribution to the shareholders, after the payment of all taxes at the corporate level, can be calculated as follows:

Fair Market Values:	
Inventories	$ 43,750
Land	1,553,750
Building	1,591,250
Gross Proceeds	$3,188,750
Tax Payable	(351,105)
Dividend Refund (Note)	203,417
Funds Available For Distribution	$3,041,062

Note The dividend refund is equal to the balance in the RDTOH account. As will be shown in a subsequent calculation, the taxable dividends paid on the wind-up are well in excess of the amount needed to trigger the refund of the entire balance in the RDTOH account.

With respect to the capital dividend account, the final balance is calculated as follows:

Balance Before Dispositions	$268,750
Disposition Of Land	387,500
Disposition Of Building	248,750
Ending Balance	$905,000

Part B - Components Of Distribution

Assuming an election has been made to declare the maximum capital dividend, the taxable dividend component of the total distribution to the shareholders can be calculated as follows:

Distribution To Shareholders	$3,041,062
Paid Up Capital	(68,750)
ITA 84(2) Deemed Dividend	$2,972,312
ITA 83(2) Capital Dividend (Balance In Account)	(905,000)
Deemed Dividend Subject To Tax	$2,067,312

As Intertel has no GRIP balance, all of this dividend will be non-eligible. The taxable amount will be $2,584,140 [(125%)($2,067,312)]. The dividend will qualify for a federal dividend tax credit of $344,552 [(25%)(2/3)($2,067,312)].

Part B - Capital Gain

With respect to capital gains, ITA 54 indicates that the proceeds of disposition for purposes of determining any capital gain on the disposition of shares does not include any amount paid out as ITA 84(2) deemed dividends. Given the preceding calculation, the capital gain to the shareholders would be calculated as follows:

Actual Distribution To Shareholders	$3,041,062
ITA 84(2) Deemed Dividend	(2,972,312)
Deemed Proceeds Of Disposition	$ 68,750
Adjusted Cost Base Of Shares	(68,750)
Capital Gain	Nil

Self Study Solution Seventeen - 8

Sale Of Assets

This calculation requires two steps. First, we must determine the after tax proceeds that will be available at the corporate level subsequent to the sale of the assets. Then, a second stage analysis is required to determine the amount that will be retained by Mr. Brock after he pays all of the taxes that are due on the proceeds that are distributed to him.

Calculation Of Corporate Income On Asset Dispositions

Net Income For Tax Purposes on the disposition of assets would be as follows:

	Active Business Income (Loss)	Taxable Capital Gains
Accounts Receivable	Nil	Nil
Inventory ($109,500 - $105,000)	$ 4,500	Nil
Land [(1/2)($70,000 - $35,000)]	Nil	$17,500
Building		
Recapture ($122,500 - $35,000)	87,500	
Capital Gain [(1/2)($136,500 - $122,500)]		7,000
Equipment (Note One)	(21,000)	Nil
Goodwill (Note Two)	82,250	Nil
Taxable Amounts	$153,250	$24,500

Note One There is a terminal loss of $21,000 ($63,000 - $42,000).

Note Two Business income in the amount of $82,250 [(3/4)($164,500)(1/2 ÷ 3/4)] will be recognized on the disposition of the Goodwill.

Taxable Income And Tax Payable

Taxable Income will total $177,750 ($153,250 + $24,500). The Tax Payable on this amount would be calculated as follows:

Federal Tax On Business Income [(28% - 17%)($153,250)]	$16,858
Federal Tax On Investment Income [(28% + 6-2/3%)($24,500)]	8,493
Part I Tax Payable	$25,351
Provincial Tax On Business Income [(4%)($153,250)]	6,130
Provincial Tax On Investment Income [(13%)($24,500)]	3,185
Total Tax Payable	$34,666

RDTOH Balance

There is no opening balance in the RDTOH account. The closing balance, which is the addition for the year, will be the least of:

- 26-2/3 Percent Of Investment Income [(26-2/3%)($24,500)] $ 6,533

- 26-2/3% Of Taxable Income, Less Income Eligible For The Small Business Deduction [(26-2/3%)($177,750 - $153,250)] $ 6,533

- Part I Tax Payable $25,351

The least of these figures and the balance in the RDTOH account is $6,533.

Funds Available For Distribution

Based on the preceding figures, the amount of cash available for distribution would be calculated as follows:

Purchase Price (Given) = Total Fair Market Value Of Net Non-Cash Assets ($561,000 - $14,000 - $70,000)	$477,000
Cash Not Purchased	14,000
Funds From Sale Of Assets	$491,000
Tax Payable	(34,666)
Dividend Refund (Balance In RDTOH)	6,533
Funds Available For Distribution	$462,867

The dividend refund is equal to the balance in the RDTOH account. As will be shown in a subsequent calculation, the taxable dividends paid on the winding-up will be well in excess of the amount required to use the full balance in the RDTOH account. In other words, the RDTOH balance is a great deal less than one-third of the dividends paid.

Capital Dividend Account

The balance in the capital dividend account would be calculated as follows:

Balance Before Dispositions	$ 70,000
Disposition Of Land	17,500
Disposition Of Building	7,000
Disposition Of Goodwill	82,250
Ending Balance	$176,750

GRIP Balance

The GRIP Balance is nil as Brock Enterprises has no Full Rate Taxable Income. As a result, any taxable dividend will be non-eligible.

Taxable Dividend Resulting From Distribution

Assuming an election has been made to declare the maximum capital dividend, the taxable dividend component of the total distribution to Mr. Brock can be calculated as follows:

Funds Available For Distribution	$462,867
Paid Up Capital	(52,500)
ITA 84(2) Deemed Dividend	$410,367
ITA 83(2) Capital Dividend (Balance In Account)	(176,750)
Deemed Dividend Subject To Tax (Non-Eligible)	$233,617

There would be no capital gain on the disposition, as demonstrated in the following calculation:

Funds Distributed	$462,867
ITA 84(2) Deemed Dividend	(410,367)
Deemed Proceeds Of Disposition For Shares	$ 52,500
Adjusted Cost Base	(52,500)
Capital Gain	Nil

Personal Tax Payable

As there is no capital gain and the PUC and the capital dividend are received tax free, the personal Tax Payable on the dividend subject to tax would be calculated as follows:

Deemed Non-Eligible Dividend Subject To Tax	$233,617
Gross Up Of 25 Percent	58,404
Taxable Dividend	$292,021
Personal Tax Rate (Given)	47%
Tax Before Dividend Tax Credit	$137,250
Dividend Tax Credit [(2/3 + 1/3)($58,404)]	(58,404)
Personal Tax Payable	$ 78,846

Sale Of Shares

The tax payable resulting from a sale of shares would be calculated as follows:

Proceeds Of Disposition	$455,000
Adjusted Cost Base	(52,500)
Capital Gain	$402,500
Inclusion Rate	1/2
Taxable Capital Gain	$201,250
Tax Rate For Mr. Brock	47%
Tax Payable	$ 94,588

Conclusion

Given the preceding calculations, the after tax, personal cash retention under both alternatives would be as follows:

	Asset Sale	Share Sale
Proceeds From Sale	$462,867	$455,000
Personal Tax Payable	(78,846)	(94,588)
After Tax Retention	$384,021	$360,412

The net proceeds resulting from the sale of shares amounted to $360,412. This compares to $384,021 that would be retained if the assets were sold. The conclusion is clear. The cash retained from the sale of assets and distribution of proceeds is $23,609 ($384,021 - $360,412) larger than the cash retained from selling the shares.

Note that the full $462,867 could be left in the business for further operations as an investment company. Given the current rate of taxation on the investment income of corporations, it is not likely that this would be an attractive alternative, even if the corporation was used to split income with other members of Mr. Brock's family.

Chapter 17 Learning Objectives

After completing Chapter 17, you should be able to:

1. Identify situations where the ITA 85.1 rollover provision is applicable (paragraph [P hereafter] 17-1 to 17-14).

2. Identify situations where the ITA 86 rollover provision is applicable (P 17-15).

3. Apply the ITA 86 rollover procedures to freeze an estate (P 17-16 to 17-17).

4. List the conditions that must be met in order to use the ITA 86 rollover provision (P 17-18 to 17-19).

5. Explain the procedures that are required in implementing an ITA 86 rollover (P 17-20 to 17-30).

6. Identify situations where the ITA 86(2) benefit rule is applicable and apply the required procedures to specific examples (P 17-31 to 17-41).

7. Describe the major tax planning considerations related to the use of ITA 86 (P 17-43 to 17-47).

8. Explain the nature of an ITA 87 amalgamation (P 17-48 to 17-51).

9. Describe the position of the amalgamated company subsequent to an ITA 87 amalgamation (P 17-52 to 17-56).

10. Describe the position of the shareholders of the amalgamated company subsequent to an ITA 87 amalgamation (P 17-57).

11. Identify the specific considerations involved in vertical amalgamations (P 17-58 to 17-63).

12. Explain both the non-tax considerations and tax planning considerations related to ITA 87 amalgamations (P 17-64 to 17-67).

13. Explain the nature of an ITA 88(1) winding-up of a 90 percent owned subsidiary (P 17-68 to 17-70).

14. Apply the procedures for recording the assets acquired by the parent company in an ITA 88(1) winding-up of a 90 percent owned subsidiary (P 17-71 to 17-86).

15. Apply the procedures required for the disposition of shares that occurs in the winding-up of a 90 percent owned subsidiary (P 17-87 and 17-88).

16. Compare the results of applying ITA 87 vs. the results of applying ITA 88(1) and any associated tax planning issues (P 17-89 to 17-95).

17. Apply the procedures required in an ITA 88(2) winding-up of a Canadian corporation (P 17-96 to 17-108).

18. Explain the procedures used under ITA 51 when there is a conversion of a corporation's preferred shares or debt securities (P 17-109 to 17-115).

19. Explain the basic alternatives for the sale of an incorporated business (P 17-116 to 17-117).

20. Explain the provisions relating to restrictive covenants (a.k.a. non-competition agreements) (P 17-118 to 17-122).

21. Describe the procedures used when the individual assets of a business are sold (P 17-123 to 17-125).

22. Describe the procedures used when the assets of a business are sold as a going concern (P 17-126 to 17-135).

23. Describe the procedures used when the shares of a business are sold (P 17-136 to 17-140).

24. Compare an offer to purchase the shares of a business and an offer to purchase its assets and determine the preferable alternative (P 17-141 to 17-155).

CHAPTER 18

How To Work Through Chapter 18

Introduction To Partnerships
❑ Read paragraph 18-1 to 18-7 (in the textbook).

Partnerships Defined
❑ Read paragraph 18-8 to 18-23.
❑ Do Self Study Problem Eighteen-1 at the end of the textbook chapter on page 928 and check the solution on page S-406 and S-407 in this Study Guide.

Co-Ownership, Joint Ventures, And Syndicates
❑ Read paragraph 18-24 to 18-36.
❑ Do Self Study Problem Eighteen-2 and check the solutions in this Study Guide.

Determining Partnership Income, Losses, And Tax Credits
❑ Read paragraph 18-37 to 18-49.
❑ Do Exercise Eighteen-1 (in the textbook) and check the solution on page S-402 in this Study Guide.
❑ Read paragraph 18-50 to 18-51.
❑ Do Exercise Eighteen-2 and check the solution in this Study Guide.
❑ Read paragraph 18-52 to 18-55.

Allocations To Partners And Partner Expenses
❑ Read paragraph 18-56.
❑ Do Exercise Eighteen-4 and check the solution in this Study Guide.
❑ Read paragraph 18-57 to 18-59.
❑ Do Self Study Problems Eighteen-3 and Eighteen-4 and check the solutions in this Study Guide.

The Partnership Interest
❑ Read paragraph 18-60 to 18-71.
❑ Do Exercise Eighteen-5 and check the solution in this Study Guide.

Adjustments To The ACB Of A Partnership Interest
❑ Read paragraph 18-72 to 18-85.
❑ Do Exercise Eighteen-6 and check the solution in this Study Guide.
❑ Read paragraph 18-86 to 18-87.
❑ Do Self Study Problems Eighteen-5 and Eighteen-6 and check the solutions in this Study Guide.

Limited Partnerships And Limited Partners
❏ Read paragraph 18-88 to 18-99.
❏ Do Exercise Eighteen-7 and check the solution in this Study Guide.
❏ Do Self Study Problem Eighteen-7 and check the solution in this Study Guide.

Transfers Of Property To And From A Partnership - No Rollover
❏ Read paragraph 18-100 to 18-105.
❏ Do Exercise Eighteen-8 and check the solution in this Study Guide.
❏ Read paragraph 18-106.
❏ Do Exercise Eighteen-9 and check the solution in this Study Guide.

Common Partnership Rollovers
❏ Read paragraph 18-107 to 18-109.
❏ Do Exercise Eighteen-10 and check the solution in this Study Guide.
❏ Read paragraph 18-110 to 18-124.
❏ Do Self Study Problem Eighteen-8 and check the solution in this Study Guide.

Specified Investment Flow Through Partnerships
❏ Read paragraph 18-125 to 18-126.

To Complete This Chapter
❏ Review the Key Terms Used In This Chapter on page 927. Consult the Glossary for the meaning of any key terms you do not know.
❏ Review the Glossary Flashcards and complete the Key Terms Self-Test for the Chapter. These features can be found in two places, on your Student CD-ROM under the heading "Key Term Practice" and on the web site.
❏ Review the Learning Objectives of the Chapter found on page S-414 of this Study Guide.
❏ As a review, we recommend that you view the PowerPoint Slides for Chapter 18 that are available on your Student CD-ROM. If you do not have access to the Microsoft PowerPoint program, the PowerPoint Viewer program can be installed from the Student CD-ROM.

Solution to Chapter Eighteen Exercises

Exercise Eighteen - 1 Solution
The following amounts would be added to Mr. Peter's 2013 Net Income For Tax Purposes:

Business Income [(50%)($55,000)]	$27,500
Taxable Capital Gains [(50%)(1/2)($40,000)]	10,000
Eligible Dividends [(50%)($10,000)]	5,000
Gross Up [(38%)($5,000)]	1,900
Total Addition	$44,400

In addition, Mr. Peters would be eligible for a federal dividend tax credit of $1,036 [(6/11)($1,900)]. The fact that he withdrew $30,000 during the year has no immediate tax consequences.

Exercise Eighteen - 2 Solution
The JL Partnership's Net Business Income would be calculated as follows:

Accounting Net Income		$262,000
Add:		
Salary To J	$45,000	
Interest To L	22,000	
Amortization Expense	26,000	
Donations	2,500	95,500
Subtotal		$357,500
Deduct:		
Maximum CCA	($42,000)	
Accounting Gain On Sale Of Land	(24,000)	(66,000)
Net Business Income		$291,500

The allocation of this Net Business Income to the two partners would be as follows:

	Partner J	Partner L
Priority Allocation For Salary	$ 45,000	N/A
Priority Allocation For Interest	N/A	$22,000
Allocation Of Residual		
[(60%)($291,500 - $45,000 - $22,000)]	134,700	
[(40%)($291,500 - $45,000 - $22,000)]		89,800
Total Business Income Allocation	$179,700	$111,800

While not required, you might note that a taxable capital gain of $12,000 [(1/2)($24,000)], as well as the charitable donations of $2,500, would be allocated to the partners on a 60:40 basis.

Exercise Eighteen - 3 Solution

The ST Partnership's Net Business Income would be calculated as follows:

Accounting Net Income	$146,000
Amortization Expense = CCA	Nil
Eligible Dividends	(12,000)
Accounting Gain On Sale Of Land	(31,000)
Net Business Income	$103,000

The addition to Net Income For Tax Purposes for each of the two partners would be calculated as follows:

	Partner S	Partner T
Net Business Income [(50%)($103,000)]	$51,500	$51,500
Eligible Dividends [(50%)($12,000)]	6,000	6,000
Gross Up [(38%)($6,000)]	2,280	2,280
Taxable Capital Gain [(50%)(1/2)($31,000)]	7,750	7,750
Net Income For Tax Purposes Addition	$67,530	$67,530

While not required, you might note that each partner would be eligible for a federal dividend tax credit of $1,244 [(6/11)($2,280)].

Exercise Eighteen - 4 Solution

Assuming these are the only charitable donations and political contributions that the partners have made, the tax credits that would be available to each of the partners would be calculated as follows:

Charitable Donations ($1,750 Each)	
[(15%)($200) + (29%)($1,750 - $200)]	$ 480
Political Contributions ($600 Each)	
[(3/4)($400)] + [(1/2)($200)]	400
Eligible Dividends ($2,100 Each)	
[(6/11)(38%)($2,100)]	435
Total Of Credits To Each Partner	$1,315

These amounts would serve to reduce the Tax Payable of each of the two partners for the year ending December 31, 2013.

Exercise Eighteen - 5 Solution

After the admission of Caitlan, Alan and Balan will each have a one-third interest in the partnership, down from the previous interest of one-half. They are each, in effect, selling one-third of their partnership interest [(1/2 - 1/3) ÷ 1/2)]. The ACB of their distribution to Caitlan is $16,000 [(1/3)($48,000)], resulting in a capital gain of $24,000 ($40,000 - $16,000). The taxable capital gain is one-half of this amount or $12,000.

The partner capital account transactions and ending balances will be:

	Alan	Balan	Caitlin
Opening Capital Accounts	$48,000	$48,000	Nil
Adjustment For Caitlin's Admission	(16,000)	(16,000)	$32,000
Ending Capital Accounts			
(Accounting Values)	$32,000	$32,000	$32,000
ACB Of Partnership Interest	$32,000	$32,000	$80,000

Exercise Eighteen - 6 Solution

The ACB of Robert's partnership interest on December 31, 2013 and January 1, 2014 would be determined as follows:

Original Capital Contribution	$12,500
Additional Contribution	7,200
Drawing	(4,000)
ACB - December 31, 2013	$15,700
Adjustment For 2013 Income	
[(40%)($11,600 + $3,100 + $46,700)]	24,560
ACB - January 1, 2014	$40,260

Robert's inclusion in Net Income For Tax Purposes would be as follows:

Taxable Capital Gain [(1/2)($11,600)]	$ 5,800
Dividends Received	3,100
Gross Up On Dividends [(38%)($3,100)]	1,178
Net Business Income	46,700
Subtotal	$56,778
Robert's Share Of Profits	40%
Inclusion In 2013 Net Income For Tax Purposes	$22,711

Note that this $22,711 addition to Robert's Net Income For Tax Purposes is not the same amount as the $24,560 that was added to the ACB of Robert's partnership interest to reflect his share of 2013 partnership income. While not required by the problem, Robert can claim a federal dividend tax credit of $257 [(40%)(6/11)($1,178)].

Exercise Eighteen - 7 Solution

ACB Of Partnership Interest		$200,000
Share Of Partnership Income (Not Loss) For 2013		Nil
Subtotal		$200,000
Amounts Owed To The Partnership	($150,000)	
Other Amounts Intended To Reduce Investment Risk (General Partner Guarantee)	(50,000)	(200,000)
At-Risk Amount - December 31, 2013		Nil

As the at-risk amount is nil, none of the loss can be deducted in 2013. The limited partnership loss at the end of 2013 is 100 percent of the $75,000 loss allocation.

Exercise Eighteen - 8 Solution

Part A Charles is considered to have disposed of the land for $100,000, resulting in a $33,500 [(1/2)($100,000 - $33,000)] taxable capital gain. LIU will be considered to have acquired the land for $100,000. Charles is considered to have made a capital contribution of $100,000 that will be added to the ACB of his partnership interest.

Part B Charles will have the same $33,500 taxable capital gain as in Part A and LIU will be considered to have acquired the land for $100,000. The capital contribution and the addition to the ACB of the partnership interest is equal to $75,000. This is the difference between the fair market value of the land transferred to LIU of $100,000 and the $25,000 in other consideration received by Charles on the property transfer.

Part C Charles will have the same $33,500 taxable capital gain as in Part A and LIU will be considered to have acquired the land for $100,000. No capital contribution is made. As Charles withdrew $12,000 ($112,000 - $100,000) more from LIU than he transferred in, Charles will be considered to have made a net withdrawal. The ACB of his partnership interest will be reduced by $12,000.

Exercise Eighteen - 9 Solution

ITA 98(2) deems DG to have disposed of the share investments for the fair market value of $94,000, resulting in a $55,000 ($94,000 - $39,000) capital gain. One-fifth of the capital gain, or $11,000, will be allocated to Darlene. One-half of this amount, or $5,500, will be a taxable capital gain that she will include in her income for 2013.

Darlene's adjusted cost base for the share investments is $18,800 [(20%)($94,000)].

The adjusted cost base of her partnership interest on December 31, 2013 and on January 1, 2014 is calculated as follows:

Partnership ACB Prior To Distribution	$30,000
Drawings [(20%)($94,000)]	(18,800)
Partnership ACB - December 31, 2013	$11,200
Allocated Capital Gain [(20%)($94,000 - $39,000)]	11,000
Partnership ACB - January 1, 2014	$22,200

Exercise Eighteen - 10 Solution

Using the ITA 85(1) rollover provision, the property would be transferred at the $156,000 ACB of the land. Given this, the transfer would not result in any current income for Samantha. The cost of the land to the partnership would be the $156,000 elected value for the transfer. This same amount would be added to the adjusted cost base of Samantha's partnership interest.

Self Study Solution Eighteen - 1

The determination of the existence of a partnership is a mixed question of fact and law, based upon the intention of the parties that may be expressed clearly through a valid written partnership agreement or inferred from actions. In Canada, the relevant provincial partnership legislation is applicable to answering this question.

In this case, an analysis of the three elements of a partnership is as follows:

1. **Was the business carried on in common by two or more persons?**

   The details of the partnership agreement contain many of the necessary ingredients that the courts will look to in support of this element. Accordingly, it appears that this element has been met.

2. **Was a business carried on by the partnership?**

   A business has a beginning and an end. Ongoing profitable activity within the business may actually only occur between these two extremes, but the activity remains a business throughout the period. In other words, profitability is generally irrelevant to a finding that a business exists. In this case, the selling off of store property will likely occur as part of the wind up process of the two stores. Accordingly, there are arguments that support the carrying on of a business.

3. **Was there a view to profit?**

   This element will be satisfied if there is a potential for profit even though one may never be realized. The facts clearly lead to a conclusion that there is no hope of profit. The additional fact that the partnership will be terminated once the property is sold and that losses are not only expected, but anticipated, speaks for itself. A tax motivation that predominates, such as this, will not invalidate a partnership as long as there is a profit potential and the other elements are met. This is not the case.

Conclusion: A partnership will not be created. As a result, no losses can be allocated to the investors. The losses belong to Wayout Ltd. only.

Self Study Solution Eighteen - 2

Part A - Partnership Results

As the original intention when the land was purchased was to develop and sell lots, the income from the sale of the lots would be reported as business income and not as a capital gain.

Using the provisions of ITA 97(2), Mr. Marrazzo could transfer the land to the partnership at its ACB of $400,000. There would be no effect on his Net Income For Tax Purposes in 2013.

His partnership income inclusion for 2014 would be calculated as follows:

Proceeds From Lot Sales	$4,400,000
Cost Of Land	(400,000)
Site Servicing Costs	(1,200,000)
Net Business Income	$2,800,000

Priority Claim Of Accrued Gain ($1,300,000 - $400,000)	$ 900,000
Allocation Of Remaining Business Income	
[(50%)($2,800,000 - $900,000)]	950,000
Addition To Net Income For Tax Purposes	$1,850,000

Part A - Joint Venture Results

No rollover under ITA 85(1) could take place because land inventory is not an eligible property. As a result, Mr. Marrazzo would recognize a 2013 gain on the transfer to Digger Inc. of $900,000 ($1,300,000 - $400,000). As previously noted, this gain would be treated as business income. The income resulting from Digger's sale of the land would be as follows:

Proceeds Of Disposition	$4,400,000
Adjusted Cost Base Of Land	(1,300,000)
Site Servicing Costs	(1,200,000)
2014 Net Business Income	$1,900,000

Mr. Marrazzo's share of this income would be $950,000 [(50%)($1,900,000)], bringing the addition to his Net Income For Tax Purposes over the two years to $1,850,000 ($900,000 + $950,000), the same total as in Part A.

Part A - Comparison

In total, Mr. Marrazzo will report the same increase in Net Income For Tax Purposes regardless of which form of organization is used. However, with the joint venture, he would have to report $900,000 of the income in 2013 and $950,000 in 2014. With the partnership, the entire $1,850,000 in income would be reported in 2014. Given that this approach provides significant tax deferral, the partnership approach appears preferable.

Part B - Adjusted Cost Base

The ACB of Mr. Marrazzo's partnership interest would be calculated as follows:

Capital Contribution - 2013	$ 400,000
Income Allocated To Mr. Marrazzo For 2013	Nil
ACB - December 31, 2014	$ 400,000
Income Allocated To Mr. Marrazzo For 2014 (Part A)	1,850,000
ACB - January 1, 2015	$2,250,000

At this point, a winding up of the partnership would have no tax consequences for Mr. Marrazzo.

The ACB of Digger Inc.'s partnership interest would be calculated as follows:

Capital Contribution - 2013	Nil
Income Allocated To Digger For 2013	Nil
Capital Contribution - 2014 = Servicing Costs	$1,200,000
ACB - December 31, 2014	$1,200,000
Income Allocated To Digger For 2014	
[(50%)($2,800,000 - $900,000) - See Part A]	950,000
ACB - January 1, 2015	$2,150,000

Self Study Solution Eighteen - 3

Partnership Net Business Income

The Net Business Income of the partnership is calculated as follows:

Net Income As Per Income Statement		$192,100
Additions:		
Partners' Salaries [(2)($44,000)]	$88,000	
Amortization Deducted	12,500	
Charitable Donations	7,200	
Closing Accounts Receivable (Note One)	56,000	163,700
Deductions:		
Opening Accounts Receivable (Note One)	($27,000)	
Capital Gains On Securities (Note Two)	(14,000)	
Dividends Received (Note Three)	(48,000)	
CCA:		
Class 8 [(20%)($26,000)]	(5,200)	
Class 50 [(55%)(1/2)($8,500)]	(2,338)	(96,538)
Net Business Income		$259,262

Note One   The addition of closing accounts receivable and the deduction of the opening accounts receivable are required to adjust the cash based income figure to an accrual based income figure.

Note Two   The total capital gain is deducted in the calculation of net business income. The taxable one-half of these gains is included on a flow through basis in the income of the individual partners.

Note Three   The dividends received are deducted in the calculation of net business income. They are flowed through as eligible dividends in the income of the individual partners.

Mr. Caldwell's Personal Income

The amount to be included in Mr. Caldwell's personal tax return would be calculated as follows:

Partnership Net Business Income	$259,262	
Mr. Caldwell's Share	50%	$129,631
Automobile Costs:		
CCA [($13,500)(30%)(75%)]		(3,038)
Operating Costs [($4,000)(75%)]		(3,000)
Net Business Income From Professional Practice		$123,593
Other Partnership Income:		
Taxable Capital Gains [(1/2)($14,000)]	$ 7,000	
Eligible Dividends Received	48,000	
Gross Up On Dividends [(38%)($48,000)]	18,240	
Subtotal	$73,240	
Mr. Caldwell's Share	50%	36,620
Net Income For Tax Purposes		$160,213

Mr. Caldwell's $3,600 [(50%)($7,200)] share of the charitable donations can be used as the basis for a credit against his personal Tax Payable. The amount of the credit would be $1,016 [(15%)($200) + (29%)($3,600 - $200)] assuming this is his only charitable donation.

He is also entitled to a federal dividend tax credit of $4,975 [(50%)(6/11)($18,240)].

Self Study Solution Eighteen - 4

Part A - Income Inclusions

CCC has three sources of income. These are business income, property income (dividends), and taxable capital gains.

The calculation of the partnership's 2013 Net Business Income is as follows:

Net Income From Coffee Roasting		$37,200
Add:		
Salaries To Partners [(3)($2,400)]	$7,200	
Interest On Capital Contributions	2,000	
Personal Partner Expenses	1,100	
Charitable Donations	1,000	
Accounting Amortization	1,450	12,750
Deduct:		
CCA		(2,000)
Net Business Income		$47,950

Income inclusions for each partner related to partnership activities would be as follows:

Net Business Income	$47,950
Eligible Dividends Received	3,440
Gross Up [(38%)($3,440)]	1,307
Taxable Capital Gains [(1/2)($6,000)]	3,000
Total To Be Allocated	$55,697
Each Partner's Share	1/3
Addition to Net Income For Tax Purposes	$18,566

Part B - Tax Credits

Charitable Donations   Each partner would be allocated $333 ($1,000 ÷ 3) in charitable donations. This would provide a federal tax credit of $69 [(15%)($200) + (29%)($133)] assuming this is their only charitable donation.

Dividends   Each of the partners would be eligible for a federal dividend tax credit of $238 [(1/3)(6/11)(38%)($3,440)].

Self Study Solution Eighteen - 5

Matt's Federal Tax Payable

The Net Business Income of the partnership would be calculated as follows:

Operating Income		$549,000
Additions:		
Amortization Expense	$12,000	
One-Half Meals And Entertainment	11,500	
Charitable Donations	17,000	40,500
Deductions:		
CCA		(19,000)
Net Business Income		$570,500

Matt's Taxable Income and share of charitable donations for the year ending December 31, 2013 would be calculated as follows:

	Partnership	Share	Taxable Income
Partnership Business Income	$570,500	1/2	$285,250
Taxable Capital Gain [(1/2)($14,000)]	7,000	1/2	3,500
Partnership Dividends Received	8,000	1/2	4,000
Dividends Received Personally	N/A		34,000
Gross Up On Dividends Received			
[(38%)($4,000 + $34,000)]	N/A		14,440
Taxable Income			$341,190
Charitable Donations	$17,000	1/2	$8,500

Based on the preceding calculations, Matt's 2013 federal Tax Payable would be as follows:

Tax On The First $135,054	$28,580
Tax On Additional $206,136 ($341,190 - $135,054)] At 29%	59,779
Tax Payable Before Credits	$88,359
Basic Personal Credit [(15%)($11,038)]	(1,656)
Dividend Tax Credit [(6/11)($14,440)]	(7,876)
Charitable Donations {[(15%)($200)] + [(29%)($8,500 - $200)]}	(2,437)
Federal Tax Payable	$76,390

Taxable Capital Gain From Sale Of Partnership Interest

The adjusted cost base of Matt's partnership interest on January 1, 2014 would be calculated as follows:

	Partnership	Share	ACB
Capital Contribution	N/A		$280,000
2012 Partnership Business Income	$180,000	1/2	90,000
2012 Drawings	N/A		(23,000)
2013 Drawings	N/A		(290,000)
December 31, 2013			$ 57,000
2013 Partnership Business Income	$570,500	1/2	285,250
2013 Capital Gain	14,000	1/2	7,000
2013 Partnership Dividends Received	8,000	1/2	4,000
2013 Charitable Donations	(17,000)	1/2	(8,500)
January 1, 2014 Adjusted Cost Base			$344,750

Given this calculation, the taxable capital gain on Matt's sale of the partnership interest would be calculated as follows:

Proceeds Of Disposition	$535,000
Adjusted Cost Base	(344,750)
Capital Gain	$190,250
Inclusion Rate	1/2
Taxable Capital Gain	$ 95,125

Self Study Solution Eighteen - 6

Part A - Adjusted Cost Base

The adjusted cost base of Eric Beam's partnership interest on the date he withdrew from the partnership is calculated as follows:

Initial Capital Contribution	$225,000
Additional Capital Contribution	54,000
Total Capital Contribution	$279,000
Drawings From Partnership	(43,000)
Income Allocations:	
Net Business Income [(1/3)($195,000)]	65,000
Capital Gains [(1/3)($66,000)]	22,000
Charitable Donations [(1/3)($12,000)]	(4,000)
Adjusted Cost Base - January 1, 2014	$319,000

Note Only one-half of the capital gain is included in the partner's income on the flow through of capital gains realized by a partnership. However, the remaining one-half is included in the assets of the partnership and, in the absence of a special provision to deal with this situation, the realization of this amount would be added to any capital gain realized on the disposition of the partnership interest and would result in double taxation.

Part B - Taxable Capital Gain On Disposition

Given the preceding calculation, the gain on the disposition of the partnership interest can be calculated as follows:

Proceeds Of Disposition [(2)($177,500)]		$355,000
Adjusted Cost Base:		
From Preceding Calculation	($319,000)	
Legal And Accounting Fees	(1,800)	(320,800)
Capital Gain		$ 34,200
Inclusion Rate		1/2
Taxable Capital Gain		$ 17,100

This amount would be included in Eric Beam's Net Income For Tax Purposes for 2014 as a taxable capital gain. He would not include any partnership income for the period January 1 to March 1, 2014, as he was not allocated any of this income.

Part C - Effect On Other Partners

Since each partner paid $177,500 to Eric in return for one-half of his interest, both John and Fred Olson would have a $177,500 increase in the adjusted cost base of their partnership interest.

Self Study Solution Eighteen - 7

Timing Of Income Inclusions For At-Risk Amounts vs. ACB

The addition of the share of the partnership income amounts to the at-risk balance as at December 31 is intended to ensure that this amount is taken into consideration in determining the amount that is actually at risk on that date. Notice, however, losses are not deducted at this time in the determination of the at-risk amount.

We would remind you that in calculating the adjusted cost base of the partnership interest, a partner's share of either a loss or a gain is not added until the first day of the following taxation year.

2013 Results

The required amounts would be calculated as follows:

ACB Of Partnership Interest - December 31, 2013	$50,000
Add: Share Of 2013 Partnership Income (Not Loss)	Nil
Subtotal	$50,000
Amounts Owed To The Partnership	(20,000)
At-Risk Amount - December 31, 2013	$30,000
Share of 2013 Loss [(10%)($400,000)]	($40,000)
At-Risk Amount - December 31, 2013	30,000
Limited Partnership Loss - December 31, 2013	($10,000)
Share of 2013 Loss [(10%)($400,000)]	($40,000)
Limited Partnership Loss - December 31, 2013	10,000
Deductible Loss For 2013	($30,000)

There is a limited partnership loss carry forward of $10,000 at the end of 2013.

2014 Results

ACB Of Partnership Interest - December 31, 2013	$50,000
Loss Deducted For 2013	(30,000)
ACB Of Partnership Interest - December 31, 2014	$20,000
Add: Share Of 2014 Partnership Income (Not Loss)	Nil
Subtotal	$20,000
Amounts Owed To The Partnership	Nil
At-Risk Amount - December 31, 2014	$20,000
Share of 2014 Loss [(10%)($70,000)]	($ 7,000)
Limited Partnership Loss Carry Forward	(10,000)
At-Risk Amount - December 31, 2014	20,000
Limited Partnership Loss - December 31, 2014	Nil
Share of 2014 Loss [(10%)($70,000)]	($ 7,000)
Limited Partnership Loss Carry Forward	(10,000)
Limited Partnership Loss - December 31, 2014	Nil
Deductible Loss For 2014	($17,000)

The $10,000 limited partnership loss carry forward from 2013 can be deducted as it is less than $13,000, the December 31, 2014 at-risk amount of $20,000 reduced by the allocated share of the 2014 partnership loss of $7,000. As a result, there is no limited partnership loss carry forward at the end of 2014.

2015 Results

ACB Of Partnership Interest - December 31, 2014	$20,000
Loss Deducted For 2014	(17,000)
ACB Of Partnership Interest - December 31, 2015	$ 3,000
Add: Share Of 2015 Partnership Income	Nil
Subtotal	$ 3,000
Amounts Owed To The Partnership	Nil
At-Risk Amount - December 31, 2015	$ 3,000

There is no limited partnership loss or deductible loss for 2015 and no limited partnership loss carry forward at the end of 2015.

Summary Of Results

The results are summarized in the following table:

	2013	2014	2015
ACB Of The Partnership Interest - December 31	$50,000	$20,000	$ 3,000
At-Risk Amount - December 31	30,000	20,000	3,000
Limited Partnership Loss	10,000	Nil	Nil
Deductible Loss	30,000	17,000	Nil
Limited Partnership Loss Carry Forward			
- December 31	10,000	Nil	Nil

Self Study Solution Eighteen - 8

Part A - Adjusted Cost Base Of Consideration

Cash With all non-share consideration, the ACB is equal to its fair market value. In the case of cash, the fair market value is equal to the face value. These amounts would be $78,000 for Porter, $222,000 for Quinn, and $422,000 for Roberts.

Adjusted Cost Base Of Preferred Shares With respect to the preferred shares received by each partner, ITA 85(3)(e) indicates that their ACB will be the lesser of:

- Their fair market value, which would be $180,000 for each of the three partners.
- The ACB of each partnership interest, reduced by the amount of non-share consideration received by the partner.

This latter value would be calculated as follows for each of the three partners:

	Porter	Quinn	Roberts
ACB	$382,000	$526,000	$726,000
Cash Received	(78,000)	(222,000)	(422,000)
Balance	$304,000	$304,000	$304,000

For each of the three partners, the lower figure would be the fair market value of $180,000 and, as a consequence, this would be the ACB of their preferred shares.

Adjusted Cost Base Of Common Shares Under ITA 85(3)(f), the ACB of the common shares received by each partner would be the ACB of their partnership interest, less the sum of the value of the non-share consideration received and the value assigned to the preferred shares received. These amounts would be calculated as follows:

	Porter	Quinn	Roberts
ACB - Partnership Interest	$382,000	$526,000	$726,000
Cash Received	(78,000)	(222,000)	(422,000)
ACB - Preferred Shares	(180,000)	(180,000)	(180,000)
ACB - Common Shares	$124,000	$124,000	$124,000

Part B - Capital Gain Or Loss

As the non-share consideration had a value that was less than the value of the assets transferred, there will be no immediate gain or loss on this rollover. This can be demonstrated with the following calculation:

	Porter	Quinn	Roberts
Proceeds Of Disposition:			
Cash	$ 78,000	$222,000	$422,000
Preferred Shares	180,000	180,000	180,000
Common Shares	124,000	124,000	124,000
Total Proceeds	$382,000	$526,000	$726,000
ACB	(382,000)	(526,000)	(726,000)
Capital Gain (Loss)	Nil	Nil	Nil

From an economic point of view the gain is still present. The partners have simply deferred recording it for tax purposes by placing a value on the common shares of $372,000 [(3)($124,000)]. This is significantly below their current fair market value of $1,080,000. Note that the difference of $708,000 ($1,080,000 - $372,000) is also the difference between the $2,342,000 fair market value of the total consideration given and the $1,634,000 value for the total ACB of the partnership interests.

Chapter 18 Learning Objectives

After completing Chapter 18, you should be able to:

1. Explain the basic approach of Canadian income tax legislation to the taxation of partnerships (paragraph [P hereafter] 18-1 to 18-7).

2. Define, for income tax purposes, a partnership arrangement (P 18-8 to 18-15).

3. List the various types of partnership arrangements that are used in Canada (P 18-16 to 18-23).

4. Describe the difference between partnership arrangements and such other forms of organization as co-ownership, joint ventures, and syndicates (P 18-24 to 18-36).

5. Explain the basic concepts that are involved in the determination of the partnership income, losses, and tax credits to be allocated to the partners (P 18-37 to 18-49).

6. Calculate the Net Business Income of the partnership (P 18-50 to 18-51).

7. Calculate the amount and type of partnership income other than business income that will be allocated to each partner under the terms of the partnership agreement (P 18-52 to 18-59).

8. Explain the concept of the adjusted cost base of a partnership interest (P 18-60 to 18-63).

9. Apply the procedures required to record the acquisition of a partnership interest (P 18-64 to 18-71).

10. Calculate the amount of the adjusted cost base of a partnership interest (P 18-72 to 18-85).

11. Apply the procedures required to record the disposition of a partnership interest because of a sale or withdrawal (P 18-86 to 18-87).

12. Define limited partner and limited partnership arrangement (P 18-88 to 18-90).

13. Apply the at-risk rules to limited partnership losses (P 18-91 to 18-99).

14. Define a Canadian partnership (P 18-100 to 18-103).

15. Apply the procedures related to transfers between a partnership and its partners when no rollover provision is used (P 18-104 to 18-106).

16. List and apply the common rollover provisions for transfers between a partnership and its partners (P 18-107 to 18-124).

How To Work Through Chapter 19

We recommend the following approach in dealing with the material in this Chapter:

Introduction To Trusts And Estate Planning
❏ Read paragraph 19-1 to 19-7 (in the textbook).

Basic Concepts
❏ Read paragraph 19-8 to 19-19.

Establishing A Trust
❏ Read paragraph 19-20 to 19-23.
❏ Do Exercise Nineteen-1 (in the textbook) and check the solution on page S-417 in this Study Guide.

Returns And Payments - Trusts
❏ Read paragraph 19-24 to 19-25.

Non-Tax Reasons For Using Trusts
❏ Read paragraph 19-26 to 19-27.

Classification Of Trusts (Personal, Testamentary And Inter Vivos)
❏ Read paragraph 19-28 to 19-38.

Taxation Of Trusts - The Basic Model
❏ Read paragraph 19-39 to 19-40.
❏ Do Exercise Nineteen-2 and check the solution in this Study Guide.

Rollovers To A Trust
❏ Read paragraph 19-41 to 19-49.
❏ Do Exercise Nineteen-3 and check the solution in this Study Guide.
❏ Read paragraph 19-50 to 19-53.
❏ Do Exercise Nineteen-4 and check the solution in this Study Guide.

Rollovers To Capital Beneficiaries
❏ Read paragraph 19-54 to 19-59.

21 Year Deemed Disposition Rule
❏ Read paragraph 19-60 to 19-63.

Net Income For Tax Purposes And Taxable Income Of A Trust
❏ Read paragraph 19-64 to 19-75.
❏ Do Exercise Nineteen-5 and check the solution in this Study Guide.

Income Allocations To Beneficiaries

❑ Read paragraph 19-76 to 19-92.
❑ Do Exercise Nineteen-6 and check the solution in this Study Guide.

Allocation Of Business Income, CCA, Recapture of CCA, And Terminal Losses

❑ Read paragraph 19-93 and 19-94.
❑ Do Exercise Nineteen-7 and check the solution in this Study Guide.

Principal Residence Exemption

❑ Read paragraph 19-95.

Tax Payable Of Personal Trusts

❑ Read paragraph 19-96 to 19-111.
❑ Do Exercise Nineteen-8 and check the solution in this Study Guide.
❑ Do Self Study Problems Nineteen-1, Nineteen-2, and Nineteen-3 at the end of the text-book chapter on pages 972 and 973 and check the solutions in this Study Guide.

Income Attribution - Trusts

❑ Read paragraph 19-112 to 19-114.
❑ Do Exercise Nineteen-9 and check the solution in this Study Guide.
❑ Do Self Study Problems Nineteen-4 and Nineteen-5 and check the solutions in this Study Guide.
❑ Read paragraph 19-115 to 19-117.

Purchase Or Sale Of An Interest In A Trust

❑ Read paragraph 19-118 to 19-123.
❑ Do Exercise Nineteen-10 and check the solution in this Study Guide.

Tax Planning Using Trusts (Family, Spousal And Alter Ego Trusts)

❑ Read paragraph 19-124 to 19-131.
❑ Do Exercise Nineteen-11 and check the solution in this Study Guide.
❑ Read paragraph 19-132 to 19-136.

Estate Planning - Tax And Non-Tax Considerations

❑ Read paragraph 19-137 to 19-141.

Estate Freeze - Objectives And Techniques, Including ITA 86 Share Exchange

❑ Read paragraph 19-142 to 19-163.
❑ Do Self Study Problem Nineteen-4 and check the solution in this Study Guide.

SIFT Partnerships And Trusts

❑ Read paragraph 19-164.

To Complete This Chapter

❑ Review the Key Terms Used In This Chapter on page 970. Consult the Glossary for the meaning of any key terms you do not know.
❑ Review the Glossary Flashcards and complete the Key Terms Self-Test for the Chapter. These features can be found in two places, on your Student CD-ROM under the heading "Key Term Practice" and on the web site.
❑ Review the Learning Objectives of the Chapter found on page S-426 of this Study Guide.
❑ As a review, we recommend that you view the PowerPoint Slides for Chapter 19 that are available on your Student CD-ROM. If you do not have access to the Microsoft PowerPoint program, the PowerPoint Viewer program can be installed from the Student CD-ROM.

Solution to Chapter Nineteen Exercises

Exercise Nineteen - 1 Solution

Case A   While Mr. Black has transferred property, it is not clear that his intention was to create a trust. No trust would be created by his transfer.

Case B   Jane's "friends" cannot be considered to be an identifiable class. As a consequence, there is no certainty as to beneficiaries and no trust would be created by her transfer.

Case C   Robert's "children" would be an identifiable class. It would appear that a trust has been created.

Case D   While Suzanne has signed the agreement, it does not appear that the property has been transferred. This means that no trust has been created.

Exercise Nineteen - 2 Solution

With respect to Joanne's transfer of her securities to the trust, the transaction would be deemed to take place at fair market value. This would result in a taxable capital gain to Joanne of $10,000 [(1/2)($220,000 - $200,000)]. There would be no tax consequences to Jocelyn or the trust as a result of this transfer.

As the trust distributed all of its income during the year, none of the interest would be taxed in the trust. All of the interest would be included in Jocelyn's income and, because she is an adult, there would be no income attribution to Joanne.

Under ITA 107(2), the transfer from the trust to Jocelyn on January 1, 2014 would take place at the trust's tax cost of $220,000. There would be no tax consequences for Joanne, Jocelyn, or the trust as a result of this transfer. However, as Jocelyn's adjusted cost base is $220,000, the sale at the fair market value of $230,000 would result in a taxable capital gain of $5,000 [(1/2)($230,000 - $220,000)].

Exercise Nineteen - 3 Solution

As there is a rollover available on transfers to a qualifying spousal trust, the accrued $30,000 gain ($90,000 - $60,000) will not be recognized until her husband or the spousal trust eventually disposes of the land. The spousal trust acquires the land (a non-depreciable capital asset) at Louise's adjusted cost base of $60,000, which will be her husband's adjusted cost base if the trust transfers the asset to him personally rather than selling it.

Exercise Nineteen - 4 Solution

In Scenarios 1, 2 and 3, the settlor has a taxable capital gain of $300 [(1/2)($1,600 - $1,000)] and the adjusted cost base to the trust is the fair market value of $1,600. In Scenarios 4 to 7, there is a tax free rollover. The results can be summarized as follows:

Scenario	Taxable Capital Gain (Settlor)	Adjusted Cost Base (Trust)
1. Inter vivos trust for adult child	$300	$1,600
2. Inter vivos trust for minor child	300	1,600
3. Testamentary trust for friend	300	1,600
4. Inter vivos qualifying spousal trust	Nil	1,000
5. Testamentary qualifying spousal trust	Nil	1,000
6. Joint spousal trust	Nil	1,000
7. Alter ego trust	Nil	1,000

Solution to Chapter Nineteen Exercises

Exercise Nineteen - 5 Solution
The required calculations are as follows:

Business Income	$220,000
Preferred Beneficiary Election	(50,000)
Distributions To Other Beneficiaries	(170,000)
Designation Under ITA 104(13.1)	
Amounts Deemed Not Paid	35,000
Net Income For Tax Purposes	$ 35,000
Business Loss Carry Forward	(35,000)
Taxable Income	Nil

The preferred beneficiary election would mean that the $50,000 would be taxed in the hands of the disabled beneficiary even though the funds are retained in the trust. Since this is an inter vivos trust, without the election, the $50,000 would be taxed at the maximum rate in the trust. As the disabled beneficiary has no other source of income, the $50,000 would be subject to tax at lower rates than would be the case if it was taxed in the trust.

By designating $35,000 as amounts not paid, the trust can absorb the loss carry forward. As a result, the beneficiaries will not pay tax on this amount even though it has been distributed to them.

Exercise Nineteen - 6 Solution
The income allocation would be as follows:

	Received By Trust	Paid To Bryan	Retained By Trust
Eligible Dividends	$100,000	$ 60,000	$40,000
Non-Eligible Dividends From CCPC	30,000	30,000	Nil
Capital Gain	20,000	20,000	Nil
Totals	$150,000	$110,000	$40,000

The Net Income For Tax Purposes of the trust would be calculated as follows:

Eligible Dividends	$ 40,000
Gross Up Of Eligible Dividends At 38 Percent	15,200
Net Income For Tax Purposes - Trust	$ 55,200

The corresponding calculation for Bryan would be as follows:

Eligible Dividends	$ 60,000
Gross Up Of Eligible Dividends At 38 Percent	22,800
Non-Eligible Dividends From CCPC	30,000
Gross Up Of Non-Eligible Dividends At 25 Percent	7,500
Taxable Capital Gains [(1/2)($20,000)]	10,000
Net Income For Tax Purposes - Bryan	$130,300

Note that the non-taxable one-half of the capital gain would be received by Bryan on a tax free basis. Both the trust and Bryan will be able to deduct a federal dividend tax credit against federal Tax Payable. The tax on split income is not applicable as Bryan is over 18 years of age.

Exercise Nineteen - 7 Solution

If the property is sold in December, 2013, no CCA can be deducted. This means that the total amount of property income to be distributed to Martin and taxed in his hands is $97,000 ($32,000 of rental income, plus $65,000 of recapture). Given this distribution, the trust's Net Income For Tax Purposes will be nil.

Alternatively, if the rental property is not sold and all of the income is distributed to Martin, he will include $6,000 ($32,000 - $26,000) in his 2013 Net Income For Tax Purposes. The trust's 2013 Net Income For Tax Purposes will be nil.

Exercise Nineteen - 8 Solution

Part A   As all of its 2013 income has been distributed, there would be no Taxable Income or Tax Payable for the trust. This conclusion would not be changed if the trust was an inter vivos trust, rather than a testamentary trust.

With respect to the beneficiary's Taxable Income, it would be calculated as follows:

Eligible Dividends Received	$100,000
Gross Up At 38 Percent	38,000
Taxable Income	$138,000

Based on the preceding, the beneficiary's federal Tax Payable would be calculated as follows:

Tax On First $135,054	$28,580
Tax On Next $2,946 ($138,000 - $135,054) At 29 Percent	854
Total Tax Before Credits	$29,434
Personal Tax Credit [(15%)($11,038)]	(1,656)
Federal Dividend Tax Credit [(6/11)($38,000)]	(20,727)
Federal Tax Payable	$ 7,051

Part B   As none of the dividends are distributed by the trust, its Taxable Income would be $138,000, as calculated in Part A. Based on this, the Tax Payable for the testamentary trust would be calculated as follows:

Tax On First $135,054	$28,580
Tax On Next $2,946 ($138,000 - $135,054) At 29 Percent	854
Total Tax Before Credits (Same As Part A)	$29,434
Federal Dividend Tax Credit [(6/11)($38,000)]	(20,727)
Federal Tax Payable	$ 8,707

Notice that the difference between the Tax Payable in Part A and the Tax Payable in Part B is $1,656 ($8,707 - $7,051). This amount is equal to the basic personal tax credit.

Part C   Once again, with no distributions to the beneficiary, the trust's Taxable Income would be $138,000. Based on this, the Tax Payable for the inter vivos trust would be calculated as follows:

Tax On $138,000 At 29 Percent	$40,020
Federal Dividend Tax Credit [(6/11)($38,000)]	(20,727)
Federal Tax Payable	$19,293

As a comparison of these examples makes clear, if a trust has beneficiaries with no other sources of income, overall tax payments will be reduced by distributing eligible dividends to beneficiaries. This is particularly true in the case of inter vivos trusts. While these examples do not illustrate this possibility, the results would be similar if non-eligible dividends were involved.

Exercise Nineteen - 9 Solution

Income on the bonds is subject to the attribution rules to the extent that the income is allocated to Trevor's spouse, Carmen, and to their minor son, Mitch. This means that two-thirds of the interest will be attributed back to Trevor. With respect to the capital gain, the attribution rules do not apply on transfers to minors. This means that only Carmen's share of the gain will be attributed back to Trevor. The increase in Taxable Income for Trevor and the trust's beneficiaries are calculated as follows:

	Carmen	Mitch	Rhonda	Attributed To Trevor
Interest Income ($27,000 ÷ 3)	$9,000	$9,000	$ 9,000	
Interest Attribution To Trevor	(9,000)	(9,000)	Nil	$18,000
Taxable Capital Gain				
[(1/2)($6,000) ÷ 3]	1,000	1,000	1,000	
Capital Gain Attribution To Trevor	(1,000)	Nil	Nil	1,000
Increase In Taxable Income	Nil	$1,000	$10,000	$19,000

Exercise Nineteen - 10 Solution

With respect to Sam, he has acquired a capital interest for consideration of $190,000. This will be the adjusted cost base of the interest he has acquired.

With respect to Mehrdad, he has disposed of a capital asset for proceeds of disposition of $190,000. Since he did not purchase the interest in the trust, his adjusted cost base as usually determined would be nil. However, for this disposition, the adjusted cost base of the capital interest is the greater of nil and the cost amount as determined under ITA 108(1). The cost amount would be $125,000, one-half of the $250,000 tax cost of the assets in the trust. The result would be a taxable capital gain of $32,500 [(1/2)($190,000 - $125,000)].

The original cost of the securities of $120,000 is not relevant in these calculations as the father was taxed on the $130,000 ($250,000 - $120,000) capital gain in the year the securities were transferred.

Exercise Nineteen - 11 Solution

As Sarah's other income places her in the maximum federal tax bracket of 29 percent, her federal tax savings resulting from transferring the assets to the family trust would be $31,900 [($110,000)(29%)]. The federal tax that would be payable on the additional $55,000 received by Jerri is as follows:

Tax On First $43,561	$6,534
Tax On Additional $11,439 ($55,000 - $43,561) At 22 Percent	2,517
Tax Before Credit	$9,051
Personal Credit	(1,656)
Tax Payable - Jerri	$7,395

The alternative minimum tax is not relevant for Jerri because the income is in the form of interest, not dividends. As Mark would be in a position to use all of his tax credits prior to receiving the additional $55,000 in income, they are not relevant to the determination of his marginal increase in taxes. The federal tax that would be payable on the additional $55,000 received by Mark is as follows:

Tax At 22 Percent ($87,123 - $45,000 = $42,123 @ 22%)	$9,267
Tax At 26 Percent ($55,000 + $45,000 - $87,123 = $12,877 @ 26%)	3,348
Additional Tax Payable - Mark	$12,615

The total tax paid by the two children would be $20,010 ($7,395 + $12,615). This is $11,890 ($31,900 - $20,010) per year less than the amount that would be paid by Sarah without the trust. When combined with a reduction in provincial taxes, the total tax savings could be significantly larger. This should be more than enough to cover the costs of establishing and maintaining this trust.

One tax planning consideration would be to have the trust pay Mark's wife rather than Mark. Since she has no income, her federal tax payable would be the same as in Jerri's calculation. Although Mark would lose the spousal credit in this case, his wife would claim the basic personal credit herself. Despite the fact that having Mark's wife as the beneficiary would result in less taxes being paid, whether this would be advantageous for Mark (and his mother) would also depend on non-tax considerations such as the state of the marriage.

Self Study Solution Nineteen - 1

Part A - Taxable Income For The Trust And Its Beneficiaries

The allocations required by the trust agreement and the Net Income For Tax Purposes and Taxable Income can be calculated as follows:

	Daughter (30%)	Son (50%)	Trust (20%)
Canadian Dividends Received	$26,100	$43,500	$17,400
Gross Up Of 38 Percent	9,918	16,530	6,612
British Interest (Gross Amount Of $110,000)	33,000	55,000	22,000
Net Rental Income ($21,000)	6,300	10,500	4,200
Net And Taxable Income	$75,318	$125,530	$50,212
British Taxes Paid* ($16,500)	$ 4,950	$ 8,250	$ 3,300

*The net interest receipt of $93,500 equals 85 percent of $110,000. This means that the taxes withheld totaled $16,500.

Part B - Federal Tax Payable For The Trust

Income that remains in a testamentary trust is taxed using the same rates as would be applicable to an individual. However, the trust would not be able to claim personal tax credits under ITA 118 to reduce the amount of Tax Payable.

Federal Tax Payable for the trust would be calculated as follows:

Federal Tax Payable:	
On First $43,561	$6,534
On Remaining $6,651 ($50,212 - $43,561) At 22 Percent	1,463
Federal Tax Payable Before Credits	$7,997
Federal Dividend Tax Credit [(6/11)($6,612)]	(3,607)
Foreign Tax Credit (See Note)	(3,300)
Federal Tax Payable	$1,090

Note The amount that can be deducted for the foreign tax credit is the lesser of the amount of foreign taxes withheld and an amount determined by the following formula:

[(Foreign Non-Business Income ÷ Adjusted Net Income)(Tax Payable Before Credits)]

= [($22,000 ÷ $50,212)($8,057)]

= $3,530

As this amount is more than the actual foreign taxes of $3,300 allocated to the trust, the actual foreign taxes paid would be the lesser amount, and would be the foreign tax credit.

You should also note that, if the foreign taxes had exceeded 15 percent of the gross amount of foreign income, the excess would have been available as a deduction under ITA 20(11), rather than as an additional amount of tax credit.

Self Study Solution Nineteen - 2

Part A - Case One

The following income allocation retains one-half of the dividend income in the trust:

Income Allocation	Trust	Spouse	Son
Business Income	$ Nil	$12,000	$ 8,000
Interest	Nil	1,800	1,200
Non-Eligible Dividends Received	25,000	15,000	10,000
Dividend Gross Up (25%)	6,250	3,750	2,500
Net Rental Income (Note)	Nil	2,400	1,600
Net Income And Taxable Income	$31,250	$34,950	$23,300
Federal Income Tax At 15 Percent	$ 4,688	$5,243	$ 3,495
Basic Personal Credit	N/A	(1,656)	(1,656)
Federal Dividend Tax Credit [(2/3)(Gross Up)]	(4,167)	(2,500)	(1,667)
Federal Tax Payable	$ 521	$1,087	$ 172

Note The $4,000 net rental income is calculated as the rent receipts of $12,000, less the operating expenses of $6,000 and CCA of $2,000. The CCA is claimed at the trust level.

Part A - Case Two

The following income allocation assumes that all of the trust's income will be allocated to Mrs. Rowand and Roger. This means that the Taxable Income and federal Tax Payable of the trust will be nil. The calculations for Mrs. Rowand and Roger are as follows:

Income Allocation	Spouse	Son
Business Income	$12,000	$ 8,000
Interest	1,800	1,200
Dividends	30,000	20,000
Dividend Gross Up (25%)	7,500	5,000
Net Rental Income	2,400	1,600
Net And Taxable Income	$53,700	$35,800

Federal Income Tax:
Son: [(15%)($35,800)] $5,370
Spouse: On First $43,561 At 15 Percent $6,534
Spouse: On Remaining $10,139
($53,700 - $43,561) At 22 Percent   2,231
Basic Personal Credit   (1,656)   (1,656)
Federal Dividend Tax Credit [(2/3)(Gross Up)]   (5,000)   (3,333)

Federal Tax Payable $2,109 $ 381

Part B
The total federal Tax Payable in Case Two is $2,490 ($2,109 + $381), which is $710 higher than the total of $1,780 ($521 + $1,087 + $172) in Case One. This difference reflects the fact that in Case Two, $10,139 of the total income was taxed at 22 percent, while in Case One, all of the income was taxed at 15 percent [(22% - 15%)($10,139) = $710].

Self Study Solution Nineteen - 3

Part A - Calculation Of Taxable Income
All amounts are allocated 30 percent to Malcolm, 50 percent to Maisy, and 20 percent to the trust. The Taxable Income of the two beneficiaries and the trust would be calculated as follows:

	Malcolm (30%)	Maisy (50%)	Trust (20%)
Interest On Government Bonds	$ 19,500	$ 32,500	$ 13,000
Eligible Dividends Received	75,000	125,000	50,000
Gross Up Of 38 Percent	28,500	47,500	19,000
Taxable Capital Gain On Land [(1/2)($2,300,000 - $1,430,000)]	130,500	217,500	87,000
Taxable Capital Gain On Building [(1/2)($4,560,000 - $3,840,000)]	108,000	180,000	72,000
Net Rental Income (Note)	183,000	305,000	122,000
Net And Taxable Income	$544,500	$907,500	$363,000

Note The net rental income, including the recapture of CCA, can be calculated as follows:

Revenues From Rental Property		$492,000
Cash Expenses On Rental Property		(342,000)
Recapture Of CCA:		
Capital Cost Of The Building	$3,840,000	
UCC	(3,380,000)	460,000
Net Rental Income, Including Recapture		$610,000

Part B - Tax Payable For The Trust
The federal Tax Payable for the trust is as follows:

Federal Tax Before Credits [(29%)($363,000)]	$105,270
Federal Dividend Tax Credit [(6/11)($19,000)]	(10,364)
Federal Tax Payable	$ 94,906

As this trust is an inter vivos trust, all of its income is subject to federal tax at 29 percent [ITA 122(1)].

Part C - Dealing With The 21 Year Deemed Disposition Rule

The 21 year deemed disposition rule will have no effect on the trust or beneficiaries in 2013. It will necessitate a deemed disposition of any capital properties still held by the trust in 11 years. To defer the recognition of capital gains, assets with significant accrued gains should be transferred to the children before the trust has been in existence for 21 years.

Self Study Solution Nineteen - 4

A. It is an inter vivos trust. In less technical terms, it could also be described as a family trust in that all of the beneficiaries are family members. In addition, it could be referred to as partially discretionary in that the trustee determines the timing of the income payments.

B. As the trust is an inter vivos trust, the year end will have to be December 31 of each year.

C. All of the income that is allocated to Mr. Dion will be subject to the income attribution rules. As a consequence, it will be included in the Net Income For Tax Purposes of Mrs. Dion. This includes interest, dividends, and capital gains earned by the trust.

   As the twins are over the age of 17, the attribution rules will not apply to their share of the trust's income. This means that the income that is allocated to them will be reported as a part of their Net Income For Tax Purposes.

   As all of the trust's income is either attributed back to Mrs. Dion or allocated to beneficiaries, the trust's Net Income For Tax Purposes will be nil.

D. The answer here will depend on the terms of the loan to the trust as the rules for non-arm's length loans apply. If it is an interest free loan, the results will be the same as in Part C. That is, the income allocated to Mr. Dion will be attributed back to Mrs. Dion, while the income allocated to the twins will be included in their Net Income For Tax Purposes. This would also be the result if the interest rate on the loan was less than the prescribed rate.

   Alternatively, if the loan paid interest at the prescribed rate or higher, the income attribution rules would not apply and the trust income allocated to Mr. Dion would be taxed in his hands. Note that the loan would have to have bona fide repayment terms and the interest would have to be paid within 30 days of the end of each calendar year.

E. ITA 74.5(3) indicates that the income attribution rules do not apply to any income or loss from property that relates to the period throughout which the individuals are living separate and apart because of a breakdown of their marriage or common-law partnership.

Self Study Solution Nineteen - 5

Part A - Trust For Daughter

The first trust created is a testamentary trust for the benefit of Mrs. Turner's daughter, Melanie. When there is a transfer of assets at death to any taxpayer other than a spouse or a spousal trust, there is a deemed disposition with proceeds equal to fair market value. Capital gains on all of the assets transferred would need to be realized along with recapture of CCA on the warehouse building.

The principal residence exemption could be used to eliminate the $165,000 [($120,000 - $20,000) + ($145,000 - $80,000)] capital gain on the principal residence. Melanie will not have a taxable benefit from use of the residence. However, since the trust pays for the upkeep and maintenance of the residence, the trust can deduct the costs and they are taxable as income to Melanie.

The capital gain and recapture on the disposition of the warehouse building would be included in Mrs. Turner's final tax return. The taxable capital gain on the warehouse land is $10,000 [(1/2)($75,000 - $55,000)]. As the fair market value of the warehouse is equal to its capital cost, there is no capital gain on the warehouse building. However, there would be $40,000 ($85,000 - $45,000) of recaptured CCA. This amount would be included in Mrs. Turner's final tax return.

The trust will be deemed to acquire all of the assets at their fair market values. In the case of the warehouse land, the adjusted cost base will be the fair market value of $75,000. In the case of the warehouse building, the capital cost and the new UCC will be the fair market value of $85,000 which is equal to its original cost.

Part A - Trust For Husband

The second trust appears to be a qualifying spousal trust. Where there is a transfer at death to a qualifying spousal trust, the transfer is deemed to be a disposition with proceeds equal to the deceased taxpayer's tax cost. This would be the capital cost of the cottage and stock portfolio and, as a consequence of using this value, the transfer of assets to the trust will have no tax consequences for Mrs. Turner's final tax return.

The trust will be deemed to have acquired all of the assets at the same capital cost values that were used as proceeds of disposition by Mrs. Turner.

Part B - Death Of Husband

Unless Mr. West has remarried with great haste and can pass these assets on to a new spouse or qualifying spousal trust, his death will result in a deemed disposition of the trust's assets for proceeds equal to fair market value. In the case of the cottage, there is a capital gain of $170,000 [($200,000 - $40,000) + ($122,000 - $112,000)], one-half, or $85,000 of which is taxable. On the stock market portfolio there will be a taxable capital gain of $30,000 [(1/2)($280,000 - $220,000)].

Chapter 19 Learning Objectives

After completing Chapter 19, you should be able to:
1. Explain the basic concepts of trusts (paragraph [P hereafter] 19-1 to 19-15).
2. Explain the difference between a trust and an estate (P 19-16 to 19-19).
3. Describe the procedures required to establish a trust (P 19-20 to 19-23).
4. Describe the procedures applicable to the filing of trust tax and information returns (P 19-24 to 19-25).
5. List the major non-tax reasons for using trusts (P 19-26 and 19-27).
6. Describe the different classifications of trusts (P 19-28 to 19-38).
7. Explain the basic model for the taxation of trusts (P 19-39 and 19-40).
8. Describe the rollovers available for contributions to a trust (P 19-41 to 19-53).
9. Describe the rollovers available to transfer assets to the capital beneficiaries of a trust (P 19-54 to 19-59).
10. Apply the 21 year deemed disposition rule (P 19-60 to 19-63).
11. Calculate the Net Income For Tax Purposes and Taxable Income of a trust (P 19-64 to 19-75).
12. Describe the provisions relating to income allocations to beneficiaries (P 19-76 to 19-95).
13. Calculate the Tax Payable for testamentary and inter vivos trusts (P 19-96 to 19-111).
14. Explain how the income attribution rules may be applicable to trusts and describe any related tax planning considerations (P 19-112 to 19-117).
15. Explain the tax treatment of the purchase and sale of an interest in a trust (P 19-118 to 19-123).
16. Describe the major tax planning factors that should be considered when evaluating various types of trusts such as family, spousal and alter ego (P 19-124 to 19-136).
17. List the non-tax and tax considerations that should be considered in estate planning (P 19-137 to 19-141).
18. Explain the objectives of an estate freeze (P 19-142 and 19-143).
19. Describe the estate freeze techniques that do not involve rollovers (P 19-144 to 19-151).
20. Describe the application of an ITA 86(1) share exchange to implement an estate freeze (P 19-152 to 19-160).
21. List the major considerations involved in choosing between a Section 85 and Section 86 rollover when implementing an estate freeze (P 19-161 to 19-163).

CHAPTER 20

How To Work Through Chapter 20

We recommend the following approach in dealing with the material in this Chapter:

Subjects Covered In Chapter
- ❑ Read paragraph 20-1 to 20-5 (in the textbook).

Residence Of Individuals, Including Part Year, Sojourner, And Deemed Residents
- ❑ Read paragraph 20-6 to 20-13.
- ❑ Do Exercise Twenty-1 (in the textbook) and check the solution on page S-428 in this Study Guide.
- ❑ Read paragraph 20-14 to 20-18.
- ❑ Do Exercise Twenty-2 and check the solution in this Study Guide.
- ❑ Read paragraph 20-19 and 20-20.
- ❑ Do Exercises Twenty-3 and Twenty-4 and check the solutions in this Study Guide.
- ❑ Read paragraph 20-21 to 20-27.
- ❑ Do Exercise Twenty-5 and check the solution in this Study Guide.

Individuals With Dual Residency
- ❑ Read paragraph 20-28 to 20-31.
- ❑ Do Exercise Twenty-6 and check the solution in this Study Guide.
- ❑ Read paragraph 20-32 to 20-34.
- ❑ Do Self Study Problems Twenty-1, Twenty-2, and Twenty-3 on pages 1,020 and 1,021 at the end of Chapter 20 in your text. Check the solutions in this Study Guide.

Residence Of Corporations
- ❑ Read paragraph 20-35 to 20-41.
- ❑ Do Exercises Twenty-7 to Twenty-9 and check the solutions in this Study Guide.
- ❑ Do Self Study Problems Twenty-4 and Twenty-5 and check the solutions in this Study Guide.

Residence Of Trusts
- ❑ Read paragraph 20-42 to 20-44.

Part I Tax On Non-Residents - Introduction
- ❑ Read paragraph 20-45 to 20-53.

Non-Residents Carrying On Business In Canada - Part I Tax
- ❑ Read paragraph 20-54 to 20-59.
- ❑ Do Exercise Twenty-10 and check the solution in this Study Guide.

Non-Residents Earning Employment Income In Canada - Part I Tax
❑ Read paragraph 20-60 to 20-64.
❑ Do Exercises Twenty-11 and Twenty-12 and check the solutions in this Study Guide.

Non-Residents Disposing Of Taxable Canadian Property - Part I Tax
❑ Read paragraph 20-65 to 20-69.
❑ Do Exercise Twenty-13 and check the solution in this Study Guide.
❑ Do Self Study Problem Twenty-6 and check the solution in this Study Guide.

Part XIII Tax On Non-Residents - Introduction And Applicability
❑ Read paragraph 20-70 to 20-76.

Part XIII Tax On Interest Income Earned By Non-Residents
❑ Read paragraph 20-77 to 20-80.
❑ Do Exercise Twenty-14 and check the solution in this Study Guide.

Part XIII Tax On Dividend, Royalty And Rental Income Earned By Non-Residents
❑ Read paragraph 20-81 to 20-91.
❑ Do Exercise Twenty-15 and check the solution in this Study Guide.

Part XIII Tax On Pension And Other Benefits Earned By Non-Residents
❑ Read paragraph 20-92 to 20-101.
❑ Do Self Study Problem Twenty-7 and check the solution in this Study Guide.

Entering Canada - Immigration
❑ Read paragraph 20-102 to 20-104.

Departing From Canada - Emigration
❑ Read paragraph 20-105.
❑ Do Exercises Twenty-16 and Twenty-17 and check the solutions in this Study Guide.
❑ Read paragraph 20-106 to 20-113.
❑ Do Exercise Twenty-18 and check the solution in this Study Guide.
❑ Read paragraph 20-114 to 20-118.
❑ Do Self Study Problem Twenty-8 and check the solution in this Study Guide.
❑ Read paragraph 20-119 to 20-127.
❑ Do Exercise Twenty-19 and check the solution in this Study Guide.

Foreign Source Income Of Residents - Introduction
❑ Read paragraph 20-128 to 20-131.

Foreign Source Income Of Residents - Reporting Requirements
❑ Read paragraph 20-132 to 20-137.
❑ Do Exercise Twenty-20 and check the solution in this Study Guide.
❑ Do Self Study Problem Twenty-9 and check the solution in this Study Guide.

Foreign Source Employment Income Of Residents
❑ Read paragraph 20-138 to 20-139.
❑ Do Self Study Problem Twenty-10 and check the solution in this Study Guide.

Foreign Source Business Income Of Residents
❑ Read paragraph 20-140 to 20-142.

Foreign Source Interest Income Of Residents
❑ Read paragraph 20-143 and 20-144.
❑ Do Exercise Twenty-21 and check the solution in this Study Guide.

Foreign Source Capital Gains Of Residents
❏ Read paragraph 20-145 and 20-146.

Foreign Source Dividend Income Of Residents - Including From Foreign Affiliates And FAPI
❏ Read paragraph 20-147 and 20-159.
❏ Do Self Study Problem Twenty-11 and check the solution in this Study Guide.
❏ Read paragraph 20-160 to 20-164.
❏ Do Exercise Twenty-22 and check the solution in this Study Guide.
❏ Read paragraph 20-165 to 20-190.
❏ Do Exercise Twenty-23 and check the solution in this Study Guide.
❏ Read paragraph 20-191 and 20-192.
❏ Do Exercise Twenty-24 and check the solution in this Study Guide.
❏ Do Self Study Problem Twenty-12 and check the solution in this Study Guide.

To Complete This Chapter
❏ Review the Key Terms Used In This Chapter on page 1018 of your text. Consult the Glossary for the meaning of any key terms you do not know.
❏ Review the Glossary Flashcards and complete the Key Terms Self-Test for the Chapter. These features can be found in two places, on your Student CD-ROM under the heading "Key Term Practice" and on the web site.
❏ Review the Learning Objectives of the Chapter found on page S-442 of this Study Guide.
❏ As a review, we recommend that you view the PowerPoint Slides for Chapter 20 that are available on your Student CD-ROM. If you do not have access to the Microsoft PowerPoint program, the PowerPoint Viewer program can be installed from the Student CD-ROM.

Solution to Chapter Twenty Exercises

Exercise Twenty - 1 Solution
While the situation is not completely clear, it is likely that the CRA would conclude that Simon is no longer a Canadian resident. By retaining his residence, he has maintained one of the primary residential ties. However, the fact that he was not able to sell the property, accompanied by the long-term lease to a third party would probably be sufficient evidence that this is not a significant residential tie. The retention of his membership in the Ontario Institute Of Chartered Accountants would be viewed as a secondary residential tie. However, S5-F1-C1 indicates that it would be unusual for a single secondary tie to be sufficient for an individual to be considered a Canadian resident.

Exercise Twenty - 2 Solution
Jane did, in fact, sever most of her residential ties with Canada. This would suggest that she would not be considered a Canadian resident during the 26 months that she worked in Florida. However, the fact that she returned frequently to visit her boyfriend might lead the CRA to assess her on the basis of being a Canadian resident during this period, but it is not clear that such an assessment would be successful.

Exercise Twenty - 3 Solution
Mark would be taxed on his worldwide income for the part of the year that he was resident in Canada. This would be the period January 1 through June 15, the date that his wife and children fly to the U.S. June 15 would be latest of: the date that Mark leaves Canada (February 1), the date that Mark establishes U.S. residency (February 1), and the date that his wife and children depart Canada (June 15). It is unlikely that the fact that his house was not sold until a later date would influence his residence status.

Exercise Twenty - 4 Solution

Mr. Kirsh will be a part year resident and liable for Canadian taxes on his worldwide income, including any income on the U.S. bank accounts, for the period September 1 through December 31 of the current year.

Exercise Twenty - 5 Solution

While Ms. Blakey is the child of a Canadian High Commissioner, it appears that she is no longer a dependant of this individual. It would also appear that she has income in excess of the base for the basic personal tax credit for 2013 of $11,038. As a consequence, she would not be considered a deemed resident under ITA 250(1).

Exercise Twenty - 6 Solution

Case 1 As it appears that Dizzy has a permanent home in Los Angeles, the tie-breaker rules would indicate that he is a resident of the United States. As he has been in Canada for more than 183 days in 2013, the sojourner rules might have made him a deemed Canadian resident. However, the tie-breaker rules in the international tax treaty would override this.

The boarding rooms and hotels would not be considered to be a permanent home given that Dizzy never intended to stay for a long period of time.

Case 2 As Donna was in Canada for more than 183 days in 2013, she is a deemed resident through the application of the sojourner rule, and therefore a dual resident. In applying the tie-breaker rules, the first factor that is considered is in which country the individual has a permanent home. With respect to this criteria, Donna would not be considered to have a permanent home in either country. She gave up her lease on the New York property and, given that she only planned to stay for a short period of time, the Toronto apartment would not be considered a permanent home. In the absence of a permanent home in either country, the next factor to consider would be the location of Donna's "centre of vital interests". This would appear to be the U.S. and, given this, the tie-breaker rules would make Donna a resident of the U.S. and a non-resident of Canada.

Exercise Twenty - 7 Solution

Roswell Ltd. is a U.S. resident because it was incorporated in that country. It is also a Canadian resident under the mind and management test. In such dual residency cases, the tie-breaker rule in the Canada/U.S. tax treaty indicates that the taxes will be assessed in the country of incorporation. That means that Roswell Ltd. would be subject to U.S. income taxes.

Exercise Twenty - 8 Solution

As the Company was incorporated in Canada after April 26, 1965, it would be deemed to be a Canadian resident under ITA 250(4).

Exercise Twenty - 9 Solution

Case 1 Taxco would be considered a deemed resident of Canada by ITA 250(4) since it was incorporated in Canada after April 26, 1965. Taxco would also be considered a factual resident of the U.S. since its mind and management are located there. Article IV(3) of the Canada/U.S. tax treaty however breaks the tie in favor of the place of incorporation. Taxco would therefore be considered a resident of Canada for treaty purposes.

Case 2 Junko would be considered a factual resident of Canada since its mind and management are situated in Canada. Junko would also be considered a resident of the U.S. since it was incorporated there. Article IV(3) of the Canada/U.S. tax treaty however breaks the tie in favor of the place of incorporation. Junko would therefore be considered a resident of the U.S. for treaty purposes and a non-resident of Canada.

Exercise Twenty - 10 Solution

Case 1 Jazzco is not carrying on business in Canada and would not be subject to Canadian taxes.

Case 2 Jazzco is carrying on business in Canada in a permanent establishment located in Toronto. Therefore, Jazzco is taxable in Canada under ITA 2(3) on the profits attributable to the Canadian factory.

Case 3 The tax treaty allows Canada to tax business income only if such income is attributable to a permanent establishment in Canada. The warehouse constitutes a fixed place of business regardless of whether it is owned or leased. However, since it appears to be used exclusively to maintain an inventory for delivery, under the Canada/U.S. tax treaty, it would be an excluded facility and would not be considered to be a permanent establishment. Jazzco would not be taxable under ITA 2(3) on its Canadian profits. The fact that the employee acts on behalf of the non-resident employer would not alter the conclusion since the employee does not have the authority to conclude contracts.

Case 4 In this Case, because the employee has authority to conclude contracts on behalf of a non-resident enterprise, the employee is deemed to be a permanent establishment. This means that Jazzco is taxable Canada under ITA 2(3) on its business profits attributable to the permanent establishment (i.e., the employee).

Case 5 Since the warehouse is not used exclusively for maintaining an inventory, the permanent establishment exception in the tax treaty would not apply with the result that profits attributable to that warehouse would be taxable in Canada.

Exercise Twenty - 11 Solution
Dawn is an individual who has become a resident of another country, but continues to receive remuneration from a resident Canadian taxpayer. Given that the tax treaty exempts her salary from taxation in Egypt, ITA 115(2) deems her to be employed in Canada and, as a consequence, she would be subject to Canadian taxes on her salary.

Exercise Twenty - 12 Solution
Case 1 The employment income is taxable in Canada. The Canada/U.S. tax treaty allows Canada to tax employment income earned in Canada unless either of two exceptions is applicable. The first exception is the $10,000 rule. This exception however does not apply since David earned $11,200 Canadian in 2013 [($2,800)(4 months)]. The second exception is the 183 day rule. Although David was in Canada for only 122 days during 2013 and therefore met the first part of the test, he failed the remaining part of the test since the employer was a Canadian resident and could deduct the payments.

Case 2 The employment income is not taxable in Canada. The 183 day rule exempts the income from Canadian taxation because the employer was not resident in Canada, did not have a permanent establishment in Canada, and could not deduct the payments for Canadian tax purposes.

Case 3 The employment income is taxable in Canada. The Canada/U.S. tax treaty would exempt the income from Canadian tax if the amount was less than $10,000 Canadian, or if Sandra spent less than 183 days in Canada in any 12 month period beginning or ending in 2013. As she earned $50,000 Canadian and spent 238 days at her job in Canada, neither of these exceptions are applicable.

Exercise Twenty - 13 Solution
Case 1 Nancy is not taxable on the gain. As a non-resident, Nancy is only taxable in Canada on the disposition of taxable Canadian property. Shares of a resident public company are only taxable Canadian property if Nancy had owned more than 25 percent of the issued shares of any class of the company in the 60 months preceding the disposition.

Case 2 Joe is taxable on the gain. The condo is taxable Canadian property since it is real property (e.g. land and buildings) situated in Canada. The Canada/U.S. tax treaty gives Canada the right to tax such gains. The property is not exempt from Canadian tax as a principal residence since Joe did not acquire the condo for his own habitation.

Case 3 Joe would be taxable on the gain on the shares. Shares of an unlisted corporation are taxable Canadian property if at any time within the preceding 60 months more than 50 percent of the fair market value of the company is derived from Canadian real property. In addition, the Canada/U.S. tax treaty allows Canada to tax the gain on the disposition of shares if the corporation is resident in Canada and the value of the shares is derived principally from real property situated in Canada.

Case 4 Joe would not be taxable on the gain on the shares. The shares are taxable Canadian property because they represent shares of an unlisted non-resident corporation that, at some time in the 60 months preceding the disposition, derived more than 50 percent of their value from taxable Canadian property. However, the Canada/U.S. tax treaty does not list this as one of the items where Canada is allowed to tax U.S. residents.

Exercise Twenty - 14 Solution
Case 1 As Jason is at arm's length from the bank and the interest is not participating debt interest, he would not be subject to Part XIII tax.

Case 2 As Janice is at arm's length with the Canadian government and the interest is not participating debt interest, the interest would not be subject to Part XIII tax. Note that interest on Canada Savings Bonds is fully exempt interest, but this fact does not affect the result in this case.

Case 3 As Julian is at arm's length from the bank and the interest is not participating debt interest, he would not have to withhold Part XIII tax.

Case 4 The Canada/U.S. tax treaty exempts U.S. residents from Part XIII tax. This means that Jasmine does not have to withhold Part XIII tax despite the fact that her brother is a non-arm's length party.

Exercise Twenty - 15 Solution
Case 1 Rentco appears to be carrying on business in Canada through a permanent establishment. As a result, no Part XIII tax is payable. However, Rentco would be subject to Part I tax on its income attributable to the permanent establishment in Saskatchewan.

Case 2 Jack would be subject to Part XIII tax of $10,500 [(25%)($42,000)]. This represents an effective tax rate of 37.5 percent on his net rental income of $28,000. Alternatively, Jack could elect under ITA 216 to be taxed under Part I on the net rental income of $28,000 ($42,000 - $14,000). Whether this is would be a good alternative depends on Jack's marginal tax rate. The break-even rate would be 37.5 percent ($10,500 ÷ $28,000). If his marginal rate is below this, taxation under Part I would be the better alternative. If his marginal rate exceeds 37.5 percent, taxation under Part XIII would be preferable.

Case 3 Jack would be subject to Part XIII tax on the gross rents received for the boats unless he would be considered to be carrying on a business. However, the Canada/U.S. tax treaty reduces the withholding tax to 10 percent of the gross rents received, or $800. Note that Jack would not be eligible to elect under ITA 216 to be taxed under Part I on the boat rents, since this election is generally restricted to real property.

Exercise Twenty - 16 Solution
There would be a deemed disposition on her departure, leaving her liable for the taxes on a $10,500 [(1/2)($49,000 - $28,000)] taxable capital gain.

Exercise Twenty - 17 Solution
As real property is exempt from the deemed disposition provision contained in ITA 128.1(4)(b), there would be no tax consequences with respect to the rental property at the time of Mr. Chrysler's departure. However, real property is Taxable Canadian Property and, as a consequence, he would be liable for Canadian taxes on both recapture and capital gains resulting from a subsequent sale of the property, even though he will be a non-resident.

Exercise Twenty - 18 Solution

With respect to the shares of the Canadian private company, there would be a required deemed disposition, resulting in a taxable capital gain of $57,500 [(1/2)($235,000 - $120,000)]. In the absence of an election on the rental property, this would be the only tax consequence resulting from her departure.

However, if Ms. Lopez elects under ITA 128.1(4)(d) to have a deemed disposition on her rental property, the results will be as follows:

Deemed Proceeds Of Disposition For Land	$30,000
Adjusted Cost Base	(60,000)
Capital Gain (Loss) On Land	($30,000)

UCC Of Building		$142,000
Lesser Of:		
Capital Cost = $160,000		
Deemed Proceeds Of Disposition = $100,000		(100,000)
Terminal Loss		$42,000

The net result would be as follows:

Taxable Capital Gain On Shares	$57,500
Allowable Capital Loss On Land [(1/2)($30,000)]	(15,000)
Terminal Loss On Building	(42,000)
Net Income Inclusion	$ 500

Exercise Twenty - 19 Solution

In the absence of ITA 128.1(4)(b)(iv), there would be a deemed disposition of both the U.K. shares and the Canadian shares at the time of Mr. Brookings' departure from Canada. As it appears that he has been in Canada for less than 60 months in the last 10 years, there will be no deemed disposition of the U.K. shares that he owned prior to his arrival in Canada. There will, however, be a deemed disposition of the Canadian shares acquired during his stay in Canada. This will result in a taxable capital gain of $8,500 [(1/2)($92,000 - $75,000)].

There will be no deemed disposition of the vacant Canadian land because real property is exempt from the deemed disposition requirement of ITA 128.1(4)(b). Note, however, that vacant land is Taxable Canadian Property. This means that any gain resulting from its disposition will be subject to Canadian taxes, without regard to whether the vendor is a Canadian resident.

Exercise Twenty - 20 Solution

Simon's total foreign investments of £85,000 (£40,000 + £45,000) push him over the $100,000 Canadian reporting limit [(£85,000)($1.55) = $131,750]. Therefore, he should report foreign investments held during the year by filing Form T1135. He is also required to report any foreign interest income that he earns on the same form.

Exercise Twenty - 21 Solution

Since there is no permanent establishment in the U.S., the income will be taxed in Canada. Jason's foreign business income tax credit is $1,800, the lesser of the $1,800 foreign tax withheld and $3,780 [($18,000 ÷ $100,000)($21,000)].

The required solution would be as follows:

Foreign Business Income Received ($18,000 - $1,800)	$16,200
Foreign Tax Withheld	1,800
Gross Income = Taxable Income Inclusion	$18,000

Canadian Tax Payable [(44%)($18,000)]	$ 7,920
Foreign Tax Credit = Foreign Tax Withheld	(1,800)
Net Canadian Tax Payable	$ 6,120
Foreign Tax Withheld	1,800
Total Taxes Payable	$ 7,920

Based on these figures, his after tax retention and overall tax rate on his foreign source income would be as follows:

| After Tax Retention ($18,000 - $7,920) | $10,080 |

| Overall Tax Rate ($7,920 ÷ $18,000) | 44% |

Exercise Twenty - 22 Solution

Forco 1   Canvest has the required 1 percent investment and, with its related subsidiary, has the required 10 percent investment. Forco 1 is a foreign affiliate.

Forco 2   Canvest has the required 1 percent investment. However, as it is not related to any of the other shareholders, the 10 percent test is not met. This means that Forco 2 is not a foreign affiliate.

Forco 3   Canvest has the required 1 percent investment and, with the controlling shareholder's spouse (a related person), has the required 10 percent investment. Forco 3 is a foreign affiliate.

Exercise Twenty - 23 Solution

Since Forco is a controlled foreign affiliate of Canco, Canco must accrue its proportionate share (100%) of Forco's investment income. The required calculations are as follows:

FAPI [ITA 91(1)]	$100,000
Deduct Lesser Of:	
• FAPI = $100,000	
• ITA 91(4) Deduction [(4)(18%)($100,000)]	(72,000)
Net Addition To Net Income For Tax Purposes	$ 28,000

Exercise Twenty - 24 Solution

Foreign Source Dividend – ITA 90(1)	$82,000
Deduct Lesser Of:	
• Previous FAPI After ITA 91(4) Deduction = $28,000	
• Dividend Received = $82,000	(28,000)
Net Addition To Net Income For Tax Purposes	$54,000

Note that the additions to Net Income For Tax Purposes for the two years total $82,000 ($28,000 + $54,000). Had there been any withholding taxes on the dividend, they would not have been eligible for a foreign tax credit.

Self Study Solution Twenty - 1

S5-F1-C1 indicates that, in general, the CRA will view an individual as becoming a non-resident on the latest of three dates:

- The date the individual leaves Canada.
- The date the individual's spouse or common-law partner and dependants leave Canada.
- The date the individual becomes a resident of another country.

As Paul's wife and daughter did not leave Canada, it would appear that the CRA would take the position that Paul did not stop being a resident of Canada.

As he purchased a house in the U.S., it is possible that he will also be viewed as a resident of that jurisdiction. If this is the case, the tie breaker rules that are contained in the tax treaty between Canada and the U.S. tax treaty must be applied. As Paul has a permanent home available in both locations, we need to apply the center of vital interests criterion. The personal ties appear to be stronger in Canada, so it is likely that the CRA would conclude that the center of vital interests is Canada. Given this, Paul would not be considered to be resident in the U.S.

Based on this conclusion, Paul should report his worldwide income in Canada, and claim a foreign tax credit for any U.S. tax paid on his employment income while he was living and working in the U.S.

Self Study Solution Twenty - 2

Mr. Aiken And Mr. Baker

Assuming that their respective moves were permanent in nature, both Mr. Aiken and Mr. Baker would be treated as part year residents. This means that they would be considered residents of Canada only for that portion of the year that they were actually in Canada. As a result, they will be liable for Canadian taxes only for a part of the current year. The prorating of deductions and credits are determined in accordance with ITA 114 and ITA 118.91.

Mr. Chase

While Mr. Chase was in Canada for the same number of days as the other individuals, the fact that he was present only on a temporary basis makes him subject to the sojourning rule. Under this rule [see ITA 250(1)(a)], he will be considered a resident for the full year if he sojourns in Canada for 183 days or more during any calendar year. As Mr. Chase was present for 192 days, he would be viewed as a Canadian resident throughout the year.

However, as he appears to also be a resident of the U.S., his dual residency status would be resolved by the tie-breaker rules in the Canada/U.S. tax treaty. As he only has a permanent home in the U.S., the tie breaker rules would deem Mr. Chase not to be a resident of Canada. This means that he would be taxed in the U.S.

Self Study Solution Twenty - 3

A. Jane Smith would be deemed a Canadian resident because she is a dependent child of a Canadian ambassador [ITA 250(1)(f)].

B. Marvin Black would not be considered a resident of Canada as he does not live in Canada. He would not be a deemed resident as S5-F1-C1 makes it clear that days spent commuting to Canada to earn employment income do not count as sojourning in Canada. However, he would be subject to Canadian taxation on the employment income earned in Canada [ITA 2(3)(a)].

C. John Leather would be considered a resident of Canada for the part of the year until September 12. As his presence in Canada during the first part of the year was not on a part time basis, he would not fall under the sojourning rules.

D. Members of the Canadian armed forces are deemed to be Canadian residents without regard to where they actually live. As Francine Donaire is exempt from French taxation due to her relationship to a deemed resident, she is a deemed resident of Canada [ITA 250(1)(g)].

E. More information would be required here. Robert would either be a part year resident of Canada or, alternatively, a non-resident earning employment income in Canada, depending on the nature of his stay in the country. If he, in fact, established residential ties in Canada, it is possible that he would be viewed as a resident during his short stay. The importance of this is that, under this interpretation of the facts, he would be subject to Canadian income tax on his worldwide income, not just his Canadian employment income.

F. The fact that Susan Allen is a Canadian citizen is irrelevant to the determination of residency. Since she appears to have no residential ties with Canada, she would not be considered a Canadian resident.

Self Study Solution Twenty - 4

A. As AMT Ltd. was incorporated prior to April 27, 1965, it is not automatically considered to be a resident of Canada. However, based on the fact that the mind and management was in Canada subsequent to that date, it was a resident of Canada subsequent to April 26, 1965. As a consequence, it would still be deemed a Canadian resident. [ITA 250(4)(a) and (c)]

B. UIF Inc. was not incorporated in Canada and its mind and management are not currently within Canada. Therefore, UIF Inc. would not be considered a Canadian resident.

C. BDT Ltd. would be deemed a Canadian resident. This is because it was incorporated in Canada subsequent to April 26, 1965. [ITA 250(4)(a)]

D. While QRS Inc. was not incorporated in Canada, it would appear that its mind and management are located in Ontario. This would result in QRS Inc. being treated as a Canadian resident.

Self Study Solution Twenty - 5

A. Molly London would be considered a part year resident of Canada until October 31, the date of her departure and would be taxed on her worldwide income for this period. As her presence in Canada during the first part of the year was on a full time basis, she would not fall under the sojourning rules.

B. Daryl Bennett would not be considered a Canadian resident. As a result, none of his income would be subject to Canadian taxes. He sojourned in Canada for less than 183 days. He would therefore not be considered a deemed resident by the sojourner rule. As his residential ties appear to be in the U.S., he would be a U.S. resident. His Canadian citizenship would not affect his residency status.

C. Tweeks Inc. would be considered resident in Canada for the full year and would be taxed on its worldwide income for the year. While Tweeks Inc. was not incorporated in Canada, it would appear that its mind and management are located in Quebec. This would result in Tweeks Inc. being treated as a Canadian resident.

D. Bordot Industries would be deemed a Canadian resident because it was incorporated in Canada subsequent to April 26, 1965 [ITA 250(4)(a)]. It would be taxed on its worldwide income for the year.

Self Study Solution Twenty - 6

Case A
Marion would be generally taxable under ITA 2(3). As her stay in Canada was less than 183 days, there is the possibility that she would be exempted from this taxation under the Canada/U.S. tax treaty. However, her employment income exceeds $10,000 and it would be deductible to her Canadian employer. Therefore, she is not exempted under the treaty and Part I tax would be applicable.

Case B
Marion would be generally taxable under ITA 2(3). However, she would be exempt under the Canada/U.S. tax treaty. She is in Canada for less than 183 days and, while her income exceeds the $10,000 threshold, it is not being deducted by a Canadian employer. This means that Part I tax would not be applicable.

Case C
The warehouse is a fixed place of business that could be viewed as a permanent establishment. However, it is used exclusively for holding inventories and, given this, it is specifically excluded from being considered a permanent establishment by the Canada/U.S. tax treaty. This means that Delcar is not carrying on business in Canada and would not be subject to Part I tax.

Case D
The warehouse is a fixed place of business that would be viewed as a permanent establishment. This would suggest the Company is earning business income in Canada and would be subject, under ITA 2(3), to Part I tax. As it is used as an office as well as a facility for holding inventories, it would not be an excluded facility under the Canada/U.S. tax treaty. Therefore, Part I tax would be applicable.

Case E
Shares of unlisted Canadian companies are viewed as Taxable Canadian Property if, within the preceding 60 months, more than 50 percent of their value is derived from Canadian real property. This means that Michael's shares would be Taxable Canadian Property and the gain would be taxable under ITA 2(3). Further, under the Canada/U.S. tax treaty, this is one of the specific types of property where gains accruing to U.S. residents are subject to Canadian tax. Therefore, Part I tax would be applicable.

Case F
Shares of unlisted companies are viewed as Taxable Canadian Property if, within the preceding 60 months, more than 50 percent of their value is derived from Canadian real property. This means that Michael's shares would be Taxable Canadian Property and the gain would generally be taxable under ITA 2(3). However, because it is not a "Canadian" corporation, it is not on the Canada/U.S. tax treaty list of Taxable Canadian Property where gains accruing to U.S. residents are subject to Canadian tax. Therefore, Michael's gain on the shares would not be taxable under ITA 2(3) and Part I tax would not be applicable.

Self Study Solution Twenty - 7

Case A
The interest she has received is not from holding participating debt and she is at arm's length with the bank. The interest would not be subject to Part XIII tax.

Case B

As the amount of interest is calculated on the basis of the corporation's revenues, it would appear that Mark is receiving interest on a participating debt security. The interest would be subject to Part XIII tax.

Case C

Because the interest is from participating debt, it would normally be subject to Part XIII tax. However, the Canada/U.S. tax treaty exempts U.S. residents from all Canadian taxation on interest income. The interest would not be subject to Part XIII tax.

Case D

As she is not a resident of a country with which Canada has a tax treaty, Darlene would be subject to Part XIII tax at a rate of 25 percent. Depending on whether she uses the available election to be taxed under Part I, the Tax Payable would be as follows:

Without Election - Part XIII [(25%)($35,000)]	$8,750
With Election - Part I [(15%)(148%)($35,000 - $27,000)]	$1,776

The use of the election is clearly desirable in this Case.

Case E

The Canada/U.S. tax treaty reduces the Part XIII rate on rental properties that are not real property from 25 to 10 percent. As Darlene is renting out real property, the 25 percent rate is applicable and the results are the same as Case D. Here again, the use of the election is clearly desirable.

Case F

Dividends from Canadian companies that are received by non-residents are subject to Part XIII tax. Under the Canada/U.S. tax treaty the statutory 25 percent rate is reduced to either 5 percent or 15 percent. Although Brian owns more than 10 percent of the voting shares of the Canadian corporation, he is an individual, not a corporation, so the applicable rate is 15 percent, not 5 percent. Brian's Part XIII tax payable would be $3,300 [(15%)($22,000)].

Self Study Solution Twenty - 8

Part A

If Holly becomes a non-resident, there will be a deemed disposition of some of her assets. The exceptions to this are her holdings of real property (home and cottage) and the "excluded right" in her RRSP. The deemed disposition of the remaining assets will result in income inclusions as follows:

Property	Fair Market Value	Capital Cost Or Adjusted Cost Base	Capital Gain
Land Rover truck (Note)	$ 15,000	$ 20,000	$ Nil
Shares in public companies	40,000	30,000	10,000
Shares in IOU Ranch Ltd, CCPC	40,000	25,000	15,000
Total Capital Gain			$25,000

Note No loss can be deducted on personal use property.

The taxable portion of this gain would be $12,500 [(1/2)($25,000)] and would have to be included in her income in the year of the departure.

Holly can pay the related tax when she files her tax return for the year of departure, but she is not obliged to pay the tax until she actually disposes of the shares [note that this deferral requires an election under ITA 220(4.5)]. Further, she is not required to post security for the estimated Tax Payable as the total taxable capital gains of $12,500 [(1/2)($25,000)] are within the $50,000 exemption.

With respect to the remaining assets, the deferred income at the time of her departure can be calculated as follows:

Property	Fair Market Value	Capital Cost Or Adjusted Cost Base	Deferred Income
Home in Cochrane, Alberta	$500,000	$200,000	$300,000
Percentage ownership	50%	50%	50%
Holly's share	$250,000	$100,000	$150,000
Cottage on Lake Manitou	165,000	145,000	20,000
Capital Gains			$170,000
RRSP	55,000	Nil	55,000
Total Deferred Income			$225,000

With respect to the capital gains on the home and cottage, they are Taxable Canadian Property and any gain on a subsequent disposition will be subject to tax in Canada, even though Holly is no longer a Canadian resident. Assuming she does not collapse her RRSP prior to departure, these amounts will be taxed under Part XIII when they are withdrawn and remitted to Holly.

Part B

Some factors that could influence Holly's residence status include:

- Whether Holly's husband and sons are moving to Brazil with her. If yes, there is a greater chance that Holly will be considered to be a non-resident of Canada.

- Whether Holly will retain her home in Canada. If she does, it is likely that she will continue to be considered a resident unless she has a long term lease with an arm's length party.

- Whether Holly plans to sell most, or all, of her Canadian assets. If so, there is a greater chance that she will be cutting her ties with Canada, and can be considered a non-resident.

- Whether Holly is severing other personal and business ties in Canada, such as her driver's licence and health care. If yes, this would be evidence that she is has become a non-resident.

Part C

Effective tax planning points in anticipation of Holly's move to Brazil are as follows:

Principal Residence Retention of the principal residence in Cochrane may influence residency. To ensure that Holly is considered a non-resident of Canada, the principal residence should be sold before she departs from Canada. This would also allow her to designate it as her principal residence and completely eliminate the capital gain on it. Even if she does not sell it, she should consider making the ITA 128.1(4)(d) election to trigger a deemed disposition. She could then use the principal residence deduction to eliminate the capital gain and increase the adjusted cost base.

RRSP   If Holly is in a high tax bracket in the current year, the move may be deferred to next year, to take advantage of lower progressive tax rates in Canada. Then, she should assess whether the 25 percent non-resident tax on withdrawals from an RRSP would be higher than the personal tax that would apply if she were to cash in the RRSP before becoming a non-resident. She should also consider non-tax factors such as what she plans to do with the RRSP proceeds, and the investment return she can expect if she reinvests the net proceeds. It may be advantageous to simply leave the RRSP intact in Canada.

Date Of Non-Residency   If there are delays between when Holly leaves Canada and when her family leaves, the latter will likely be considered the date of cessation of residence. Any employment earnings in the intervening period will be taxable in Canada.

Moving Expenses   Any moving expenses incurred in the move to Brazil will not be tax deductible in Canada. Will the Brazilian government pay for moving expenses? If not, it may be preferable to arrange for reimbursement of moving expenses (not taxable) rather than a compensating salary, which would likely be taxable (in Canada or Brazil).

Self Study Solution Twenty - 9

A. No foreign investment reporting is required as the total amount is less than $100,000.

B. Foreign investment reporting is not required. Since the cottage is personal use property, the fact that the cost is greater than $100,000 is not relevant. The fair market value is also not relevant.

C. Foreign investment reporting is not required. The cost of the one-half of the shares in the trading account is less than $100,000 [(1/2)($112,000) = $56,000]. The current fair market price is not relevant. The shares in the RRSP would not be included as a self-directed RRSP does not have to report foreign investments.

D. No foreign investment reporting is required as the assets are used in an active business.

Self Study Solution Twenty - 10

A. Because he is a resident of Canada, the hockey player will have all US$14,000 of hockey school income subject to tax in Canada. With respect to U.S. taxation, he would not have a tax obligation in that country because his total earnings are only $7,000. The Canada/U.S. tax treaty exempts non-residents from U.S. taxation when their earnings in that country are less than $10,000.

B. Because the expert is a resident of Canada, the full $150,000 of income would be subject to tax in Canada. He would not be taxed in the U.S. because the provisions of the Canada/U.S. tax treaty exempt Canadian residents from U.S. taxation provided they are in the U.S. less than 183 days, their employer does not have a permanent establishment in the U.S., and their employer does not deduct the compensation in computing U.S. taxes. The expert was in the U.S. for only 180 days [(3)(60)], and his compensation is paid by a Canadian company.

Self Study Solution Twenty - 11

The Hispanic Ltd. tax withholding equals 25 percent ($5,750 ÷ $23,000) of the dividend paid. The Deutsch Inc. tax withholding equals 10 percent ($1,400 ÷ $14,000) of the dividend paid. As the foreign non-business tax credit is limited to 15 percent, the additional 10 percent ($2,300) withheld by Foreign Country 1 will have to be deducted in the determination of Mona's Net Income For Tax Purposes.

Net Employment Income	$ 87,000
Hispanic Ltd. Gross Dividends (No Gross Up)	23,000
Deutsch Inc. Gross Dividends (No Gross Up)	14,000
Excess Withholding [(25% - 15%)($23,000)]	(2,300)
Net Income For Tax Purposes And Taxable Income	$121,700

Using this result, her federal Tax Payable would be calculated as follows:

Tax On First $87,123		$16,118
Tax On Next $34,577 ($121,700 - $87,123 At 26%)		8,990
Tax Payable Before Credits		$25,108
Basic Personal Credit	($11,038)	
EI	(891)	
CPP	(2,356)	
Canada Employment	(1,117)	
Total Credit Amount	($15,402)	
Applicable Rate	15%	(2,310)
Tax Otherwise Payable		$22,798
Foreign Tax Credits (See Note)		
Hispanic Ltd.		(3,450)
Deutsch Inc.		(1,400)
Federal Tax Payable		$17,948

Note The foreign non-business tax credits are calculated on a country by country basis (see Chapter 11).

The tax credit on the Hispanic Ltd. shares would be the lesser of:

- Amount Withheld (Limited To 15%) = [(15%)($23,000)] = $3,450

- $\left[\dfrac{\text{Foreign Non-Business Income}}{\text{Adjusted Division B Income}} \right] (\text{Tax Otherwise Payable})$

$$= \left[\frac{\$23,000}{\$121,700} \right] (\$22,798) = \$4,309$$

The tax credit on the Deutsch Inc. shares would be the lesser of:

- Amount Withheld (Less Than 15%) = $1,400

- $\left[\dfrac{\text{Foreign Non-Business Income}}{\text{Adjusted Division B Income}} \right] (\text{Tax Otherwise Payable})$

$$= \left[\frac{\$14,000}{\$121,700} \right] (\$22,798) = \$2,623$$

Self Study Solution Twenty - 12

Alta Inc. Dividends

As BK Inc. owns more than 10 percent of the Alta Inc. shares, Alta Inc. is a foreign affiliate of BK Inc. Alta Inc. is operating in a country with which Canada has a tax treaty. In addition, all of its income is from active business activities. Given this, all of the dividend is being paid from Exempt Surplus. This means that, while the pre-withholding amount of the dividend will be included in Net Income For Tax Purposes, this amount can be deducted in full under ITA 113(1)(a).

Bolt Ltd. Dividends

While Bolt Ltd. earns all of its income through active business activities, it is not located in a country which has a tax treaty or a TIEA with Canada. Given this, the dividend will be paid from Taxable Surplus. It will be included in Net Income For Tax Purposes and not deductible under ITA 113(1)(a). However, it will be eligible for a deduction under ITA 113(1)(b) for taxes paid by Bolt Ltd. in the foreign jurisdiction, as well as a deduction under ITA 113(1)(c) for taxes withheld on the distribution to BK Inc.

Taxable Income And Tax Payable Calculation

The required calculations for Taxable Income and Tax Payable would be as follows:

Alta Inc. Dividends (Before Withholding)	$ 34,000
Bolt Ltd. Dividends (Before Withholding)	76,000
Addition To Net Income For Tax Purposes	$110,000
Deductions:	
ITA 113(1)(a) Alta Dividends	(34,000)
ITA 113(1)(b) - Note 1	(12,000)
ITA 113(1)(c) - Note 2	(45,600)
Taxable Income	$ 18,400
Rate	25%
Canadian Tax Payable	$ 4,600

Note 1 Given Bolt's local tax rate of 5 percent, the pre-tax income that formed the base for the dividend to BK Inc. was $80,000 [$76,000 ÷ (1 - 5%)]. This means that the local taxes paid by Bolt were $4,000 [(5%)($80,000)] and that the ITA 113(1)(b) deduction would be $12,000 [($4,000)(3)]. See the text for an explanation of the relevant factor of 3.

Note 2 Taxes withheld were $11,400. Given this, the ITA 113(1)(c) deduction is equal to $45,600 [($11,400)(4)]. See the text for an explanation of the relevant factor of 4.

Reconciliation

As indicated in the text, the goal here is to have foreign affiliate dividends paid from Taxable Surplus subject to total Canadian and foreign taxes at a rate of 25 percent. The preceding calculation has achieved this goal as supported by the following calculation.

Bolt's Pre-Tax Income [$76,000 ÷ (1 - 5%)]	$80,000
Rate	25%
Total Tax At 25% Rate	$20,000
Foreign Tax Paid On Bolt's Income [(5%)($80,000)]	$ 4,000
Taxes Withheld From Dividend	11,400
Canadian Tax Payable	4,600
Total Tax Paid	$20,000

Chapter 20 Learning Objectives

After completing Chapter 20, you should be able to:

1. Determine the residence of an individual based on an evaluation of primary and secondary residential ties (paragraph [P hereafter] 20-1 to 20-13).

2. Evaluate the residency status of an individual who is temporarily absent from Canada or is only resident for part of the year (P 20-14 to 20-20).

3. Identify the types of individuals who will be deemed to be Canadian residents without regard to their actual physical location (P 20-21 to 20-34).

4. Determine the residence of corporations and trusts (P 20-35 to 20-44).

5. Describe the liability for Part I tax of non-residents earning Canadian source income from business, employment and the disposition of taxable Canadian property (P 20-45 to 20-69).

6. Describe the liability for Part XIII tax of non-residents earning Canadian source property income including income from interest, dividends, royalties, rents and pensions (P 20-70 to 20-101).

7. Describe the deemed disposition/reacquisition provisions related to immigration to Canada (P 20-102 to 20-104).

8. Describe the tax provisions related to emigration from Canada, including those related to elective dispositions and security for departure tax (P 20-105 to 20-118).

9. Describe the provisions available for unwinding a deemed disposition on departure from Canada (P 20-119 to 20-124).

10. Explain the rules applicable to short-term residents of Canada (P 20-125 to 20-127).

11. Apply the appropriate tax treatment for Canadian residents of foreign source employment income, business income and capital gains (P 20-128 to 20-146).

12. Describe the basic concepts behind the taxation of foreign source dividends received by resident individuals (P 20-147 to 20-159).

13. Describe the taxation of dividends received by resident corporations from non-affiliated corporations (P 20-160).

14. Identify foreign affiliates (P 20-161 to 20-164).

15. Describe the tax treatment of dividends received from non-controlled foreign affiliates, including identification of their various types of surplus balances (P 20-165 to 20-178).

16. Explain the concept of a controlled foreign affiliate (P 20-179 to 20-182).

17. Apply the rules associated with, and the appropriate tax treatment of, foreign property accrual income (FAPI) (P 20-183 to 20-190).

18. Describe the tax treatment of dividends paid from FAPI (P 20-191 to 20-192).

CHAPTER 21

How To Work Through Chapter 21

We recommend the following approach in dealing with the material in this chapter:

Introduction To The GST/HST
❏ Read paragraph 21-1 to 21-10 (in the textbook).

The Current Situation And How We Will Deal With The Complexity
❏ Read paragraph 21-11 to 21-19.

Transaction Tax Concepts, Including VATs
❏ Read paragraph 21-20 to 21-43.
❏ Do Exercise Twenty-One-1 (in the textbook) and check the solution on page S-444 in this Study Guide.
❏ Do Self Study Problem Twenty-One-1 at the end of the textbook chapter on page 1070 and check the solution in this Study Guide.

Liability For GST/HST And The Concept Of Supply
❏ Read paragraph 21-44 to 21-48.

Supply Categories (Fully Taxable, Zero-Rated And Exempt)
❏ Read from the Note before paragraph 21-49 to 21-62.

Applying the GST/HST Rate Using the Place Of Supply Rules
❏ Read paragraph 21-63 to 21-71.

Responsibility For Collection And Remittance Of GST/HST
❏ Read paragraph 21-72 to 21-75.

Registration - Including The Small Supplier Exemption
❏ Read paragraph 21-76 to 21-90.
❏ Do Exercise Twenty-One-2 and check the solution in this Study Guide.
❏ Read paragraph 21-91 to 21-94.
❏ Do Self Study Problem Twenty-One-2 and check the solution in this Study Guide.

Input Tax Credits
❏ Read paragraph 21-95 to 21-114.
❏ Do Exercises Twenty-One-3 to Twenty-One-5 and check the solutions in this Study Guide.
❏ Do Self Study Problems Twenty-One-3 and Twenty-One-4 and check the solutions in this Study Guide.

Relief For Small Businesses (Quick Method And Streamlined ITC Method)
❑ Read paragraph 21-115 to 21-126.
❑ Do Exercises Twenty-One-6 and Twenty-One-7 and check the solutions in this Study Guide.
❑ Do Self Study Problems Twenty-One-5 and Twenty-One-6 and check the solutions in this Study Guide.
❑ Read paragraph 21-127 to 21-132.
❑ Do Exercise Twenty-One-8 and check the solution in this Study Guide.

GST/HST Procedures And Administration, Including GST/HST Returns And Payments
❑ Read paragraph 21-133 to 21-159.

Employee And Partner GST/HST Rebate
❑ Read paragraph 21-160 to 21-168.
❑ Do Self Study Problem Twenty-One-7 and check the solution in this Study Guide.

Residential Property And New Housing Rebate
❑ Read paragraph 21-169 to 21-175.
❑ Do Self Study Problems Twenty-One-8 and Twenty-One-9 and check the solutions in this Study Guide.

Sale Of A Business
❑ Read paragraph 21-176 to 21-189.

Specific Applications Including Charities, Not-For-Profits And MUSH
❑ Read paragraph 21-190 and 21-191.

Partnerships And GST/HST
❑ Read paragraph 21-192 to 21-200.

Trusts And GST/HST
❑ Read paragraph 21-201 to 21-203.

To Complete This Chapter
❑ Review the Key Terms Used In This Chapter on page 1069. Consult the Glossary for the meaning of any key terms you do not know.
❑ Review the Glossary Flashcards and complete the Key Terms Self-Test for the Chapter. These features can be found in two places, on your Student CD-ROM under the heading "Key Term Practice" and on the web site.
❑ Review the Learning Objectives of the Chapter found on page S-452 of this Study Guide.
❑ As a review, we recommend that you view the PowerPoint Slides for Chapter 21 that are available on your Student CD-ROM. If you do not have access to the Microsoft PowerPoint program, the PowerPoint Viewer program can be installed from the Student CD-ROM.

Solution to Chapter Twenty-One Exercises

Exercise Twenty-One - 1 Solution
Account Based System Under an account-based system, the 5 percent would be applied to the value added, resulting in a tax of $7,600 [(5%)($416,000 - $264,000)].

Invoice-Credit System Alternatively, under an invoice-credit system, $20,800 [(5%)($416,000)] would be owing on sales, but would be offset by an input tax credit of $11,650 [(5%)($233,000)] on purchases. The net tax owing in this case would be $9,150. The fact that the tax is larger under the invoice-credit system reflects the fact that the cost of goods sold exceeded the purchases of goods by $31,000.

Exercise Twenty-One - 2 Solution

As Ms. Salome's sales **exceed** $30,000 in the October to December, 2013 quarter, she will be required to begin collecting GST on the first sale in that quarter that exceeds the $30,000 threshold. This means she will have to begin collecting GST sometime between October 1 and December 31. She will be required to register within 30 days of that date.

As Mr. Laughton's sales **accumulate** to more than $30,000 ($8,000 + $13,000 + $4,000 + 17,000 = $42,000) by the end of the January to March, 2014 quarter, he will have to begin collecting GST on May 1, 2014 the first day of the second month following the January to March calendar quarter. He will be required to register by May 31, 2014.

Exercise Twenty-One - 3 Solution

The HST payable would be calculated as follows:

HST On Sales [(13%)($1,223,000)]	$158,990
Input Tax Credits:	
Purchases [(13%)($843,000 + $126,000)]	(125,970)
Salaries	Nil
Interest	Nil
Amortization	Nil
HST Payable For The Quarter	$ 33,020

Exercise Twenty-One - 4 Solution

The HST payable would be calculated as follows:

HST On Sales [(13%)($224,000)]	$29,120
Input Tax Credits:	
Rent [(13%)($25,800)]	(3,354)
Assistant's Salary	Nil
Capital Expenditures [(13%)($36,000 + $20,000)]	(7,280)
HST Payable For The Year	$ 18,486

Exercise Twenty-One - 5 Solution

The pro rata input tax credit for the land and building acquisition would be $24,000 [(5%)(40%)($1,200,000)]. There would be no input tax credit for the office equipment as it is used less than 50 percent for taxable supplies.

Exercise Twenty-One - 6 Solution

The purchases made do not affect the Quick Method calculation since they are non-capital. The GST payable under the Quick Method would be calculated as follows:

Basic Tax [(1.8%)(105%)($42,500)]	$803
Credit On First $30,000 [(1%)($30,000)]	(300)
GST Payable For The Quarter	$503

Exercise Twenty-One - 7 Solution

If the Quick Method is not used, the HST payable (refund) would be calculated as follows:

HST On Sales [(13%)($56,100)]	$7,293
Input Tax Credits:	
Current Expenditures [(13%)($23,400)]	(3,042)
Capital Expenditures [(13%)($42,000)]	(5,460)
HST Payable (Refund) For The Quarter - Regular Method	($1,209)

Alternatively, under the Quick Method, the calculation would be as follows:

Basic Tax [(4.4%)(113%)($56,100)]	$2,789
Credit On First $30,000 [(1%)($30,000)]	(300)
Subtotal	$2,489
Input Tax Credits:	
Current Expenditures	Nil
Capital Expenditures [(13%)($42,000)]	(5,460)
HST Payable (Refund) For The Quarter - Quick Method	($2,971)

As the Quick Method produces a larger refund, it would be the preferable method. Note that input tax credits on capital expenditures are available, even when the Quick Method is used.

Exercise Twenty-One - 8 Solution

To apply the streamlined method, we need to know the tax inclusive amounts of current expenditures (given in the problem), as well as the tax inclusive amounts of personal capital property expenditures. This latter figure is $52,500 [(105%)($50,000)]. Using the streamlined method, the GST payable (refund) would be calculated as follows:

GST Sales [(5%)($315,000 ÷ 1.05)]	$15,000
Input Tax Credits On Purchases And Personal Capital Property	
[(5/105)($189,000 + $52,500)]	(11,500)
Input Tax Credits On Real Capital Property [(5%)($150,000)]	(7,500)
GST Payable (Refund) For The Year	($ 4,000)

Self Study Solution Twenty-One - 1

GST Calculation

Under the normal GST system, an 8 percent provincial tax would be charged on the selling price at each stage and each business would get an input tax credit for the tax paid on purchased inputs. The net result is that all payments of GST by vendors are refunded as input tax credits, so there is no net out-of-pocket cost (other than administration) to vendors from the GST.

Vendor	Cost	Selling Price	GST Charged	ITC Claimed
Raw Materials Supplier		$ 200	$ 16.00	Nil
Manufacturer	$200	280	22.40	$ 16.00
Wholesaler	280	392	31.36	22.40
Retailer	392	549	43.92	31.36
Totals		$1,421	$113.68	$69.76

The net GST charged for all stages is $43.92 ($113.68 - $69.76). The consumer bears the full cost of the tax by paying GST of $43.92 [(8%)($549)] with no opportunity to get an input tax credit.

Turnover Tax Calculation

The turnover tax is similar to the GST, as it applies to revenue. However, the turnover tax is significantly different as there is no input tax credit for tax paid at each stage on purchased goods (inputs). The tax is passed on to the purchasers in the chain, resulting in pyramiding of the tax. Because of the multiple times goods get taxed, to raise the same amount of tax revenue, the turnover tax rate of 3.09 percent (as shown in the following calculation) is much lower than an 8 percent provincial GST rate.

[($200)(X%)] + [($280)(X%)] + [($392)(X%)] + [($549)(X%)] = $43.92
[($200 + $280 + $392 + $549)(X%)] = $43.92
[($1,421)(X%)] = $43.92
X% = $43.92 ÷ $1,421
X% = 3.09%

As verification, the total of the selling price in the above table is $1,421. If the rate of 3.09 percent is applied to this total (the equivalent of each stage charging a turnover tax), the total tax collected would be equivalent to $43.91 ($.01 rounding error).

Self Study Solution Twenty-One - 2

Calendar Quarter Test   Under this test, persons are required to register for the GST if taxable revenues exceed $30,000 in any single quarter. Under this test, Chantelle is not required to register.

Four Calendar Quarters Test   Under this test, persons are required to register for the GST if their taxable revenues accumulate to more than $30,000 in any four consecutive calendar quarters. In this example four quarters of sales accumulate to $36,500 ($29,000 - $4,000 + $11,500) by the end of the quarter ending December 31, 2013. As a result, Chantelle Chance is required to start collecting GST on February 1, 2014, the first day of the second month following the quarter in which the $30,000 threshold is reached. However, she has until March 2, 2014 to register (30 days after February 1, 2014).

Self Study Solution Twenty-One - 3

The GST refund for Lassen Ltd. for the current year would be calculated as follows:

GST Collected [(5%)($5,700,000 - $1,200,000 - $2,400,000)]	$105,000
Input Tax Credits:	
Purchases [(5%)($2,600,000 - $200,000)]	(120,000)
Amortization Expense	Nil
Salaries And Wages	Nil
Interest Expense	Nil
Other Expenses {[5%][$370,000 - (50%)($40,000)]}	(17,500)
Building [(5%)(40%)($3,000,000)]	(60,000)
Other Capital Expenditures	Nil
GST Payable (Refund)	($ 92,500)

Notes:

- The fact that GST is paid on all purchases is not unreasonable, despite the fact that the Company provides both zero-rated and exempt supplies to its customers. Some zero-rated supplies, for example exports, involve selling items on which GST is paid. Exempt supplies could include the provision of certain types of services for which no purchases are required.

- Amortization expense does not affect the GST calculation.

- No GST is paid on salaries and wages, or interest. As a result no input tax credits are available.

- The recovery of GST on meals and entertainment expenses is limited to 50 percent.

- Input tax credits on real property are available based on a pro rata portion of their usage in providing taxable supplies.

- No input tax credits are available on capital expenditures other than real property if less than 50 percent of their usage is in providing taxable and zero-rated supplies.

Self Study Solution Twenty-One - 4

For Part A and Part B, the HST refund for the year would be calculated as follows:

	Part A	Part B
HST Collected [(13%)($1,955,000)]	$254,150	$254,150
Input Tax Credits:		
Purchases [(13%)($1,356,000 - $212,000)]	(148,720)	(148,720)
Amortization Expense	Nil	Nil
Salaries And Wages	Nil	Nil
Interest Expense	Nil	Nil
Other Expenses [(13%)($162,000 - $5,000)]	(20,410)	(20,410)
Equipment [(13%)($725,000)]	(94,250)	Nil
Building [(13%)(($1,450,000)]	(188,500)	
[(13%)(73%)($1,450,000)]		(137,605)
HST Payable (Refund)	($197,730)	($ 52,585)

In both Part A and Part B, no input tax credit is allowed for HST paid on membership fees or dues in any club whose main purpose is to provide dining, recreational, or sporting facilities.

In Part A, input tax credits are available on both the equipment and the building because 100 percent of their usage is for taxable supplies (fully taxable and zero-rated).

In Part B, there is no input tax credit available on the equipment as it is used less than 50 percent to provide taxable supplies. The building's input tax credit is limited to 73 percent of the HST paid.

Self Study Solution Twenty-One - 5

The required GST remittance for Bombardeaux is based on Canadian GST included sales of $73,500 and is calculated as follows:

Basic Tax [(3.6%)($73,500)]	$2,646
Credit On First $30,000 [(1%)($30,000)]	(300)
Subtotal	$2,346
Input Tax Credit On Capital Expenditures [(5%)($20,000)]	(1,000)
GST Remittance	$1,346

Self Study Solution Twenty-One - 6

Part A

Using the regular calculations, the HST payable for Konzak Inc. for the current year would be calculated as follows:

HST Collected [(13%)($226,700)]		$29,471
Input Tax Credits On Current Expenditures:		
Purchases [(13%)($104,300 + $14,600)]	($15,457)	
Amortization Expense	Nil	
Salaries And Wages	Nil	
Interest Expense	Nil	
Other Operating Expenses [(13%)($41,800)]	(5,434)	(20,891)
Total Payable Before Capital Expenditures		$ 8,580
Input Tax Credits On Capital Expenditures		
[(13%)(100%)($98,310 ÷ 1.13)]		(11,310)
HST Payable (Refund)		($ 2,730)

Notes:

- Amortization expense does not affect the HST calculation.
- No HST is paid on salaries and wages, or interest. As a result no input tax credits are available.
- Full input tax credits are available on capital expenditures other than real property if more than 50 percent of their usage is to provide fully taxable supplies.

Part B

When Konzak's HST included taxable sales of $256,171 [(113%)($226,700)] are combined with the associated company's HST included taxable sales of $180,800 [(113%)($160,000)], they total $436,971. As this is greater than $400,000, neither Konzak nor the associated company is eligible to use the Quick Method.

Part C

In order to determine the Quick Method remittance rate, the following amounts are required:

2012 GST Inclusive Purchases Of Goods For Resale [($92,500)(113%)]	$104,525
2012 GST Inclusive Sales Of Taxable Supplies [($190,000)(113%)]	$214,700

Since $104,525 ÷ $214,700 equals 49 percent and this is greater than 40 percent, Konzak Inc. would use the reseller's remittance rate of 4.4 percent.

The Quick Method calculations would be as follows:

Basic Tax [(4.4%)(113%)($226,700)]	$11,272	
Credit On First $30,000 [(1%)($30,000)]	(300)	
Total Payable Before Capital Expenditures	$10,972	
Input Tax Credit On Capital Expenditures		
[(13%)(100%)($98,310 ÷ 1.13)]	(11,310)	
HST Payable (Refund)	($ 338)	

If Konzak could use the Quick Method (which it cannot), it would produce a smaller HST refund than the regular HST calculation. As a consequence, even if Konzak could use the quick method, it would not be a good choice for the company.

Self Study Solution Twenty-One - 7

The opening UCC includes the HST paid. The maximum CCA that Mr. Lord can claim for 2013 is as follows:

Opening UCC ($27,120 - $4,068)	$23,052
GST/HST Rebate Claimed On Car CCA In Preceding Year	(468)
Adjusted UCC	$22,584
Class 10 Rate	30%
Maximum CCA	$ 6,775

The 2013 employee GST/HST rebate for Mr. Lord would be calculated as follows:

Total Expenses Other Than CCA	$19,020	
GST/HST Exempt Purchases		
Interest	(2,100)	
Insurance)	(1,100)	
Eligible Expenses Other Than CCA	$15,820	
Rate	13/113	$1,820
Eligible CCA	$6,775	
Rate	13/113	779
Employee GST/HST Rebate		$2,599

Self Study Solution Twenty-One - 8

Since in all three Cases, the purchase price is less than $350,000, the new housing rebate is calculated at 36 percent of the GST paid.

Case A
To determine the total GST included in the purchase price, multiply the $200,000 price by 5/105, to arrive at the total GST amount of $9,524.

The new housing GST rebate would be $3,429 [($9,524)(36%)].

As it appears that the purchaser will be paying the GST, that individual would be entitled to the rebate.

The net GST paid would be $6,095 ($9,524 - $3,429).

Case B
The total GST that would be charged is calculated by multiplying the purchase price of $200,000 by 5 percent, to arrive at $10,000 total GST.

The new housing rebate would be $3,600 [($10,000)(36%)].

As it appears that the purchaser will be paying the GST, that individual would be entitled to the rebate.

The net GST paid would be $6,400 ($10,000 - $3,600).

Case C
Since $200,000 is equal to the price of the house including GST net of the new housing rebate, the GST excluded price can be calculated by solving the following equation for x.

$$\$200,000 = [(105\%)(x) - (36\%)(5\%)(x)]$$

The GST excluded price of the new house would be $193,798 {$200,000 ÷ [105% - (36%)(5%)]}. The total GST amount is $9,690 [($193,798)(5%)].

The new housing rebate would be $3,488 [($9,690)(36%)].

A verification of these numbers is as follows: $193,798 + $9,690 - $3,488 = $200,000.

The only GST that will be remitted is being paid by the vendor so it can be assumed that the vendor has been assigned the rights to the GST rebate. As a consequence, the $3,488 rebate would be claimed by the vendor.

The net GST paid would be $6,202 ($9,690 - $3,488).

Self Study Solution Twenty-One - 9

GST Consequences

As used residential properties are not subject to GST, the renovator would not have paid any tax on the $85,000 purchase.

With respect to the sale, the GST treatment will depend on whether the upgrading was a substantial or non-substantial renovation. Given that 100 percent of the interior was replaced, it would be considered a substantial renovation. As a result, the sale would be treated as a taxable supply of a new home and would be subject to GST. This, in turn, means that GST paid on the costs of renovations can be claimed as input tax credits.

These credits can be claimed when the expenses are incurred, without regard to when the house is sold. The renovator could also claim input tax credits on GST that would be paid on commissions and transfer fees.

Cost Of House And Net Profit

For the purchaser, the usual 5 percent rate applied to the sales price of $200,000 would result in a basic GST figure of $10,000. However, as the house has a purchase price below $350,000, the purchaser would be eligible for a rebate equal to 36 percent of the GST paid. This rebate would be $3,600 [(36%)($10,000)], leaving a net GST payable of $6,400 ($10,000 - $3,600). The net cost of the house to the purchaser would then be $206,400.

The net profit on the transaction for the renovator, calculated net of GST payment and input tax credits, would be calculated as follows:

Selling Price		$200,000
Less Costs:		
Purchase Price	$85,000	
Subcontractors - No GST Included	10,700	
Subcontractors (Net Of $1,000 GST)	20,000	
Materials (Net Of $1,500 GST)	30,000	
Employee Wages - No GST Included	6,000	151,700
Net Profit		$ 48,300

GST Remittance

The contractor will have a liability for GST as follows:

GST Charged (Net Of Rebate)		$ 6,400
Less Input Tax Credits:		
Subcontractors [($21,000 ÷ 105%)(5%)]($ 1,000)		
Materials [($31,500 ÷ 105%)(5%)]	(1,500)	(2,500)
GST Remittance		$ 3,900

This solution assumes the purchaser assigns the rebate to the builder on closing. If this is not the case, the purchaser would apply personally for the $3,600 GST rebate, and the renovator's GST remittance would be $3,600 larger.

Chapter 21 Learning Objectives

After completing Chapter 21, you should be able to:

1. Describe, in general terms, the current transaction tax situation (GST/HST) in all of the provinces (paragraph [P hereafter] 21-1 to 21-19).

2. Describe the different ways in which transaction taxes can be assessed and the approach the GST/HST uses (P 21-20 to 21-43).

3. Explain the basic charging provision for GST/HST and the concept of supply (P 21-44 to 21-48).

4. Outline the difference between fully taxable supplies, zero-rated supplies, and exempt supplies (P 21-49 to 21-62).

5. Explain the place of supply rules and how the GST/HST is applied to tangible goods, real property and services (P 21-63 to 21-71).

6. Explain who is responsible for collecting and remitting the GST/HST (P 21-72 to 21-75).

7. Determine whether an entity is required to register for GST and if so, at what point in time registration is required (P 21-76 to 21-94).

8. Apply the rules for calculating input tax credits on current and capital expenditures (P 21-95 to 21-101).

9. Explain some of the basic restrictions on claiming input tax credits (P 21-102 to 21-104).

10. Discuss input tax credits as they relate to vendors of exempt supplies (P 21-105).

11. Describe the relationship between amounts determined for accounting, income tax and GST/HST purposes (P 21-106 to 21-110).

12. Calculate the GST/HST payable or refund when fully taxable, zero-rated and exempt supplies are provided (P 21-111 to 21-114).

13. Apply the quick method of accounting for GST/HST (P 21-115 to 21-126).

14. Apply the simplified method of accounting for input tax credits (P 21-127 to 21-132).

15. Outline the basic procedures and administration of the GST/HST (P 21-133 to 21-159).

16. Calculate the employee and partner GST/HST rebate (P 21-160 to 21-168).

17. Calculate the effects of GST/HST on the acquisition and disposition of residential property, including new homes (P 21-169 to 21-175).

18. Describe the possible GST/HST implications resulting from the sale of a business (P 21-176 to 21-189).

19. Briefly describe how the GST/HST applies to certain types of organizations such as those included in MUSH (P 21-190 and 21-191).

20. Describe the GST/HST implications related to partner expenses, dispositions of partnership interests, transfers between a partnership and its partners and the reorganization of partnerships (P 21-192 to 21-200).

21. Explain the applicability of GST/HST legislation to trusts (P 21-201 to 21-203).

GLOSSARY

Note that this Glossary is also available on the Student CD-ROM
as part of the Folio version of Canadian Tax Principles in FITAC.

A

Accrual Basis   A method of accounting for Income based on recording assets when the right to receive them is established and liabilities when the obligation to pay them arises.

Acquisition Of Control   Acquisition of sufficient voting shares of a corporation, by a Person, or Group Of Persons, that they have the right to elect a majority of the board of directors of the Corporation.

Active Business   A business carried on by a Taxpayer, other than a Specified Investment Business or a Personal Services Business.

Active Business Income   Income earned by an Active Business.

Additional Refundable Tax On Investment Income (ART)   A 6-2/3% tax on the Aggregate Investment Income of a CCPC.

Adjusted Active Business Income   A term used in calculating the M&P Deduction, defined as the excess of a Corporation's Income from Active Business, less a Corporation's losses from Active Business. It does not appear to be a different concept than Active Business Income of a Corporation.

Adjusted Cost Base   For depreciable capital property it is the cost of the property to the Taxpayer. For non-depreciable capital property it is the cost of the property to the Taxpayer, subject to ITA 53 adjustments (e.g., deduction of government grants on land purchase).

Adjusted Taxable Income   Regular Taxable Income, adjusted to remove certain tax preferences. Used to calculate the Alternative Minimum Tax.

Adoption Expenses Tax Credit
A credit against Tax Payable that is available to individuals with eligible adoption expenses.

Advance Tax Ruling   Interpretations provided, at the request of a taxpayer, by the Income Tax Rulings Directorate as to how a particular transaction will be treated for tax purposes. Such interpretations are not binding on the CRA.

Affiliated Group Of Persons
A Group Of Persons each member of which is affiliated with every other member.

Affiliated Person [ITA 251.1(1)]
For an Individual, an Affiliated Person is that individual's Spouse or Common-Law Partner. For a Corporation, an Affiliated Person is a Person or an Affiliated Group Of Persons who Controls the Corporation, or the Spouse or Common-Law Partner of either the Person who Controls, or a member of the group that Controls. More complex rules apply to determine affiliation between two Corporations.

Age Tax Credit   A credit against Tax Payable that is available to Individuals who are 65 years of age or older.

Aggregate Investment Income   As defined in ITA 129(4), this concept of investment income includes net Taxable Capital Gains for the year reduced by any Net Capital Loss carry overs deducted in the year, Interest Income, rents, and royalties.

Alimony   A term that was used at an earlier point in time to refer to both Spousal Support and Child Support.

Allowable Business Investment Loss
The deductible portion (currently one-half) of a Business Investment Loss.

Allowable Capital Loss   The deductible portion (currently one-half) of a Capital Loss.

Allowance   An amount paid by an employer to an Employee to provide for certain types of costs incurred by the Employee, usually travel costs or automobile costs.

Alter Ego Trust An Inter Vivos Trust established by an Individual aged 65 years or more, subject to the conditions that the Individual must be entitled to all of the Trust's Income during his/her lifetime, and the Individual must be the only Person who can access the capital of the Trust during his/her lifetime.

Alternative Minimum Tax (AMT) A tax, calculated at the minimum federal rate on Adjusted Taxable Income, less a basic $40,000 exemption.

Amalgamation A Rollover provision which allows two Taxable Canadian Corporations to be combined into a single Taxable Canadian Corporation, without tax consequences.

Annual Business Limit The maximum amount of Active Business Income that is eligible for the Small Business Deduction in a particular taxation year (currently $500,000).

Annual Child Care Expense Amount The annual per child limit for deductible Child Care Expense. The amount is $4,000, $7,000, or $10,000, depending on the age and health of the child.

Annual Gains Limit Taxable Capital Gains for the current year on qualified assets, less the sum of Allowable Capital Losses and Net Capital Loss Carry Overs deducted during the current year, plus Allowable Business Investment Losses realized during the current year. Used to determine the Lifetime Capital Gains Deduction for the current year.

Annuitant This term is used to describe a Person who is receiving an Annuity. However, in tax publications this term is often (and incorrectly) used to refer to the Beneficiary of an RRSP or RPP.

Annuity A series of periodic payments that continues for a specified period of time, or until the occurrence of some event (e.g., the death of the Annuitant).

Anti-Avoidance Provision A provision in the *Income Tax Act* that is designed to prevent a Taxpayer from taking some action that would allow him to avoid taxes.

Apprenticeship Job Creation Tax Credit An Investment Tax Credit that is available to eligible employers (individuals and corporations) for salaries and wages paid to qualifying apprentices.

ART An acronym for "additional refundable tax on investment income".

Assessment A formal determination of taxes to be paid or refunded. A Reassessment is a form of Assessment.

Associated Corporations Two or more Corporations that have an ownership/control arrangement that falls into one of the categories described in ITA 256(1) (e.g., two Corporations controlled by the same Person).

At-Risk Amount A defined measure that limits the amount of deductions that can be flowed through to a Limited Partner.

At-Risk Rules A set of rules, directed largely at Limited Partners, designed to prevent an investment from creating tax deductions that exceed the amount invested (the At-Risk Amount).

B

Basic Federal Tax Payable An amount of individual Tax Payable that has been reduced by some, but not all of the Tax Credits available to individuals. Used in the calculation of Tax Payable of Canadian Residents who do not live in a province.

Beneficiary The Person who will receive the benefits from a Trust.

Billed Basis A method of determining Net Business Income based on recording inclusions when the relevant amounts are billed. Can only be used by certain specified types of professionals (e.g., accountants).

Bonus Arrangement As used in this material, a tax planning arrangement for Employees. A Corporation declares and deducts a bonus near the end of its fiscal year. It is usually designed to be paid to the Employee early in the following calendar year. As Employment Income is taxed on a Cash Basis, the bonus will not be taxed in the employee's hands until that year.

Bonusing Down A process of paying deductible salary to the owner-manager of a CCPC, or related parties, in order to eliminate corporate Taxable Income that is not eligible for the Small Business Deduction.

Boot A colloquial term used by tax practitioners to refer to Non-Share Consideration.

Business A business is a self-sustaining integrated set of activities and assets conducted and managed for the purpose of providing a return to investors. A business consists of (a) inputs, (b) processes applied to those inputs, and (c) resulting outputs that are used to generate revenues.

Business Combination A transaction in which an enterprise acquires net assets that constitute a business, or acquires an equity interest in a Corporation that gives the enterprise Control over the operating, financing, and investing decisions of that Corporation.

Business Income   Income that is earned through Active Business activity. This would include amounts earned by producing goods, selling goods or services, or delivering services. While usage is not always consistent, this term usually refers to a net amount (i.e., inclusions less deductions, or revenues less expenses).

Business Investment Loss   A loss resulting from the Disposition of shares or debt of a Small Business Corporation.

C

Canada Disability Savings Bonds   A system of grants under which the federal government makes contributions to an Individual's RDSP based on family net income.

Canada Disability Savings Grants   A system of grants under which the federal government makes contributions to an Individual's RDSP based on a percentage of the contributions to that Individual's RDSP that have been made by others.

Canada Education Savings Grants
A system of grants under which the federal government makes contributions to an Individual's RESP based on a percentage of the contributions to that Individual's RESP that have been made by others.

Canada Employment Credit   A credit against Tax Payable that is available to individuals with employment income.

Canada Learning Bonds   A system of grants under which the federal government makes contributions to an Individual's RESP based on the number of years in which the Individual's family is eligible for the National Child Benefit supplement.

Canada Pension Plan (CPP)   A pension plan sponsored by the federal government. Individuals with Employment or Business Income must make contributions based on their income and, in return, receive benefits in future years.

Canada Pension Plan Tax Credit   A credit against Tax Payable that is available to Individuals making contributions to the Canada Pension Plan.

Canadian Controlled Private Corporation
A Corporation that is controlled by Persons Resident in Canada and that does not have any of its shares listed on a designated stock exchange.

Canadian Corporation   A Corporation that is resident in Canada.

Canadian Partnership   A Partnership, all of the members of which are Residents of Canada at the time the term is relevant.

Capital Asset   An asset that is held for the purpose of producing Income.

Capital Cost   The amount paid to acquire a depreciable asset. The tax equivalent of acquisition cost in accounting.

Capital Cost Allowance (CCA)   A deduction in the determination of Business or Property Income based on the capital cost of capital assets. The tax equivalent of accounting amortization.

Capital Dividend   A Dividend paid out of a Private Corporation's Capital Dividend Account. It is received on a tax free basis.

Capital Dividend Account   An account that tracks a group of items, defined in ITA 89(1), that can be distributed by Private Corporations to shareholders as a tax free Capital Dividend (e.g., the non-taxable portion of realized Capital Gains).

Capital Gain   The excess of proceeds resulting from the Disposition of a capital asset, over the sum of the Adjusted Cost Base of the asset plus any costs of disposition.

Capital Gains Reserve   A Reserve that is deductible against Capital Gains. It is available when some part of the Proceeds Of Disposition is not collected in the period of disposition.

Capital Gains Stripping   Procedures designed to allow a Corporation to convert a taxable capital gain resulting from the Disposition of investment shares to an arm's length party, into a tax free intercorporate Dividend.

Capital Interest (In A Trust)   All rights of the Taxpayer as a Beneficiary under the trust, other than those that are an Income Interest in the Trust.

Capital Loss   The excess of the sum of the Adjusted Cost Base of a capital asset plus any costs of disposition, over the proceeds resulting from the Disposition of the asset.

Capital Tax   A tax assessed on the capital of a Corporation, without regard to its Income.

Caregiver Tax Credit   A credit against Tax Payable that is available to an Individual who provides home care for an adult relative.

Carry Over   As used in tax work, the ability to apply current year losses against Income in earlier or later years.

Cash Basis   A method of accounting for Income based on cash receipts and cash disbursements.

Cash Damming   Situations in which a separate bank account is established to receive all deposits of borrowed funds. Expenditures from this account are then limited to those which qualify for interest deductibility. This procedure facilitates linking the borrowed money to income producing investments.

CCPC An acronym for "Canadian controlled private corporation".

Charitable Donations Tax Credit A credit against Tax Payable that is available to Individuals making donations to qualifying charitable organizations.

Charitable Gifts Donations to a registered charity, a registered Canadian amateur athletic association, a housing corporation resident in Canada that is exempt from tax under ITA 149(1)(i), a Canadian municipality, the United Nations or an agency thereof, a university outside of Canada which normally enrolls Canadian students, and a charitable organization outside of Canada to which Her Majesty in right of Canada has made a gift in the year or in the immediately preceding year.

Child Care Expenses Costs associated with caring for an Eligible Child.

Child Care Spaces Tax Credit An Investment Tax Credit that is available to Taxpayers who have incurred costs to create new child care spaces for the Taxpayer's employees.

Child Fitness Tax Credit A credit against Tax Payable that is available to individuals for fees paid for the enrollment of a child under 16 in an eligible program of physical activity.

Child Support A Support Amount that is not identified as being for the benefit of a Spouse or Common-Law Partner, or a former Spouse or Common-Law Partner.

Child Tax Benefit A monthly payment that is available to Individuals with children. The payments may be reduced or eliminated if Income is in excess of a threshold amount.

Child Tax Credit A credit against Tax Payable that is available to the parent of a child who is under the age of 18 years at the end of a taxation year.

Children's Arts Tax Credit A credit against Tax Payable that is available to individuals for fees paid for the enrollment of a child under 16 in an eligible program of artistic, cultural, recreational or developmental activities.

Class As used in tax work, a defined group of depreciable assets for which the *Income Tax Regulations* specify the CCA rate to be applied, as well as the method to be used in applying the rate.

Clawback An income tested taxing back, or reduction, in the payment of Old Age Security benefits and Employment Insurance benefits.

Commercial Activity This is a GST term which refers to any business or trade carried on by a Person, or any supply of real property made by a Person. Commercial Activity does not include any activity involved with making an exempt supply or any activity engaged in by an Individual without a Reasonable Expectation Of Profit.

Commodity Tax A type of Transaction Tax that is applied to the sale of certain types of commodities (e.g., taxes on the sale of tobacco products).

Common Shares Corporate shares that normally have all of the rights which are provided for under the relevant corporate enabling legislation. While there may be variations in the rights of such shares, at a minimum, voting rights would have to be present for the shares to be considered Common Shares.

Common-Law Partner A Person who cohabits in a conjugal relationship with the Taxpayer and (a) has so cohabited with the Taxpayer for a continuous period of at least one year, or (b) is a parent of a child of whom the Taxpayer is also a parent.

Comparable Uncontrolled Price A Transfer Pricing method that bases transfer prices on the prices used in comparable transactions between arm's length buyers and sellers, operating in the same market and under the same terms and conditions.

Competent Authority An authorized representative of a country's tax organization that helps resolve taxpayer disputes by negotiating with the other country on matters not adequately addressed by the tax treaty.

Connected Corporation Corporation A is connected with Corporation B if Corporation B Controls Corporation A, or if Corporation B owns more than 10% of the voting shares of Corporation A and more than 10% of the fair market value of all issued shares of Corporation A.

Consent Form A form that is used when a taxpayer wishes to have a different person represent him in dealing with the CRA. This form (T1013) authorizes the CRA to disclose information to, and deal with, a specified representative.

Consumption Tax A tax levied on the consumption of some product or service. This type of tax is also called a sales tax.

Contributed Capital In accounting usage, the amount of a Corporation's Shareholders' Equity that was received in return for issuing the shares that are currently outstanding.

Control [ITA 256(1.2)(c)] A Corporation, Person or Group Of Persons has Control of a Corporation if that Corporation, Person or Group Of Persons owns either more than 50% of the Common Shares of that Corporation or, alternatively, owns shares (common and/or preferred) with a fair market value that exceeds 50% of the fair market value of all of the outstanding shares of that Corporation.

Control (IAS 27) Control is the power to govern the financial and operating policies of an entity so as to obtain benefits from its activities.

Controlled [ITA 251.1(3)] Under ITA 251.1(3), Controlled means controlled, directly or indirectly in any manner whatever. [The reference here is to de facto control, which does not necessarily require majority ownership of shares.]

Controlled Foreign Affiliate A Foreign Affiliate of the Taxpayer that was controlled by (a) the Taxpayer, (b) the Taxpayer and not more than four other Persons Resident in Canada, (c) not more than four Persons Resident in Canada, other than the Taxpayer, (d) a Person or Persons with whom the Taxpayer does not deal at arm's length, or (e) the Taxpayer and a Person or Persons with whom the Taxpayer does not deal at arm's length.

Convertible Property A debt or equity financial instrument of a Corporation that can be exchanged for an equity financial instrument of the same Corporation, without the payment of additional consideration.

Co-Ownership Ownership of a single real or personal property by two or more Persons.

Corporation An artificial legal entity created through either federal or provincial legislation.

Cost Of Capital (M&P) For purposes of calculating the M&P Deduction, this amount is 10% of the Gross Cost of Capital Assets used by the corporation, plus 100% of rents paid for Capital Assets used by the Corporation.

Cost Of Labour (M&P) For purposes of calculating the M&P Deduction, this is the total cost of salaries and wages, plus non-salary amounts paid for employee-like services.

Crown Gifts Gifts made to Her Majesty in right of Canada or to Her Majesty in right of a province.

Cultural Gifts Gifts of objects that the Canadian Cultural Property Export Review Board has determined meet the criteria of the *Cultural Property And Import Act*.

Cumulative Eligible Capital (CEC) This term is used to refer to the amortized balance of Eligible Capital Expenditures. The amortization of this amount that is deducted under ITA 20(1)(b) is usually referred to as the cumulative eligible capital amount.

Cumulative Gains Limit Taxable Capital Gains on qualified assets that have been realized since 1984, less the sum of Allowable Capital Losses and Net Capital Loss Carry Overs deducted after 1984, plus Allowable Business Investment Losses realized after 1984, capital gains deductions claimed in previous taxation years, and the Cumulative Net Investment Loss at the end of the year. Used to determine the Lifetime Capital Gains Deduction for the current year.

Cumulative Net Investment Loss (CNIL) The amount by which the aggregate of investment expenses for the current year and prior years ending after 1987, exceeds the aggregate of investment income for that period.

Customs Duties A tax imposed on the importation or exportation of certain goods or services.

D

Death Benefit All amounts in excess of $10,000 that are received by a Taxpayer in a taxation year, on or after the death of an Employee, in recognition of the Employee's service in an office or employment.

Declining Balance Method A method of calculating CCA in which a specified rate is applied to the ending UCC balance in a depreciable asset Class in order to determine the CCA for the period.

Deemed Disposition A requirement to assume that a Disposition has taken place when, in fact, a disposition transaction has not occurred (e.g., a change in use is deemed to be a Disposition).

Deemed Dividends A group of capital transactions and distributions, as specified in ITA 84(1), that are deemed to be Dividend payments.

Deemed Resident An Individual who is considered a Resident of Canada because of some factor other than physical presence in Canada (e.g., members of the Canadian armed forces are deemed to be Canadian Residents under ITA 250 without regard to where they are physically located).

Deemed Year End A requirement to have a taxation year end at a specified date, or as the result of a specified event.

Deeming Rules Rules that are used to require that an item or event be given a treatment for tax purposes that is not consistent with the actual nature of the item or event (e.g., members of the Canadian armed forces are deemed to be Canadian Residents even if they are not present in Canada at any time during the year).

Deferred Income Plans   A group of plans that allow Individuals to receive Income on a tax deferred basis.   These include Registered Pension Plans, Deferred Profit Sharing Plans, Registered Retirement Savings Plans, and Registered Retirement Income Funds.

Deferred Profit Sharing Plan (DPSP)
A trusteed plan to which employers can make deductible contributions, the amount of which is related to the profits of the enterprise, and which do not create a Taxable Benefit for the recipient employees. Earnings accumulate tax free within the plan. Withdrawals from the plan are subject to tax.

Defined Benefit Plan   A retirement savings plan in which the plan sponsor (usually an employer) promises a known or determinable retirement benefit and assumes financial responsibility for providing that benefit.

Defined Contribution Plan (a.k.a., Money Purchase Plan)   A retirement savings plan in which the plan sponsor (employer or individual) makes known or determinable contributions. The retirement benefit is based on the accumulated contributions and earnings on investments within the plan.

Dependant   As defined in ITA 118(6), an Individual who, at any time during the year, is dependent on the taxpayer for support and is the child or grandchild of the Individual or of the individual's Spouse or Common-Law Partner, the parent, grandparent, brother, sister, uncle, aunt, niece, or nephew, if resident in Canada at any time in the year, of the Individual or of the individual's Spouse or Common-Law Partner.

Depreciable Capital Property   Capital property, such as equipment or furniture and fixtures, that is subject to depreciation or amortization.

Designated Stock Exchange
A stock exchange that has been designated as such by the Minister of Finance. Replaces the term "prescribed stock exchange".

Disability Supports Deduction   A deduction available to individuals for attendant care and other disability support expenses, incurred to allow the disabled individual to work or to attend a designated educational institution.

Disability Tax Credit   A credit against Tax Payable that is available to Individuals with a doctor certified severe mental or physical disability. Can be transferred to a supporting Individual.

Disability Tax Credit Supplement   A supplement to the Disability Tax Credit that is available for individuals who are under 18 years of age at the end of the year.

Disappearing Source Rules   Rules designed to provide relief to investors who have borrowed money to make an investment and subsequently sold the investment for less than the related borrowings. These rules provide that any amount of debt that remains after the proceeds of the sale are used to pay off a portion of the total balance is deemed to be debt that is used to produce income.

Discretionary Trust   A Trust for which the Settlor has given the Trustee discretion to decide the amounts of income or capital to be allocated to each Beneficiary.

Disposition   The disposal of an asset through sale, gift, physical destruction, conversion, expropriation, or other means.

Dividend Gross Up   An amount that is based on a percentage of the Dividends from Taxable Canadian Corporations that have been received by an Individual or Trust. This amount must be included in the Net Income For Tax Purposes of the Individual or Trust.

Dividend Stripping   Procedures designed to allow an Individual to remove accumulated Income from a Corporation in the form of tax-free capital gains, while still retaining Control of the Corporation.

Dividend Tax Credit   A credit against the Tax Payable of an Individual or Trust. The amount is based on a fraction of the Dividend Gross Up that has been included in Net Income For Tax Purposes.

Dividends   Amounts declared and paid, at the discretion of management, as a return on equity investments.

Dividends In Kind   Dividends, other than Stock Dividends, paid in corporate assets other than cash.

Division B Income   An alternative name for Net Income For Tax Purposes.

Double Taxation   A reference to situations in which the same stream of Income is subject to tax a second time.

Dual Resident   A taxpayer who is considered to be a Resident of two countries.

E

Earned Capital (a.k.a. Retained Earnings)
In accounting usage, the amount of a Corporation's Shareholders' Equity that resulted from the retention of earnings in the corporation.

Earned Income (Child Care Expenses) For purposes of determining the deductible amount of Child Care Expenses, Earned Income is defined as Employment Income (gross), Business Income (not losses), and Income from scholarships, training allowances, and research grants.

Earned Income (RRSP Deduction Limit) The sum of Employment Income (without the RPP deduction), Business Income (losses), royalties (if the taxpayer is the author, inventor, or composer), taxable (deductible) support payments, supplementary unemployment benefits, income (loss) as an active partner, net rental income (loss), research grants (net of certain expenses), and CPP disability benefits.

Earned Surplus An archaic accounting description of what now is called Retained Earnings. However, the term continues to be found in the *Income Tax Act*.

Ecological Gifts Gifts of land certified by the Minister of the Environment to be ecologically sensitive land, the conservation and protection of which is important to the preservation of Canada's environmental heritage.

Education Tax Credit A credit against Tax Payable that is available to Individuals attending a designated educational institution on a full or part time basis.

Election A choice that is available to a Taxpayer with respect to a particular tax outcome (e.g., a Taxpayer can elect to have the spousal Rollover provision not be applicable).

Eligible Capital Expenditure An amount expended to acquire an intangible asset that is not eligible for either write-off through CCA deductions or as a deduction in the period in which it is incurred.

Eligible Capital Property An intangible asset that results from making an Eligible Capital Expenditure.

Eligible Child With respect to the deductibility of Child Care Expenses, a child of the Taxpayer, his Spouse, or a child who is dependent on the Taxpayer or his Spouse, and whose Income does not exceed the basic personal tax credit base amount. An Eligible Child must either be under 16 years of age at some time during the year, or dependent on the Taxpayer or his Spouse by reason of physical or mental infirmity.

Eligible Dependant Tax Credit A credit against Tax Payable that is available to a single Individual supporting a Dependant in a self-contained domestic establishment.

Eligible Dividends Dividends that have been designated by the payor as eligible for the enhanced gross up and tax credit procedure.

Emigration Leaving a country, usually in order to establish permanent residency in another country.

Employee An Individual who has an employment relationship with an entity that provides remuneration. Whether or not an Individual is working as an Employee or a Self-Employed Individual is dependent on factors such as control, ownership of tools, chance of profit or risk of loss, and the ability to subcontract or hire an assistant.

Employee and Partner GST Rebate A provision that allows employees and partners to recover the GST paid on their employment or partnership related expenses.

Employer/ Employee Relationship A written, verbal, or tacit agreement in which an Employee agrees to work on a full-time or part-time basis for an employer for a specified or indeterminate period of time, in return for Salary or wages. The employer has the right to decide where, when, and how the work will be done. In this type of relationship, a contract of services exists.

Employment Income The Salary, wages, and other remuneration, including gratuities, received by an Employee in the year (see Employer/Employee Relationship).

Employment Insurance (EI) A federal insurance plan designed to provide benefits to unemployed Individuals. In order to receive benefits, Employees must make contributions when they are employed.

Employment Insurance Tax Credit A credit against Tax Payable that is available to Employees making payments to the federal Employment Insurance plan.

Estate As the term is used in the *Income Tax Act*, the property of a deceased Individual.

Estate Freeze Procedures undertaken by an Individual in order to fix a tax value for all or part of the Individual's property, and to Transfer future growth in the value of this property to other Individuals.

Estate Planning Tax planning directed towards the distribution of an Individual's property at death.

Excessive Eligible Dividend Designation (EEDD) A balance, subject to Part III.1 tax, which reflects an inappropriate designation of an amount of dividends paid as an Eligible Dividend.

Exchange Of Shares In A Reorganization (ITA 86) A Rollover provision that allows one class of shares in a Corporation to be exchanged for a different class of shares, without tax consequences.

Executor   A Person appointed by an Individual in their Will to oversee the administration of the Estate on their death in accordance with the terms of that Will.

Exempt Goods And Services   Goods and services that are not subject to the GST. Registrants who sell Exempt Goods And Services are not eligible for Input Tax Credits for GST paid. Examples include sales of used residential housing, most medical services, and most financial services.

Exempt Surplus   A surplus account that tracks certain sources of income of a Foreign Affiliate.

F

Fairness Package   Replaced by the Taxpayer Relief Provisions.

Family Caregiver Tax Credit   An addition to the base for the spousal, eligible dependant, child, and (regular) caregiver tax credits. It is available in those situations where the dependant has a disability for a long and continuous period of indefinite duration.

Family Trust   An Inter Vivos Trust, established by an Individual, with family members as Beneficiaries.

Farm Property   Farm Property includes real estate and property that is used in farming activities, a share of a Corporation that is carrying on a farming business, or an interest in a Partnership that is carrying on a farming business.

Federal Tax Abatement   A 10 percentage point reduction in the federal tax rate on Corporations, applicable to Income earned in a province.

Final Tax Return   A term used to describe the tax return filed for an Individual for the year of their death.

First Time Home Buyer's Tax Credit
A credit against Tax Payable equal to 15% of $5,000 of the cost of an individual's first Principal Residence.

First Time Donor's Super Tax Credit
A temporary addition to the charitable donations tax credit. The amount is equal to 25 percent of the first $1,000 of qualifying donations. It is available if neither the individual nor the individual's spouse or common-law partner has claimed a charitable donations tax credit since 2007.

First Year Rules   See Half-Year Rules.

Fiscal Period   A taxation year that does not exceed 53 weeks.

Fishing Property   Fishing Property includes real estate and property that is used in fishing activities, a share of a Corporation that is carrying on a fishing business, or an interest in a Partnership that is carrying on a fishing business.

Fixed Term Annuity   An Annuity that is paid for a specified number of periods.

Flat Tax System   A tax on Income that is applied at the same rate to all Taxpayers, without regard to the level of their Income.

Foreign Accrual Property Income (FAPI)
Income of a Controlled Foreign Affiliate from property (interest, Dividends, rents, royalties), Income from inactive businesses, Taxable Capital Gains from properties not used in an Active Business, and Income from an investment business, defined as a business the principal purpose of which is to earn Property Income.

Foreign Affiliate   A non-resident Corporation in which a Canadian Taxpayer has an equity percentage of at least 1 percent. As well, the aggregate equity percentages of the Taxpayer and each Person related to the Taxpayer must be at least 10 percent.

Foreign Taxes Paid Credit   A credit against Tax Payable based on taxes withheld by a foreign taxing authority on foreign source income.

Former Business Property   Real property that is used in the operation of a business.

Fringe Benefits   Non-cash benefits provided to Employees by an employer (e.g., contributions to an Employee's Registered Pension Plan).

Full Rate Taxable Income   For purposes of calculating the General Rate Reduction, Taxable Income reduced by amounts which have received preferential treatment under some other provision (e.g., the Small Business Deduction).

Fully Taxable Goods And Services   Goods and services that are taxable at the full 5% GST rate. Registrants who sell Fully Taxable Goods And Services are entitled to Input Tax Credits for GST paid. Examples include clothing, furniture, legal fees, hydro services, building materials, and restaurant meals.

G

GAAP   An acronym for "generally accepted accounting principles".

GAAR   An acronym for "general anti-avoidance rule". This ITA 245 provision attempts, in a very generalized manner, to limit the ability of Taxpayers to avoid tax through certain types of transactions that have no bona fide purpose other than to obtain a tax benefit.

General Partner   A Partner whose personal liability for the debts and obligations of the partnership are not limited.

General Partnership   A Partnership, all of the members of which are General Partners.

General Rate Income Pool (GRIP)   A notional account that tracks amounts of a CCPC's income that can be used for the payment of Eligible Dividends.

General Rate Reduction   A percentage point deduction in the calculation of corporate Tax Payable that is designed to reduce the general corporate tax rate of 38 percent.

Gift   A voluntary Transfer of goods or services without remuneration.

Goods And Services Tax (GST)   A type of Transaction Tax that is assessed on the sale of goods and services.   As it is assessed at all stages of the production/distribution chain, the tax that an enterprise must collect and pay to the government is offset by Input Tax Credits for the tax paid on the various inputs required to produce or distribute the goods and services.

Goodwill   The excess, if any, of the total fair value of a business enterprise, over the sum of the fair values of its identifiable tangible and intangible assets.

Gross Cost   For purposes of calculating Capital Cost in the determination of the M&P Deduction, this is the cost of Capital Assets, without the deduction of government grants or Investment Tax Credits.

Group Of Persons   For purposes of determining Control of a Corporation, a Group Of Persons is any two or more Persons, each of whom owns shares in the Corporation.

GST   An acronym for the "goods and services tax".

GST Tax Credit   A Refundable Tax Credit that is available to all Resident Individuals aged 19 or older who file a T1 tax return. May be reduced or eliminated by a deduction of Income in excess of a threshold amount.

H

Half-Year Rules (a.k.a. First Year Rules)   A group of rules which require, for most CCA Classes, the subtraction of one-half of the year's net additions (additions, less the amount subtracted from the class because of disposals) from the Class, prior to calculating the CCA for the year.

Harmonized Sales Tax (HST)   A combined federal/provincial sales tax that is generally assessed on the same basis as the federal Goods And Services Tax (GST). The combined rate varies across the provinces and is notionally a combination of the 5% GST plus a provincial sales tax ranging from 7% to 10%.

Head Tax   A tax levied on the Individuals that are included in a specified classification.

Hobby Farmer   A part-time farmer who does not have a Reasonable Expectation Of Profit.

Home Buyers' Plan (HBP)   A provision that allows Individuals to make a temporary, non-taxable withdrawal from their RRSP for purposes of acquiring a residence.

Home Relocation Loan   A loan provided by an employer to an Employee to assist that Employee in acquiring a home at a new work location.

I

Identical Property Rules   Rules which require that, for a group of identical Capital Assets (e.g., Common Shares) acquired at different prices, the Adjusted Cost Base used to determine the gain or loss will be the average cost of the group. The rules are used when there is a partial Disposition of the group.

Immigration   Entering a new country, usually for purposes of establishing permanent residence.

Imputed Interest   Interest on outstanding debt calculated at a specified interest rate without regard to the actual interest rate being paid. This concept is used to determine the Taxable Benefit on loans to Employees and Shareholders.

Inadequate Consideration   A term used to refer to a situation where a non-arm's length transfer of property has been made and the Proceeds Of Disposition are not equal to the fair market value.

Income   A measure of either how much an entity has earned during a period or, alternatively, how much its net worth has increased during a period. As the term is used in accounting and tax, it is a rules-based calculation. In the case of accounting, the rules are referred to as generally accepted accounting principles (GAAP), while in tax the rules are found in the *Income Tax Act* and other sources.

Income Attribution   The allocation of some types of Income, on assets that have been transferred to a Spouse or related minors, back to the Transferor for inclusion in the Transferor's Net Income For Tax Purposes.

Income Interest (In A Trust)   A right of the Taxpayer as a Beneficiary under a Personal Trust to receive all or any part of the Income of the Trust.

Income Splitting   A group of Tax Planning techniques designed to divide a given stream of Income among family members or other related parties. The value of these techniques is based on progressive tax rates which means that, if a stream of Income can be divided into a group of smaller streams, a larger portion of it will be taxed at lower rates, resulting in aggregate tax savings.

Income Tax   A tax on the Income of certain defined entities.

Income Tax Application Rules   A set of rules designed to deal with transitional problems associated with the introduction of Capital Gains taxation in 1972. While these rules were very important in the years immediately after 1971, they are of declining importance at this point in time.

Income Tax Folios   A CRA publication providing their interpretation of various technical issues related to income taxes. These will gradually replace the CRA's Interpretation Bulletins.

Income Tax Regulations   A set of rules concerning administration and enforcement of the *Income Tax Act*. One of the major issues covered here is Capital Cost Allowance rates and procedures.

Income Tax Technical News   An irregularly published newsletter prepared by the Income Tax Rulings Directorate.

Income Trust   A Trust that has sold its beneficial interest units to the public in order to raise funds to acquire a business operation. All cash flows from the business are distributed to the unit holders.

Indexation   The process of adjusting tax brackets and some Tax Credits to reflect changes in the consumer price index.

Individual   A single human being.

Individual Pension Plan   A defined benefit pension plan established for one individual.

Infirm Dependant Over 17 Tax Credit
A credit against Tax Payable available to individuals who have a Dependant over the age of 17 who is mentally or physically infirm.

Information Circulars   A group of separate publications that provides information regarding procedural matters that relate to both the *Income Tax Act* and the provisions of the Canada Pension Plan.

Information Return   ITA 221(1)(d) gives the CRA the right to require any class of Taxpayer to file a return providing any class of information that it would like to have. A common example of an Information Return would be the T4 which employers are required to file in order to provide information on their Employees' earnings and withholdings.

Input Tax Credit (ITC)   An amount, claimable by a registrant, for GST paid or payable on goods or services that were acquired or imported for consumption, use, or supply in the course of the Registrant's Commercial Activity.

Instalment Threshold   An amount, currently $3,000 of net tax owing for Individuals or taxes payable for Corporations that is used to determine the need to make Instalment payments (i.e., Individuals are required to make Instalment payments if their Net Tax Owing in the current year and one of the two preceding years exceeds the Instalment Threshold of $3,000).

Instalments   Payments made during a taxation year by both Individuals and Corporations. They are designed to accumulate to an amount sufficient to cover the tax liability for the year. Individuals and Small CCPCs make quarterly Instalments. Corporations that are not Small CCPCs are required to remit monthly.

Integration   An approach to the taxation of Corporations that attempts to ensure that amounts of Income that are flowed through a Corporation to its Individual shareholders, are subject to the same amount of tax as would be the case if the Individuals had received the Income directly from its source.

Inter Vivos Transfer   A Transfer made by a living Individual, as opposed to a Transfer made subsequent to that Individual's death.

Inter Vivos Trust   A Trust that is not a Testamentary Trust.

Interest Income   An amount that represents compensation for the use of money, is calculated with reference to a principal sum, and that accrues on a continuous basis.

International Tax Treaty (a.k.a., International Tax Convention)   A bilateral agreement between two countries which establishes rules for dealing with cross-jurisdictional tax issues.

International Taxation   Income and other types of taxation related to transactions and events that take place in multiple jurisdictions.

Interpretation Bulletins   A group of over 500 individual publications which provides the CRA's interpretation of the various laws that they administer.

In-The-Money   A term that is used to describe stock options in situations where the fair market value of the stock exceeds the option price.

Inventory   Property, the cost or value of which is relevant in computing a taxpayer's income from a business for a taxation year. The property is being held for resale, as opposed to being held to produce income.

Investment Tax Credit   A credit against Tax Payable, calculated as a percentage of some specified type of expenditure made by the Taxpayer.

Involuntary Disposition   A Disposition of a capital property resulting from theft, destruction through natural causes, or expropriation by a statutory authority.

J

Joint Spousal Or Common-Law Partner Trust   An Inter Vivos Trust established by an Individual aged 65 years or more, subject to the conditions that the Individual and his/her Spouse or Common-Law Partner must be entitled to all of the Trust's Income during their lifetimes, and the Individual and his Spouse or Common-Law Partner must be the only Individuals who can access the capital of the Trust during his/her lifetime.

Joint Tenancy   A holding of property, either real or personal, by two or more Persons with each sharing the undivided interest that cannot be sold without the consent of all joint tenants.

Joint Venture   An arrangement in which two or more Persons work together in a limited and defined business undertaking, which does not constitute a Partnership, a Trust, or a Corporation, the expenses and revenues of which will be distributed in mutually agreed portions.

L

Labour Sponsored Funds Tax Credit
A credit against Tax Payable that is available to Individuals making investments in prescribed labour sponsored venture capital corporations.

Legal Stated Capital   An amount that is specified in corporate enabling legislation. In general, it is equal to the amount of consideration received for the issuance of shares.

Life Annuity   An Annuity that continues until the death of the Annuitant.

Lifelong Learning Plan (LLP)   A provision that allows Individuals to make temporary, non-taxable withdrawals from their RRSP when they are enrolled in a qualifying education program at a qualifying educational institution.

Lifetime Capital Gains Deduction   A deduction in the calculation of the Taxable Income of an Individual. It permits the deduction of a cumulative lifetime amount of up to $750,000 in Capital Gains resulting

from the Disposition of Qualified Small Business Corporation shares or Qualified Farm or Fishing Property.

Limited Liability   A reference to the fact that the liability of investors in equity shares of a Corporation is limited to the amount of their invested capital.

Limited Liability Partnerships   A Partnership, all of the members of which are legislatively specified professionals. The members of such Partnerships are relieved of any personal liability arising from the wrongful or negligent action of their professional Partners, as well as Employees, agents, or representatives of the Partnership who are conducting partnership business.

Limited Partner   As defined in most provincial legislation, a Partner whose liabilities for partnership debts is limited to the amount of his contribution to the Partnership, and who is not permitted to participate in the management of the Partnership.

Limited Partnership   A Partnership composed of at least one General Partner and at least one Limited Partner. To be considered a Limited Partnership, the Partnership has to be registered as such under the appropriate provincial registry.

Limited Partnership Loss   The excess of losses allocated to a Limited Partner (other than farming or capital losses), over his At-Risk Amount.

Liquidating Dividend   A Dividend that represents a return of invested capital, as opposed to a distribution from earnings.

Listed Personal Property   A defined subset of Personal Use Property. The included items are works of art, jewelry, rare books, stamps, and coins.

Loss Carry Back   The application of a loss incurred in the current taxation year against the Income reported in a previous taxation year, resulting in a refund of taxes paid in that previous year.

Loss Carry Forward   The application of a loss incurred in the current taxation year against Income reported in a subsequent taxation year, resulting in a reduction of Tax Payable in that subsequent year.

Low Rate Income Pool (LRIP)   A notional account that tracks amounts of a non-CCPC's income that cannot be used for the payment of Eligible Dividends.

Lump-Sum Payments   Retroactive payments for Spousal or Child Support, pension benefits, EI benefits, and Employment Income (including payments for termination), that relate to prior years. Qualifying amounts of such payments are eligible for an alternative Tax Payable calculation.

M

M&P An acronym for "manufacturing and processing" usually used in connection with the calculation of the Manufacturing And Processing Profits Deduction.

M&P Capital 100/85 of the Cost Of Capital related to Qualified Activities for M&P.

M&P Labour 100/75 of the Cost Of Labour related to Qualified Activities for M&P.

M&P Profits A concept of Income based on M&P Capital and M&P Labour, applied in a formula contained in ITR 5200.

Manufacturing And Processing Profits Deduction (M&P Deduction) A deduction in the calculation of corporate Tax Payable. It is equal to the General Rate Reduction rate applied to M&P Profits.

Median Rule A rule applicable to Capital Assets acquired before 1972. For purposes of calculating Capital Gains on Dispositions of these assets, the Adjusted Cost Base is equal to the median of the cost of the asset, the Valuation Day value of the asset, and the Proceeds Of Disposition.

Medical Expense Tax Credit A credit against Tax Payable that is available to Individuals with qualifying medical expenses.

Merger A combination of two or more business enterprises. While widely used in the *Income Tax Act*, this term does not have a formal definition in that legislation.

Money Purchase Limit An amount, specified in tax legislation that represents the maximum amount of Employee and employer contributions that can be added, for the benefit of a given Employee, to an RPP in the specified taxation year.

Money Purchase Plan (a.k.a., Defined Contribution Plan) A retirement savings plan in which the plan sponsor (employer or Individual) makes known or determinable contributions. The retirement benefit is based on the accumulated contributions and earnings on investments within the plan.

Moving Expenses Costs, as described in ITA 62(3), that can be deducted when an Individual is moving; to a new work location, to commence full-time attendance at a post-secondary institution, to a new work location after ceasing to be a full-time student at a post-secondary institution, or to a new location to take up employment, if unemployed prior to the move.

MUSH An acronym for "municipalities, universities, schools, and hospitals". It is used in GST work to refer to the special rules applicable to these organizations.

Mutual Fund A taxable entity, either a Trust or a Corporation, that manages a portfolio of investments on behalf of its unitholders or shareholders.

N

"Negative" Adjusted Cost Base A term used to refer to situations where negative adjustments to the Adjusted Cost Base of a Capital Asset exceed its original cost plus positive adjustments. While, in general, such amounts must be taken into Income, an exception is made for Partnership Interests, for which such amounts can be carried forward.

Net Assets Assets minus the liabilities of a business enterprise.

Net Business Income As used in this text, the net of inclusions less deductions, related to Business Income, with all amounts determined as per Division B, Subdivision b, of the *Income Tax Act*.

Net Capital Loss The excess of Allowable Capital Losses over Taxable Capital Gains for the current year.

Net Income As used in this text, the net of revenues plus gains, less expenses plus losses, with all amounts determined through the application of GAAP.

Net Income For Tax Purposes The sum of Employment Income, Business and Property Income, net Taxable Capital Gains, other sources of income, and other deductions from income, determined using income tax procedures and concepts. These amounts are combined as per the rules in ITA 3. This amount is also referred to as Division B Income or simply Net Income. However, we tend to use the full Net Income For Tax Purposes title in order to avoid confusion with Net Income as determined by accounting rules.

Net Property Income As used in this text, the net of inclusions less deductions, related to Property Income, with all amounts determined as per Division B, Subdivision b, of the *Income Tax Act*.

Net Tax Owing A term, applicable to Taxpayers who are Individuals, used to describe the sum of federal and provincial taxes owing for the year, less amounts withheld for the year.

NETFILE An electronic filing system that requires the use of an approved software program. An Individual uses the Internet to transmit their return directly to the CRA, without the use of a third party.

New Housing GST Rebate A provision that allows an individual to recover a portion of the GST paid on the acquisition of a new residence.

Non-Capital Loss   The sum of employment losses (for Individuals), business losses, property losses, Net Capital Losses deducted, and deductible Dividends received (for Corporations), less Income as calculated under ITA 3(c).

Non-Depreciable Capital Property   Capital property, such as land or holdings of securities, that is not subject to depreciation or amortization.

Non-Discretionary Trust   A Trust for which the Trust documents have specified the amounts of Income and capital to be allocated to each Beneficiary.

Non-Eligible Dividends   Dividends that have not been designated by the payor as eligible for the enhanced gross up and tax credit procedure.

Non-Portfolio Property   (Definition relevant only to SIFT entities) These properties are made up of (1) securities of a subject entity (corporation, trust, or partnership) where the securities held have a value that is greater than 10% of the equity value of the subject entity or, the securities held, along with securities of entities affiliated with the subject entity, have a fair market value that is greater than 50% of the equity value of the trust or partnership, (2) real estate and resource properties where such properties total more than 50% of the equity value of the trust or partnership, and (3) property used in the course of carrying on a business in Canada.

Non-Refundable Tax Credit   A Tax Credit that can only be used against the Tax Payable of an Individual. It will not be "refunded" to Individuals without sufficient Tax Payable to make use of it.

Non-Resident   A Corporation, Trust, or any other type of entity that exists, was formed or organized, or was last continued under the laws of a country, or a political subdivision of a country, other than Canada.

Non-Share Consideration   Consideration received by a Taxpayer from a Corporation that is in the form of assets other than shares of the Corporation.

Northern Residents Deductions   Deductions from the Taxable Income of residents of prescribed areas in northern Canada, designed to compensate them for the higher costs of living in these regions.

Notice Of Assessment   A form that the CRA sends to all Taxpayers after they process their returns. It tells Taxpayers whether there were any changes made to the returns and, if so, what they are. It also informs Taxpayers of the amount of their additional tax payable or their refund.

Notice Of Objection   A statement made to the CRA which provides a statement of facts and reasons, detailing why a Taxpayer or GST Registrant disagrees with an Assessment. The notice can be filed using Form T400A or by simply writing a letter to the CRA.

O

OAS Clawback   A taxing back, or reduction, in the payment of Old Age Security benefits. The federal government taxes back, or retains, an amount of these payments equal to 15% of the Individual's Income in excess of an indexed threshold amount.

Old Age Security Benefits (OAS)   A monthly payment to Residents of Canada who are 65 years of age or older (see also OAS Clawback).

Operating Cost Benefit   A Taxable Benefit assessed to Employees whose employers pay the operating costs of an automobile provided to the Employee. It is designed to reflect, on a notional basis, the value of these operating costs.

Ordering Rule   Rules which establish the sequence or order in which a group of deductions must be made.

P

Paid Up Capital (PUC)   A balance that is, in general, equal to Legal Stated Capital as determined under the legislation governing the particular Corporation. The equivalent of Contributed Capital in accounting usage.

Parent Company   A Corporation that Controls one or more Subsidiaries.

Part IV Tax   A refundable tax, applicable to Private Corporations and Subject Corporations, and assessed on Portfolio Dividends received as well as some Dividends received from Connected Corporations.

Part Year Resident   An Individual who either enters Canada during the year and becomes a Resident or, alternatively, an Individual who departs from Canada during the year and gives up their Resident status. In either case, the Individual will be taxed on their worldwide income for the part of the year that they were considered to be a Resident of Canada.

Partner   A Person who is a member of a Partnership.

Partner and Employee GST Rebate   A provision that allows partners and employees to recover the GST paid on their partnership or employment related expenses.

Partnership   Two or more Persons who combine forces to carry on a business together for the purpose of making a profit by contributing their skills, knowledge, labour, experience, time, or capital.

Partnership Interest A Non-Depreciable Capital Property that reflects the Partner's original cost, adjusted for earnings, withdrawals, and other factors.

Past Service Cost The cost of starting a pension plan and extending the benefits/contributions to years of service prior to the inception of the plan or, alternatively, amending the benefit/contribution formula of an existing plan and extending the change retroactively to years of service prior to the amendment.

Past Service Pension Adjustment (PSPA) An adjustment to reflect the past service benefits/contributions allocated to an Employee for years of service prior to the current year.

Penalties Amounts taxpayers or GST registrants must pay if they fail to file returns or remit or pay amounts owing on time, or if they try to evade paying or remitting tax by not filing returns. Penalties must also be paid by people who knowingly, or under circumstances amounting to gross negligence, participate in or make false statements or omissions in their returns, and by those who do not provide the information required on a prescribed form.

Pension Adjustment (PA) An adjustment reported by employers which reflects, for an individual Employee, the Employee and employer contributions to RPPs and DPSPs for the previous year (in the case of Defined Benefit RPPs, benefits are converted to an equivalent amount of contributions).

Pension Adjustment Reversal (PAR) An adjustment for amounts of benefits/contributions that were included in previously issued Pension Adjustments, but have subsequently been lost to the Individual (e.g., benefits earned during a pre-vesting period that did not ultimately vest).

Pension Income Tax Credit A credit against Tax Payable that is available to Individuals with qualifying pension income.

Periodic Child Care Expense Amount A weekly limit on deductible child care costs, defined as 1/40 of the Annual Child Care Expense Amount.

Permanent Establishment A fixed place of business of a Corporation, including an office, a branch, a mine, an oil well, a farm, a timberland, a factory, a workshop, or a warehouse.

Person A term used in the *Income Tax Act* to refer to taxable entities. For income tax purposes, the three taxable entities are Individuals, Corporations, and Trusts.

Personal Capital Property For GST/HST purposes, any capital property other than Real Property.

Personal Services Business A Corporation that provides the services of a Specified Shareholder [ITA 248(1)] who could reasonably be regarded as an officer or Employee of the business, and that does not have five or more other full time Employees throughout the year.

Personal Tax Credits A group of credits against Tax Payable that are specified in ITA 118(1). They include credits for Individuals, Spouses, Common-Law Partners and various Dependants, as well as credits for types of income such as pension or employment.

Personal Trust A Testamentary or Inter Vivos Trust in which no beneficial interest was acquired for consideration paid to the Trust or to a Person who contributed property to the Trust.

Personal Use Property Any property that is owned by the Taxpayer and used primarily for his enjoyment, or for the enjoyment of one or more Individuals Related to the Taxpayer.

Phased Retirement A term used to refer to situations where an individual over 55 years of age continues to earn partial pension benefits, despite the fact that he or she has started to receive pension benefits from that employer.

Political Contributions Tax Credit A credit against Tax Payable that is available to Individuals who have made contributions to a registered federal political party or to a candidate at the time of a federal election.

Pooled Registered Pension Plan A registered pension plan established by a financial institution. Eligible registrants would be employees and other individuals who are not members of a registered pension plan established by an employer.

Portfolio Dividend A Dividend received from a Corporation to which the recipient is not connected (see Connected Corporation). Usually applicable if 10% or less of the voting shares are owned.

Post-1971 Undistributed Surplus Amounts earned by a Corporation after 1971 and retained in the Corporation.

Pre-1972 Capital Surplus On Hand Capital Gains accrued before 1972 that have been realized as the result of a Disposition after 1971, less Capital Losses that accrued before 1972 that have been realized as the result of a Disposition after 1971.

Pre-1972 Undistributed Surplus Amounts earned by a Corporation prior to 1972 and retained in the Corporation.

Pre-Acquisition Surplus   A surplus account that tracks certain sources of Income of a Foreign Affiliate.

Preferred Beneficiary   An Individual who is a Beneficiary of a Trust and who is either eligible for the Disability Tax Credit or, alternatively, 18 years of age or older and can be claimed by another Individual for purposes of the dependant tax credit for Individuals who are dependant because of mental or physical infirmity.

Preferred Beneficiary Election   An Election which allows trust income to be allocated to a Preferred Beneficiary without being distributed to that Beneficiary by the Trust.

Preferred Shares   Shares that do not have all the rights which are provided for under the relevant corporate enabling legislation. While there are many variations in the rights that such securities have, Preferred Shares would normally have a fixed or determinable Dividend and would not have voting rights.

Prescribed Debt Obligations   A group of non-standard debt contracts that are defined in ITR 7001 (e.g., a debt contract with no interest stipulated as payable).

Prescribed Proxy Amount   An alternative basis for calculating Scientific Research And Experimental Development overhead costs. Instead of calculating actual overhead costs, a Prescribed Proxy Amount, based on 65% of the Salaries and wages of Employees involved in Scientific Research And Experimental Development activities, can be used.

Prescribed Rate   An interest rate which, as described in ITR 4301, changes quarterly and is based on the average interest rate paid on 90 day Treasury Bills during the first month of the preceding quarter. The basic rate is used for a variety of purposes (e.g., calculation of the Taxable Benefits on interest free loans to Employees). The basic rate, plus 2 percentage points, is used to calculate interest owing from the government to Taxpayers (e.g., interest on late payment of a tax refund). The basic rate, plus 4 percentage points, is used to calculate interest owed by Taxpayers to the government (e.g., interest on late Instalment payments).

Prescribed Stock Exchange
This term has been replaced by "designated stock exchange".

Principal Residence   Any accommodation owned by the Taxpayer that was ordinarily inhabited in the year by the Taxpayer, his Spouse, a former Spouse, or a dependent child, and is designated by the Taxpayer as a Principal Residence.

Private Corporation   A Corporation that is a resident of Canada, but is not a Public Corporation.

Proceeds Of Disposition   Amounts received as the result of a Disposition. Usually related to a capital property Disposition.

Profit Sharing Plan   A trusteed plan to which employers can make deductible contributions, the amount of which is related to the profits of the enterprise. Both the contributions and the earnings resulting from their investment are taxed in the hands of the Employees as they occur. Payments from the plan are received by the Employees on a tax free basis.

Progressive Tax System   A tax system that applies higher effective rates for Individuals with higher Incomes and lower effective rates for Individuals with lower Incomes (e.g., personal income taxes).

Property Income   Income that is earned through the passive ownership of property. It would include rents, interest, Dividends, and some royalties (i.e., royalties paid on assets that have been purchased). While usage is not always consistent, this term usually refers to a net amount (i.e., inclusions less deductions, or revenues less expenses).

Property Tax   A tax on the ownership of some particular set of goods.

Public Corporation   A Corporation that has at least one class of its shares listed on a designated stock exchange in Canada.

Public Transit Pass Tax Credit
A credit against Tax Payable that is available to individuals who purchase monthly or longer public transit passes.

PUC   An acronym for "paid up capital".

Purification Of A Small Business Corporation   A process of disposing of corporate assets that are not being used to produce Active Business Income, so that the Corporation meets the 90% of assets test required to qualify as a Small Business Corporation.

Q

Qualified Activities   Types of activity, as defined in ITR 5202, that are considered to be manufacturing and processing activities.

Qualified Farm Property   A Qualified Farm Property is a Farm Property that, prior to its Disposition was owned by the Taxpayer, his Spouse, or his Common-Law Partner, or their children for a period of 24 months or more.

Qualified Fishing Property
A Qualified Fishing Property is a Fishing Property that, prior to its Disposition was owned by the Taxpayer, his Spouse, or his Common-Law Partner, or their children for a period of 24 months or more.

Qualified Property   Certain specified types of property that, when acquired, qualify the Taxpayer for an Investment Tax Credit.

Qualified Scientific Research And Experimental Development Expenditures
Scientific Research And Experimental Development expenditures that qualify the Taxpayer for Investment Tax Credits.

Qualified Small Business Corporation
A Small Business Corporation that, at the time of its Disposition, has been owned by no one other than the Taxpayer or a related party during the preceding 24 months, and during that 24 month period, more than 50% of the fair market value of its assets were used in an Active Business carried on primarily in Canada.

Qualifying Corporation   A CCPC throughout the year with Taxable Income in the immediately preceding year of no more than $500,000 and previous year Taxable Capital Employed In Canada of $10 million or less, thereby qualifying for the additional 15% tax credit on the first $3,000,000 of Qualified Scientific Research And Development Expenditures.

Qualifying Spousal Or Common-Law Partner Trust   A Spousal Or Common-Law Partner Trust that qualifies for the Rollover of assets into the Trust under ITA 73(1.01) for Inter Vivos Trusts or ITA 70(6) for Testamentary Trusts.

Qualitative Characteristics   This term is used in our text to refer to non-quantitative characteristics of a tax system that are considered to be desirable (e.g., fairness).

Quick Method   A method of determining GST amounts payable or receivable that is available to Registrants with annual GST taxable sales, including those of associated businesses, of $400,000 or less. Specified percentages are applied to the GST inclusive sales figures to determine the GST payable or the refund. Accounting for Input Tax Credits on non-capital expenditures is not required. Input Tax Credits on capital expenditures are tracked separately.

R

RDTOH   An acronym for "refundable dividend tax on hand".

Real Property   Land and all appurtenances to it, including buildings, crops, and mineral rights, a.k.a. real estate.

Reasonable Expectation Of Profit (REOP)
A test that involves the determination of whether a business or an investment is likely to have a profit. The CRA has tried to use this test to limit the ability of Taxpayers to deduct losses resulting from businesses and investments that fail their REOP test.

Reassessment   A revision of an original Assessment (see Assessment and Notice Of Assessment).

Recapture Of CCA   An inclusion in Business and Property Income that arises when deductions from a CCA Class, engendered by disposals, leave a negative balance in that Class at the end of the taxation year.

Redemption Of Shares   A transaction in which a Corporation purchases some of its own outstanding shares, either in the open market, or through a direct purchase from shareholders.

Refundable Dividend Tax On Hand (RDTOH)   A balance made up of refundable taxes paid, less refunds received as the result of paying Dividends.

Refundable Investment Tax Credit
An Investment Tax Credit that will be paid to the Taxpayer, even if the amount resulting from the Investment Tax Credit exceeds the Taxpayer's Tax Payable.

Refundable Medical Expense Supplement
A refundable credit against Tax Payable that increases the amount available to certain low income individuals for their eligible medical expenses.

Refundable Part I Tax   The portion of Part I tax that is applicable to a notional amount of Aggregate Investment Income earned by a CCPC.

Refundable Part XI.3 Tax   A 50% tax that is assessed on contributions to a Retirement Compensation Arrangement and on the earnings of amounts invested in the plan. It is fully refundable when amounts are distributed from the arrangement and taxed in the hands of the recipient Employees.

Refundable Tax Credit   An amount, based on a Tax Credit calculation, that will be paid to an Individual even if the amount resulting from the Tax Credit calculation exceeds the Individual's Tax Payable.

Registered Disability Savings Plan (RDSP)
A trusteed arrangement that allows Individuals to make non-deductible contributions that will be invested on a tax-free basis, with the accumulated funds being used to make distributions to an individual who qualifies for the disability tax credit.

Registered Education Savings Plan (RESP) A trusteed arrangement that allows Individuals to make non-deductible contributions that will be invested on a tax-free basis, with the accumulated funds being used to provide for the post-secondary education of a child.

Registered Pension Plan (RPP) A retirement savings plan sponsored by an employer, to which the employer will make contributions which are not taxable to the Employee, and the Employee may make contributions which are deductible. Earnings accumulate tax free within the plan. Withdrawals from the plan are subject to tax.

Registered Retirement Income Fund (RRIF) A trusteed plan to which a Resident Individual can transfer balances from retirement savings plans on a tax free basis. Earnings accumulate tax free within the plan. Withdrawals from the plan are subject to tax. Unlike RRSPs, a minimum withdrawal is required each year.

Registered Retirement Savings Plan (RRSP) A trusteed plan to which a Resident Individual can make deductible contributions. Earnings accumulate tax free within the plan. Withdrawals from the plan are generally subject to tax.

Registrant An entity who is registered to collect and remit the GST.

Regressive Tax System A tax system that applies higher effective rates for Individuals with lower Incomes and lower effective rates for Individuals with higher Incomes (e.g., most sales taxes).

Related Persons ITA 251(2)(a) indicates that two Individuals are related if they are connected by blood relationship, marriage or common-law partnership, or adoption. ITA 251(2)(b) describes various situations in which a Corporation would be related to other Persons (e.g., a Corporation is related to the Person who Controls it). ITA 251(2)(c) describes various situations in which two Corporations would be related to each other (e.g., the two Corporations are controlled by the same Person).

Reorganization Of Capital (ITA 86) A Rollover provision that allows one class of shares in a Corporation to be exchanged for a different class of shares, without tax consequences.

Replacement Property Rules A set of rules which provide for the deferral of both Recapture and Capital Gains on Involuntary Dispositions and some voluntary Dispositions of capital property. Deferral is conditional on replacing the property within a specified period after the Proceeds Of Disposition are received.

Resale Price Method A Transfer Pricing method generally used where fair market value comparables are

unavailable because of the uniqueness of the products. It also applies to situations where the purchaser adds little or no value and effectively acts as a distributor or sales agent.

Reserve A deduction in the calculation of net Business Income or net Taxable Capital Gains.

Resident A Person who is located in a place. This is the basis on which Canadian income taxes are assessed. That is, Canadian Resident Persons are liable for the payment of Canadian income tax, without regard to their citizenship or the source of their Income. While not defined in the *Income Tax Act*, IT-221R3 provides guidance on the determination of residency for Individuals and IT-447 provides similar guidance for Trusts.

Residential Ties Factors that will be considered in determining whether or not an Individual is a Resident of Canada. While there are many such ties, IT-221R3 indicates that the most commonly used would be the maintenance of a dwelling in Canada, having one's Spouse or Common-Law Partner remain in Canada, and having one's Dependants remain in Canada.

Restricted Farm Loss A farmer whose chief source of Income is not farming or a combination of farming and some other source of Income, but who has a reasonable expectation of long-run profitability, can only deduct losses to the extent of the first $2,500, plus one-half of the next $12,500. Losses in excess of this deductible amount are referred to as Restricted Farm Losses.

Restrictive Covenant An agreement entered into, an undertaking made, or a waiver of an advantage or right by the Taxpayer. This would include, but would not be limited to, non-competition agreements.

Retained Earnings (a.k.a. Earned Capital) In accounting usage, the amount of a Corporation's Shareholders' Equity that resulted from the retention of earnings in the Corporation.

Retirement Compensation Arrangement An unregistered plan to which employers make deductible contributions to provide Employees with benefits subsequent to their retirement. Both contributions and earnings are subject to a Refundable Part XI.3 Tax.

Retiring Allowance Amounts received at retirement as recognition for long service, or as the result of loss of employment.

Revenue Jurisdiction Approach An international taxation approach under which a country taxes all Income earned by its Residents, without regard to the country in which that Income is earned.

Reversionary Trust A trust agreement under which the property held by the Trustee can revert to the Settlor.

Rights Or Things With respect to a deceased Taxpayer, these are amounts that are due, but have not been received (e.g., wages to the end of a pay period prior to death, but not yet received).

Rollover As this term is used in tax work, it refers to a tax free Transfer of assets under circumstances that, in the absence of a special Rollover provision, would be considered a taxable Transfer.

RRSP Deduction Limit The amount that is the sum of the Unused RRSP Deduction Room at the end of the preceding year, plus the amount by which the lesser of the RRSP Dollar Limit and 18% of Earned Income for the preceding year exceeds the Pension Adjustment for the preceding year. This sum is adjusted for any Past Service Pension Adjustment or Pension Adjustment Reversal. In simplified terms, it represents the maximum amount of contributions that have been made to an RRSP that can be deducted for a year.

RRSP Deduction Room The excess of the RRSP Deduction Limit, over the amount of RRSP contributions that have been deducted.

RRSP Dollar Limit Generally, the Money Purchase Limit for the preceding year.

S

Safe Income For purposes of applying ITA 55(2) to Capital Gains Stripping, Safe Income is made up of amounts earned by a Corporation after 1971, or if the investment shares in that Corporation were acquired after that date, amounts earned after the acquisition.

Salary The amount an employer pays an Employee for work done. An employer records this type of Employment Income on a T4. A common component of Employment Income.

Salary Deferral Arrangement An arrangement, whether funded or not, under which an Individual who has the right to receive compensation postpones the receipt of that compensation, and it is reasonable to assume that one of the main purposes of this postponement was to defer the payment of taxes.

Scientific Research And Experimental Development (SR&ED) Activities related to basic or applied research, and for the development of new products and processes.

Self-Employed Individual An Individual who has a business relationship with an entity. Whether or not an Individual is working as an Employee or a Self-Employed Individual is dependent on factors such as control, ownership of tools, chance of profit or risk of loss, and the ability to subcontract or hire an assistant.

Separate Class Rules Rules that require certain types of assets that would, in the absence of these special rules, be included in a single Class, be allocated to a separate balance for that Class (e.g., each rental property with a cost greater than $50,000 must be placed in a different Class 1).

Settlor The Individual who creates a Trust by contributing property to be managed and administered by a Trustee for the Beneficiaries.

Share For Share Exchange (ITA 85.1) A Rollover provision that allows one Corporation to acquire shares in another Corporation by issuing its own shares, without tax consequences to either of the Corporations or their shareholders.

Shared Use Capital Equipment Capital Assets that are used more than 50 percent, but less than 90 percent, in Scientific Research And Experimental Development activities.

Shareholders' Equity The residual interest of the shareholders of a Corporation in the Net Assets of the Corporation.

Short Fiscal Period A taxation year that is less than 12 months in duration. Can occur in the first and last years of operation, as well as certain other situations.

SIFT Partnership To be a Specified Investment Flow-Through (SIFT) partnership, (1) the partnership must be a Canadian resident partnership; (2) investments in the partnership must be publicly traded; and (3) the partnership must hold one or more non-portfolio properties.

SIFT Trust To be a Specified Investment Flow-Through (SIFT) trust, (1) the trust must be resident in Canada; (2) investments in the trust must be publicly traded; and (3) the trust must hold one or more non-portfolio properties.

Simplified ITC Accounting An alternative designation for "Streamlined ITC Accounting".

Small Business Corporation A Corporation that is a Canadian Controlled Private Corporation that uses all or substantially all (90% or more) of the fair market value of its assets in an Active Business that is carried on primarily (more than 50 percent) in Canada.

Small Business Deduction A deduction in the calculation of corporate Tax Payable equal to 17 percentage points on the first $500,000 of Active Business Income earned by a CCPC.

Small CCPC   A Canadian Controlled Private Corporation that has (1) Taxable Income in the current or previous year of $500,000 or less, (2) has Taxable Capital Employed In Canada in the current or previous year of $10 million or less, (3) is able to claim some amount of the Small Business Deduction in the current or previous year, and (4) has a perfect payment compliance record for the last 12 months.

Small Suppliers Exemption   An exemption from the requirement to register for the collection and remittance of GST for those entities with less than $30,000 in taxable supplies.

Social Benefits Repayment (a.k.a., Clawback)   An income tested taxing back, or reduction, in the payment of Old Age Security Benefits and Employment Insurance Benefits.

Soft Costs   Costs, such as interest and property tax, on land and buildings that are incurred prior to the capital asset being used for business or income producing purposes.

Sojourner   An Individual who is deemed under ITA 250 to be a Canadian Resident for the full taxation year as the result of having sojourned (i.e., been temporarily present) in Canada for 183 days or more.

Source Deductions   Amounts that are withheld by an employer from the Income of Employees. The withholdings for income taxes, Canada Pension Plan contributions, and Employment Insurance premiums must be remitted to the government.

Source Jurisdiction Approach   An international taxation approach under which a country taxes all Income earned within its borders, without regard to whether it is earned by Residents or Non-Residents.

Specified Class [ITA 256(1.1)]   A class of shares that has certain specified terms and conditions, including a fixed or determinable Dividend and an absence of voting rights. Would generally be referred to as Preferred Shares.

Specified Employee   An Employee who owns 10% or more of the shares of the Corporation, or who does not deal at arm's length with the Corporation.

Specified Individual   An Individual who has not attained the age of 17 before the beginning of the year and who has a parent who is Resident in Canada.

Specified Investment Business   A Corporation that does not have five or more full time Employees throughout the year, whose principal purpose is to derive Income from property.

Specified Non-Resident Shareholder   A specified shareholder who is a non-resident Person or non-resident investment company.

Specified Shareholder [(ITA 18(5)]   A shareholder of a Corporation who owns, either alone or together with other related persons, more than 25% of the voting shares of a corporation or, alternatively, shares that have more than 25% of the market value of all of the corporation's shares.

Specified Shareholder [ITA 248(1)]   A shareholder of a Corporation who owns, directly or indirectly, at any time in the year, not less than 10% of the issued shares of any class of the capital stock of the Corporation, or of any other Corporation that is related to the Corporation.

Split Income   Certain types of Income received by a Specified Individual from non-arm's length sources that will be taxed at the maximum federal rate of 29 percent.

Spousal Or Common-Law Partner Trust   An Inter Vivos or Testamentary Trust that has an individual's Spouse or Common-Law Partner as a Beneficiary (see also Qualifying Spousal Or Common-Law Partner Trust).

Spousal RRSP   An RRSP to which the Spouse or Common-Law Partner of the Annuitant (i.e., Beneficiary of the RRSP) has made contributions that the Spouse or Common-Law Partner can deduct in calculating Net Income For Tax Purposes.

Spousal Support   A Support Amount that is for the benefit of a Spouse or Common-Law Partner, or a former Spouse or Common-Law Partner.

Spousal Tax Credit   A credit against Tax Payable that is available to individuals who have a Spouse or Common-Law Partner.

Spouse   An Individual to whom a Taxpayer is legally married.

Standby Charge   A Taxable Benefit assessed to Employees who have been provided with an automobile by their employer. It is designed to reflect, on a notional basis, the value of having the car available on a standby basis for personal usage.

Stock Dividend   A pro rata distribution of a Corporation's shares to its existing shareholders.

Stock Option   A contractual arrangement which gives the holder the right to purchase a specified number of shares for a specified period of time at a specified acquisition price.

Stop Loss Rules   A group of rules which, under specified conditions, prevent the deduction of a loss.

Straight-Line Method A method of calculating CCA in which a specified or determinable rate is applied to the Capital Cost of acquired assets in order to determine the CCA for the period.

Streamlined ITC Accounting A method of determining Input Tax Credits available to small businesses, charities, not-for-profit organizations, and certain public service bodies. The organization must have annual GST taxable sales, including those of associated businesses, of $1,000,000 or less and annual GST taxable purchases of $4,000,000 or less. Input Tax Credits are determined by multiplying all GST inclusive purchases, except real property purchases, by 5/105 rather than using the actual GST paid. Input Tax Credits on real property are tracked separately.

Student Loan Interest Tax Credit A credit against Tax Payable that is based on the amount of interest on a loan under the *Canada Student Loans Act*, or the *Canada Student Financial Assistance Act*.

Subject Corporation For purposes of the Part IV Tax, a Public Corporation that is controlled by, or for the benefit of, an Individual or a related group of Individuals. Also used in the determination of Dividend Stripping (ITA 84.1) and share sales to non-residents (ITA 212.1) to describe a Corporation, the shares of which have been sold.

Subsidiary An enterprise that is controlled by another enterprise (the Parent Company). The Parent Company has the right and ability to obtain future economic benefits from the resources of the Subsidiary and is exposed to the related risks.

Superficial Loss (ITA 54) A loss on the Disposition of property that is disallowed for tax purposes because the Taxpayer has acquired an identical property, either 30 days before the Disposition or, alternatively, 30 days after the Disposition.

Supply A broad range of transactions between Persons. To "make a supply of property or a service" means to provide it in any way, including sale, transfer, barter, exchange, licence, rental, lease, gift, or Disposition.

Support Amount Amounts paid as the result of the separation or divorce of two Individuals who were Spouses or Common-Law Partners. Can be divided into Spousal Support and Child Support.

Surtax An additional or extra tax on something already taxed.

Syndicates A group of Persons combined or making a joint effort to undertake some specific project or to carry out a specific transaction.

T

Tariffs A tax imposed on the importation or exportation of certain goods or services.

Tax Avoidance The undertaking of transactions or arrangements with a view to avoiding or minimizing the payment of taxes. As the term is generally used, it refers to legitimate procedures that could also be described as Tax Planning.

Tax Base The income source, class of transaction, type of property, or other factor on which tax is assessed (e.g., sales tax is assessed on sales).

Tax Court Of Canada A court that hears appeals about income tax and GST/HST assessments. In addition, the Court has jurisdiction to hear appeals under the Canada Pension Plan Act, Employment Insurance Act, and several other Acts. The Tax Court maintains four offices (Vancouver, Ottawa, Toronto, and Montreal) and regularly conducts hearings in major centres across Canada.

Tax Credit A credit against Tax Payable.

Tax Deferral An important type of Tax Planning. The basic idea here is to find procedures that will put off the payment of taxes until a later taxation year. The value of these procedures reflects the time value of money. That is, there is a value associated with making a payment later, rather than sooner.

Tax Evasion This typically involves deliberately ignoring a specific part of the law or willfully refusing to comply with legislated reporting requirements. Tax evasion, unlike tax avoidance, has criminal consequences.

Tax Expenditures Foregone tax revenues due to special exemptions, rate reductions, rebates, and credits that reduce the amount of tax that would otherwise be payable. Often designed to encourage certain kinds of activities or to serve other objectives, such as providing assistance to lower-income or elderly Canadians.

Tax Free Savings Accounts (TFSAs) A trusteed arrangement that allows Individuals to make non-deductible contributions that will be invested in qualified assets. Earnings accumulate on a tax free basis within the plan and can be distributed to the Individual who established the plan on a tax free basis.

Tax Haven A foreign country used to avoid or reduce income taxes, especially by investors from another country.

Tax Incidence   The Person who ultimately pays a tax, regardless of the legal basis of assessment (e.g., taxes paid by Corporations may be passed on to either Employees or customers).

Tax Planning   The undertaking of legitimate transactions or arrangements with a view to avoiding or minimizing the payment of taxes. Some or all of such efforts could also be referred to as Tax Avoidance.

Tax Shelter (ITA 237.1)   The acquisition of a property, in respect of which it is represented that the acquisition of the property, or the donation or contribution of the property under a gifting arrangement, would generate any combination of tax credits or deductions that in total would equal or exceed the cost of acquiring the property.

Tax Shelter (Other Meanings)
An investment that shelters Income from other sources (e.g., Employment Income) by producing tax losses, or an investment with a positive cash flow that is sheltered by sufficient non-cash deductions (e.g., CCA) to produce a nil Taxable Income.

Taxable Allowance   An allowance provided by an employer to an Employee that must be included in the Employee's Employment Income. The amount is included on the Employee's T4.

Taxable Benefit   An amount of money, or the value of goods or services, that an employer pays or provides in addition to Salary.

Taxable Canadian Corporation   A Canadian Corporation that is not exempt from Canadian income tax by way of a statutory provision.

Taxable Canadian Property   A group of assets that are listed under the definition of Taxable Canadian Property in ITA 248(1). These assets are distinguished by the fact that gains on their Disposition are taxable without regard to the residence of the selling Taxpayer. For example, if a U.S. Resident sells Canadian real estate, Canadian income tax will be assessed on any gain resulting from the sale.

Taxable Capital Employed In Canada
This amount is the GAAP-determined capital of the Corporation, less the allowance for investments in other Corporations, multiplied by the percentage of the Corporation's activity at Permanent Establishments in Canada as determined under ITR 402. It is used in a number of calculations, including the determination of a small CCPC and the calculation of the reduction of the Small Business Deduction.

Taxable Capital Gain   The taxable portion (currently one-half) of a Capital Gain.

Taxable Entity   A defined organization or Individual that is subject to tax (e.g., Corporations are taxable entities for income tax purposes).

Taxable Income   Net Income For Tax Purposes, less certain deductions that are largely specified in Division C of Part I of the *Income Tax Act*. These deductions include loss carry overs, the Lifetime Capital Gains Deduction, and for Corporations, Dividends and Charitable Gifts.

Taxable Surplus   A surplus account that tracks certain sources of Income of a Foreign Affiliate.

Taxation Year   The period that is covered by a Taxpayer's return. As defined in ITA 249, it is equal to a calendar year for Individuals and Inter Vivos Trusts, and a Fiscal Period for Corporations and Testamentary Trusts.

Taxpayer   An entity that is required to file a tax return and pay taxes. For income tax purposes, a Taxpayer is an Individual, a Corporation, or a Trust.

Taxpayer Relief Provisions   Information Circular 07-01 contains guidelines on the discretionary authority the Minister has to grant relief based on a Taxpayer's situation. An example would be a waiver of late filing interest and penalties because the Individual suffered a serious illness. It replaces the fairness provisions.

Tenancy In Common   A holding of property, either real or personal, by two or more Persons, with each having a divisible interest that can be sold.

Term Preferred Shares   Preferred Shares which have a provision which allows them to be redeemed by the issuer or redeemed at the request of the holder.

Terminal Loss   A deduction in the calculation of Business and Property Income which arises when the last asset in a CCA Class is retired and a positive balance is left in the Class.

Testamentary Trust   A Trust that arises on, and as a consequence of, the death of an Individual.

Textbook Tax Credit   A credit against Tax Payable that is available to Individuals who qualify for the Education Tax Credit.

Thin Capitalization   A reference to situations where a non-resident Specified Shareholder is receiving interest on an amount of debt that exceeds two times the sum of his share of contributed capital plus 100% of Retained Earnings.

Tie-Breaker Rules   Provisions in International Tax Treaties that are designed to prevent the Double Taxation of Dual Residents.

Transaction Tax A tax that is assessed on specified types of transactions. Such taxes are most commonly applied to transactions involving the sale of goods or services.

Transfer To convey or move from one Taxpayer to a different Taxpayer.

Transfer Pricing An expression used to describe the price at which services, tangible property, and intangible property are traded across international borders between related or non-arm's length parties.

Transfer Tax A tax on the Transfer of property from one owner to another.

Transferee A Taxpayer to whom a Transfer is made.

Transferor A Taxpayer who makes a Transfer.

Trust A relationship in which one Person holds the title to property for the benefit of another Person.

Trustee An Individual or trust institution that holds legal title to property in trust for the benefit of the Trust Beneficiaries.

Tuition Fees Tax Credit A credit against Tax Payable that is available to Individuals making qualifying tuition payments. The base includes specified ancillary fees and fees and ancillary costs associated with writing university examinations and required examinations in professional programs.

Twenty-One (21) Year Deemed Disposition Rule A requirement, applicable to some types of Personal Trusts, that requires a deemed disposition of the Trust's capital property at the end of every twenty-one years.

U

Undepreciated Capital Cost (UCC) The Capital Cost of a depreciable asset class, less the cumulative CCA that has been taken to date. The tax equivalent of net book value in accounting.

Universal Child Care Benefit A $100 monthly payment that is available to Canadian families for each of their children under the age of 6 years.

Unused RRSP Deduction Room The cumulative total of all RRSP Deduction Limits, less amounts deducted in those years. The end of the preceding year balance is used when calculating the RRSP Deduction Limit.

V

Valuation Day (V-Day) December 22, 1971 for publicly traded assets and December 31, 1971 for other assets.

Value Added Tax (VAT) A tax based on the value added to a product at each stage of production or distribution by a particular entity. It is generally based on some accounting measurement of Income.

Vertical Amalgamation An Amalgamation of a Parent Company and one or more of its Subsidiaries.

Vested Benefit A benefit is vested if the beneficiary has an irrevocable right to receive it.

Vested Contribution A contribution is vested if the Individual making the contribution has an irrevocable right to either the amount of the contribution or a benefit of equivalent value.

Volunteer Firefighters Tax Credit A credit against Tax Payable that is available to volunteer firefighters who perform at least 200 hours of volunteer firefighting services during a taxation year.

W - Z

Wholly Dependent Person A Dependant who lives with the Taxpayer (this requirement is not applicable if the Dependant is the Taxpayer's child) in a self-contained domestic establishment and is eligible for the Eligible Dependant Tax Credit.

Will A document that is a legal declaration of an Individual's wishes as to the Disposition of his or her property after death.

Winding-Up Of A 90% Owned Subsidiary A Rollover provision that allows the asset of a 90% or more owned Subsidiary to be combined with the assets of its Parent Company, without tax consequences.

Winding-Up Of A Canadian Corporation A series of transactions that result in substantially all of the assets of a Canadian Corporation being distributed to the shareholders of that Corporation.

Working Income Tax Benefit A refundable credit available to low income individuals who are earning employment and business income.

Zero-Rated Goods And Services Goods and services that are taxable at a zero GST rate. The fact that they are designated as "taxable" means that Registrants who sell such goods and services are eligible for Input Tax Credits for the GST that they pay. Examples include basic groceries (e.g., milk, bread, and vegetables), prescription drugs, and exports.